by the
Bomb's
Early Light

Also by Paul Boyer

Urban Masses and Moral Order, 1820–1920

Salem Possessed: The Social Origins of Witchcraft (with Stephen Nissenbaum)

Purity in Print: Book Censorship in America

Paul Boyer

by the Bomb's Early Light

*American
Thought and Culture
at the Dawn of the Atomic Age*

Pantheon Books/New York

All rights reserved under International and Pan-American Copyright
Conventions. Published in the United States by Pantheon Books, a
division of Random House, Inc., New York, and simultaneously in
Canada by Random House of Canada Limited, Toronto. Originally
published in hardcover by Pantheon Books, a division of Random
House, Inc., in 1985.

Since this page cannot legibly accommodate all acknowledgments,
they appear on the following two pages.

Library of Congress Cataloging-in-Publication Data
Boyer, Paul S.
By the bomb's early light.
Includes bibliographic notes and index.
1. United States—Civilization—
1945-   . 2. Atomic bomb. 3. Atomic bomb—
Moral and ethical aspects. I. Title.
E169.12.B684   1985   973.92   85-42844
ISBN 0-394-74767-4 (pbk.)

Manufactured in the United States of America

First Paperback Edition

Grateful acknowledgment is made to the copyright holders for their kind permission to reprint the following previously published material:

Excerpt from William Rose Benét, "God's Fire." Reprinted by permission of Harold Ober Associates Incorporated. Copyright 1935, 1942, 1943, 1944, 1945, 1946, 1947 by William Rose Benét.

Excerpt from John Berryman, "The Dispossessed," from *Short Poems* by John Berryman. Copyright 1948 by John Berryman. Reprinted by permission of Farrar, Straus, and Giroux, Inc.

Robert Frost, "U.S. 1946 King's X," from *The Poetry of Robert Frost,* edited by Edward Connery Lathem. Copyright 1947, © 1969 by Holt, Rinehart and Winston. Copyright © 1975 by Lesley Frost Ballantine. Reprinted by permission of Holt, Rinehart and Winston, Publishers.

Excerpt from Randall Jarrell, "1945: The Death of the Gods," from *The Complete Poems* by Randall Jarrell. Copyright 1946, renewed 1974 by Mary Von Schrader Jarrell. Reprinted by permission of Farrar, Straus, and Giroux, Inc.

Excerpt from Milton Kaplan, "Atomic Bomb." Reprinted from *Commentary,* March 1948, by permission. All rights reserved.

Excerpt from Karl and Harty, "When the Atomic Bomb Fell" (1945). Reprinted by permission from Rounder Records, Somerville, Massachusetts 02144.

Excerpt from Aaron Kramer, "Night Shift, Detroit." Reprinted by permission of the author from *Thru our guns: a group of war poems* (Astoria, New York, January 1945), p. 10. Also published in Aaron Kramer, "Hiroshima: A 37-Year Failure to Respond," NER/BLQ [*New England Review/Bread Loaf Quarterly*], vol. 5 (Summer 1983).

Excerpt from C. S. Lewis, "On the Atomic Bomb: Metrical Experiment," from *Poems* by C. S. Lewis. Copyright © 1964 by the executors of the estate of C. S. Lewis. Reprinted by permission of Harcourt Brace Jovanovich, Inc.

Excerpt from Robert Lowell, "Where the Rainbow Ends," from *Lord Weary's Castle.* Copyright 1946, © 1974 by Robert Lowell. Reprinted by permission of Harcourt Brace Jovanovich, Inc.

Excerpt from Robert Lowell, "Fall 1961," from *For the Union Dead* by Robert Lowell. Copyright © 1962, 1964 by Robert Lowell. Reprinted by permission of Farrar, Straus, and Giroux, Inc.

Excerpt from Irene Orgel, "Sonnet: To Lise Meitner." Reprinted from *The American Scholar,* vol. 15, no. 2 (Spring 1946). Copyright 1946 by the United Chapters of Phi Beta Kappa. By permission of the publishers.

Excerpt from Karl Shapiro, "The Progress of Faust," from *Collected Poems, 1940–1978* by Karl Shapiro. © Random House, Inc. Reprinted by permission.

Excerpt from Frank Zappa, "Be in My Video." © 1984 by Munchkin Music, ASCAP.

Some of the material in the Epilogue originally appeared in different form in Paul Boyer, "From Activism to Apathy: The American People and Nuclear Weapons, 1963–1980," *The Journal of American History,* vol. 70, no. 4 (March 1984). © 1984 The Organization of American Historians.

For Katie and Alex

Contents

Photo sections begin on pages 17, 85, 155, and 309.

Acknowledgments

A great many people, including longtime friends and colleagues as well as others I have met through this project or in some cases know only through letters, have been generous in helping shape my understanding of this vast topic. At the beginning of the Notes section I have listed those participants in the events of 1945–1950 who granted interviews or graciously responded to written queries. I would like to thank them again here.

Here at Wisconsin I am particularly indebted to my colleagues James Baughman, John Dower, James Gustafson, J. Rogers Hollingsworth, Carl Kaestle, Stanley Kutler, Gerda Lerner, Thomas McCormick, Jr., Ronald Numbers, Dick Ringler, and Stephen Vaughn. Students in my graduate and undergraduate courses have contributed significantly to this work as well, both in their discussion comments and in steering me toward important source materials. Among them are Christopher Berkeley, Carolyn Brooks, JoAnne Brown, Maureen Fitzgerald, Joyce Follett, Stephen Kretzmann, Brian Ohm, Andrew Patner, Susan Rusch, Deborah Reilly, and Douglas Swiggim.

Thoughtful critiques of papers based on this study were offered by James Gilbert and Lawrence Wittner. Fellow researchers in the fields of nuclear-weapons history, civil defense, and peace studies have been most supportive, offering encouragement, ideas, and in some cases access to their unpublished work in progress. Thanks, then, to Barton Bernstein, Charles DeBenedetti, Lloyd Graybar, Martin Sherwin, William Vandercook, Spencer Weart, and Allan Winkler.

Stanley Katz was not only one of my early mentors in the study of history, but at a late stage in the writing of this book he supplied helpful information on his grandfather-in-law, John Haynes Holmes. Jean Toll, archivist of the General Mills Corporation, Minneapolis, Minnesota, and Nathan M. Kaganoff of the American Jewish Historical Society, Waltham, Massachusetts, provided valuable research assistance.

Others who commented on my initial prospectus or have otherwise shared their thinking and insights with me include the following, to all of whom I extend my gratitude: Loren Baritz, Robert Beisner, Leonard Berkman, Barry Childers, Alan Clive, Richard Elias, Joseph Ellis, James Farrell, Michael Fellman, Robert Griffith, Erwin Hiebert, David Hollinger, Robert Holsworth, Michael Howard, Michael Kazin, Robert Kelley, Edward Linenthal, Elaine Tyler May, Richard Minear, Lewis Perry, Kenneth Roseman, Howard Schoenberger, Ronald Sider, Kenneth Taylor, David Thelen, Robert Westbrook, R. Jackson Wilson, David Wyman, and Dorothy Zinberg. Thanks, as well, to those persons at a number of colleges and universities from Maine to Minnesota, as well as at the Woodrow Wilson Center of the Smithsonian Institution, who have made it possible for me over the past four years to meet a large number of people who share my interest in these matters.

Generous grants from the Rockefeller Foundation Humanities Fellowship program and the University of Wisconsin Research Committee provided invaluable freedom from teaching duties for the research and writing of this book. The University of Trondheim, the Nobel Institute of Norway, the Norwegian Foreign Policy Institute, and the Nordic Committee for International Studies in Stockholm jointly underwrote a Scandinavian lecture tour in the spring of 1983 that provided many opportunities to meet with scholars working in this area. My sincere thanks to Jarle Simensen of the University of Trondheim for initiating and coordinating this tour, and to Jarle and his gracious wife Aud Marit for their hospitality.

Tom Engelhardt, my editor at Pantheon, is keeping alive the great Maxwell Perkins tradition of editors who become genuinely engaged with the work their authors are struggling to bring to fruition. Tom richly deserves the praise one finds in the acknowledgment section of books he has been involved with; certainly this one is much improved for his ministrations. I also appreciate the cheerful assistance of Dan Cullen at Pantheon in the preparation of the manuscript.

Special thanks, also, to the fine secretarial staff of the Unversity of Wisconsin History Department, and particularly to the departmental secretary, Jane Mesler, and those who so efficiently and cheerfully typed successive drafts of this manuscript and related materials: Carla Jabs, Kathleen Kisselburgh, and Anita Olson.

I wish to express particular appreciation to my friend and admired senior colleague Merle Curti, a pioneer in two fields relevant to this study: intellectual history and peace studies. He has not only given unstinting encouragement, but also the benefit of his insight and experience.

Finally, my father, C. W. Boyer, shared with me his memories of a meeting with Albert Einstein in 1947, and my son Alex his extensive knowledge of science fiction. My entire family, including Katie and Alex, to whom this book is dedicated, and my wife Ann, have been most supportive and generous of spirit during my work on this book. This generosity is doubly impressive because this particular project not only involved the familiar but never easily resolved stress between family life and writing a book, but also for four years kept a difficult and threatening subject closer to the center of their awareness than they sometimes might have preferred.

Introduction

If a scholar a thousand years from now had no evidence about what had happened in the United States between 1945 and 1985 except the books produced by the cultural and intellectual historians of that era, he or she would hardly guess that such a thing as nuclear weapons had existed. We have studies of the evolution of nuclear strategy and some superb explorations of the political and diplomatic ramifications of the nuclear arms race, but few assessments of the bomb's effects on American culture and consciousness. We have somehow managed to avert our attention from the pervasive impact of the bomb on this dimension of our collective experience. As the journalist Robert Manoff recently observed: "Nuclear weapons have not and never will be an inert presence in American life. Merely by existing they have already set off chain reactions throughout American society and within every one of its institutions." [1]

Early in 1981, when I decided to attempt such a study, I was influenced, too, by what seemed a profound public apathy toward the threat of nuclear war. I hoped that the book I envisioned would help counteract that apathy. But almost immediately, the climate changed. The level of public attention and activist energy directed to the nuclear menace surged, and my own motivation shifted somewhat. I felt I might contribute a dimension of historical understanding to an issue whose origins often seemed as obscure as its present reality seemed inescapable. My students were clearly anxious about the nuclear threat, yet almost totally innocent of its history. In this respect, I sensed, they were not much different from the rest of society.

But no sooner did I begin to think about trying to fill in some of the gaps in our nuclear awareness than I found myself drawing back from the magnitude and amorphousness of the topic. How could one possibly define the nature and limits of such a study? The full dimensions of the challenge became vividly evident to me as I tried to sort out the ways that the nuclear reality had affected the consciousness of one individual: myself.

Of course, I had no delusions that I was Everyman. There were peculiarities in my background that might plausibly be seen as having particularly "sensitized" me to the issues of war and peace. Reared in the pacifist beliefs of the Brethren in Christ Church, a small denomination in the German Anabaptist tradition, I had early heard stories from my father of the harassment and even physical abuse he had experienced as a war resister in 1917–1918; later, when my turn came, I took the same route, spending two years with the Mennonite Central Committee in Europe in the 1950s as a conscientious objector.

Yet, despite my background, the nuclear arms race had not been a particular focus of attention for me since the late 1950s and early 1960s, when like others of my generation I was drawn into the campaign to stop nuclear testing. Indeed, I suspect it is not my particular upbringing, but experiences I share with most Americans of the postwar generation, that are relevant here. Even a few random probes of my nuclear consciousness have made clear to me how significantly my life has been influenced by the ever-present reality of the bomb.

The most obvious of these influences are those having to do with everyday life: the hours spent reading about the nuclear threat in the newspapers, hearing about it on television, being confronted with it even at the most unexpected moments. On a family camping trip to the West Coast in 1977, for example, we found in some of the most isolated regions of the country vast tracts marked "Off Limits" on the map. These, we soon realized, were missile installations. Closer to home, radioactive waste is now regularly transported across Wisconsin, and the northern part of the state, an area of lakes and woods where French *coureurs de bois* once roamed and where Menominee and Chippewa still live, is a prospective nuclear waste dump site. In these same woods, work is well along on the quaintly named Project ELF, an extra-low-frequency communications system for nuclear submarines. The earth itself, even in its most remote reaches, is being transformed into a nuclear landscape. As E. B. White wrote at the time of the first postwar atomic test in 1946: "Bikini lagoon, although we have never seen it, begins to seem like the one place in all the world we cannot spare. . . . It all seems unspeakably precious, like a lovely child stricken with a fatal disease."[2]

Or take another example. A few years ago, my family and I went to a local outfitters to investigate canoes. The salesperson recommended one made of Du Pont's Kevlar, a remarkably strong new synthetic. We followed his advice and have since spent many hours paddling Madison's lakes and surrounding rivers. Soon after, in an article about the MX missile, I noticed that the second-stage motor casings will be made of—guess what—*Kevlar,* which turns out to be a strategic product highly useful in missile technology. The same material that makes our canoe so durable will assure the smooth functioning of the missiles as they streak toward Moscow.

But the bomb's corrosive impact on the externals of life pales in comparison to its effect on the interior realm of consciousness and memory. As I probed this level of my nuclear experience, I discovered a whole locked roomful of recollections, beginning with the afternoon of August 6, 1945, when I read aloud the ominous-looking newspaper headline, mispronouncing the new word as "a-*tome*" since I had never heard anyone say it before.

Once the door is unlocked, other memories tumble out: Standing in a darkened room early in 1947, squinting into my atomic-viewer ring, straining to see the "swirling atoms" the Kix Cereal people had assured me would be visible. . . . Coming out of a Times Square movie theater at midnight on New Year's Eve, 1959, having just seen the end of the world in *On the Beach,* overwhelmed by the sheer *aliveness* of the raucous celebrators. . . . Feeling the knot tighten in my stomach as President Kennedy, in that abrasive, staccato voice, tells us we must all build fallout shelters as quickly as possible. . . . Watching the clock in Emerson Hall creep up toward 11 A.M. on October 25, 1962—Kennedy's deadline to the Russians during the Cuban missile crisis—half expecting a cataclysmic flash when the hour struck. . . . Overhearing my daughter's friend recently telling how her little sister hid under the bed when searchlights probed the sky a few nights earlier (a supermarket was having its grand opening), convinced the missiles were about to fall. And on and on and on . . .

But one's "nuclear consciousness" is not just a matter of isolated memories set apart because of their particular intensity. It is also a matter of perceptions more gradually arrived at. I have, for example, come to realize that the home town of my memory, Dayton, Ohio, the city to which my grandparents moved in the 1890s, where my parents spent most of their lives, and where I grew up, no longer exists. This happens to everyone, of course, but in my case it came with a nuclear twist: Dayton has become another node on the vast R&D grid that propels the nuclear arms race to new levels of menace. As its old enterprises—refrigerators, tires, automotive parts, tool-and-die-making—declined, nearby Wright-Patterson Air Force Base emerged as a major center of nuclear weapons research. With thirty-two thousand workers, the Pentagon is now Dayton's biggest employer, pumping $1.6 billion annually into the local economy.[3]

Even my sense of ancestral rootedness is now interwoven with images of nuclear menace and danger. In the summer of 1978, my brother Bill and I, finding ourselves together in Pennsylvania, took a little excursion to find the cemetery where some of our forebears who had migrated from Germany in the 1750s were buried. As we drove southward from Harrisburg along the Susquehanna, the looming concrete bulk of a nuclear power plant—Three Mile Island—suddenly hove into view. Almost literally in the shadows of those squat, hideous—and soon to be famous—towers, we found the small burial plot we were seeking.

Obviously more is involved in understanding one's nuclear experience than compiling lists of memories. So fully does the nuclear reality pervade my consciousness that it is hard to imagine what existence would have been like without it. It is as though the Bomb has become one of those categories of Being, like Space and Time, that, according to Kant, are built into the very structure of our minds, giving shape and meaning to all our perceptions. Am I alone in this feeling? I think not.

If even a superficial exploration of a single nuclear consciousness led in so many unexpected directions, how could I possibly presume to discuss the impact of the bomb on an entire culture? Would not a history of "nuclear" thought and culture become indistinguishable from a history of all contemporary thought and culture? My mind buzzed with interpretive possibilities. The wave of UFO sightings in the 1950s, for example: surely they were a manifestation of the fear of nuclear attack that had gripped America since August 1945. And what of the theories of extraterrestrial cataclysm recently advanced by some paleobiologists to account for the sudden disappearance of dinosaurs and certain other mass extinctions? Would they have emerged without our cultural preoccupation with the possible extinction of our own species through nuclear holocaust?

On a different plane, I found myself wondering how the large-scale psychological changes of our day are related to nuclear fear. Psychiatrists report an increasing incidence of narcissism among their patients: total self-absorption coupled with the lack of a strong self-image and the inability to commit oneself to long-term relationships or goals. Cultural observers, generalizing from such clinical observations, begin to speak of a "narcissistic society." Surely such profound psychological changes, if they are indeed occurring, must be dealt with in any study of the cultural impact of nuclear weapons.

Increasingly, the project I had mapped out threatened to slip out of control and flow off in all directions. If, as the *New Boston Review* has recently put it, "contemporary culture grows in a dark place, beneath the shadow of the nuclear threat," how could one deal adequately with this topic without dealing with the whole of contemporary culture?[4]

I responded to these unsettling reflections by making some fairly radical decisions about the limits of my study. First, I would build my work on the kinds of evidence historians are trained to use: the vast literature in which Americans directly and explicitly discussed the atomic bomb and its meaning, the wealth of cultural material—from the most rarified to the most ubiquitous—clearly influenced by the bomb. Such a foundation, I hope, will provide a grounding for ventures into even more tantalizingly speculative realms. Second, rather than trying to survey forty years of nuclear culture, I would go back to the beginning, 1945 through 1950, the years when Americans first confronted the bomb, struggled against it, and absorbed it into the fabric of the culture.

But even when I placed these limits on my study, I soon found myself overwhelmed by the wealth of evidence. Wherever I dipped into the early postwar cultural record, from any big glossy picture magazine to scholarly conferences to country music to the black press, I encountered the bomb. The problem was not finding material, but deciding when to turn off the tap. The real challenge was how to organize and interpret this Niagara of evidence. This book is interpretive as well as descriptive, but I certainly do not see my interpretive schema as definitive. I hope what I have written will be viewed not as the last word, but as a point of departure for further work.

Another surprise as I narrowed my focus to 1945–1950 was the realization of how quickly contemporary observers understood that a profoundly unsettling new cultural factor had been introduced—that the bomb had transformed not only military strategy and international relations, but the fundamental ground of culture and consciousness. Anne O'Hare McCormick's comment in the *New York Times* on August 8, 1945, that the atomic bomb had caused "an explosion in men's minds as shattering as the obliteration of Hiroshima" was echoed by literally scores of observers in these earliest moments of the atomic age.[5] The fallout from this "explosion in men's minds," then, became my subject.

I have been repeatedly struck, too, at how uncannily familiar much of the early response to the bomb seems: the visions of atomic devastation, the earnest efforts to rouse people to resist such a fate, the voices seeking to soothe or deflect these fears, the insistence that security lay in greater technical expertise and in more and bigger weaponry. I gradually realized that what I was uncovering was, in fact, the earliest versions of the themes that still dominate our nuclear discourse today. All the major elements of our contemporary engagement with the nuclear reality took shape literally within days of Hiroshima. (On August 26, 1945, for instance, the *Washington Post* was already vigorously discussing whether some type of Star-Wars-like defense could be developed to destroy incoming nuclear missiles. A science writer felt sure such a defense was possible—he spoke of "rays" that would disrupt the missile's control system. The *Post*'s editorial writers, however, were skeptical: "The possibility of discovering any defense against atom bomb rockets shot from thousands of miles away seems . . . out of the question. . . . As far as we can discover, there is no loophole or joker in this new contract with the devil."[6]) This sense of déjà vu was both an unexpected and in some ways a profoundly discouraging discovery whose implications I shall return to at the end of this book.

By the Bomb's Early Light, then, is an effort to go back to the earliest stages of our long engagement with nuclear weapons. Unless we recover this lost segment of our cultural history, we cannot fully understand the world in which we live, nor be as well equipped as we might to change it. Again the *New Boston Review* editors put the matter well: The struggle to escape this dark place, they continued, will ultimately "not be just political. It will be cultural. Nuclear weapons, after all, are a product of our culture. . . . As artists, writers, critics, and readers, we have to recognize that our history and culture created and perfected nuclear weaponry. . . . American artists must face the present danger and give voice to it." I would add historians to this list as well.

As is appropriate, this book will be read and judged by my professional peers as a piece of scholarship like any other. I hope it will not seem presumptuous to say that it is also intended as a contribution, however flawed, to the process by which we are again, at long last, trying to confront, emotionally as well as intellectually, the supreme menace of our age.

Henry Adams once wrote: "No honest historian can take part with—or against—the forces he has to study. To him, even the extinction of the human race should merely be a fact to be grouped with other vital statistics."[7] I readily confess that I have not achieved Adams's austere standard of professional objectivity. This book is a product of experiences outside the library as well as inside, and it is not the work of a person who can view the prospect of human extinction with scholarly detachment.

One

First
Reactions

1.

"The Whole World Gasped"

Just as people recall the circumstances under which they first heard the news of the attack on Pearl Harbor, so they will remember how the atomic bomb first burst upon their consciousness.

—*Scientific Monthly*, September 1945

August 6, 1945. President Truman was aboard the U.S.S. Augusta, steaming across the Atlantic on his way home from the Postdam conference, when he received the word: an American atomic bomb had been successfully detonated over Hiroshima, Japan. Excitedly Truman rushed to the officers' wardroom and told them the news. The navy men burst into cheers.

At the White House, it was a slow news day and only a few reporters were on duty. In mid-morning, assistant press secretary Eben Ayres strolled into the press room and told the reporters something might be coming later. At 10:45 A.M., Eastern War Time, Ayres released the story. At first the reporters seemed to hesitate, then they rushed for the telephones. The first bulletin went out over the Associated Press wire at 11:03.

John Haynes Holmes, minister of the Community Church of New York City, was vacationing at his summer cottage in Kennebunk, Maine, that day. Soon after, he described his feelings on hearing the news: "Everything else seemed suddenly to become insignificant. I seemed to grow cold, as though I had been transported to the waste spaces of the moon. The summer beauty seemed to vanish, and the waves of the sea to be pounding upon the shores of an empty world. . . . For I knew that the final crisis in human history had come. What that atomic bomb had done to Japan, it could do to us." [1]

How does a people react when the entire basis of its existence is fundamentally altered? Most such changes occur gradually; they are more discernible to historians than to the individuals living through them. The nuclear era was different. It burst upon the world with terrifying suddenness. From the earliest moments, the American people recognized that things would never be the same again.

Perhaps the best way to convey a sense of the earliest days of what almost immediately began to be called the "Atomic Age" is not to impose too much order or coherence on them retrospectively. Out of the initial confusion of emotions and welter of voices, certain cultural themes would quickly emerge. But first, the Event.

The first to hear the news that distant Monday were those who happened to be near a radio at midday—housewives, children, the elderly, war workers enjoying a vacation day at home:

> This is Don Goddard with your news at noon. A little less than an hour ago, newsmen were called to the White House down in Washington, and there they were read a special announcement written by President Truman. . . . This was the story of a new bomb, so powerful that only the imagination of a trained scientist could dream of its existence. Without qualification, the President said that Allied scientists have now harnessed the basic power of the universe. They have harnessed the atom.[2]

As the sultry August afternoon wore on, the news spread by word of mouth. The evening papers reported it in screaming headlines:

ATOMIC BOMB LOOSED ON JAPAN
ONE EQUALS 20,000 TONS OF TNT
FIRST TARGET IS ARMY BASE OF HIROSHIMA
DUST AND SMOKE OBSCURE RESULT.

On his six o'clock newscast, Lowell Thomas of CBS radio, already assuming that everyone had heard the story, began in his folksy, avuncular voice:

> That news about the atomic bomb overshadows everything else today; and the story of the dropping of the first one on Japan. The way the Japanese describe last night's raid on Hiroshima indicates that this one bomb was so destructive that the Japs thought they had been blasted by squadrons of B-29s.[3]

Meanwhile, over at NBC, the dean of radio news commentators, H. V. Kaltenborn, was preparing the script of his 7:45 P.M. broadcast. The first draft began by describing the atomic bomb as "one of the greatest scientific developments in the history of man." Hastily, Kaltenborn penciled in a punchier opening: "Anglo-Saxon science has developed a new explosive 2,000 times as destructive as any known before."[4]

Continuing in his stern, professorial voice, Kaltenborn struck a somber note: "For all we know, we have created a Frankenstein! We must assume that with the passage of only a little time, an improved form of the new weapon we use today can be turned against us."

Kaltenborn was far from alone in perceiving the nightmarish possiblities. Science may have "signed the mammalian world's death warrant," warned the *St. Louis Post-Dispatch* on August 7, "and deeded an earth in ruins to the ants." A *Milwaukee Journal* editorial on the same day speculated about "a self-perpetuating chain of atomic destruction" that, like "a forest fire sweeping before high winds," could obliterate the entire planet.

In a broadcast that evening, Don Goddard added a chilling concreteness to these ominous forebodings:

> There is reason to believe tonight that our new atomic bomb destroyed the entire Japanese city of Hiroshima in a single blast. . . . It would be the same as Denver, Colorado, with a population of 350,000 persons being there one moment, and wiped out the next.[5]

Thus in the earliest moments of the nuclear era, the fear that would be the constant companion of Americans for the rest of their lives, and of millions not yet born in 1945, had already found urgent expression.

The carefully orchestrated government press releases, illustrated with a set of officially approved photographs, only partially allayed the gathering fear and uncertainty. Hiroshima itself was enveloped in an eerie silence that the outside world only gradually penetrated. "As for the actual havoc wrought by that first atomic bomb," said Lowell Thomas on August 7, "one earlier report was that the photographic observation planes on the job shortly after the cataclysmic blast at Hiroshima had been unable to penetrate the cloud of smoke and dust that hung over that devastated area." An air force spokesman on Okinawa said Hiroshima "seemed to have been ground into dust by a giant foot."

At a hectic news conference on Guam, Col. Paul Tibbets, Jr., pilot of the *Enola Gay,* the atomic-bomb plane, compared the cloud over the city to "boiling dust." Navy captain William S. Parsons, the scientist responsible for the final bomb assembly aboard the plane, extended an open palm to represent Hiroshima and said that only the fingers—the docks jutting into Hiroshima Bay—had been visible after the blast. The news conference was continually interrupted by a cigar-chomping Gen. Curtis LeMay with a terse, "No, you better not say that."[6]

Speculation and "human interest" stories supplemented the tightly controlled official releases. Newsmen compared the atomic bomb to the 1917 explosion of a munitions ship in the harbor of Halifax, Nova Scotia, that had killed eighteen hundred people. They interviewed the wife of Gen. Leslie R. Groves, military chief of the Manhattan Project ("I didn't know anything about it until this morning, the same as everyone else"). They sought out Eleanor Roosevelt, who gave FDR's posthumous benediction to the atomic bomb: "The President would have been much relieved had he known we had it."

Journalists strove for a local angle: "DEADLIEST WEAPONS IN WORLD'S HISTORY MADE IN SANTA FE VICINITY" was the headline carried by the *Santa Fe New Mexican* over its story about tiny Los Alamos, nerve center of the Manhattan Project. Tennessee papers played up what the *New York Times* dramatically called the "secret empire" at Oak Ridge, where work on the atomic bomb had been conducted in a vast "labryinthine concrete fortress." In Hanford, Washington, reporters found the local residents surprised to learn that the vast secret facility nearby had been making plutonium; they had assumed poison gas. The Albany newspapers noted that General Groves was the son of a Presbyterian minister who had once had a church in that city.[7]

The secret atomic-bomb test conducted at Alamogordo, New Mexico, on July 16, 1945, was now revealed. Lowell Thomas quoted a railway engineer who had been in the cab of the *Santa Fe* over 100 miles away at the moment of the predawn test: "All at once, it seemed as if the sun suddenly appeared out of the darkness. . . . The glare lasted about three minutes, then all was dark again." Newspaper stories told of Georgia Green, a blind girl in Albuquerque, 120 miles from Alamogordo, who at the moment of detonation had cried out, "What was that?"[8]

On August 9, with Hiroshima still dominating the nation's consciousness, came a further shock: a second atomic bomb had been dropped on the Japanese city of Nagasaki. "It is an awful responsibility which has come to us," intoned President Truman on nationwide radio the next day. "We thank God that it has come to us instead of to our enemies; and we pray that He may guide us to use it in His ways and for His purposes."[9]

Amid the stupefying rush of events, people could only assure each other that something momentous, almost unfathomable, had occurred. "[One] forgets the effect on Japan . . . ," said the *New York Herald Tribune*, "as one senses the foundations of one's own universe trembling." The papers were full of such observations. The bomb, commented *Christian Century* magazine, had "cast a spell of dark foreboding over the spirit of humanity." In the *New York Times*'s first letter-to-the-editor about the atomic bomb (forerunner of thousands that would appear in the years to follow), A. Garcia Diaz of New York City spoke of the "creeping feeling of apprehension" pervading the nation. (With characteristic understatement, the *Times* cap-

tioned this letter: "Atomic Bomb Poses Problem.") In the *New York Sun,*
correspondent Phelps Adams described the mood in Washington: "For forty-
eight hours now, the new bomb has been virtually the only topic of conversation and discussion. . . . For two days it has been an unusual thing to see
a smile among the throngs that crowd the streets. The entire city is pervaded
by a kind of sense of oppression." Political cartoonist D. R. Fitzpatrick of
the *St. Louis Post-Dispatch* pictured a tiny human figure desperately clinging
to a pair of reins attached to an awesome lightning bolt streaking across the
skies. The caption was: "Little Man, Where To?" [10]

On August 10, a day after the Nagasaki bombing, the Japanese offered
to surrender if Emperor Hirohito could keep his throne. The Allies agreed,
and on August 14, World War II ended. The nation's cities erupted in
frenzied celebration, but the underlying mood remained sober and apprehensive. In Washington, the *New Republic* reported, the war's end did nothing
to mitigate the post-Hiroshima gloom or the "curious new sense of insecurity, rather incongruous in the face of military victory." Thanks to the atomic
bomb, wrote an official of the Rockefeller Foundation a few weeks later, the
nation's mood at the moment of victory was bleaker than in December 1941
when much of the Pacific Fleet had lain in ruins at Pearl Harbor. [11] "Seldom,
if ever," agreed CBS radio commentator Edward R. Murrow on August 12,
"has a war ended leaving the victors with such a sense of uncertainty and
fear, with such a realization that the future is obscure and that survival is
not assured." [12]

On August 17, amid stories of the surrender ceremonies in Tokyo Bay,
H. V. Kaltenborn reported a sobering assessment by air force general H. H.
("Hap") Arnold of what an atomic war would be like. "As we listen to the
newscast tonight, as we read our newspapers tomorrow," said Kaltenborn,
"let us think of the mass murder which will come with World War III." A
few days later he added, "We are like children playing with a concentrated
instrument of death whose destructive potential our little minds cannot
grasp."

"The knowledge of victory was as charged with sorrow and doubt as
with joy and gratitude," observed *Time* in its first postwar issue.

> In what they said and did, men are still, as in the aftershock of a great
> wound, bemused and only semi-articulate. . . . But in the dark depths
> of their minds and hearts, huge forms moved and silently arrayed
> themselves: Titans, arranging out of the chaos an age in which victory
> was already only the shout of a child in the street.

The war itself had shrunk to "minor significance," *Time* added, and its
outcome seemed the "most grimly Pyrrhic of victories." [13]

The best known of these early postwar editorials, Norman Cousins's

"Modern Man Is Obsolete," which appeared in the *Saturday Review* four days after the Japanese surrender, exuded this spirit of apprehension. "Whatever elation there is in the world today," wrote Cousins,

> is severely tempered by . . . a primitive fear, the fear of the unknown, the fear of forces man can neither channel nor comprehend. This fear is not new; in its classical form it is the fear of irrational death. But overnight it has become intensified, magnified. It has burst out of the subconscious and into the conscious, filling the mind with primordial apprehensions.[14]

Among book publishers, the post-Hiroshima race was won by Pocket Books, which on August 17 published *The Atomic Age Opens,* a 256-page paperback compendium of news stories, editorials, and pronouncements by world leaders intended to help those who were "grasping for solid ideas through the haze of the first excitement." The general tenor of these utterances is summed up in one chapter title: "The Whole World Gasped."[15]

Perhaps the most important print medium through which the American people formed their initial impressions of the atomic bomb was Henry Luce's photo magazine *Life,* with its five million-plus circulation. *Life* devoted much of its August 20, 1945, issue to the bomb; here, in full-page photographs of Hiroshima and Nagasaki, many Americans encountered for the first time the towering mushroom-shaped cloud that would become the quintessential visual symbol of the new era. Hiroshima, said *Life,* had literally been "blown . . . off the face of the earth." Nagasaki, it added, choosing its words carefully, had been "disemboweled."

Underscoring a point made frequently in this early postwar period, *Life* noted that the atomic bombings were simply an extension of the massive B-29 "fire-bomb missions" under General LeMay that had already "ripped the guts out of Japan's great cities." These raids, *Life* explained, relied on

> the newly developed "jelly" bombs, which were aimed at different spots in a city and calculated to merge into one huge conflagration. Airmen called them "burn jobs" and a good-sized "burn job" did almost as much damage to property as the atomic bomb did and it also killed almost as many people.

In a lengthy background feature, *Life* insisted that the most important story concerning the debut of atomic energy was the scientific one: "Even the appalling fact that some 100,000 Japanese had died seemed incidental to the fact—which touched the destiny of everyone alive—that a way had been found to release the forces which killed these 100,000." Through several pages of simplified text and drawings, *Life* introduced its readers to the mysteries of the atom, uranium, and nuclear fission.

But what did it all mean? In an editorial titled "The Atomic Age" and in an essay, "The Atom Bomb and Future War," by *New York Times* military analyst Hanson W. Baldwin, *Life* tried to place the devastating events in context. Baldwin minced no words. As soon as the long-range rockets developed by the Germans were fitted with atomic warheads capable of "destroy[ing] cities at one breath," he wrote, echoing H. V. Kaltenborn, mankind would have "unleashed a Frankenstein monster." If conventional infantrymen had any future role at all, Baldwin continued, it would be as "an army of moles, specially trained in underground fighting."

In its editorial, by contrast, *Life* strove for a hopeful note: Atomic fission was a major breakthrough in humankind's long struggle to understand and subdue nature, and the world should be grateful that "Prometheus, the subtle artificer and friend of man, is still an American citizen." The future would be different, certainly, but it need not terrify. Even Hanson Baldwin's grim predictions could be viewed in an optimistic light. After all, "consider the ant, whose social problems much resemble man's":

> Ants have lived on this planet for 50 times as many millions of years as man. In all that time they have not committed race suicide and they have not abolished warfare either. Their nations rise and fall and never wholly merge. Constructing beautiful urban palaces and galleries, many ants have long lived underground in entire satisfaction.

But whatever the long-range reassurance offered by entomology or Greek mythology, the compelling immediate fact was that atomic fission had just been used to vaporize two cities. To its credit, *Life* confronted this fact squarely. The increasing ferocity of strategic bombing since the late 1930s, it said, "led straight to Hiroshima, and Hiroshima was, and was intended to be, almost pure *Schrecklichkeit* [terror]." All the belligerents, the United States no less than Nazi Germany, had emerged from World War II "with radically different practices and standards of permissible behavior toward others."

Despite these bleak reflections, the editorial concluded on a note of moral elevation. Above all else, the atomic bomb raised "the question of power. The atomic scientists had to learn new ways to control it; so now does political man":

> Power in society has never been controlled by anything but morality. . . . Our sole safeguard against the very real danger of a reversion to

barbarism is the kind of morality which compels the individual conscience, be the group right or wrong. The individual conscience against the atomic bomb? Yes, there is no other way.

No limits are set to our Promethean ingenuity, provided we remember that we are not Jove.[16]

Many readers responded with lavish praise. The editorial was a reminder, said one, that "the simplest language is the best vehicle for the profoundest thoughts."[17] But what was *Life* actually saying? Evidently this: the same individuals who had acquiesced in the degradation of warfare into *Schrecklichkeit* were now being exhorted to confront the atomic bomb with consciences finely tuned to moral considerations. The American Prometheus who had assumed Jove's mantle and obliterated two cities with his newly discovered atomic thunderbolts was now being sternly told that he must resist the temptation ever again to play god.

After the initial shock, Americans seemingly rallied and took the atomic bomb in stride. Comedians (not all of them professionals) strained to find humor in the new weapon. A radio newscaster commented that Hiroshima "looked like Ebbetts Field after a game between the Giants and the Dodgers." Others joked that Japan was suffering from "atomic ache." Only one radio entertainer—Milton Berle—explicitly refused to make jokes about the atomic bomb.[18]

Within hours of Eben Ayres's announcement, the bar at the Washington Press Club offered an "Atomic Cocktail"—a greenish blend of Pernod and gin. A letter in the *Philadelphia Inquirer* suggested that atomic vitamin pills be given to the slumping Athletics. *Time* said the Alamogordo test had "proved the bomb a smash-hit." Updating an old joke, *Life* reported that Oak Ridge workers, when asked what they were building, had replied: "We're making the fronts of horses, and shipping them to Washington for final assembly." One of the odder of the post-Hiroshima headlines appeared in the *Milwaukee Journal* on August 8: "The New Bomb Is So Staggering to the Mind, One Doesn't Dare Pun 'Up and Atom!' " *Stars and Stripes,* the military newspaper, reported one GI's comment: "Wait a minute, I got a gag for you. Just put in your paper: 'Now we're cooking—with atomic bombs!' and don't forget to credit me." On August 13, the *Chicago Tribune* ran an entire column of "Atomic Anecdotes." The *New Yorker,* while taking a dim view of all this "humor," dutifully recorded some of it "for the benefit of future social historians."[19]

Nor could American business resist the bomb's commercial possibilities. Within days of the Hiroshima bombing, department stores were running "Atomic Sales" and advertisers offering "Atomic Results." Somewhat later, a jewelry company on New York's Fifth Avenue advertised:

BURSTING FURY—Atomic Inspired Pin and Earring. New fields to conquer with Atomic jewelry. The pearled bomb bursts into a fury of dazzling colors in mock rhinestones, emeralds, rubies, and sapphires. . . . As daring to wear as it was to drop the first atom bomb. Complete set $24.75.

Other enterprising entrepreneurs gathered the greenish, glass-like fused sand at the Alamogordo test site and (oblivious to the danger of radioactivity) fashioned it into costume jewelry, which they advertised nationally. The Atomic Age Publishing Company of Denver announced a new magazine, *The Atom,* with a goal of one hundred thousand subscribers. By 1947, the Manhattan telephone directory listed forty-five businesses that had appropriated the magic word, including the Atomic Undergarment Company.

In 1946 the General Mills Corporation offered an "Atomic 'Bomb' Ring" for fifteen cents and a Kix cereal boxtop. Look into the "sealed atom chamber" in "the gleaming aluminum warhead," the advertisement said, and "see genuine atoms SPLIT to smithereens!" "Based on a scientific principle used in laboratories," the ring was "perfectly safe" and "guaranteed not to blow everything sky high." It was loaded with extras, including "bombardier's insignia embossed on cylindrical bomb grip." In fact, this little promotional premium managed to anticipate several cultural themes that would obsess America in the years ahead. Behind the bomb warhead was a space for secret messages: "You can outwit enemies by concealing a message of 100 words in this strategic compartment," the cereal-box copy promised; "It's so deceptive that anyone plotting to spy against you will be thrown off guard." Some 750,000 American children deluged General Mills with orders for their very own "Atomic 'Bomb' Ring." [20]

In Hollywood, writers rushed to incorporate the atomic bomb into their movie scripts. The first film to accomplish this feat, *The House on 92nd Street,* was released in late September 1945. A spy thriller about Nazi agents operating in New York City early in World War II, it was revised at the last minute to make the object of the agents' quest be "Process 97, the secret ingredient of the atomic bomb."

The music industry was quick to cash in on the new national preoccupation as well. The Slim Gaillard Quartet recorded "Atomic Cocktail" in December 1945. The following year brought "Atom Buster" and "Atom Polka." In the interesting "Atom and Evil" by the San Francisco–based Golden Gate Quartet, a black gospel group, atomic energy is portrayed as an innocent, well-intentioned man seduced by a jaded "Miss Evil." A California company marketed a line of jazz recordings under the "Atomic" label complete with the picture of a mushroom-shaped cloud. [21]

The complex psychological link between atomic destruction and Eros (a link that at the time of America's first postwar atomic test in 1946 led a French fashion designer to christen his new bathing suit the "Bikini") was established very early. Within days of Hiroshima, burlesque houses in Los Angeles were advertising "Atom Bomb Dancers." In early September, putting aside its pontifical robes for a moment, *Life* fulfilled a Hollywood press agent's dream with a full-page cheesecake photograph of a well-endowed MGM starlet who had been officially dubbed "The Anatomic Bomb." In "Atom Bomb Baby," a pop song of 1947, the bomb became a metaphor for sexual arousal.[22]

Despite the outpouring of post-Hiroshima atomic ephemera, it would be wrong to conclude that Americans took the bomb casually or that its impact quickly faded. Just below the surface, powerful currents of anxiety and apprehension surged through the culture. As one cultural observer noted in January 1946, the attempts to make light of the atomic bomb were simply a by-product of the more profound underlying reaction: "paralyzing fear."[23]

Some observers found this reaction rather contemptible. "Fantasy is running wild," complained Maj. Alexander de Seversky in the February 1946 *Reader's Digest*. "The hysteria with which Hiroshima was greeted . . . does not reflect credit on the United States," agreed a Yale University military strategist later that year.[24] But whatever they thought of it, contemporary social observers agreed that the news of the atomic bomb had had a devastating effect, the impact made all the more traumatic by the unexpectedness of Truman's announcement. A flurry of journalistic stories in 1939 had publicized breakthroughs in the esoteric field of nuclear fission (arousing sufficient uneasiness that physicist Enrico Fermi went on CBS radio to assure the country there was "no cause for alarm"), but then a blanket of secrecy had descended and the atom largely disappeared from the public consciousness.[25]

The spring and summer of 1945 had brought vague talk of new and terrible secret weapons, and the Postdam Declaration of July 26 had threatened the Japanese with "complete and utter destruction." Such isolated and generalized allusions, however, had prepared Americans no better than the Japanese for August 6. Except to a tiny circle of scientists and government officials, Truman's announcement came as a bolt from the blue.

To be sure, the immediate reaction was also influenced by the fact that for nearly four years Japan had been the hated, treacherous enemy. Vengeance was on many minds. "The Japanese began the war from the air at Pearl Harbor," said President Truman grimly; "They have been repaid manyfold." The moral symmetry of this equation appealed to many commentators and editorial writers. "No tears of sympathy will be shed in America for the Japanese people," said the *Omaha Morning World Herald* on August 8. "Had they possessed a comparable weapon at Pearl Harbor, would they have hesitated to use it?" The *New York Times's* first editorial comment on the bomb, "Our Answer to Japan," was no less vindictive. The devastation of Hiroshima, it said, was "but a sample" of what lay ahead. More atomic bombs were being built and could be "dropped on Japan at any time our military leaders choose."

"We are lucky to have found The Thing and are able to speed the war against the Japanese *before the enemy can devise countermeasures,*" observed the Communist Party's *New York Daily Worker.* "Nip propagandists" protesting the atomic bomb should recall who started the war, said the *Los Angeles Times* on August 8. The "whining, whimpering, complaining" Japs, agreed the *Philadelphia Inquirer* three days later, were "good at dishing it out," but with the tables turned, "they now want to quit." "The Jap Must Choose," proclaimed *Newsweek* on August 13, "between surrender and annihilation." Outweighing the bomb's "wholesale slaughter," agreed the *Nation* on August 18, was its "spectacular success" in forcing the Japanese surrender. Two billion dollars, it added, "was never better spent."

"When the Atomic Bomb Fell," a country-music song of December 1945, praised the bomb for giving the enemy just what he deserved:

> Smoke and fire it did flow,
> Through the land of Tokyo.
> There was brimstone and dust everywhere.
> When it all cleared away,
> There the cruel Jap did lay,
> The answer to our fighting boy's prayer.[26]

Many political cartoonists quickly assimilated this new motif into propagandistic anti-Japanese cartoons. A *Philadelphia Inquirer* cartoon of August 7 portrayed a grotesque, apelike brute staring up in dumb wonder as an atomic bomb exploded overhead. The cartoon in *PM,* the liberal New York City daily, was totally blank except for the words "So sorry" in a balloon at the top. The *Chicago Tribune* pictured the dove of peace flying over Japan, an atomic bomb in its beak. An *Atlanta Constitution* cartoon showing bodies flying into the air over Hiroshima was captioned: "Land of the Rising Sons."[27]

But given the heavily racist wartime climate, post-Hiroshima vindictiveness proved surprisingly short-lived and was quickly overshadowed by a growing fear of what might lie ahead. The bomb might indeed force Japan to her knees, wrote Hanson W. Baldwin in the *New York Times* on August 7, but it would also bring incalculable new dangers. "We have," he concluded bleakly, "sowed the whirlwind."[28]

Nor did the promise of a peacetime atomic Utopia initially do much to diminish post-Hiroshima fear. Typically, the editor of a religious periodical noted in September 1945 that such speculations were being advanced, but confessed that "at the moment we can visualize only the unutterably shattering effect upon civilization and the wholesale destruction of millions of human beings." [29]

The darkening national mood was intensified by the reaction from abroad. While the news of Hiroshima and Nagasaki did not have as sharp and immediate an impact in Europe (itself devastated and prostrate) as it did in the United States, awareness of the bomb's ominous implications came quickly. In a statement that somehow gained force from its stilted, Latinate English, the Vatican newspaper *Osservatore Romano* declared on August 7: "The last twilight of the war is colored by mortal flames never before seen on the horizons of the universe, from its heavenly dawn to this infernal era. This war gives us a catastrophic conclusion that seems not to put an end to its apocalyptic surprises." In contrast to President Truman's gloating, Winston Churchill struck a somber note: "This revelation of the secrets of nature, long mercifully withheld from man," he declared, "should arouse the most solemn reflections in the mind and conscience of every human being capable of comprehension." [30]

Reinforced by such pronouncements from abroad, the "Great Fear" was open, palpable, and starkly literal in its expression. Newsman Don Goddard, as we have seen, quickly transmuted the devastation of Hiroshima into visions of American cities in smoldering ruins, and millions of Americans soon made the same imaginative leap. Physically untouched by the war, the United States at the moment of victory perceived itself as naked and vulnerable. Sole possessors and users of a devastating new instrument of mass destruction, Americans envisioned themselves not as a potential threat to other peoples, but as potential victims. "In that terrible flash 10,000 miles away, men here have seen not only the fate of Japan, but have glimpsed the future of America," wrote James Reston in the *New York Times*.

The *Milwaukee Journal* on August 8 published a large map of the city overlaid by concentric circles of destruction. And worse lay ahead. The primitive atomic bombs of 1945, observed the *New York Times* on August 12, were analogous to "the steam engine of James Watt, the telegraph of Morse, the flying machines of the Wrights." As soon as the atomic bomb was paired up with the guided missile, speculated the *Detroit News* on August 17, the threat to civilization would rise to "a new pitch of terror." In an interview with the *New Yorker,* John W. Campbell, Jr., the editor of *Astounding Science Fiction,* offered a similar vision of World War III: "Every major city will be wiped out in thirty minutes. . . . New York will be a slag heap. . . . Radioactive energy . . . will leave the land uninhabitable for periods ranging from ten months to five hundred years, depending on the size of the bomb." Speaking on a New York radio station days after Hiroshima, the sociologist Harvey W. Zorbaugh (a member of the wartime Committee for National Morale) predicted "an armament race such as the world has never seen." [31] The life expectancy of the human species, said the *Washington Post* on August 26, had "dwindled immeasurably in the course of two brief weeks."

From our contemporary perspective, such fears seem so familiar as to be almost trite, but it is important to recognize how *quickly* Americans began to articulate them. Years before the world's nuclear arsenals made such a holocaust likely or even possible, the prospect of global annihilation already filled the national consciousness. This awareness and the bone-deep fear it engendered are the fundamental psychological realities underlying the broader intellectual and cultural responses of this period.

This primal fear of extinction cut across all political and ideological lines, from the staunchly conservative *Chicago Tribune,* which wrote bleakly of an atomic war that would leave Earth "a barren waste, in which the survivors of the race will hide in caves or live among ruins," to such liberal voices as the *New Republic,* which offered an almost identical vision of a conflict that would "obliterate all the great cities of the belligerents, [and] bring industry and technology to a grinding halt, . . . [leaving only] scattered remnants of humanity living on the periphery of civilization." [32]

This fear pervaded all society, from nuclear physicists and government leaders to persons who barely grasped what had happened, but who sensed that it was deeply threatening. Indeed, the more knowledgeable and highly placed the individual, it seemed, the greater the unease. The "strange disquiet" and "very great apprehension" the atomic bomb had left in its wake, wrote theologian Reinhold Niebuhr, was particularly intense among "the more sober and thoughtful sections of our nation." Eugene Rabinowitch, a Manhattan Project chemist at the University of Chicago, later recalled walking the streets of Chicago in the summer of 1945 haunted by visions of "the sky suddenly lit by a giant fireball, the steel skeletons of skyscrapers bending into grotesque shapes and their masonry raining down into the streets below, until a great cloud of dust rose and settled over the crumbling city." As the members of the U.S. Strategic Bombing Survey probed the ruins of Hiroshima and Nagasaki in September 1945, an "insistent question" formed itself in their minds: "What if the target for the bomb had been an American city?" [33]

So palpable was the depression in Washington, D.C., wrote newsman Phelps Adams, that many were admitting "they would be happier if this $2,000,000,000 gamble had failed," or if the new knowledge could be "bundled up in a sack and lost in the river like an unwanted kitten." The malaise gripping the capital, agreed the *New Republic,* was not rooted in dismay over what the atomic bomb had already done, but in "thoughts of its future use elsewhere and specifically against ourselves or our children." Even if the secret remained secure for fifteen years, said radio commentator

Elmer Davis on December 30, 1945, that was a short time "for people who are raising children."[34]

Children were on many minds in these unsettled weeks. *Life* flippantly suggested that a generation weaned on Flash Gordon would be unfazed by the atomic bomb; but within days of Hiroshima, the *New Yorker* reported this moment observed among children at play in Manhattan:

> For years the playground in Washington Square has resounded to the high-strung anh-anh-anh of machine guns and the long-drawn-out whine of high-velocity shells. Last Saturday morning a great advance was made. We watched a military man of seven or eight climb onto a seesaw, gather a number of his staff officers around him, and explain the changed situation. "Look," he said, "I'm an atomic bomb. I just go 'boom.' Once. Like this." He raised his arms, puffed out his cheeks, jumped down from the seesaw, and went "Boom!" Then he led his army away, leaving Manhattan in ruins behind him.

Some time later, another observer of juvenile life in New York City noted a change in the Broadway penny arcades: "Where during the war for a nickel you could try your luck shooting at a helpless parachutist as he drifted toward the ground, you can now try your luck at wiping out a whole city, with an atomic bomb—all for five cents."[35]

As the historian shifts focus to the level of individual experience, the evidence becomes tantalizingly fragmentary: the child who, in a prayer shortly after Hiroshima, asked God to let his family all die together; the little girl who, when asked what she wanted to be when she grew up, replied "alive"; the young mother in Pelham Manor, New York, who had just given birth to her second son when the Hiroshima news came and who three days later recorded her feelings in a letter to H. V. Kaltenborn:

> Since then I have hardly been able to smile, the future seems so utterly grim for our two little boys. Most of the time I have been in tears or near-tears, and fleeting but torturing regrets that I have brought children into the world to face such a dreadful thing as this have shivered through me. It seems that it will be for them all their lives like living on a keg of dynamite which may go off at any moment, and which undoubtedly will go off before their lives have progressed very far.[36]

Such scattered evidence gives us a glimpse into the consciousness and culture of childhood, as well as the concerns of adults trying to fathom the bomb's impact on the generation that would grow up in its shadow. It is perhaps noteworthy that John Hersey chose to conclude his influential 1946 work *Hiroshima* with the recollections of a ten-year-old survivor. The lad's

Enter the mushroom cloud. Photographs like this one taken over Nagasaki and described in *Life* as "a big mushroom of smoke and dust" were widely reprinted in newspapers and magazines in August 1945, quickly becoming the universally recognized visual symbol of atomic-age menace.

Des Moines could be next. Newspapers brought the word in stark headlines: a single bomb could now destroy a city. In the editorial cartoon, a newly unleashed atom menaces a terrified world.

"...and then the next thing, some general comes out and says the first _atom_ bomb is obsolete!"

Within two weeks of Hiroshima, a *New Yorker* cartoon envisioned a nuclear arms race with weapons that would make the 1945-model atomic bomb seem antiquated.

The many faces of nuclear fear. This illustration from John W. Campbell's 1947 popularization *The Atomic Story* was captioned: "In a cave or forgotten cellar, an atomic bomb can soon be set up."

For a brief, intense moment, world government or the international control of atomic energy seemed to offer an escape from terror. But as this 1947 Herblock cartoon illustrates, such hopes proved short-lived.

Dreamscapes of the nuclear future. At the end of *Life*'s "36-Hour War" (November 19, 1945), technicians measure radioactivity in the rubble of Manhattan as the marble lions of the New York Public Library direct their unblinking gaze over the devastated city.

account is terse and noncommital, but Hersey does not assume that the emotional effects of the experience were therefore negligible. "It would be impossible to say," he observes, "what horrors were embedded in the minds of the children who lived through the day of the bombing in Hiroshima."[37] Comparable fears about American children contributed to the larger uneasiness that seeped through the culture in the weeks after August 6, 1945.

Rather than diminishing, this mood deepened as weeks stretched into months. America was in the grip of a "fear psychosis," said anthropologist Robert Redfield in November 1945; atomic anxiety had become "a nightmare in the minds of men." *The First One Hundred Days of the Atomic Age,* a paperback published in late November, offered yet another potpourri of statements still "pouring forth from all sides" and reflecting "ever widening concern and alarm." Despite the passage of several months, wrote Hertha Pauli in the December *Commentary,* the bomb seemed to "weigh more and more heavily on the minds of more and more men." When *Time* named Harry Truman "Man of the Year" on December 21, 1945, the president's picture on the cover was dwarfed by a mushroom-shaped cloud and a hand gripping a lightning bolt. All the year's great events, said *Time,* including the deaths of FDR and Hitler and the surrender of Germany and Japan, paled before the awesome reality of the bomb:

> What the world would best remember of 1945 was the deadly mushroom clouds over Hiroshima and Nagasaki. Here were the force, the threat, the promise of the future. In their giant shadows . . . all men were pygmies. . . . Even Presidents, even Men of the Year, [were] mere foam flecks on the tide. . . . In such a world, who dared be optimistic?[38]

Nor did the new year bring relief. In January, a State Department official commented on the undiminished "hysteria" and "poisonous fog" of suspicion and fear still pervading the country. Talk of the bomb was continuing to "boom on unceasingly from radio, press, and platforms," wrote another observer. A mental-health writer who made a national lecture tour that spring found "general fear and confusion." Bob Hope joked about this fear. "Have you noticed the modern trend in verses this year?" he said on his radio show on Valentine's Day 1946. "No more of this 'Roses are red, violets are blue.' I picked up one and it showed an atom bomb exploding, and under it a verse that read: 'Will you be my little geranium, until we are both blown up by uranium?' " The strain in such humor was apparent.

As late as 1948, a speaker before a New York City business and professional club began:

> The atomic age is here, and we're all scared to death; you, I, and everyone else. And no wonder. We woke up one morning, and either

heard over the radio or read in big, black headlines, that an atomic bomb had been delivered, when we didn't even suspect the possibility of such a thing. Our very first contact was a shock, particularly since it told of the death of a great city.[39]

But how accurate were all these comments? Were these cultural observers perhaps simply quoting each other, parroting what had quickly become conventional wisdom? Was the culture indeed in shock, or was this simply an instant media cliché? Some at the time wondered the same thing. "We know what the atomic bombs did to Hiroshima and Nagasaki," commented *Fortune* in December 1945. "What did they do to the U.S. mind?"[40]

Conclusions must be tentative, but the evidence does suggest quite strongly that the atomic-bomb announcement was, indeed, a psychic event of almost unprecedented proportions. In the first place, the news spread with amazing rapidity. "Never before," said the American Institute of Public Opinion (the Gallup poll) in November 1945, had it found "such *continuous* public interest in one particular subject or issue." Not since opinion polling began, commented *Time* in December, 1945, had one topic evoked such "prolonged [and] intense public concern." The report of an exhaustive 1946 opinion study conducted under the auspices of the Social Science Research Council similarly emphasized the bomb's "phenomenal" impact: 98 percent of the adult population knew of it, including "even the most isolated."[41]

But did this intense preoccupation with the atomic bomb also reflect, as many cultural observers claimed, incipient dread and barely controlled terror? Here the public-opinion data become confusing and to some extent contradictory. Attitudes on the subject seem to have been remarkably volatile. Different pollsters reported different findings; the same poll sometimes produced seemingly conflicting results.

The earliest post-Hiroshima polls reveal a considerable will to think positively about the bomb. In a September 1945 Gallup poll, 69 percent of the respondents considered it "a good thing" the atomic bomb had been developed, while only 17 percent took the contrary view and 14 percent expressed no opinion. A *Fortune* survey of the same period confirmed the positive view—though less decisively—with 47 percent saying the atomic bomb had decreased the chances of world war, 16 percent asserting it had increased the chances, and 24 percent seeing no change.[42]

But in the most comprehensive early survey of public attitudes toward the bomb, the study conducted in the summer of 1946 by Leonard S. Cottrell, Jr., and Sylvia Eberhart for the Social Science Research Council, the results were far less clear-cut. A two-stage study yielding very similar results in polls taken before and after the Bikini Atoll atomic tests, it employed in each segment a general opinion survey of a representative sample of some three thousand adult Americans, and an hour-long interview with about six hundred subjects selected from the larger sample.

Some of the findings tend to confirm the hopeful spirit revealed by the early Gallup poll data. For example, when subjects in the intensive interviews were asked "How worried are you about the atomic bomb?" only about 25 percent would admit to being "greatly worried," while 65 percent claimed they were either not worried at all or not much worried. Asked to list unsettling world issues, only one in six spontaneously mentioned the atomic bomb.[43]

But other results of the 1946 study add a degree of ambiguity to the picture. For example, a strong majority agreed that America's nuclear monopoly would be short-lived. In the in-depth interviews, when asked how soon other countries would be able to make an atomic bomb, nearly 80 percent of those willing to venture an opinion thought that other nations either already *had* bomb-building capability, or would achieve it within five years or so. In the general survey, 60 percent said they believed the bomb secret was already known to other countries. More tellingly, nearly half the subjects expressed the fear that another world war was either certain or possible within twenty-five years. (Other polls of 1946 and 1947 reveal even deeper apprehensions on this score.) Nor was there much doubt that this would be a nuclear war. Sixty-four percent of those polled perceived a "real danger" that atomic bombs would someday be used against the United States.[44]

Puzzled by findings that paradoxically revealed both a widespread assumption of eventual atomic war and a low level of openly acknowledged worry about the bomb, Cottrell and Eberhart offered several explanations. They noted, for example, that a majority (56 percent) of those polled believed an effective atomic-bomb defense would soon be developed. (This confidence, Cottrell and Eberhart suggested, was rooted less in specific knowledge than in a generalized faith in "the inexhaustibility of scientific invention.") Further, they reported, many of the in-depth interviewees seemed fatalistically convinced that it was pointless to brood about such a cosmic threat. The very magnitude of the danger, in other words, led them (at least when talking with a pollster) to deny it a place among the issues they spent time consciously worrying about. "If you were living in a country where there were earthquakes," said one, "what good would it do you to go to bed every night worrying whether there would be an earthquake?"[45]

Others linked their reported lack of anxiety to a generalized confidence in the nation's leaders. "I know the bomb can wipe out cities," said one interviewee, "but I let the government worry about it." Agreed another: "I let the people who are qualified in these things do the worrying. I . . . accept circumstances as they are." This reliance on "the authorities" emerges strongly in three representative in-depth interviews Cottrell and Eberhart reprinted verbatim. "Some people are worried, hysterically so," a young university-trained chemical engineer acknowledged, but of himself he said: "As long as our government is continuing atomic research so we won't be caught by new and more drastic developments, I'm not particularly worried. . . . Let's call it 'apprehension' rather than 'worry.' " "I feel that the government will work out some method of defense," said a fifty-six-year-old skilled worker from Pennsylvania. "I am placing my trust in these great master-minds that are working on it now."[46]

What conclusions does this public opinion data suggest? First, that generalizations about the nation's post-Hiroshima mood must be sensitive to the passage of time. A statement by a contemporary observer that accurately caught the mood of, say, October 1945 might be contradicted by a poll taken a few months later—and both could be accurate. This point is illustrated by the changing responses to the Gallup poll's query about whether development of the atomic bomb was a "good thing" or a "bad thing." By October 1947, the percentage considering it a "good thing" had dropped to 55 percent, while the "bad thing" contingent had more than doubled, to 38 percent. Confirming a significant shift in attitudes, another 1947 Gallup poll showed an almost equal division on the question whether people everywhere would in the long run be "better off because somebody learned to split the atom."[47] In the immediate post-Hiroshima period, one might speculate, relief over the war's end and the emotional high brought on by Japan's surrender inclined Americans to downplay their atomic-bomb fears and to endorse "for the record" President Truman's insistently positive view of the bomb. But as the wartime climate faded and people turned increasingly to thoughts of the future, they may have become more willing to express openly the deep anxiety that many cultural observers insisted was present from the beginning.

Even taking the passage of time into account, how much do the polls really tell us? In dealing with the cultural ramifications of so profound an event as this, are we perhaps confronting a reality to which this useful instrument of social investigation is ill-suited? Significantly, Cottrell and Eberhart themselves speculated that American culture in 1946 may have been suffused with "much more anxiety than people admit, but that it is repressed." "Listening to the people talk," concluded *Time,* in its December 1945 summary of various opinion surveys, "the pollsters found awe, fear, cynicism, confusion, hope—but mostly confused fear and hopeful confusion."[48]

Perhaps one should not try to put a finer point on such limited and ambiguous evidence. Shaken and disoriented by an awesome technological development of almost unfathomable implications, Americans grasped at straws, searched for hopeful signs, and tried to arrange scary new facts into familiar patterns.

Somber pronouncements and opinion polls are not our only window on the nation's mood at the dawn of the atomic era. Popular culture offers a sometimes overwhelming wealth of additional evidence far removed from the world of the *American Scholar* and the American Institute of Public Opinion. In the country-music field, for example, a brief vogue of "atomic bomb" songs produced what musicologist Charles Wolfe has called "some of the most bizarre country songs ever written." Some of these simply cashed in on the "atomic" theme in their titles or carried on the vindictive wartime mood. Others, however, expressed deep fear and uncertainty about the future. Certainly this is true of the most successful song of this genre, "Atomic Power," by coutry-music star Fred Kirby. A frequent guest on CBS radio's "Carolina Calling," Kirby during the war had toured radio stations as the government's "Victory Cowboy," singing patriotic songs. He wrote "Atomic Power" on August 7, 1945, after a sleepless night brought on by the Hiroshima news. An immediate hit, the song was recorded by at least seven country-music groups, including the Buchanan Brothers, Chester and Lester, whose 1946 version on the Victor label enjoyed several weeks near the top of *Billboard*'s listing of "Most-Played Juke Box Folk Records." Kirby himself performed the song thousands of times in churches, on the radio, and at country-music festivals.[49]

"Atomic Power" is squarely in the tradition of country-music songs that for decades had both celebrated and deplored the inroads of technology; memorialized train wrecks, ship disasters, and hotel fires; and evoked the fundamentalist religious beliefs of Southern Protestantism. While the human toll at Hiroshima and Nagasaki elicits no particular regret ("they paid a big price for their sins"), the fact of two great cities literally "scorched from the face of the earth" arouses horror-struck awe. Atomic power is seen as coming from "the mighty hand of God" ("They're sending up to Heaven to get the brimstone fire,")—but as a fearsome destroyer and apocalyptic omen rather than a benevolent gift. In the concluding verse, atomic destruction is again linked to a divinely ordained ending to human history that will come as a bolt from the blue; "We will not know the minute, and will not know the hour."[50] Fear, trembling, brimstone, images of cosmic destruction: the themes of "Atomic Power" are wholly in keeping with the national mood so frequently described by cultural observers in the months after the atomic bomb burst upon the American consciousness.

Clearly, then, the weeks and months following August 6, 1945, were a time of cultural crisis when the American people confronted a new and threatening reality of almost unfathomable proportions. Equally clearly, the dominant immediate response was confusion and disorientation. But interwoven with all the talk of uncertainty and fear was another, more bracing theme: Americans must not surrender to fear or allow themselves to be paralyzed by anxiety; they must rally their political and cultural energies and rise to the challenge of the atomic bomb.

Two

Overture

The World-Government Movement

2

The Summons to Action

Americans . . . have been set down in the years of the world's
Great Decision. . . . This is no time for thoughtless or trivial
living.

—Malvina Lindsay in the *Washington Post* (1946)[1]

Of the various radio news commentators of the 1940s, Elmer Davis was
particularly noted for his calm, reassuring manner and the matter-of-fact,
commonsense tenor of his broadcasts. It is thus doubly interesting to note
the portentous, almost apocalyptic terms in which Davis discussed the
atomic bomb's public-policy implications. "Decisions made now, in the next
two or three years," said Davis in December 1945, "may determine the
entire foreseeable future."[2]

Elmer Davis was only one of hundreds of post-Hiroshima opinion-molders
who dinned such a message into the ears of the American people. The dense
cloud of fear that enveloped the nation after August 6, 1945, produced
a massive fallout of hortatory talk informing Americans of their solemn
duty to rise to the atomic challenge. From the people, the message went,
must come a political response commensurate with the awful new danger.
This insistent theme began to take shape from the moment of President
Truman's announcement. The "new age" born on August 6, wrote Norman Cousins in the *Saturday Review,* would transform "every aspect of
man's activities, from machines to morals, from physics to philosophy,
from politics to poetry." The shaping of atomic policy, agreed columnist
Dorothy Thompson in the *Ladies' Home Journal* that October, "is not a
scientific question, but a political, moral, and even religious question.
And it has to be answered by you and by me." The bomb, insisted a popularized 1946 account of the Manhattan Project, was "the most important
matter for all of us to think about today, tomorrow, and in the years to
come."[3]

Chancellor Robert M. Hutchins of the University of Chicago and others
carried the word to the nation's teachers. "There is only one subject of really
fundamental importance at the present moment," proclaimed Hutchins in

the National Education Association's *Journal* early in 1946, "and that is the atomic bomb." Global survival, wrote an education professor at Temple University later that year, depended "more than anything else upon the American people. . . . We must hold meetings. We must talk with everyone we can persuade, or force, to listen."[4]

Another influential leader who echoed this theme was David E. Lilienthal. A brilliant and personable Chicago lawyer, Lilienthal rose to fame in the 1930s as head of the Tennessee Valley Authority, one of the best-known —and most controversial—of the New Deal programs. He figures prominently in this history in three capacities: as a policymaker and head of the Atomic Energy Commission from 1946 to 1950, as a frequent public speaker on atomic-energy matters, and as a diarist whose private thoughts on the atom were often strikingly at variance with his usually ebullient public pronouncements.

In his public role, Lilienthal tirelessly called for citizen engagement in atomic-energy matters. The challenge of turning "the awful strength of atomic power away from destruction . . . directly affects every man, woman, and child in the world," he declared in a typical speech early in 1946. "We all share in the responsibility for a wise, a humane, and a morally sound conclusion."[5]

These exhortations were not merely routine calls for more public discussion on a matter of current interest. They had about them an urgency that is difficult to recreate after the passage of forty years. The same urgency is conveyed in an October 1945 address by Nobel Prize–winning chemist Harold C. Urey of the University of Chicago. In the face of "the most devastating weapon of all times," said Urey, everything else paled to insignificance. All other problems would be "solved some way, and their solution, whatever it may be, will not affect any of us very greatly. But atomic bombs are a different matter entirely."[6]

Via newspapers, magazines, sermons, speeches, and radio broadcasts, the same pressing message echoed throughout the land. "Over and above all else you do," readers of the *Ladies' Home Journal* were told early in 1946, the prevention of atomic war is "the thought you should wake up to, go to sleep with and carry with you all day." "At this very minute," began the script of a 1946 public-affairs program produced at the University of Denver and heard on radio stations throughout the Midwest, "a time bomb is under your home—is under this radio studio. It is ticking slowly away. Even while I talk, even while you listen, time is running out. America must *act,* if we are to choose the road of atomic peace rather than atomic war." That June, in "Exploring the Unknown," a Mutual network series narrated by Clifton Fadiman, a program on the atomic bomb contained this segment:

Fadiman:	It's as though the entire world were under sentence.
Sound:	Gavel.
Judge:	I sentence you to a few short years—in which to solve the problems posed by nuclear fission. Penalty for failure—death![7]

Spurred by such exhortations, the nation's media and opinion-molding institutions did indeed devote massive attention to atomic issues. The months after Hiroshima saw something approaching a national town meeting on the atomic bomb and its meaning. News magazines like *Time, Newsweek,* and *United States News;* general publications such as *Life, Collier's,* and the *Saturday Evening Post;* and specialized magazines for educators, businessmen, women, ministers, and countless other groups published so many articles on the subject that the unwary researcher quickly finds himself drowning in a sea of print. One scholar, compiling a "fever chart" of America's nuclear consciousness, has counted over three hundred articles on the atomic bomb in major American periodicals in 1946 alone. Magazines as diverse as *Business Week* and the *Saturday Review* set up special "Atomic Energy" departments.[8]

This was the golden age of radio, and the networks as well as local stations contributed to the national discourse with special features, lectures, and extensive coverage on regular news programs. On August 24, 1945, for instance, commentator Raymond Gram Swing of NBC's "Blue Network" (later ABC) announced that henceforth every Friday's broadcast would be devoted to bomb-related issues, with the other four weekday broadcasts given over to news of the pre-atomic world "while it dawdles off the stage."[9]

Journals such as the *American Scholar,* the *Antioch Review,* and the *Annals of the American Academy of Political and Social Science* published special issues on the bomb. The American Philosophical Society, the *Nation,* and the *New York Herald Tribune* organized symposia on the subject and published extensive reports of the proceedings. "You can scarcely take a step without stumbling over an atom-bomb conference," wrote columnist Max Lerner in November 1945. "If there is any general group today that is not discussing atomic bombs," agreed an official of the Rockefeller Foundation, "I have not heard of it."[10]

The quickened pace of national discourse assumed many forms, as citizens took the exhortations to heart. A Manhattan delicatessen owner set up an "atomic" display in his window, including actual samples of radioactive ores and photographs of Hiroshima and Nagasaki. "There won't even *be* any delicatessens if somebody starts dropping these bombs," he said, explaining his activism. A small businessman in Dayton, Ohio, hitherto little involved in politics, became so caught up in the mood of the moment that he subscribed to the newly founded *Bulletin of the Atomic Scientists*, gave talks to local church groups on the dangers of atomic war, and on a 1947 trip east even detoured to Princeton to meet Albert Einstein.[11] "One kind of letter comes to me more often from listeners than any other," observed Raymond Gram Swing in December 1945, "one which asks, almost in prayer, 'What can I *do*?'"[12]

The initial response of the American people to the atomic bomb, then, was shaped by two intertwined cultural moods: intense fear and a somewhat unfocused conviction that an urgent and decisive public response was essential. But precisely *what* response? Here the stark clarity of the summons to action became murky and vague; the initial generalized exhortations to public engagement offered few specifics. This led to considerable frustration, intensifying the sense of a culture in disarray. As Harold C. Urey put it in 1946: "The advent of the atomic bomb has caused endless confusion in the thinking of men. And the confusion spreads to more people as they come to realize all the implications of this weapon."[13]

With a high level of anxiety feeding into a diffuse but strong impulse to action, earnest advocates of a bewildering variety of causes, projects, and points of view now began to compete for the public ear. The stakes were high: to shape, at the very dawn of the atomic age, the fundamental contours of national attitudes toward the bomb and influence the course of the nuclear future. What were some of the visions that competed for public attention as Americans took their first hesitant steps into the trackless atomic wilderness?

3

Atomic-Bomb Nightmares and World-Government Dreams

Raymond Gram Swing, Oberlin College dropout turned newspaperman turned radio reporter, was an extremely influential opinion-molder in the early postwar period. As principal news commentator for the American Broadcasting Company, he ranked slightly behind his CBS and NBC rivals Lowell Thomas and H. V. Kaltenborn, but seems to have been particularly attractive to well-educated and politically knowledgeable listeners who responded to his intelligence and generally liberal commentary.[1]

So it is significant indeed that Swing was not only shaken to the core by the news of Hiroshima and Nagasaki, but that he freely communicated this reaction to his listeners. "I was as greatly affected by the atomic bomb as by any event in my lifetime," he later wrote. "I felt that along with every member of the human race, I was personally involved, and . . . had a personal responsibility." Having long followed developments in nuclear fission, Swing initially reacted to Truman's announcement with elation over the "new freedom now in wait for mankind." But, as for so many others, excitement soon gave way to fear. Atomic war was inevitable, Swing concluded, unless dramatic steps were taken quickly. And what were these steps? For Swing, the answer seemed crystal clear: "Internationally, I was sure [the atomic bomb] meant world government, for that would be the only way to abolish war, which had to be abolished if civilization were to endure." On an early-morning walk in late August 1945, near the end of his summer vacation, Swing vowed to devote his energies, on the air and off, to the cause of world government. And so he did, in broadcast after broadcast, some of which were reprinted in his 1946 book, *In the Name of Sanity*. He reported on various world-government conferences (in several of which he himself participated), called attention to public-opinion polls that seemed to indicate a groundswell of popular support for the idea, and collaborated with Albert Einstein in an appeal for world government, published under Einstein's name.[2]

Swing was only one of a number of influential Americans who became convinced after Hiroshima that a radically new international order was not only imperative but attainable. So awesome was the danger, the equation went, that the political response had to be equally dramatic. As J. Robert Oppenheimer put it, atomic bombs called for—and by their very existence would help create—"radical and profound changes in the politics of the world." "At last," wrote Methodist bishop G. Bromley Oxnam in his diary on August 10, 1945, "we have power to remake a world." The bomb, wrote Anne O'Hare McCormick in the *New York Times* while the mushroom cloud still hung over Hiroshima, was "the most unanswerable argument yet" for a world state. Columnists Dorothy Thompson and Max Lerner reached the same instantaneous conclusion. "The bomb at Hiroshima was the bell that tolled for us all," wrote Lerner on August 20. "Its message rang out clearly: world state or world doom." Looking back, Lerner has recently recalled: "Hiroshima crystallized my own commitment to collective security, moving it—by its sheer dramatic impact—a final step into [support for] a world state." [3]

The dream of world government—from Tennyson's great parliament of mankind to Wendell Willkie's visionary 1943 bestseller *One World*—was hardly a new one in 1945. But for its longtime champions, that year brought two events that seemed of portentous significance: the United Nations charter was adopted at the San Francisco conference in June, and in August came the atomic bomb. What more compelling stimulus could one imagine for a radically new world system? As one veteran world-government advocate wrote that autumn: "Something much greater than Hiroshima was smashed . . . on August 6, 1945": also demolished were the "pompous fantasies" of national sovereignty. "Hiroshima was, of course, a tremendous stimulus," observed another activist in 1947. While dramatizing the need for world government, Hiroshima had also created the political conditions favorable for achieving it: with its atomic monopoly, some of these advocates openly boasted or discreetly implied, America could now impose on the world its vision of a new international order. [4]

Capitalizing on the suddenly favorable climate, fifty longtime world-government advocates gathered at Dublin, New Hampshire, in October 1945 to map strategy and draft a manifesto. This pronouncement, published as an advertisement in the *New York Times* on October 17, warned of the devastation of atomic war and called for a "World Federal Government" as the only alternative. In April 1947, a new national organization, the United World Federalists, emerged to spearhead the movement. Cord Meyer, a well-connected young Yale graduate, was elected its first president. [5]

A remarkably diverse group of post-Hiroshima opinion-molders endorsed world government as the answer to the atomic threat. "Nuclear energy insists on global government," wrote the humorist E. B. White in the *New*

Yorker's unsigned "Notes and Comments" column in late August 1945. Nationalism had always been "bloody business," he added later; "reinforced with the atom, it may be fatal business." The solemn duty of "this generation and of the next, if there is one," agreed the editors of the *Antioch Review* that December, "is world government." In an age of atomic menace, said political columnist Walter Lippmann early in 1946, nations would be "compelled" to create a world state not by the rhetoric of its advocates but by "the inevitability of the truth."[6]

Some influential churchmen offered their blessings. "There is a defense against the atomic bomb," observed the Catholic journal *Commonweal* in November 1945. "It is simple. It consists of creating . . . a world state; . . . If we do not wish to be morally guilty of suicide, the establishment of such a world power is the only thing left to us."[7]

Like the Great Fear, this surge of support for world government cut across the usual boundaries of political ideology. Only those who had "not yet grasped the meaning of the new discovery" could fail to realize the urgency of world government, wrote Freda Kirchwey in the liberal *Nation* on August 18. "We face a choice between one world or none." "Science has killed isolationism," said Mrs. Ogden Reid, wife of the editor of the staunchly Republican *New York Herald Tribune*, in welcoming delegates to the October 1945 world-affairs conference. "Responsibility for one world has come sooner than its protagonist Wendell Willkie ever dreamed." The atomic bomb, she continued, had fused "a common kinship overriding national boundaries." Even the *Reader's Digest*, then as now a bastion of conservatism and patriotism, succumbed briefly to the prevailing internationalist mood. "The atomic bomb has made political and economic nationalism meaningless," declared a November 1945 article. "No longer merely a vision held by a few idealists, *world government has now become a hard-boiled, practical and urgent necessity*."[8]

Some scientists who had been involved with the bomb project provided influential support as well. Even before the war's end, through an informal "Committee on Social and Political Implications" at the University of Chicago, Manhattan Project scientists James Franck and Eugene Rabinowitch had pushed their colleagues to embrace world government, and after the war, they and other "atomic scientists" went public with their internationalist convictions. "A superior world government of some kind . . . ," declared Harold C. Urey in an October 1945 address, "is the only way out."[9]

Another scientist who lent his prestige to the cause was Leo Szilard, who gained fame in 1945 as the author of the 1939 letter, signed by Albert Einstein, alerting President Roosevelt that the atomic bomb was theoretically possible. In the early postwar period Szilard worked on a number of political fronts, but fundamentally he saw a world state as the only hope.

"Permanent peace cannot be established without a world government," he declared in a May 1947 *Saturday Review* article urging that this goal be made "the cornerstone of our national policy."

Szilard proposed an elaborate complex of new international agencies to supervise disarmament and atomic energy, control strategic raw materials, and create a new world economic order through large-scale capital transfers from richer to poorer nations and "the building up of a vast consumers goods industry" in Russia and other countries. The United States, he said, should at once allocate 10 percent of its national income to these purposes—a modest sum, he noted, compared to the cost of a nuclear arms race. To promote the shift in loyalties a world government would require, Szilard suggested a vast increase in international student exchanges and a vaguely described global propaganda agency that would be "given jurisdiction over one page of every newspaper in the world" including *Pravda,* the *New York Times,* and the *Chicago Tribune.* (The reaction of the *Tribune*'s irascible owner Robert R. McCormick to this idea is not recorded.)

Though some of these proposals may have been intended mainly to provoke discussion, the seriousness of Szilard's general purpose is evident: to stimulate support for new international structures that "within one or two generations" could be transformed "into a genuine world government." Equally serious were Szilard's reflections on how this internationalist crusade might be launched. The trick, he said, was to reach and convince the world's intellectual elite. "Many of the men who influence public opinion by speaking or writing come from a small class of people—the class of people who have the advantage of higher education," he wrote. "Their attitudes and their loyalties will, in the long run, affect the set of values accepted throughout the whole community." [10]

Of all the scientists who called for world government in these months, the most famous was Albert Einstein. With his shambling walk, benevolent smile, rumpled sweaters, and unkempt hair, Einstein was for many Americans the visual embodiment of the brilliant if eccentric scientific genius. Though his scientific link with the bomb lay in theoretical work done decades before, he was for many the quintessential "atomic scientist." His views were solicited as soon as the Hiroshima bombing became known, and he responded with such epigrams as: "The atomic bomb has changed everything except the nature of man." The most comprehensive of Einstein's various pronouncements on world government was the one prepared in collaboration with Raymond Gram Swing. First excerpted by Swing on his radio broadcast, it was published in the November 1945 *Atlantic Monthly.* The very simplicity of Einstein's political ideas made them highly quotable. Scores of sermons, speeches, and magazine articles in this period included the potent incantation: "As Professor Einstein says . . ."

What Professor Einstein said was, in essence, that only a "supernational organization" with sweeping powers could prevent atomic war. The prospects for such a transformation might have seemed "illusory, even fantastic" before August 1945, but so urgent was the atomic crisis that mankind could not wait for "a gradual historical development"; under the spur of "harsh necessity," world government must come *now*. No longer merely "desirable in the name of brotherhood," it had become "necessary for survival." The United States, Great Britain, and the USSR should take the lead and invite the other nations to join. Further, "since the United States and Great Britain have the secret of the atomic bomb and the Soviet Union does not, they should invite the Soviet Union to prepare and present the first draft of a Constitution for the proposed World Government." [11]

For these post-Hiroshima partisans of world government, the United Nations represented a dilemma. Some gave the UN qualified support as a step in the right direction, but many insisted that the atomic bomb had so transformed the political landscape that the UN had to be radically overhauled, if not abandoned altogether. "Had we known at San Francisco that atomic bombs were only a few weeks away," declared the Rockefeller Foundation's Raymond B. Fosdick in a national radio address a few days after Hiroshima, "it is possible that the institution would have been greatly strengthened. It must be strengthened now—with imagination and daring." To Cord Meyer, the bomb made the United Nations charter an "elaborate charade." In the shadow of the bomb, agreed E. B. White, the San Francisco charter seemed like "the preparations some little girls might make for a lawn party as a thunderhead gathers just beyond the garden gate." The Hiroshima blast, wrote Dorothy Thompson in the October 1945 *Ladies' Home Journal*, "did more than blow up landscapes, buildings, and populations. It blew up the San Francisco charter . . . and made it as obsolete as the Holy Alliance created after the Napoleonic wars." [12]

How widespread was the post-Hiroshima enthusiasm for world government? The limited evidence available suggests that in this period when the shock of Hiroshima and the fear of atomic war were most intense, the idea won at least passive support from a third to a half of the American people. An Ohio survey publicized by Raymond Gram Swing early in 1946 showed overwhelming support for world government—but in response to a question which promised that such a reform would "abolish war." An August 1946 Gallup poll found 54 percent of Americans in favor of transforming the UN into "a world government with power to control the armed forces of all nations, including the United States." By contrast, however, a poll conducted that same month by Cottrell and Eberhart for the Social Science Research Council found only 36 percent in favor of a world organization in which the U.S. "would have to follow the decisions of the majority of nations." This same poll found that only 25 percent of the respondents thought it possible to organize the nations of the world in the same way as the United States "with a government over them all to make laws that they would have to obey." Opinion on the subject was uncrystallized, Cottrell and Eberhart cautiously concluded, and much depended on the phrasing of the question. When specifics were offered as to aspects of national sovereignty that might actually have to be surrendered, they noted, support for world government dropped sharply.[13]

Despite such ambiguous public-opinion data, there can be no doubt that "world government" was, from 1945 through 1947, an enormously important cultural motif, symbolizing for many the need to devise policy responses equal to the magnitude of the atomic threat. Of the opinion-molders who embraced this cause, two of the most influential were Robert M. Hutchins, chancellor of the University of Chicago, and Norman Cousins, editor of the *Saturday Review of Literature.* The responses of Hutchins and Cousins cast a revealing light on the broader group propelled by news of Hiroshima into enthusiastic public advocacy of world government.

Like Raymond Gram Swing, Robert Hutchins attended Oberlin College, where Hutchins's father taught in the school of theology. He went on to Yale Law School, where he became a teacher and then dean. In 1929, still only thirty, he was installed as the "boy president" of the University of Chicago. Committed to the ideal of general education, he reorganized the Chicago curriculum around the study of "Great Ideas," generating turmoil and controversy in the process. As the *enfant terrible* of American higher education, Hutchins exerted an influence far beyond the Chicago campus. Tall, handsome, articulate, and totally self-assured, he reached a national audience through speeches, magazine articles, and a weekly radio program, the *Chicago Roundtable.*[14]

"Up to last Monday," Hutchins told his radio audience on August 12, 1945, "I must confess I didn't have much hope for a world state. I believed that no moral basis for it existed, that we had no world conscience and no sense of world community sufficient to keep a world state together." But the shock of Hiroshima had changed all this, making crystal clear "the necessity of a world organization." In the months following this political epiphany, Hutchins created and served as figurehead president of a "Committee to Frame a World Constitution" and tirelessly promoted the cause in public forums and media outlets available to him at that time.

Unlike some world-government advocates, Hutchins recognized that changes in the organic relationships of the world's peoples and nations would have to come first, and he saw this "moral, intellectual, and spiritual revolution" as a fundamental task of educators. Nevertheless, commenting in 1947 on a *New York Times* editorial that had tepidly endorsed world government as an "ultimate" goal, he observed with asperity: "I do not understand the use of the word 'ultimate' in this connection. . . . What is ultimately required of us is required of us now. If what is ultimately required of us is the abolition of war through a world government, then we had better set about trying to get war abolished through world government now."[15]

It is not without irony that Hutchins' world-government pronouncements gained such a hearing in part because of his connection with an institution whose history had been inextricably linked to that of the atomic bomb since the day in 1942 when Enrico Fermi, working under the bleachers of Stagg Field, had achieved the first self-sustaining chain reaction in uranium. Indeed, some contemporary observers even suggested that Hutchins's vocal internationalism in the later 1940s reflected his desire to replace Chicago's "bomb factory" image with a more positive one in the public mind.[16]

Of all the high-visibility converts to world government, Norman Cousins had perhaps the most dramatic immediate impact. The twenty-eight-year-old Cousins had become editor of the staid *Saturday Review* in 1940. Prior to August 1945 he had given little hint of what would in fact be a long career as a publicist for various causes, but like Raymond Gram Swing and Robert Hutchins, he was profoundly shaken by Truman's announcement. On the night of August 6 (while a sleepless Fred Kirby in Charlotte was composing "Atomic Power"), Cousins wrote an impassioned editorial, "Modern Man Is Obsolete," which appeared in the *Saturday Review* on August 18. An expanded version was published in book form that October.[17]

The problem in the past had not been the lack of strategies for attaining the age-old goal of world peace, Cousins insisted, but of the will to implement them. What he called the "Atomic Solvent" would change all that. Stimulated by atomic fear, the instinct for survival would arouse world public opinion to demand a new international system. To those who considered a world government beyond the human capacity to devise, Cousins pointed to the Manhattan Project as proof that man "can extend and over-extend himself when pressed." The awesome event at Hiroshima had opened the door not only to unimaginable horrors, but also to the possibility of a thrilling new era in human relations! "This is a propitious moment, the grand moment . . . to take the moral leadership." By an ironic stroke of fate, America's possession and use of the most awful weapon in human history had thrust into her hands the scepter of leadership in the march toward a world state.

Writing within hours of the Hiroshima announcement, Cousins recognized the powerful appeal of what would later be called deterrence theory, but rejected it as a very weak reed indeed. "The tempting but dangerous notion . . . that the atomic bomb is so horrible and the terror of retaliation so great that we may have seen the last of war," he wrote, was "quasi-logical, but war is no respector of logic. . . . If history teaches us anything, it is that the possibility of war increases in direct proportion to the effectiveness of the instruments of war."

Making a point that would be echoed by many world-government advocates, Cousins found a heartening historical precedent in the union formed by the thirteen American colonies in 1776. If the British threat had been sufficient to draw these separate governments together then, he argued, surely the vastly more dangerous atomic menace would now have the same effect on the nations of the world.[18]

Modern Man Is Obsolete had a tremendous impact. Newspapers reprinted the editorial verbatim; the book sold many thousands of copies. The phrase entered the stream of public discourse, cropping up everywhere. Like Thomas Paine's *Common Sense* in its clarity, assurance, and simplicity, Cousins's manifesto was profoundly appealing at a moment of great fear and uncertainty.

The reviews of the book were mixed, but generally favorable. The *New Yorker* noted the "high rhetorical content" of Cousins's essay, but still praised it enthusiastically. *Social Studies* offered somewhat ambiguous praise: The atomic crisis "requires that we examine . . . every possible crumb of constructive thinking. *Modern Man Is Obsolete* offers several not insignificant crumbs." No such reservations marked the reaction of the physicist Hans Bethe, who hailed Cousins's "very impressive arguments." Veteran world-government proponents were, of course, delighted. Cousins's work, said former Supreme Court justice Owen J. Roberts, was "the best thing I have seen since the atomic bomb came to light."[19]

Despite the "high rhetorical content" and intellectual weaknesses apparent at the time and no less evident in retrospect, *Modern Man Is Obsolete* remains a central cultural document of the immediate post-Hiroshima moment. The intensity of Cousins's response to the bomb, the passion of his insistence on its revolutionary implications, and the urgency of his call for a radical response both reflected and helped shape the nation's mood in these months.

From the first, the world-government cause aroused criticism, ranging from cautious reservations to open contempt and ridicule. *Time,* describing the atomic bomb as "new, energized, vitaminized oats for every old hobby," found "no signs [of] . . . any deep spring of world statism in the U.S." *Newsweek* columnist Ernest K. Lindley accused the world-government advocates of simply manipulating post-Hiroshima fear to give this hoary idea a contemporary cachet. David Lawrence, editor of *U.S. News and World Report,* attributed the whole thing to "hysteria." One skeptic, pointing out that in a world government based on popular sovereignty India would be among the most powerful states, proceeded to spin out an elaborate scenario in which a coalition of India and the Moslem states, combining their respective dietary codes, impose a worldwide ban on beef and pork. The *New York Times* acknowledged the "desperate urgency" of Norman Cousins's appeal, but found his case for world government unpersuasive.[20]

In their panicky reaction to the bomb, news commentator Elmer Davis argued, Cousins and others had embraced the world-government idea without really assessing its difficulties or implications. Commenting on Cousins's comparison of humanity's situation to that of a man poised at the edge of a deep canyon ten feet wide while a forest fire rages behind him, afraid to jump yet realizing he will be burned to death if he doesn't, Davis said: "But suppose . . . the canyon is not ten feet wide but forty. It might then make sense . . . to see if there isn't some other way out before he tries that standing broad jump." David E. Lilienthal, by now chairman of the newly formed Atomic Energy Commission, was unimpressed by his 1947 meeting with world-government champion Robert Hutchins. His "logical oversimplifications . . . and his notion that we are dealing with fixed factors," wrote Lilienthal in his diary, "reminded me more of a college debate than a serious discussion among men who have decisions to make."[21]

Would a world government be any more conducive to human well-being than the present arrangement of national sovereignties, and would it be immune to the evils classically associated with the exercise of power? "Even in a world state," drily observed Herbert W. Briggs, professor of government at Cornell, early in 1947, "there may be such a thing as politics." So long as people continued to hold "deeply entrenched views on nationalism, politics, and economics," he went on, the shaping of policy in a new world order would remain "a matter of power politics." Further, he asked, after pointing out that at least 75 percent of the world's population lived under dictatorships or other authoritarian regimes, where did the proponents of world government "ever pick up the notion that a world state would be a democracy?"[22]

Writing in the *Partisan Review,* cultural critic Robert Warshow characterized E. B. White's *New Yorker* pieces advocating world government as primarily exercises in prescribing a proper *attitude* toward the possibility of atomic annihilation—morally serious, yet also sophisticated and mildly ironic—rather than genuine calls to political activism or engagment. In the "humane and yet knowing" ambience of the *New Yorker*'s pages, he went on, "history and destruction and one's own helplessness become small and simple and somehow peaceful. . . . History may kill you, it is true, but you have taken the right attitude, you will have been intelligent and humane and suitably melancholy to the end." Indeed, added Warshow, enlarging the point, the essential function of the *New Yorker* was to provide "the intelligent and cultured college graduate with the most comfortable and least compromising attitude he can assume toward capitalist society without being forced into actual conflict."[23]

The world-government cause came in for criticism by several participants at a symposium on "Atomic Energy and Its Implications" organized by the American Philosophical Society in November 1945. "I see no hope of world government by formula," said Joseph H. Willits, director for the Social Sciences of the Rockefeller Foundation, as part of a larger rejection of all "unitary, mechanistic" solutions to the atomic dilemma. The Princeton economist Jacob Viner dismissed Norman Cousins's apocalyptic call for world government as a substitution of "hysteria for history." The patient exercise of "mutually conciliatory diplomacy," while less "spectacular, revolutionary, soul-stirring, or exciting," he suggested, was more likely in the long run to prevent nuclear war.[24]

From the diplomatic establishment itself, the counterattack was led by Sumner Welles, a former undersecretary of state. Writing in the January 1946 *Atlantic Monthly,* Welles dismissed as "wholly impracticable" the Einstein-Swing proposals for world government. All such scenarios, Welles insisted, ignored the realities of world politics—and one reality in particular: "I cannot imagine that the Soviet Union would participate in a world government upon any other basis" than that of "a World Union of Soviet Socialist Republics with the capital . . . located in Moscow." Writing in the Spring 1946 *American Scholar,* Nathaniel Peffer, professor of international relations at Columbia University, readily conceded that the bomb had given "a new [and] terrible urgency" to the prevention of war, and even acknowledged that if one were to ask "an extra-planetary commission or a commission composed of Confucius, Aristotle, and Bacon" to propose the best means to that end, "the answer would be found quickly enough: world government." He insisted, however, that in the real world of 1946 "only a negligible minority of men in the Western world have any disposition to waive national sovereignty in favor of a world state—a minority even among the educated and privileged classes."[25]

Nor, despite some exceptions, did the world-government reform find much favor in the nation's religious press. A *Christian Century* writer ridiculed the churchmen who were loudly proclaiming the imminent arrival of a world state at a time when Christianity itself remained divided into hundreds of competing denominations and sects. The 1946 report of a commission of the liberal Protestant Federal Council of Churches appointed to formulate a position on atomic weapons was also extremely skeptical on the issue of world government:

> Exclusive trust in a political structure of any sort to solve the problems posed by atomic warfare would be a dangerous illusion. In particular, the hope for world government, useful as a guiding principle, cannot be turned into a program for immediate action without very serious confusion of aim. . . . Rigid insistence on full world government now is in effect a vote for continued international anarchy.

United Evangelical Action, the magazine of the National Association of Evangelicals, warned darkly against all plans for "a conglomerate world citizenry —half pagan and half Christian." [26]

Of all these religious critics of the world-government idea, one of the harshest was the Protestant theologian Reinhold Niebuhr. A 1930s Marxist disillusioned by the Stalin show trials and the Nazi-Soviet pact, Niebuhr by late 1945 was moving rapidly toward the tough anti-Soviet stance and bleak view of sinful human nature that would characterize his postwar thought. With Soviet-American tensions increasing, he wrote as early as October 1945 in his journal *Christianity and Crisis,* the world-government idea seemed increasingly unrealistic. To Niebuhr, this crusade was only the latest manifestation of the characteristically American belief that intelligence and goodwill could end social injustice and international conflict—a belief he had criticized in 1932 in his seminal work *Moral Man and Immoral Society.* In the same issue of *Christianity and Crisis,* another writer, arguing from theological rather than *Realpolitik* premises, dismissed the "secularist" world-government assumption "that changes in political institutions by themselves would assure human survival." [27]

Critics like Niebuhr and Sumner Welles may have appeared to be swimming against the tide in 1945 and 1946, but in fact their attacks on the advocates of world government proved prophetic. With dramatic suddenness, this idea that had fleetingly attracted so much respectful attention fell victim to its internal weakness and, perhaps more importantly, to a worsening Cold War climate of suspicion and conformity. Membership in the United World Federalists fell off rapidly after 1949 as the idea became, in the words of historian Charles DeBenedetti, a "fast-fading dream." [28]

The drumfire of critical attack intensified. Reinhold Niebuhr remorselessly dissected "The Illusions of World Government" once again in a 1949 *Foreign Affairs* article. The "fear of mutual annihilation" was indeed a powerful new element in the world consciousness, he agreed, but history offered no record of "peoples establishing a common community because they feared each other, though there are many instances when the fear of a common foe acted as the cement of cohesion." (Decoded, this meant: NATO, yes; world government, no.) The entire idea, Niebuhr said, was a tissue of delusions and fallacies boiling down to two fundamentally erroneous beliefs: that far-reaching changes in the world order could be achieved by fiat, and that new forms of governance could create a world community. World-government advocates who favored imposing the new order by atomic threats, Niebuhr went on, "walk bravely up the hill of pure idealism and down again into the realm of pure power politics." Their sweeping proposals and paper constitutions only illustrated the "illusions of omnipotence which infect the thought of this kind of political idealism." Niebuhr's final judgment on the world-government cause was unsparing. "The trustful acceptance of false solutions for our perplexing problems," he said, only added "a touch of pathos to the tragedy of our age. . . . We may have pity upon, but can have no sympathy with, those who flee to the illusory security of the impossible from the insecurities and ambiguities of the possible." [29]

As the world-government movement faded, its leaders, so visible and voluble a few years earlier, turned to other issues or fell silent. Robert M. Hutchins involved himself with issues of academic freedom and his chairmanship of the *Encyclopedia Britannica* corporation. Raymond Gram Swing retired from broadcasting in 1948 to be replaced at ABC—appropriately enough—by Elmer Davis, one of the more outspoken critics of the world-government movement. Reflecting in 1968 on the cause that had so absorbed him twenty years earlier, Swing wrote: "As I now look back, . . . I think it would have been wiser and indeed more accurate not to have used the far-reaching phrase 'world government.' " Like many other Americans, Swing now placed his hopes in nuclear deterrence. Thanks to the great powers' arsenals of atomic weapons, he wrote, "a nuclear world war is unlikely—one hopes that it is highly unlikely." [30]

Cord Meyer, too, soon moved on. By 1949, he would later write, "I had ceased to enjoy my role as Cassandra. My repetitive warnings of approaching nuclear doom echoed hollowly in my head, and I came to dislike the sound of my own voice as I promised a federalist salvation in which I no longer had real confidence." Meyer ceased to be active in the United World Federalists that autumn, and soon he joined the Central Intelligence Agency. "Our most serious miscalculation," he concluded in 1980, "was the assumption that the danger of devastating nuclear war could be used to bridge the gap between differing institutions and ideologies." [31]

Norman Cousins came closest to keeping the faith, but even he could not sustain the confidence and assurance of his initial manifesto. In 1961, Cousins sadly admitted that the world powers had "resisted the need to subordinate their sovereignty to a world organization" and conceded the improbability of any such development in the foreseeable future. Cousins now spoke in cautious, muted terms of gradually reshaping individual and community values over a long span of time as a way of creating "a new context for the human situation." [32]

Short-lived though it was, the world-government crusade remains an interesting and significant phenomenon. Politically, it was something of a hybrid, briefly bringing together people of vastly different orientations to whom the atomic crisis gave, at least superficially, a common outlook. Some, in their fear of atomic war, were clearly drawn into the world-government camp by genuinely idealistic and internationalist motives. Most of these, whatever their apparent standing or cultural influence, were political outsiders, totally cut off from the power centers in Washington (and certainly Moscow), where critical decisions were being made that were far removed from their vision of a liberal, cooperative postwar world order.

Others, however, justly criticized by Reinhold Niebuhr, were far from being starry-eyed innocents. They viewed America's moment of absolute atomic supremacy as the opportune occasion for establishing a global *Pax Americana*. Confronted with Soviet intransigence, they proposed to proceed with a "world" government excluding Russia, or even spoke ominously of using atomic threats to impose their new order. Some at this end of the spectrum moved easily from their world-government phase to support for Washington's Cold War program of global anticommunism and atomic supremacy. From this perspective, Cord Meyer's rapid progression from the World Federalists to the CIA is not as anomalous as it seems. Another eloquent world-government advocate of 1945–1946, the New York corporation lawyer Thomas K. Finletter, joined the Truman administration in 1950 as secretary of the air force.

Culturally, the world-government movement is illuminating as well, and provides the perfect starting point for our survey of the larger contours of post-Hiroshima American thought. It was one of the earliest and, in some respects, most characteristic manifestations of both the fear that spread across America after August 1945 and the conviction that the gravity of the crisis demanded a response of equally dramatic magnitude.

Three

The Atomic Scientists

From Bomb-Makers to Political Sages

4

The Political Agenda of the Scientists' Movement

On September 1, 1945, three weeks after Hiroshima, seventeen University of Chicago scientists, all veterans of the Manhattan Project, gathered at the nearby Shoreland Hotel for a luncheon. When it was over, tall and heavy-set Samuel K. Allison, newly appointed as head of the university's Institute for Nuclear Studies, offered some extemporaneous remarks in which he tried to sum up the emotional roller coaster that he and his colleagues had been riding in recent months. "All of us," he said, "had a momentary elation when our experiment met with success, but that feeling rapidly changed to a feeling of horror and a fervent hope that no more bombs would be dropped. When the second bomb was released, we felt it was a great tragedy." [1]

Allison's comments were echoed over and over again in this period by a great many scientists who had been associated with the bomb project. Indeed, so ubiquitous was this theme that one must be careful not to assume that *all* Manhattan Project scientists felt this way. Some, no doubt, had few qualms about their wartime role and quietly resumed their war-interrupted careers. But time and again in contemporary accounts and later reminiscences, one finds evidence that for many scientists involvement in the Manhattan Project was a traumatic experience that turned their lives inside-out. Some were dismayed that the bomb had been used; others reluctantly approved. Nearly all shared an intense fear of what lay ahead. Out of fear, and in some cases guilt, came activism. Many scientists concluded after August 6, 1945, that it was their urgent duty to try to shape official policy regarding atomic energy. So began the "scientists' movement" that for a brief but intense period was a seminal force in American life. Many of the post-Hiroshima cultural developments we shall be examining cannot be fully understood without attention to the remarkable public role played by the atomic scientists.

The story of this role—well told in Alice Kimball Smith's superb study, *A Peril and a Hope*—had its beginnings in the spring and summer of

1945, when some Manhattan Project scientists at Chicago worked feverishly to delay the full military use of the bomb at least until a demonstration shot could be arranged. This last-ditch effort culminated in the so-called Franck Report of June 11, 1945, signed by James Franck and six other scientists. Also playing a catalytic role was Niels Bohr, a highly respected, even beloved figure in the tight little world of theoretical physics. First in his native Denmark and then from 1943 to 1945 in the United States, Bohr worked to alert the leaders of the wartime alliance to the implications of atomic energy, and to prod the social consciousness of his fellow scientists. Though Bohr's influence on the postwar movement was indirect, the inspiration of his example was critical. In a sweepingly comprehensive statement published by the *Times* of London shortly after Hiroshima, Bohr declared that every scientist who had worked on the bomb must now be "prepared to assist, in any way open to him, in bringing about an outcome of the present crisis of humanity that is worthy of the ideals for which science through the ages has stood."[2]

In the short run, Bohr's optimism seemed disastrously ill-timed. The Franck Report had failed to prevent the obliteration of two Japanese cities. The impulse behind it, however, intensified in the postwar period, as several thousand scientists were drawn into intense political activity. One can link this activism to a longer tradition of scientific involvement in public issues (In the activist 1930s, for instance, a few scientists, including Arthur H. Compton, formed the American Association of Scientific Workers and issued pronouncements on current social issues.) But the most striking feature of the postwar scientists' movement was its sudden and spontaneous emergence. Its source was not some theoretical commitment to social involvement, but direct experience and emotion: the magnitude of the blasts at Alamogordo, Hiroshima, and Nagasaki; the casualty figures and observers' reports that filtered out of the devastated cities; and the oppressive knowledge that it could all happen again on a vastly greater scale. In the words of the University of Chicago sociologist Edward Shils, himself a friend of several leading figures in the scientists' movement, it was rooted in the scientists' "worried conviction that they alone possessed an awful knowledge which, for the common good, they must share with their fellow countrymen and, above all, with their political leaders."[3]

Shils's interpretation is borne out by those activist scientists who sought to explain their motivation. Eugene Rabinowitch, for example, joined with two other scientists to write in *Life* magazine in October 1945: "Having helped man to make the first step into this new world, [scientists] have the responsibility of warning and advising him until he has become aware of its perils as well as its wonders." In a world menaced by atomic holocaust, they insisted, politics and science could no longer inhabit separate realms, if indeed they ever had. Harold C. Urey offered a compelling analogy: "It is as if a bacteriologist had discovered a dread disease which might lead to a disastrous epidemic. He would not be a 'politician' if he asked that the city health commission take measures to deal with a plague. He would merely be demonstrating common decency and social awareness."[4]

Nor were such statements merely for public consumption; they expressed deeply held feelings. As a chemist wrote in 1946 in the technical journal *Chemical and Engineering News,* far from the public eye: "Because chemists had a major share in bringing the bomb into being, chemists have a special responsibility . . . to educate the public and especially our politicians of the necessity for intelligent action before it is too late."[5]

The phrase "intelligent action" is revealing. Underlying the scientists' movement was a belief in the power of fact to compel assent in the political realm no less than in the laboratory. As one veteran of the movement later recalled, "I had faith that once public officials realized the enormity of the weaponry, they would agree that an equally enormous change had to come about in politics." The movement was also sustained by a prevailing belief, among scientists and nonscientists alike, that a commitment to science almost automatically gave one a global perspective and a unique ethical vantage point. As James Franck put it, scientists were members of "a kind of international brotherhood, comparable in many ways to a religious order," whose public activities were "dictated solely by our social conscience." If any group could resolve the atomic dilemma, wrote Christian Gauss, dean of Princeton College, in 1946, it would be those engaged in the practice of science, "the greatest cooperative global enterprise known to man."[6]

Organizationally, the scientists' movement first took shape as small groups of atomic scientists at Chicago, Los Alamos, and Oak Ridge came together to share and act upon their common concerns. (The other major Manhattan Project installation, the plutonium factory at Hanford, Washington, was never a major center of activism.) In those doom-obsessed days, the initials of one group, the Association of Los Alamos Scientists—ALAS—attracted mordant notice. In November 1945, representatives of these local groups formed a national organization, the Federation of Atomic (later "American") Scientists. Early in 1946, FAS assessed dues, launched a newsletter, and opened a Washington office. The "scientists' movement" was fully underway. Closely interwoven with the world-government movement, it was nevertheless distinct. While many of the activist scientists no doubt believed in some form of world government as an ideal, most directed their primary energies to more immediate political objectives.[7]

The first objective was defeat of the May-Johnson bill, a measure drafted by the War Department and introduced in Congress in October 1945 that would have placed all atomic research and development under military control. Most scientists were appalled by the measure, both for its militarization of the atom and for its stringent secrecy provisions. As one rather poetically put it: "Scientific research is like a porcelain egg. Catch it too tightly, it shatters—and you have nothing."[8]

The staff of the embryonic FAS threw itself into the campaign to defeat the bill, drafting statements, coordinating speakers, and briefing the stream of scientists shuttling into Washington to testify or lobby against it. Particularly active was the ever-energetic Leo Szilard, who, from his base of operations at the Wardman Park Hotel, alerted scientist friends around the country (running up massive phone bills in the process), met with senators and congressmen, and testified at hearings. ("Who was that man Liz-*ard?*" asked a puzzled legislator after one of the Hungarian's lightning forays on Capitol Hill.)[9]

The scientists' first major break came in late October when the Senate created the Special Committee on Atomic Energy under the chairmanship of Connecticut's Brien McMahon, who turned it into a forum for scientists and others critical of the May-Johnson bill. Full victory seemed to come the following July with the passage of the Atomic Energy Act of 1946—the so-called McMahon Act—establishing a civilian Atomic Energy Commission. This was not the unalloyed triumph it seemed, however. In its final form, the much-amended act contained security provisions nearly as stringent as those of the May-Johnson bill and embedded a powerful Military Liaison Committee into the basic framework of the AEC. In fact, the military got essentially all it wanted in the McMahon Act. As Alice Kimball Smith concludes, the new law was at best "a qualified triumph . . . full of ironies."[10] But at the time it appeared to be a significant achievement; the activist scientists, it seemed, had made the transition to successful political lobbyists with ease.

As the struggle over the domestic management of the atom proceeded to its ambiguous conclusion, another issue surged to the fore: international control of atomic energy. For many scientists, this was *the* cause. In October 1945, 515 scientists at Harvard and MIT signed a five-point statement that summed up a rapidly evolving consensus:

1. "Other nations" would soon be able to produce atomic bombs.
2. No effective defense was possible.
3. Mere numerical superiority in atomic weaponry offered no security.
4. A future atomic war would destroy "a large fraction of civilization."
5. Therefore, "International cooperation of an unprecedented kind is necessary for our survival."[11]

Embodying the basic message of the scientists' movement, these five points soon took on a certain formulaic quality, as they were reiterated in countless speeches and articles.

The high point of the international-control movement came early in 1946. That January, Secretary of State James F. Byrnes named a top-level committee headed by Undersecretary Dean Acheson to prepare a plan for presentation to the United Nations Atomic Energy Commission, whose first meeting was scheduled for June. Acheson's committee in turn appointed a five-man board of consultants, chaired by David E. Lilienthal and including J. Robert Oppenheimer, to undertake actual drafting of the proposal. Working feverishly, the consulting committee produced its *Report on the International Control of Atomic Energy* on March 28. Beginning with the scientists' familiar five points, the report went on to sketch in broad strokes a scheme for world cooperation in the peaceful development of atomic energy led by a United Nations atomic energy authority that would survey and control all known fissionable ore deposits on earth; license, construct, and monitor all national atomic-energy facilities; and have broad inspection powers to detect any diversion of atomic resources to military purposes. [12]

Viewed in the most favorable light, the "Acheson-Lilienthal Report," as it was quickly dubbed, can be seen as reflecting the drafters' belief in the power of reason, goodwill, and the spirit of scientific cooperation. Rather than spelling out every detail in advance, it offered, in Lilienthal's words, "a place to begin, a foundation on which to build." Woven through the hopeful prose was a dark thread of warning: "Only if the dangerous aspects of atomic energy are taken out of national hands . . . is there any reasonable prospect of devising safeguards against the use of atomic energy for atomic bombs." [13]

The report was greeted with enthusiasm by the politically active atomic scientists—and small wonder, for it seemed to give an official imprimatur to what they had been saying for months. Edward Teller called it "the first ray of hope that the problem of international control can, actually, be solved." To Harold Urey it was "the most statesmanlike pronouncement . . . on the subject since the atomic bomb fell on Hiroshima."

These were heady and exciting days for the activist scientists. One young activist, the physicist David Inglis, has recalled several encounters with J. Robert Oppenheimer in Washington during this period, and Oppenheimer's head-shaking comments: "David, I'm finding these guys receptive. They're getting the idea that we've really got to do something drastic." "For the first time since the end of the war, we began to feel hopeful," the director of FAS's Washington office later recalled. "We clasped the new bible in our hands and went out to ring doorbells." [14]

On June 14, 1946, the eleven-member United Nations Atomic Energy Commission (UNAEC) gathered for its first session in the elaborately redecorated Hunter College gymnasium in the Bronx. In the packed hall were J. Robert Oppenheimer, Arthur Compton, and Harold Urey representing the atomic scientists. Delivering the opening address was the United States delegate, Bernard M. Baruch, seventy-five-year-old financier and perennial presidential advisor. Drawing himself up to his full six feet, four inches, the silvery-haired Baruch began on an apocalyptic note: "We are here today to make a choice between the quick and the dead. That is our business." Evoking the fear that had enveloped America in the ten months since Hiroshima, he wove it into a larger message of promise: "Behind the black portent of the new atomic age lies a hope which, seized upon with faith, can work our salvation. If we fail, then we have damned every man to be the slave of Fear." After outlining the American plan, Baruch soared to his peroration:

> All of us are consecrated to making an end of gloom and hopelessness. It will not be an easy job. The way is long and thorny, but supremely worth traveling. All of us want to stand erect, with our faces to the sun, instead of being forced to burrow into the earth like rats. . . .
> We say we are for Peace. The world will not forget that we say this. . . . We shall nobly save, or meanly lose, the last, best hope on earth.[15]

Except for a few isolationist newspapers like the *Chicago Tribune,* the journalistic reaction—from the *New York Times* to small-town newspapers—was overwhelmingly enthusiastic. Said the *Toledo Blade:* "There is not type enough in any newspaper office anywhere big enough to emphasize the importance of the American proposal today." Fitzpatrick, the political cartoonist of the *St. Louis Post-Dispatch,* who in August 1945 had drawn a puny human figure vainly trying to rein in the streaking lightning bolts of atomic energy, now offered a more hopeful image of a powerful arm labeled "Control Plan" actually gripping and restraining the nuclear lightning. A parade of civic groups and other national organizations endorsed the Baruch proposals.[16]

However, insiders familiar with the shaping of American atomic policy did not share the exalted hopes aroused by Baruch's lofty rhetoric. During the drafting of the Acheson-Lilienthal Report, differences had developed over precisely when the United States would relinquish its atomic monopoly to an international authority, and a covering letter appended to the report upon its public release insisted on America's freedom to continue building and testing atomic bombs until the plan became fully operational. Even then, it added, the United States could reject it and carry on with its atomic-weapons program: "That decision, whenever made, will involve considerations of the highest policy, affecting our security, and must be made by our government under its constitutional processes and in the light of all the facts of the world situation." The United States thus preserved a de facto veto over the entire plan: not until Washington agreed that the raw-materials survey was complete and the inspection system satisfactorily in place would the international-control arrangement begin. While the Soviets gave up critical information about their fissionable resources and their progress in atomic-weapons research, in other words, the United States could retain and enlarge its stock of bombs, conduct its tests, and in general maintain its massive lead in the field. Viewed from Moscow, this "generous" and "idealistic" plan seemed a formula for perpetuating American nuclear superiority into the indefinite future.[17]

From the first, knowledgeable supporters of international control were dismayed by these qualifications. Writing in the *Nation,* the Washington journalist I. F. Stone warned that "newspaper hoopla" and David Lilienthal's high reputation had "led many people to read the [Acheson-Lilienthal Report] much less critically than its importance warrants." Focusing on the report's covering letter, Stone warned that no plan that insisted on the United States' right to stockpile atomic bombs and "change our minds four or five years hence about handing over the secret" offered any hope of forestalling an atomic-arms race. For all the high hopes riding on it, Stone concluded, the report "may turn out to be a prize phony, a slice of atomic pie in the sky."[18]

In "U.S. 1946 King's X," the poet Robert Frost evoked a familiar children's game to express a similar skepticism toward America's atomic-energy proposals:

Having invented a new Holocaust,
And been the first with it to win a war,
How they make haste to cry with fingers crossed,
King's X—no fairs to use it any more![19]

These apprehensions had deepened immeasurably with the appointment of the vain and publicity-hungry Bernard Baruch as the American delegate to UNAEC. Not involved in the drafting of the Acheson-Lilienthal Report, Baruch insisted as a condition of his appointment that he be free to formulate his own negotiating position. Surrounding himself with a coterie of Wall Street conservatives deeply suspicious of the Soviet Union, Baruch imposed his own heavy imprint on the American position and solicited the opinion of the joint chiefs of staff, who predictably stressed the enormous military importance of America's atomic monopoly. More broadly, he brought to the negotiating process a jingoistic tone, an a priori suspicion of the Soviet Union, and a penchant for playing to the gallery that was quite alien to the spirit in which the consulting committee had pursued its mandate.

Despite the warning signals, Americans awaited the Soviet response to Baruch's speech. The night before the Soviet delegate Andrei Gromyko was to deliver the Russian reply, Baruch in a typically grandiose gesture took the entire UNAEC membership to dinner at the Stork Club and then to the heavyweight championship fight between Joe Louis and Billy Conn; afterwards he and Gromyko retreated to Baruch's hotel suite for private conversation over drinks. But all to no avail. In his speech the next day, June 19, 1946, Gromyko bluntly insisted that a world moratorium on the production and use of atomic weapons must precede any agreement on international control. With this speech, the climate of hope that had been sustained for six months sharply altered. Though the talks dragged on, they increasingly degenerated into propaganda harangues. Baruch resigned his UNAEC post at the end of 1946. By May 1948, when UNAEC finally expired, the international-control effort launched with such optimism two years before was long since dead.[20]

Was any other outcome possible? Might a more persistent and forthcoming American approach, and a different chief negotiator, have achieved a different result? Was international control ever in the cards at a time when the Soviet Union was working feverishly to build its own atomic bomb? Probably not. But we shall never know for certain—and that alone is surely tragedy enough.

As an episode in American statecraft, this depressing story has been well told in a number of excellent historical works. But how did the American people feel about international control during these critical months when hopes were raised and then dashed? If one looks only at the statements of public figures and activist scientists, the resolutions of civic organizations like the League of Women Voters, or newspaper and magazine editorials, one does get the sense of overwhelming support for the Acheson-Lilienthal plan. Even after Gromyko's tough speech of June 19, hope died hard among the nation's editors. The *New York Times* insisted that the Gromyko and Baruch proposals could be reconciled. The editors of *Business Week* issued an almost desperate call for redoubled effort at the United Nations:

> We cannot see anything in either the Baruch or the Gromyko statements that . . . make[s] the task completely impossible. We can still look at the New York skyline without shuddering for its future. . . . Literally the fate of the world hangs on this attempt. . . . Unless the United Nations Commission can arrest the drift of events, we are moving toward a horrible war. The Commission must succeed. . . . There is no alternative except atomic chaos.[21]

But when one turns from media pronouncements to the public-opinion polls, a rather different and somewhat puzzling picture emerges. *Some* polls did indicate a high level of at least generalized support for the international-control idea, but such support tended to evaporate when the wording of the question implied the sacrifice of some perceived American advantage. In a Gallup poll of October 1945, only 17 percent of the respondents thought "the secret of making atomic bombs" should be put under United Nations control, while 71 percent said the United States should "keep the secret" to itself. Significantly, when Cottrell and Eberhart asked the same question in June 1946, after the heavy publicity given the Acheson-Lilienthal plan and before Gromyko's negative response, the results were almost identical: 21 percent were prepared to turn the bomb secret over to the UN, with 72 percent advocating a continuation of the American monopoly. (In Cottrell and Eberhart's follow-up survey in August, after Gromyko's speech and the Bikini tests, the margin in favor of clinging to the secret widened still further.) Those citizens least informed on world affairs were the most opposed to UN control, Cottrell and Eberhart reported, but even among the most knowledgeable, over half opposed such control, with a little more than a third in favor. A survey conducted in Iowa in the summer of 1946 carefully avoided any references to America's atomic "secrets," but even so, only 40 percent endorsed the international-control plan, while 50 percent rejected it as a bad idea.[22] Even when the movement for international control was at its apogee, in short, the idea never won more than lukewarm popular support.

Clearly disturbed by these findings, Cottrell and Eberhart speculated about their meaning. Perhaps, they suggested, Americans were operating on the principle that "A bird in the hand is worth two in the bush," concluding that it was preferable to hold on to whatever temporary security the bomb "secret" offered, rather than surrender it for an untried alternative.[23] Accepting this explanation for the moment, one might compare the situation to that of a shipwrecked man clinging to a waterlogged piece of debris in a stormy sea. He sees what *appears* to be a lifeboat in the distance, but to swim for it would be to surrender the precarious and temporary safety of his bit of flotsam on the gamble that he could make it to the lifeboat—a lifeboat that might be only a mirage. One might wish that Americans of 1946 had rallied behind the more daring option, but one can understand the more cautious choice. And since the choice against taking *any* risks on behalf of international control was precisely what the nation's military leaders— the joint chiefs—were advocating, the fact that most Americans agreed should hardly surprise us.

A second, rather different, explanation suggested by Cottrell and Eberhart was that the comparatively weak support for international control reflected the public's lack of more than the most cursory information about the issues involved:

What stands out in any detailed survey of public opinion is that much of the business that so deeply preoccupies their leaders goes on above people's heads. . . . The government [and] its problems . . . are remote and shadowy, not only among the poor and uneducated but also to a large extent among those who according to socio-economic norms must be classed as at least average Americans.

While people recognized the bomb's "almost unbelievable destructiveness," Cottrell and Eberhart continued, they needed "a much more adequate grasp of the world situation"—not only more information about specific issues, but the kind of comprehensive overview that would enable them to see issues "in meaningful contexts" and "grasp the implications of alternative courses of action."[24] A much more comprehensive effort at public education was necessary, they insisted, if the American people were to understand and support new and untested approaches to resolving the atomic crisis. The belief that if only "the people" can be made to understand "the issues" they will surely choose wisely and well is, of course, a tenacious one in the American reform tradition. But what were "the issues"? In the volatile political climate of the later 1940s, a number of voices offering very different messages were competing for the public ear. The message increasingly emanating from Washington, where Cold War ideology was rapidly becoming the new orthodoxy, was far removed from the internationalist one assumed to be desirable by Cottrell and Eberhart. Nevertheless, it was the assumptions formulated by Cottrell and Eberhart that underlay the urgent public phase of the atomic scientists' campaign: that of bringing home to the American people the sobering facts about the atomic bomb and the consequences of nuclear war, as a way of building grassroots support for the program they believed in.

5

"To the Village Square":
The Public Agenda of the Scientists'
Movement

> To the village square we must carry the facts of atomic energy. From there must come America's voice.
>
> —Albert Einstein, June 1946[1]

An evening shortly after the war, in Taos, New Mexico: A mixed audience of artists, craftspeople, local citizens, and blanket-clad Indians from the nearby pueblo has come together for a public meeting. The speakers are young Edward Teller and Cyril Smith, two Manhattan Project scientists from nearby Los Alamos. The audience listens intently as Teller and Smith discuss the principles of atomic fission, the effects of an atomic blast, and the importance of international control. When it is over, they thoughtfully drift off into the desert night.[2]

Scenes like this—in churches, clubrooms, school auditoriums, radio studios, and conference halls—were repeated many times over in the early post-Hiroshima months. For a brief but crucial interval, scientists played a central role in molding the public's earliest nuclear perceptions and attitudes.

To a public for whom the bomb was still an awesome mystery, the stature of the "atomic scientists" grew to gargantuan proportions after August 6, 1945, and so politically active scientists found themselves speaking with voices amplified many times over by the continuing awe their exploits had aroused. Even decades later, one could occasionally catch echoes of that magnified respect when a magazine writer or a television interviewer spoke with one of the dwindling band of men who were actually *there* with Fermi at Stagg Field, with Ernest O. Lawrence at Berkeley, or with Oppenheimer at Alamogordo. Of course, since the days of the alchemists, an aura of mystery has surrounded scientists—an aura nurtured in more recent times by writers like Jules Verne and H. G. Wells, by science popularizers like

Paul de Kruif and his *Microbe Hunters* of 1928, and by movies and magazine features that offered highly romanticized accounts of the exploits of Pasteur, Edison, Steinmetz, Curie, and other wizards of the laboratory. Now, reality had truly outrun fantasy! The power of the sun itself had been unleashed on earth by the practitioners of that most arcane and rarified of sciences, nuclear physics.

The near-veneration of atomic scientists in the later 1940s is one of the most striking features of this period. "The prestige of the physical scientist as the creator of these marvels was never higher," observed Robert Redfield in November 1945. "What a physical scientist says on almost any subject is thought more important than what anybody else says." Even Alice Kimball Smith, a friend and admirer of many members of this fraternity, has written of their "over-inflated prestige" in the post-Hiroshima days. Political cartoonists rang every possible change on the theme of the omnipotence of science. In a *Chicago Tribune* cartoon of August 11, 1945, for instance, a small figure representing the "U.S. Fighting Man" raises aloft the flag of victory, his feet firmly planted on a massive book labeled "SCIENCE." A Fitzpatrick cartoon in the *St. Louis Post-Dispatch* pictured two dwarflike "Statesmen" staggering under the weight of an atomic bomb given them by "The Scientists," represented by a figure of such towering height that only his lower legs are visible.[3]

Journalists became almost starry-eyed when they described the atomic scientists' postwar role as political activists. Max Lerner wrote of "the almost miraculous clarity" with which they were analyzing "the social and political consequences of what they created." The cultural critic Lewis Mumford called them "the Awakened Ones." Most rhapsodic of all was Raymond Gram Swing's description of the youthful atomic scientists who descended on the capital in 1945 and 1946: "Their faces are open and clear, their eyes look steadily, and as witnesses before the Senate and House committees, and in their newspaper conferences, they were quiet, modest, lucid, and compellingly convincing." Looking back in 1949, physicist and Manhattan Project administrator Samuel K. Allison evoked a postwar mood that had already faded:

> Suddenly physicists were exhibited as lions at Washington tea-parties, were invited to conventions of social scientists, where their opinions on society were respectfully listened to by life-long experts in the field, attended conventions of religious orders and discoursed on theology, were asked to endorse plans for world government, and to give simplified lectures on the nucleus to Congressional committees. No wonder heads were turned.

In the same vein, MIT physics professor Bernard Feld recalled his experience as a young FAS volunteer in postwar Washington: "We were the fair-haired boys, and when we said something, people listened. We knocked on some-body's door, and the door would be wide open, and you'd say, 'I'm from Los Alamos. . . .' "[4]

For many Manhattan Project veterans suddenly thrust into the lime-light, the glare of attention seemed a heaven-sent opportunity, and they quickly capitalized on their celebrity to promote the cause of peace as they understood it. A 1947 address by Arthur H. Compton helps illuminate the motives that impelled them. A Nobel Prize–winning physicist and director of the wartime atomic-bomb group at Chicago, Compton enthusiastically welcomed the postwar scientists' movement. Indeed, he said, the building of the atomic bomb was merely "an incident" in the larger "atomic crusade" through which scientists would become "a significant factor in [America's] political and social life." In Compton's view, the fundamental meaning and importance of the Manhattan Project lay in the vast public influence it had given to the scientists associated with it. They must now, he insisted, use this influence to help society move toward a brighter, more harmonious, more peaceful future. "It is this great goal that the atomists hold before them," he declared. "Atomic energy gives perhaps the greatest opportunity they will ever have to work effectively toward that goal."[5] Like General Groves the son of a Presbyterian minister, Compton brought some of the eloquence and fervor of the pulpit to his description of the atomic scientists' postwar mission.

Besides, of course, it was exciting and flattering to be courted by radio and newspaper reporters, summoned to testify before congressional commit-tees, and invited to address large public gatherings. In contrast to Comp-ton's grand vision, the Hungarian émigré Leo Szilard, who wore his "atomic scientist" halo rather awkwardly, offered in 1947 a somewhat more jaun-diced perspective on this sudden celebrity. In 1939, he said, he had grasped what physicists were about to do to the world, but only later had he realized "what, by way of revenge, the world would do to the physicists":

> I did not foresee that scientists would be crowding into Washington to see Congressmen and Senators, that they would be interviewed, pho-tographed, made into movie characters; that they would feel impelled to write and to talk on subjects other than their own, and, generally speaking, to make a circus of themselves.

Szilard then acknowledged the salient fact that was not much spoken of amidst the hectic activity of the scientists' movement: the reason for their cultural celebrity and political influence was their role in constructing a doomsday weapon that had killed more than a hundred thousand human beings. "It is remarkable," he marveled, "that all these scientists . . . should be listened to. But mass murders have always commanded the atten-tion of the public, and atomic scientists are no exception to this rule."[6]

Listened to they were! "It is no exaggeration to say," wrote the philosopher Sidney Hook in 1950, "that American atomic scientists molded the opinions of the entire Western world on the subject of nuclear energy." The first, eagerly reprinted public statements by scientists after Hiroshima came from individual notables of high visibility: Bohr, Einstein, Oppenheimer, Compton. Oppenheimer's initial statement, for example, appeared in the *New York Times* on August 9; the Manhattan Project scientists had been "sustained by hopes for the future," he said, and were now convinced that world "cooperation and understanding" were a "desperate necessity." Then the lesser-known scientists at Los Alamos, Chicago, and Oak Ridge began to put out newsletters, issue public statements, and speak to civic groups and radio audiences. "We as physicists held the limelight," Ralph Lapp has recalled. "We could say something and even though we didn't know much about it, it would get press."[7]

A key role in this public-information effort was played by the National Committee for Atomic Information (NCAI), a "lay" organization closely linked to the Federation of American Scientists. Set up in November 1945, NCAI was a coordinating agency sponsored by nearly fifty religious, labor, professional, and civic organizations. NCAI distributed a regular newsletter, *Atomic Information;* a widely circulated pamphlet, *Education for Survival*; and reprints of articles and speeches by scientists. It sponsored a touring exhibit, "Atomic Energy: Force for Life or Chaos" and held "atomic education" institutes in a number of cities. By arrangement with Metro-Goldwyn-Mayer Studios, NCAI set up informational literature tables in the lobbies of theaters showing *The Beginning or the End*—a 1946 MGM movie about the atomic bomb.[8]

For a group of supposedly absentminded scholars fresh from the laboratory, these scientist-activists showed considerable savvy in the techniques of public relations. Establishing links to Bruce Bliven of the *New Republic,* Freda Kirchwey of the *Nation,* Norman Cousins of the *Saturday Review,* and other well-placed editors, they generated many columns of publicity for their cause. Utilizing the drawing power of well-known names and aided by a skillful writer and publicist named Michael Amrine, they placed articles by big-name scientists in periodicals as diverse as *Collier's, Popular Science,* the *Rotarian,* and the *New York Times Magazine.* Through Raymond Gram Swing, Clifton Utley, and others, the scientists reached a vast radio audience. The Advertising Council promoted the scientists' cause with radio plugs and public-service ads for insertion in magazines and newspapers. By the end of 1946, the council proudly reported, over six million "listener impressions" had been registered. Several leading atomic scientists, including Urey, Oppenheimer, James Franck, and Hans Bethe spoke on the regular intermission program of the New York Philharmonic's network broadcasts. "Nobel Prize winners have made themselves nearly as accessible as politicians," marveled one observer. To help finance these varied endeavors, a prestigious Emergency Committee of Atomic Scientists raised about $100,000 in its initial fund drive in the summer of 1946.[9]

The atomic scientists showed great resourcefulness, too, in tailoring their appeal to specific groups. To build support for the Acheson-Lilienthal plan, the Association of Los Alamos Scientists gave the mayors of the nation's forty-two largest cities enlarged photographs of devastated Nagasaki and glass paperweights made of melted sand from the Alamogordo blast. The Federation of American Scientists asked the American Psychological Association for its views on the psychological aspects of human aggressiveness. "To our knowledge," said the APA proudly, "this is the first time that physical scientists have called upon psychologists to pool information." For Washington politicians, FAS organized a lecture series on nuclear physics. Sixty congressmen showed up for the first lecture, reported *Time,* and "listened in absolute stillness." This series proved shortlived, the "absolute stillness" apparently being in some cases sleep, as the legislators found even simplified physics far over their heads; but the "Seminar for Senators" quickly became enshrined in the lore of the scientists' movement. For classroom use, the FAS prepared informational packets and a cartoon filmstrip illustrating the themes of the scientists' movement. The first frame, showing an innocent-looking man cradling a bomb, was captioned: "Here we are, halo shining, holding our sacred trust, the Atom Bomb. . . . We wouldn't hurt anyone." But everyone dashes for cover all the same, and in the final frame the world's statesmen, having adopted an international-control plan, happily shake hands above a fresh grave where the atomic bomb lies safely buried.[10]

In this campaign to carry the word of atomic danger and the need for action "to the village square," the Atomic Scientists of Chicago were especially active. The yellowing files of this small and loosely knit organization —bulging with memos on speeches to be delivered, articles to be written, phone calls to be answered, and conferences to be organized—can still evoke, after the passage of forty chastening years, the urgency, excitement, and earnestness of the scientists who decided in 1945 to go public with their message.[11] The Chicagoans were also responsible for one of the most effective —and certainly the most durable—of the scientists' attempts to influence public opinion: the *Bulletin of the Atomic Scientists.* The outgrowth of conversations over coffee in the autumn of 1945 among physicist Hyman Goldsmith, chemist Eugene Rabinowitch, and sociologist Edward Shils, the *Bulletin* was launched in December 1945. From modest beginnings, it soon emerged as the leader among the "bulletins" and "newsletters" that had sprung up at the various Manhattan Project sites after Hiroshima. By 1946, circulation stood at 10,000. From the first, the aim was to reach both scientists and nonscientists with articles in layman's language exploring the bomb's political and social implications. Highly regarded by newspaper editors, public officials, educators, and other opinion-molders, it exerted an influence out of all proportion to its circulation.[12]

From 1945 to 1973, the *Bulletin* was edited by Eugene Rabinowitch, a man of enormous energy and broad-ranging interests. Rabinowitch left Russia as a youth in 1917; studied chemistry at Berlin; worked with James Franck at Göttingen; and then, with the rise of nazism, came in the late 1930s to the United States. Though a full-time university professor, first at Chicago and then at the University of Illinois, Rabinowitch never flagged in his commitment to the *Bulletin*. "After many others lost faith or patience," Alice Kimball Smith has written, "he continued to explore ways in which science and scientists could contribute to international understanding and to encourage his colleagues to educate themselves in the broader implications of their work." Rabinowitch infused the magazine with his own social concern and essentially moral response to the bomb. As he wrote in 1949, "The *Bulletin* has always been a creation of conscience."[13]

The *Bulletin*'s most famous feature was the clock that appeared on the cover of each issue, the hands forever approaching—but never quite reaching —midnight. Together with the mushroom-shaped cloud itself, this clock would eventually become one of the best-known visual symbols of the atomic age. It was a remarkably apt representation of the fear and urgency felt by many atomic scientists as they sought to awaken the public to the perils their research had unleashed upon an unsuspecting world.

6

The Uses of Fear

Radio listeners who happened, on June 30, 1946, to tune in to *Exploring the Unknown,* a popular science show on the Mutual network, were in for a frightening experience. The entire program that summer Sunday evening was devoted to the atomic bomb. After an account of the Manhattan Project and the bomb's role in ending World War II, it quickly proceeded to a chillingly realistic depiction of the outbreak of a future atomic war. As a metronome ticked in the background, narrator Clifton Fadiman recreated the casual, workaday activities of a typical American in the final ten seconds before the first bomb strikes. This was followed, according to the script directions, with an "Unearthly Roar," which quickly faded out as Fadiman said: "Silence—complete and total silence. The infinite silence of death. In a fraction of a second—you and thousands of your neighbors . . . vaporized . . . blown to bits . . . to nothingness." As the scene shifted to a farmer working in the fields six miles from the center of the city, listeners heard:

> *Sound:* Unearthly Roar
> *Fadiman:* The unearthly blast sweeps over the fields, flattening farmhouses and buildings like grotesque toys . . . striking you with staggering force. . . .
> *Man:* Oh! (*Gasping cry*)
> *Sound:* Body smacks down.

Later in the program, a gavel banged three times and a somber voice intoned: "I sentence you to a few short years—in which to solve the problems posed by nuclear fission. Penalty for failure—death!" At the end, an announcer speaking for the program's sponsor, the Revere Copper and Brass Company, urged listeners to write for information on the Lilienthal report and the Baruch plan.[1]

America's airwaves, pulpits, and lecture halls were full of such frightening fare in the early post-Hiroshima period, as the nation's atomic fears were manipulated and exacerbated by the media and by political activists. In their effort to use grass-roots pressure to shape public policy, atomic scientists, world-government advocates, and international-control advocates played upon the profound uneasiness pervading the nation. The politicization of terror was a decisive factor in shaping the post-Hiroshima cultural climate.

It is important to reiterate at the outset, however, that America's atomic fear in this immediate postwar period was in no sense a synthetic creation of activists or the media. The surge of fear that swept America after August 6, 1945, was a spontaneous and authentic response to the horror of Hiroshima and Nagasaki. It continued to find powerful expression as weeks turned to months; indeed, with the passage of time it became, if anything, more concrete and specific. In December 1945, the *Wall Street Journal* published a lengthy feature article that vividly pictured an attack by planes and missiles that could wipe out 98 percent of the population of the United States. In February 1946, Brig. Gen. Thomas F. Farrell, commander of the first U.S. Army investigating team to enter Hiroshima, testifying before the McMahon Committee, declared that eight Nagasaki-type bombs would demolish New York City. In such an attack, Farrell added, the city's skyscrapers "would fly apart as though they themselves were bombs and someone had lighted their fuse." Concluded General Farrell soberly: "This isn't a bomb at all. The use of the word 'bomb' carries with it a completely inaccurate picture of what this thing does." *Collier's* was soon on the stands with "What the Atomic Bomb Really Did," an article that quoted liberally from Farrell's testimony and went on to predict that the atomic bombs of 1945 would compare to those of 1965 "much as the first feeble flight of the Wright brothers contrasts with the performance of today's aircraft."[2]

Even the generally up-beat *Reader's Digest* reflected the raw fear so starkly apparent in post-Hiroshima America. "The energy released in a uranium explosion is beyond imagination," noted an October 1945 article. "Everything within a mile of the explosion is vaporized." The *Digest's* military editor, Francis Vivian Drake, struck an even more alarming note that December: "The Hiroshima bomb is already dated," he wrote. "It is now in the power of the atom-smashers to blot out New York with a single bomb. . . . Such a bomb can burn up in an instant every creature, can fuse the steel buildings and smash the concrete into flying shrapnel."[3]

It is true that the *Digest* also published, in February 1946, "Atomic Bomb Hysteria," an article by Alexander de Seversky pooh-poohing the threat. "If dropped on New York or Chicago," declared de Seversky in a much-quoted sentence, "one of these bombs would have done no more damage than a ten-ton blockbuster." Three months later, however, the magazine in effect repudiated the de Seversky article with Robert Littel's "What the Atom Bomb Would Do to Us." To equate an atomic bomb with a World War II blockbuster was ludicrous, said Littel; it would do at least eighty times as much damage. Atomic scientists and other experts were unanimously agreed, he declared, that de Seversky had "dangerously minimized the menace of atomic bombing and tended to lull people into a false sense of security at a critical time."[4]

"Mist of Death Over New York," a 1947 *Reader's Digest* article, described in realistic detail an atomic explosion in New York harbor that sends a deadly radioactive cloud drifting over the city and beyond. "Within six weeks," noted the article with chilling precision, "389,101 New Yorkers were dead or missing," including persons drowned when they threw themselves into rivers, looters shot by the National Guard, and thousands killed fleeing the city in "the worst panic known in all human history." Continued this vividly explicit account:

> Most of the survivors suffered from some form of radiation sickness. In addition, many thousands outside of Manhattan were stricken, particularly in the Bronx and Westchester County, and great numbers of them died. The casualties most distant from the explosion were in the upstate town of Watkins Glen, about 180 miles away, where the vagaries of the air currents dropped a large concentration of fission products.[5]

In May 1947, Francis Vivian Drake sent a draft of a similar article to J. Robert Oppenheimer with a request for comments. "I think that we are both agreed that a sense of *fear* is probably necessary to break public apathy," wrote Drake in his covering letter, "I would therefore like to keep the Radioactive Warfare sequence as dramatic or sensational as I possibly can, to the utmost limit of underlying facts which are true or *which could be true.*"[6]

The most vivid of these scenarios of atomic destruction, "The 36-Hour War," appeared in *Life* in November 1945. It was illustrated with realistic drawings, including one of a mushroom cloud rising over Washington, D.C. and another panoramically depicting missiles descending on thirteen major American cities. (Interestingly, *Life* in 1945 identified no *source* for this hypothetical attack, tracing it only to equatorial Africa where "an enemy of the U.S." had secretly built rocket-launching sites in the jungle.)

After this surprise attack kills ten million Americans, according to *Life*'s scenario, the enemy lands airborne troops wearing antiradiation gear to complete its conquest. Attempting an upbeat ending, *Life* concluded its grim fantasy: "As it is destroyed, the U.S. is fighting back. The enemy airborne troops are wiped out. U.S. rockets lay waste the enemy's cities. U.S. airborne troops successfully occupy his country. The U.S. wins the atomic war." But the hollowness of this conclusion was revealed in the final full-page drawing of a rubble-strewn New York, in which only the great stone lions guarding the public library are left to gaze impassively as heavily shielded technicians "test the rubble of the shattered city for radioactivity."[7]

If the atomic scientists and other postwar activists did not create a pervasive, nationwide terror of atomic annihilation, they did contribute powerfully to sustaining and intensifying it. The public appeals of the scientists' movement were based almost wholly on fear. "Five years from today, if we are in a serious war crisis," wrote W. A. Higinbotham, executive secretary of the Federation of American Scientists, in a 1946 *New York Times Magazine* article, "you will be haunted by the overpowering knowledge that if war is declared, you, your house, or your business, may disappear in the next second." An article ghostwritten by FAS publicist Michael Amrine and published by *Collier's* under Harold Urey's name bore the arresting title "I'm a Frightened Man." It began: "I write this to frighten you. I'm a frightened man, myself. All the scientists I know are frightened—frightened for their lives—and frightened for *your* life. . . . [We] who have lived for years in the shadow of the atomic bomb are well acquainted with fear, and it is a fear you should share if we are intelligently to meet our problems." This article was illustrated with a photograph of a hollow-eyed Urey looking very frightened indeed.[8] (Photographs of J. Robert Oppenheimer, with his gaunt, solemn face and staring eyes, lent themselves especially well to the iconography of fear in these years.)

These doom-laden pronouncements had an enormous cultural and media impact, as newspapers and magazines liberally quoted the scientists' descriptions of what an atomic attack would do. The *Reader's Digest*'s 1947 article describing an atomic-bomb explosion in New York harbor was clearly inspired by the speeches and congressional testimony of various atomic scientists and it concluded with a blunt statement of the scientists' basic message: "We must do everything in our power to bring about international control of atomic energy. The men who have worked with the bomb feel that the United States plan, as presented to the United Nations by Bernard M. Baruch, is the best answer to the problem." "Old Man Atom," a 1947 song by the Sons of the Pioneers, even brought the scientists' message to the world of country music. After grim warnings of atomic destruction it concluded:

So listen folks, for here's my thesis,
Peace in the world, or the world in pieces.[9]

The many radio programs of the early postwar years that offered chillingly realistic descriptions of an atomic attack were often prepared in close collaboration with scientists. Indeed, the Atomic Scientists of Chicago offered to radio stations a recorded program in which physicist Philip Morrison described his firsthand observations of the destruction of Hiroshima. In "The War That Must Not Come," another program written with ASC cooperation and broadcast on Chicago station WMAQ in April 1946, NBC newsman

Clifton Utley offered yet another description of a hypothetical atomic bombing, this one of Chicago:

> Most of those in the center of the city were violently killed by the blast or by the following vacuum which explosively burst their stomachs and intestines, and violently ruptured their tissue. Those few who escaped the blast, but not the gamma rays died slowly but inevitably after they had left the ruined city. . . . No attempt at identification of bodies or burial ever took place. Chicago was simply closed, and the troops did not allow anyone to return.

After further discussion of mass sterility and a precipitous decline in the birth rate as long-term consequences of atomic war, the program characteristically concluded with a plea for support of the Acheson-Lilienthal plan.[10]

These orchestrations of fear were undertaken quite consciously and deliberately. To many post-Hiroshima social observers, *fear* represented a potent lever of social change. From mass terror would spring a mass demand for the radical transformation of the international order upon which survival depended. "Fear," wrote *Commonweal* in August 1945, "may do what sheer morality could never do." If humankind managed to avoid atomic war, this Catholic journal speculated, "not conscience but the most basic of instincts will probably get the credit." The psychiatrist Franz Alexander agreed. Fundamental psychic changes might in the remote future lead the human race to an ethical renunciation of war, he wrote in 1946, but the best short-run hope was that fear would "activate the forces of self-preservation and bring nations to their senses." In her speech welcoming delegates to the *New York Herald Tribune* world-affairs forum in October 1945, Mrs. Ogden W. Reid articulated the same hope:

> Children are trained by fear to use intelligent caution and fear of death has given inspiration for the cure and prevention of disease. All religions have been nurtured through fear of punishment before or after death. . . . If a united fear of the atomic bomb [can be] . . . transform[ed] into determined action, it may become the greatest benefactor of mankind.[11]

The energizing power of fear, as historian Lawrence S. Wittner has noted, had special significance for those activists who were promoting specific reform agendas. World-government advocate Robert M. Hutchins set the theme as early as August 12, 1945, when, on his *Chicago Roundtable* broadcast, he speculated that the atomic bomb, like hell in Christian theology, could be "the good news of damnation" that would frighten people into "the creation of a world society." In his *Saturday Review* editorial, "Modern

Man Is Obsolete," Norman Cousins similarly argued that the "primordial apprehensions" the atomic bomb had aroused could, if properly channeled, lead mankind to accept the inexorable logic of world government: "Once the instinct for survival is stimulated, the basic condition for change can be met. That is why the quintessence of destruction . . . must be dramatized and kept in the forefront of public opinion." [12]

The post-Hiroshima writings and pronouncements of the atomic scientists are full of references to the potency of fear as a catalyst of political action. As Philip Morrison put it in testimony before the McMahon Committee: "We have a chance to build a working peace on the novelty and terror of the atomic bomb." One aim of the *Bulletin of the Atomic Scientists,* wrote Eugene Rabinowitch, was "to preserve our civilization by scaring men into rationality." Albert Einstein expressed hope that the atomic bomb would "intimidate the human race into bringing order into its international affairs." Writing for the *Rotarian,* Arthur H. Compton made the same point: "Creators of the bomb have done what Alfred Nobel thought he had achieved when he invented dynamite: make war so terrible and destructive that men would be frightened into peace. . . . Science is forcing the hand of the statesman." [13]

Fleshing out the rhetoric, other activists candidly discussed the tactical considerations that underlay the use of fear. The aim, said one scientist, was to "scare the pants off" the public to build support for international atomic control and the outlawing of atomic weapons. "Only one tactic is dependable —the preaching of doom," a Chicago atomic scientist told the *New Yorker;* anything else was "met with yawns." In July 1946, writing to a physicist who had composed a pamphlet carefully setting forth the case for international control and world government, Bernard Iddings Bell, an Episcopal churchman and social activist with close links to the atomic scientists' movement, observed that the pamphlet's very reasonableness and rationality were its central flaws. "We are going to get nowhere by a campaign of education," insisted Bell. "What we need," he continued,

> is a campaign of shameless propaganda . . . which will appeal to emotion and prejudice rather than to the mind. Hitler was able to change the attitude of the German people . . . but he was able to do it only by ruthless propaganda. What we need for our purpose now is slogans, shibboleths, comic strips, motion pictures centering around glittering stars and crooners. The last thing that we can depend upon is an appeal to common sense. [14]

In the activists' day-to-day planning, this campaign to arouse and intensify the public's fears of nuclear destruction found practical expression. "The program should have speed and a lot of wallop," one wrote to the producers of a planned radio program on the bomb; "Such sound effects as the Geiger counter, etc., can be worked in nicely." Drafting an article aimed at labor leaders, a Chicago scientist wrote: "Unless we act quickly, twenty to fifty percent of our union members may have less than five years to live." (In a penciled revision, the "five" was changed to "ten.") Beth Olds, office manager for the Atomic Scientists of Chicago, repeatedly stressed the fear theme in advising scientists on their public speeches. "Scare them a little, and incidentally give them some scientific background," she told one. To another, scheduled to address a meeting of radio executives in New York, she wrote:

> It would probably be most useful to our cause to make this a blood and thunder speech about no defense and the horrible consequences of another world war. After you have thoroughly frightened the people . . . the afternoon will be devoted to a discussion of just what the radio networks can contribute to maintaining world peace.

Another speaker preparing for the same meeting was advised to "scare the living hell out of them" while incidentally giving them "some off-the-record inside dope or . . . what seems to be information of that nature." [15]

Though the atomic scientists consciously manipulated the public's fears, they did not do so cynically. They were genuinely convinced that the atomic devastation they described was a strong liklihood, if not a near certainty; that time was desperately short; and that the remedies they proposed offered at least a slim hope. The emphasis on fear in the scientists' campaign, the Manhattan Project metallurgist Cyril Smith has observed, was "a pretty spontaneous thing." In a recent interview, Smith recalled his own feelings when he addressed general audiences in the early postwar period:

> I remember finding myself quite emotionally involved, more emotional than I meant to be, on the level of the terror and the horror and so on. But this was by no means a planned approach, it was just that in the talking I found myself getting worked up and of course ended with the usual story about [how] we must do something about it. . . . I don't remember ever being told what I should say. [16]

A few scientists resisted the prevailing tendency to use doomsday talk to build support for international control. Niels Bohr, for one, consistently advocated a positive, hopeful emphasis. Bohr did not deny the danger of world disaster, but he stressed the "prosperity and cultural development" that international control could bring. The atomic bomb should not be presented to the public solely as a potential destroyer, insisted Bohr in an

October 1945 message to the American scientific community, but as a "forceful reminder of how closely the fate of all mankind is coupled together," and as "a unique opportunity to remove obstacles to peaceful collaboration between nations and to . . . enable them jointly to benefit from the great promises . . . held out by the progress of science." [17]

Such hopeful visions were rare among the atomic scientists as they charted their post-Hiroshima course. More characteristic was the position of J. Robert Oppenheimer, who in November 1945 warned against any tendency among scientists to downplay the horror of atomic war. "It will not help to avert such a war," he said with characteristic understatement, "if we try to rub the edges off this new terror that we have helped to bring to the world." He continued:

> If I return so insistently to the magnitude of the peril . . . it is because I see in that our one great hope. . . . As a vast threat, and a new one, to all the peoples of the earth, by its novelty, its terror, its strangely promethean quality, it has become, in the eyes of many of us, an opportunity unique and challenging. [18]

Not everyone agreed with the fear-inducing tactics employed by the atomic scientists and other activists of the early postwar period. A few shared Alexander de Seversky's view that the fears were exaggerated. Military analyst Stefan T. Possony of Georgetown University, for example, wrote caustically of the "League of Frightened Men" who were spreading unjustified "fear and despair" with their predictions of "the demise of mankind in an earth-shattering chain-reaction." Others who did not question that the atomic bomb was a fearful thing nevertheless warned that the manipulation and exacerbation of those fears for political purposes was a dubious and potentially counterproductive strategy. The attempt to panic people into support for internationalist remedies, wrote Reinhold Niebuhr in October 1945, reflected a serious misreading of human nature. American-Soviet relations were likely to have a greater impact on public attitudes than fear of atomic war, Niebuhr presciently observed, since "ultimate perils, however great, have a less lively influence upon the human imagination than immediate resentments and frictions, however small by comparison." [19]

Niebuhr's reservations were shared by other observers as well. "The atomic bomb presents an ominous alternative . . .," observed the New York minister Harry Emerson Fosdick in a post-Hiroshima radio sermon, "but no man or nation was ever yet frightened into real brotherhood and peace." "I am amazed . . . that so many of my contemporaries . . . seem to believe that the sheer frightfulness of atomic energy's potentialities will somehow scare us all into being good," wrote columnist Eduard C. Lindeman in November 1945. "If the fear theory of morality were sound, we should have eliminated war and crimes long ago." "Some who have cried loudest for world government have built their case on the shakiest of arguments," said *Fortune* in January 1946; "They have appealed to fear." A few activists agreed. "Those who contend that the horrible prospect of future warfare will cure man of his bad habits," the longtime world-government champion Senator Elbert D. Thomas told the American Society for International Law in October 1945, "reckon without the ability of man to live carelessly, blindly, and nonchalantly in the midst of a physical situation that may threaten to destroy him at any time." G. A. Borgese, head of the Chicago-based Committee to Frame a World Constitution, writing in June 1946, criticized the "psychological and political simplicity" of those who were pushing the nation "toward a state of near panic" in the pursuit of their political objectives.[20]

Even those sympathetic with the idea of rousing the public to political commitment through fear sometimes questioned the strategy's assumptions. Might not its ironic ultimate effect, in fact, be a *numbing* of awareness? "The louder they shout to us, the more inaudible their voices become," observed Lewis Mumford early in 1946. "The very abundance of these reminders," commented another cultural observer that August, seemed to be "conditioning a resistance in our minds to their import." Conversely, if fear *did* remain at a high pitch, the result might be not a determination to act, but feelings of helplessness and futility—an effect suggested in the headline of a December 1945 *Newsweek* story on some particularly alarming testimony before the McMahon Committee: "BLACK LESSON OF THE ATOM BOMB: ITS AWFUL FURY KILLS EVEN HOPE." This, in turn, could lead to consequences far different from those the activists sought. Debilitating atomic fear was as likely to lead to calls for a preemptive attack on a potential enemy, observed Richard M. Fagley in the October 1945 *Christianity and Crisis,* as to support for international control.

Elaborating the point in the Spring 1946 *American Scholar,* historian Erich Kahler wrote:

> The general fear, on which so many people count as a restraining influence, is a very questionable defense. Between fear and its object there exists a menacing and magic interaction which tends to gradual intensification, and eventually to a panic merging of the two. In a crisis, help has never come from fear, but only from calm and careful consideration.

And even if the effects of long-sustained fear were not cataclysmic, they could insidiously undermine society, leading to a national orgy of hedonism and self indulgence—or so some feared. As one scientist warned at the February 1946 conference for religious leaders sponsored by the Atomic

Scientists of Chicago: "We must be wary lest we scare people so that they will become cynical about the whole thing. . . . If this reaction develops, we will destroy all we want to accomplish in our role as amateur teachers of morals." [21]

By 1947, amidst a rapidly changing political climate, the tempo of skeptical criticism quickened. "Human psychology is such that it is completely impossible to scare people collectively or for any length of time," insisted John W. Campbell, Jr., in *The Atomic Story*, as he discussed the cultural response to the bomb. "Every human being has a subconscious and unalterable conviction that death is something that happens to other people, but never to him." In a widely reprinted speech of June 1947, David E. Lilienthal complained that for nearly two years the public had been "fed a publicity diet of almost nothing else but horror stories," and warned: "Scaring the daylights out of everyone so no one can think, inducing hysteria and unreasoning fear . . . .is not going to get us anywhere . . . we want to go." Continued the Atomic Energy Commission chairman:

> To those who have given little thought to such matters, it might have seemed like a good idea to scare the world into being good, or at least sensible. But fear is brother to panic. Fear is an unreliable ally; it can never be depended upon to produce good. . . . Public thinking that is dominated by great fear . . . provides a sorry foundation for the strains we may find it necessary to withstand. [22]

Confronted with such criticisms, some who had initially advocated the fear approach had second thoughts. Robert M. Hutchins soon was criticizing the scare approach as fallacious:

> After each war it is said that the next one will be so horrible that nobody will ever start it. Atomic war will be the most horrible we have known, and both the victor and the vanquished will lose it. But since men have been willing to involve themselves in conflicts in which 5 million human beings were killed in 4 years, it seems unlikely that they will abstain in the future merely because 40 million human beings may be killed in half an hour.

Even J. Robert Oppenheimer, who in November 1945 had insisted that scientists must keep the horrors of nuclear war forever fresh in the public mind as part of their larger political program, was advising by 1947 that as Hiroshima and Nagasaki receded from the nation's consciousness, the scientists' role could no longer be that of "prophets of doom coming out of the desert." [23]

Though it failed, however, the strategy of manipulating fear to build support for a political resolution of the atomic menace helped fix certain basic perceptions about the bomb deep in the American consciousness, and it set a precedent for activist strategy that would affect all later anti-nuclear crusades.

Despite the unique features of the immediate post-Hiroshima cultural moment, the conviction that if only the full horror of atomic war were made vivid enough mankind would surely take radical steps to avoid it had deep cultural roots. Time and again throughout history, the advent of new and more terrible weapons—the crossbow, the submarine, TNT, aerial bombing —had stirred similar hopes. Indeed, even with reference to the atomic bomb, this theme far antedated 1945. It is the message of H. G. Wells's "The World Set Free," a 1914 story that understandably became famous after August 1945 for its explicit prediction of the atomic bomb. According to Wells's scenario, a European war set in the 1950s is about to end in German victory when a young aviator attached to the French army's "special scientific corps" seeks out his nation's secret stockpile of atomic bombs, loads three of them in his airplane, and sets out for Berlin filled with "the happiness of an idiot child that has at last got hold of the matches." Not only is Berlin wiped off the map, but the area where the city once stood is made permanently radioactive. Terrified, the nations of the world outlaw war and set up an international organization to enforce peace. Warfare had already become anachronistic as a means of settling international disputes, Wells says, but people "did not see it until the atomic bombs burst in their fumbling hands."[24] The similarity between this passage and countless pronouncements of 1945–1946 is striking. Not only in his prediction of the atomic bomb, but also in his anticipation of the uses to which its horror would be put by advocates of peace and international cooperation, Wells in 1914 proved himself an uncanny prophet. Only in his conclusion—that all the talk of peace, disarmament, and world harmony through atomic fear would actually produce that result—did Wells miss the mark.

7

Representative Text:
One World or None

In March 1946, seven months after World War II ended in fiery atomic bursts over Hiroshima and Nagasaki, the Federation of American Scientists published *One World or None,* an eighty-six-page paperback that immediately became a national bestseller. It remains a document of intense cultural interest for the way it epitomizes the themes we have been exploring: the political activism of the atomic scientists, the post-Hiroshima interest in world government and international control of atomic energy, the manipulation of fear.

The book's title itself sums up an interesting bit of cultural history. As with "Manifest Destiny," "New Deal," "Cold War," and other phrases that have entered the language, its exact provenance is uncertain. Wendell Willkie, as we have seen, had popularized the phrase "One World" by choosing it as the title of his 1943 book reporting on a world tour he had undertaken at FDR's request. After Hiroshima, the phrase took on an added sense of urgency. On August 12, 1945, Edward R. Murrow referred to "the editorial writers who have been saying that we are faced with a choice between a new world or none at all." Raymond Gram Swing used a slight variant, "One World or No World" in an August 1945 radio broadcast, but the first use in precisely this form I have noted is "One World or None" by Freda Kirchwey, an article in the August 18 *Nation.*[1]

Priced at a dollar, the FAS *One World or None* sold a hundred thousand copies. Reviews were respectful and highly favorable. "Americans who would like to die a natural death can read it with profit," said *Time.* Another reviewer called it "illuminating, powerful, threatening and hopeful" and said it would "clarify a lot of confused thinking." *Business Week* found it "eloquent." The authors of a 1947 popularization called *Atomics for the Millions* pronounced it "the outstanding book on this problem to date." WMCA, a major commercial radio station in New York City with a public-service orientation, broadcast a thirteen-part series based on it.[2]

One gets the sense that a great many Americans *wanted* this book to be a definitive guide to the atomic era, and that the wish was father to the thought. In fact, though its fifteen contributors included five Nobel laureates and other distinguished personages, *One World or None* is a very disjointed affair. Much of it is a scissors-and-paste compilation of brief pieces written for other purposes—such as Niels Bohr's August 11, 1945, statement to the *Times* of London—and pulled together by the editors, Dexter Masters of *Science Illustrated* magazine and Katherine Way, a physicist who in the early postwar period doubled as office manager for the Atomic Scientists of Chicago.

One World or None is divided into two major sections, the first describing the hazards of the atomic era, the second discussing what could be done. The first is by far the more compelling. "Catastrophe lies ahead if war is not eliminated," warned Arthur H. Compton in the introduction, and one by one a succession of atomic scientists documented Compton's stark assertion. Physicist Louis Ridenour demolished any hope of adequate defense against atomic attack. Edward U. Condon, associate director of the Westinghouse Research Laboratory during the war and now head of the National Bureau of Standards, painted a scary picture of nuclear sabotage: "In any room where a file case can be stored, in any district of a great city, near any key building or installation, a determined effort can secrete a bomb capable of killing a hundred thousand people and laying waste every ordinary structure within a mile."[3] Frederick Seitz and Hans Bethe estimated that "other nations" could develop an atomic bomb in five or six years. The Nobel laureate chemist Irving Langmuir of the General Electric laboratory, just back from a trip to the Soviet Union, reported that the large-scale Russian atomic program would probably produce a bomb "within about three years." Langmuir's estimate would prove accurate. An atomic-arms race on which the United States was budgeting half a billion dollars was already underway, Langmuir wrote. Air force general H. H. ("Hap") Arnold warned that if international control failed, the alternatives would be draconian indeed: population dispersal, the burial of key industries, and (an early articulation of deterrence theory) a massive build-up of atomic weapons to deter attack through the threat of retaliation. Harlow Shapley of the Harvard College Observatory implied in his contribution that extraterrestrial civilizations may already have failed the atomic challenge now facing the human species. "The well-known Crab Nebula in Taurus," he wrote, "is now recognized as the wreckage of the supernova of July 4, A.D. 1054 . . ., the result, apparently, of the mishandling by a star of its resources in atomic energy." In keeping with the book's general tone of pessimism, Gale Young offered a discouraging assessment of the atom's peacetime uses.[4]

By far the most gripping chapter of *One World or None* was "If the Bomb Gets Out of Hand" by Philip Morrison, a Cornell physicist who had worked on the Manhattan Project at Chicago and Los Alamos, participated in the final bomb assembly on Tinian Island, and after the war been among the first to inspect Hiroshima. The best prose stylist among the atomic scientists, Morrison had already won attention for his gripping testimony before the McMahon Committee in December 1945 describing, in understated but memorable specificity, the destruction he had witnessed. With twenty-six of Hiroshima's thirty fire stations demolished, he reported, "Debris filled the streets, and hundreds, even thousands of fires burned unchecked among the injured and the dead. No one was able to fight them." Eight months before John Hersey's *Hiroshima*, Morrison's testimony brought the numbing abstraction of megadeaths down to the level of a single human being:

> I remember seeing one man, a patient, who had worn a railway-worker's uniform. This uniform in Japan is a dark serge with an insigne to designate his grade. This man wore, as insigne, a kind of cross-shaped emblem over the left breast.
> His whole body was burned very badly and blackened, with the exception of the region under this cross. That was because the white clothing passed the heat somewhat less than the dark clothing did. The dark clothing absorbed the heat and caught fire and burned him.

Morrison's discussion of the effects of radiation on blood-forming tissue in the bone marrow was equally graphic: "The blood does not coagulate, but oozes in many spots through the unbroken skin, and internally seeps into the cavities of the body." At a moment when the initial shock of Hiroshima and Nagasaki was beginning to fade somewhat, Morrison's McMahon Committee testimony brought it rushing back. Raymond Gram Swing quoted from it liberally in his radio broadcast. *Newsweek* printed extensive extracts. The *New Republic* published the text verbatim under the title "Beyond Imagination."[5]

In his contribution to *One World or None*, Morrison drew upon his Hiroshima observations to describe a hypothetical atomic-bomb attack on New York City, reasoning that a "clearer and truer understanding can be gained from thinking of the bomb as falling on a city, among buildings and people, which Americans know well." Many journalists and writers offered such scenarios in these months, but none matched Morrison's. In moment-by-moment detail, he described the effect of a single Hiroshima-type bomb dropped at 12:07 P.M. and detonated at twenty-six hundred feet "just above the corner of Third Avenue and East 20th Street, near Gramercy Park":

> From the river west to Seventh Avenue and from south of Union Square to the middle Thirties, the streets were filled with dead and dying. The old men sitting on the park benches in the square never knew what had happened. They were chiefly charred black on the side toward the

bomb. Everywhere in this whole district were men with burning clothing, women with terrible red and blackened burns, and dead children caught while hurrying home to lunch.[6]

Bellevue Hospital is demolished. As radiation disease spreads, many thousands die of "unstoppable internal hemorrhages, of wildfire infections, of slow oozing of the blood into the flesh." Morrison even offered a Manhattan variant of the railway worker with the insignia outlined in his flesh: a man "who saw the blast through the netting of the monkey cage in Central Park and bore for days on the unnatural ruddy tan of his face the white imprint of the shadow of the netting." Estimating total deaths of three hundred thousand in such an attack, Morrison minced no words in his conclusion: "If the bomb gets out of hand, if we do not learn to live together so that science will be our help and not our hurt, there is only one sure future. The cities of men on earth will perish."[7]

In one way or another, all the contributors to *One World or None* echoed Morrison's sentiments. The danger was great; the need for action urgent. The only alternative to catastrophe, said Arthur Compton, was "adjusting the pattern of our society on a world basis." J. Robert Oppenheimer, as noted earlier, foresaw "radical and profound changes in the politics of the world" as a result of the bomb. The book's "eloquent and unanswerable argument," declared the FAS in a concluding summation, was that atomic power would "bring death to the society that produced it if we do not adapt ourselves to it."[8]

But how was the average citizen to "adapt" to the bomb, much less (as Harold Urey put it) "vigorously grasp the situation and take the offensive"? What was one to do to avoid the horrendous fate so grimly spelled out in *One World or None?* Here the book faltered. For all their eloquence, the contributors were much better at evoking the atomic nightmare than at prescribing remedies. The final chapters, intended to chart a course of action, were confused and ill-focused. Most contributors agreed in a general way on the need for international control, but with sharp differences of emphasis and varying degrees of confidence. The most outspoken was Albert Einstein, who, in a short piece adapted from a recent *New York Times* article, dismissed all talk of "gradual historical development" and called for the immediate creation of a world government. For Walter Lippmann, by contrast, gradualism was the great hope. "The world state is inherent in the United Nations," Lippmann proclaimed, "as an oak tree is in an acorn." Nevertheless, with a rather labored extension of the analogy, Lippmann qualified his optimism: "Not all acorns become oak trees; many fall on stony ground or are devoured by the beasts of the wilderness. But if an acorn matures it will not become a whale or an orchid."[9] Precisely where these insights left the world-government argument was not clear.

Leo Szilard offered another of what Alice Kimball Smith has called his "successive schemes for resolving the atomic crisis." The long-term goal, he said, was world government. The short-term goal was an international inspection system to insure that atomic energy was used only for peaceful purposes. To staff this inspection system he proposed using recent college graduates in the sciences, "who would welcome the opportunity to serve for a year after graduation as inspectors in some foreign country, to broaden their knowledge and gather experience in a technical field of their own choosing." Szilard further proposed an expanded program of international exchange of scientists *and their families,* so the scholarly visitors could report any violations of the proposed international-control agreement by their own government "without endangering their lives or the safety of their families." [10]

As Szilard's contribution suggests, *One World or None* exemplified both the tension in the scientists' movement between the advocates of world government and those who argued for less ambitious schemes of international control, and the compromise formula which sought to paper over that tension: that international control of the atom would be a first step toward world government and universal peace. As Harold C. Urey put it: "Control of atomic bombs must inevitably lead to the control of all weapons of war. . . . Nothing less than the total abolition of war will prevent their use." The FAS, in its summation, expressed the same vision of Utopia achieved in stages, with international atomic control as stage one. In a key passage whose subtle shift from the imperative to the declarative mood epitomized the confusedly hopeful thinking so characteristic of this period, it said: "The nations must collaborate for the development of the new force. . . . Out of the success of such collaboration . . . will emerge a greater success. The common possession of atomic energy and the prevention of atomic war will lead to the end of war itself." The FAS closed its appeal—and the book—with an earnest call for public engagement:

> The facts are out. They are visible in the rusted rubble of Hiroshima. They are here, in this book, in your hands. Unless these facts become real to you, unless you learn from them as we have learned from them —that we all must act—there will be no answer ever to our problem. . . . Now that you have read this book, discuss it with your friends— don't lay it aside. . . . Make sure that your Senators and Congressmen know that you are aware of the unprecedented gravity of the problem. . . . Time is short. And survival is at stake. [11]

Read, discuss, act! *One World or None* was the quintessential expression of the sense of desperate urgency and febrile optimism that characterized one strand of the early reaction to the atomic bomb. If only the American people could be awakened and informed, surely they would rally behind enlightened internationalism. In the earnest rhetoric of the FAS, one hears echoes of the Depression era's faith in the Common Man. One sees images of millions of decent, goodhearted, ordinary Americans—the kind played by Gary Cooper or James Stewart in Frank Capra's movies—reading this book and, convinced by its inexorable logic, calling on their leaders to eliminate the atomic danger in a high-minded, but commonsensical, fashion. Unfortunately, America in 1946 was not a Capra movie. The people never rallied behind the movement for international control with anything resembling unanimity. *Vox populi* was heard not only in support of the scientists' movement but in *Chicago Tribune* editorials demanding that the United States build more atomic bombs than anyone else. It was heard in this 1946 letter to the editor of the *New York Daily News:* "Russia shows by its spy activities in Canada that it badly wants the atom bomb, so I say give the bomb to Russia the same way we gave it to the Japs." [12] Already in 1946, social and political forces had been unleashed by the atomic genii that neither dire warnings nor calm reasonableness could easily return to the bottle.

These points were made very forcibly in one of the few hostile reviews of *One World or None,* by ABC news commentator Elmer Davis. While amply documenting the bomb's horrors, he said, it failed utterly to confront the key question: "What shall we do to be saved?" While calling for international cooperation and "One World," he charged, the contributors had offered "virtually no examination, of the sort that you might expect from scientists used to dealing with practical problems, of the possible methods of reaching this objective or of the difficulties in the way." Raising a point that soon would totally dominate the discussions of the atomic-weapons issue, Davis noted that the contributors had practically ignored the question of Soviet-American relations. "You cannot intelligently discuss the atomic bomb except against the background of present political realities," he declared, "and the biggest . . ., most enigmatic, and most ominous [of those realities] is Russia." These well-meaning activists, Davis concluded, exhibited "a terrifying unawareness of politics, [and] of the difficulty of getting things done in a field more complex than nuclear science." [13]

Though ominously anticipatory of future trends, Elmer Davis's pessimistic and skeptical tone was sharply at variance with the prevailing mood of 1946. The generally enthusiastic reviews accorded to *One World or None* marked the high-water mark of the brief interlude when atomic scientists were looked to as gurus who would lead the world out of the valley of darkness and confusion.

8

The Mixed Message of Bikini

Early in 1946, with the scientists' movement and the international-control campaign in full swing, a terse announcement emanated from Washington: the United States would conduct a series of atomic tests later that year at Bikini Atoll in the Marshall Islands. America's fears of the atom's destructive power soon focused on the forthcoming tests.

These fears found much support from seemingly authoritative sources. Some scientists publicly cautioned that the tests could produce "almost unbelievable damage"; others speculated that the blasts might cause fissures in the earth's crust, allowing the Pacific Ocean to rush into the molten interior; a French scientist warned of a global chain reaction.[1]

On a quite different plane, E. B. White wrote evocatively in the *New Yorker* in March 1946 of his feelings about the approaching tests:

> Bikini lagoon, although we have never seen it, begins to seem like the one place in all the world we cannot spare; it grows increasingly valuable in our eyes—the lagoon, the low-lying atoll, the steady wind from the east, the palms in the wind, the quiet natives who live without violence. It all seems unspeakably precious, like a lovely child stricken with a fatal disease.[2]

The dire predictions of global disaster were pooh-poohed by public officials and government scientists, but as the July 1 test date approached, the world was clearly jittery. "Can you do anything to stop the atomic tests?" a Vancouver listener asked H. V. Kaltenborn. "We here on the coast don't feel any too good about a 100-foot tidal wave plunging over our city and drowning thousands." The mood in Paris, reported a correspondent, was "Eat, drink, and be merry, for tomorrow we atomize."[3]

Proponents of one form or another of international control, including Secretary of State James F. Byrnes, warned that the tests could jeopardize the UN negotiations then under way. As Raymond Gram Swing put it on the eve of the test: "So we strive to save civilization, and we learn how to wreck it, all on the same weekend." Returning to this theme several weeks later, Swing observed:

This was a war game, the first of the atomic era war games. But in a situation in which we alone have the bomb, and are continuing to make it, this war game will appear to others, as not being defensive in its ultimate meaning. It is a notice served on the world that we have the power and intend to be heeded." [4]

President Truman turned aside all proposals that the Bikini tests be canceled or postponed. Indeed, on the eve of the first test, three top military leaders, Gen. Dwight D. Eisenhower, Adm. Chester W. Nimitz, and Secretary of the Navy James V. Forrestal, went on nationwide radio to emphasize their urgency. (Commented *New York Times* critic John Crosby: "The phrases 'save American lives' and 'national defenses' ran through the program with the persistence of a Pepsi-Cola jingle. . . . Fear advertising no longer carries the old punch in selling mouthwashes, but it still works fine to sell a national policy." [5])

The media, caught off guard in 1945, made massive efforts to recoup in 1946. Test Able, the first Bikini test, was surely the most thoroughly covered of all the world's atomic blasts. (A few reporters, getting a jump on their colleagues, even wrote their full stories the day before.) The chief of the air force photographic crew boasted that it would be "the most photographed event in history." Indeed, the test was nearly swamped in publicity, ballyhoo, and sensationalism. A Hollywood studio announced plans to film the explosion and incorporate it into a forthcoming movie. A picture of Rita Hayworth, the ubiquitous pin-up girl of World War II, was stenciled on the bomb. Arrangements were made for live radio transmission from observation ships and planes. A metronome on one of the target ships was wired to a worldwide radio hook-up. It would stop ticking, listeners were told, at the moment of the blast. Straining for human interest, one reporter described the commander of the Bikini task force, Vice Adm. W. H. P. Blandy, as pacing the deck "like an expectant father"—a phrase that infuriated at least one woman listener. "Of all the lousy metaphors!" she exclaimed. "This is a death watch, not a maternity ward." According to public-opinion surveys, the live broadcast from Bikini drew a "tremendous audience." [6]

After all the build-up, Test Able was a letdown. The air-dropped bomb fell about two miles off target, and on-the-scene observers saw and heard little. One called the blast a "giant firecracker"; another dismissed it as "a sneeze in a windstorm." Radio listeners, waiting breathlessly, heard nothing. "The sound of the explosion was not nearly what people had expected," observed a San Francisco commentator lamely. In a parody, a Buenos Aires station, after a dramatic build-up, represented the actual blast with the toot of a child's whistle. Test Baker, the underwater blast of July 25, was far more impressive visually and (as we shall see) far more ominous in its long-term implications. But by July 25, the army of reporters had largely dispersed, and world attention had shifted away from the tiny atoll in the South Pacific.[7]

The short-term effect of the 1946 test series, then, was to dampen fears of the atomic bomb. "The reports from Bikini reflect some sense of disappointment," noted the ever-skeptical Elmer Davis on July 1; "So far from disintegrating the ocean as had been predicted by a few wild prophets . . . , the explosion didn't even knock over the palm trees on the islands around the lagoon." *Time* magazine struck the same note. "The Thing [grew] a little less awful as a result of Bikini," it observed; "its apparently infinite power was finite after all." *Time* went on to poke fun at the French, among whom pre-Bikini fear had been so intense: "The Eiffel Tower still stood," but "Frenchmen felt that it had been a close call." Scientists returned from Bikini to a bored and inattentive public. "We were surprised at first to find so little interest," one wrote. In November, news magazines published photographs of a smiling Admiral Blandy and his wife at a Washington party cutting a large cake in the shape of a mushroom cloud. Bikini, one historian has concluded, "soothe[d] the fears of the American people almost as much as the bombs dropped on Japan had aroused them."[8]

For government spokesmen and others seeking to mute "excessive" and "hysterical" atomic-bomb fears (an effort we shall examine more closely in a later chapter), the apparent "failure" of the Bikini test was a godsend. Several civil-defense books of the late 1940s reminded readers of the tests' superficially reassuring results. Of the 42,000 servicemen at Bikini, noted one such manual, *"not a single one . . . was hurt by atomic rays."*[9]

Some observers were dismayed by the public's apparent readiness to stop worrying about the bomb on the basis of such slim evidence. The "feeling of awe has largely evaporated and has been supplanted by a relief unrelated to the grim reality of the situation," wrote William L. Laurence of the *New York Times*. "Having lived with a nightmare for nearly a year, the average citizen is now only too glad to grasp at the flimsiest means that would enable him to regain his peace of mind."[10]

But relief was not the only reaction to the tests, for Bikini became a kind of ideological battleground, as its symbolism was appropriated for different polemical purposes. While some saw it as a useful antidote for imaginations overheated by fears of the bomb, others tried to use it to sustain such fears. "Keep in mind those newsreel pictures of the second Bikini test," urged the chairman of the Federation of American Scientists in November 1946. In peacetime, wrote Anne O'Hare McCormick in the *New York Times,* the atomic bomb seemed even "more reverberant" than it had "as the final thunderbolt of war." The mice used in the test, she went on, were "just substitutes for men" and a "grisly reminder . . . that human beings are as helpless as mice before the Frankenstein they have let loose." Norman Cous-

ANATOMIC BOMB

Starlet Linda Christians brings the new atomic age to Hollywood

Almost before ink was dry on headlines announcing the crash of the first atomic bomb, Hollywood had turned the event to good publicity. At the Metro-Goldwyn-Mayer studio Miss Linda Christians, a hitherto obscure starlet, was solemnly proclaimed the Anatomic Bomb. Half-Mexican, half-Dutch, Linda was born in Tampico, Mexico, thinks it was 22 years ago. Her real name is Blanca Rose Welter. Her father, an oil executive, traveled widely, taking his family with him. They were in Palestine in 1941 during a bomb scare. Linda was evacuated to Mexico with a bad case of malaria, recovered, went to Hollywood to join her brother, got a job modeling hats, was seen and signed by M-G-M. So far she has been in no pictures, the publicity role of the Anatomic Bomb being her first important assignment. With long residence in Holland, Italy, France and Switzerland, Linda thinks Hollywood is wonderful.

The mass culture's response to the bomb took many forms. A few weeks after Hiroshima, *Life* joined forces with MGM studio to launch Linda Christians's Hollywood career as "The Anatomic Bomb." In an oddly passive, almost deathlike pose, she soaks up solar radiation at poolside.

October 1945: With a punning banner and dummy "bodies" strewing the lawn, an Indiana University fraternity adopts an atomic-bomb motif in its decorations before a big football game with Nebraska. (*Life,* November 5, 1945.)

Within days of Truman's announcement, Tennessee land speculators were jockeying to cash in on an expected real estate boom in the vicinity of the Manhattan Project's vast secret facility at Oak Ridge.

ATOMIC HOUSING will be confined exclusively to abandoned coal mines, of which there are few.

Cartoonists had a field day speculating about the coming Atomic Age. But as these cartoons from the August 9, 1945, *San Francisco Examiner* (1.) and the February 1949 *Science Illustrated* (r.) make clear, even such stabs at humor often revealed an underlying uneasiness.

At a Washington, D.C., party celebrating the completion of the 1946 atomic tests at Bikini, the commander of the operation, Vice Admiral W. H. P. ("Spike") Blandy, and his wife cut an angel-food cake in the shape of an atomic-bomb cloud. In the spirit of the occasion, Mrs. Blandy's hat also bears a striking resemblance to a mushroom cloud.

Late in 1946 General Mills offered the children of America a genuine Atomic "Bomb" Ring for fifteen cents and a Kix cereal boxtop. Some 750,000 kids mailed in their orders.

In this publicity still from MGM's 1946 movie *The Beginning or the End*, Robert Walker, Audrey Trotter, Tom Drake, and Beverly Tyler face the atomic future with resolution, though they seem a bit confused about which direction the menace is coming from.

ins detailed the extensive damage to ships at Bikini in the *Saturday Review,* and reminded his readers that a future world war would be fought "not with two atomic bombs, but with hundreds, perhaps thousands."

Such cautionary, fear-inducing interpretations of Bikini gained reenforcement as word began to filter out that Test Baker had pumped massive quantities of deadly radioactive material into the water and the atmosphere. Under the headline "Bikini Breath of Death," *Science News Letter* noted that if the target ships had had full crews, "they would surely be manned only by corpses" after their exposure to the "clinging, persistent lethal fog of radioactive water droplets and fission byproducts that the bomb spewed into the air over the whole target area." [12]

In the months that followed, these disturbing accounts intensified rather than diminished. It was Bikini, rather than Hiroshima and Nagasaki, that first brought the issue of radioactivity compellingly to the nation's consciousness. "It is now generally agreed," strategic thinker Stefan T. Possony could write in April 1947, "that radiation is the most dangerous aspect of the atomic bomb." The *Reader's Digest*'s "Mist of Death over New York," which appeared the same month, brought this disturbing message to a mass audience. In the August 1947 *Collier's,* Edward P. Morgan offered a somber, alarming account of the radiation found in ships, test animals, and surrounding fish and algae after Test Baker. Despite intensive efforts at decontamination, he reported, the Bikini test ships were still radioactive. [13]

Bikini-induced radiation fears are evident in "What Science Learned at Bikini," a special feature published by *Life* on the first anniversary of the test. *Life* strove for a positive tone as it surveyed the scientific findings—the careful mapping of the Bikini lagoon, the studies of its ecology and origins —that had resulted from this "rare opportunity to survey the life of a Pacific atoll." And it exploited the human-interest angle, telling, for example, of a pig locked in an officers' toilet aboard a test ship before the blast and later unaccountably found swimming in Bikini lagoon. But the tone turned somber as *Life* reflected on "the awful ubiquity of radioactive elements" and documented, with graphic photographs, the high death rates from radiation sickness among the hundreds of rats, goats, pigs, mice, and guinea pigs aboard the test ships. [14]

This special *Life* feature concluded with an article (later condensed in *Reader's Digest*) by Dr. Stafford Warren, dean of the UCLA medical school and a prominent radiologist who had led research teams at the sites of all five atomic blasts since 1945. To a culture already in the grip of atomic jitters, Warren's message was a chilling one. The radioactive spray of Test Baker—"an entirely new danger of atomic war"—had so saturated every crevice of the target ships that scientists and military personnel could visit them only on hurried forays. (Years later, long-classified government records would reveal the dismay of Warren's staff at the "hairy chested" attitude toward radiation warnings on the part of Bikini naval commanders, who even permitted sailors to sleep in their shorts on the decks of contaminated ships.) Radioactive algae had been eaten by larger fish, which had died in turn, their decaying bodies passing the radioactivity back to the algae. Were a Bikini-type bomb dropped in New York harbor under meteorological conditions favorable to the maximum diffusion of radioactive particles, he wrote, two million people would die. "The only defense against atomic bombs still lies outside the scope of science," Warren concluded. "It is the prevention of atomic war." [15]

The delayed but intense fear of radioactivity aroused by the Bikini tests reached its peak in 1948 with the publication of *No Place to Hide* by David Bradley, a physician who had served with the Radiological Safety Unit of Operation Crossroads at Bikini. The work of a writer with journalistic experience, Bradley's book was no scientific treatise but a deceptively casual narrative of his experiences and impressions before, during, and after the Bikini tests, with extended extracts from his journal.

No Place to Hide, which was an immediate success, made the *New York Times* best-seller list for ten weeks and was selected by the Book-of-the-Month Club. Prepublication extracts appeared in the *Atlantic Monthly,* and a condensation was published in the *Reader's Digest.* By the end of 1949, some 250,000 copies had been sold. In scientific circles, it aroused a cautious response. One leading radiologist was sharply critical, charging that Bradley's popularized treatment risked creating a national hysteria reminiscent of the notorious Orson Welles "War of the Worlds" broadcast. Most reviews, however, were highly favorable. Bradley's narrative, wrote E. B. White in the *New Yorker,* was "like a chapter in a dream book. His laboratory was a paradise, and the experiment in which he was involved was an experiment in befouling the laboratory itself." [16]

Published, as we shall see, at a critical point when the postwar international-control movement was nearly moribund and when official attention was shifting to atomic superiority and civil defense, *No Place to Hide* was especially welcomed by demoralized activists for the boost it gave their embattled cause. Norman Cousins spoke for these groups:

At a time when the world has virtually accepted the inevitability of another war, and when [civil] defense commissions in the United States are devising elaborate plans to "reduce vulnerability" . . . in the event of war, Bradley states flatly, as other atomic scientists have done, that there is no defense against atomic attack.

At the Pentagon, Bradley's book was greeted with dismay. "You can't imagine the trouble you have caused us with that book of yours," one official told him. [17]

But *No Place to Hide* was no political tract; it was, in fact, a work of considerable literary merit—one scholar has recently called it "a lost classic of nuclear weapons literature." It gains its emotional force from the contrast between the idyllic, almost dreamlike South Pacific setting and the author's gradual realization of the extent and seriousness of the ecological damage done by the tests. This awakening is conveyed subtly, through a series of impressions: the coral reefs gradually bleaching white as the algae that gave them color die off; the radioactive fish that take their own pictures when placed on photographic plates; the navy's determined, frustrating, and ultimately futile efforts to decontaminate the surviving ships by scrubbing, scraping, and sandblasting; the pariah fleet of ghostly radioactive ships anchored off Kwajalein Atoll after the tests, including "the beautiful *Prinz Eugen,* once the pride of the German fleet and as sleek and cavalier a ship as ever sailed the seas," physically undamaged by the blasts but "nevertheless dying of a malignant disease for which there is no help." [18]

Another low-keyed but memorable section records Bradley's September 1946 visit to Rongerik Island, where some 160 Bikini natives had been "temporarily" relocated. Reflecting on this visit, Bradley wrote: "The Bikinese . . . are not the first, nor will they be the last, to be left homeless and impoverished by the inexorable Bomb. They have no choice in the matter, and very little understanding of it. But in this perhaps they are not so different from us all." [19]

Bradley summed up his conclusions in a series of stark propositions underscoring "the devastating influence of the Bomb and its unborn relatives" not only on the immediate population but on future generations and on the planet itself for centuries to come, through the persistence of radioactivity. His final assessment of the meaning of the Bikini tests was a bleak one: "Hastily planned and hastily carried out, they may have only sketched in the gross outlines of the real problem; nevertheless, these outlines show pretty clearly the shadow of the colossus which looms behind tomorrow." [20]

9

The Scientists' Movement in Eclipse

Eugene Rabinowitch was in a somber mood as he wrote his editorial "Five Years After" for the January 1951 *Bulletin of the Atomic Scientists*. Not only were the world-government and international-control movements moribund, but the preceding fifteen months had brought a succession of jolting developments: the testing of an atomic bomb by the Soviet Union, the American decision to proceed with development of a hydrogen bomb, the outbreak of the Korean War, and mounting evidence that a full-scale nuclear arms race was underway.

From this ominous perspective, Rabinowitch looked back on the scientists' movement, tracing the shattering impact of the bomb on the scientists who had created it and recalling the dedication with which many had carried the message of international control to the nation. But he refused to sentimentalize this undertaking. "Scientists—whose profession requires a recognition of facts, however unpleasant," he wrote, "cannot but admit the fact that their campaign has failed." Dissecting the propaganda campaign in which he himself had played a prominent role, Rabinowitch concluded that it had been worse than a failure: it had actively encouraged the very reliance on atomic weapons the scientists had hoped to avoid. The scientists' endless insistence on the awesome destructive potential of the atomic bomb had left the American people "half educated": the lesson of the bomb's terrible power had been well learned, the lesson of international control and cooperation as a means of escaping that terror had not, leaving a net effect of "despair and confusion." "While trying to frighten men into rationality, scientists have frightened many into abject fear or blind hatred." The alarming developments that had come with a rush at the end of the decade—President Truman's hydrogen-bomb decision, the demands for American atomic superiority, the "clamor for the use of atomic weapons in Korea"—he said, were rooted, in part, in five years of "indoctrination by scientists" who had drummed into the public consciousness the bomb's irresistible power.

Concluding his bleak editorial, Rabinowitch salvaged a few scraps of consolation. Insisting that the scientists' movement had been justified even though it failed, he vigorously denied the charges of those who had dismissed the activist scientists as naïve dreamers. They had recognized only too clearly, he said, that their objectives "were *almost* unattainable, and the fight *almost* lost, even before it began." But no doctor would abandon a patient who had even a 5 percent chance of survival, and the scientists, too, had launched their campaign against similarly desperate odds. And he took some slight comfort in the thought that despite the immediate failure, the scientists' public-education campaign might prove influential in the long run in shaping the ideas of future leaders and of the voters who would choose those leaders. Perhaps decades hence, he mused, when the Cold War no longer blotted out all other considerations, the value of the seemingly futile campaign of 1945–1947 might become apparent. This slim hope, he concluded, would have to provide "the justification of our efforts." In the meantime, he advised a "patient and humble" scientific community to make what modest contributions it could toward national security and slowing the drift toward war.[1]

This obituary for the scientists' movement merely made official, as it were, a process of decline and disintegration that had been underway for years. Criticism had begun early. Even in November 1945, for example, one hostile government official could caricature their message this way: "The atomic bomb is just too dreadful, too awful, too—too—too—Everybody must do something about it quick. What are you doing? What am I doing? We must all get together right away and do more." The reactionary *Oakland Tribune* had predictably dismissed the activist scientists as "tub thumpers," but from the beginning such criticism was not limited to the Far Right. On issues of foreign policy and international relations, the *New York Times* observed with asperity in October 1945, an atomic scientist carried no more authority than an "intelligent doctor or lawyer or carpenter."[2]

Especially sharp criticism came from a group of political scientists at Yale's Institute of International Studies. Frederick S. Dunn attacked the scientists' "mechanical answers" to the problems posed by the atomic bomb. "Man's alleged choice between one world or none," insisted another Yale strategist, was "romantic exaggeration." The most extended critique came from Bernard Brodie, an early exponent of deterrence theory. Speaking early in 1946, Brodie rejected "the notion that our safety depends on a complete revolution in the hearts and minds of men" and dismissed as "meaningless and useless" the scientists' insistent formula that mankind's only choices were international control or catastrophe. "Absolute security against the atomic bomb lies irretrievably in the past," Brodie concluded, "and neither panic nor incantations will help us to reinvoke it."[3]

Other critics questioned the atomic scientists' motives and their moral right to offer themselves as political guides. Reinhold Niebuhr suggested that their activism sprang less from an informed understanding of international realities than from unacknowledged guilt over Hiroshima and Nagasaki. A reflective silence, Niebuhr implied, might be a more appropriate stance for the makers of the bomb than eager volubility. When the Emergency Committee of Atomic Scientists spoke in 1946 of its "heavy responsibility" to warn of the horrors of atomic war and the need for international control, *Commonweal* magazine responded sarcastically: "Now that we are enlightened by the scientists, how do we achieve the goals they have set?" Rather than prescribing for the future, *Commonweal* went on, the scientists might better "talk about the past and tell us where was their feeling of 'heavy responsibilty' when they handed over the bomb to the generals *after* the German defeat."[4]

Even within the scientific community, the assumptions underlying the scientists' movement did not go unchallenged. One sharp critic was Percy W. Bridgman of Harvard, winner of the 1946 Nobel Prize for his work in high-pressure physics. Addressing the American Association for the Advancement of Science in December 1946, Bridgman denied that scientists had a particular "social responsibility" for the consequences of their research. "The assumption of the right of society to impose a responsibility on the scientist which he does not desire," he said, was no more than "the right of the stupid to exploit the bright." The plunge of scientists into politics, he suggested, reflected their "youthful philosophy," and "eagerness for self-sacrifice."[5]

Ultimately more damaging to the scientists' movement than such criticism, however, was the mounting evidence, in the opinion polls and elsewhere, that their campaign was failing. "It is a bitter thing to report," wrote columnist Max Lerner in November 1945, "that thus far all the meetings and resolutions" of the atomic scientists and other "men of goodwill" had had little effect on Washington policymakers. The McMahon Committee hearings attracted little press coverage (except for dramatic testimony like that of Philip Morrison or General Farrell) and very few daily visitors—"about as many people . . . as could be expected to escape alive if an atomic bomb were dropped over the Capitol," commented the *Antioch Review*. The authors of an early history of the Atomic Energy Commission called the hearings a "dismal fizzle."[6]

From this perspective, the rather exaggerated praise given to *One World or None* seems less a triumph for the atomic scientists than a fleeting interruption in the general pattern of waning influence. By the fall of 1946, writes Alice Kimball Smith, the scientists' initial fervor was giving way to "a growing sense of futility." Noting that "colorful blasts from Szilard or Urey" could still command notice, Smith saw that the organized scientists' movement was not being attended to in a careful and sustained way. With the failure of the UN negotiations, the movement collapsed like a punctured balloon. "I am bankrupt of further ideas," Oppenheimer confessed as early as July 1946 in a mood of "deep despair." Soon after, he advised his fellow scientists to cut back on their public activities and remember that they were "after all, intellectuals and not politicians."[7]

By early 1947, pessimism and disillusionment pervaded the movement. In May, Michael Amrine wrote Oppenheimer that he was "much depressed by news of confusion and discouragement among the scientists." When the FAS polled its membership at about this time on the question, "Do you think the United States should proceed with the production of atomic bombs?" the response was affirmative by a startling 242 to 174 margin. To General Groves, this meant that, for Manhattan Project veterans, weapons research had proven stronger than the temporary appeal of politics: "After they had this extreme freedom for about six months, their feet began to itch. . . . Almost every one of them has come back into government research, because it was just too exciting."[8]

Even the ebullient Leo Szilard was affected by the spreading malaise. While still devising elaborate schemes of world cooperation and gamely insisting, for example, that a dedicated cadre of voters committed to international atomic control could make the difference in a close presidential election, Szilard's mood by the spring of 1947 was decidedly bleak:

> To me it seems futile to hope that 140 million people of this country can be smuggled through the gates of Paradise while most of them are looking the other way. . . . Nothing much can be achieved now or in the very near future until such time as the people of this country undersand what is at stake. . . . Maybe God will work a miracle—if we don't make it too difficult for him.[9]

A few voices urged redoubled effort in the face of setbacks, but such calls went unheeded as young activists picked up the threads of their interrupted careers. "For many of us it has meant the postponement or complete loss of two years of valuable research time out of the productive part of our lives," wrote FAS leader John A. Simpson in September 1947. "We feel this has been justified in the past two years, but cannot be justified over longer periods of time." J. Robert Oppenheimer, writing to Niels Bohr that autumn, tried to put the best face on a bad situation: "It seems important for all our future hopes that the wrong lessons should not have been learned by the failure of the past year, but that on the contrary there may be a renewed courage for a somewhat deeper attack on the problem."[10]

From 1945 through 1947, the prevailing attitude toward the activist scientists had been approval and admiration. By the end of 1947 this reservoir of goodwill was clearly diminishing. The hostility of David Lilienthal intensified as he recognized the conflict between the scientists' message and the efforts of the Atomic Energy Commission to promote a more positive public attitude toward atomic energy. The citizenry's view of atomic energy would be more balanced, Lilienthal complained in his diary in February 1948, "if the scientists had not (ironically) underlined its bad side with such vigor, picturesqueness, and skill at time when no one else knew enough to weigh their arguments." The activist scientists, he went on, "were driven forward by a notion that their vehemence could effect political change— [and] that the amount of change toward supra-national government was in direct proportion to the vehemence with which they said this was the only way out." [11]

By this time, even the warmest supporters of the scientists' movement were conceding its collapse. Early in 1948 Lewis Mumford denounced the "moral inertness" of the American people for ignoring the scientists' advice. Even the perennially hopeful Albert Einstein was forced to a bleak assessment: "The public, having been warned of the horrible nature of atomic warfare, has done nothing about it, and to a large extent has dismissed the warning from its consciousness." [12]

By the end of the decade, social observers vied with each other in pronouncing the demise of the scientists' movement and retroactively criticizing it. In *Must We Hide?*—a 1949 book about civil defense—Ralph Lapp dismissed the scientists' movement with patronizing condescension. After Hiroshima, he said,

> scientists suddenly became very vocal. Thrust into the limelight, the more eloquent discoursed at length on the atom and on world affairs. They met in small groups, with the best of intentions, and soon came forth with the pronouncement that there was no defense against the A-bomb and that soon other countries would have the bomb. They said that there must be One World or None. . . . This was a dictum in black and white, unrelieved by any tone of gray. [13]

In *The Christian Response to the Atomic Crisis* (1950), Edward L. Long, Jr., could already write of the scientists' movement (in a chapter titled "The Failure of Activism") as an ephemeral phenomenon that had quickly faded. Summing up what was rapidly becoming the conventional wisdom, Long praised the scientists' ethical earnestness but criticized the "persistent utopianism" of their failed quest for "a new and more perfect age." When "the awakening did not occur as was expected," he wrote, "the crusaders became lonely prophets." Despite "great publicity," the scientists' call to action had "disintegrated into general apathy." Even from the first, Long added, it should have been evident that the scientists, for all their prestige, were in no position "to reform a culture that has ignored other seers and prophets for many ages." [14]

Harsher criticism came from Sidney Hook, who in 1950 sharply challenged the respectful hearing that had been accorded the atomic scientists on matters beyond their expertise. On such issues, said Hook (elaborating the point made earlier by the *New York Times*), the scientist was no more qualified than any other informed and thoughtful citizen to offer political guidance. Indeed, he went on, the very skills of precision, exactitude, and logic that were essential to their professional work made scientists particularly ill-adapted to the ambiguous and emotional realm of politics.[15]

Burnt out, disillusioned, and stung by the intensifying criticism, more and more activist scientists drifted away from political engagement. The National Committee on Atomic Information collapsed. Membership in the Federation of American Scientists declined sharply. The FAS took no official position on the question of the use of the atomic bomb in Korea and accepted the hydrogen-bomb decision as "inevitable under the circumstances," though it did urge a counterbalancing effort for peace. Assessing the state of the organization in January 1951, two of its leaders described it as "struggling against a powerful tide running counter to original FAS objectives."[16]

As the decade ended, some scientists even criticized their colleagues' presumption in entering the political arena in the first place. In his November 1949 address to the American Physical Society, Samuel K. Allison echoed the earlier conclusions of Reinhold Niebuhr and Leo Szilard: the scientists' postwar celebrity had simply reflected popular awe at their achievement in the realm of doomsday weaponry, not a willingness to accept their political judgments. In the long run, Allison suggested, this war-related celebrity might come back to haunt them. Noting how the corporations involved in the Manhattan Project, mindful of the "Merchants of Death" tag of earlier years, had kept a low postwar profile, Allison observed: "It is my feeling that the physicists might have done well to use a bit of this caution." J. Robert Oppenheimer acknowledged the problem in a 1950 address. "Is there anything in the methods of science itself, or in the spirit of science, which can help in the making of [political] decisions? . . . Is there anything we can learn from the relevance of science to politics? If we are to answer these questions, and answer them honestly, we must recognize important and basic differences between problems of science and problems of action, as they arise in personal or in political life. If we fail to recognize these differences, we shall be seeking magic solutions and not real ones."[17]

To be sure, even after the "scientists' movement" as a highly visible phenomenon had faded, a few scientists continued to speak out, in the *Bulletin of the Atomic Scientists* and elsewhere. This remnant, wrote Edward Shils in 1957, "installed themselves into the conscience and intelligence of the upper levels of American public life" and continued to influence "the whole politically interested population." Concluded Shils's appreciative assessment: "Backbones have been stiffened and hearts have been cheered in many quarters by the scientists' movement, and many minds have been made more thoughtful on all the issues of public policy in which science is involved."[18] Certainly, too, the movement established an important precedent not only for scientists but also physicians, educators, and other groups that in future years would go public with their nuclear concerns.

One may readily grant all this, however, and still recognize that as a cohesive movement of central cultural significance, the postwar scientists' movement was essentially over by the end of the 1940s. Never again would scientists speak with such clarity or such apparent unanimity, and never again would their pronouncements receive such wide and respectful attention.

How, then, shall we assess the movement? Unquestionably some of the atomic scientists did display considerable political naïveté, seeming not to grasp the fundamental differences between the political realm and that of the laboratory and the classroom. The more extreme pronouncements of a few who insisted that world government could be created *now*, today, in response to the atomic emergency revealed a profoundly ahistorical consciousness. Reinhold Niebuhr was right: The exaggerated hopes many of them placed in political formulas and structural changes in government vastly underestimated the intractable problem of human nature and its well-known propensity for spawning mischief and evil even under the best-conceived and most benign social arrangements.

Yet in assessing the scientists' hopes and pronouncements, one must keep in mind the historical context. The atomic-bomb project itself was a technological achievement of staggering magnitude. In such a climate, it is hardly surprising that at least some scientists became convinced that comparable wonders might be possible in the political realm. As Henry DeWolf Smyth wrote in December 1945: "Anyone who has been associated with the Manhattan Project for five years must believe that anything is possible."[19]

Nor should one judge the movement by the pronouncements of a few. Certainly idealistic hopes for greater international harmony and an end to war helped give the movement its distinctive flavor, but, as Eugene Rabinowitch made clear in 1951, many of the scientists who became politically active after August 1945 had no illusions that Utopia could be achieved overnight. They advocated what seemed to them moderate and realistic steps toward the international control of atomic energy under adequate safeguards and inspection—the only alternative, they were convinced, to ultimate nuclear cataclysm. (That the world has managed to survive for several decades without such a cataclysm is, of course, no proof that their analysis was wrong.)

One's assessment of the program of the "mainstream" scientists' movement depends in part on one's view of the viability of the postwar effort for international atomic control. In *The Nuclear Question* (1979), Michael Mandelbaum dismisses the entire attempt as misconceived from the first. Not only was the United States' proposal doomed on practical grounds, since it would have forced the Soviets into a permanent second-class status in the nuclear realm, Mandelbaum argues, but it was also a deluded venture in Wilsonian-style "liberal diplomacy." In its global scope, its theatrical presentation, its assumption that agreement could be reached under the kleig lights of publicity, and—above all—its challenge to the principle of national sovereignty, says Mandelbaum, the United States initiative of 1946–1947 ran deeply counter to the canons of traditional diplomacy, in which limited agreements are hammered out between sovereign states far from the public eye. Only when the United States abandoned the utopian dream of abolishing atomic weapons under the aegis of the United Nations and returned to the established paths of diplomacy—bargaining with the Soviets over nuclear tests, force levels, and so on—he argues, did it choose the approach that held out any hope of avoiding nuclear war. This traditional approach did not achieve "the best of all imaginable nuclear worlds," he concludes, but it did achieve "the best of all possible nuclear worlds." [20]

One can hardly disagree with Mandelbaum's argument that the fishbowl and propagandistic aspects of the UNAEC negotiations seriously and perhaps fatally damaged the movement for international control. But his basic point about the immutability of national sovereignty rests on an idealized conception of world order that is ultimately unprovable. Mandelbaum assumes not only that national sovereignty is deeply rooted in human history, but that it is a fundamental and unalterable condition of human existence. Building on this assumption, he further argues that international control of atomic energy would not simply have modified, but actually destroyed the principle of national sovereignty. "For nuclear weapons to be abolished," he writes, "sovereignty would have to be abolished." [21] One can only ask: why? Is not this all-or-nothing approach a classic example of what Arthur M. Schlesinger, Jr., once called the fallacy of the excluded middle?

Writing from the vantage point of the late 1970s, Mandelbaum clearly finds utopian and unrealistic the widespread post-Hiroshima conviction "that international politics had changed dramatically, that a new age was at hand, and that entirely new measures were required for nations to survive and prosper." [22] Nothing in his argument, however, proves that the movement for international control was foreordained to fail; that only "traditional diplomacy" offered any hope; or that it was demonstrably fallacious, on a priori grounds, to conclude in 1945 or 1946 that the threat of atomic war was such a radical new reality that radical changes in the international order might occur in response.

Certainly there are grounds for criticizing the scientists' movement. Much of its rhetoric implicitly saw atomic-energy control as an *event*, or series of events, rather than a *process*. Defeat the May-Johnson bill! Adopt the Acheson-Lilienthal plan! Such were the directives urged by the atomic scientists. Attention to the immediate and the specific was essential, of course, especially in this early period, when the basic framework of atomic policy was being established. But in the midst of these hectic ad hoc efforts, few scientists showed much awareness that passage of a particular bill or adoption of a particular international-control plan would be only the beginning of a complex and probably unending effort. As Edward Shils has written, what began as an emergency soon "established itself as a chronic condition."[23] With rare exceptions, the atomic scientists were not prepared for this transition. Few showed the kind of political endurance that could absorb defeat and return to the fray. As some noted at the time, their intellectual orientation, with its emphasis on defining and rationally confronting arbitrarily delimited problems, was ill-suited to the world of politics, where few issues are ever disposed of once and for all, where most problems are maddeningly tangled and amorphous, and where proximate solutions are often the most one can reasonably hope for.

This orientation toward the intense, precisely targeted campaign rather than the patient, long-term effort became a fatal liability when the UNAEC negotiations bogged down and finally collapsed. For months, the scientists had focused their lobbying efforts and public appeals almost entirely on the Acheson-Lilienthal plan. When that effort failed, the scientists had no fallback position, and many seemed, like Oppenheimer, bankrupt of further ideas. For months they had preached the either/or message of international control or chaos, one world or none, and now they fell victim to their own rhetoric. One can see the possible consequences of this mind-set most plainly in the career of Edward Teller. Initially Teller welcomed the Acheson-Lilienthal plan enthusiastically and worked to arouse support for it. But when the UNAEC negotiations collapsed, Teller lost all further interest in political efforts to control atomic weapons. The one great moment had passed; further effort was pointless. As Teller wrote in 1962: "The United States, immediately after World War II, had a unique opportunity to ensure peace. . . . But we let the opportunity slip by, and it never can return."[24] Succumbing increasingly to an all-encompassing suspicion of the Soviet Union, Teller championed development of the hydrogen bomb, challenged nearly all arms-control efforts as naïve and dangerous, and advocated a nuclear arms build-up almost without control or limit.

But to focus one's criticisms narrowly on the scientists themselves is to miss critical dimensions of the story. As Teller's history suggests, the scientists' movement did not occur in a political void. It was played out during a period of rapid political change in America, a period when powerful figures in government, the foreign-policy elite, the media, and ultimately the American people succumbed to an intense and all-pervasive anticommunist ideology that perceived communism as a monstrous and monolithic global conspiracy centered in Moscow and bent upon absolute world domination.

Historians like Daniel Yergin, Stephen Ambrose, Lloyd Gardner, and Walter LaFeber have documented in compelling detail the process by which this ideology became dominant in elite circles in the immediate postwar period, shaped American foreign policy, and saturated the rhetoric in which that policy was presented to the American people. As early as June 1946, just as the Baruch plan was being presented at the United Nations, John Foster Dulles published an alarming two-part article in Henry Luce's *Life* magazine warning of Russia's plan for world domination. "I can think of no articles in my experience in journalism," an admiring Luce wrote the future secretary of state, "which so definitely accomplished a job. For a great many people, directly and indirectly, your article ended all doubts as to the inescapable reality of the Russian-Communist problem." "There has been a tremendous change in public attitude toward Russia," wrote Baruch that August, in a memo discussing how the stalemated international-control talks could best be terminated. [25]

Militarily, the rapidly solidifying anticommunist consensus found expression in proposals for streamlining the Pentagon and building up the nation's arsenal, including atomic weapons. "If there are to be atomic weapons in the world, we must have the best, the biggest and the most," wrote General Groves in 1946, and Pentagon planning reflected this simple premise. The number of nuclear cores for atomic bombs grew from thirteen in 1947 to nearly three hundred in 1950, with a corresponding increase in delivery capability. Historian Gregg Herken has described in chilling detail the evolution of the Pentagon's atomic-war plans in these years—plans bearing such code names as Pincher, Broiler, Grabber, and Sizzle. [26] As we proceed to examine the earnest discussions that were pursued in many cultural forums in these years, we must keep constantly in mind that far from the public eye, the strategic planning and bomb-making that would embed atomic weapons at the very center of all American military and diplomatic calculations were moving inexorably forward.

Early in 1947, as President Truman was preparing to ask Congress for funds for military aid to aid a corrupt and repressive Greek regime in defeating its opponents in a bitter and murky civil war, his advisers and Republican congressional leaders alike warned him that only a rousing, heavily rhetorical speech would win over wary legislators. As Republican Senator Arthur Vandenberg put it, Truman would have to "scare hell out of the American people." Truman did just that; his address to a joint session of Congress on March 12, 1947, spoke in sweeping, apocalyptic terms of communism as an insidious world menace that lovers of freedom must struggle against at all times and on all fronts. A population that for a year and a half had been in the grip of atomic fear was now told to turn its fear in a new direction: not vaporization but communization was the great menace confronting mankind. A few weeks later, the Senate and House overwhelmingly approved Truman's appropriation request. [27]

The anticommunist ideology that now ruled Washington had broad ramifications in the arena of domestic opinion. Truman's speech forged a powerful link between anticommunism abroad and anticommunism at home. If communism was indeed such an insidious, all-encompassing menace, it could crop up in one's own neighborhood just as easily as in some foreign land! As historians David Caute and Athan Theoharis have shown in their work on this period, a pervasive fear of communism gripped the nation. Norman Thomas, making one of his periodic trips to California in the spring of 1947, was amazed at how quickly a "hysterical anti-Communism" had spread through the state. That June, the valedictorian of a high-school senior class in New Jersey chose as the topic of her graduation address the international control of atomic energy; it was vetoed by her principal as "too controversial." [28]

In another important action of March 1947, Truman set up a federal loyalty-review program. Over the next five years, about 20,000 government employees were investigated, some 2,500 resigned "voluntarily," and 400 were fired. Between 1945 and 1952, the House Un-American Activities Committee, the Senate Internal Security Subcommittee, and other legislative committees conducted over eighty inquiries into domestic subversion. [29] When Whittaker Chambers told HUAC in 1948 that Alger Hiss had been a Soviet spy, many concluded that this was only the tip of the iceberg of a vast conspiracy. In the *New York Times Index* for 1949, the entry for "U.S. —Espionage, Sabotage, Treason, and Subversive Activities" fills seventeen pages of very small print.

With Washington setting the pace, political paranoia swept the nation. Views that seemed in any way deviant or heterodox became suspect, if not downright dangerous. Hollywood writers were blacklisted; professors were forced to sign loyalty oaths. (Over 150 faculty members at the University of California were fired in 1949 for refusing to sign.) The National Education Association voted that no Communist should be permitted to be a teacher. "Labor leaders, liberals, Democrats, Republicans, and leading newspapers and journals," writes historian James Gilbert, "all contributed to defining rejected ideas as treasonous acts." In a Gallup poll of 1945, 38 percent of the American people had viewed the Soviet Union as "aggressive"; two years later, the figure stood at 66 percent. Of course, Soviet pronouncements and actions in Iran and elsewhere influenced this dramatic shift, but so, too, did the strident, insistent anticommunist rhetoric reverberating across America. Well before 1950—the year of the notorious Internal Security Act, the Rosenberg trial, and the emergence of Senator Joe McCarthy—what David Caute calls "the Great Fear"—not of nuclear destruction, this time, but of communism—held the nation in its grip. The 1951 science-fiction movie *The Day the Earth Stood Still*—in which government authorities, news commentators, and ordinary citizens alike react with suspicion and violence to a benign alien who arrives in Washington, D.C., by spaceship to plead for world harmony and an end to the atomic-arms race—in fact accurately reflected a change in the cultural climate that had been underway for several years. As the brilliant Professor Barnhart (Sam Jaffe), modeled on Albert Einstein, tells the sympathetic extraterrestrial: "We scientists are too often ignored, or misunderstood." [30]

The decline of the scientists' movement cannot be understood without awareness of this larger climate. What Lewis Mumford in 1948 called the "moral inertness" of the American people on the nuclear issue was not some inexplicable, spontaneous phenomenon, but rather an almost inevitable corollary of the climate of anticommunist suspicion and fear that for months had been deliberately encouraged by governmental leaders and powerful figures in the media.

The drumfire of criticism directed at the scientists' movement as the decade ended was often far from disinterested. Some of the sharpest attacks came from individuals who were themselves Cold War ideologues (Hook and Niebuhr, for example); strategists urging a very different response to the atomic danger (Brodie and Possony); or spokesmen for a Pentagon civil-defense perspective (Lapp).

While the atomic scientists' lingering aura of prestige may have spared them some of the cruder forms of attack, they were by no means immune to the national obsession with disloyalty and subversion. Well before the famous Oppenheimer case of 1954, many scientists with radical pasts or associations, or who for whatever reason aroused suspicion, found themselves subject to harassment. AEC "loyalty investigations" were triggered by the flimsiest charges. (One Oak Ridge scientist was investigated because a copy of the *New Masses* was found in his wastebasket.) Physicist Edward U. Condon, associate director at Los Alamos for a brief period in 1943 and head of the National Bureau of Standards from 1945 to 1951, was subjected to a massive AEC security investigation in 1948 involving FBI interviews with over three hundred people. When the Justice Department refused HUAC's demand for Condon's file, Congressman Richard Nixon and other committee members blasted the administration. "ATOM CHIEF LINKED TO SPY RING," a Chicago newspaper headlined. Condon was eventually cleared, but the attack continued. In September 1948, HUAC announced plans to investigate atomic scientists, Hollywood, and black leaders. [31]

Scientists and their supporters reacted to all this with alarm and anger. The *Bulletin of the Atomic Scientists* protested. MIT President Karl Compton denounced the publicity circus surrounding hearsay charges against reputable scientists. During the 1948 presidential campaign, eight prominent atomic scientists telegraphed candidates Truman and Dewey warning of widespread demoralization in the scientific community. The Federation of American Scientists set up a special committee to assist scientists faced with government investigation. In *Security, Loyalty, and Science* (1950), Columbia University law professor Walter Gellhorn eloquently warned of the deadening effect of governmental snooping on scientists' willingness to speak out on controversial public issues. At a New York dinner sponsored by 150 scientists to show support for Edward Condon, Robert M. Hutchins declared: "If Ed Condon, whose Americanism sticks out all over him and all over his record, could be linked to a spy ring, anybody could be linked to a spy ring. . . . Nobody is safe." [32] Even when they were not investigated, scientists who failed to fall in quickly enough with the new consensus were increasingly dismissed as "naïve," indulgently patronized, or simply drowned out by the anticommunist ideologues in full cry.

As Eugene Rabinowitch observed in his 1950 editorial, this larger context added a dimension of almost tragic irony to the skill and effectiveness with which scientists wielded their most powerful and reliable instrument of persuasion: fear. For years prior to 1945, "fear" had been a potent rhetorical theme in American political life. FDR told Americans in 1933 that they had nothing to fear but fear itself, and in January 1941 he listed Freedom from Fear as one of the Four Freedoms for which America stood. Yet within a few years, a new and terrible fear of unfathomable magnitude had insinuated itself into American culture and consciousness. The activist scientists deliberately intensified this fear in pursuit of goals they deeply believed in. If only the reality of atomic destruction could be made vivid enough, surely grass-roots America would rise up and demand that their leaders take measures to eliminate the danger. As Harold Urey put it at the end of his October 1945 address detailing the bomb's awful potential:

> I pass the problem to you now. Do you see any way to avoid the threat of an atomic war? . . . After all, it is the people of the United States who face destruction and death, and they should have the privilege of making their own decisions.

Endlessly in 1945–1947 the American people were told that they could influence the direction of atomic policy—indeed, that human survival depended on such public engagement. Ignore those who claim the individual citizen "exercises little power or control," exhorted the *Ladies' Home Journal* in a 1946 article on the atomic bomb. "That's not the way a democracy is run. The opinions of individuals make the opinions of communities. . . . Man can change his world, almost overnight. It's been done repeatedly." [33] Many thousands responded to this challenge. They debated atomic issues, studied the Acheson-Lilienthal Report, read *One World or None*, and wrote their congressmen and their newspaper editors. What was the result? Except for the ambiguous McMahon Act, practically nothing. The international-control movement collapsed; the nuclear arms race began.

From the vantage point of the 1980s, the scientists' manipulation of fear, rather than the particular causes they espoused, seems their principal legacy. Indeed, they may have served as unwitting advance agents of the very anticommunist hysteria most of them deplored. The emotions they worked so mightily in 1945–1947 to keep alive and intensify created fertile psychological soil for the ideology of American nuclear superiority and an all-out crusade against communism. The scientists' political agenda was overwhelmed by larger forces, but their rhetoric of fear continued to echo through the culture, to be manipulated by other people pursuing other goals. The scientists offered one avenue of possible escape from atomic fear; Truman offered another. Truman won.

This fear remains with us still, a potent source of political energy struggled over by advocates of competing visions of the future. During periods of antinuclear activism, one hears in the fear-inducing rhetoric of eloquent leaders echoes of the scientists' warnings of 1945–1947. More frequently, as in the years after 1947, it has been those in the Pentagon, the think tanks, the military industries, and the White House who have played upon our fear to win us over to their conviction that somewhere down an endlessly receding road—or somewhere out in space—exists the definitive technological solution that will free us of our fear at last and make us safe and secure in a nuclear world.

Four

Anodyne
to Terror

Fantasies of a Techno-Atomic Utopia

10

Atomic Cars, Artificial Suns, Cancer-Curing Isotopes: The Search for a Silver Lining

"Imagination leaps forward to visualize the use of atomic power for man's comfort and enjoyment in generations to come." So declared the *St. Louis Post-Dispatch* on August 7, 1945, a little more than twenty-four hours after the world's second atomic bomb had obliterated a city. At about the same time, the *New York Herald Tribune* was proclaiming that atomic power, if wisely used, could be "a blessing that will make it possible for the human race to create a close approach to an earthly paradise." On the twelfth, the *Dallas Morning News* published a large editorial cartoon depicting a skeleton labeled "CANCER" fleeing in terror as lightning bolts of "ATOMIC ENERGY" rain down upon it from the skies. Another newspaper cartoon pictured a beneficent goddess opening the locked chest of "ATOMIC ENERGY," revealing untold treasures inside; still another half-humorously, half-seriously offered a collage of peacetime wonders, from atomic cars to atomic toothpaste.[1]

These spontaneous journalistic effusions within hours of Hiroshima clearly represent a very different response to the atomic bomb from those we have examined so far. Along with the shock waves of fear, one also finds exalted prophecies of the bright promise of atomic energy. The more euphoric of these predictions soon faded, but the upbeat theme proved remarkably tenacious. These two responses that seem so contradictory—the terror of atomic war and the vision of an atomic Utopia—were in fact complexly interwoven.

The Manhattan Project may have been a secret, and Hiroshima a shock, but Americans of 1945 were prepared in a general way for news of atomic breakthroughs that would transform their lives. As one atomic scientist noted in 1946: "It has often been said that man would someday 'unlock the energy of the atom' and . . . this goal has been frequently described in fiction." As a result, he observed, the news of August 6, 1945, had been "more or less expect[ed] . . . for a considerable length of time."[2]

As early as 1928, a General Electric scientist wrote in *Scientific Monthly* that if science ever achieved atomic fission, the world's "whole economic system and daily life might be revolutionized."[3] Such speculations had peaked in 1939–1941. In 1939, building on the theoretical and experimental work of Ernest Rutherford, Niels Bohr, and Enrico Fermi, the German physicists Otto Hahn and Fritz Strassman successfully achieved fission in the U-235 (uranium) atom. In popular parlance, they had "split the atom." Soon other physicists, including John R. Dunning at Columbia University, were duplicating these experiments.

These exciting developments were soon transmitted to the outside world by science writers who speculated freely about their practical applications. In what he always considered his greatest scoop, John O'Neill of the *New York Herald Tribune* reported Dunning's experiments in a June 1940 *Harper's* article prophetically titled "Enter Atomic Power." Later that year, William L. Laurence described uranium's "fabulous power" in the *New York Times* and the *Saturday Evening Post*. A *Reader's Digest* article hailed "The World-Shaking Promise of Atomic Research," and similar articles appeared in other popular magazines before the blanket of secrecy descended.[4]

The most visionary of these prewar articles, by physicist Rudolph M. Langer of the California Institute of Technology, appeared in *Collier's* in July 1940. Though Langer warned vaguely of the "destructive potentialities" of U-235, the article's tone was set by the editors: "Science unleashes a tremendous new source of energy. Here are the things, fantastic only yesterday, that you'll probably live to see." "Despite current headlines," declared Langer as Europe plunged into war, "we are about to enter an era of unparalleled richness and opportunities for all"—the era of the atom. In Langer's 1940 vision, the populace lives underground in climate-controlled atomic houses, surfacing only for a dip in the above-ground swimming pool (which also provides insulation), for trips in large, transparent atomic-powered automobiles suspended from overhead tracks, or in airplanes propelled by high-speed particles emitted by U-235, just as "the ejection of a stream of water can be made to cause a lawn sprinkler to rotate." The subterranean houses are heated and cooled by walls of radioactive uranium and illuminated by translucent panels aglow with the "fluorescence which occurs around U-235." Each family is a self-sufficient unit, subsisting on fruits and vegetables grown underground hydroponically with light supplied by U-235 and cooked instantaneously in microwave ovens. (Another new discovery helped shape Langer's brave new world: "We shall be able to satiate ourselves with all the plastic our ingenuity can discover.")[5]

Pearl Harbor rudely interrupted such fantasizing, but in August 1945, it quickly revived. Almost immediately, as one observer put it, "wonders and portents too numerous to mention" filled the media.[6] The earliest discussions of the atom's peacetime uses drew heavily on the prewar speculations. John J. O'Neill's *Almighty Atom: The Real Story of Atomic Energy,* which appeared within days of Hiroshima, for example, was simply an updated version of a book he had been working on since 1940. After a historical and theoretical survey of nuclear physics, O'Neill offered some sweeping and rather breathless reflections on the applications of atomic energy. Acknowledging that only a "superhuman imagination" could anticipate them all, he nevertheless made a valiant attempt. Without spelling out details, he predicted fantastically cheap power; "atomic-energy vitamin tablets"; the mining and smelting of various metals through radioactive beams; and the imminent availability of atomic-powered rockets, airplanes, ships, and automobiles.

Of all these marvels, the atomic automobile most fired O'Neill's imagination: "Drive the car as long as it holds together, and you will never have to stop for refueling." Offering an "idealized concept" that he conceded might "require some modification" in practice, O'Neill described how such a dream car might work: "Each cylinder will contain a complete atomic-power unit. . . . When the piston reaches the top of the cylinder, a small block of uranium 235 located like a central spark plug would be immersed in . . . water, causing the atomic-energy chain reaction to burst into action, instantly vaporizing the surrounding film of water into steam and thus supplying the pressure to the piston for its downward power stroke." As to radioactivity, O'Neill suggested an oil or paraffin shield. The economic upheaval would be great, since the nation's thirty million cars would suddenly become obsolete, but the benefits would far outweigh the drawbacks. Individual car owners would enjoy vast savings, automobile travel would be quieter and more relaxing, world competition for petroleum would end, and the elimination of exhaust fumes would do wonders for the urban environment.

Pursuing the environmental-improvement theme, O'Neill suggested that the polar ice cap might be melted through a continuous bombardment of atomic bombs in the Arctic region, giving "the entire world a moister, warmer climate." Since this would also raise ocean levels and produce "important changes in the outlines of many countries and the continents," O'Neill cautioned against hasty interference "with nature's processes in establishing climatic conditions," but the thought was exciting all the same as an indication of "the gigantic tasks which man can undertake as an unlimited source of energy now becomes available." The idea of melting the polar ice cap with atomic explosions particularly captured the public imagination. War hero Eddie Rickenbacker threw his prestige behind it. While improving the world's climate, proponents claimed, it would also open vast tracts for development.[7]

Another visionary post-Hiroshima book was *Atomic Energy in the Coming Era* by David Dietz, science and technology writer for the Scripps-Howard newspaper chain. Like other prophets in these heady days, Dietz anticipated truly amazing transformations: the era of atomic energy would be "as different from the present as the present is from ancient Egypt." Atomic airplanes, he predicted, would carry "several thousand passengers, with as much cabin space as a luxury liner." As to surface travel: "Instead of filling the gasoline tank of your automobile two or three times a week, you will travel for a year on a pellet of atomic energy the size of a vitamin pill." (Noting the diversity of small objects being used to designate the minuscule quantity of fuel atomic cars and planes would need—aspirins, vitamin pills, bricks, fingernails, and so on—the *New Yorker* humorously suggested that the pea be designated the official unit of measurement.)[8]

Dietz also anticipated atomic weather control, not by melting the polar ice cap, but through "artificial suns mounted on tall steel towers."

> No baseball game will be called off on account of rain in the Era of Atomic Energy. No airplane will bypass an airport because of fog. No city will experience a winter traffic jam because of heavy snow. Summer resorts will be able to guarantee the weather, and artificial suns will make it as easy to grow corn and potatoes indoors as on the farm. . . . For the first time in the history of the world, man will have at his disposal energy in amounts sufficient to cope with the forces of Mother Nature.

He acknowledged that these atomic suns would have to "screen out" lethal radioactivity, but insisted that this matter—like all the other technical problems associated with harnessing the atom—was "merely one of detail."[9]

O'Neill and Dietz were but two voices among many. Atomic energy, proclaimed Robert M. Hutchins in September 1945, could "usher in a new day of peace and plenty," bring universal health and leisure, and "carry to the most backward places of the earth the means of developing their material and their human resources." At an atomic-energy forum that December, a Canadian uranium official predicted that man would soon, by simulating cosmic radiation, be able to "convert any kind of matter into energy." And if this could be achieved, why not the reverse? Man in the Atomic Age would learn "not only how to decompose matter but also how to construct it; . . . [how] to produce artificially any kind of material needed, because we will have at our disposal tremendous energies necessary for the artificial production."[10] Truly this was a world of unlimited power, unlimited abundance—a world limited only by man's capacity to imagine new wants and needs.

The news media avidly jointed in the speculation about the peacetime promise of the new force. As early as August 7, for instance, the *Milwaukee Journal* catalogued the amazing predictions that would soon become clichés:

Atoms in an amount of matter spread out the size of a fingernail, say the scientists, could supply sufficient energy to propel an ocean liner across the sea and back. An automobile, with a microscopic amount of matter from which atomic energy could be released, could be driven around for a lifetime if it didn't wear out, never stopping at a gas station.

A few days later, after cautioning that the atom's "miraculous powers" would not be available immediately, *Newsweek* hastened to report that "even the most conservative scientists and industrialists" were talking of a new era that would "make the comic-strip prophecies of Buck Rogers look obsolete." The *New York Times* reported that French officials planning the country's winter fuel requirements were now wondering whether they need bother, "if a few atoms could be pulverized between now and winter and the released energy distributed in heat." [11]

The Atomic Age Opens, the hasty compilation of media comment issued by Pocket Books within days of Hiroshima, offered in a section called "A New World" a rich sampling of such early speculation. Typical was an editorial reprinted from *PM:* "The power behind the atomic bomb" could "change the face of the earth in peace as well as war," it said, producing "the Utopia that men have dreamed of through centuries of war, depression, famine, and disease." [12]

Encouraged by the seemingly authoritative pronouncements of some scientists and well-known science writers, such speculation intensified in late 1945 and into 1946. "Heat will be so plentiful that it will even be used to melt snow as it falls," declared Robert M. Hutchins. Novelist Philip Wylie, writing in the September 29, 1945, *Collier's,* hailed the "great day" —"probably in your lifetime!"—when bulky hydroelectric plants would be replaced by "small, neat energy-producing buildings" and by compact household atomic-energy units able to "heat, cool, and air-condition a home for a decade." In atomic-energy research, Wylie declared, "we stand where Benjamin Franklin stood with his key and kite in relation to electricity." Economist Stuart Chase, writing in the *Nation* that December, cautioned against excessive optimism, but went on to speculate that atomic energy would make possible the "lavish production of plastics"; revolutionize highway construction (through controlled explosions that would fuse earth into lava, as at Alamogordo); "air-condition cities in the tropics, and warm up polar housing for the comfort of man"; and "by the electrification of soils" possibly "change the whole crop pattern." (While awaiting such wonders, another *Nation* writer had earlier suggested, atomic bombs could be used immediately "to dig canals, to break open mountain chains, to melt ice barriers, and generally to tidy up the awkward parts of the world." [13]

Like the atomic fear, this post-Hiroshima euphoria respected no ideological bounds. The splitting of the atom, exulted a 1946 Socialist Party pamphlet on "The Atomic Age," had "made it possible to transform nature into the servant of man, giving him food infinitely beyond the capacity of the human appetite, clothing far more abundant than he can wear, homes for all to fill our streets with palaces." *Business Week,* meanwhile, had as early as August 11, 1945, proclaimed that while there were no new words left to describe the atomic bomb's destructiveness, it would take "billions of other words" to tell the positive side "of the new creative force." Getting a start on those billions of words, *Business Week* reflected in awe on the massive energy that could be released from "an aspirin-like tablet of U-235" to generate power in stationary plants, automobiles, trains, ships, and airplanes that would soar into the wild blue yonder "virtually without the incubus of a fuel load, giving them a radius of operation well nigh incalculable." [14]

Such pronouncements, ranging from the merely unrealistic to the totally bizarre, quickly took on a formulaic, almost hypnotic quality, as if the entire nation were caught up in a kind of collective trance about the nuclear Utopia ahead. The atomic bomb's disorienting cultural effect, already noted in other contexts, is dramatically evident as well in the diversity of opinion on the positive uses of atomic energy—a diversity approaching incoherence. For even as the most fanciful utopian dreams were being spun out, one also begins to find a persistent undercurrent of doubt on the subject that quickly turned to deep skepticism. Business analysts soon translated the predictions into dollars and cents, with discouraging results. For all the talk of incredibly cheap atomic power, coal, oil, and public-utility stocks showed no noticeable drop on Wall Street. The *Journal of Commerce* very early warned investors that the cost factor would probably rule out atomic power except for "highly specialized purposes." *Business Week,* its accustomed sobriety restored, was soon cautioning that only "painful, piecemeal research" would unlock the atom's peacetime potential and criticizing the "unreasonable hopes" aroused by "popular writers on the subject." [15]

Surveying "The Atom and the Economy" in the Winter 1947 *American Scholar,* economist Walter Isard of MIT and political scientist Vincent Whitney of Brown University offered a very restrained appraisal of atomic energy's "far from revolutionary" economic potential. Compared to the earlier impact of coal, canals, or railroads, they predicted, it would ultimately rank as a "minor force." On the basis of available scientific evidence, they wrote, "dreams of atomic pellets for our gas tanks and of radioactive particles to light our Adirondack cabin must remain for some time—if not forever—the sole property of the comic books." As for fixed-site atomic-power plants, they noted that energy costs represented less than 3 percent of the total cost of American manufactured goods, so that, even if atomic power cut energy costs by half, the overall cost of manufactured goods would drop only about 1 percent. While atomic energy might marginally affect economic development, they concluded, "it is not, unfortunately, the wand of the fairy godmother which overnight will bring us unparalleled abundance."[16]

A succession of scientific pronouncements seemed further to deflate exaggerated atomic-energy hopes. In the immediate aftermath of Hiroshima, a few scientists had offered euphoric predictions, but most had remained aloof from the prophecy game. This restraint was evident in the circumspection of President Truman's August 6th announcement—drafted in consultation with his scientific advisors—on this point: "Atomic energy may in the future supplement the power that now comes from coal, oil, and falling water, but at present it cannot be produced on a basis to compete with them commercially. Before that comes there must be a long period of intensive research."[17]

In the waning months of 1945, one scientist after another cautioned against atomic-energy daydreams. No practical benefits should be expected "for a long time" said Albert Einstein in November. Arthur H. Compton warned that the massive quantity of fissionable material needed to sustain a chain reaction made stationary power plants the only plausible application. The technical journal *Chemical and Metallurgical Engineering* criticized the discussion of peacetime applications in O'Neill's *Almighty Atom* as "badly distorted" and "most misleading."[18]

Another early cautionary voice, interestingly, was that of John W. Campbell, Jr., the editor of *Astounding Science Fiction*. An MIT-trained physicist, Campbell had long been campaigning to make science fiction more scientifically plausible. Interviewed shortly after Hiroshima, Campbell reported that for years he had rejected stories involving atomic-powered vehicles. Radiation hazards would make them far too dangerous, he argued, especially in the event of accident: "If an atomic-powered taxi hit an atomic-powered streetcar at Forty-second and Lex," he said, "it would completely destroy the whole Grand Central area."[19]

By 1946, the atomic scientists' initial reticence on the question of peacetime applications had progressed to a full-scale counterattack. Several of the scientific contributors to *One World or None* poured cold water on the feverish predictions of an atomic Utopia. In *Atomic Energy in Cosmic and Human Life* (1946), for instance, physicist George Gamow not only insisted that the many tons of lead shielding required in any nuclear reactor ruled out atomic cars or airplanes, but also pointed out the "serious disadvantages" of nuclear power, including accidental radiation leakage. In May 1946, *Science Digest* marshalled impressive scientific opinion against melting the polar ice cap through atomic bombing. Even if technically possible, said a professor at the Brooklyn Polytechnic Institute, such a project would cost $660,000 billion, or about 2,500 times the national debt of that time.[20]

Bleakest of all was *Scientific American*'s authoritative survey of "Industrial Uses of Atomic Energy" published early in 1946 at the instigation of the Atomic Scientists of Chicago. The idea of small, portable atomic-power sources was scientifically absurd, the magazine said, since the minimum quantity of uranium and uranium oxide needed for a sustained chain reaction was about eleven tons, and when one added the graphite necessary to control the reaction, the total approached twenty tons. The essential cooling system and radiation absorbing shield, it went on, would add further bulk and weight. In short, hard realities ruled out the dreams of atomic cars, planes, and individual household power plants. The only conceivable source of atomic energy was from "stationary, high-power units" and even these, it added, because of high costs, technical complexities, and the risk of accident and malfunction, should be "reserved for the special purposes for which other types of power are not so well suited."[21]

Warning of the "jungle of difficult scientific and engineering problems" blocking the way, David E. Lilienthal cautioned in a widely publicized speech of October 1947 that industrial applications of atomic energy were "NOT just around the corner" and indeed, not even "around two corners." "Don't expect a pellet of uranium 235 to drive your car for a year," cautioned physicist Otto Frisch in his 1947 popularization *Meet the Atoms.* "A few minutes' ride in this car would be enough to kill you."[22]

Confronted by such a barrage of cautionary pronouncements from economists and scientists, most social prognosticators soon moderated their tone. Stuart Chase, for example, did concede that scientific opinion was against "those bright dreams of lump-of-sugar prime movers, to drive a plane from Chicago to Shanghai." A similar caution spread through the popular literature on atomic energy. After describing the visions of atomic cars and household atomic-power plants promulgated by "adventurous science writers" after the war, the authors of *Atomics for the Millions* (1947) concluded flatly: "Nothing could be further from reality." Atomic power might supplement conventional power sources, they acknowledged, but even here, they emphasized "the highly dangerous radiation" associated with atomic fission and warned that an accident at an atomic-power plant "could render a large area uninhabitable." John W. Campbell, Jr., predictably, minced no words in *The Atomic Story,* an exceptionally bleak 1947 book aimed at a popular market: "For the general public the much advertised atomic age is about to open with a dull thud of disappointment and a growing conviction that it has been badly oversold."[23]

In a reasonably quick progression, then, at least one strand of discourse on the promise of atomic energy evolved from exalted hopes to cautious skepticism to something approaching scorn for anyone gullible enough to have been taken in by such utopian fantasies. "Almost two years have dribbled away since Hiroshima," complained the author of a *Collier's* article in May 1947, and we have still to get beyond the starting line in our search for new atomic knowledge and applications." What happened, *Time* asked plaintively in August 1948, "to the nation's glamorous program for peacetime uses of nuclear energy?"[24] Reflecting the shift, a satirical note crept into journalistic treatments of atomic-energy predictions. An August 1947 *Harper's* short story told of a man in Arizona who after months of tinkering at last achieves fission in *frijolium,* a new element synthesized from Mexican beans, and puts the new energy source to all kinds of household uses. ("BEAN ATOM BUSTED," headlines one newspaper; "Frijole Fission Runs Washer for Basement Einstein; Clean Undies Prove Plutonium Now Obsolete.") *Science Illustrated* in 1949 published two pages of cartoons suggesting new uses for atomic energy, including atomic dry cleaning, atomic housing ("confined exclusively to abandoned coal mines"), and atomic dental equipment ("When accidents happen, keep calm, don't lose your head").[25]

Discussing "The Atom in Peace and War" in 1950, the editor of *Scientific American* conceded the theoretical possibility of important nonmilitary applications in the future, but concluded that for the present, harsh reality belied all such bright visions. Not only were most of the known applications of atomic energy "of questionable value for any peaceful purpose," but as the world's nuclear arsenals grew, it would prove increasingly difficult to persuade "the military and its chauvinistic supporters in all countries to yield up their stockpiles." "Nothing could be more illusory," he concluded bleakly, than the earlier "complacent feeling" that a technology of hideous destructiveness developed in the crucible of one global conflict and now being increasingly drawn into another would somehow, someday, be turned to "the uses of peace."[26]

The vision was not easily relinquished, however. The tension between the experts' increasingly cautious assessments and the strong impulse of journalists and popularizers to magnify the atom's peaceful potential (and perhaps the public's will to believe such claims) produced some interesting ambiguities in the popular literature on atomic energy. This ambiguity is strongly evident in the postwar writings of William L. Laurence. As official reporter for the Manhattan Project, Laurence had written the first newspaper stories about the bomb project, gaining in the process a considerable reputation as an authority on matters related to atomic energy. In his 1946 book *Dawn Over Zero,* as well as in several magazine articles with titles such as "Is Atomic Energy the Key to Our Dreams?," Laurence tried to salvage some of the optimism of his prewar writings on the wonders of "atomic power," describing it as "the philosopher's stone" that would "transmute the elements and create wealth far greater in value than gold," and comparing post-atomic man to Moses on Mount Pisgah, "gazing at a land of promise." But Laurence was also aware of the growing body of scientific literature on the subject, and he realized that the exaggerated claims of popularizers like O'Neill and Dietz were being ridiculed by knowledgeable scientists. Accordingly, he undercut his own bright generalities by debunking the "fantastic fairy tales" of his journalistic competitors. Citing the *Scientific American* report and other studies, he ridiculed talk of atomic cars, airplanes, and power pills, and asserted that even stationary atomic-power plants were unlikely to challenge traditional energy sources "for many years to come."[27]

As Laurence's obvious ambivalence makes plain, however, the will to believe that the development of the atomic bomb would somehow produce vast benefits for mankind proved remarkably tenacious. As the authors of the 1947 debunking article in the *American Scholar* observed, "visions of a new world in which atomic energy is harnessed as the great servant of mankind die hard." Despite gloomy pronouncements from experts, the level of media and public interest in the atom's peacetime promise remained high throughout the late 1940s. In part, this reflected the fact that, as we shall see, in these years the Atomic Energy Commission and other government agencies worked determinedly to sustain public interest, in the face of mounting negative evidence, in the vast and exciting potential of the "peaceful atom." In addition, beneath the post-Hiroshima hoopla lay a kernel of truth: in certain limited and specific areas, atomic energy and its research by-products did have significant civilian applications.

But more than governmental manipulation or a realistic appraisal of actualities was involved. One almost senses at times a willful determination not to acknowledge the increasingly pessimistic conclusions of the experts. As late as December 1947, a Columbia University dean could still in a public address invoke visions of atomic power "about as cheap as water, sunlight, and air"; of an atomic agricultural revolution in which "animals will grow bigger [and] quicker"; and of meteorological wonders through which "the desert can be made to blossom like the rose, arctic climes made habitable, and weather and climate . . . bent to human control." In a 1948 book entitled *The Art of Staying Sane,* a Unitarian minister described the marvels of atomic energy in phrases reminiscent of the most euphoric pronouncements of the earliest post-Hiroshima days. From the grass roots, one Vernon Snodgrass wrote to Robert M. Hutchins in November 1948 proposing that the Rocky Mountains be leveled by atomic bombs to increase rainfall in the Great Plains. "You are at liberty to plug this idea in any way you see fit," he generously offered; "It has unlimited possibilities as a thought-provoker."[28]

For *Time,* the dream of an atomic airplane died hardest. In July 1948, *Time* reported a lecture by an engineer with a corporation doing secret AEC research on the project that "sounded hopeful, as if he had items of progress which he wished he could crow about." That October, *Time* quoted an Oak Ridge engineer who claimed the theoretical work for an atomic-powered airplane was "99 percent perfected"; all that remained, he said, was for "the slide-rule men" to translate theory into reality.[29]

By the later 1940s, the early postwar fantasies of vast benefits from atomic energy were in eclipse. The most durable—that of cheap and abundant power—would revive, of course, with the actual inauguration of a nuclear power plant in Shippingsport, Pennsylvania, in 1957, but for the moment, the bright dreams had faded. As the decade wore on, the will to salvage a vestige of hope from the deepening atomic gloom increasingly centered on the promise of radioactive isotopes. Initially, these fission by-products had not received much journalistic attention. As other hoped-for peacetime applications were discredited or downgraded, however, they gained more and more notice. In the writings of William L. Laurence, for instance, his increasingly candid discussions of the poor prospects for atomic cars, atomic airplanes, and atomic power are balanced with glowing descriptions of the medical and research potential of isotopes. The usefulness of "tagged atoms" in locating certain forms of cancer, he suggested, was only the beginning of their role as "a lantern in the dark labyrinth of life." Isotope research, he predicted, would enable scientists to duplicate photosynthesis, supplying all the world's food needs and perhaps eventually converting solar rays into energy more efficiently than nature herself. In this way, Laurence concluded with a characteristic flourish, atomic know-how would "bring the sun down to earth as its gift to man." [30]

Similarly, in a bleak assessment of atomic energy's peacetime applications in the February 1946 *New Republic,* physicist Alvin Weinberg's one speculative flight focused on isotopes. If their research potential could be realized, he wrote, "the bountifulness of the earth would be multiplied indefinitely" and mankind's fuel and food requirements assured "as long as the sun continues to emit light." The potential of isotopes, agreed *Life* in December 1946, was "almost unlimited." They would, for example, help scientists "learn more about the processes of life, and thereby postpone death." The medical applications of radioactive isotopes in the treatment of cancer and other human ills, reported *Collier's* in May 1947, offered "cures for hitherto incurable diseases" and opened the door to a "golden age of atomic medicine." As soon as hospitals were equipped "to offer atomic medicine to all who need it," this article concluded, "much of the pain and premature death which now face so many of us may prove to be avoidable." Writing in the *American Magazine* about the same time, Robert M. Hutchins gave his imagination full rein: "The atomic city will have a central diagnostic laboratory, but only a small hospital, if any at all, for most human ailments will be cured as rapidly as they are diagnosed." [31]

By 1948, radioactive isotopes had absorbed the full magical aura that earlier surrounded the atomic automobile, the artificial atomic sun, and the household atomic-power pack. Thanks to atomic energy, declared *Operation Atomic Vision,* a high-school study unit published that year by the National Education Association, "it is unlikely that you or any of your classmates will die prematurely of cancer or heart disease, or from any contagious diseases, or from any other human ills that afflict us now. Many of your generation will reach the century mark." In an enthusiastic article called "Atom: Key to Better Farming," *U.S. News and World Report* that June described the amazing agricultural breakthroughs isotopes would make possible, including vastly increased crop yields through radioactive fertilizer; the use of man-made photosynthesis to produce gasoline, coal, and food by entirely artificial means; and further benefits "bigger and more important than the scientists themselves can imagine right now."[32]

The same impulse to view isotopes as the one authentic atomic age miracle was clearly at work in a 1948 article in *Coronet* magazine entitled "A World Worth Waiting For," which offered a "glimpse into the future of the Atomic Age" as visionary as anything published in 1945. It predicted that isotopes would soon yield agricultural and industrial wonders, amazing medical applications such as a possible cure for diabetes, "a basic understanding of the heart and its disorders," "the control of one or more types of cancer," and ultimately "a real cure that will eradicate [cancer] or even eliminate it before it appears." Echoing other writers, he predicted within a decade "one of the greatest scientific triumphs of all time": the artificial duplication of photosynthesis.

But even this would be only the beginning, this *Coronet* article continued. If added to plant nutrients at the proper moment in the reproductive cycle, isotopes could produce "millions of plant mutations" that could be bred to produce giant new species "beyond all the dreams of yesterday's science." And such genetic tinkering need not be limited to plants! Isotope tracers could decode the metabolic process of animals, leading to "the fantastic possibility . . . of directing that growth into channels most useful to man. And then may come the control of growth in man himself!" Like so many other articles on atomic energy in these years, this article ended on a note of high inspiration and promise: "Atomic energy is to us what the Atlantic Ocean was to Columbus when he sailed from Spain. He set out to find India but discovered the Western Hemisphere instead. Who can tell where our voyage into this unknown realm will lead?"[33]

The imagination and eloquence with which radioactive isotopes were promoted in the later 1940s, after the earlier surge of enthusiasm for atomic energy had faded, helps explain the persistence with which a great many Americans, even in the face of a stream of discouraging pronouncements from scientists, economists, and others, remained confident of the potential benefits of atomic energy. In late 1948, for example, the Gallup poll asked whether "in the long run" atomic energy would do more good than harm. While a significantly large proportion of respondents (35 percent) expressed "no opinion," about two-thirds of those who did felt that atomic energy would be more beneficial than harmful. (In Holland, Sweden, England, and Australia, where the same question was asked, the percentage of positive responses was substantially lower.)[34] Broken down by educational level, this poll revealed the results shown in the table. The more highly educated, the more likely an American of 1948 was to hold a hopeful view of atomic energy; the lower the educational level, the less likely to view atomic energy favorably—or to express an opinion at all.

"Do you think that, in the long run, atomic energy will do more good than harm?"
(Gallup poll, 1948)

	More Good	**More Harm**	**No Opinion**
College educated	61%	18%	21%
High-school educated	47%	25%	28%
Grade-school educated	31%	23%	46%

These results are intriguing. They may reflect a cultural "lag" at different educational (and perhaps social-class) levels. Among the less educated, the most compelling associations with the words "atomic energy" may have remained the fearsome ones dramatically implanted in August 1945 and massively reinforced during the heyday of the "scientists' movement." Among better-educated Americans at the middle and upper socioeconomic levels, by contrast, the elemental fear of 1945–1947 may have been more affected by subsequent cultural and political developments: the diminished public emphasis on the horror of atomic war with the failure of the international-control campaign; the growing entanglement of the nuclear weapons issue with the intensifying struggle with the Soviet Union; and (of particular relevance in this context) the sustained media attention to the peacetime promise of atomic energy, now focused especially on radioactive isotopes and, to a limited extent, on nuclear power. As the 1940s ended, then, it seems to have been the least educated, least "well-informed," perhaps poorest Americans who remained the most deeply skeptical about the probable impact of atomic fission on mankind's future, while the more highly educated were the most inclined to the view, powerfully reinforced by the government and important voices in the media, that the atomic future was bright with promise. As an omen for the future, this pattern suggested some disturbing possibilities.

11

Bright Dreams and Disturbing Realities: The Psychological Function of the Atomic-Utopia Visions

Fascinating in their own right, the early pronouncements hailing the exciting peacetime uses of atomic energy also illuminate our central concern in this study: the impact of the atomic bomb on American thought and culture. Nuclear power, radioactive isotopes, and other civilian applications of atomic energy were, of course, matters of legitimate interest in these years. But the obsessive preoccupation with these applications right after Hiroshima, and the exaggerated hopes they aroused, also tell us something about the bomb's larger effect on the national consciousness. Dreams of a "new world" of atomic energy just around the corner were a way of dealing with —or avoiding—unsettling immediate realities: America's use of two atomic bombs to obliterate two cities and the prospect that even more terrible atomic weapons might someday devastate the earth.

With striking frequency, predictions of the atom's beneficent promise were explicitly linked to references to Hiroshima and Nagasaki. One finds this, for example, in a rather misty *New York Times* editorial within days of the war's end:

> In this shock that ran like an earthquake around the world, there is room for hope, room for dreams of a nobler future for mankind. The atomic bomb was perfected for war, but the knowledge which made it possible came out of . . . the deathless yearning to know and to use the gifts of nature for the common good. . . . This new knowledge . . . can bring to this earth not death but life, not tyranny and cruelty, but a divine freedom. What dazzling gifts the science which split the atom can offer the heavily laden everywhere! . . . What cannot this science do for the millions of China and India, bound for so many ages in sweat and hunger to the wheel of material existence.[1]

Magazine writers, too, forged a similar rhetorical link between the atomic bombing of Japan and a glorious atomic future. "Through medical advances alone," asserted the *Atlantic* in 1946, "atomic energy has already saved more lives than were snuffed out at Hiroshima and Nagasaki." At last, proclaimed *Christian Century* in a report on isotope research on algae being conducted at Stanford University, atomic energy was "beginning to give promise of doing something besides destroy life." "Control of cancer," predicted *Science News Letter* in 1946, while "not as spectacular at first glance as atomic power or atomic bombs, will undoubtedly, in the long run, be the great achievement of the atomic age."[2]

Sometimes it was further implied that the Japanese bombings were, in some way, an essential step in unlocking the atom's peacetime promise. A writer discussing the agricultural applications of atomic energy, for example, passed along reports that the crops in Hiroshima in 1946 and 1947 were exceptionally good—"bigger and more fruitful than ever before." A radiologist with close ties to the AEC reported in a medical journal that a cancer patient in Nagasaki had "enjoyed prolonged remission as a result of the radiation received at the time of the blast." The U.S.-sponsored Atomic Bomb Casualty Commission study of the genetic effects of radiation exposure on survivors and their offspring, said *Coronet* magazine in 1948, could be "one of the most important scientific reports in history," providing the key to "the elimination of inherited disease and . . . other profound secrets of human creation." A 1947 *Collier's* feature on "the positive side of the atom" generalized the point: "The blast at Hiroshima," it said, "illuminated hitherto impenetrable continents of human knowledge." A physician discussing "Medical Care in the Atomic Age" in 1950 established the link even more firmly: "Out of the ashes of Hiroshima and Nagasaki," he wrote,". . . a beneficent atomic energy . . . will rise phoenix-like to benefit the health and welfare of our nation."[3]

The importance of Hiroshima and Nagasaki to the unfolding of the larger promise of atomic energy was eloquently portrayed by Arthur H. Compton in the January 1947 *Annals of the American Academy of Political and Social Science*. The atomic-bomb project, Compton insisted, was "only the wartime aspect of a much greater vision"—the vision of physicists who had for decades "dreamed of a more abundant life, of greater knowledge to control disease, of greater freedom to build a better world." In Compton's vision, the scientists' immersion in the Manhattan Project was somewhat like Jesus' time in the desert before the beginning of his ministry:

The years they spent at making atomic bombs prepared those who were making them to burst into a vast missionary call for peace as soon as the war was won. . . . The whole world shall have peace and, as far as the new advances of science and technology can bring it, prosperity and a more complete life. . . . Such is the spirit of the atomic crusade.[4]

As such pronouncements make clear, speculation about atomic energy's glorious promise enabled Americans to turn from the immediate reality of its military use, and even to view that use as a necessary stage in a larger, beneficent process. These "roseate dreams of the future" (as the *New Republic* called them on August 20, 1945) facilitated the process by which Americans absorbed Hiroshima and Nagasaki into their moral history.[5]

They also made it easier for Americans to cope with their fears of atomic dangers ahead. This process was noted as early as December 1945 by a writer in the *Nation*. The immediate reaction to Hiroshima and Nagasaki had been fear, he said, but "what a change has occurred during the last few weeks! . . . [People] have at last seen the light. Suddenly from all sides, and sometimes even from the same people who were so pessimistically inclined only a month ago, we have heard that the applications of atomic energy to civilian life are possible, imminent, and even unavoidable."[6]

This shift of outlook was neither so instantaneous nor so total, but it did happen and it was a shaping cultural force. That atomic energy had been first introduced as a destructive force, some argued, was simply an unfortunate twist of history that distorted its true significance—as though, a 1949 article in a psychological journal noted, electricity had initially become known through the mass electrocution of a hundred thousand people. As the Baltimore newspaperman and political writer Gerald W. Johnson wrote in the *American Scholar* early in 1946: "Atomic fission seems to open the way to such improvement in the conditions of life as the race has never known. It also opens the way to sudden, violent death, but what of that? So did steam; so did electricity. Yet we have made use of them, in spite of their dangers." Deluged by hundreds of such postwar pronouncements, one is tempted to find at least symbolic significance in the fact that one of the most visionary evocations of the atom's bright promise in these years appeared in a book entitled *The Art of Staying Sane.*[7]

Some opinion-molders were quite explicit about the importance of accentuating the positive. "World reaction to the atomic bomb has been too largely limited to a feeling of terror," wrote Philip Wylie in September 1945. "Atomic energy is *only incidentally* a military weapon. As a source of power it will be more important to human beings than all the wars recorded." A committee of the American Psychological Association, advising public officials and educators on how to deal with the nation's nuclear fears, made the same point in June 1946: *"The possible benefits of atomic energy must be emphasized and developed.* The atmosphere of demoralizing fear which surrounds the phrase atomic energy can be reduced by presenting the facts in honest, unexaggerated *peacetime* terms." Discussing "The Teacher and

Atomic Energy" in 1948, an educator wrote: "The job of the teacher is not to scare the daylights out of people by regaling them with the horrors of atomic destruction." The dangers of atomic war should not be ignored, he said, but the schools' major effort should be "in stimulating thinking and guiding analysis on the positive aspects of atomic energy control in the service of mankind."[8]

Such pronouncements sometimes reflected an almost mystical belief in the power of positive thinking, a conviction that mere discussion of the atom's peacetime promise—whatever the actual achievement—was a significant social good. The way people "keep returning to the theme of 'peaceful uses' of atomic energy," said *Life,* "is a tribute . . . to their innate decency." The psychological value of atomic energy as a "stimulus to the imagination, an awakening force," observed David E. Lilienthal in a 1947 diary entry, was much more important than any specific practical use. After an address to forty-five hundred delegates at a Farm Bureau convention in Chicago later that year, Lilienthal reflected, "It was wonderful to see how profoundly moved these people are when one talks about eliminating this as a weapon, putting it to beneficial uses. . . . I added a conclusion, reverting to the note of 'service to humanity and the Kingdom of God,' and that audience seemed to merge into a single picture, . . . a unified presence, you might say; it was like uttering a benediction."[9]

This magnification of the atom's hypothetical peacetime benefits as a way of avoiding the reality of the atomic threat was encouraged by the "either/or" structure of many post-Hiroshima pronouncements: either civilization would vanish in a cataclysmic holocaust, or the atomic future would be unimaginably bright. As Dwight Macdonald observed as early as September 1945 in his one-man journal of opinion, *Politics*: "The official platitude about Atomic Fission is that it can be a Force for Good (production) or a Force for Evil (war), and that the problem is simply how to use its Good rather than its Bad potentialities."[10]

Macdonald's jaundiced summary aptly characterizes a flood of post-Hiroshima pronouncements. "We face the prospect either of destruction on a scale which dwarfs anything thus far reported," editorialized the *New York Times* within hours of Truman's announcement, "or of a golden era of social change which would satisfy the most romantic utopian." The bomb might be the signal of "the crack of doom," observed the *Dallas Morning News* a few days later, or of mankind's entry into paradise. Raymond Gram Swing on August 13 offered an equally stark alternative: "The choice before men is simple: . . . either live fabulously well, or . . . commit suicide as a race." The "either/or" theme of Philip Wylie's September 1945 *Collier's* article is summed up in the title chosen by the editors: "Deliverance or Doom."[11]

Presented this way, the issue did have a certain symmetry and simplicity—certainly more symmetry and simplicity than the alternative view, rarely heard in these years, that atomic energy might be *both* mankind's scourge and benefactor. The "either/or" formulation was powerful—so powerful that it even found its way into *One World or None,* despite that book's generally skeptical view of the peacetime atom. "If the terror of the bomb is great . . . ," said the Federation of American Scientists in its concluding statement, "the hope for man in the release of nuclear energy is even greater. . . . We cannot now see more than the faint shadow of what such a new force can mean for man. But it is our faith as scientists and our experience as citizens of the twentieth century that it will mean much." [12]

The "either/or" polarity found imaginative expression in William L. Laurence's 1946 eyewitness accounts of the Alamogordo test and the Nagasaki bombing. At Alamogordo, wrote Laurence, the cloud that surged over the predawn desert reminded him of a great Statue of Liberty, "its arm raised to the sky, symbolizing the birth of a new freedom for man." At Nagasaki, by contrast, the cloud seemed like a grotesque totem pole suggesting "an atavistic throw-back to primitive savagery and barbarism." Which would it be, asked Laurence, echoing scores of other writers: atomic energy as destroyer or as "the gateway to a new world" that would "set man on the road to the millennium"? [13]

Mankind's allegedly simple yet momentous choice between bliss or horror was strongly emphasized by the Acheson-Lilienthal Report. The key to escaping the nightmare of an atomic arms race and ultimate atomic war, insisted this influential document, was cooperative world research "to develop the beneficial possibilities of atomic energy and encourage the growth of fundamental knowledge, stirring the constructive and imaginative impulses of man rather than merely concentrating on the defensive and negative." [14]

For the next four years, in dozens of speeches, AEC reports, and articles for mass-circulation magazines, David E. Lilienthal rang the changes on exactly this theme. Indeed, he almost came to personify the desperate hope that atomic energy would prove to be mankind's friend. "It's natural enough, remembering the bomb," to think of atomic energy "as a terrible, destructive force," he told an audience in October 1946, "but as a matter of fact, it's one of the most magnificent discoveries of all time. It can be put to many uses beneficial to humankind." "Genuine security and peace of mind" in the atomic age, he wrote in *Collier's* in 1947, would come only with "full-scale realization of the promise and possibilities of the use of nuclear science, and the coming new industries, professions and skills that will grow up in this nourishing soil of nuclear knowledge." The true meaning of the "atomic adventure" was as "a towering symbol of one of the faiths that makes man civilized, the faith in knowledge." [15]

Lilienthal himself grew increasingly discouraged as the international-control movement failed, the nuclear arms race began, and the coming of the "peaceful atom" receded ever further into the distance. He confined his doubts mainly to the privacy of his journal, however, continuing in public to proclaim with almost shrill optimism the vast promise of atomic energy.

Other AEC commissioners naturally echoed Lilienthal's theme. In 1947, in an open letter to two schoolchildren who had written asking how "a person can live happily in the atomic age," Commissioner W. W. Waymack advised them to recognize that all human discoveries posed "terrible dangers, if used badly," but also "magnificent opportunities for making a better and happier world, if used wisely." The fate of Hiroshima had made the dangers of atomic energy all too evident; the challenge now was to make it "a benevolent servant" to produce for mankind "more comforts, more leisure, better health, more of real freedom [and] a much happier life." [16]

The preoccupation with the atom's peacetime promise in the months after Hiroshima thus was part of the process by which the nation muted its awareness of Hiroshima and Nagasaki and of even more frightening future prospects. Taking the lead from respected scientists like Compton and public figures like Lilienthal, columnists, commentators, and other opinion-molders offered the American people a hopeful scenario: support peaceful development, and the threat of atomic war will diminish. This promise at times became almost touchingly explicit. Noting the symbolism of the creation of the civilian AEC and the first shipment of research isotopes from Oak Ridge for scientific research almost precisely one year after Hiroshima, *Science News Letter* concluded hopefully: "These steps should mark the turning of atomic power from the ways of war to the paths of peace." The development of a pilot nuclear power plant at Los Alamos in 1947 and the promise of still more peacetime applications, observed another journal, would do much "to re-establish [America's] reputation as the champion of a better world" and its determination to make atomic-energy research "less dangerous and nihilistic." [17] In the May 1947 *Collier's* feature on "Man and the Atom," even the illustrations emphasized the theme that concentration on peacetime uses would diminish the threat of atomic destruction. Over paired photographs of a devastated city and a humming industrial plant supposedly run by atomic energy were printed the words: "Not This . . . But This." An article on the medical benefits of radioactive isotopes was illustrated with two photographs superimposed to create a single image: that of a pajama-clad man, obviously a recently recovered invalid, standing erect and smiling in the midst of a mushroom-shaped cloud, his empty wheelchair in the background. [18]

One of the more ingenious elaborations of the theme was offered in a February 1948 address to a New York City professional club by William R. Foulkes, editor of a current-affairs digest widely used by college debaters. The "unlimited power and . . . other benefits" promised by atomic energy, as symbolized by the miraculous isotope, Foulkes predicted, would be the social force that would dissuade the nations of the world, and especially the Soviet Union, from a nuclear arms race:

> It is one thing for a bitter, impoverished nation to be willing to risk its own suicide to encompass the destruction of enemies it hates for their possessions. It is something else to commit suicide when you are standing—materially at least—at the entrance of Paradise. . . . So let's add this final credit to atomic energy, that out of its own accomplishments it may create the political conditions that will save it from being used for the destruction of the world.[19]

A few observers at the time recognized—and deplored—the narcotizing effect of the "peaceful atom" dream. "The ultimate benefits of nuclear energy may well surpass its present terrors," observed *Business Week* on the first anniversary of Hiroshima, "but the terrors are here now in awful dimension, and man must face them." The ubiquitous speculation about the atom's future promise, wrote Walter Isard and Vincent Whitney in 1947, was, in part, a form of "whistling to keep up our courage in the darkness of the political night." "How much more pleasant," wrote David Bradley in 1948, to push aside radiation worries in favor of fantasies about "the coming miracles of healing, the prolongation of life, the days of sunny leisure. . . . Why let in the bogeyman to the sweet dreams of atomic energy for peacetime purposes." Whatever the peacetime promise of atomic energy, declared Bernard Brodie in 1948, it "must count as nothing compared to the awful menace of the bomb itself."[20]

A particularly sharp criticism of these post-Hiroshima visions of atomic wonders ahead came from radicals who challenged them not on scientific but on ideological grounds. Writing in the Marxist journal *Science and Society* in 1946, John K. Jacobs dismissed all such euphoric fantasies as "nonsense"—but nonsense that served the interests of the ruling class by spreading "all kinds of illusions as to the abilities of capitalism to solve the problems of humanity." These "comic strip utopias," he added, were pathetically deficient in social vision when compared to the "naive but courageous and principled picture" of a socialist future found in Edward Bellamy's 1889 classic *Looking Backward*.[21]

The leaders of the scientists' movement were quick to recognize the implicit tension between their own insistent emphasis on the threat of atomic war and the hopeful visions of the peaceful atom. "Since I do not forsee that atomic energy is to be a great boon for a long time," wrote Albert Einstein in his November 1945 plea for world government, "I have to say that for the present, it is a menace." The choice was not "either/or," J. Robert Oppenheimer told the American Philosophical Society in November 1945. In "a world committed to atomic armament," fear, guilt, and great danger would continue to overshadow the entire nuclear enterprise. Speculation about peacetime applications, he insisted, must not be allowed to divert attention from "the immediacy and the peril of atomic weapons." Oppenheimer reiterated the point early in 1946: "The development of atomic energy for peace," he told a Westinghouse Corporation forum, "cannot be separated from its development for war."[22]

Editors and writers who approached atomic issues from a religious or ethical perspective seemed particularly acute at recognizing how the publicity being lavished on the "peaceful" atom was deadening awareness of more immediate issues. "The picture, conjured up by some of our writers, of vast power and plenty made possible by atomic energy," observed Richard M. Fagley in *Christianity and Crisis* as early as October 1945, was, in fact, a "tragic reflection of the present crisis."

> How distorted is our vision to see so easily the vista of mechanical progress in this Atomic Age, and to fail to see clearly the greed, pride, and fear in ourselves which have now brought us to the doorstep of doom! . . . Only if man has a new spirit within him can he pass over into this Promised Land. The Atomic Age is otherwise almost certain to be extremely short and extremely brutish.[23]

Even the liberal Protestant journal *Christian Century*, though itself hardly immune to the siren song of the peaceful atom, could also express bleak pessimism. Noting in August 1947 that the second anniversary of Hiroshima had aroused "little indication of public interest," *Christian Century* concluded that for all the rhetoric to the contrary, America's atomic effort was "centered on the production of bigger and better bombs," and that research on peacetime uses was really "the stepchild of the whole enterprise."[24]

The most devastating of these early attacks in the religious press on the seductive visions of an atomic Utopia came in an embittered editorial in the Catholic journal *Commonweal* early in 1946. "When something is very painful and complicated to think about," said *Commonweal*, "it is convenient to have it put away somewhere in the past or held off somewhere remotely in the future, hoping that you may never catch up with it. . . . That is what we have been doing about the atomic bomb." Rather than facing reality, this editorial continued, Americans were indulging in pipe dreams about a misty future of atomic marvels:

> Would it not be wonderful to use atomic energy to make Africa green —no more lean years, no more thirsty camels. And all the cities everywhere heated for nothing, the factories running by themselves, the steamships propelled by a little bottle kept in the Captain's safe. There

is plenty to talk about if you talk about the future. . . . Very few people talk about the present.

And what of the present? Citing budget figures which made clear that America's postwar atomic-bomb research and production had already moved into high gear even as proponents of the peaceful atom spun out their fantasies, *Commonweal* concluded: "The government of the United States is actively engaged, *now*, in linking the horror of the past to an inevitably horrible future."[25]

By 1950, the Protestant writer Edward L. Long, Jr., could pen a bleak and perceptive epitaph to five years of wishful thinking about the wonders of the peaceful atom. As always in history, he said, these utopian fantasies reflected, like an inverted mirror image, the culture's darker preoccupations: a bad conscience about the past, bleak discouragement over present trends, brooding fear of what lay ahead: "A brighter future is dreamily pictured," wrote Long, "in order to overcome the problem of the dark present, and the peaceful plenty of atomic energy is stressed to offset a sense of frustration resulting from the fact that nuclear fission first destroyed a city. . . . We talk of an atomic Utopia, supposing that promise of such rosy prospects can dispel the gloom and insecurity of present darkness." But in the long run, self-delusion would exact a fearful toll. Whatever else it might hold in store, Long concluded, "the atomic age will not be Utopia."[26]

Five

The Social Implications of Atomic Energy

Prophecies and Prescriptions

12

Optimistic Forecasts

E. B. White was one of the first to capture the mood. "For the first time in our lives," he wrote in the *New Yorker* on August 18, 1945, after a fortnight that had brought news of Hiroshima, Nagasaki, Alamogordo, and the Manhattan Project, "we can feel the disturbing vibrations of complete human readjustment. Usually the vibrations are so faint as to go unnoticed. This time they are so strong that even the ending of a war is overshadowed." The disturbing vibrations White sensed were soon resonating through the culture.[1]

In the last two chapters we looked at the prophecies of technological and medical marvels in the era of the atom. But such predictions represent only a small fraction—and, except as a psychological barometer, the least significant fraction—of the post-Hiroshima cultural discourse about the coming atomic age. The more revealing speculation centered not on technological change per se but on its social, cultural, and political ramifications. How would the atom affect the consciousness and character of the American people? How would society, culture, and governmental structures be altered? Such issues were under intense and urgent discussion in the early postwar years. Some speculation was wildly off base; some uncannily prophetic. Some was hopeful; much bleakly pessimistic. But taken as a whole, this torrent of social discourse offers a revealing glimpse of a people struggling to come to terms with changes of almost unfathomable magnitude.

As E. B. White's comment suggests, the advent of the atomic bomb was very quickly recognized as one of those rare events that forever alter the human landscape. "In an instant, without warning," as *Time* put it, a headline, a radio bulletin, or a chance remark brought the realization that "the present had become the unthinkable future." Hiroshima bisected history. In its aftermath, historian Allan Nevins observed in 1946, people found themselves "beholding a new heaven and a new earth, to which they somewhat dazedly tried to adjust themselves." When the cloud rose over Alamogordo, William L. Laurence was soon telling Americans, "your world and mine, the world we knew, came to an end."[2]

Indeed, the news that came on August 6, 1945, remains unique in

American history for its combination of profound importance and shocking immediacy. The Declaration of Independence was a fundamental turning point, to be sure, but it required a long war to establish that fact decisively. The Civil War's transforming impact unfolded only gradually. The full impact of the railroad, the automobile, the computer, and other protean forces of change only slowly penetrated the national consciousness. (There had, of course, been other moments when the nation's attention had been riveted upon a single event—Lincoln's assassination, Lindbergh's flight, the attack on Pearl Harbor, FDR's death—but few claimed that these events marked a new stage of human history.) The sociologist Louis Wirth made this point in 1947, contrasting the "startling suddenness" of the atomic bomb's advent with the more familiar pattern of cultural perception by which even "the most startling technological innovations . . . made their way slowly into the ways of living and into the minds of men," allowing ample time for "the thinking of the social scientists, the statesmen, and the public to catch up with them."[3]

How different in 1945! In dramatic contrast to the typical pattern of slowly developing awareness described by Wirth, social commentators and opinion-molders were insisting within hours of Truman's announcement that a fresh page had been turned in the book of human history; that human existence was about to be radically altered. The atom's potential social effects, insisted a Rockefeller Foundation official in a typical comment from those first months, "can only be judged as the size of an iceberg is judged with seven-eighths of its whole below the surface of visibility." The unleashing of the atom, agreed a *Nation* writer in December, "moves humanity forward several centuries."[4]

This insistence that sweeping social transformations were imminent persisted even after the initial shock of Hiroshima had faded. In the atomic era, wrote *Time*'s science editor assuredly in 1946, "few present institutions can survive unchanged." Even skeptics who doubted that the social effects would be as drastic as predicted acknowledged the ubiquity of such speculation. "Few current statements are more often repeated and more readily accepted," observed the psychiatrist Franz Alexander early in 1946, "than the assertion that with [atomic energy] we have entered a new era in history." Such pronouncements, commented a *Christian Science Monitor* correspondent in 1947, had "become almost axiomatic" in American cultural discourse.[5]

Another point of agreement among early commentators was the solemn obligation of every citizen to think seriously about the atom's social implications, to bring fresh ideas to bear, and in general to help out with what John J. O'Neill called "the task of organizing an entirely new economic structure and a new social structure." As President Truman himself put it in an October 1945 message to Congress: "The release of atomic energy constitutes a new force too revolutionary to consider in the framework of old ideas."[6]

An impressive number of Americans did, indeed, try to rise to the challenge. In the weeks and months after Hiroshima, wrote Allan Nevins in 1946, a universal theme of conversation was "what the new world and the new era would be like." *Business Week* observed in July 1946: "Atom Year I has probably been marked by more debate on a single subject than any other twelve months in the world's history. Social, economic, and political as well as purely technical issues have been pressing for realistic solution." Ministers, columnists, commentators, editors, civic groups, schoolchildren, labor leaders—nearly everyone, it sometimes seemed, was caught up in this national discussion of the social implications of atomic energy. The Social Science Research Council secured foundation grants to investigate the subject. At the University of Chicago, Chancellor Robert M. Hutchins organized an "Office of Inquiry into the Social Aspects of Atomic Energy," which brought together economists, sociologists, political scientists, religious leaders, and others whose insights might conceivably shed light on the topic.[7]

But precisely *what* social changes were in store, and how ought one go about preparing for them? The answers to these key questions were frustratingly imprecise and contradictory. As an Ohio college professor wrote in December 1945, the average American was "bewildered" by the "dramatic injunction to live and think and feel differently because he has entered a new era," since few of the sweeping pronouncements gave any indication "exactly what the new era requires of him."[8]

When broad generalization gave way to specificity, the unanimity and assurance of these social prognosticators ended, and their ideas trailed off in all directions. A few, indeed, were uneasy about offering any detailed social forecasts, believing that confident prediction was foolhardy. "It is as though we had opened a tiny door and found an infinity of black space behind it," commented one cautious observer. "At present our eyes are able only to penetrate about six inches of this Stygian darkness." For others, the most striking immediate social effect of the "new era" was precisely the diverse, contradictory, and sometimes bizarre social comment it elicited! "Early public statements about the problem of the atomic bomb," said the editors of the *Antioch Review* late in 1945, "have given as much evidence of psychic shock as of intelligent consideration." The advent of the bomb had caused "endless confusion," agreed Harold C. Urey in 1946. "And the confusion spreads to more people as they came to realize all the implications of this weapon." Gerald W. Johnson, writing in the *American Scholar* of Hiroshima's effect on social thought, voiced the sentiments of many:

Not houses and factories only, but concepts and convictions as well, have gone where Hiroshima went. . . . For the moment, the lines of thinking are hopelessly snarled. . . . We have been spun in the vortex of the atomic bomb until our sense of direction is lost.[9]

But few opinion-molders let the prevailing confusion inhibit them from speculating about the social contours of atomic-age America. This speculation is noteworthy precisely because of its general banality and lack of originality. What is most striking, if perhaps unsurprising, about American social thought as the nation self-consciously prepared to enter a "new era" is the extent to which it reflected prior concerns, values, and ideological presuppositions. For most of these thinkers, the atom's probable social, political, and cultural effects meshed remarkably well with their engrained social views and political ideology. As the *Antioch Review* perceptively observed late in 1945, "It has been somewhat as though the explosion over Hiroshima merely set our leaders of opinion talking at a faster tempo and a higher pitch of whatever was on their minds at the moment."[10]

The best way to approach this considerable body of social thought is to look first at that which anticipates generally positive social and cultural consequences from the advent of atomic energy, and then at that which exudes pessimism and apprehension. (Some of the most penetrating comments, of course, did not fall unequivocally in either category.) Just as the early postwar period brought innumerable predictions of the material transformation of American life thanks to atomic energy, so too, with no less confidence, others foresaw equally breathtaking social and cultural changes. Indeed, the post-Hiroshima months brought a tidal wave of expansive predictions that the whole of human society would be transformed for the better as a result of the global prosperity and harmony the peaceful application of atomic energy would bring. One such visionary foresaw a dramatic easing of world tensions as atomic energy brought universal prosperity, erased the old distinction between "have" and "have not" nations, and ushered in an age of "equality, peace, and happiness." In the same vein, *Coronet* magazine pointed out in 1946 that with "unlimited wealth" now available to all nations through atomic energy, no country would ever again be impelled by economic factors to invade its neighbors, thus eliminating "the basic reason for war." Anticipating Marshall McLuhan's "global village," a journalist predicted in 1947 that the atomic age would bring a "shrinkage of the globe . . . into a single neighborhood with virtually equal opportunity for all." Domestically, science writer John J. O'Neill predicted, the industrial decentralization made possible by atomic power would promote social harmony by fostering "a greater uniformity of interests in all parts of the nation."[11]

Others discerned shimmering spiritual and cultural promise in the new social world of the techno-atomic Utopia. Such a world would give man "the limitless opportunities that can come with time to think," predicted Norman Cousins, and make possible "a revolution . . . in his leisure-time activities . . . , so far . . . associated almost entirely with the commodities of vended amusement." (Fewer honky-tonk and amusement-park customers; more *Saturday Review* subscribers!) In another of those effusions produced at white heat within hours of Hiroshima, a euphoric professor at a Connecticut teachers' college predicted that cheap and unlimited energy would at last "release man from daily toil and give him time to live creatively in the world of mind and spirit." [12]

A particularly inspiring vision of the social contours of the future age was offered in 1946 by Gerald Wendt, science writer for *Time* magazine. In an analysis that echoed Simon N. Patten's 1904 work *The New Basis of Civilization,* Wendt predicted that in the atomic era, physical labor would be practically eliminated, releasing vast human energies for cultural and spiritual pursuits: "Then at last science will have freed the human race not only from disease, famine, and early death, but also from poverty and work. Then at last science will enable humanity to *live,* as well as to earn a living. . . . Then materialism and mechanism will be merely the servants of the spiritual life. . . . Educators, artists, clergymen, and governments," Wendt declared, should cooperatively share the task of preparing "the coming generation for a golden age." [13]

Reaching his optimistic conclusion by a somewhat different route, Philip Wylie argued that the very experience of grappling with the terrors of the atomic age could itself have a revitalizing effect upon the American spirit. For decades, Wylie suggested, with the wilderness subdued and material prosperity achieved, zest and excitement had gradually been draining from American life, producing cultural and spiritual malaise:

> Some of us have lost hope. Many of us . . . have been unable to discern in the future a proper heritage for Americans—a thing of sufficient challenge and possibility to give us endless incentive and the dignity that belongs to a race which pays its respects alike to Thomas Jefferson and Paul Bunyan.

When the bombs burst over Hiroshima and Nagasaki, Wylie went on, this insipid cultural climate changed overnight. What greater challenge than to wrestle the fundamental powers of the universe into submission! "This is the dream we yearned for. This is . . . the main chance. This is the superlative responsibility which, if shouldered, promises a paradise men can make with their own hands and their own minds." Like John Winthrop on the *Arabella* reminding his fellow Puritans that the eyes of mankind were upon them, Philip Wylie told Americans that world attention was once again riveted upon them as they faced this latest and grandest of history's challenges. Indeed, they were at the center now not merely of the global but the cosmic stage. "We, who have gone so far in two centuries, now own infinity and eternity." [14]

Some who spoke most hopefully of the atom's social implications drew particular inspiration from the vast undertaking that had successfully developed the atomic bomb. Emulate the Manhattan Project, and learn its social lessons, they suggested, and the positive social effects could be dramatic indeed. For John Sembower, director of industrial relations at the Hanford plutonium plant, the wartime bomb project represented a triumphant vindication of American democracy. We won the race for the atomic bomb, he boasted, while "the supposedly real specialists in the creation of horror machinery and terror, the Axis warmongers, never succeeded in putting to use this greatest destroyer of all." To some, this line of thought might have occasioned sober reflection, but to Sembower it proved the superiority of a democratic society even under the stress of war. A Nazi atomic-bomb project, he said, would have been brutally totalitarian: arbitrary property seizures, slave labor, terror-enforced secrecy. In the United States, by contrast, land was acquired legally with fair compensation, workers recruited (and allowed to quit) in normal fashion, and secrecy maintained through voluntary cooperation. In short, the atomic bomb

> came into being under the general framework of democracy as we know it. Great and awesome as this new force may be, . . . it has not conquered our basic institutions. . . . We decided that the end, however urgent or vital, does not justify the means of tyranny. . . . Thus we may already have laid one chain of restraint about the atomic Frankenstein. We did not even let the prized promise of the atomic bomb make us totalitarian." [15]

To other observers, the Manhattan Project offered an uplifting model of social endeavor at its best—not only a "striking example of international cooperation in science" (as the *New York Times* put it) but also a great shared venture with implications for society as a whole. The development of the atomic bomb by "many minds belonging to different races and different religions . . . ," declared Eleanor Roosevelt in a radio broadcast a few days after Hiroshima, "sets the pattern for the way in which in the future we may be able to work out our difficulties." Proponents of this theme stressed the diverse national origins of the key Manhattan Project scientists: the Italian Fermi, Bohr from Denmark, the Hungarian Szilard, Einstein and Franck from Germany, Oppenheimer, Compton, and others from the United States, and so on. *Time,* in a passage reminiscent of a Norman Rockwell painting, described how differences of education, race, region, and social status had been submerged in the great common effort: "Professors, including Nobel Prize winners, deserted their campuses to live in dusty deserts. Workers trekked in their trailers—careful New England craftsmen, burly Southern Negroes, all the races and types of the great U.S." [16]

The selflessness that had welded a heterogenous assortment of individuals into a smoothly functioning unit pursuing a common goal was endlessly praised in the press accounts of the Manhattan Project. In this postwar period when the nation was faced with numerous strikes, writers dwelled on the labor harmony that had prevailed in the project. John Sembower noted "the almost total absence of work stoppages through labor difficulties" at Hanford. "Never has a job so vast and so complicated been carried through with less friction. . . ," reported *Business Week*; "Thousands of corporation executives, engineers, production men, technicians, clerks, and just plain laborers in hundreds of companies gave themselves to the job with a tight-lipped devotion." For *Business Week,* as for Eleanor Roosevelt, the lesson for the atomic era was clear: social unity must replace divisiveness and conflict; progress in exploiting the atom's vast promise depended on recapturing "the whole-souled cooperation of individuals, companies, and governments that marked the wartime development of the atomic bomb." [17]

Of all those who proposed the Manhattan Project as a relevant social model for postwar America, none was more articulate or more assured than Arthur H. Compton, Nobel laureate in physics and wartime director of the Manhattan Project team at the University of Chicago. In speeches and in publications ranging from the *Annals of the American Academy of Political and Social Science* to the *Rotarian,* Compton tirelessly peddled his hopeful message: the Manhattan Project epitomized values essential to any social endeavor—cooperation, the spirit of service, dedication to a common ideal. Indeed, he insisted, this venture represented one of history's greatest cooperative endeavors. Personal ambition and social antagonisms had been thrust aside as "individual scientists, leaders of the Government, the Army, universities and great industrial organizations successively caught the vision of . . . a chance to share in what was instinctively recognized as one of the great human adventures of all time."

Ethnic, national, and racial distinctions had been forgotten in the quest for a common goal. Linking the Nazis' repudiation of "Jewish science" to their failure to develop the atomic bomb, Compton cited the Manhattan Project's freedom from prejudice as a major factor in its success. Distinctions of race and social class had been rejected as well: a "dozen Negro scientists" had "worked in complete equality with their white colleagues"; "skilled and unskilled labor of all kinds" had shared tasks harmoniously with brilliant scientists. In countless ways, in short, the wartime project illustrated the growing influence of the social ideal, as opposed to mere individual aggrandizement, in human affairs.

For Arthur Compton, the social meaning of the Manhattan Project vastly transcended the mundane fact that several atomic bombs had been constructed. It represented an important step in the "steady progression of science that is compelling man to become human." The task now was to apply this lesson to the larger society—a task doubly important in the atomic age. Combining his ethical idealism with a Social Darwinian argument reminiscent of Lester Ward, Compton offered his reading of the central challenge facing America in the atomic era:

> The evolutionary law of the survival of the fittest applies to societies as well as to individuals. According to this law, the society of the future will inevitably advance along these lines of cooperativeness . . . and . . . service toward the common welfare. If selfish interests or an ill-adapted form of government should prevent the growth of one nation along these lines, some other nation or group . . . will pass it by. . . . What the society of an atomic age cannot permit is the development of antagonisms between . . . groups that will prevent effective cooperation.[18]

In Arthur Compton's moral calculus, the same wartime project whose lethal product made a higher ethic so urgent also offered a practical example of the harmony, selflessness, and intelligent planning the new cooperative order would demand.

Such a scenario undoubtedly offered reassurance to many trying to find their spiritual way through the manifold uncertainties of an atomic world. But while Compton and others offered their optimistic social visions, other commentators were reaching very different conclusions about what American society would be like in the age of the atom.

13

Darker Social Visions

I saw General Wainwright in his parade here—from behind,
and 20 floors up. Even at that distance it was a good sight.
The whole city has a kind of love-feast warmth of thousands
of great and small homecomings; this keeps up by the day
and week. It is lovely. And God, what most of the homecom-
ers and those they come home to, are in for!

      —James Agee, New York City, to James Harold Flye,
      September 19, 1945[1]

Agee was in good company in feeling vaguely apprehensive as the war ended,
and much of that apprehension focused on the social impact of atomic
energy. Among thoughtful observers, many who wished (as columnist Max
Lerner put it) that the bomb could be "erased forever from the human eye
and mind" were thinking not only of the obvious danger of atomic war but
also of the nature of American life in an age of atomic bombs.[2]

Even the much-heralded "peaceful applications" of atomic energy,
some warned, could prove disastrous. If, as the *New Republic*'s Bruce Bliven
and countless others were predicting, the work week were cut to a "small
fraction" of its present forty hours, they suggested, the resulting disruption
could be catastrophic.[3] The bomb, in fact, unleashed the first wave of speculation about what would come to be called "post-industrial" society. And,
like the handwringing over the catastrophic effects of "automation" and
"robotization" in the early 1960s, it generally involved radical overestima-
tions of the economic disruption the new technology would bring. "Mass
leisure" was simply a euphemism for mass unemployment, wrote James
Reston of the *New York Times,* warning that the coming of atomic energy
had heightened the danger (already the subject of apprehensive discussion)
that the end of the war would bring back the hard times of the 1930s. "How
are men to be employed in an era of atomic power," Reston worried, "when
we could not even employ them in an age of electricity?" For others, the
social and moral consequences of this envisioned mass leisure seemed at least
as serious as the economic ones. "Upon a people already so nearly drowned
in materialism," warned *Time,* "the good uses of [atomic] power might easily

bring disaster as prodigious as the evil." Atomic energy might indeed free people to pursue higher things, observed Stuart Chase in December 1945— if, he added sardonically, "enough higher things can be found." For Gerald W. Johnson, a drastic reduction in labor needs would starkly pose

> the danger of idleness, against which the race has been warned from time immemorial. . . . The possibility exists that our triumph over nature might lead to our moral ruin, for a slave population suddenly released with no preparation for liberty is a fearful thing. The experience of the American southern states right after the Civil War is sufficient evidence. The experience of Russia after 1917 corroborates it. The sudden release of atomic energy, not in explosive, but merely in propulsive force, might make those incidents seem mere child's play by comparison.[4]

Robert M. Hutchins, though capable of the most euphoric predictions, was beset by deep apprehension as well. "If atomic power . . . becomes overwhelmingly cheap and plentiful," he mused to a visiting journalist in 1946, "what would happen to the doctrine that life is a process of salvation by work?" By 1947, Hutchins was predicting mass boredom and "suicidal tendencies" unless the problems of "the new era of leisure and abundance" were intelligently and quickly confronted. Relentlessly, Hutchins spun out his bleak prognosis:

> If we survive, the leisure which the atomic age will bring may make peace more horrible than war. We face the dreadful prospect of hour after hour, even day after day, with nothing to do. After we have read all the comic books, travelled all the miles, seen all the movies, drunk all the liquor we can stand, what shall we do then? At the age of forty-seven, I can testify that all forms of recreation eventually lose their charm.[5]

The implications of leisure had preoccupied social thinkers for decades, but what had been viewed as a chronic, perhaps gradually worsening problem related to long-term industrial trends now suddenly, in the aftermath of Hiroshima, appeared to some a threat pointing to imminent social collapse.

While some thinkers worried about mass leisure, others speculated that the emergence of a highly complex technocratic economy based on atomic energy would inevitably give rise to massive concentrations of economic and political power, with a corresponding threat to the integrity of the individual. This, too, was a fear with deep historical resonance in American social thought. For some, the threat lay in the vast increase in corporate power atomic energy would likely involve. "It will tend to strengthen the big industries," flatly declared the University of Chicago sociologist William F. Ogburn a week after Hiroshima, and, if not resisted, "reinforce movements toward monopoly and . . . cartels." To the Left, predictably, this danger seemed especially acute. "We dare not permit the emergence now of an atom king, shaped in the pattern of the steel baron, the railway magnate, the auto czar . . . ," declared a 1946 Socialist Party pamphlet. "The slaves of the machine must not now become the slaves of the atom." Max Lerner posed a nightmarish vision of all-powerful corporations gaining control of atomic energy and ruling the globe. "The world of which the fascists have been long dreaming, in which a small pitiless elite could hold the power of life and death over the large mass of mankind," Lerner wrote in *PM* on August 19, 1945, had come a big step closer on August 6.[6]

Others saw the threat of centralization in terms of massively enhanced governmental power. "Atomic energy looms as a giant new force propelling us towards the organization of society from the center," declared Joseph H. Willits of the Rockefeller Foundation in November 1945. "When atomic power is developed for commercial purposes, it will . . . be developed in Federal central stations, and the system will be a Federal system." Inevitably, Willits concluded, this expansion of authority would diminish the individual. Indeed, he said, this process was underway already: "At the various conferences on atomic energy which I have attended, controls at the international level were discussed, and controls at the national level, but . . . the individual [was] not mentioned even when representatives of theological seminaries were present. The individual, seemingly, had become too small change to matter."

Virgil Jordan's *Manifesto for the Atomic Age* (1946) combined both fears, mass leisure and centralized power, in a single vision of indolence and control. In an atom-based economy of such abundance and effortless productivity that the masses drifted into boredom and demoralization, he predicted, the government's principal function would be social control. Lacking the spur of work, individual initiative would atrophy, and only officially generated activities, amusements, and incentives would prevent society from total ossification.[7]

A different but no less ominous scenario of centralized governmental power in the atomic age was offered in 1947 by Charles Edison, former governor of New Jersey and president of the National Municipal League. In a vision of the future that would prove (though for different reasons) remarkably accurate, Edison foresaw dire consequences if unlimited atomic power resulted in the dispersal of industries and urban centers: "Cities will move closer to bankruptcy as their higher income residents quit the tax rolls, . . . the vacated dwellings sink into the slum class, [and] . . . unplanned, jerry-built subdivisions are thrown up by speculative builders." Such a chaotic social situation, Edison went on, could exacerbate a trend that was already "an ominous part of American life": "The danger is that frustrated citizens and officials, believing it impossible to solve the new problems, will . . . surrender their sovereignty to big, centralized government. . . . The vast and still unknown dimensions of atomic energy might suggest that only the central government is big enough to control it."[8]

Another glum warning that the advent of atomic energy was bad news for American freedom came in a May 1946 *Collier's* article by Robert DeVore. Not only did the Atomic Energy Commission hold something close to a state monopoly on this new source of power, DeVore warned, but the security provisions of the Atomic Energy Act—requiring FBI clearance of all AEC employees from custodians on up, including everyone doing AEC-funded research—posed a major threat to civil liberties: scientists would no longer be able to teach freely; political dissidents could be muzzled by overzealous investigators. "Slowly," DeVore observed bleakly, "men are beginning to learn that the price of admission to the Golden Age of the Atom will be paid in freedom."[9]

While some called attention to social and political hazards in the peacetime development of atomic energy, others focused on the bomb itself, arguing that its mere existence—quite apart from the obvious danger of atomic war—could have the most catastrophic social consequences. In a world of atomic bombs, in which "survival depends upon beating [one's] opponents to the draw," declared New York University sociologist Harvey Zorbaugh in a radio broadcast a few days after Hiroshima, "the power of government [will] inevitably be heightened and centralized." A University of Chicago social scientist underscored the point a few weeks later: "Total war is now the only way war can be waged, and this calls for total defense and fosters totalitarian conceptions of life and government. It is not a good situation for democracy." Norman Cousins and Thomas K. Finletter, writing in the *Saturday Review,* agreed:

> An atomic armaments race means more than the manufacture of atomic bombs. . . . Every American will be directly affected, [and] the required controls will of necessity be in the hands of the military. . . . It is a real question whether free institutions as we understand them can be maintained.

Cousins and Finletter made clear that they were not anticipating a deliberate military plot to seize power, but that the rise of the military to an all-powerful role would simply be an inevitable social by-product in a nuclear armed world. They focused particular attention on the social implications of the massive population dispersal some civil-defense advocates were already proposing. The "powerful momentum" of such fear-spawned schemes, they predicted, would "inevitably force the War Department to carry out the biggest and most complicated physical changeover of a nation in the world's history—with all that that implies in the way of political and social readjustment and control."[10]

Fears of military domination were particularly acute in 1945–1946 when the May-Johnson bill was being debated. *Time* asked, "Is the military about to take over U.S. science lock, stock, and barrel, calling the tune for U.S. universities and signing up the best scientists for work fundamentally aimed at military results . . . ?" Harold Urey attacked the bill in *One World or None* as "similar in intent and effect to the transfer of power from the German Reichstag to Hitler," and said its enactment would be "the beginning of the end of our representative government and of the Bill of Rights." The May-Johnson controversy, he went on, was symptomatic of deeper concerns: How would American democratic values fare in an era when the nation's arsenals contained weapons of world-destroying capabilities? How could the political process function meaningfully when life-and-death issues were muffled in secrecy? "From our beginnings," he wrote, "we have known the extent of our armed forces. Today we and our elected representatives do not know the extent of these forces. Atomic bombs are being manufactured in an amount unknown to us." The compulsions of atomic secrecy, he predicted, would eventually undermine the very structure of democratic government:

> The citizens of the country will know less and less in regard to vital [strategic] questions and finally must accept decisions in regard to public affairs blindly and from a few men in power . . . , decisions previously made through their elected representatives. Men on horseback will rapidly appear on the public scene. . . . Freedom . . . will be seriously threatened.

Ultimately, Urey concluded, sustained fear of atomic war could give rise to calls for "frantic and desperate" defense measures that only a dictatorship could fulfill.[11]

Such forebodings were on many minds in these months. Chronic public anxiety over the menace of atomic subterfuge, wrote Edward Condon in his contribution to *One World Or None,* could readily lead to a "police state." In "Nightmare" (1946), science-fiction writer Chandler Davis imagined an American society torn apart by uncontrollable fears that atomic bombs were being secretly assembled in major cities by enemy agents.[12]

Nor was the speculation about the domestic consequences of a protracted atomic-arms race all of the apocalyptic variety. If the United States became involved in an atomic competition with the Soviet Union, asked Joseph Willits in November 1945, how long would the civil liberties of domestic Communists and other radicals be secure? In the same vein, Ryland W. Crary of Columbia University Teachers College speculated in 1948 that the "general insecurity" associated with a permanent nuclear arms race could lead to government control of the mass media and a severe abridgement of constitutional liberties: "To be known as a liberal, to espouse peace, or to desire to vote for a political rearrangement may be ranked as heretical and unpatriotic." Crary also predicted (in a striking anticipation of the political climate of the Reagan years) that the requirements of the military in a full-scale nuclear arms race would not only determine the nature and location of industrial development, but also have a disastrous impact on domestic social programs: "The cost . . . would be so great that either taxes would need to be raised to new heights or current tax rates diverted from welfare services, social security, agricultural research, conservation, education, and the many other services expected of a democratic government." [13]

Still another perspective on the social implications of the development of atomic weapons was offered by Edward L. Long, Jr., in his 1950 book, *The Christian Response to the Atomic Crisis.* To Long, the Manhattan Project, this secret and highly compartmentalized undertaking carried out by thousands of workers most of whom perceived its purpose only dimly or not at all, offered a disturbing preview of a technocratic society in which individuals would increasingly function as cogs in vast projects they could neither understand nor control. Without denying the moral differences between the politico-technocratic processes that had produced Dachau and Auschwitz, on the one hand, and Hiroshima and Nagasaki, on the other, Long nevertheless insisted that in a structural sense there were similarities that had sobering implications for the notion of individual moral responsibility in complex modern social organizations. [14]

"No matter what shape it may assume," commented one observer, the atomic future "will be an uncomfortable place for the individual." Whether in the form of bombs or power plants, wrote E. L. Woodward, professor of international relations at Oxford University, in the *New York Times Magazine* in 1946, "this new source of energy . . . must increase enormously the power of the state over the citizen." Indeed, Woodward foresaw a kind of neofeudal system in which an elite of technocrats, strategists, and corporate barons would control atomic energy, with the rest of the populace effectively denied a meaningful decision-making role. [15]

Whatever the nuances of the argument, or the particular focus of discussion, such gloomy forebodings, rooted in the oppressive sense that the unleashing of the atom may have sounded the death knell for basic American values, pervaded much post-Hiroshima social commentary. "Unless the greatest care is taken . . ." wrote the University of Chicago political scientist Charles E. Merriam in a March 1946 discussion of the implications of atomic energy, "human liberty may be lost at this point in the toils of a concentrated dictatorship such as has never been seen before." [16] The full contours of the dawning atomic era may still have been obscure, but some observers, at least, were dismayed by the dim outlines they thought they already discerned.

While a great many post-Hiroshima social thinkers speculated briefly about atomic-age American society, a few offered more extended reflections. Two such efforts were those by William Liscum Borden and the influential political columnists Joseph and Stewart Alsop.

A law student and international affairs specialist at Yale, Borden would later play a critical role in a major historical drama when his 1953 letter accusing J. Robert Oppenheimer of being a Soviet espionage agent triggered the governmental proceedings that resulted in the removal of Oppenheimer's security clearance. He figures here, however, as the author of *There Will Be No Time* (1946), an early work of nuclear strategy and speculation about the social changes to be expected in the age of atomic weapons. The book's point of departure is the assumption that in the atomic future, the nation's military needs would be radically altered. Within months of V-J Day, Borden betrayed a touch of nostalgia for a kind of warfare that he believed had been rendered anachronistic by the atomic bomb: "G.I. Joe, with his beard and muddy boots, is the symbol of an age gone past. . . . Not the bravest fighters, but the ones who control the best rockets and atomic bombs will win another war." The altered character of war would in turn affect the civilian population as well. The era when war engaged the energies and passions of a whole people were gone forever:

> America may never again experience war-bond campaigns, victory gardens, anti-enemy movies, swing shifts, and radio commentators who discuss strategy for listeners remote from danger. The twenty-year-old youth who would have been good draft material in 1942 will become merely another refugee along with the older men who might have been on his draft board. Housewives who once would have operated a riveting machine in the local aircraft plant may also swell the ranks of atomic refugees, and their main concern will be to find food and shelter through an Office of Civil Defense. The mission of everyone not on active duty with the armed forces when hostilities commence will be to stay alive, and no more.

Though Borden was here discussing American society under actual conditions of atomic war, he also insisted that even in peacetime, the presence of atomic weapons in the nation's arsenals would have profound social effects:

A relatively small, well-trained elite may come to hold a monopoly on future warfare. The grade school graduate who was learned enough to drive a tank or fire a carbine may be barred from the select fraternity of those who preside over V-2s and atomic bombs. The last effective monopoly on warfare was held by knights in armor, a monopoly which reinforced the feudal social structure.

Elaborating the point made by E. L. Woodward and others, Borden saw the bomb as a fundamental turning point not only in military strategy, but also in the organization of society. The most salient social change of the atomic era, he suggested, would be devaluation of the individual, an explicit undermining of the egalitarian premises of American political ideology, and a reversal of the democratic thrust of the vaunted "century of the common man." A society shaped by atomic energy (in whatever guise) would be rigidly stratified between a secular priesthood adept in the atom's technological, strategic, economic, and diplomatic ramifications, and the great mass outside the charmed circle whose primary social obligation, in peace as in war, would be "to stay alive, and no more." [17]

"Your Flesh *Should* Creep," the Alsop brothers' discussion of these matters, appeared in the June 13, 1946, *Saturday Evening Post*. If the international-control negotiations failed, they wrote, a full-scale atomic-arms race was sure to ensue, bringing "radical changes in the character of our national life." Strategic considerations, for example, would dictate the uprooting and resettlement of the urban masses:

> We cannot . . . tolerate a situation in which fifty or sixty million Americans may be killed in an instant. Therefore, we shall be forced to replan our urban pattern. The great cities will become ghost towns. Population and industry will be dispersed in new urban communities, planned either on the ribbon or the cellular principle.

Paralleling these physical and social upheavals would be sweeping governmental changes that would fundamentally affect the democratic process. Internal security procedures would be "immensely increased" to guard against atomic sabotage or the smuggling in of bombs. To assure the continuity of government in the event of attack, a new "line of succession" would be established, not necessarily confined to "democratically elected officials." Indeed, they speculated, civil-defense authorities might "organize a complete, specially trained emergency government as a sort of spare, and . . . keep it in a cavern until needed." A vast program of civilian emergency training would be essential to prepare for

the time when all our great cities will be reduced to radioactive shards;

when the whole overland communications network will be put out of operation; when tens of millions of dead will await burial; when tens of millions of casualties will need care and hospitalization; and when half the nation will be deprived of light, heat, water and the other essential services. . . . If panic strikes in these conditions, the end will be at hand.

Nuclear fear, in short, would "act as a sort of chemical solvent, attacking the very foundations of our state."

The Alsops' account was, indeed, calculated to make the flesh creep. Nor, they insisted, was this merely a nightmarish fantasy: "The picture which has been painted is not drawn from science fiction; on the contrary, it is based on the serious, informed, and expert thinking of very hard-headed, highly trained men." Concluding their recital, the Alsops hammered home their central point: the decision to base the nation's defenses on atomic weapons had far more than purely military ramifications; it would, in fact, destroy democratic government:

> No true democracy can maintain an immense and powerful armament in a state of twenty-four-hour alert for years and decades on end. No true democracy can confide to a single individual, the rocket controller, such responsibilities as would be his. . . . No true democracy can enforce military discipline among all its people, or suspend the right of freedom from search and seizure, or condemn by dictate all its great cities and bodily transplant their inhabitants to new homes. . . . By painful stages, we shall sink into the mood which begets Fascism.[18]

Few of the issues raised by these post-Hiroshima social prognosticators, either the optimists or the pessimists, were new. Indeed, practically every theme central to American social thought since the turn of the century figured at least implicitly in these speculations: the fear of class conflict and racial unrest; concern over vast concentrations of power—whether corporate or political; forebodings about mass leisure; worry that the individual would be lost in an impersonal technocratic order; uneasiness about the rise of a technological elite; apprehension about the role of the military in a society that liked to think of itself as essentially pacific; even a long-standing uneasiness over the rise of great cities.

But if the issues were not new, the context surely was. Social questions that had been hashed over for decades, often in a rather perfunctory fashion, were now infused with new urgency. Amidst the reverberating aftershocks of Hiroshima, and the grim warnings that this was only an inkling of what lay ahead, it seemed totally plausible to conclude that American society was, indeed, about to change in the most fundamental ways imaginable.

On the whole, it was the pessimists who proved the more accurate prophets. Some of their predictions, the forced depopulation of cities, for example, did not come about. But it is sobering to consider how many of these predictions in fact proved remarkably prophetic in the decades that followed.

14

Experts and Ideologues Offer Their Prescriptions

On a balmy southern California evening in early September 1945, just four weeks after Hiroshima, the lawyers of Beverly Hills gathered for their regular bar association meeting. The speaker for the occasion was Judge Frank G. Tyrrell of the Los Angeles municipal court. Rather than discuss municipal-court overcrowding or some other topic of immediate concern, Judge Tyrrell chose a far weightier theme: the legal profession's solemn duty to prevent atomic war. The organized bar, he said, must take the lead in the campaign to substitute the rule of law for the "international anarchy" that in an era of atomic bombs could lead to catastrophe. If the 170,000 American lawyers would mobilize their "intelligence, force, and statecraft" in support of international atomic control, Tyrrell proclaimed, success would be assured: "Do you for a moment think that anything which the united bar has resolved upon could long be successfully opposed? If you do, you do not know lawyers."[1]

In this conviction, Judge Tyrrell was in fact representative of a broad-scale cultural phenomenon. In the early post-Hiroshima period, spokesmen for a quite amazing diversity of professions and ideological persuasions argued passionately that their particular expertise or ideology had suddenly become crucial to mankind's survival.

Indeed, could it have been otherwise? The atomic bomb may have ushered in a "new era," but people confronted that new era with ideas and professional identities formed over many years in the old, pre-atomic age. Thus it is hardly surprising that many Americans joined Judge Tyrrell in concluding that their particular ideology or profession had become especially relevant in the age of the atom. (Social scientists seem to have felt their new responsibility especially keenly—so keenly, in fact, that their response will be reserved for separate consideration.)

To public-opinion experts, the basic message of the bomb was the need for a more informed public opinion. While nearly all Americans had heard of the atomic bomb, said Leonard Cottrell and Sylvia Eberhart in summarizing their 1946 Social Science Research Council survey, atomic-energy policy issues remained "remote and shadowy" for most. Policymakers in this field should work with media and public-opinion experts, they advised, "to close the serious gap . . . between what they are thinking and trying to do and the . . . understanding of these matters on the part of the people."[2]

Discussing "Newspapers and the Bomb" in 1947, a group of reporters and editors who were recipients of the prestigious Harvard Nieman Fellowship concluded that most papers had "fumbled the atom badly" with stories that were either trivial or overly technical. As for the 1946 Bikini tests, they continued, most of the hundreds of reporters on the scene had "no idea of what had happened, except that there was a big beautiful explosion." In the atomic age, this report concluded, it was the nation's newspapers that would "set the pattern and pace" of the public's scientific knowledge and hence determine its ability to make informed decisions on life-and-death issues.[3]

City planner Tracy B. Augur told the American Institute of Planners in 1946 that the planning profession had a crucial role to play in guiding the urban dispersal being widely advocated as a civil-defense measure. If properly conducted, he said, such a project would involve not just piecemeal resettlement, but a wholly new urban planning approach. The starting point, he went on, was for experts to define "the qualities of social life that are worth having" and then to "plan the kind of urban structure that will make them more fully possible." Demonstrating the readiness of his profession to rise to this challenge, Augur presented a series of charts showing how a "typical city of half a million could be rearranged from a concentrated to a dispersed form without weakening its capacity to function as a single metropolitan unit."

Such a systematic attack on the problems of the city, Augur insisted, was in any case overdue. "Long before the threat of the atom-bomb," he said, urban planners had warned of the need for comprehensive programs to save the American city from "the blight . . . gnawing at its innards" and to convey to the larger society their dream of a totally planned urban environment. Now suddenly Hiroshima and Nagasaki had propelled the question of the urban future to the top of the public's agenda. In the realm of city planning, Augur concluded hopefully, "the threat of atom bombing may prove a useful spur to jolt us forward!" At long last, city planners would assume the central social role they had long sought. Having lost the public ear after their heyday in the Progressive Era, city planners, under the spur of the atomic threat, would finally take charge of urban development and guide it along rational lines.[4]

In a 1947 address to the National Recreation Association, a longtime activist in the park and playground movement painted the familiar grim picture of mass leisure in the atomic age, but hastened to offer a solution: "The answer to all this is, of course, EDUCATION and RECREATION." The government must take the lead, he said, in expanding the nation's recreational resources, including "parks and playgrounds, game reserves, public theaters, opera houses, orchestras, [and] hobby centers." Echoing Tracy Augur's message to the city planners, this speaker assured the recreation specialists that their profession would be crucial to society's survival in the era of atomic energy. "Unless ability to make wise use of leisure increases," he insisted, "there is no doubt that our civilization is doomed." However implausible and even comic such views seem in retrospect, they were advanced in all earnestness in the perfervid post-Hiroshima cultural climate.[5]

Of all the groups whose role seemed enhanced by the coming of the atomic bomb, none was more convinced of the fact than the intellectuals: those whose self-defined function was to think critically about social issues and propose courses of action. In the atomic era as never before, wrote Christian Gauss, the dean of Princeton College, early in 1946, "scholars . . . must move forward in the faith . . . that there is no problem the human reason can propound which the human reason cannot reason out." An editor of *The American Scholar,* introducing a special postwar issue on the atomic bomb, underscored Gauss's point: "The 'people' have a right to look to the 'scholar,' " she wrote, "for that wisdom without which the people perish." Robert M. Hutchins emphatically concurred. "We cannot look to the politicians for the vision, the knowledge, or the detachment which the crisis demands," he declared early in 1946, but to "that much maligned race, the intellectuals. Now is the time for the intellectuals to show whether they have intellects equal to the task."[6]

In actual practice, the urgent but somewhat amorphous duty of "intellectuals" and "scholars" to guide mankind out of the atomic wilderness often reduced itself to the obligation of the nation's teachers to rethink their function in light of the atomic crisis. Endlessly in these volatile months, America's educators were told that the younger generation, and older citizens as well, must be trained to play their proper role in the atomic era. Surveying thirteen American educational journals of the immediate postwar period, historian Charles DeBenedetti found them all deeply engaged in the effort "to define their unique professional responsibility" in the atomic age. Another researcher found 260 articles on the atomic bomb and atomic energy in education journals between 1945 and 1950![7] Only a "profound consciousness of the great crisis which faces humanity," declared one educator early in 1946, could form an adequate basis of "an education for Americans which is suited to the modern era." The very fate of mankind, wrote a Temple University education professor in a 1946 article in a teachers' journal, depended on whether America's educators, with other concerned citizens, could rise to the challenge that confronted them: "We have an appointment with Destiny. For a brief, precarious moment we are playing the major role on the world's stage. What happens in the next few years will shape the course of history for decades, perhaps centuries to come."[8] Even after the high hopes of 1946 for international atomic-energy control faded, conviction concerning the crucial role of education in the atomic age did not. Atomic energy had made "the unintelligent man obsolete," Charles Edison told the National Municipal League in 1947. "We have got to strive to make our heads more potent than uranium. . . . Our public schools and our colleges must do a great deal more."[9]

The specific role assigned educators in the atomic age tended to vary markedly depending on the writer's academic specialty or pedagogical philosophy. Science teachers, understandably, insisted that more and better science education was necessary. Social studies teachers saw their specialty as crucial. Teachers at religious schools looked at matters from their distinctive vantage point. At a moment when "the end of civilization" suddenly loomed as a real possibility, wrote a professor at a Massachusetts theological seminary in 1946, the nation's church-related schools and colleges, with their concern for "ultimate things," had a newly vital mission to perform.[10] Others insisted that in the coming age of leisure, the humanities must take precedence. Discussing "Atomic Energy and the Liberal Arts" in 1946, a University of Denver professor argued that the new era of abundance could open the door to "esthetic experiences unlimited in quantity or quality." But if the young were to be readied for this cultural paradise, public education at all levels must be radically reoriented, emphasizing "history, literature, religion, the classics, [and] philosophy," as well as music, drama, painting, and the other creative arts.[11]

Other champions of the humanities were even more specific. "When atomic power . . . overwhelms us, wholly unprepared, with an enormous access of leisure," a high-school classics teacher in Connecticut rhetorically inquired in 1947, who would be better prepared to minister to "the spiritual well-being of mankind [than] the proponents and guardians of the classics?" Classics teachers were "the ones to take the matter in hand," he insisted, and serve as "the spearhead and vanguard in preparing to meet the challenges of the new world that atomic energy has so suddenly foisted upon us." (Perhaps a bit overwhelmed at the magnitude of the cultural responsibility he had just volunteered for, this classicist did call upon the "teachers of English and the modern languages to join our ranks."[12])

Not everyone was convinced that educators, and humanities teachers in particular, would play so crucial a social role in the atomic era. One somewhat surprising dissenter was Princeton's Christian Gauss. Despite his belief that the social role of intellectuals had been vastly enhanced by the atomic crisis, Gauss held a rather jaundiced view of the role of humanists and social scientists in the new age. Confronted by a "staggering problem of readjustment, reconstruction, and re-education," he said, society could not "remain anchored to its past . . . it must orient itself toward the future. It must

Automobile . . .

. . . jet plane . . .

Visions of an atomic Utopia as an anodyne to fear. On August 20, 1945, *Newsweek* pictured an atomic automobile, jet plane, ocean liner, and kitchen. In each drawing, a tiny dot represented "the approximate size of atomic power plants they would need."

—Extension Service, Iowa State College

IN THE FIELD: RADIOACTIVE FERTILIZER APPLIED TO TEST PLOT

Atomic-age agriculture. An Iowa experimenter applies radioactive fertilizer to a test plot in 1948. *U.S. News and World Report* captioned the story: "Atom: Key to Better Farming."

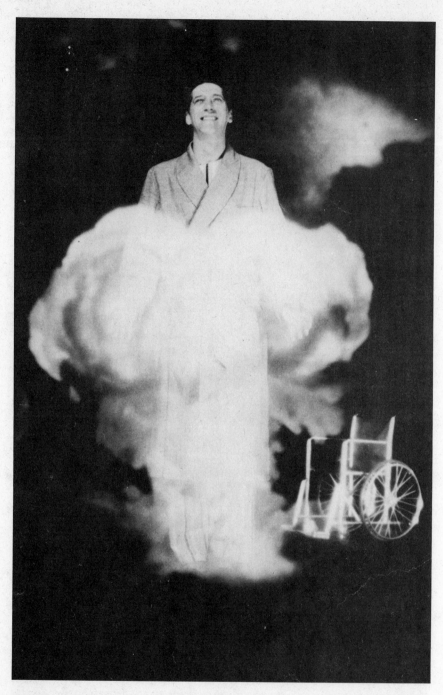

Healed by atomic energy. In this photo montage from a May 3, 1947, _Collier's_ article on the atom's medical promise, a recovered paraplegic emerges smiling from a mushroom cloud, his abandoned wheelchair in the background.

Land of the Rising Sons

Bishop in The St. Louis Star-Times.
"Do You Recognize Me Now?"

Racist wartime propaganda helped shape early responses to the atomic bombing of Japan. In the *Atlanta Constitution*'s August 8, 1945, cartoon, "Land of the Rising Sons," bodies fly whimsically through the air above Japan. The *St. Louis Star-Times* cartoonist pictured a grotesque stereotyped "Jap" snarling back as death bearing an atomic bomb looms above him.

'But for the Grace of God—'

It saved American lives. A post-Hiroshima editorial cartoon in the *Memphis Commerical Appeal* illustrates the Truman administration's claim that the only alternative to the atomic bombing of Japan was an invasion that could have cost many hundreds of thousands of casualties.

The bomb and attitudes toward science. Admiration, awe, and pride were the most powerful immediate reactions. On August 18, 1945, the *Chicago Defender* offered a black variant of the prevailing response.

"Baby Play with Nice Ball?"

But from the beginning, feelings about the atomic scientists were also tinged with edginess and fear, as in the widely reprinted cartoon by the Britisher David Low (above). By 1948, as the Herblock cartoon below suggests, the scientist-heroes of 1945 had become the object of increasing public and governmental hostility.

From The Herblock Book (Beacon Press, 1952)

reverse its time sense." Parochial and nationalistic thinking would have to give way to broader perspectives. And what would be the role of the academy in this transformation? Except for natural scientists already accustomed to thinking globally, said Gauss, most academics were ill-suited to this process of cultural reorientation. Rather than emphasizing the timeless and universal qualities of a Shakespeare or a Cervantes, for example, literature teachers had dwelt on each writer's most time-bound and culture-bound characteristics, and in the process "nationalized and over-historicized" the field. If the social adjustments Hiroshima and Nagasaki required were "in any sort of proportion to the power released," he said, most scholars "would do well to realize that figuratively speaking, the bomb has fallen on their own heads as well." [13]

By and large, though, academia readily succumbed to the flattering suggestion that its role would be significantly enhanced in the atomic age. Of all the educators who exploited the post-Hiroshima cultural disarray to promote their particular vision, the most visible was surely Robert M. Hutchins. Through a long and in many respects remarkable career, Hutchins earned a reputation for cosmic pronouncements and sweeping social prescriptions delivered with an assurance that bordered on arrogance. At no time in that long career was the larger culture more receptive to his brand of visionary utterance than in the turbulent months when America first sought to come to terms with the atomic bomb. For a time after August 1945, Hutchins gained a remarkable public visibility. Though his great hobbyhorse in this period was world government, he insisted that this radical transformation would never come without a "moral, intellectual, and spiritual revolution"—and this was a job for the schools and colleges. "Since the great aim is a world community," he declared, "the great task is education." Education in the atomic era would assume "a scope of which our ancestors could not dream."

But not just any education would do. What America needed in the atomic era, Hutchins declared, was "neither the frivolity of liberal arts colleges nor the single-minded materialism of vocational training," but "a liberal education worthy of the name"—in other words, education by the Hutchins formula. When be became president of the University of Chicago in 1929, Hutchins had launched a series of controversial reforms. He emphasized adult education, and in place of the elective system, imposed a strictly prescribed curriculum. Criticizing narrow specialization, he insisted that Chicago undergraduates ponder broad philosophical questions and immerse themselves in the "Great Books." After August 1945, he promulgated his educational creed to a vastly enlarged audience. Colleges in the atomic era must not stress disciplinary specialization or narrow professional training, but preparation for world citizenship. A common curriculum, Hutchins claimed, would give college students the experience of being a part of a cohesive academic community, thereby preparing them for membership in the world community. In the coming era of mass leisure, educators must also urgently pursue an objective they had long acknowledged rhetorically: adult education. "If we want to save adults in the atomic age from suicidal tendencies which boredom eventually induces, . . . we must regard the continuing education of our people throughout life as our principal responsibility." [14] Once American higher education had transformed itself in the Hutchins image, in short, the atomic future need hold no terrors.

Just as spokesmen for a wide variety of professions viewed the dawning atomic era from their particular perspective, so, too, did adherents of a broad spectrum of political creeds, from Marxists to passionate believers in laissez-faire capitalism. For the former, the challenge was to analyze the probable effect of atomic energy on the unfolding class struggle. Some true believers argued that the Soviet Union, as a socialist state, would prove much more efficient at exploiting this new technology, thereby convincing workers everywhere of the superiority of socialism. This position was sharply challenged in 1946, however, by a writer in the American Marxist journal *Science and Society*. If workers were not convinced by the evidence already available, he suggested, whatever changes atomic energy brought would not likely persuade them. Indeed, he said, the coming of atomic energy might well in the short run strengthen world capitalism:

> Backward peoples, particularly in colonial and semi-colonial countries which will be unable to develop atomic energy themselves, may find themselves receiving equipment from Du Pont and General Electric along with capital from the Chase Bank. It is quite possible that atomic energy may become a powerful means of imperialist exploitation in the hands of American monopoly. The super-profits from such ventures might even provide a new, if temporary, "lease on life" for American imperialism.

In the long run, however, whatever its technological innovations, capitalism would eventually be brought down by its own internal contradictions, as Marx had predicted:

> Capitalism . . . long ago developed all of the productive forces contained within it. . . . The rate of growth of productivity in America reached its peak at around 1915. No technological discovery can of itself make capitalism very much more obsolete than it now is. . . . It is not the application of atomic energy which will "blow the capitalist system to pieces," but the working class that will do so. [15]

The noncommunist Left, by contrast, was more inclined to see atomic energy as at least a potential instrument of radical social change. If the correct political decisions were made quickly, insisted the 1946 Socialist Party pamphlet cited earlier, it could be the means of achieving a transformed social and economic order. With energy universally available, the economic conditions that underlay human want and international conflict could be eliminated. Nations would no longer need compete for scarce raw materials, or go to war to alleviate domestic unemployment. The standard of living of the masses could be raised dramatically, assuring that no child ever again need "carry the grime of poverty on his face and soul." But only if atomic energy were dealt with according to socialist principles would these good results be assured: "The people must be the owners of atomic energy. . . . The atom can be socialized. It can be made the property of the people of the United States and, through the internationalism of our world parliament, the property of the people of the world." Taking advantage of the sudden celebrity of the atomic scientists, this pamphlet reminded Americans that the great Einstein himself had in his young days been an ardent socialist.

The stakes were high, this socialist tract made clear: if atomic energy fell under the control of the militarists and the capitalists, the consequences for mankind would be disastrous. Like the public-opinion experts, urban planners, educational reformers, and other professional groups, the Socialist party concluded that a role of transcendent importance had suddenly been thrust upon it: "Until now, Socialism, with its promise that all men would share in the potential goodness of the earth seemed like a desirable dream. The atom bomb has made it an urgent necessity. We cannot delay." [16]

Others on the Left had similar views. "Domestically, I was sure it meant socialism," wrote Raymond Gram Swing in 1946, describing his first reactions to the bomb. "Atomic energy may prove to have undercut the basis of private ownership of the essentials of power and life," wrote PM columnist Max Lerner. "No longer can we afford a social system which would permit private business, in the name of freedom, to control a source of energy capable of creating comfort and security for all the world's people," wrote Freda Kirchwey in the Nation on August 18, 1945. This "self-evident" fact, she went on, "calls for changes so sweeping that only an immense effort of will and imagination can bring them about. . . . The people must establish public ownership and social development of the revolutionary force war has thrust into their hands." [17]

New Deal supporters who had long advocated government economic planning quickly concluded that the unleashing of atomic energy clinched their argument. An Antioch College professor called in December 1945 for a reconstituted National Planning Resources Board (a New Deal agency terminated in 1943) to develop a comprehensive economic plan incorporating atomic energy. To the economist Stuart Chase, a longtime advocate of planning, the message of the atom was plain. Economic chaos and mass unemployment would inevitably follow if atomic-energy developments were left to the workings of the free market. The nationalization of atomic energy as part of a comprehensive federal program of economic planning, Chase insisted late in 1945, had become an urgent necessity: "How can any community endure the . . . shock of this new energy without planning for it? On the practical level, how could a wildly disorganized America hope to compete with other powers when they had organized the flow of neutrons." [18]

Those who feared big government and centralized planning predictably took a very different position. Charles Edison of the National Municipal League, for example, exhorted local communities to resist all proposals to turn the entire matter over to the federal government. "American communities . . . have a rare opportunity to show that local government and citizenship can keep pace with scientific discovery," he declared. "We, the people, still have the power to stem the tide toward complete centralization. . . . The control of atomic energy is the battleground." [19]

For those businessmen and their ideological allies convinced that the free-enterprise system must be safeguarded from creeping socialism, the crucial challenge of the atomic era was to assure a role for private corporations in exploiting this new energy source. Despite growing skepticism toward the atom's peacetime potential, more rather than less publicity was given to capitalism's stake in atomic development as the 1940s wore on, not only in business magazines like *Fortune* and *Nation's Business,* but also in *Time, Newsweek, Collier's,* and the like. "Atom Becomes Big Business," proclaimed *U.S. News and World Report* early in 1950. Here David Lilienthal, reflecting the AEC's policy of giving maximum publicity to "peaceful" development, played a crucial role. In addresses and articles with titles like "Free the Atom," Lilienthal urged that American business be given more scope to develop the atom's nonmilitary potential. This was a major theme, too, in the 1948 presidential campaign of Thomas E. Dewey. "The genius that split the atom was not furnished by government," Dewey proclaimed, and American capitalism must be given "a chance to turn this power to production and peaceful account." (In its first postelection issue, prepared when a Dewey victory seemed certain, *Christian Century* gloomily brooded that this speech boded ill for the atomic-energy policy of the new Republican administration that would soon take office!) [20]

One of the more labored yet interesting of these early efforts to assess the ideological implications of atomic energy was that of Gerald W. Johnson, a longtime editorial writer for the *Baltimore Sun* who by the postwar period had turned from daily journalism to a career as a free-lance political writer and biographer. Discussing "The Liberal of 1946" in the *American Scholar* that spring, Johnson reflected on the appropriate liberal stance toward atomic energy. For Johnson, postwar liberalism was defined less by a distinct political ideology or economic program than by its mood and temperament: a spirit of optimism; receptivity to new ideas; and flexibility in adapting to new social, political, and technological realities:

> Find a man in 1946 [Johnson wrote] who is . . . aware of perils ahead and therefore alert, but who is convinced that the opportunity is greater than the danger, and you will find a liberal. . . . If while not ignoring the possibility of the destruction of civilization, he is much more fascinated by the possibility of its reformation—he is essentially a liberal. . . . Never mind the projects and programs, then. Find a man unterrified, and you have found the liberal of 1946.

This adaptable, unterrified liberal outlook, Johnson went on, was just what was needed at a moment when a vast new force whose ramifications were only dimly discernible had suddenly burst upon the scene. Indeed, Johnson suggested, in the circumstances of 1946, it was the height of self-delusion to pretend that anyone could confidently formulate a detailed program for dealing with the political and economic challenges of the atom or to proclaim, as many were doing, that any single political ideology or area of professional expertise had all the answers. The true liberal, said Johnson, must simply remain hopefully receptive to an unknown future, prepared to deal with specific problems as they came along. Since no one knew what the future held, the ideologically unencumbered liberal was the best equipped to confront it!

Having said all this, however, Johnson did offer some speculations about issues that might emerge in the atomic era, and possible liberal responses. Accepting a massive increase in leisure as a probability, Johnson suggested that here, perhaps, was an opportunity to make real progress on "the goal of all true liberalism throughout history . . . the democratization of culture." The prospect of sudden mass leisure held its dangers, but for that very reason represented a supreme challenge to the liberal imagination. Since "we have never tried giving the masses any considerable amount of leisure," he wrote, "our conviction that it would be a bad thing is purely hypothetical." If American liberals would seriously address the task of elevating the cultural and intellectual level of the masses, he suggested, "the bogey of the evil of idleness would be exorcised in an instant." In a "liberalism" nearly devoid of ideological content, here at least was one substantive goal: "Liberalism has ever been based on belief in the possibility of raising the general level of civilization of the masses. It is not belief in the perfectibility of human nature, but it is belief in the possibility of its improvement."[21]

As long ago as 1910, in *The Promise of American Life,* Herbert Croly had lain down a demanding agenda for liberals: to create an American culture worthy of the nation's material abundance. Now, in a very different era,

Gerald W. Johnson tried to revive Croly's vision. At a moment when post–New Deal liberalism seemed exhausted, he shifted attention once again to the cultural arena. Under the new social conditions atomic energy was likely to create, liberals could again concentrate on Croly's long-deferred agenda. He thus joined a large company of otherwise very diverse post-Hiroshima social thinkers who shared a common conviction: that the atomic bomb and the prospect of a world transformed by atomic energy had massively enhanced the social relevance of their particular professional skill, reform cause, or political belief. As Albert Einstein said in a different context, the atomic bomb changed everything except the way men thought.

15

Social Science into the Breach

Lewis Paul Todd was a young instructor at a Connecticut teachers' college when he heard the news of Hiroshima. Within hours, he began an impassioned essay published a few weeks later in a journal for high-school social-studies teachers. The news of August 6, he wrote, had made vividly apparent the chasm "between man's ability to solve the problems of the physical universe and his utter inability to solve social problems." The imperative response, Todd continued, must be to match the unleashing of atomic energy with "a revolution of equal force in the world of human relations." In an age of atomic bombs every other activity must be subordinated to "the job of *social engineering*." [1]

Todd was far from alone in this conclusion. Indeed, it crops up with almost hypnotic frequency in post-Hiroshima social commentary. Hiroshima, commented Lyman Bryson in a CBS radio broadcast soon after the event, underscored the urgency of applying "the same kind of thinking in managing men as we can show in managing atoms." It was high time, said the *New Republic* on August 27, for "the science of human personality and . . . society" to receive the same urgent attention "hitherto devoted to discovering the secrets of matter." The atomic scientists had done their job, added the *Antioch Review* in December; society now awaited "the guidance of the social scientists."

The philosopher John Dewey, who for decades had urged the application of scientific method to social problems, renewed his plea in the aftermath of Hiroshima. Writing early in 1946, Dewey lamented the "tragically one-sided development of knowledge" that had left man's social knowledge "in an infantile state" relative to his "discoveries, inventions, and technologies." "Natural science has far outstripped social science," agreed Harvard historian Sidney B. Fay in his 1946 presidential address before the American Historical Association. "We have discovered how to split the atom, but not how to make sure it will be used for the improvement and not the destruction of mankind." [2]

What was to be done? Many commentators insisted that the teaching of the social sciences, and especially history, must be radically revised to reflect atomic-age realities. The ferocity of World War II, culminating at Hiroshima and Nagasaki, wrote E. B. White in the *New Yorker* a few weeks after the war's end, underscored the irrelevance, if not the actual meretriciousness, of the traditional patriotic classroom approach to history, with its focus on nation-states, and their wars and conflicts. "We take pains to educate our children at an early age in the rituals and mysteries of the nation," White observed, ". . . but lately the most conspicuous activity of nations has been the blowing of each other up, and an observant child might reasonably ask whether he is pledging allegiance to a flag or to a shroud." In the same vein, Princeton's Christian Gauss paused in his *American Scholar* attack on the parochialism of literature teachers to take on the historical profession as well. In a misguided attempt to be "scientific," he charged, historians had "refrain[ed] from passing moral or 'value' judgments" and emphasized disembodied "historic forces" over individual choice and responsibility. Yet for all the profession's pretensions to objectivity, he went on, echoing E. B. White, textbook history remained narrowly nationalistic at a time when global thinking had become essential. Gauss even implied that all history prior to August 6, 1945, had been rendered irrelevant by the atomic bomb. Would "even the most accurate and dispassionate account of every stage that led to the invention and dropping of the bomb," he asked, "help us very much in reaching a wise solution of the problem with which science has confronted us?" If historians were to play any meaningful role in the atomic era, he concluded, they would have to rethink radically the nature of their enterprise.[3]

Some social-science teachers were themselves reaching the same conclusion. These subjects would have to undergo a thorough "reconstructing and revitalizing," warned Alonzo B. May of the University of Denver, to be of much value in a society transformed by atomic energy. If a comprehensive revision of "the social studies curriculum . . . was necessary a year ago," agreed the headmaster of a New Hampshire high school early in 1946, " it is even more so today." Though the bomb seemed overwhelming, he insisted, educators in the nuclear era must "strive to break down old cultural fears and shibboleths and encourage a more fearless questioning of the social order . . . in the hope that a new generation may be adaptable to social change." In an age of atomic bombs, declared Lewis Paul Todd, "the social sciences must become the keystone . . . of public education. And . . . the increased time we devote to the study of human relations must be taken from the physical sciences." Todd insisted that if the social-studies curriculum were to prove equal to the crisis created by the bomb, it must be organized around a "directing moral principle" to provide the rising generation the ethical orientation it would urgently need in the atomic era.[4]

While social-studies teachers pondered the pedagogical implications of the atomic bomb, others spoke expansively of a vastly enlarged public role for social science. In his 1939 book *Knowledge for What?* sociologist Robert S. Lynd had called for an activist, engaged social science, and in 1945 Lynd's summons seemed more germane than ever. Within forty-eight hours of the Hiroshima news, a group of five prominent social scientists including sociologist Talcott Parsons and political economist Lincoln Gordon submitted a lengthy letter to the *Washington Post* asserting that world peace had become society's most urgent challenge in light of "the startling news of the atomic bomb" and that in this task the social sciences had a vital role to play. Cooperative human intelligence could solve "human problems as well as . . . those of atomic physics," they insisted, provided it proceeded according to a method, and "this method must be social science." They urged a high-level study to "explore the needs which social sciences must fill in a world equipped for suicide, and the means to put social science brains in harness." The planning advocate Stuart Chase quickly caught the mood. "As the first item on the educational agenda," Chase wrote late in 1945, "I respectfully suggest that another two billion dollars be allocated, this time to the *social scientists*. An equally urgent directive should go along with it: [to] show us how to live with the unbelievable power the physical scientists have loosed upon us."[5]

One of the strongest expressions of this exalted view came from John S. Perkins, professor of management at Boston University. Sitting at his typewriter on the evening of V-J Day, Perkins wrote an article that soon appeared in *School and Society,* "Where Is the Social Sciences' Atomic Bomb?" "Man's behavior and that of his institutions must now be harnessed just as the behavior of atoms has been harnessed. This is the result the social scientists must produce. This is their atomic bomb. Can they come through?" The social scientists would succeed at this task, Perkins went on, only if they emulated the organizational genius of the atomic scientists in mobilizing "the ideas of men all over the world" in a coordinated attack on an urgent problem. "Only by the same kind of . . . concerted, all-out effort where past procedures are thrown by the board can the social scientists produce their atomic bomb." Swept up in the excitement of his vision, Perkins summoned social scientists to something akin to a religious crusade. "The top minds of the world must be commandeered," he said, to "harness the complex and powerful aspirations, actions, and attitudes of men and channel them into the ways of peace. This is their Manhattan District Project. Upon their success now rests the fate of all mankind." Such a crusade, he went on, would surely win for social scientists "respect in the halls of government and in the minds of the people—respect which has been missing to a notable extent in the past. . . . The physical scientists . . . have deservedly won the praise which a still incredulous world is pouring out to them. . . . Now it is the social scientists' turn."[6]

A similarly expansive vision of the social scientists' role in the atomic era came in a 1946 *New York Times Magazine* article, "We Need a New Kind of Leader," by psychologist A. M. Meerloo. Man's only hope in the atomic era, he said, was "scientific long-range social planning," and this would require experts: "We are desperately in need of social scientists today—instead of the atomic physicists who try to give social advice." Only "a united social science—embracing economics, sociology, and psychology," and led by "free intellectuals with original thoughts, who will not bend to authority" would be adequate to the atomic crisis. The United Nations should at once set up "a scientific social board," Meerloo concluded, "to lead the world into sane and workable channels of peace."[7]

Though rarely with such soaring rhetoric, many social scientists in this post-Hiroshima period embraced the view that they possessed knowledge and expertise essential to mankind's survival. With humanity "haunted by the uneasy fear that an unconquerable monster has been released," a sociologist stated in *Science* early in 1946, social science must devise "an economic, social, and political organization" that would promote "human values, health, love, emotional adjustment, and security." At a moment when the bomb had made the threat of extinction real and immediate, social psychologist Kenneth Clark told the National Committee for Mental Hygiene in 1947, "the retardation in the development of the social sciences" must be urgently addressed.[8]

Three outspoken advocates of a major social-science response to the atomic crisis were faculty colleagues at the University of Chicago, the institution that gained so much postwar attention for its role in the Manhattan Project. They were anthropologist Robert Redfield, famed for his work on folk cultures and in 1945 dean of social sciences at Chicago; sociologist William Ogburn, author of a classic study of social change that had introduced the phrase "cultural lag" to the language; and urban sociologist Louis Wirth.

Discussing the "Consequences of Atomic Energy" at a symposium of educators in November 1945, Redfield struck the by-now familiar note: the social sciences must catch up with man's advancing mastery of physical forces. In an age of atomic bombs, he said, survival depended upon "the understanding and control of human relations. . . . It has always been so . . . now it is fatally so." Turning to specifics, Redfield revived a proposal first advanced in Walter Lippmann's *Public Opinion* of 1922: the creation of a high-level, permanent, and generously funded public agency, presumably made up largely of social scientists, to function as "a sort of auxiliary brain for policy forming." This "Commission of Inquiry," enjoying a prestige "comparable, perhaps, to that of the courts," would advise government officials and the public "in a semi-authoritative way" on the issues of social policy "made acute by the advent of atomic energy."

William Ogburn, discussing "Sociology and the Atom" in the January

1946 *American Journal of Sociology,* impatiently dismissed the atomic scientists, religious leaders, and journalists who were trying to think about the social ramifications of the atomic bomb. On this subject, he said, "the ready advice of editorial writers, lecturers, preachers, columnists, and radio commentators is not worth very much, perhaps even less than the advice of natural scientists on the social implications of their discoveries." Such matters should be left to the experts: "It is the function of the natural scientist to make the atomic bomb," Ogburn testily insisted, "but of the social scientist to say what the social consequences are likely to be."

Ogburn readily conceded that the social-research task would be monumental: "Over one hundred and fifty different social effects of radio" had been discovered, he wrote, and the atomic bomb's social effects might even exceed that number! Simply to investigate one small facet of the problem—the effects of the threat of atomic war on urban development—would require "a great deal of sociological research, perhaps hundreds of large projects" and governmental funding of Manhattan Project proportions:

> For every subsidized piece of research in natural science there should be corresponding financial aids to research in social science. . . . Since two billion dollars were spent on making the atomic bomb which will produce many social problems, an intelligent society would aid social research to solve the problems the bomb creates.[9]

Invest as much in social-science research as was spent on the Manhattan Project, and the results for mankind would be as breathtakingly dramatic.

Ogburn's article elicited a heated response from another sociologist, Donald R. Taft of the University of Illinois, who described it as an unintentional example of Ogburn's own concept of "cultural lag." Faced with a technological breakthrough of unfathomable and potentially horrendous implications, Ogburn had proposed long-term research projects on possible social effects. The "ponderous lethargy" of Ogburn's business-as-usual academic response to the bomb, Taft suggested, compared unfavorably to the social activism of the atomic scientists. Observed Taft sarcastically:

> The social effects of the bomb on the structure of our cities and on family and community life may conceivably be studied at leisure by visiting sociologists from Mars, as they paw over the ruins of the University of Chicago or of New York or of Moscow. Today's challenge of the bomb is more immediate.

Taft, however, questioned only the nature of the sociologists' post-Hiroshima public role, not the assumption that they had such a role. In the shadow of the bomb, he insisted, sociologists must direct their research to urgent issues bearing directly on mankind's survival: the roots of war, social conflict, and international tension. And they must go beyond research to social action, developing specific strategies for bringing about the "radical changes in attitudes and even in social institutions" the atomic crisis demanded, and then promoting them through political lobbying, adult education, and other "opinion-forming efforts." Sociologists must not only learn "the facts of social relations" but also "how to 'sell' these facts and their implications to policy makers"; they must, in short, "use the atomic bomb crisis for such an organized large-scale development of, and application of, social science . . . as has never before been dreamed of." [10]

Louis Wirth echoed Ogburn's conclusions—while also showing a degree of affinity with Donald Taft's more radical perspective—in a 1947 essay on "The Responsibility of Social Science." Highly regarded for his work in urban sociology, Wirth in 1947 was president-elect of the American Sociological Society. In this essay, Wirth agreed that the atomic bomb posed an unprecedented challenge to social science—a challenge "not only to discover ways and means of preventing civilization from committing suicide by means of this new weapon, but also . . . ways and means by which the beneficent potentialities of this new discovery can be fully exploited."

The task was a daunting one. Social scientists would have to develop new research techniques ("If social science as it now is cannot help us in this predicament, then we must create a better social science"), recruit more talented students, secure large-scale public funding, and overcome the skepticism of a public chronically unable to grasp "the difference between social science and common sense." And they must confront a still more fundamental problem: the most significant social research inevitably threatened the status quo; "only the innocuous and the irrelevant are completely neutral." To expose entrenched social institutions to investigative scrutiny was "to court the displeasure, if not the outright hostility, of the dominant elements in society." This problem would become especially acute as social scientists investigated the implications of atomic energy, Wirth predicted, because experience taught that a society's "economic, social, and political arrangements" often impeded "the full utilization of scientific discoveries" for the general good. Despite the risks, social science "must . . . discharge its social responsibility by answering the larger and more important questions which society raises"—and in 1947 there seemed to be no larger or more important question than the social impact of atomic energy.

One reason sociology remained so "stunted and inadequate" and sociologists' prescriptions were so often ignored by those in authority, Wirth went on, was that in the past they had "lacked the power to persuade or compel others to put [their] program into operation." In the fearful post-Hiroshima climate, however, this situation might change. Sociologists might at last be granted the functional role in social control they had long envisioned. To prepare for this enlarged role, said Wirth, they must not only investigate the social implications of atomic energy, but also explore the means of stimulating in the popular mind the will to use the new technology for "the achievement of a good society." In a more general cultural sense, too, Wirth concluded, the atomic bomb could enhance the status of social scientists. The very fact of their engagement with an issue of such urgent public concern might in itself bring increased prestige and be the "catalytic agent" leading to "the development of a more adequate and publicly supported social science." [11]

Questions of status, prestige, and public acceptance were never far from the minds of sociologists as they speculated on the role of their discipline in the age of the atom, but something more concrete was also involved. The issue of federal support for social-science research was of immediate concern to sociologists in the 1945–1950 period. During the war, scientific research on military projects had been funded through the Office of Scientific Research and Development, headed by Vannevar Bush of MIT. (The atomic-bomb project itself was under OSRD until 1943, when it was transferred to the army.) As the war drew to a close, Bush began to campaign for a continued flow of federal dollars to scientific research in the postwar period. In *Science: The Endless Frontier* (1945), an OSRD report to President Roosevelt, Bush called for the creation of a new federal agency, the National Science Foundation, as a conduit for such support. In the early postwar months—and intermittently for the next five years—this proposal generated heated debate in Washington and in the press.

Would the proposed foundation support the social as well as the natural sciences? Psychologists, sociologists, economists, and other social scientists had engaged in federally funded research through President Herbert Hoover's Research Committe on Social Trends (1929) as well as various New Deal and World War II agencies, and many now insisted that social-science research be included in any postwar program of federal support of science. Vannevar Bush disagreed, however, and the original NSF bill (introduced in July 1945 by Senator Warren Magnuson) reflected his views. Influential social scientists at once raised objections. The Social Science Research Council—established in 1923 by the professional societies of the various social sciences to promote interdisciplinary cooperation, more rigorous research standards, and a larger public role for these disciplines—took the lead in the campaign to incorporate the social sciences in the proposed legislation. In October, Senator Harley Kilgore of West Virginia introduced an alternative NSF bill that did, indeed, include the social sciences. [12]

In the early post-Hiroshima years, then, discussion of social science's role in the atomic age frequently became enmeshed in the debate over the scope of the National Science Foundation. Not only leading social scientists, but also influential natural scientists, vocally supported the Kilgore bill in the fall of 1945. Forming the Committee for a National Science Foundation, astronomer Harlow Shapley and chemist Harold Urey secured the signatures of hundreds of scientists, including Albert Einstein, Enrico Fermi, and other notables, to a petition calling for the inclusion of "all fields of fundamental scientific inquiry relevant to national interest without arbitrary exclusion of any area." A poll of some six hundred leading members of the American Association for the Advancement of Science revealed that nearly 70 percent favored federal funding of social-science research. President Truman let it be known that he supported the Kilgore bill.[13]

The issue came to a head in October 1945, when a subcommittee of the Senate Committee on Military Affairs conducted hearings on the various NSF bills then before the Congress. While a few witnesses, including the spokesman for the American Chemical Society, explicitly opposed inclusion of the social sciences, most of those who addressed the matter, including J. Robert Oppenheimer, President Karl Compton of MIT, President James Conant of Harvard, and, of course, the big guns of the Social Science Research Council, favored such inclusion.[14]

Many of these witnesses couched their support for federal funding of social-science research explicitly in terms of the social crisis the atomic bomb had created. "Ignorance of the science of humanity will lead us inevitably to destruction," declared Commerce Secretary Henry A. Wallace. "Our great problems . . . are not the problems of the natural sciences," added the Princeton physicist Henry D. Smyth. "They are the problems of the social sciences, and of politics and of ethics, if you like." Federally funded research that simply made possible "bigger and better atomic bombs" without helping society learn "how to live without using these new weapons," said historian John Milton Potter, president of Hobart and William Smith Colleges, would betray "the aspirations of most Americans."[15]

This theme was stressed, too, in the extended plea for federal funding of social-science research made in 1946–1947 by Talcott Parsons. The atomic bomb, wrote Parsons in the December 1946 *American Sociological Review,* had dramatically underscored "the potentialities of modern scientific technology for destruction and disruption of social life," and a social-science response was imperative. While the physical scientists' "enormous popular prestige" gave an "oracular" quality to "their pronouncements on almost any subject, whether or not it falls within their field of special competence," he said, social scientists were in fact the best qualified to confront the social problems science had created. Acknowledging social science's "distressing history of ineffectuality" in contrast to the physical sciences, he insisted that in several areas—organization theory, public opinion, demography, the business cycle—it could already "deliver results of first-rate practical importance" and that on all fronts it was rapidly progressing toward full scientific legitimacy.[16]

Pursuing the theme in the January 1947 *Bulletin of the Atomic Scientists,* Parsons developed his argument by stressing the unity of science and rejecting any definition that would exclude the study of society. "It simply is not possible to draw sharp, clear-cut lines between the natural and the social sciences," he insisted, citing medicine as an example. "Each side needs the contributions of the others, and many of the most important problems fall across the line." Public funding of social-science research, he concluded, would be a symbolically important acknowledgment that "science" was "not a mere isolated technical tool in modern western society" but a mode of thinking whose "roots penetrate to the deepest levels of our cultural and moral motivations." [17]

A few critics, however, challenged the assertion that social-science research represented America's greatest hope in the nuclear age. As early as November 1945, the director for social sciences of the Rockefeller Foundation deplored the fact that "many intelligent people" seemed convinced that the problems of the atomic age could be solved by some "mechanistic solution" offered by social scientists. No single, comprehensive "answer" from social science, he said, would eliminate the continuing threat posed by the bomb. Another skeptic, at least in the privacy of his journal, was David E. Lilienthal. In a series of annoyed entries from 1946 to 1948, Lilienthal fulminated against the widespread view that all would be well as soon as social science could "catch up" with the natural sciences. Social and political change did not come about through any "process of pure reasoning" by social scientists, he wrote. Indeed, it was "not affected by social scientists at all" but by technological and scientific developments. The social scientists "merely record changes that have occurred, or predict ones to come, or analyze the facts, etc." It was therefore vain, Lilienthal insisted, to look for an answer to the atomic dilemma through the accumulation of social-science data. [18]

Religious writers were also particularly acute in criticizing the hopes some were investing in the social sciences. Writing in 1948, L. Harold DeWolf of the Boston University School of Theology rejected the widespread assumption that mankind's plight was "due to a cultural lag in which the physical sciences have too far outstripped the social sciences." He also challenged the belief (implicit in this assumption) that while technological and scientific advances had both positive and negative potential, social-science research would be used only in beneficent ways. Pointing out that Hitler and Stalin had perfected sophisticated techniques of social control, DeWolf insisted that "the power given by the study of man," no less than the power given by nuclear physics, "can be used for either good or ill." Volumes of social research might accumulate on the shelves, but the question of the ends and purposes of that knowledge would remain, and social science could never in itself provide the answer. [19]

Meanwhile, as the debate continued, the proposal for a National Science Foundation had become involved in numerous other controversies and political crosscurrents, and not until the spring of 1950 was the enabling legislation finally passed. As ultimately set up, the NSF was mandated to support basic research in the "mathematical, physical, medical, biological, [and] engineering" sciences, though a loophole reference to "other sciences" opened the door to the social sciences at least a crack.[20]

Despite the scattered notes of caution, the conviction that social science could resolve the atomic dilemma found many adherents in these years. Indeed, a few social scientists went beyond broad generalizations and actually tried to apply their expertise to specific atomic-bomb-related issues. The results were not encouraging. In his 1946 essay on "Sociology and the Atom," for example, William F. Ogburn devoted considerable attention to a single issue: the relocation of city dwellers as a response to the danger of atomic attack. Ogburn simply began with the premise that such an urban dispersal project was necessary and desirable. Downplaying the daunting practical difficulties of such an undertaking, as well as the warnings of some that such an exercise in forced relocation would turn America into a police state, Ogburn discussed this bizarre idea as though it were, in fact, a serious policy option. Tapping into the nightmarish visions of urban destruction that had swept over America, Ogburn built a case for breaking up the nation's cities into hundreds of small towns scattered across the countryside. Those who found such ideas "utterly impracticable," said Ogburn, should consider that an atomic war could wipe out "fifty million city dwellers in a few minutes." Citing his own institution as an example, he acknowledged that "to move the University of Chicago a hundred miles away" might seem "a very difficult task," but insisted that it must be viewed in the context of the fact that

> within twenty-five years an atomic bomb may melt down all the buildings now on campus and all the equipment, books and laboratories. . . . A crisis great enough to spur us to dismember our cities is almost sure to come sometime. But then it will be too late. Are we farsighted enough to act in advance?"

In an imposing display of analytical precision, Ogburn calculated that the cost of breaking up America's cities into a thousand smaller ones would be $250 billion, "less than the cost of the second World War to the United States and perhaps less than the cost of a third world war." He also introduced historical precedent to buttress the feasibility of his project:

> The Pueblo Indians once moved their cities from the plains, where they were the prey of their warlike enemies, and set them in caves scooped

out of canyon walls high above the river. This was a task as difficult for them, perhaps, with their simple tools, as a decentralization of our big cities would be for us, with all our technology and wealth.

Further, he pointed out, urban dispersal would simply restore city dwellers to the state their ancestors had known since time immemorial: "We lived as a race for hundreds of thousands of years without cities. In fact, we have lived in cities scarcely a century; seventy-five million of us in the United States live away from cities now." While abandoning the cities might involve a "possible loss of advantage from our urban civilization"—museums, universities, orchestras, metropolitan newspapers, "aggregations of intelligentsia"—Ogburn suggested that with adequate social planning, these advantages might be equally attainable in smaller places. In fact, he wrote, the quality of life might be

> much better with well-planned smaller cities and towns. . . . We could have better health, fewer accidents, wider streets for automobiles, landing places for helicopters, more sunlight, space for gardens, more parks, less smoke, more comfortable homes, efficient places of work, and, in general, more beauty.[21]

While serious discussion of the urban dispersal option was widespread in the late 1940s, William Ogburn's pronouncements illustrate yet again how the early discussions of the bomb's implications often moved in well-worn grooves, involving, in this case, two familiar themes in American social thought: hostility to the city, and a strong social-control impulse toward the urban masses.[22]

The most significant cooperative social-research projects inspired by the atomic bomb in the immediate post-Hiroshima years were those sponsored by the Social Science Research Council. Early in 1946, the SSRC set up a Committee on Social Aspects of Atomic Energy funded by the Carnegie and Rockefeller foundations and chaired by Winfield W. Riefler, an economist at Princeton's Institute for Advanced Study. The other members were sociologists Rensis Likert of Michigan and William Ogburn; demographer Frank W. Notestein of Princeton; economist Jacob Marschak of Chicago; strategist Bernard Brodie of Yale; and, representing the atomic scientists, I. I. Rabi and Henry D. Smyth.[23]

This panel sponsored two studies published in 1947: *American Opinion on World Affairs in the Atomic Age,* the 1946 opinion survey discussed in Chapter 1, and *The Problem of Reducing Vulnerability to Atomic Bombs,* a strategic essay by Ansley J. Coale, a young economist and demographer who would go on to a distinguished career at Princeton. The former, with its internationalist flavor and presumption in favor of the Baruch plan, reflected the political climate of early 1946. The public-opinion data revealed a frightened and confused public, but offered little of value to policymakers. The Coale essay, by contrast, reflected scant confidence in international control and urged American atomic superiority and a vigorous program of civil defense as the most promising avenue of security. These two studies reflect in their contrasting emphases the political sea change already underway in 1946–1947. Neither, however, bore out the oft-repeated claim of these months that social science had profound and original insights to offer a society terrified of the bomb.

Whether intimidated by the very grandiosity of the post-Hiroshima summonses to the social scientists, or chastened by the disappointing results achieved by those who heeded that summons, few American social scientists followed in the footsteps of William Ogburn. Writing in the *New York Times Magazine* on the fifth anniversary of Hiroshima, the former Federation of American Scientists publicist Michael Amrine observed: "In the first reverberations of Alamogordo, [the atomic scientists] knew that the questions raised there would not be answered by physical science. Still devout in their belief in progress and reason, they waited for the answer from social scientists. They are still waiting." Despite all the postwar calls for research on the social implications of the bomb, agreed Chicago sociologist Edward Shils in 1957, practicing social scientists had with a few exceptions "remained aloof." "Sociologists took no interest in these matters," he has recently reiterated. Nor did the calls for a reformation of social-studies teaching bear much fruit. A 1949 U.S. Office of Education study concluded that while the "Atomic Age" phrase had been widely adopted by authors and editors as "a good interest-catcher . . . which proves their book is 'up-to-date,'" few books went beyond "generalities" in dealing with the subject. While insisting that "American democracy must 'meet the challenge of the Atomic Age,'" this study concluded, few textbooks offered any specifics "about what the Atomic Age means or what kinds of challenges we should prepare to meet"—which, in itself, is a fair summary of the results of the postwar surge of enthusiasm for research on the social implications of the atom.[24]

Six

The Crisis of Morals and Values

16

Justifications, Rationalizations, Evasions: Hiroshima, Nagasaki, and the American Conscience

Navy Day, October 27, 1945, ten weeks after the end of World War II. One hundred thousand people gathered in the Los Angeles Coliseum that evening for one of those extravaganzas at which southern California excels: a "Tribute to Victory" pageant reenacting the war in the Pacific. Searchlights stabbed the sky; the resonant voice of narrator Edward G. Robinson filled the vast open-air coliseum. Toward the end came the *pièce de résistance:* the atomic bombing of Hiroshima. The *Los Angeles Times* described the scene:

> At a signal, a low-flying B-29 skimmed over the bowl, the multi-colored search light beams tinting its gleaming silver with pastels. As the big bomber roared over the peristyle, a terrific detonation shook the ground, a burst of flame flashed on the field and great billows of smoke mushroomed upward in an almost too-real depiction of devastation.
>
> As the smoke snaked skyward, red and blue lights played over the white column with magic effectiveness.

The searchlights then shifted to the American flag and a reenactment of the Japanese surrender aboard the U.S.S. *Missouri* (with Walter Pidgeon as Douglas MacArthur). One hundred thousand people (a number of some resonance when one thinks of the atomic bomb) went wild: "It was a thrilling sight, and one that set the crowd cheering long and loudly."[1]

It takes an act of will to recapture the mood. When Hiroshima and Nagasaki were still the stuff of headlines, editorials, articles, sermons, and Hollywood-style pageants, how did Americans deal with the fact that an awesome new force developed and employed by their lawfully chosen representatives had wiped out two great cities in a few moments of time? How do we deal with it today? Without confronting Hiroshima and Nagasaki, the pacifist A. J. Muste has written, "no political or moral appraisal of our age is adequate, no attempt to find an answer to its dilemmas and destiny offers hope." As early as 1947, James Conant anxiously asked J. Robert Oppenheimer how he now viewed the atomic bombing of Japan. "I feel," Conant wrote, "that a great deal turns on this point in regard to the future."

As recently as 1983, in their pastoral letter on nuclear weapons, the American Catholic bishops circled back to the events of August 1945.

> After the passage of nearly four decades . . . we must shape the climate of opinion which will make it possible for our country to express profound sorrow over the atomic bombing in 1945. Without that sorrow, there is no possibility of finding a way to repudiate future use of nuclear weapons.

In a recent interview, the Manhattan Project physicist and later activist Ralph Lapp, discussing what he called the "great void" in American responses to the nuclear threat, said: "If the memory of things is to deter, where is that memory? Hiroshima . . . has been taken out of the American conscience, eviscerated, extirpated."[2]

This chapter, then, is about official deeds that seem at once remote and restlessly alive. "Hiroshima" and "Nagasaki" stand as signposts marking both a gash in the living flesh of our historical consciousness and a turning point in our ethical history: the concluding events of a "good" war, the opening events of a murky era of moral ambiguity and uncertainty through which we still wander.

The question of how Americans reacted to the atomic bombing of Japan, while fundamentally important, is far from easy to answer. Discussion of Hiroshima and Nagasaki in the immediate postwar period was often subordinated to other, seemingly more urgent, questions: Would American cities suffer the same fate? What were the future implications of atomic energy? Could the threat of atomic war be contained through international control? As Americans apprehensively eyed the atomic future, the events of the recent past were often blurred and obscured. Did this obsessive preoccupation with the atomic future provide an excuse for avoiding what had already happened? This argument was, in fact, made as early as 1946 by the Dutch psychologist A. M. Meerloo, who, at the end of his American lecture tour, linked the pervasiveness of "vague, ill-defined fear" to "hidden feelings of guilt."[3] Such psychological generalizations about an entire society are, by their very nature, unprovable. Even so, the very lack of evidence, like "the dog that didn't bark" in the Sherlock Holmes story, may prove suggestive.

In a study of early reactions to the use of the atomic bomb, historian Michael J. Yavenditti found "little public remorse." "No one that I have talked with seems shocked over Hiroshima or Nagasaki," observed Senator

Elbert Thomas in April 1946. Hiroshima, wrote novelist Mary McCarthy that August, had already become "a kind of hole in human history." Soon after, Edward Teller had a conversation with a minister who insisted that America would never drop the atomic bomb. When reminded that America had already dropped two, Teller later wrote, the minister "said no more, leaving me with the indelible impression that he wanted to forget Hiroshima."[4]

Public-opinion data support such impressionistic evidence. When the Gallup poll in late August 1945 asked the straightforward question "Do you approve or disapprove of the use of the atomic bomb?" 85 percent approved. (The corresponding figure for Great Britain was 72 percent.) Later that autumn, pollster Elmo Roper obtained the following results when he asked a representative sample of Americans which of four statements best expressed their opinion about the dropping of atomic bombs on Japan.[5]

1. We should not have used any atomic bombs at all 4.5%
2. We should have dropped one first on some unpopulated region, to show the Japanese its power, and dropped the second one on a city only if they hadn't surrendered after the first one 13.8%
3. We should have used the two bombs on cities, just as we did 53.5%
4. We should have quickly used many more of the bombs before Japan had a chance to surrender 22.7%
   Don't know 5.5%

Among the poor and "the traditionally fire-eating people of the southwestern states," Roper reported, nearly 30 percent wished "many more" atomic bombs had been dropped, while support for the two milder courses of action was highest among blacks and the "well-to-do and the well-educated." These findings raise a host of intriguing questions. Were the white poor more suceptible than the well-to-do to the cruder forms of anti-Japanese war propaganda, and perhaps less attuned to the longer-term political implications of the use of the bomb? Did they have a higher proportion of sons and husbands in combat units likely to have been involved in an invasion of Japan? Did the greater bloodthirstiness of the southwestern states reflect higher levels of anti-Oriental prejudice? And what of black Americans' lower support for the use of the bomb? Had blacks already concluded, as others would in later years, that racism was a factor in America's readiness to use this new instrument of horror against nonwhite peoples?

One glaring fact certainly does emerge from such early polls: in the early postwar period, upwards of 80 percent of Americans approved the atomic bombing of Hiroshima and Nagasaki, and what *Fortune* magazine called "a considerable minority of disappointed savagery" wished that even more Japanese cities had been wiped out. An analysis by historian Maureen Fitzgerald of some 225 letters about the bomb published in sixteen major American newspapers in August 1945 reveals about the same ratio of approval.[6]

Between 1945 and 1947, as the table shows, the Gallup poll did find an increase in negative feelings about the atomic bomb in general. But these results may only reflect declining hopes for international control, rather than proving that public approval of the use of atomic bombs against Japan was diminishing. Indeed, when four thousand New Yorkers were asked in 1948: "Which one of these words best describes your feelings when you hear the phrase 'atomic energy': Awe, Boredom, Fear, Guilt, Hope, Insecure, Justified, Secure," only about 1 percent chose "Guilt."[7] This is admittedly inconclusive (a person might have felt guilt and still chosen some other word to express his or her primary emotional response), yet it hardly suggests a nation overcome with remorse.

"Do you think it was a good thing or a bad thing that the atomic bomb was developed?"

	September 1945	October 1947
Good thing	69%	55%
Bad thing	17%	38%
No opinion	14%	7%

In this respect, the nation's opinion-molders mirrored the attitude of the larger public. According to a study of all atomic-bomb references by fourteen leading American political columnists through 1948, only Dorothy Thompson made more that "fleeting mention . . . of the opinion that the bombing of Japanese cities had been an immoral act, or that it might be so regarded by others." The nation's newspapers, Michael Yavenditti concludes, "almost unanimously applauded" Truman's decision.[8]

Is this surprising? The nation was, after all, at war. Pearl Harbor, Bataan, and the brutal island campaigns of the Pacific were fresh in memory. For years, news reports and propaganda (much of it involving racist stereotypes of striking crudity) had stressed Japanese savagery, barbarity, and fanaticism. Such was the climate of opinion in which Truman's announcement was received and in which crucial first judgments about the dropping of the atomic bomb were formed. The brutal hatred of the Japanese evident in many post-Hiroshima newspaper cartoons was matched in the letters Americans wrote to newspapers and radio commentators. Many urged that Tokyo be the next target. "Hirohito is the representative of the devil," a North Dakota listener wrote H. V. Kaltenborn. "He and his palace should be blowed off the map with an atomic bomb." Letters in the *Philadelphia Inquirer, Louisville Courier-Journal, Milwaukee Journal,* and other papers expressed regret that atomic bombs had not been used to destroy all human life in Japan. A Milwaukee woman expressed her genocidal impulses this way: "When one sets out to destroy vermin, does one try to leave a few alive in the nest? Certainly not!" A letter in the *Washington Post* on August 17 from a woman who said the atomic bomb made her ashamed to be an American elicited a torrent of bitter, abusive letters.[9]

Many who supported the decision to drop the bomb saw it as fair retribution for Japanese treacheries and atrocities. A *Chicago Tribune* cartoon of August 8 pictured a long fuse running from Pearl Harbor to Hiroshima over which flies debris and various body fragments including a severed head murmuring "So Sorry." "If it were not for the treachery of Pearl Harbor; the horrible cruelties of the Death March . . . the stories told by the starved, filth-encrusted, dazed American prisoners coming out of Japanese prison camps," said the *Atlanta Constitution* on September 1, "we might feel sorrow for the Japanese who felt the atomic bomb." William L. Laurence struck the same note in *Dawn Over Zero* (1946) as he described his feelings while flying toward Nagasaki: "Does one feel any pity or compassion for the poor devils about to die? Not when one thinks of Pearl Harbor and of the Death March on Bataan."[10]

The major official justification offered for the use of the atomic bomb was that it shortened the war and saved American lives. President Truman stressed this consideration in his initial announcement, and it clearly weighed heavily in the public's initial reaction. The psychiatrist Robert Jay Lifton, for example, has described his reactions as a young medical student: "I remember telling a friend that, if a single American life were saved, dropping the bomb was the right thing to do. . . . I wanted very much, like other Americans, for the war to end quickly in victory." As Lifton suggests, his views in 1945 were probably shared by the overwhelming majority of his fellow citizens. In a post-Hiroshima cartoon in the *Louisville Courier-Journal,* an American G.I., captioned "Bloodless Invasion," strides ashore in Japan as a phantom corpse representing "Avoided Costs" sprawls on the sand beside him. Historian Allan Nevins summed up this prevailing outlook in 1946: "The Army was ready in the Pacific, but happily it never had to meet its most fearful test—a death grapple with the still unbeaten two million Japanese warriors mustered in the home islands, and the million on the Asiatic continent. Navy, air power, and the atomic bomb saved us from that bloody ordeal."[11]

One group found this argument particularly compelling: the G.I.s in the Pacific who would have fought in any invasion of Japan. Now in their sixties or older, these men remain unshakably convinced that the atomic bomb saved their lives. In retrospect, one can see that this justification must be evaluated in the context of other considerations: the United States' "unconditional surrender" policy, Washington's lack of response to Japanese peace feelers, the practicality of a blockade as an alternative strategy for ending the war, the various proposals for a "demonstration shot" that were being advanced. At the time, however, such complexities were rarely considered.

Some went further. Not only did the bomb spare the lives of American boys, insisted Secretary of State James Byrnes in an early post-Hiroshima statement, but also those of "hundreds of thousands of Japanese boys and millions more of Japanese people." The same argument was made by Freda Kirchwey in the *Nation* and Bruce Bliven in the *New Republic*. The "humanitarian impulse" to pity the victims of Hiroshima and Nagasaki, wrote Bliven, "is complicated by the realization that the loss of these lives, by hastening the end of the war, probably in the long run saved more lives by helping to compel Japan's fanatical rulers to capitulate." A *Chicago Tribune* editorial on the American leaders who had made the decision expressed the point succinctly: "Being merciless, they were merciful." [12]

Pursuing this line of thinking to its logical conclusion, some insisted that the atomic bombs visited upon Japan were a positive good, "a blessing in disguise," as an American University law professor wrote late in 1945, "the Divine Wind that saved Japan from national *hara-kiri*." Thanks to the atomic bomb, observed Vannevar Bush, "we were free to begin the rehabilitation of the Japanese people rather than forced to undertake the conquest of a starving desert inhabited by a broken lot of physical and mental wrecks." From this perspective, the principal cause for regret was that one bomb had been insufficient to divert the Japanese warlords from their fanatical course. "Jap slowness of comprehension cost them dearly," Harold Urey wrote early in 1946. "At Hiroshima, men were killed. At Nagasaki, they committed suicide." [13]

The argument that the atomic bomb saved hundreds of thousands of American and Japanese lives is, of course, speculative. One should note, however, that it was decisively rejected in the authoritative United States Strategic Bombing Survey of 1946. On the basis of a detailed study of the state of the Japanese war effort in the summer of 1945, and exhaustive interviews with high Japanese officials, the USSBS concluded that Japan would have surrendered "certainly prior to 31 December 1945, and in all probability prior to 1 November 1945 . . . even if the atomic bombs had not been dropped, even if Russia had not entered the war, and even if no invasion had been planned or contemplated." [14] Of course, if this USSBS projection assumed the continued terror bombing of Japanese cities such as had been practiced since March 1945, the loss of Japanese, if not American, lives might indeed have been in the additional hundreds of thousands, even without the atomic bomb. Whatever its validity, the belief that the atomic bomb "saved American lives" (and, to a lesser extent, Japanese lives) quickly became an article of faith after August 6, 1945, and fundamentally shaped Americans' responses to the destruction of Hiroshima and Nagasaki.

The overwhelming public approval of the dropping of the atomic bomb was also influenced by the way the news was reported. In the earliest, officially approved accounts, radiation was scarcely mentioned. From the beginning, the entire Hiroshima/Nagasaki story was carefully stage-managed by the American military. The first accounts, written by William L. Laurence, who was in effect functioning as the Manhattan Project's pub-lic-relations man, simply recorded the visual observations of the bomb crews. The first team of American reporters actually to visit Hiroshima, a carefully screened group flown out from Washington by the Pentagon, ar-rived on September 3. They were shepherded around by American officials, briefed by Manhattan Project scientists, and plied with government-approved information.

The first reporter to visit the city apart from this select group was Wilfred Burchett of Australia, who also arrived on September 3. Visiting the few surviving hospitals, talking to victims and local Japanese authorities, and watching fish die in the Ota River, Burchett, in a dispatch transmitted to Tokyo by Morse code and published in a front-page story in the London *Daily Express* on September 5, reported that survivors were falling ill of a mysterious malady. "In Hiroshima, thirty days after the first atomic bomb," he wrote, "people are still dying, mysteriously and horribly—people who were uninjured in the cataclysm from an unknown something which I can only describe as the atomic plague."

But Burchett's report stood alone, and American authorities soon moved to counter its impact, convening yet another briefing for their hand-picked reporters in Tokyo. When Burchett arrived unexpectedly and de-scribed what he had seen, the briefing officer repeatedly denied any radiation aftereffects. When Burchett persisted, the officer told him curtly: "I'm afraid you've fallen victim to Japanese propaganda." Burchett was whisked off to a hospital for examination, and when he was released, discovered that his camera, containing an entire roll of film from Hiroshima, and the original of his Hiroshima dispatch were missing.

Another journalist who was not part of the officially selected team, George Weller of the *Chicago Daily News,* made his way to Nagasaki and filed a series of stories on his observations in the hospitals. Weller's report was held up by American Occupation press officials in Tokyo, however, and never published.

In this carefully managed news environment, little word of radiation filtered through to the American public. Indeed, quite the reverse. In two major stories on September 12 and 13, both bearing William Laurence's byline and quoting high Manhattan Project officials, the *New York Times* categorically denied that radiation sickness was occurring as a result of the atomic-bomb attacks. All reports to the contrary, said the *Times,* echoing the official line, were "Japanese propaganda." In short, the long history of official lying and misrepresentation on the issue of radiation—a history that includes the notorious advice of President Eisenhower to AEC officials in 1953 to keep the public "confused" about different types of radiation hazards —dates from the very beginning of the atomic era.[15]

The public's initial failure to grasp this critical aspect of the new weapon's importance was related, also, to the so-called "Jacobson incident." On August 7 and 8, 1945, many newspapers published an International News Service story in which Dr. Harold Jacobson of Columbia University, a low-level Manhattan Project scientist, described the bomb's probable long-term effects: "Hiroshima will be a devastated area not unlike our conception of the moon for nearly three-quarters of a century. . . . Rain falling on the area will pick up the lethal rays and will carry them down to the rivers and the sea. And animal life in these waters will die." The very land on which Hiroshima had once stood, he said, would remain "a vast, inorganic mass . . . until a geological process takes place in which the sun and the rain . . . create a new earth." Jacobson's nightmarish predictions made scary reading indeed. "Death Will Saturate Bomb Target For 70 Years," headlined the *Atlanta Constitution.*[16]

The reaction was swift. J. Robert Oppenheimer and other scientists ridiculed Jacobson's lurid scenario. Under pressure from the War Department and after hours of grilling by the FBI, a shaken Jacobson announced that his statements represented personal opinion and were not based on any confidential information. In the aftermath of this incident, the entire radiation issue became hopelessly muddled. A few papers expressed cautious concern. The *Boston Globe* in late August said that reports of radiation effects should be fully investigated. The *New York Times* agreed, but suggested that such stories were probably being spread by the Japanese "in an effort to arouse world sympathy." *Science News Letter* took the same position, while the *New Republic* jeered. "If radioactivity is present in the soil, such plants will be marked by an unusual number of . . . mutations. Here is the ideal job for Emperor Hirohito, an amateur geneticist. . . . Let him go to Hiroshima, sit among the ruins, and watch the mutations grow."[17] In the immediate postwar period, then, the subject of radiation damage was typically dismissed as the product of overheated imaginations or of Japanese propaganda. The bomb's effects, while awesome in scale, were not initially perceived as radically different in kind from the blast and heat produced by conventional explosives.

Further, Truman's initial announcement downplayed the civilian casualties. Said the president: "The world will note that the first atomic bomb was dropped on Hiroshima, a military base. That was because we wished in this first attack to avoid, insofar as possible, the killing of civilians." Though soon contradicted by compelling evidence, Truman's initial assurances helped shape crucial first impressions. H. V. Kaltenborn's August 6 broadcast began with a reference to Hiroshima as "an important Japanese Army Base," though he later noted that it was also a city of over 300,000 people.[18]

The American people were also encouraged to believe that the residents of the two doomed cities were given explicit advance warning. Lowell Thomas, for example, in his characteristically telegraphic style, said: "The American-British-Chinese warning to Japan was deliberately given in advance of the atomic bomb. The Japs warned in time. They did not yield, and then according to schedule, elemental devastation hit them." Again, the truth was more ambiguous. The "advance warning" was a clause in the July 26 Potsdam Declaration threatening "prompt and utter destruction" unless the Japanese surrendered unconditionally—words utterly debased by years of wartime propaganda.[19]

Finally, the overwhelming approval of the Hiroshima and Nagasaki bombings reflects the fact that Americans had already been conditioned to accept the terror bombing of cities as a legitimate military strategy. In its early edition of August 6, 1945, before the news of Hiroshima broke, the *Atlanta Constitution*'s lead headline proclaimed: "580 B-29s RAIN FIRE, TNT ON 4 MORE DEATH-LIST CITIES." Similar headlines had screamed from American newspapers for months. Thus, while the atomic bomb came as a shock, the destruction of entire cities did not. A letter in the *New Orleans Times Picayune*, for instance, reminded the "self-appointed moralists" who were condemning the atomic bomb that it was, after all, only the equivalent of a thousand of the conventional bombs that had long been used to such good effect. *Scientific American* claimed in October 1945 that at Hiroshima and Nagasaki "the Japanese learned what 'all out' war meant," but in fact both they and the Americans had learned that grim lesson well before the *Enola Gay* took off from Tinian Island.[20]

The spontaneous impulse of most Americans to support their government's decision to use the atomic bomb was reinforced in subsequent months as key participants justified and defended that decision. One of the earliest of these pronouncements was Karl Compton's "If the Atomic Bomb Had Not Been Used," in the December 1946 *Atlantic Monthly*. President of MIT since 1930 (and brother of Arthur Compton), physicist Karl Compton had served on the Interim Committee and other high-level wartime bodies. Compton's purpose in this article, he said, was to counter the "wishful thinking" of "after-the-event strategists" who were criticizing the use of the atomic bomb as "inhuman or . . . unnecessary." His essay, a skillful lawyer's brief, gave authoritative voice to many of the arguments we have already examined. Emphasizing how many lives were saved, Compton vigorously denied that Japan was already beaten by early August. Certainly "the fortunes of war had turned," but the Japanese were "still fighting desperately and there was every reason to believe . . . [they] would defend their homeland with even greater fanaticism than when they fought to the death on Iwo Jima and Okinawa." Compton concluded: "The atomic bomb introduced a dramatic new element into the situation which strengthened the hands of those who sought peace and provided a face-saving argument for those who had hitherto advocated continued war."[21]

Following shortly upon Compton's article was Henry L. Stimson's "The Decision to Use the Atomic Bomb" (Harper's, February 1947). As secretary of war from 1940 to 1945, Stimson was at the center of atomic-bomb decision-making. After FDR's death, it was he who told President Truman of the Manhattan Project. Stimson proposed to offer an "exact description" of the "thoughts and actions" leading up to that decision "as I find them in the records and in my clear recollection." (In a letter to Truman, Stimson was more explicit. His aim, he said, was to answer the "Chicago scientists" and "satisfy the doubts of that rather difficult class of the community which will have charge of the education of the next generation, namely educators and historians."[22]) Compared to Karl Compton, Stimson was far more sensitive to the larger contours of the topic. He included, for example, a memorandum prepared for an April 1945 meeting with Truman about the bomb in which he had observed somberly that the world might eventually find itself "at the mercy of such a weapon" and warned that all decisions relating to it involved "very serious responsibility for any disaster to civilization which it would further."

But despite his sense of the bomb's somber implications, Stimson, like Compton, vigorously defended the decision to use it against Japan: "The destruction of Hiroshima and Nagasaki put an end to the Japanese war. It stopped the fire raids, and the strangling blockade; it ended the ghastly specter of the clash of great land armies." Step by step, Stimson reviewed the events leading up to the Interim Committee's recommendation that the atomic bomb be used as soon as possible against a combined military-civilian target, with no advance warning. Japan had put out peace feelers, he acknowledged, but they were "tentative" and "vague" and included unacceptable conditions. A "tremendous shock" was necessary to "extract a genuine surrender from the Emperor and his military advisors." An invasion of Japan, he went on, would probably have met a resisting citizenry united in "fanatical despair" as well as "an armed force of five million men and five thousand suicide aircraft, belonging to a race which had already amply demonstrated its ability to fight literally to the death." The war would have lasted at least through 1946 and cost upwards of a million American and many more Japanese casualties.

As between this awful prospect and the use of the atomic bomb, said Stimson, only one choice was possible. No one in his position, eager to force

Japan's surrender without a costly invasion and "holding in his hands a weapon . . . for accomplishing this purpose . . . could have failed to use it and afterwards looked his countrymen in the face." The Potsdam ultimatum, Stimson insisted, made plain to the Japanese what lay in store, and once it had been rejected, the dropping of two atomic bombs—coupled with demoralizing hints that more were on the way—administered the therapeutic "shock" that jolted Japan into surrender. The alternative courses of action proposed by some Manhattan Project scientists during the final period of decision-making were carefully considered, he claimed, but each was judged too risky. Only one bomb had been tested, he reminded his readers, and that on a stationary tower, not in a drop from an airplane. The "real possibility" that any given bomb might not detonate, he insisted, argued compellingly against either a demonstration shot or an explicit advance warning.

The most powerful part of the article was its conclusion, in which the eighty-year-old statesman who had started his governmental career as William Howard Taft's secretary of war, reflected on the moral ambiguity and even anguish involved in all wartime decision-making:

> As I read over what I have written, I am aware that much of it, in this year of peace, may have a harsh and unfeeling sound. It would perhaps be possible to say the same things . . . more gently. But I do not think it would be wise. As I look back over the five years of my service as Secretary of War, I see too many stern and heartrending decisions to be willing to pretend that war is anything else than what it is. The face of war is the face of death; death is an inevitable part of every order that a wartime leader gives. The decision to use the atomic bomb was a decision that brought death to over a hundred thousand Japanese. No explanation can change that fact and I do not wish to gloss it over. But this deliberate, premeditated destruction was our least abhorrent choice. . . . In this last great action of the Second World War we were given final proof that war is death. War in the twentieth century has grown steadily more barbarous, more destructive, more debased in all its aspects.[23]

For all its detail and eloquence, Stimson's account fell short of a full discussion of all the calculations in the minds of American policymakers in the spring and summer of 1945. Specifically, he did not confront the question of the place of the Soviet Union in American calculations—a question already in the air at the time he wrote. "I have heard it argued," Raymond Gram Swing told his listeners in April 1946, "that the bomb dropped on Hiroshima was in effect dropped on the Russians, since it was not needed to bring the Japanese war to a close, but to establish and demonstrate a vast margin of power superiority over the Soviet Union." Norman Cousins and

Thomas K. Finletter raised the same point in a *Saturday Review* article that June, and in 1947, the pacifist A. J. Muste wrote: "There seems no escape from the conclusion that the Hiroshima and Nagasaki atrocities were in one important aspect a move in the power struggle between the United States and Russia."[24]

The Nobel Prize—winning British scientist P. M. S. Blackett elaborated the argument in his 1948 book *Fear, War, and the Bomb,* in which he described the military prospect as it must have appeared to Washington strategists in the early summer of 1945. Russia, pledged to enter the Japanese war by early August, might well defeat the Japanese armies on the Asian mainland and provide the final impetus for Japan's surrender—all while American ground forces were "no nearer to Japan than Iwo Jima and Okinawa." Russia would thus emerge as a major force in postwar Japan and America's powerful rival for world dominance. The Alamogordo test transformed the situation: "One can imagine the hurry with which the two bombs —the only two existing—were whisked across the Pacific to be dropped on Hiroshima and Nagasaki just in time, but only just, to insure that the Japanese Government surrendered to American forces alone." The targeting of two crowded cities, rather than exclusively military objectives, Blackett went on, vastly increased the value of the attack as a demonstration of the new weapon's power. "The dropping of the atomic bombs," he concluded, "was not so much the last military act of the Second World War, as the first major operation of the cold diplomatic war with Russia now in progress."[25]

Not until the very different cultural and political climate of the 1960s, however, would this view get a serious hearing. Between 1945 and 1950, it was ridiculed, denounced, or ignored. Blackett's book, in particular, was heavily attacked. One of the few reviewers to give it serious attention was physicist Philip Morrison, who called Blackett's argument "admittedly conjectural" but "fascinating" and "cogent" and offered a bit of corroborating firsthand testimony: "I can testify personally that a date near August tenth was a mysterious final date which we, who had the daily technical job of readying the bomb, had to meet at whatever cost in risk or money or good development policy. That is hard to explain except by Blackett's thesis." Most reviewers cited Blackett's leftist politics and dismissed his book as communist propaganda. Manhattan Project veteran I. I. Rabi, for instance, briskly dismissed Blackett's suggestion that the targeting of a large city may have involved *Realpolitik* calculations: "The wailing over Hiroshima finds no echo in Japan. The Japanese know that Hiroshima was an important headquarters and staging area and a legitimate target. They are very glad that something, anything, happened to stop the insane war. However, with sufficient propaganda, they might in time be induced to feel that they were greatly wronged. Hiroshima, by the way, is largely rebuilt."[26]

Turning a deaf ear to unsettling questions, most Americans appear to have found persuasive the justifications articulated by Truman, Compton, Stimson, and others. These authoritative accounts strongly reenforced the position of those who insisted that the United States had taken the only proper course in opting to drop the atomic bomb on two Japanese cities. So widely accepted was this view that, by 1949, Gen. Leslie R. Groves could recite it like a familiar incantation: "The use of the bomb against Japan brought to a sudden end the greatest war in history and thus saved hundreds of thousands of American casualties as well as untold suffering to the people of Japan." [27]

The man who bore ultimate responsibility for the decision, Harry S. Truman, never veered in public or private from this basic argument. From the first he rejected any suggestion that the decision may have had a tragic or morally ambiguous dimension. When J. Robert Oppenheimer suggested to him that some atomic scientists felt they had blood on their hands, Truman contemptuously offered him a handkerchief and said: "Well, here, would you like to wipe off your hands?" After Oppenheimer left the Oval Office, Truman turned to Dean Acheson, who was also present, and said: "I don't want to see that son of a bitch in this office ever again." The passing years only deepened his certainty. Near the end of his life, when the producers of a television series on his career suggested a pilgrimage to Hiroshima, Truman replied: "I'll go to Japan if that's what you want. But I won't kiss their ass." [28]

While public figures from Truman on down explicitly defended the atomic-bomb decision, other opinion-molders reenforced public acceptance of that decision in more indirect ways. The activist scientists and other international-control advocates, for example, simply avoided any discussion of it for tactical reasons. As the *Bulletin of the Atomic Scientists* put it early in 1946, the bomb decision was "water over the dam," and there seemed "no reason to risk disagreements on past events" when scientists were united on what the nation's future course should be. A Federal Council of Churches official wrote a sharply critical letter to pacifist A. J. Muste, an outspoken critic of the decision to drop the bomb, urging him not to "divide our forces" by raising the matter in his writings. [29]

Further, in early comment on the dropping of the atomic bomb, one time and again finds the focus shifting abruptly from the immediate reality to some more generalized context. The destruction of two cities was less significant, these commentators typically insisted, than the events' symbolic meaning. "Far more important to humanity . . . [than] what has happened in Hiroshima," said H. V. Kaltenborn on August 6, 1945, "is how [these bombs] will affect mankind's destiny." The atomic bomb had not only blasted two cities, *Business Week* noted in early September, but also (and clearly more importantly) "flashed across the world a light of such glaring intensity that even blind eyes could glimpse the forked road that is presented to humanity's choice and destiny." "What is happening to men's minds is more important than what has happened in the physical realm," Senator Elbert Thomas observed shortly after Hiroshima. If only people would "look under the ashes of all those dead Japs," A Texas subscriber wrote *Time* in September 1945, they would realize that the atomic bomb represented a "most powerful deterrent to future wars of aggression." Merely to treat the atomic bomb in terms of "measurable destruction," wrote the novelist Mary McCarthy in 1946, was "in a sense, to deny its existence"; it was actually in a different realm, "the moral world," she went on, "that the atom bomb exploded." [30]

The particular "meaning" ascribed to Hiroshima varied, depending on the writer's orientation. Some emphasized the gain in scientific knowledge. In *Atomic Energy in Cosmic and Human Life* (1946), physicist George Gamow expressed regret that "from the point of view of pure knowledge (or curiosity?)," the second bomb had not been dropped in Nagasaki harbor, so scientists could have observed the effects of an underwater detonation. This section of Gamow's book was illustrated with a whimsical pen-and-ink sketch of such a harbor explosion, with toy-like ships and planes tossed about in the air. Others, like the *New York Times* editors, stressed the peacetime prospects of atomic power. The bomb "did far more than disintegrate the homes, the industries, and the very bodies of the Japanese," said *Scientific American* in October 1945. It proved that man had at last discovered "the means of unleashing the locked-up power of the atom and putting it to work." [31] World-government advocates viewed Hiroshima and Nagasaki from their particular ideological vantage point. "Something much greater than Hiroshima was smashed when the atomic bomb was dropped . . . ," wrote one world-government publicist late in 1945: "The fiction of [national] sovereignty had its false crown and robes blown right off." [32]

An almost lyrical mood overtook some writers as they contemplated the larger truths illuminated at Hiroshima and Nagasaki. "Never in all the long history of human slaughter," declared *Reader's Digest* in November 1945, "have lives been lost to greater purposes." All mankind, it continued, was now joined "by bonds . . . fused unbreakably in the diabolical heat of those explosions." [33] In passages like these, one hears distant echoes of 1914–1918, when statesmen and propagandists alike had seen in the carnage of war the seedbed of a brave new world of peace and democracy. Like those who were insisting that the bomb's apparent role in shortening the war settled all questions of its use, these commentators who so confidently discussed the bomb's "larger meaning" and "true significance" contributed to the process by which thick layers of psychic keloid tissue gradually came to overlay the still unhealed moral wounds of Hiroshima and Nagasaki.

A mass-culture product that typifies the view of the atomic bombing of Japan being fed to Americans in these months was *The Beginning or the*

End, an MGM movie about the bomb that premiered in Washington, D.C., in February 1947, starring Hume Cronyn as J. Robert Oppenheimer. (The role of General Groves, rejected by Spencer Tracy, went to Brian Donlevy.) Though ostensibly a documentary, the film contained many insidious distortions of the atomic-bomb decision. President Truman is portrayed as agonizing over the decision when, in fact, as he himself frequently boasted in later years, he made it quickly with no qualms. The movie falsely suggests that the Japanese were nearing completion of their own atomic bomb. (For moviemakers, Louis B. Mayer explained in a 1946 letter to Albert Einstein about the film, "dramatic truth is just as compelling a requirement . . . as veritable truth is on a scientist.") The most blatant distortion, however, is the claim that the people of Hiroshima were given explicit advance warning. "We've been dropping warning leaflets on them for ten days now," comments an *Enola Gay* crew member. "That's ten days' more warning than they gave us before Pearl Harbor." [34]

On the moral issue, a colonel sums up the movie's dominant view: "Get it done before the Germans and Japs, then worry about the bomb." A fictional scientist, Matt Cochran, expresses some qualms, but in a farewell letter delivered to his widow after his death in a radiation accident, Matt concludes that his superiors were better judges than he of the ethical issues and expresses confidence that atomic energy will vastly benefit mankind.

The Beginning or the End was neither a critical nor a box-office success. Reviewers comments ranged from "cheery imbecility" *(Time)* to "horrible falsification" *(Bulletin of the Atomic Scientists).* [35] In intent, however, it heavily underscored the message of Compton, Stimson, and countless other opinion-molders: the decision to use the bomb against Japan was entirely justified and morally praiseworthy. To this extent, Hollywood contributed its bit to the larger cultural process by which Hiroshima and Nagasaki gradually sank, unconfronted and unresolved, into the deeper recesses of American awareness.

17

"Victory for What?"—
The Voice of the Minority

It was a few days after the war's end, and the victory celebration that had surged through downtown Chicago was still a fresh memory. But Fred Eastman of the Chicago Theological Seminary was not in a celebratory mood. "King Herod's slaughter of the innocents—an atrocity committed in the name of defense—destroyed no more than a few hundred children," he wrote bitterly to *Christian Century;* "Today, a single atomic bomb slaughters tens of thousands of children and their mothers and fathers. Newspapers and radio acclaim it a great victory. Victory for what?" The poet Randall Jarrell, stationed at an air-force base in Arizona, had a similar reaction: "I feel so rotten about the country's response to the bombings at Hiroshima and Nagasaki," he wrote a friend in September 1945, "that I wish I could become a naturalized cat or dog."[1]

Eastman and Jarrell were not alone. From the moment the news of Hiroshima flashed across the nation, isolated voices of protest, ranging from troubled uneasiness to anguished dismay, could be heard. One must not exaggerate this response, but neither may one ignore it. Though a minority viewpoint, it has survived tenaciously, becoming more pronounced as the nuclear arms race—the bitter fruit of decisions taken in 1945—has grown in magnitude and menace.

This protest was not coordinated or organized, nor did it reflect a distinct ideological coloration. It was simply a spontaneous, anguished cry which some Americans, even at the end of a ferocious war, felt compelled to utter. Many were obscure; a few were prominent. Socialist Norman Thomas deplored the "pious satisfaction" of most commentators—including those on the Left—at Truman's announcement. The atomic destruction of a second city, Thomas wrote, was "the greatest single atrocity of a very cruel war." Stuart Chase, even as he speculated on the atom's peacetime role, warned that the obliteration of Hiroshima and Nagasaki, "whatever the rationalization," could "handicap the moral leadership of the United States . . . for generations to come." Surely, Chase insisted, Washington could have found a way to achieve its objectives "without this appalling slaughter of school children." [2]

In the nation's newspapers, the general editorial approval for the atomic bombing of Japan was moderated by a few expressions of moral uneasiness. The *Hartford Courant* credited the bomb for ending the war, but added: "We cannot disregard the voice of our own conscience, which tells us that the new bomb is just as bestial and inhuman as the Japanese say it is." The *New York Herald Tribune* found "no satisfaction in . . . the greatest simultaneous slaughter in the whole history of mankind, and [one that] in its numbers matches the more methodical mass butcheries of the Nazis." The *Omaha World Herald* criticized as "almost sacrilegious" the unctuous tone of Truman's announcement "in using the name of a merciful God in connection with so Satanic a device." Far from being a reason for "exultation," this editorial continued, the Hiroshima news only underscored "that war is a degrading, dirty business." [3]

A few columnists struck a similar note. Marquis Childs, writing in the *New York Post* on August 10, called it a "supreme tragedy . . . that the new discovery . . . had to be used first for the destruction of human life." "Surely we cannot be proud of what we have done," wrote David Lawrence in the *U.S. News and World Report.* "If we state our inner thoughts honestly, we are ashamed of it." Richard L. Strout of the *Christian Science Monitor* posed troubling questions: "How can the United States in the future appeal to the conscience of mankind not to use this new weapon? . . . Has not the moral ground for such an appeal been cut away from under our feet?" [4]

From the grass roots, too, came a faint but distinct cry of dismay. Newspapers all over the country, noted one observer a few days after Hiroshima, were receiving letters "protesting the killing of the noncombatant civilians in Japan, calling it inhuman, and protesting our disregard of moral values." The letters of this dissident minority were often extremely bitter. One called the bombing "a stain upon our national life"; another said it was "simply mass murder, sheer terrorism." An appalled reader of *Time* wrote:

> The United States of America has this day become the new master of brutality, infamy, atrocity. Bataan, Buchenwald, Dachau, Coventry, Lidice were tea parties compared with the horror which we . . . have dumped on the world. . . . No peacetime applications of this Frankenstein monster can ever erase the crime we have committed. [5]

The letters on the atomic bomb written to H. V. Kaltenborn included several of moral protest. "Why . . . did we choose to drop our first bomb on a crowded city, where 90% of the casualties would *inevitably be civilian?*" asked a St. Paul listener. "True, there were war industries in Hiroshima, but there are war industries in most of our American cities, and what would we think of an enemy who would wipe out our fair cities, *hospitals and all,* on such a pretext?" The expressions of moral outrage from Kaltenborn's listeners ranged from the articulate and thoughtful to the barely literate:

Phooey America. That blood will scream up to our dear God—What will come next? . . . Burry the bomb and all the papers, it is too shocking news what America did with that knowledge. If we destroy innocent civilians we will be destroyed in return—that was a devlish act against Japan.[6]

Isolated and weak in contrast to the overwhelming chorus of approval for the atomic bombing of Japan, such expressions were nevertheless an authentic part of the larger mosaic of response to the bomb. In a 1946 epic poem called *The Bomb That Fell on America*, a California writer named Hermann Hagedorn included a section called "The Conscience of America" in which he attempted to convey the ethical unease that at least some were feeling. "The dead lie across our hearts," he wrote, "and fall in a black rain upon our souls."[7]

Opposition to the bombing of Hiroshima and Nagasaki surfaced, too, in the pages of the black press. This is not to say, however, that the black reaction was unambiguously hostile. By 1945, leading black newspapers like the *Washington Afro-American* and the *Chicago Defender* were celebrating the exploits of black combat troops against the "Japs" on Okinawa and elsewhere, and when the atomic-bomb story broke they reported with pride that seven thousand blacks had been employed at Oak Ridge and that black chemists and mathematicians had been part of the Manhattan Project at the University of Chicago. "NEGRO SCIENTISTS HELP PRODUCE 1ST ATOM BOMB," headlined the *Defender* on August 18.[8]

But the dominant response of black opinion-molders quickly turned to hostility and skepticism. The seven thousand black workers at Oak Ridge, the *Washington Afro-American* noted in a follow-up story, had lived in segregated, inferior housing; performed menial jobs only; and had not (unlike the white workers) had a school provided for their children. In a variation of a familiar proposal, the *Defender* suggested that another $2 billion be allocated to social-science research "to isolate and destroy the venom of racial hate."[9]

The top leadership of the National Association for the Advancement of Colored People was uniformly critical. Executive Secretary Walter White, commenting on Winston Churchill's determination to keep the bomb in "Anglo-Saxon" hands, observed that Chinese, Russians, Indians, and others could learn nuclear physics as well, and speculated that some day "an atomic bomb might be launched against London from the remote fastness of some part of the British Empire." A few weeks after Hiroshima, W. E. B. DuBois, the NAACP's director of research (and America's leading black intellectual), described Japan as "the greatest colored nation which has risen to leadership in modern times" and predicted that the humiliation of her spectacular defeat would slow the advance of dark-skinned peoples everywhere. Roy Wilkins, editor of the NAACP magazine *The Crisis,* linked the atomic bomb to other wartime tactics such as roasting Japanese soldiers alive with flamethrowers and attributed such barbarities to racist attitudes that viewed the Japanese as subhuman. Asked Wilkins in a September 1945 editorial on the bomb: "Who is bad and who is good? Who is barbarian and who is civilized? Who is fit to lead the world to peace and security, and by what token?" [10]

Woven through this black commentary was the suspicion that the bomb had been deliberately reserved for use against Asians rather than Europeans. The Hiroshima news, said the *Washington Afro-American,* "revived the feeling in some quarters that maybe the Allies are fighting a racial war after all." American military planners may have spared the Germans, who, "after all, represent the white race," this editorial suggested, and "saved our most devastating weapon for the hated yellow men of the Pacific." [11]

The black poet Langston Hughes developed all these themes in a bitter *Chicago Defender* column on August 18, 1945, putting his harshest comments in the mouth of "Simple," the uneducated but shrewd black he used as a journalistic persona in these years. "Them atom bombs make me sick at the stomach," says Simple. Why wasn't the bomb used against Germany? "They just did not want to use them on white folks. Germans is white. So they wait until the war is over in Europe to try them out on colored folks. Japs is colored." The $2 billion spent on the bomb, Simple concludes, would have been better spent on decent housing, playgrounds, and education for the nation's poor—including education for whites who persisted in electing racists to Congress. [12]

And what of the churches? The response of the religious press and church bodies to the dropping of the atomic bomb was far from uniform. Evangelicals who stressed individual conversion and downplayed engagement with social issues remained comparatively silent on the bomb, or viewed it simply as further evidence of the need for personal evangelism. This response is illustrated in the pages of *United Evangelical Action,* the magazine of the National Association of Evangelicals, an organization of conservative Protestant denominations. While denouncing the "wholesale excesses of drunkenness and lust" on V-J Day, the editors made no comment on the atomic bombing of Japan. When a reader questioned this silence, they responded with a classic statement of the evangelical position:

> Our concern is not so much about the atomic bomb as about the people who control it. If the people are saved Christians, it will do the world no harm. If they are pagan, beware. . . . Our business is to preach the

gospel. . . . We are unwilling to take any blame for the shortcomings of our social order beyond our own personal conduct.[13]

Nor can one assume that the church leaders and editors who did condemn the atomic bombing of Japan spoke for the great mass of the laity. Indeed, the findings of the public-opinion polls suggest that they probably spoke for only a minority even of their own constituencies. When these caveats have been noted, however, the fact remains that the greatest concentration of critical comment on the Hiroshima and Nagasaki bombings came from the churches. Though a minority viewpoint, this response laid the groundwork for and added a sharp intensity to the debate over the general moral implications of nuclear weapons.

One of the first responses came from the Federal Council of Churches, an association of liberal Protestant denominations. On August 9 (before news of the Nagasaki bombing was released), the president of the FCC, Methodist bishop G. Bromley Oxnam, and John Foster Dulles, chairman of its Commission on a Just and Durable Peace, issued a joint statement urging that no further bombs be dropped. "If we, a professedly Christian nation, feel morally free to use atomic energy in that way," they said, "men elsewhere will accept that verdict. Atomic weapons will be looked upon as a normal part of the arsenal of war and the stage will be set for the sudden and final destruction of mankind." To refrain from dropping additional bombs, they went on, was "the way of Christian statesmanship" and would be viewed not as evidence of weakness, but of "moral and physical greatness."[14]

Two weeks after Hiroshima, thirty-four prominent Protestant clergymen, including several well-known pacifists, addressed a letter to President Truman condemning the decision. One of the signers, Harry Emerson Fosdick of New York's Riverside Church, was particularly outspoken. In an early postwar sermon broadcast nationally Fosdick declared: "When our self-justifications are all in, every one of us is nonetheless horrified at the implications of what we did. Saying that Japan was guilty and deserved it, gets us nowhere. The mothers and babies of Hiroshima and Nagasaki did not deserve it." To argue that the "mass murder of whole metropolitan populations is right if it is effective," Fosdick went on, was to abandon "every moral standard the best conscience of the race ever has set up."[15]

Another independent religious voice of protest was that of John Haynes Holmes of the nonsectarian Community Church of New York. The atomic bomb, wrote Holmes in the September 1945 issue of his magazine *Unity*, was "the supreme atrocity of the ages; . . . a crime which we would instantly have recognized as such had Germany and not our own country been guilty of the act." The claim that the decision had hastened the end of the war, he added, was simply the familiar "end-justifies-the-means" argument and "as great and dangerous a fallacy as ever." Even on practical grounds the utilitarian argument might prove fallacious: "The atomic bomb is not going to stop here. What if it 'Speeds the end' not only of this war, but also of civilization? . . . The long range view in this case is a thing to chill the soul." [16]

In the publications of the mainstream Protestant denominations, one finds, even in the flush of victory, expressions of moral unease. The Baptist *Watchman-Examiner* on August 16, 1945, condemned the "ghastly slaughter of women and children who have not the remotest connection with a military objective." The response of the Methodist *Christian Advocate,* initially tentative, grew stronger with time. In September 1945 the editor, Roy L. Smith, wrote that the bomb illustrated the need to find alternatives to war, but found no basis for condemning its use against Japan so long as one accepted other forms of terror bombing. By March 1946, however, Smith was expressing growing qualms: "The moral conscience of the American people continues restless in the memory of the awful effects of the explosion, and as more detailed and dependable information comes in, this sense of uneasiness deepens." Quoting a proposal by David Lawrence, Smith concluded: "Let's rebuild Hiroshima as a symbol of spiritual reawakening." [17]

Other Methodist periodicals were even more outspoken. "There is no religion, however primitive, or law that can sponsor the horrors of this war," declared the *Central Christian Advocate,* published in Chicago, on August 30, 1945. "Hate and kill, kill without hate; any method, anybody, or better still, every method and everybody. This was a wonderful war." *Motive,* the magazine of the Methodist Student Movement, expressed its "unmitigated condemnation" of the atomic-bomb "atrocity" in an editorial titled: "We Have Sinned." *Motive* also published a list of the Methodist churches, schools, and social-welfare agencies in Hiroshima and Nagasaki as well as a play involving a dialogue between Satan and the Angel Gabriel that was, in effect, a bitter attack on the dropping of the atomic bomb. It "was ruthless and needless," says Gabriel. "One side was already defeated and helpless. . . . Do the Americans boast of it? Soldiers save their own lives by taking the lives of children? What courage, what honor is that?" Gloats Satan: "Dr. Gallup indicates that 85 percent of the American people approved . . . which gives me the largest majority I've had since prohibition." [18]

The interdenominational liberal weekly *Christian Century* not only took a strong initial stand against the decision to drop the bomb, but published several pages of letters from readers who shared its view. The obliteration of two cities by atomic bombs, it said on August 15, had brought to "perfect flower" von Clausewitz's doctrine of war without limit or restraint. "Short of blowing up the planet, this is the ultimate in violence," this editorial declared. "Instead of congratulating ourselves . . . we should now be standing in penitence before the Creator of the power which the atom has hitherto kept inviolate." *Christian Century's* August 29 editorial, "America's Atomic

Atrocity," was even more outspoken in condemning the "brutal disregard of any principle of humanity" that had placed the United States in an "indefensible moral position" and "sadly crippled" its "influence for justice and humanity." Predicting a reaction against Christianity in Japan, *Christian Century* called on the churches to "disassociate themselves and their faith from this inhuman and reckless act of the American government." (Deluged by critical letters, *Christian Century* tempered its stand a few weeks later. While still describing the atomic-bomb decision as "impetuous" and "wanton," the magazine now insisted that it had not condemned the action categorically, but only pointed out that the government had not persuasively shown that its use was essential to Japan's defeat. [19])

The closest thing to an authoritative Protestant response to the atomic bombing of Japan was "Atomic Warfare and the Christian Faith," the report of a blue-ribbon commission presented to the Federal Council of Churches in March 1946. Chaired by Robert L. Calhoun, professor of historical theology at Yale, this twenty-two-member commission included an impressive array of theologians, philosophers, and church historians drawn from prominent seminaries, universities, and such colleges as Oberlin and Haverford. Among its well-known members were Roland H. Bainton and H. Richard Niebuhr of Yale and John C. Bennett, Reinhold Niebuhr, and Henry P. Van Dusen of Union Theological Seminary. Like the council itself, the membership was drawn almost exclusively from Protestantism's liberal, "modernist" wing. The commission divided over whether the use of atomic bombs could ever be morally acceptable, but on the use already made of them, it was unanimous and unequivocal:

> We would begin with an act of contrition. As American Christians, we are deeply penitent for the irresponsible use already made of the atomic bomb. We are agreed that, whatever . . . one's judgment of the ethics of war in principle, the surprise bombings of Hiroshima and Nagasaki are morally indefensible.

The commission gave reasons for this damning indictment: the atomic attacks on two cities involved "the indiscriminate slaughter of noncombatants" in a particularly "ghastly form"; the first bomb had been dropped without specific warning or advance demonstration, and the second before Tokyo had been given a reasonable opportunity to react to the first; the bombs were dropped despite Japan's "hopeless" strategic position and the virtual certainty that she herself did not possess such weapons. Even if the atomic bomb shortened the war, the commission concluded, "the moral cost was too high. . . . We have sinned grievously against the laws of God and the people of Japan." Aid by American Christians to "the survivors of those two murdered cities," the Calhoun Commission said, would be "a token of repentence . . . cherished as long as men remember the first atomic bomb."

This call for repentance was not well received, however. The main result, commented one well-placed observer in 1950, was to produce "a barrage of arguments trying to apologize for our use of the atomic bomb in such a way as to deny any need for contrition." [20]

The leading voices of American Roman Catholicism were even more uniformly critical of the atomic bombing of Japan. Indeed, concludes historian Robert C. Batchelder, Catholic theologians and journals of opinion were "nearly unanimous in condemning the bomb's use." "The name Hiroshima, the name Nagasaki, are names for American guilt and shame," declared *Commonweal* in August 1945. This editorial sarcastically dismissed the justifications being offered ("To secure peace, of course. To save lives, of course") and the peaceful avowals being made by leaders who had just brought "indescribable death to a few hundred thousand men, women and children." [21]

Catholic World, the voice of the Paulist Fathers, called the surprise use of the atomic bomb against civilians "atrocious and abominable" and "the most powerful blow ever delivered against Christian civilization and the moral law." All "civilized people," this September 1945 editorial continued, should "reprobate and anathematize" this "horrible deed." Of the argument that the two doomed cities had been given sufficient advance warning, *Catholic World* said: "Let us not combine cruelty with hypocrisy, and attempt to justify wholesale slaughter with a lie." [22]

The judgment of the influential Jesuit journal *America,* while longer in coming, was no less devastating. If the justifications being given for America's decision to drop the bomb were morally sound, wrote a Jesuit theologian in *America* in 1947, then *any* belligerent in *any* just war could use atomic weapons with impunity; but if they were not, "then the United States committed an enormous wrong at Hiroshima, and duplicated it at Nagasaki." This author left no doubt of his view. The argument that the bomb had shortened the war, he said, "collapses against a primary principle of sound morality: no end—however good, however necessary—can justify the use of an evil means." The evil deeds of August 1945 were "of the gravest concern," he declared, because they sanctioned the substitution of "national pragmatism" for "the transcendence of the moral order." This writer sharply criticized the "obfuscation" of those who had responded to the destruction of Hiroshima and Nagasaki with calls for the abolition of war. While this was "a consummation devoutly to be wished," he said, no one should suppose "that by turning to it we have resolved the question of our past performance and proved our conscience clear." [23]

While theologians debated, the moral discourse over the atomic bombing of Japan emerged in an unlikely quarter. Readers of the *New Yorker* had little reason to suspect that the August 31, 1946, issue would not offer the magazine's usual urbane mélange of cartoons, humorous pieces, cultural comment, and reviews. The cover was a lighthearted collage of summer fun and games: swimming, sunbathing, tennis, croquet. In fact, however, the entire issue was devoted to a single long journalistic account entitled simply "Hiroshima." The author, thirty-one-year-old John Hersey, was born in China in 1914 and spent his first ten years there. Graduating from Yale, he joined *Time-Life* publications and during World War II produced many stories and three books based on his reportorial experiences in Europe. The best-known of his war stories, "A Bell for Adano," appeared in *Liberty Magazine* in 1944; by early 1945 the book version had gone through fifteen printings. Planning a journalistic trip to Japan late in 1945, Hersey discussed with *New Yorker* editor William Shawn a possible piece on the atomic bomb. "Hiroshima" was the result.[24]

Hersey's essay had an immediate and profound impact. The book version became a runaway best-seller. The Book-of-the-Month Club distributed free copies to many of its 848,000 members. A reading of the entire work, in four half-hour segments, over the ABC radio network won the Peabody Award for the outstanding educational broadcast of 1946.[25]

A seasoned reporter and successful popular writer, Hersey in *Hiroshima* adopted a tried-and-true journalistic technique, describing in minute detail the activities of six Hiroshima residents before, during, and after the bomb fell: a young secretary; a widowed seamstress; a German Jesuit missionary; a Japanese Methodist minister; a young physician affiliated with a large, modern hospital; and an older physician who operated a small private clinic. This was a form familiar to American readers. Photographers like Dorothea Lange, novelists like John Steinbeck, and journalists like James Agee had explored the impact of the Great Depression by focusing on individuals, and the genre had been transferred to the battlefront in the war dispatches of Ernie Pyle, the London broadcasts of Edward R. Murrow, and the cartoons of Bill Mauldin. In books like Richard Wright's *Native Son* or James Farrell's Studs Lonigan trilogy, this form of individualized social realism could be tough, hard-boiled, and even brutal. But in the hands of other writers—Erskine Caldwell, William Saroyan, Thornton Wilder—it took on a sentimental and picaresque quality.

Hersey was closer to the latter school. Indeed, his *Hiroshima* was modeled on Wilder's *The Bridge of San Luis Rey,* which offered biographical vignettes of several ordinary people randomly united in death by the collapse of a bridge in Peru, while *A Bell for Adano* sentimentally described a liberated Italian village and the efforts of an American occupation official, one Major Joppolo, to replace a church bell melted down by the Fascists. To be sure, occasional grim details give the story an authentic wartime flavor: "At the corner . . . the two men came on a dead Italian woman. She had been dressed in black. Her right leg was blown off and the flies for some reason preferred the dark sticky pool of blood and dust to her stump." But such passages are rare amid the descriptions of picturesque village life and encounters between simple local folk and friendly, well-meaning Americans. The publisher's promotional copy made clear how readers should approach *A Bell for Adano*, describing it as a story of "THE HUMAN SIDE OF WAR: . . . the wonderful, simple people of Adano—the fishermen, the officials, the pretty girls, the children who ran in the streets shouting to the American soldiers to throw them caramels, . . . the American who broke through red tape and discovered the heart of Italy." [26]

Given Hersey's journalistic background, and his weakness for the sentimental and melodramatic, the restraint with which *Hiroshima* unfolds is striking. The book is remarkably free of either sentimentality or sensationalism. It begins in a quiet, understated fashion: "At exactly fifteen minutes past eight in the morning, on August 6, 1945, Japanese time, at the moment when the atomic bomb flashed above Hiroshima, Miss Toshiko Sasaki, a clerk in the personnel department of the East Asia Tin Works, had just sat down at her place in the plant office and was turning her head to speak to the girl at the next desk." As in *A Bell for Adano*, there are scenes of horror that embed themselves in the memory, such as the description of a group of some twenty soldiers in a park some distance from the blast's epicenter: "Their faces were wholly burned, their eyesockets were hollow, the fluid from their melted eyes had run down their cheeks. (They must have had their faces upturned when the bomb went off; perhaps they were anti-aircraft personnel.) Their mouths were mere swollen, pus-covered wounds, which they could not bear to stretch enough to admit the spout of the teapot." [27] But such scenes were not heightened for dramatic effect. Indeed, they receive no more emphasis than the everyday details of uninjured persons coping with all-encompassing disaster. In a style so uninflected it struck some readers as heartless, Hersey gave the same weight to horror, heroism, and mundane banality.

In general, the reception of *Hiroshima* was overwhelmingly approving. Of hundreds of letters, postcards, and telegrams that poured into the *New Yorker* offices, the vast majority were favorable. Most reviews were enthusiastic. "Nothing that can be said about this book can equal what the book has to say," wrote Charles Poore in the *New York Times;* "It speaks for itself, and in an unforgettable way, for humanity." The *Christian Century* reviewer could hardly contain himself: "Once in a lifetime you read a magazine article that makes you want to bounce up out of your easychair and go running around to your neighbors, thrusting the magazine under their noses and saying: 'Read this! Read it now!' " [28]

To many reviewers, Hersey's unemotional prose was a distinct asset, heightening the impact of his account. "The calmness of the narrative," said anthropologist Ruth Benedict in the *Nation,* "throws into relief the nightmare magnitude of the [bomb's] destructive power." A few, however, were sharply critical. "Mr. Hersey's . . . excessively subdued effect . . . left the facts to speak for themselves, and they have not spoken loudly enough," wrote the anonymous reviewer in the (London) *Times Literary Supplement.* The living "occupy all the foreground, and the mounds of dead are only seen vaguely in the background." Dwight Macdonald, editor of the one-man journal of opinion *Politics,* attacked the book's "suave, toned-down, under-played kind of naturalism"—a stylistic flaw he blamed on both the *New Yorker's* influence and Hersey's defects as a writer: "no style, no ideas, no feelings of any intensity, and no eye for the one detail that imaginatively creates a whole." If only Hemingway could have written the account, he lamented! Ultimately, said Macdonald, *Hiroshima's* stylistic shortcomings sprang from a "moral deficiency" in Hersey's vision: "The 'little people' of Hiroshima whose sufferings Hersey records in antiseptic *New Yorker* prose might just as well be white mice, for all the pity, horror, or indignation the reader—or at least this reader—is made to feel for them." Perhaps, Macdonald concluded, "naturalism is no longer adequate, either esthetically or morally, to cope with the modern horrors."[29]

No such tentativeness moderated the negative judgment of novelist Mary McCarthy. Far from being an indictment of atomic war, McCarthy wrote, Hersey's piece actually diminished the atomic bomb by treating it as one would a natural castastrophe—a fire, flood, or earthquake—solely for its "human interest" value. To recreate the Hiroshima bombing by inter-viewing survivors, she said, was "an insipid falsification of the truth of atomic warfare. To have done the atom bomb justice, Mr. Hersey would have had to interview the dead." Hersey, she charged, had filled his bomb-scape "with busy little Japanese Methodists; he has made it familiar and safe, and so, in the final sense, boring." Hersey had also failed, she went on, to confront "the question of intention and guilt" or even to identify the source of the disaster that overwhelms his subjects. Hersey's failure, she said, reflected the inevitable constraints of the elite magazine for which he was writing. "Since the *New Yorker* has not, so far as we know, had a rupture with the government . . . it can only assimilate the atomic bomb to itself, to Westchester County, to smoked turkey, and the Hotel Carlyle."[30]

These criticisms offer a mélange of insightful and highly questionable judgments. It is doubtful, for example, that Hersey's failure to dwell on the United States as the source of the catastrophe means that the book must be relegated to the genre of hurricane and earthquake stories. Readers were only too aware of the source of the cataclysm. The *Christian Century* reviewer found it "excruciating" to identify himself, "as every American must, with the hand that tripped the bomb release that sent compound tragedy hurtling into the unsuspecting city."[31] Nor does even a cursory reading sustain McCarthy's charge that the focus on a few individual survivors obscures the magnitude of the disaster. No one could finish *Hiroshima* without confronting a catastrophe of horrendous proportions. "A hundred thousand people were killed by the atomic bomb," says Hersey on page 4, and this stark fact reverberates through the numerous references to vast devastation, piles of bodies, throngs of dazed and wounded survivors, and hordes of victims inundating shattered hospitals. "Of a hundred and fifty doctors in the city," he writes, "sixty-five were already dead and most of the rest were wounded. Of 1,780 nurses, 1,654 were dead or too badly hurt to work." [32]

If Hersey's technique underplayed some facets of the truth of Hiroshima, it cast others in sharper relief. He gave careful attention to the lingering effects of radiation exposure—still in 1946 a little-understood phenomenon and one that most early accounts barely touched upon. And he sensitively explored the varied psychological responses of people finding themselves still alive in the midst of mass death: the man who deliberately turned back toward the burning city, never to be seen again; the young mother who crouched motionless for hours, cradling her dead baby; the lassitude and passivity of many survivors; the guilt of others like the Methodist minister Kiyoshi Tanimoto, murmuring apologies to the dead and dying; the mingled fear and excitement of the children. As we have seen, the book ends with a matter-of-fact account by a ten-year-old survivor: "I saw a light. I was knocked to my little sister's sleeping place. . . . The neighbors were walking around burned and bleeding. . . . My girl friends Kikuki and Murakami . . . were looking for their mothers." [33]

Hersey was not writing in a cultural vacuum, or bringing first news of some unknown event. For a year, the obliteration of Hiroshima and Nagasaki had been the subject of enormous public attention. What one might call the panoramic background of an atomic attack—the sheets of flame, the mushroom cloud, the mass destruction, the instantaneous death of thousands —was already vividly present in the consciousness of Hersey's readers. But that unearthly panorama had been largely devoid of human content. Of course, the human reality was always implicit in the casualty statistics and the photographs of endless rubble. And sometimes it was made explicit: a March 1946 *Collier's* article, "What the Atomic Bomb Really Did," included graphic details such as dress fabric imprints burned into the skin of women survivors; in May 1946 the *Saturday Review* published a survivor's account that in some respects anticipated Hersey's. [34] More typically, however, the statistics of devastation and death were simply recited as prefatory to a plea for international control, civil defense, or some other cause. On a canvas whose broadbrush background scenes were already familiar, Hersey etched several vividly realized foreground figures. In isolation, his account does seem limited and incomplete; in the context of his readers' experience, its great impact becomes more understandable.

As for McCarthy's (inaccurate) complaint that the book is dominated by "busy little Japanese Methodists," this contains its own unpleasant whiff of racial, religious, and class prejudice. Commenting in 1976 on the Macdonald-McCarthy reaction to *Hiroshima,* critic John Leonard offered a harsh judgment:

> The literary intellectual tries to cope by appropriating the abyss for himself. . . . Not even the survivors of the unimaginable will be allowed to possess it. It is too big, too important, for them; they are irrelevancies. This, of course, isn't really coping; it is striking an attitude. It is, moreover, greedy and elitist, a kind of critical imperialism: my categories are better than your categories, and what do ordinary people know anyway, unworthy as they are of their tragedy? [35]

Macdonald's suggestion that Hersey's brand of naturalism was inadequate to the "modern horrors" was undeniably true. But would any style have been "adequate"? Hersey himself gives perhaps unconscious hints in *Hiroshima* of his awareness of this inadequacy. Whenever *books* are mentioned, it is as an absurd irrelevancy. The secretary Toshiko Sasaki nearly dies when the blast topples a bookcase over on her. "There in the tin factory, in the first moment of the atomic age," observes Hersey, "a human being was crushed by books." Another survivor recalls: "I started to bring my books along, and then I thought, 'This is no time for books.' " [36] Perhaps Hersey was merely the hapless target of Macdonald's larger realization that the "modern horrors" had undermined not just a particular style, but the entire literary enterprise.

John Hersey himself always contended that he had deliberately chosen the understated, reportorial style of *Hiroshima* not to diminish but to heighten the emotional impact. "The flat style was deliberate, and I still think I was right to adopt it," Hersey wrote early in 1985. "A high literary manner, or a show of passion, would have brought *me* into the story as a mediator; I wanted to avoid such mediation, so the reader's experience would be as direct as possible." Without making inflated literary claims, one may still credit his considerable achievement in transforming the subhuman "Japs" of wartime propaganda back into Japanese: human beings who loved their children, bled when they were cut, and spent their time in life's ordinary routines. Hersey achieved this by a journalist's eye for telling detail: the hand-lettered signs in the rubble with such queries as "Sister, where are you?"; the school girls singing to keep up their spirits as they lay pinned under a fence; the small boat on the shore of the Ota River, its five-man crew sprawled dead around it in various positions of work. [37]

Hiroshima may have left Dwight Macdonald cold, but others found the book profoundly affecting. "I had never thought of the people in the bombed cities as individuals," one young reader wrote. A veteran of the Manhattan Project found himself weeping as he read the book, and "filled with shame to recall the whoopee spirit" with which he had welcomed the bombing of

Hiroshima. The definitive response, perhaps, was that of the Catholic journal *America:*

> Despite the miles of print, and endless reels of photographs . . . it is this *New Yorker* report which most shudderingly brings home to the reader the utter horror of the atom bomb. . . . One curse of the modern world is that individuals are becoming . . . mere faceless ciphers. . . . We may escape the atom bomb because men with souls will realize that it dooms men with souls.

Hersey, in short, reminded Americans of what Rev. Tanimoto forced himself to repeat over and over as he aided hideously burned victims: "These are human beings." [38]

But what was the larger effect of this heightened awareness? Some have suggested, in the words of one historian, that Hersey "laid the groundwork" for a fundamental moral reassessment of the bomb decision and "contributed to a continuing dialogue over the justification for atomic warfare." Indeed, it is true that during the periods of intense engagement with the nuclear threat that have occurred at intervals since 1945, *Hiroshima* has always been rediscovered as a primary text. One must also acknowledge, however, that its immediate effect seems curiously ephemeral and elusive. Published just as a long cycle of diminished public engagement and activism on the nuclear front was beginning, it did little to reverse that trend. *Hiroshima* neither reenergized the international-control movement nor launched a vigorous public debate over the bombing of Hiroshima and Nagasaki. Of hundreds of letters in which readers reported how deeply Hersey's account had moved them, only a handful expressed feelings of guilt or a determination to work politically to prevent future atomic war. [39]

For the minority already politically engaged or disturbed by the moral questions surrounding the atomic bomb, Hersey's book intensified their commitment or concern. For most readers, however, it seems to have had no such effect. Providing a deeper understanding of Hiroshima's human meaning, it did not lead further. Indeed, for many, the very act of reading seems to have provided release from stressful and complex emotions. Like the funeral rituals that provide a socially sanctioned outlet for grief and mourning, *Hiroshima* may have enabled Americans of 1946 both to confront emotionally what had happened to the people of Hiroshima and Nagasaki and, in a psychological as well as a literal sense, to close the book on that episode. Perhaps in this sense, it was less a stimulus to action and reflection than a cathartic end point.

This effect was intensified by Hersey's emphasis on the victims' patience and resignation. This was war, he reported survivors as saying, and such things must be expected. He described the eerie silence of Hiroshima's

Asano Park where hundreds of the grievously injured quietly endured their suffering. (Describing *Hiroshima* as "a capsule of Japanese life" and "a source-book on Japanese behavior," anthropologist Ruth Benedict assured *Nation* readers that "patient fortitude" and a helpless passivity suggestive of "sheep without shepherds" was absolutely in character, reflecting behavior patterns "inculcated for centuries.") Here was implicit expiation for Americans. The Japanese themselves had accepted their fate. They did not rage against those who had dropped the bomb. One could empathize with their ordeal, even admire their stoic endurance, and still maintain one's personal moral distance.

Hiroshima is sometimes linked with other American books that had a profound cultural impact—Thomas Paine's *Common Sense,* Harriet Beecher Stowe's *Uncle Tom's Cabin,* Upton Sinclair's *The Jungle,* Rachel Carson's *Silent Spring.* In fact, it is very different. These other words were energizing, spurring readers to engagement and activism. One can trace their social and political ramifications in a quite direct fashion. *Hiroshima* was not such a ringing call to action. Its closest psychological parallel in American literature, perhaps, is to a classic from another war, *The Red Badge of Courage.* Like *Hiroshima,* Stephen Crane's novel was praised for its realism, its freedom from cant, and its delineation of the experiences and feelings of individuals overwhelmed by death and destruction. But, again like *Hiroshima,* it induces an almost elegiac mood. The reader is not stirred to action, but left with the feeling that he has gained a deeper understanding of war's human meaning, and through understanding, emotional release. The ending of *The Red Badge of Courage* might almost stand as an epigraph to *Hiroshima:*

> The youth smiled. . . . He had rid himself of the red sickness of battle. The sultry nightmare was in the past. He had been an animal blistered and sweating in the heat and pain of war. He turned now with a lover's thrust to images of tranquil skies, fresh meadows, cool brooks—an existence of soft and eternal peace.
>
> Over the river, a golden ray of sun came through the hosts of leaden rain clouds.

In the intense but strictly circumscribed engagement with the Hiroshima reality offered by John Hersey, it was as though Americans were saying: "We have now faced what we did. We have been told. We have experienced its full human horror. But we must get on with our lives. We can now put all that behind us." It is perhaps not irrelevant to note that, for all its success, *Hiroshima* was not the number one bestseller of 1946. That honor went to *The Egg and I,* a lighthearted comedy about life on an Oregon chicken farm.

18

Atomic Weapons and Judeo-Christian Ethics: The Discourse Begins

The atomic age was opened with prayer. A chaplain on Tinian Island invoked divine blessing on the crew of the *Enola Gay* as it took off for Japan. In his initial announcement, President Truman intoned: "We thank God that it has come to us, instead of to our enemies; and we pray that He may guide us to use it in His ways and for His purposes."[1]

Such benedictions were undoubtedly intended to enfold atomic weapons within America's moral and religious tradition, and, in truth, for some the bomb posed no ethical difficulties: God had given America the secret, and its further development would reflect the divine plan. Had not President Truman himself, after all, offered just such assurance? As the rhymester Edgar Guest put it in September 1945:

> The power to blow all things to dust
> Was kept for people God could trust,
> And granted unto them alone,
> That evil might be overthrown.

Among the nation's newspapers, the Hearst press fully shared Truman's confidence that American military strategy and God's cosmic plan coincided. "Divine providence," the *New York Journal American* assured its readers, "has made the United States the custodian of the secret of atomic energy as a weapon of war."[2]

This conviction that the Manhattan Project represented "a direct intervention of the Almighty in human affairs" (as a *Life* reader put it) emerges in many post-Hiroshima letters to newspapers and magazines. A *Time* subscriber expressed gratitude for "this blessed bomb." A serviceman at Camp Shelby, Mississippi, wrote *Life:* "Thank God for the atomic bomb, which has proved so essential and valuable already." From Shawano, Wisconsin, Mrs. Winfred Bossell wrote the *Milwaukee Journal:* "God, our Father, is still in His Heaven. And just as in ages past He made the sun to stand still, so also has He stayed the hand of the war devil. In the perfecting of the atomic bomb, I feel all is well with the world, just so long as it stays in the hands of the people who believe in and practice the principles of Christ."[3]

In the same spirit, others anticipated striking moral advances in the atomic age. It offered an unparalleled opportunity for "spiritual creativeness" and an enhancement of "life-elevating ideals," promised a University of Wisconsin philosophy professor. The business magazine *Fortune*, discussing the impact of the bomb early in 1946, predicted a "religious awakening" and a "reaffirmation of Christian values" that would sweep away the secularism, materialism, and political radicalism of the prewar years.[4]

Arthur H. Compton, a leading Protestant layman, was particularly sanguine in discussing the bomb's ethical and theological implications. Exploring "The Moral Meaning of the Atomic Bomb" in a 1946 symposium organized by the Episcopal Church, Compton proclaimed: "Atomic power is ours, and who can deny that it was God's will that we should have it?" In the beginning, Compton suggested, human development was in God's hands alone. But then dawned the age of science, and henceforth man became God's partner, "sharing with Him the great task of making life what they wanted it to be." "With the growth of human knowledge more and more of the responsibility is being shifted to man's shoulders." The discovery of atomic fission represented simply "one further step in this transfer of authority." America had thus far used its divinely bestowed power properly, Compton went on, to win a war fought to assure the freedom of all people "to become the children of God." Unquestionably, the future held grave risks. A "rapid growth in moral stature" was essential to survival in the nuclear era, and it was "yet too early to say whether the moral historian, if there be one a thousand years hence, will record the use of the atomic bomb as the work of the world's guardian angel or . . . of the devil bent on man's destruction." But, for Compton, confidence in God's overarching plan won out: Mankind would meet the challenge and "advance in human justice, sympathy, and understanding." From the struggle to master this new power, "inevitably there must result a growth of the human spirit."[5]

Few who grappled with the bomb's ethical implications found the matter either quite as hopeful or as clear-cut as did Arthur Compton. Confusing the issue for many was the fact that well before August 1945, "total war" had come to include the terror bombing of civilian populations. German planes aiding Franco bombed the Spanish town of Guernica in 1937. The Japanese did the same in China, and in 1940 the German *Luftwaffe* conducted massive raids against British shipping, military installations— and cities. At first vehemently condemning such raids, the Allied governments soon responded in kind. Early in the war, the RAF conducted massed raids against Cologne, Bremen, Hamburg, and other German cities. In a well-known 1942 directive, British bombers were explicitly instructed to target working-class neighborhoods, with a goal of rendering one-third of the German population homeless by 1943. In 1944, German V-1 and V-2 rockets began to fall on London and other English cities. American bombing was initially limited to precision attacks on military targets, but this policy was never strictly observed in practice, and by early 1945 it had for all practical purposes been abandoned. In February 1945, some 25,000 Berliners died in a single raid. This was followed by the fire-bombing of Hamburg and beautiful, refugee-swollen Dresden, the latter an Anglo-American operation memorialized by novelist Kurt Vonnegut in *Slaughterhouse-Five*. The destruction at Hamburg equaled that of two Hiroshima-type bombs. By the end of February, American newspapers were proclaiming as new air force policy: "the deliberate terror bombing of the great German population centers." In Operation CLARION, launched at this time, small towns and villages were added to the target lists to spread demoralization through the entire German population.

In the Pacific, large-scale terror bombing was introduced in March 1945. Under the command of General Curtis LeMay, armadas of up to a thousand low-flying B-29s roamed the Japanese islands almost at will, raining incendiary bombs on Tokyo, Nagoya, Kobe, Osaka, Yokohama, and other cities. Scores of thousands perished in the ensuing fire storms. Some were incinerated by walls of flame that engulfed entire sections of Japan's tinderbox cities; others were asphyxiated as all available oxygen was consumed. By early August 1945, an estimated 190,000 Japanese civilians had died in these raids. A single air attack on Tokyo on the night of March 9–10, 1945, killed over one hundred thousand people.[6]

These raids were enthusiastically welcomed by the American press. Magazines from *Collier's* to *Harper's* criticized the restraints of the early war years and demanded *more* bombing of civilian targets. "It seems brutal to be talking about burning homes," conceded *Harper's* in 1943; "But we are engaged in a life and death struggle for national survival, and we are therefore justified in taking any action which will save the lives of American soldiers and sailors." The March 1945 raid on Tokyo was a "dream come true," *Time* said, showing that "properly kindled, Japanese cities will burn like autumn leaves."[7]

Only a few religious publications questioned terror bombing on moral grounds. *Christian Century* consistently deplored the practice, though viewing it as an unavoidable part of "the hell of war." "It appalls us to say this, but it must be said," wrote *Christian Century* in April 1943: "bombing, if it contributes to victory, is here to stay as long as war lasts. Those who merely raise the moral and humanitarian questions are talking in a vacuum."[8] A similar ambivalence is evident in a 1944 report of the Calhoun Commission, the Federal Council of Churches committee whose 1946 report on atomic warfare we have already noted. In its 1944 report, responding to such atrocities as the Nazis' reprisal execution of all the males in the Czech village of Lidice, the Calhoun Commission denounced the killing or torturing of prisoners or hostages as well as "the massacre of civilian populations." "The Church cannot acquiesce," it said, "in the view that modern war may properly, even in case of extreme peril to nation, church, or culture, become total war." The majority, however, supported "all needful measures" necessary to defeat the Axis powers, while "some"—the number was not specified in the report—explicitly endorsed the obliteration bombing of cities as "essential to the successful conduct of a war that is itself justified."[9]

The far more explicitly condemnatory Catholic reaction to the bombing of civilians was rooted in the Augustinian doctrine of the "just war," which held that war, though intrinsically evil and contrary to God's will, could be justified morally if fought for a just cause and circumscribed by clearly defined moral restraints, including the duty of belligerents to spare civilians. The "total-war" strategy that emerged after 1942 largely erased the combatant-noncombatant distinction and thus directly challenged the just-war dogma. In a series of wartime pronouncements, Pope Pius XII rejected the total-war mentality and even questioned whether modern warfare could still be seen as "an apt and proportionate means of solving international conflicts." While the pope's condemnation had little effect on the course of the war or even, perhaps, on the views of the average American Catholic, it did influence the major Catholic journals of opinion. *Commonweal* rejected terror bombing in 1942 as "indefensible morally, no matter how efficacious militarily," while *America, Catholic World,* and the Jesuit *Theological Studies* echoed the same conclusion.[10]

The issue briefly entered the larger arena of public discourse in March 1944, when an American pacifist organization, the Fellowship of Reconciliation, published "Massacre by Bombing" by the English pacifist Vera Brittain, together with an endorsement by twenty-eight American clergymen and others, including Harry Emerson Fosdick and former *Nation* editor Oswald Garrison Villard. Brittain's tract won qualified support in parts of the religious press. *Christian Century* urged that it be read, though again questioning the value of such moral protests in wartime. *Commonweal* reprinted it, noting that pacifists should not be forced to bear the entire burden of challenging the morality of terror bombing. Many critics, however, accused Vera Brittain and her American supporters of aiding the enemy. Among the most vitriolic were Protestant evangelicals. "We protestants repudiate the un-American pacifism of Dr. Fosdick and associates," declared Harold J. Ockenga of the National Association of Evangelicals. "God has given us the weapons." added Presbyterian fundamentalist Carl McIntyre, "let us use them."[11]

The initial ethical confrontation with the atomic bomb, then, occurred in the context of a war in which the terror bombing of civilians had already become accepted practice. As *Life* observed on August 20, 1945, "The very concept of strategic bombing . . . led straight to Hiroshima." The *Central Christian Advocate,* in its August 1945 editorial protesting the atomic bomb, commented: "The increasing frightfulness of the war has stupefied the religious sensibilities of people. . . . The whole thing has sunk into a slough of brutality and cruelty." J. Robert Oppenheimer, in his characteristically elliptical fashion, made the same point in *One World or None:*

> Nothing can be effectively revolutionary that is not deeply rooted in human experience. If, as I believe, the release of atomic energy is in fact revolutionary, it is surely not because its promise of rapid technological change, its realization of fantastic powers of destruction, have no analogue in our late history. It is precisely because that history has so well prepared us to understand what these things may mean.

Years later, Philip Morrison put it more simply as he recalled the mood at Los Alamos: "From our point of view, the atomic bomb was not a discontinuity. We were just carrying on more of the same, only it was much cheaper. . . . We had already destroyed sixty-six [cities]; what's two more?" [12]*

Having accepted terror bombing as essential to the nation's purposes, most Americans seem to have viewed the atomic bomb as a fearsome but ethically indistinguishable technical means to a legitimate strategic purpose. As the *Chicago Sun* put it on August 9, 1945: "There is no scale of values which makes a TNT explosion right and a uranium explosion wrong." The *New Republic,* dismissing moral arguments against the atomic bomb, commented: "It is objected that such a weapon cannot be loosed without murdering thousands of non-combatants, including women and children. The same objection, however, applied with equal force to the strategic bombing of enemy cities." Modern war was "wholesale slaughter," declared Judge Frank Tyrrell in his September 1945 address to the Beverly Hills bar association; "What difference to those killed, whether they are annihilated by big guns, blockbusters, or atomic bombs? Indeed, the last may be the most merciful." Responding to those raising ethical objections to the atomic

---

* The Catholic moralist William V. O'Brien has offered an interesting observation bearing on this point. "It is now clear," he wrote in 1967, "that we were laying the basis in World War II for a major part of our present moral dilemma. In World War II the United States seems to have accepted the proposition that *all* means are permissible in total conflict with a truly evil enemy. This may turn out to be the most tragic of the many bitter legacies left us by the Axis powers—an adversary so patently evil that the habit of unlimited response was inordinately encouraged." The German Lutheran theologian Dieter Georgi, who as a fifteen-year-old boy lived through the fire-bombing of Dresden, has recently made the same point: "The most demonic success of Hitler was his ability to Hitlerize his enemies, sealed by two atomic bombs." [13]

bomb, Vannevar Bush wrote in 1949: "The moral question was hardly raised regarding the fire raids, yet that question is substantially identical in the two cases."[14]

The same point was made by readers who disagreed with *Christian Century*'s criticism of the atomic bombing of Japan. "Wars are not fought . . . with pea-shooters, but with whatever weapons the wit of man can devise," insisted a tough-minded correspondent from California; "It was no worse to kill a hundred thousand [Japanese] in a split second than to kill the same number over a period of weeks by a lingering death."[15]

Responding editorially to these letters, *Christian Century* agreed that no essential moral distinction could be drawn between the atomic bomb and other weapons of mass destruction. Ignoring the combatant-noncombatant distinction in the just-war tradition, *Christian Century* declared:

> In the regime of war—that is, in the regime ruled by military necessity —the bombing of cities, whether by an atomic bomb or by B-29s, is on the same plane as the killing of an enemy soldier with a rifle. . . . War has no moral character. When a nation commits its destiny to the arbitrament of sheer might, it abandons all moral constraints.[16]

Essentially the same argument was advanced by Yale strategist William Liscum Borden in his 1946 work *There Will Be No Time*. War is war, insisted Borden, and the technical means a moral irrelevance. "All weapons are alike in that they destroy human life. . . . Hiroshima furnishes novelty only in the rapidity of its destruction." Dismissing the notion that any "special horror" attached to the atomic bomb, he insisted that its use was consistent with the evolution of Allied bombing strategy from military targets to "the indiscriminate phase." Future decisions to use atomic weapons, like the decision of 1945, would be based strictly on military considerations; the ethical gloss was mere rationalization: "The first users of the nuclear bomb were Christians and democrats. They used it because it was to their advantage. They excused it on the grounds that it shortened the war and thus saved thousands of lives on both sides. This logic is unimpeachable, and a future aggressor will probably be pleased to borrow it." All talk of "ethical limitation on war" was pointless, Borden said, and merely illustrated "the extreme to which responsible thinkers" were being driven "in search of a formula for optimism." In Borden's dark vision, another world war was almost certain, and when it came atomic bombs would be used "in any way, however terrible, which offers profit to the user."

Borden further agreed that the soldier-civilian distinction had for all practical purposes disappeared. In Japan, for example, "the homefront worker was no less a soldier than the man who carried a gun. Even the mothers of Hiroshima were caretakers of children who would soon fill a place on the firing line. If taking human life is ever morally defensible, then the presence or absence of a uniform made no substantial difference." The urgent task, in Borden's view, was civil defense; those paralyzed by "moral revulsion at man's inhumanity to man" were simply "distracting attention" from this challenge. [17]

Carrying the argument further, some insisted that the crucial distinction, ethically, was not between one weapon or another, but the motive for the use of any weapon. John Dewey had taken this position as long ago as 1917, in justifying his support for America's intervention in World War I, and it was updated now in 1945. From a moral perspective, Max Lerner argued, the key distinction was "not so much the mechanism as the spirit in which it is used." If employed with "hatred and sadism," he went on, "it brutalizes the user," but if used, "as I think we used the atom bomb, to end the war quickly, and with a loathing for its needs, then the heart that uses it may be salvageable." The author of a 1947 article on the ethics of the atomic bomb in *Military Affairs* made the same case: "We can kill in war and still disapprove of killing. This is the necessary compromise we have to make for the survival of our civilization." [18]

But if some found nothing novel in the ethical issues posed by the bomb, for others it did raise important new issues, or at least infused with new urgency the ongoing discourse over the morality of modern war. Even if the atomic bomb raised "no new moral questions," observed Haverford College physicist Richard Sutton in 1946, "many old problems are thrown into high relief by the threat of its devastating power." The ethical issues of modern war would be profound even "if Hiroshima were standing, and Nagasaki as busy a center of commerce as ever," acknowledged the British Catholic churchman Ronald Knox, but he nevertheless insisted on the bomb's unique moral significance as "a kind of signature tune" to the five-year "orgy of destruction" and "a symbol which has struck the public imagination and deepened its sense of doom." *Catholic World* summed up its position in a terse common-sense observation: when dealing with military methods that violated just-war principles, "The more destructive the instrument, the more grievous the crime." [19]

While some used the earlier terror bombings to legitimize the atomic bomb, others drew the opposite lesson, concluding that any strategy that could justify Hiroshima and Nagasaki must itself be reexamined. "Many consciences have winced at the indiscriminate bombing our planes have conducted over Japan," a Pennsylvania Methodist pastor wrote *Christian Century,* "but the [atomic bomb] leaves no room for conscience at all." "We Christians have been too slow, too afraid, perhaps," agreed a minister from Orono, Maine, "to speak and act conscientiously as the war has progressed in its downward spiral of scientific ghastliness." [20]

This conclusion was supported by at least a few influential opinion-molders. "We started the war in horror over the brutality of the Germans," observed Raymond Gram Swing in an April 1946 broadcast. "We ended it on a plane of conduct indistinguishable from theirs, insofar as the use of air power was concerned." More disturbing still, continued Swing, the change in moral outlook seemed permanent. "Since the end of the war there has been no snapping back to the prewar attitude of condemning a war waged against civilians, no nationwide or worldwide campaign to restore the thinking of past times."

Reviewing the stages that had led up to the "indescribable horror" of Hiroshima, David Lawrence, in an August 1945 *U.S. News and World Report* editorial, similarly dated the nation's loss of moral bearings much earlier. America had entered the war professing horror at the Nazi murder of civilians in Rotterdam and Warsaw, he recalled, but was soon itself "bombing men, women, and children in Germany." To Reinhold Niebuhr, the entire total-war mentality, including the insistence on unconditional surrender, that lay behind the dropping of the atomic bomb, reflected both a "nauseous self-righteousness" and the vain hope that from utter ruin "a more ideal social structure" could emerge.[21]

Moral revulsion against the bomb sometimes surfaced in unexpected quarters, including not only John Foster Dulles but also former President Herbert Hoover. "Despite any sophistries," Hoover told a conference of newspaper editors in September 1945, America had introduced to the world a weapon whose only conceivable purpose was "to kill women, children, and civilian men of whole cities." Moral queasiness occasionally overtook David Lilienthal as well, though as usual he kept his darker moods to himself. Lilienthal in a December 1947 diary entry brooded about the bomb's effect on moral sensibilities and reviewed the long process by which war had evolved from a kind of game—deadly, but with recognized rules—to indiscriminate slaughter culminating in the atomic bomb. "The fences are gone," he concluded bleakly, "and it was we, the civilized, who have pushed standardless conduct to its ultimate."

In 1948, Lilienthal even held several informal meetings with Bishop G. Bromley Oxnam to discuss the "moral problems of mass weapons." At one point the two men agreed on the need for an AEC advisory committee to address the issue in a more formal way. Lilienthal soon backed off, however, informing Oxnam early in 1949 that the idea had met with opposition from within the commission.[22]

In a remarkable 1948 essay, Lewis Mumford lashed out at both the "genocide" that had now become accepted American practice and the hypocrisy of those who euphemistically termed it "total war." The only novelty of the atomic bomb, he said, was that it "wrapped up this method of extermination in a neater, and possibly cheaper package." Mumford was appalled not only by the "moral nihilism" that had permitted the descent into mass extermination, but by the public's apathetic response: "It is as if the Secretary of Agriculture had authorized the sale of human meat during the meat shortage, and everyone had accepted cannibalism in daily practice as a clever dodge for reducing the cost of living." It was not the atomic bomb alone, he concluded, "but our willingness to use any instruments of genocide, that constitutes the all-enveloping danger."[23]

Pacifists, of course, strongly supported the view that the atomic bomb offered final proof of modern war's fundamental immorality. If accepting war meant accepting the atomic bomb, then so much the worse for war. The atomic bomb's legacy of "charred bodies and . . . pulverized cities," said the Women's International League for Peace and Freedom, in a statement echoed by many pacifist groups, symbolized America's "shattered moral authority"and the bankruptcy of war itself.[24]

The most powerful statement of the post-Hiroshima case for pacifism was A. J. Muste's *Not by Might* (1947). Dutch-born Muste grew up in Grand Rapids, Michigan, where he trained for the Reformed church ministry. Absorbed by labor activism and Trotskyite politics in the 1920s and early 1930s, he grew disillusioned with Marxism and by 1935 had returned to the Christian pacifism he had initially espoused during World War I. In 1940, he became national secretary of the Fellowship of Reconciliation. (Already in his sixties when World War II ended, he would survive to play a vigorous role in the 1960s antiwar movement.)

Muste minced no words in *Not by Might*. "If Dachau was a crime," he wrote, "Hiroshima is a crime." The nadir of an increasingly brutalized war, this "ultimate, atomic atrocity" had exposed America's moral pretensions, spawned a climate of fear, and breached the final barriers separating warfare from mass murder. Atomic war was "sin of the most hideous kind," he insisted, but still only an aspect of the sin of war itself. We must ponder the meaning of the bomb "steadfastly [and] relentlessly," he wrote, "until it has burned its way into our consciousness and in doing so has burned away all illusions about war, including World War II." Not fear (as many activists hoped), but the conviction of sin was the only hope of preventing atomic holocaust. Even before political remedies must come "moral conversion and spiritual rebirth": "People who know no peace in their own spirits do not really want peace in the outward order and their fitful and distracted efforts to achieve it will be constantly thwarted. . . . The reordering of our lives and of society, the establishment of control over atomic energy, must begin with the individual spirit."

Muste sharply challenged the so-called "Christian realist" position, most fully articulated by Reinhold Niebuhr in *Moral Man and Immoral Society* (1935), which held that the Christian ethic of love, while the standard for individuals, was inapplicable to nations and social classes. Since considerations of power, calculation, and self-interest would prevail among nations and classes while human history continued, Niebuhr had argued, it was a matter of moral indifference whether the struggle of oppressed peoples and exploited social classes were pursued through politics or revolutionary violence.

Not so, said Muste. "The notion that there is or can be one law for the individual and another for society," he insisted, found "no support whatever in the Jewish-Christian scriptures." Readily conceding that "violence and the struggle for power are indubitable facts," he denied that they must therefore be "accepted . . . as normative for Christian thought and practice." On the contrary, he insisted, "they are the great taproot of evil, and must be radically dealt with." To Niebuhr, Muste went on, "the tensions between the historical and the transcendent" meant that one's social and political choices were usually contingent and relative, lacking an absolute moral dimension. Yet the very concept of "tension," Muste insisted, acknowledged the continual claim of the transcendent and further implied that, at certain historical moments, that claim becomes absolute and "the Church must take a final stand." Such a point had been reached in the slavery controversy, he said, and now it had come in the Church's long struggle over war. In the shadow of the atomic bomb, the ancient Christian compromise with war as sometimes "the lesser of two evils" was simply no longer tenable. "The contention that something could be more evil than a total, global, atomic war," he wrote, "seems so obviously absurd that we do not need to spend time discussing it."

Invoking the war resisters of earlier days—Thoreau during the Mexican War, Randolph Bourne during World War I—Muste called for a moral rebellion not only against the atomic bomb, but against war itself. Only the radical pacifist position—"better to suffer than to inflict suffering . . . to be killed than to kill, to have atomic bombs dropped on you than to drop them on others"—he said, offered an alternative to complicity in ultimate atomic destruction. He concluded with a plea to religious leaders and opinion-molders: "Men are waiting to have the Church tell them in Christ's name whether making atomic war is right or wrong. Simply that. The ethical evaluation of atomic bombing is what they ask for. Not the effects of being bombed, but whether it is right or a sin to bomb others. . . . Any hesitation, any qualification they will take as conclusive evidence that nobody knows; relativity rules; therefore, anything goes." [25]

Muste's eloquent manifesto posed profound dilemmas for the nonpacifist Christian who held with the just-war tradition that some conflicts were morally justifiable, and who believed that World War II fell in this category, but who recognized that it had ended in a orgy of killing almost beyond restraint or limit, culminating in the ultimate horror of Hiroshima and Nagasaki. For such a person was offered an agonizing choice: accept total war in all its horror, including the atomic bomb, or embrace a pacifist position that since the third century had existed on the fringes of mainstream Christian thought. One might admire the Quakers and other "peace churches" and respect the witness of individual pacifists like Muste, yet still draw back from committing oneself to their radical position. But in the other direction lay Coventry, Hamburg, Dresden, Tokyo—and Hiroshima.

The issue was posed starkly by a German Jesuit, John A. Siemes, himself a Hiroshima survivor. A professor of philosophy at Tokyo's Catholic University, Siemes with his fellow Jesuits had been transferred to the supposed greater safety of a monastery near Hiroshima. Here he witnessed the bomb blast and ministered to hundreds of victims. In an account published in the United States in May 1946, Siemes concluded:

> We have discussed among ourselves the ethics of the use of the bomb. Some consider it in the same category as poison gas and were against its use on a civil population. Others were of the view that in total war, as carried on in Japan, there was no difference between civilians and soldiers, and that the bomb itself was an effective force tending to end the bloodshed, warning Japan to surrender and thus to avoid total destruction. It seems logical to me that he who supports total war in principle cannot complain of war against civilians. The crux of the matter is whether total war in its present form is justifiable, even when it serves a just purpose. Does it not have material and spiritual evil as its consequences which far exceed whatever the good that might result? When will our moralists give us a clear answer to this question? [26]

Some attempted to escape this moral conundrum by a breathtaking leap of faith: so horrible was the atomic bomb, they reasoned, that mankind would surely renounce war forever. Muste's pacifistic millennium would be achieved, but effortlessly, almost automatically. Moral revulsion against atomic weapons would transform the human race's ethical consciousness, providing the impetus for a new order of peace and harmony. A "moral transformation . . . no matter how arduous," wrote a contributor to the *American Scholar*'s 1946 symposium on the atomic bomb, was "the only course that remains to us." Even if the atomic threat did not bring universal peace, it might at least revitalize the battered principle of limited war. In light of the bomb, wrote David Lawrence, the nations must again assert "the rule of conscience" in war and confine hostilities to "strictly military installations." Of those who discerned the glow of world spiritual regeneration in the mushroom-shaped clouds over Japan, few described their vision more fervently than the editor of the *Ladies' Home Journal*, who in January 1946 discussed the bomb's meaning in explicitly Christian imagery:

> The atomic bomb, born in hate, has been released in a world appalled at the destruction which awaits us all unless we learn to love one

another. . . . Out of the crucifixion of those who died at Nagasaki and Hiroshima (as well as of our own men who died in Europe and the Pacific) may come the final redemption of the world.[27]

What of the American Jewish response to the bomb? Like other Americans, Jews welcomed Japan's surrender and many hailed the atomic bomb as the means to that end. The V-J Day statement of the head of the Jewish War Veterans echoed countless other end-of-the-war pronouncements: the atomic bomb, he said, had "hastened the end of the war and saved the lives of an untold number of men of the United States."[28]

Similarly, many editorials in Jewish periodicals reiterated the prevailing formula of 1945–1946: atomic energy could be used for good or evil, and the great challenge was to choose wisely. "As Jews," wrote editor Elliott E. Cohen in the inaugural issue of the Jewish magazine of opinion *Commentary* in November 1945, "we share with the rest of humanity the deep unease of breathing air almost visibly clotted with fantastic utopias or unimaginable cataclysms." A Michigan rabbi expressed the formula in a sermon written in the style of a divine prophecy. After describing the wonders of the atom's peacetime uses, the Lord foresees the consequences of atomic war: "All the living will be blotted out, and I will have before me the endless silence of millennium after millennium in which to try to forget My offspring, man, to whom I gave a portion of My spirit, and whom I did really love." With the discovery of atomic energy, this sermon concluded, humanity was at the end of its childhood and poised at the edge of adulthood—the moment of the Bar Mitzvah: "This is the day of your majority, O My son—Man! You are an infant no more. You have come to man's estate. Today, I set before you life and death, the blessing and the curse. Choose life, I beseech you, choose life!"[29]

In this spirit, the American Jewish leadership strongly supported the movement for international control. Both the Synagogue Council of America and the Central Conference of American Rabbis endorsed the Acheson-Lilienthal plan in 1946. The *National Jewish Monthly,* the magazine of the B'nai B'rith service organization, observed of Jewish scientists who were taking a leading role in the international-control movement: "We don't know how Jewish they are in the formal sense, but in their courageous insistence for the beneficent control of the monster they helped to create they are expressing the ethical ideals of Judaism, just as in the same way the non-Jewish scientists are expressing Christianity."[30]

In the immediate aftermath of Hiroshima, a number of Jewish periodicals noted with pride the many Jewish scientists involved in bringing the bomb into being. "FOUR JEWISH REFUGEE SCIENTISTS LAUDED FOR THEIR CONTRIBUTION TO THE DISCOVERY OF ATOMIC BOMB," headlined the *Jewish Advocate* of Boston on August 9, 1945. "Thanks in good measure to the genius of Jewish scientists," wrote Bernard Postal in the journal *Liberal Judaism,* "the world has entered a new epoch of civilization which history will know as the atomic era." Not only were many of the atomic scientists Jewish, Postal went on, but so was the Manhattan Project reporter William L. Laurence and even a crew member of the Nagasaki plane: Sgt. Abe Spitzer of the Bronx.[31]

The prominent role of Jewish scientists in the atomic-bomb project, some suggested, would help wipe out anti-Semitism in America. "The credit of Jewish refugees in this country has reached a new high since the discovery of the atom bomb," wrote a columnist in the *Jewish Record* of St. Louis on August 17, 1945. "Now even the most rabid 'refugee-haters' admit that the United States has benefited greatly from the fact that many of the Jewish scientists who were driven out by the Nazis from Germany came to this country." This fact, he predicted, would "add to the credit of the Jewish refugees as well as to the glory of the Jews in the United States."[32]

But even at the moment of victory, one finds among at least some Jewish religious leaders a significant undercurrent of ethical queasiness and apprehension. "Mankind should join us Jews in chanting fervent prayers of atonement," proclaimed Rabbi Beryl D. Cohon of Temple Sinai, Brookline, Massachusetts, in his Yom Kippur sermon of September 1945. "We have drawn from the infinite storehouse of God's world enormous powers, and have converted them into instruments of destruction. . . . Unless we discipline the revelation of atomic power by the revelation of Mount Sinai, making it subservient to the Moral Law, we shall . . . reduce our earth to a dead cinder spinning in space in infinite futility."[33]

Mordecai Kaplan, editor of the respected Jewish religious periodical *The Reconstructionist,* addressing the issue of the atomic bomb in October 1945, acknowledged that it seemed to forebode "a tragic reversion to chaos, an uncreating of the moral order," but took comfort in those moments in Jewish history when disaster came as a retribution for sin but also served to "restore the moral balance." Perhaps the bomb, too, he speculated, would "recall mankind to its senses, and . . . clear the way for the eventual establishment of God's kingdom on earth." Specifically, if it hastened the arrival of an international order "founded on justice and peace," it could "prove the salvation of mankind." In any event, there was no turning back. An inevitable condition of growth was greater danger: the infant confronts more hazards than the fetus in the womb. Atomic menace was the price of the enlargement of human knowledge.[34]

In a December 1945 editorial in *The Jewish Spectator,* an independent journal of opinion based in New York, editor Trude Weiss-Rosmarin cautioned Jews against taking excessive pride in the Jewish atomic scientists: "Frankly, we cannot see what all this jubilation is about. . . . The mathematical genius of Einstein and Lise Meitner is in no way related to their

Jewishness." Rather than boasting of nuclear physicists who happened to be Jewish, she went on, Jews should reassert their religious and ethical tradition, which had now become more timely than ever:

> Jewish ethics must become the norm of national and international human relations if we are to save ourselves from perishing by the weapons which our own hands have forged. . . . Now if ever Judaism is called upon to face the task which is the meaning of its existence and survival: to perfect the mundane sphere in accordance with the Divine attributes of goodness, justice and peace.

Offering a specific example of her point, Weiss-Rosmarin noted that the ancient Jewish prohibition against "graven images" condemned not only idol worship, but any value system that would place material achievement above spiritual and moral concerns. This ethical principle, she insisted, had taken on a compelling new urgency at a moment when so many were in awe of the stunning technological achievement that had unlocked the secret of the atom.[35]

Overshadowing the Jewish response to the atomic bomb was the destruction of European Jewry, the full horror of which was unfolding just as the reports of Hiroshima and Nagasaki arrived. "When the news of the atomic bomb first came to my neighborhood," wrote another columnist in the *Jewish Record* on August 17, 1945, "the general reaction of my friends was—wouldn't it have been fine if this had happened before, so that it might have been used on the Nazis." From this perspective, the prominence of refugees from Nazism in the bomb project took on added resonance. Without this forced brain drain, this columnist continued, the bomb might have ended in Hitler's hands "and half of the world would have been exterminated instead of merely the Jews of Europe." Discerning a divine pattern in these events, he concluded:

> The world was saved by the fact that Germany lost through the Nazi persecution of Jews, her principal workers in the field of atomic energy. . . . How deeply the master race had to pay for driving out the inferior Jews! . . . God did not want the Germans to find the secret of the bomb so he caused the Jewish scientists to shake the dust of Germany off their feet.

It was a supreme "irony of history," agreed Bernard Postal, that the "anti-Jewish crusade" of Hitler and Mussolini "presented the United States with some of the best scientific brains of Germany, Italy, and the occupied countries" and thereby "enabled American and British science to outpace all German efforts and to usher in the atomic era."[36]

For many Jews (as for many non-Jews), the overriding ethical issue to emerge from World War II was not the means used to defeat Hitler or his Japanese ally, but how such a phenomenon as nazism could have arisen in the first place, what it boded for the future, and how Hitler's brutal assault on the Judeo-Christian ethical tradition could be repaired. All hope that ethical restraint could prevent atomic war was undermined, said the *National Jewish Monthly* in October 1945, by nazism's demonstration of the fragility of such restraint, and by awareness of "the holocaust Hitler brought upon the world" even without such cosmic weapons.[37]

In his November 1945 *Commentary* editorial, Elliot Cohen acknowledged that the atomic bomb was "shadowing every moment of our thinking and feeling" and agreed with "ten thousand editorial writers the world over" that the bomb represented mankind's ultimate ethical challenge. But for Jews, he went on, reflection about the atomic future was inevitably influenced by their particular awareness of how mankind had responded to that other ethical challenge: the Jewish Holocaust. The Jews of Europe, he reminded his readers, were "not killed in battle, not massacred in hot blood, but slaughtered like cattle, subjected to every physical indignity—*processed.*" And what was the response? "There were men and women in other lands who raised their voices in protest, who lent helping hands. But . . . the voices were not many, the hands were not many. There was a strange passivity the world over in the face of this colossal latter-day massacre of innocents." The anti-Semitism and other forms of prejudice that had spawned the Holocaust were far from dead, Cohen concluded, and if again unleashed could "wreak destruction comparable to the atomic bomb itself." To reaffirm "the sanctity of the human person" and eradicate the malignity that had given rise to Nazism, he suggested, posed an ethical challenge at least as great as that of the atomic bomb.[38]

Revealing in this context is a resolution adopted by the Central Conference of American Rabbis in 1949 in support of a United Nations convention against genocide: "Our generation has seen the Divine image in man degraded and desecrated by furnace and gas chamber. Every believer in the Sovereignty of God, in the oneness of humanity, must feel a personal sense of shame and guilt at the mass slaughter of the innocent. This can never be fully erased from our consciousness. Wholesale extermination of human beings must be forever ended."[39] With its imagery of furnaces and gas chambers, this powerful and eloquent statement evoked only the Holocaust. It did not confront (except perhaps implicitly) the other instrument of efficient and indiscriminate extermination to emerge from World War II: the atomic bomb.

What one sees in this early postwar period is a divergence in the ethical response to the two events of World War II that did most to undermine humanity's fragile ethical tradition: the mass extermination of the Jews, and the mass extermination of city dwellers, culminating at Hiroshima and Nagasaki. This divergence would widen in the years that followed. Some ethical writers addressed the Jewish Holocaust; others addressed the potential world holocaust of atomic war or the actual holocaust visited upon two Japanese cities in August 1945 and other cities earlier. Only a few like Dwight Macdonald and John Hersey (whose 1950 novel *The Wall* dealt with the uprising of the Jews of Warsaw's ghetto) bridged the gap that had quickly opened between the two issues.

Can the gap be bridged? Robert Jay Lifton has moved from writing about Hiroshima and nuclear numbing to examining another form of numbing: that of the German doctors who conducted the notorious "medical experiments" in the Nazi death camps. From the other side, the remarkable Japanese artists Iri and Toshi Maruki have moved from powerful murals of the Hiroshima horror to equally powerful murals of the Auschwitz horror. Perhaps after the passage of four decades, we are ready for a more comprehensive understanding of the moral disintegration wrought by World War II—an understanding that will at least consider in the same context (without necessarily equating) the atomic bomb and the gas chamber.

For Protestants, the ethical dilemma posed by the atomic bomb is perhaps best illustrated in the 1946 report of the Calhoun Commission. As we saw in the previous chapter, the commissioners eloquently and unanimously condemned the bombing of Hiroshima and Nagasaki. They even retracted their somewhat ambiguous 1944 approval of civilian bombing: "Wholesale obliteration bombing as practiced at first by the Axis powers and then on a far greater scale by the Allies. . . .[and] culminating in the use of atomic bombs against Japan," they now declared, "is not defensible on Christian premises."

On the fundamental issue of the ethics of atomic war in general, however, their response was uncertain and divided. A crucial footnote revealed basic differences over the reasons for the condemnation of the Hiroshima and Nagasaki bombings. Without identifying individuals or even indicating relative strength, it reported that the commission was divided among three positions. One, anticipating A. J. Muste's pacifist stance, held that "the atomic bomb has revealed the impossibility of a just war, and has shown the necessity for repudiation of all support of war by the Church." A second faction, while holding back from an explicitly pacifist position, nevertheless unqualifiedly condemned "obliteration bombing and the atomic bomb as utilized for that purpose." The third faction based its condemnation of Hiroshima and Nagasaki primarily on the circumstances under which these particular attacks had been carried out. "The way should be left open to regard the use of atomic weapons under some circumstances as right," this group held, for "in the present state of human relations, if plans for international control of aggression should fail, the only effective restraint upon would-be aggressors might be fear of reprisals, and . . . this possible restraint should not be removed in advance."[40]

Commenting on the Calhoun Commission report in May 1946, one of the dissident members, Ernest Fremont Tittle, pastor of the First Methodist Church of Evanston, Illinois, vehemently insisted that under no conditions could atomic bombs ever be used morally. Even the stockpiling of such weapons, he argued, would produce "a world of fear, suspicion, and almost inevitable final catastrophe." The Christian church, he went on,

> should not itself be a party to the coming of Armageddon. It should put its trust in the power of God . . . not in the power of the atomic bomb or in a human wisdom that inclines to think, against all the protests of the heart, that *perhaps* the merciless incineration of millions upon millions of men, women, and children may be regarded in some circumstances as right.

Thus in the dawn of the atomic era, a question that would continue to trouble consciences forty years later—the morality of threatening atomic retaliation (or "deterrence," as it would come to be called)—had surfaced as a fundamental and divisive issue.[41]

The Calhoun Commission report, and particularly its relegation of the fundamental moral issue to a footnote, deeply disappointed A. J. Muste. "If responsible people are going to say such things," he wrote, "they rest under a very solemn obligation to say just what they mean." Talk of preventing atomic war by the threat of reprisal not only had "an ugly and sinister sound, especially when it comes from Christian lips," he said, but such a strategy could easily edge over into advocacy of a preventive first strike. To believe that a "no first use" pledge (one of the commission's recommendations) would restrain a nuclear-armed nation if it thought itself threatened, he said, was "utterly sentimental." If Christian leaders continued to equivocate on the ethical issue, Muste concluded, they would be "handing a blank check to the militarists" and their ultimate guilt could well be "far greater than that which rests upon the Nazis."[42]

Muste had at least one outspoken adherent. In *The Christian Response to the Atomic Crisis* (1950), Edward L. Long, Jr., reviewed the respective positions of Muste and the Calhoun Commission and found the former more persuasive and biblically defensible. The impulse to retain a retaliatory capability, Long insisted, reflected secular expediency, not Christian discipleship. "When all considerations except those of ultimate religious obedience are eliminated," Long wrote, "it seems that the ultimate principle of love would demand a pacifist position." The only hope of breaking the "vicious cycle" of the nuclear arms race, he wrote, lay in the religious and ethical realm. "The cost of Christian faith is not cheap," he concluded, "but reliance upon political schemes may be costlier still."[43]

And what of the Roman Catholic position? In view of the condemnation of wartime terror bombings and the Hiroshima and Nagasaki attacks in the major Catholic journals, one might have expected a categorical rejection of any conceivable future use of the atomic bomb. In fact, the response was more qualified and ambivalent. The atomic bomb raised "numerous and extremely grave" moral issues, said *America* on August 18, 1945, but precisely for this reason, it went on, "moral theologians will hesitate to give a forthright decision as to whether or not its use as a weapon of war can be justified for any reason or on any ground." *Commonweal* and *America* had little to say on the ethical aspects of atomic weapons in the later 1940s. *Catholic World,* having emotionally deplored the use of the bomb in its first post-Hiroshima issue, offered a rather different view in May 1946. In "God, Man, and the Atom Bomb," Francis X. Murphy, Catholic chaplain at the U.S. Naval Academy, insisted that the development and use of the atomic bomb was "in accordance with the divine plan." With "Christian concepts of morality ignored or denied over a large section of the globe," he wrote, the nation's only safeguard was a strong military force, including nuclear missiles. (Of course, he carefully added, "there always will be a navy.") Murphy vigorously denied that reliance on an atomic arsenal contradicted the just-war doctrine. "It has always been possible to be a warrior and a good Christian at the same time," he said, and it would continue to be so in the era of atomic weapons.[44]

A more comprehensive formulation of a Catholic position on the bomb was "The Ethics of Atomic War" (1947), published by the Catholic Association for International Peace, a body chaired by the Jesuit theologian Wilfred Parsons and including such well-known churchmen as John Courtney Murray and Fulton J. Sheen. This document began by reiterating the conclusion of Catholic moral commentators during the war that the terror bombing of cities—even in a just war—was "not allowable ethically" because the means were not proportionate to the end. "No matter what the end sought," a "deliberate and direct attack" on civilians was "simple murder." As for the argument that in modern warfare the strategic contribution of soldiers and civilians was indistinguishable, the association noted that even under total mobilization, as much as 60 percent of the homefront population—the aged, children, housewives, civilian service workers, farm laborers—could not by any reasonable definition be viewed as war workers.

Turning to the specific issue at hand, the association concluded that an atomic attack on a civilian population "would fall under the same condemnation" as other forms of terror bombing. But having gone this far, this body of Catholic moralists, like the Protestant Calhoun Commission the year before, drew back from a categorical moral condemnation of the use of atomic bombs under any circumstances. Insisting that reason, not emotion, must be the guide in such matters, the association posed a hypothetical situation in which an enemy had already launched an atomic attack against the United States, and was poised to invade. In such a situation, it concluded, one could reasonably find it "morally defensible" to launch an atomic attack against the enemy's cities, "even though it meant the loss of millions of civilian lives," provided the purpose was not "mere retaliation, but defense in the true sense," and the bombs were not deliberately targeted against civilians but against the enemy's "military productive capacity." Intent, then, distinguished this situation from the "total war" so firmly condemned earlier. Millions of men, women and children would die, but as a side-effect, not a primary objective; and thus their deaths would be "outweighed by the good obtained, the salvation of the innocent country. This is not total war in the condemned sense."[45]

By 1947, then, both the Protestant and Catholic branches of American Christendom had formally addressed the moral issues posed for them on August 6, 1945. Both had roundly condemned the concept of total war, the deliberate terror bombing of civilians, and the destruction of Hiroshima and Nagasaki. But each had drawn back from a categorical condemnation of the atomic bomb as an instrument of war, granting moral legitimacy to the retaliatory use of atomic weapons under certain conditions—precisely the theory that would provide the ethical foundation of the nation's nuclear policies for the next generation. One may respect the earnestness with which these theologians undertook their task, and acknowledge the daunting complexity of the issues they faced, and still agree in retrospect with A. J. Muste that in the last analysis they gave a blank check to the militarists—a check that would be used to make very large drafts upon mankind's slim reserves of moral restraint in the realm of war.

Had the churches condemned the atomic bomb as categorically as A. J. Muste and a few others urged, the nuclear arms race might well have unfolded precisely as it did. Yet it is surely not without significance that at the dawn of the atomic era, when values and attitudes were still in a formative stage, the nation's religious leaders, while clearly deeply troubled by the ethical implications of atomic weapons, failed to render a clear and unequivocal no to these new instruments of mass destruction.

19

Human Nature, Technological Man, the Apocalyptic Tradition

> The atomic crisis is a historical illumination of life's deepest
> issues; it forces each individual to re-examine his basic in-
> terpretation of reality.
>
> —Edward L. Long, Jr. (1950)[1]

While church commissions and religious periodicals wrestled with the morality of dropping the bomb on Japan and with the larger ethical dilemma
posed by atomic weapons, others were speculating on what the advent of the
bomb, with its potential for human annihilation, revealed about the condition of modern man. As a New York Methodist minister put it in an August
1945 sermon about the bomb: "Before us on the stage of history is a panorama of the soul."[2]

What did this panorama reveal? The consensus was exceptionally bleak.
To Senator Elbert Thomas, the public's largely unquestioning acceptance of
the atomic bombing of Japan was evidence of a "new callousness toward
life"; the bomb's most important moral effect, he suggested, would be "to
brutalize the men who wield it." The very fact that the new weapon was the
creation of the "good" side in World War II—which many viewed as clear
evidence of divine favor—struck others as full of menacing implications.
"The ghastly thing about this bomb is that it was released not by Hitler in
some mad mania of lust," wrote New York minister John Haynes Holmes,
"but by sane and good men who knew what it could do. *Our* leaders, . . .
the self-appointed custodians of civilization, were the ones to strike this
blow."[3]

Similarly, the intellectual brilliance of the achievement, which some
saw as a model for a comparable leap forward in the social and political
realm, seemed to others the definitive refutation of the Enlightenment belief
that greater human knowledge would inevitably bring greater happiness and
ethical advances. In the November 1945 morality play about the bomb in
the Methodist magazine *Motive*, "Satan" observes: "This atomic plaything is

doing what Hitler—that stupid fool—was never able to do. His open attack on men aroused Americans' noblest instincts. My more subtle appeal to their glory and scientific acumen made them vulnerable. Now they are mine." *Commonweal,* while praising the "democratic optimism" of David E. Lilienthal's call for informed public decisions about atomic matters, observed that knowledge was no guarantee of right action. Even the fully informed could make evil decisions: "Being but human, we are inclined to go astray in our choices even when we realize we are doing wrong. A good choice requires . . . not only knowledge, but also good moral character, and, sometimes, Grace." Protestant theologian Richard M. Fagley similarly rejected the "secularist" assumption that political adjustments could assure mankind's safety in the nuclear age. Such panaceas, he wrote in October 1945, did not confront the problem of evil: "No form of government is foolproof. No system of international control can provide a final answer. Political institutions can be corrupted. Controls can break down. . . . Twist and turn as we may, we cannot escape from this crisis by secularist means."[4] To the Harvard philosopher William E. Hocking, Americans' fitful response to the bomb revealed fundamental deficiencies in society's agencies for transmitting moral values. The news had shocked "an easygoing public into a moment of sobriety," Hocking wrote in 1946, but the anxious discussion that ensued had no firm moral grounding. This Hocking attributed to the failure not only of the churches, but of all traditional sources of ethical direction:

> The search for moral guidance is half the battle of world peace . . . and the pertinent guides are our natural authorities, those with which our first moral insights are reached . . . , the home, the school, and the church. One reason for our present fumbling . . . is that all of these institutions are derelict in their duty.

The ill-focused ethical response to the bomb, Hocking concluded bleakly, suggested that "little can be expected in the way of a trained moral intuition in the next generation."[5]

Catholic moralists, whose predecessors had for several centuries deplored the inroads of secularism, readily saw the atomic bomb as the culmination of this long process. The development and use of the bomb reflected the breakdown of "the universal and everlasting moral law" under the pressures of modern relativism and was final proof of the "ethical anarchy" of the contemporary world, wrote the editor of *Catholic World* in September 1945. "Nothing remains but nihilism." The bomb was the natural culmination of a materialist view of life, agreed Archbishop Richard J. Cushing of Boston in 1948: "That theory has uttered its last word of Power—and has produced its ultimate reaction: Fear."[6]

While some engaged in sweeping generalizations about the "moral meaning" of the bomb, others explored a somewhat more limited question: What did the development and use of the atomic bomb by the United States government reveal about the relationship between the individual conscience and the demands of the state in the modern era? Again, the answers were bleak. For A. J. Muste, the fact that the dutiful German functionaries who had run the Nazi extermination camps and the Americans who had bombed Hiroshima had both acted "under orders" raised the most somber moral issues. "We have to abandon as evil and the source of evil the notion that the individual is not responsible for what is done in war and under orders," he insisted. "The need of our day is for conscientious objectors, no-sayers."[7]

Edward L. Long, Jr., elaborated the point in his 1950 work *The Christian Response to the Atomic Crisis.* A 1945 physics graduate from Rensselaer Polytechnic Institute, Long went on to New York's Union Theological Seminary where he studied with Reinhold Niebuhr and John C. Bennett (who "tempered but never dissolved away" his pacifist beliefs). In 1951 Long received a Ph.D. in the philosophy of religion and ethics from Columbia University, having written a dissertation on the religious beliefs of American scientists. The separation of persons from the consequences of their actions in modern society "so amply illustrated in the atomic bomb project," wrote Long in 1950, "raises the possibility that history may produce a 'technocrat'"—a skilled functionary oblivious to and unconcerned about the larger purpose or outcome of his activity. (A few hours after the Hiroshima bombing, Col. William S. Parsons described to reporters his thoughts as he had activated the bomb aboard the *Enola Gay:* "I knew the Japs were in for it, but I felt no particular emotion about it.") While not equating the atomic-bomb project and the Nazi death camps morally (as A. J. Muste came close to doing), Long saw distinct parallels in their ethical significance. "There is something alarming in the power of large-scale and organized evil," he observed, "whether arising from 'necessity' as in the case of the atomic weapon, or from distorted motives, as in the case of Nazi power."

While insisting that the question of individual responsibility was central to understanding the moral dimensions of the atomic crisis, Long rejected the position of some who were pointing an accusatory finger at specific scientists. (Writing in *Fellowship* magazine in 1948, the moralist Milton Mayer described Albert Einstein and Harold Urey as "a pair of unlovely characters indeed, with whom I do not hope, ever, to shake hands, since their hands, in the words of Isaiah, are full of blood.") While there were degrees of responsibility, said Long, whatever guilt attached to the dropping of the atomic bomb must be collectively shared. "The scientists' sense of guilt does not come from knowledge of having done a specific wrong," he said, but rather "from a sense of having been involved in a great, perhaps unavoidable, tragedy." Indeed, he went on, the atomic-bomb project offered "a clear and convincing illustration" of the Christian doctrine of original sin, which involved not "some external quality passed from generation to generation in an entirely mystical way," but rather "the inevitable enmeshing of every human life in the corporate evil of the world, and the inability of any life, by its own power alone, to avoid that evil completely."

The problem was hardly a new one. As early as 1905, in *Sin and Society,* the economist Edward A. Ross had argued that the notion of "sin" needed to be updated to encompass corporate structures in which countless small individual actions could add up to a great social evil. How could society deal with corporate evil? In the moral realm of 1905, the answer lay in tenement codes, child-labor laws, and pure-food acts. The sudden emergence of the atomic bomb from a vast, secret, compartmentalized technological project involving many thousands of people posed the dilemma in far more urgent and complex terms.

Pursuing the question from a Christian theological perspective, Long described two approaches to ethics: the secular one—experimental, calculative, problem-oriented—and the religious one, defining its purposes in "obedience to a transcendent power" and taking "its ultimate standards of right and wrong from revelation, particularly in the life and teachings of Jesus." The ethical problem of the atomic bomb, he went on, could best be approached on the basis of the latter. "Calculative morality becomes less and less useful as the issue at stake becomes more and more momentous." While "the trial and error that underlie an experimental ethic" might be tolerable "when a mistake can be survived," he concluded, "an ethic that would . . . depend solely upon historical accomplishment for its vindication, does not make sense in an atomic age." Only an ethic rooted in obedience to the Christian imperative of self-forgetting love was defensible in an era when the consequences of a wrong choice were so incalculably high.[8]

The bleakest assessment of the bomb's larger moral import came, however, not from the religious realm at all, but from the secular journalist and critic Dwight Macdonald. A veteran of the political wars of the 1930s whose experiences in the Depression decade had ranged from Henry Luce's business magazine *Fortune* to Trotskyite politics to the anti-Stalinist journal *Partisan Review,* Macdonald by 1945 was an intensely individualistic cultural observer whose personal commitments ran toward pacifism and a nonmilitant anarchism. His journalistic outlet was his small but influential one-man magazine *Politics.*[9]

Macdonald's first reaction to Hiroshima was unequivocal: "This atrocious action places 'us,' the defenders of civilization, on a moral level with 'them,' the beasts of Maidanek," he wrote in August 1945, alluding to a notorious Nazi death camp in Poland. The justifications being advanced for the decision to drop the bomb—it shortened the war, the Japanese had struck first, and so on—he added later, could be used to rationalize "*any* atrocious action, absolutely *any* one." In subsequent months, Macdonald returned several times to the issue of the bomb. The events of August 1945, he wrote, had blasted once and for all the fatuous faith in "Science" and "Progress" and with it "the whole structure of Progressive assumptions on which liberal and socialist theory has been built up." As for the "official platitude" of post-Hiroshima public discourse—that atomic energy had potential for either good or evil, and that mankind must now make sure that it was used only for good—he wrote: "Atomic Fission is something in which Good and Evil are so closely intertwined that it is hard to see how the Good can be extracted and the Evil thrown away." The Marxists who were proclaiming that only under socialism could atomic energy serve the common good, he added, were equally mesmerized by the "potentialities-for-Good-or-for-Evil platitude" and the blind faith in "Science and Progress" that underlay it. All such talk of future benefits, he said, "blunts our reaction to the present horror by reducing it to an episode in an historical schema which will 'come out all right' in the end." Such wishful thinking "makes us morally callous" and "ignores the fact that such atrocities as The Bomb and the Nazi death camps are right now brutalizing, warping, [and] deadening the human beings who are expected to change the world for the better."

Deepening the horror, in Macdonald's view, was the fact that the atomic atrocity was the product of an elaborately organized bureaucratic undertaking involving the uncoerced labor of many thousands of workers. Some found the bureaucratic, "ordinary" quality of the project reassuring. Thanks to "supremely careful planning" and the compartmentalization of work and knowledge, *Life* had observed shortly after Hiroshima, "thousands of workers spent the war working on something that was assuredly tremendous but completely unknown." "The weapon has been created not by the devilish inspiration of some warped genius," commented Henry D. Smyth of Princeton in his report on the Manhattan Project, "but by the arduous labor of thousands of normal men and women working for the safety of their country."

To Dwight Macdonald, however, this aspect of the atomic-bomb project revealed how readily a modern technocratic state could organize large-scale undertakings whose end result was horrendous beyond all imagining. The project had been initiated by scientists who only dimly grasped its long-range implications but who, functioning as specialists rather than as "complete men," had pushed ahead with this greatest of all experiments "with cities as the laboratories and people as the guinea pigs." And it had been carried out by 125,000 willing workers of whom "only a handful . . . knew what they were creating." "There is something askew with a society in which vast numbers of citizens can be organized to create a horror like The Bomb without even knowing they are doing it," observed Macdonald. "What real content, in such a case, can be assigned to notions like 'democracy' and 'government of, by and for the people'?" The Manhattan Project, in short, chillingly illustrated "that perfect automatism, that absolute lack of human consciousness or aims which our society is rapidly achieving." The fact that not Roosevelt and Churchill but "colorless mediocrities" like Truman and Atlee presided over the project's spectacular denouement simply underscored the interchangeability of the human components: "The more commonplace the personalities . . . , the more grandiose the destruction." It was *"Götter-dämmerung* without the gods." [10]

Returning to the theme in "The Root Is Man" (*Politics,* July 1946), Macdonald used Hiroshima and other wartime atrocities as points of departure for broader ethical reflections. Noting the ease with which governments in wartime flouted supposedly fundamental ethical values, Macdonald concluded that the officially espoused moral code was little more than a thin veneer. "Evils are rejected only on a superficial, conventional, public-oration and copy-book-maxim plane, while they are accepted or at least temporized with on more fundamental, private levels." Ethics had become a matter of conventional pieties: "The fact that 'everybody' agrees that war, torture, and the massacre of helpless people are Evil is not reassuring to me. It seems to show that our ethical code is no longer *experienced* but is simply *assumed,* so that it becomes a collection of 'mere platitudes.'"

How could one combat the ethical numbness that had allowed the Manhattan Project to roll to its conclusion so easily and the majority of Americans to accept Hiroshima and Nagasaki so readily? On what basis could an ethically sensitive culture be constructed? Here Macdonald rejected the faith in science as an ethical resource central to both Marxism and John Dewey's Instrumentalism. In fact, he said, ethics and science inhabited different realms. (Macdonald's friend A. Dwight Culler elaborated the distinction in a *Politics* essay of the same period. Science, he wrote, involved incremental advances in knowledge and mastery of the natural world, while "moral and social and artistic development" was not cumulative, but involved a series of successive states of human consciousness: the difference was between "an activity and a quality." The only "scientific" ethics would be one based on the quantification of actual human behavior—and that would be a very depressing exercise indeed.)

What, then, was the answer to the moral issues posed by the atomic bomb? "Once we have divorced value judgments from scientific method . . . , where in the world, or out of it, do they come from?" Here, Macdonald parted company from theologians like Edward L. Long, Jr., who were calling for repentence and a revival of religious faith. Since adolescence, he said, religion had neither attracted nor interested him. Further, to root ethics in supernatural imperatives seemed to him a resort to moral authoritarianism as objectionable as the Marxists' appeal to scientific materialism.

And what of the quasi-religious belief in the building of a "better world" that had inspired countless ethical pronouncements and reformist proposals in the past? All, he said, had been drastically undercut by the bomb:

> Scientific progress has reached its end, and the end is turning out to be the end of man himself. . . . Now that we confront the actual, scientific possibility of The End being written to human history and at a not so distant date, the concept of the future, so powerful an element in traditional socialist thought, loses for us its validity.

Nor did Macdonald accept another favorite post-Hiroshima formula: that the folly of atomic war was so obvious, and the promise of atomic energy so vast, that mankind must somehow "summon" or "discover" the intellectual and moral resources to avoid the former and realize the latter. Macdonald did acknowledge "an authentic sweetness and divinity in life that we would not willingly let die" and he did not categorically dismiss the "wild possibility" that "in the urgency of our fear the needed idea may come, though it come in advance, so to speak, of our mind's capacity to house it." But his overall assessment of the human prospect was reminiscent of Henry Adams at his most pessimistic:

> Sometimes . . . the hideousness of the world rises up and almost chokes us. At such moments it does seem fitting that man should stretch his fossil out beside that of Tyrannosaurus and let the mosquitoes have the next try. The Creator might then set down in His book that the experiment of the brain was not a success.

For Macdonald, the only anodyne to despair was the capacity of the individual conscience to resist massive social pressure. "The only way we have ever learned anything essential about ethics," he observed, was through the intuitions of individuals—intuitions that sometimes "strike common chords that vibrate respondingly in other people's consciences." That this "subjective, personal, even arbitrary process . . . should appear such a mysterious business today, if not downright childish," he added, simply underscored "the disproportionate place scientific method has come to occupy in our consciousness."

Applying this insight to the atomic crisis, Macdonald drew a measure of encouragement from the isolated individuals whose consciences had rebelled against the atomic bomb and all it signified. He praised the handful of scientists who had refused to join the Manhattan Project. "This is 'resistance,' this is 'negativism,' " he wrote, "and in it lies our best hope." Only this stubborn insistence "on acting as a responsible individual in a society which reduces the individual to impotence," he went on, offered "a chance of changing our present tragic destiny."[11] This emphasis on the individual conscience as ethical arbiter is reminiscent of the writings of Jane Addams, Randolph Bourne, and a handful of other World War I pacifists who had stood up in 1917–1918 against the sweeping rhetorical justifications for the war and the exalted predictions of the finer age that would emerge from the carnage. In a similar vein, Macdonald scornfully dismissed the official rationalizations being advanced for the decision to drop the bomb and the soothing predictions of a better world ahead.

While the atomic bomb turned Dwight Macdonald to speculations about the individual and the state, it set other Americans to thinking about last things. Among some religious writers, these reflections took an explicitly theological turn as they explored the ancient Christian doctrine that God would someday bring human history to an end, judge mankind, and institute a new era of righteousness. The early Church had been convinced that these events were imminent, but over the centuries the eschatological vision had grown dim. In the aftermath of Hiroshima and Nagasaki, however, such prophetic biblical passages as "The heavens shall pass away with a great noise, and the elements shall melt with fervent heat, the earth also and the works that are therein shall be burned up" (II Peter 3:10) took on a chilling resonance. For generations, wrote Wesner Fallaw of the Andover Newton Theological Seminary in 1946, the moral obligation of Christians "to make preparation for world's end" had been "ignored or relegated to the subconscious." But now, he continued, "eschatology confounds us at the very center of consciousness." Others were even more explicit. "The end of human existence on earth was regarded by the early Christians as near at hand [and] by modern Christians as far in the future," observed the Methodist leader Ernest Fremont Tittle in a 1946 lecture on the radical changes in consciousness the bomb had wrought. "We have now, apparently, to reckon with the possibility of a speedy end to man's life on earth. . . . What is new in the present situation is not the possibility of a last generation but the possibility . . . that *ours* may be the last generation!"[12]

But what ethical meaning could one derive from this renewal of the eschatological vision? To some, it suggested the need for a redoubled commitment to social justice. The journalist and critic James Agee, in a letter to his spiritual mentor, the Episcopal priest James Flye, in September 1945, commented on the way atomic fear seemed to be numbing Americans to the suffering in war-devastated Europe. Man might indeed be doomed, he said, "but in that case there is everything to be said for dying as near in a state of grace as possible." For Wesner Fallaw, the prospect of an imminent end to history meant that Christians should emulate the early Church and concentrate on "the sacrificial reapportionment of material goods, while there is time, so that . . . the world's miserable ones may have succor." Ernest Fremont Tittle struck a similar note. The renewed awareness among Christians that history "is not limited to this passing world but will have its consummation in the eternal Kingdom of God" could serve as "an antidote to panic," he observed, but it must not be seen "as a substitute for faithful effort to prevent a world-destroying catastrophe brought on by human sin and folly." [13]

This atom-induced revival of eschatological thinking also encouraged in some a tendency to turn from social concerns toward issues of individual salvation and personal morality. This tendency appeared even in some ostensibly secular responses to the bomb. A 1946 *Saturday Evening Post* story by Philip Wylie offered a series of vignettes of the moment when a global atomic blast destroys all life, and in the process echoed countless evangelical sermons in which the last trump catches heedless sinners unawares. In Wylie's story a murderous wife is vaporized as she raises the knife over her sleeping husband, and "the carefree, stay-out revelers in Hollywood, California" are struck down in the midst of their debauchery. Wesner Fallaw, while urging continued social activism, also exploited the mood of approaching apocalypse to reenforce an individualistic moral message. Those most likely to survive a world-shattering catastrophe, he wrote in 1946, would not be the "people who are sedentary, lovers of deep cushions and rich pastries," but "toughened athletes" and those "skilled in working with their hands as craftsmen and tillers of the soil"; the survivors would need to know medicine and other basic skills to assure their own well-being and aid others. Accordingly, he said, Christian schools and colleges should concentrate on the "physical conditioning" and "complete rigorous training" of the young for their post-holocaust mission. [14]

As the decade closed and the larger pattern of cultural-political responses to the bomb shifted, this tendency to derive a personalistic moral and religious message, rather than a social-activist one, from the revived eschatological strain in Christian thought increased sharply. One can see it, for example, in the insistence of Edward L. Long, Jr., in 1950 that not only secular ethics, but the entire secular worldview—with its belief in progress, its faith in "history" as giving meaning to human endeavor, and its assurance that "the life of the individual [would] always be outlasted by the life of the group"—had been "blasted by the atomic flash." Only the New Testament eschatological vision, Long concluded, with its contingent sense of history and its understanding "that all achievement can be quickly lost, and that life does not inevitably grow better," was adequate to the nuclear age. For Long, the prospect of atomic annihilation reaffirmed the central themes of evangelical Christianity: individual repentence and redemption beyond history:

The precondition of any healthy response to the atomic crisis begins with a creative experience of Christian redemption. . . . No destruction of the world can destroy the free will of the faithful by which they believe in God and partake of his eternity. God's will is supreme, and those who serve him need not be caught in any final emptiness.[15]

No one was more successful at translating the revived Protestant apocalyptic vision from the pages of religious periodicals and theological works into the popular mind than the young Baptist evangelist Billy Graham. On September 25, 1949, the unknown Graham opened a tent revival in Los Angeles. Two days earlier, President Truman had announced the first Soviet atomic test. With his keen sense of current events, his shrewd reading of the popular mood, and his riveting, staccato delivery, Graham at once gave the ominous news a prominent place in his sermons. "On Friday morning . . . our President . . . announced to the startled world that Russia had now exploded an atomic bomb. An arms race unprecedented in the history of the world is driving us madly toward destruction!"

For centuries, evangelists had evoked images of sudden death and hellfire to frighten their listeners into repentence. Graham now had available the most potent scare tactic of all: atomic war. If he dwelt less on the terrors of hell than his predecessors, it was perhaps because it now seemed superfluous: People "are afraid of war, afraid of atomic bombs, fearful as they go to bed at night. . . . trembling because they feel that we are on the verge of a third world war, a war which could sweep civilization back into the Middle Ages." Graham documented his warnings with the pronouncements of government leaders and accounts of private conversations with the world's power-wielders: "Mr. Truman said in yesterday's press conference that we must be prepared for *any* eventuality at *any* hour. . . . Three months ago, in the House of Parliament, a British statesman told me that the British government feels we have only five to ten years and our civilization will be ended." Graham added concrete, if fanciful, particulars that gave the generalized threat a vivid immediacy: "Do you know the area that is marked out for the enemy's first atomic bomb? New York! Secondly, Chicago; and thirdly, the city of Los Angeles! We don't know how soon, but we do know this, that right now the grace of God can still save a poor lost sinner."

In contrast to the characteristic theological pronouncements of the 1945–1947 period, Graham made no comment on the morality of atomic weapons. He offered no ideas for reducing the atomic threat which Christians might support. His only answer to the coming holocaust was the age-old evangelical cry: Repent! "Time is desperately short. . . . I say to you, the message of the Lord has not changed! The message is still the same—prepare to meet thy God!"[16]

While Billy Graham and other churchmen underscored their calls for repentence and righteousness with visions of atomic holocaust, some cultural observers expressed skepticism about the long-term effectiveness of such tactics. In a 1950 lecture at Rutgers University entitled "The End of the World," historian Perry Miller traced Anglo-American apocalyptic literature from Michael Wigglesworth's *Day of Doom* (1662) to Jonathan Edwards's *History of the Work of Redemption* (1739), noting the efforts of successive authors to give their lurid visions a scientific basis. In *The Sacred Theory of the Earth* (1681), for example, Thomas Burnet had speculated that "Seeds of Fire" were sealed within the atoms at the center of the earth and that on the Last Day God would release the "Chains" holding these atomic fires in check and they would burst forth, consuming the earth. (A staunch Protestant, Burnet further predicted that the initial conflagration would break out in Rome.) Fifteen years later, by contrast, William Whiston, influenced by Isaac Newton's newly published work on gravity, predicted in his *New Theory of the Earth* that the final holocaust would come when a comet brushed the Earth in its orbit of the sun.

Miller went on to describe the decline of apocalyptic thinking under the advance of science in the eighteenth and nineteenth centuries and its sudden and unexpected revival after 1945. The account of the Hiroshima bombing published in 1946 by the United States Strategic Bombing Survey, he noted, uncannily paralleled the classic apocalyptic prophecies: the sequence of sudden flash, blast, and all-consuming fire; the heedless unconcern of the populace; the lack of any hiding place.

Many of the earlier apocalpytic writers, Miller observed, had believed that the fear of earth's final destruction could have dramatic spiritual effects. William Wriston, for example, predicted that after the comet's devastating visit the survivors would at once reform, leading to a millennium of righteousness, peace, and harmony. Out of destruction and death would come Utopia. But Miller also noted a persistent skepticism toward such hopeful expectations. He cited, for example, Jonathan Swift's response to Wriston's book. If people actually knew that the end of the world was certain and imminent, Swift argued, the result would not be mass repentence, but orgies of debauchery. Imagining the reaction of Londoners to the arrival of a destroying comet, Swift wrote: "They drank, they whored, they swore, they lied, they cheated, they quarrelled, they murdered. In short, the world went on in the old channel."

From *The Day of Doom* to nightmarish descriptions of atomic destruction, Miller suggested, the apocalyptic vision had had little effect on human behavior. "Men cannot be scared into virtue," he wrote. "Catastrophe, by and for itself, is not enough." [17] Like their secular counterparts who hoped that atomic fear would produce a new world order, Billy Graham and other churchmen anticipated that the prospect of global destruction would stir a great religious awakening. Perry Miller, for one, citing historical evidence, viewed all such hopes with a jaundiced and skeptical eye.

Seven

Culture and Consciousness in the Early Atomic Era

20

Words Fail: The Bomb and the Literary Imagination

James Agee was living in New York, a thirty-six-year-old aspiring novelist, screenwriter, and movie critic for *Time,* when he heard the news of Hiroshima and Nagasaki. Profoundly shaken, he began a novel about the atomic bomb. "In some respects," he wrote Father James Flye, "this seems the only thing much worth writing or thinking about." But he soon bogged down. In November 1945, he wrote Father Flye that he had not returned to the project for nearly a month. Except for an incomplete fragment, Agee's atomic-bomb novel remained unwritten.

That five-thousand-word fragment, which Agee eventually described as a "rough sketch for a moving picture," is a highly revealing document. "Dedication Day" is a disturbing and in some ways brilliant work of surreal satire reminiscent of Nathanael West's *Day of the Locust* or Ralph Ellison's *Invisible Man.* It describes the dedication in Washington, D.C., of a soaring "fused uranium" Arch designed by Frank Lloyd Wright in commemoration of the atomic bomb. Beneath the Arch burns the Eternal Fuse, a strand of chemically treated cotton which unrolls from an elaborate underground mechanism through a platinum orifice designed as a replica of Martha Washington's wedding ring.

It is a glorious occasion. Flags wave in the breeze under a brilliant sun. Top government officials and foreign dignitaries are on hand. Vendors sell Good Humor ice cream to the vast throng of onlookers. Arturo Toscanini leads the choral movement of Beethoven's Ninth Symphony. Representatives of the major religious faiths offer appropriate prayers. By a special hook-up, the new electronic marvel, television, carries the ceremony to New York City, where more notables are assembled. A beautiful little girl named Lidice, "her bladder a trifle unstabilized" by all the attention, unveils the Arch's commemorative plaque. It bears only the cryptic inscription: "THIS IS IT."

Darkening the festivities, however, is an undercurrent of menace. The Eternal Fuse burns with a faint crackling sound "not unlike that which a snake elicits as he retires among dead leaves." A bugler struggles against the impulse to play Taps rather than the Reveille he has been assigned. At the moment of dedication, a pregnant woman faints and miscarries.

The menace deepens as the story shifts to the workroom beneath the Arch where the Keepers of the Flame—crippled war veterans and maimed victims of Hiroshima and Nagasaki—work around the clock manufacturing the Eternal Fuse, which burns at a constant rate of one inch per second. Among the Keepers of the Flame is an elderly atomic scientist whose mind has become unhinged. He constantly weeps, pulls at his hair, claws at his face until the blood drips over his starched laboratory jacket, and babbles of a religious pilgrimage to Tibet.

On Dedication Day, this deranged scientist asks to turn on the machine that will operate the Eternal Fuse, and out of deference for his past achievements his wish is granted. Just as he turns the switch, however, he swallows prussic acid and falls dead. In a suicide note he says that by his death he hoped to atone for his wartime role and to "endow the triumphal monument with a new and special significance." Despite public anger at his bizarre and unseemly act, he is buried with full honors at ground zero of the Alamogordo test site in New Mexico.

A tantalizingly incomplete work, "Dedication Day" makes plain the intensity and bitterness of Agee's feelings about the atomic bomb. The story's topographical structure—official celebrations above ground contrasting with strange and disturbed goings-on underground—metaphorically suggests his sense of the complexity and partially hidden nature of the American response to the bomb. But, above all, this fragmentary draft offers eloquent evidence of Agee's difficulty in translating anguish and dread into literature.[1]

James Agee was not alone among serious writers in finding the bomb profoundly daunting as a subject. At one level, to be sure, the atomic bomb unleashed a flood of literary productivity. The newspapers were full of the kind of doggerel verse that all heavily publicized events seem to call forth. Edgar Guest wrote a poem; the crew of the *Enola Gay* commemorated its moment in the limelight with a laboriously produced verse that began:

It was the 6th of August, that much we knew,
When the boys took off in the morning dew,
Feeling nervous, sick, and ill at ease
They flew at the heart of the Japanese,
With a thunderous blast, a blinding light,
And the 509th's atomic might.[2]

Numerous didactic plays, poems, and short stories were also produced in the early post-Hiroshima years to warn of the dangers of atomic war and build support for international control. The 1947 *Harper's* story in which a schoolteacher develops a new energy source from Mexican beans was, for all its farcical aspects, a serious comment on the dangers of nuclear proliferation. In his one-act play *Pilot Lights of the Apocalypse* (*Fortune,* January 1946), atomic scientist Louis Ridenour first raised the specter of atomic cataclysm through human error and technological failure. An underground missile-launching site in California is struck by sharp tremors that cut it off from the Washington command center. Signal lights indicate that San Francisco has been attacked, and a panicky crew member launches the retaliatory missiles. Moments too late, the men learn the truth: San Francisco has been destroyed not by enemy missiles, but by an earthquake. In Philip Wylie's 1946 short story "Blunder," a fable about the danger of secrecy in atomic research, two isolated Norwegian scientists are testing a new fission process by which they hope to supply all of Scandinavia's power needs. One of their early theoretical articles contains a horrendous error that could lead to catastrophe if the tests proceed. Frantic scientists in other countries try desperately to warn the two, but are foiled by their governments' obsession with atomic secrecy, and the experimenters proceed to blow up the planet.[3]

Similarly, the late 1940s saw the publication of numerous hortatory poems underscoring the message that mankind must master the atom or face annihilation. Hermann Hagedorn's *The Bomb That Fell on America* (1946) took nearly sixty pedestrian pages to make its point:

> The heart and the soul must be as great as the brain if the work of the brain is not to wreck the world.

> We are one hundred and thirty-five million people, and we must grow up, overnight, or make the world one final Hiroshima.[4]

Aaron Kramer's "On the Harnessing of Atomic Energy" warned scientists against hubris in their moment of triumph, while William Rose Benét's "God's Fire" viewed atomic energy with deep apprehension:

> Raging inferno, consuming lava pit,
> Fury of flame, with life's foundations split

> Time was, Time is! How fatefully the sound
> Time shall be! tolls. Prometheus is unbound.

While Benét wrote of Prometheus, the poet Karl Shapiro invoked another of the great myths of the darker side of knowledge. In "The Progress of Faust" (1947), Shapiro imagined the demonic Dr. Faustus—the man willing to sell his soul to the devil for the secrets of the universe—reincarnated as a pioneer of Baconian science, an Enlightenment *philosophe,* a physicist expelled from Nazi Germany in 1939—and a builder of the bomb:

> Five years unknown to enemy and friend
> He hid, appearing on the sixth to pose
> In an American desert at war's end
> Where, at his back, a dome of atoms rose.[5]

Apart from a few isolated voices, however, the initial literary response to the atomic bomb was, to say the least, muted. This was not from any lack of urging. With "collective suicide" a distinct possibility, wrote Lewis Mumford, artists had a "special task and duty" to remind men and women "of the depths of their humanity and the promise of their creativity." "If our civilization is not to produce greater holocausts, our writers will have to become something more than merely mirrors of its violence and disintegration; they . . . will have to regain the initiative for . . . the forces of life, chaining up the demons we have allowed to run loose." The socially responsible writer should not merely chronicle modern man's spiritual confusion, agreed William Faulkner in his much-quoted Nobel Prize address of 1950, but help him "endure and prevail."[6]

Such summonses, however, had scant effect. Indeed, one critic in examining the initial response of American writers to the bomb was moved to reflect on "how dimly literature reflects and comprehends the actual." In the same vein, Alfred Kazin wrote in 1959: "I don't care for novelists who ignore what H. G. Wells himself called the 'queerness' that has come into contemporary life since the bomb." The "dimness," "flatness," and "paltriness in so many reputable novelists," Kazin suggested, represented so many "ways of escape" from the nuclear reality.[7]

Indeed, it was true that while some writers like James Agee struggled unsuccessfully to deal with the bomb, others seemed almost deliberately to ignore it. In a long letter to William Faulkner on August 9, 1945, the critic Malcolm Cowley made no reference to the world-shaking event of three days earlier. The published correspondence of Archibald MacLeish is similarly mute on the subject. In a letter to T. S. Eliot shortly after Hiroshima, MacLeish discussed Ezra Pound's legal problems at length, but did not mention the atomic bomb. The only reference to the bomb in Edmund Wilson's voluminous journal and random jottings for 1945 is a casual one: In an Athens nightclub in mid-August he reports the comment of the master of ceremonies to a sexy female performer: "I wish you were the town of Hiroshima and I *la bomb atomique pour tomber dessus.*"[8]

In most of the major novels of the immediate post-Hiroshima years— Lionel Trilling's *The Middle of the Journey;* Saul Bellow's *The Victim;* Norman Mailer's *The Naked and the Dead*—the atomic bomb is notable by its absence.

The same is true of the early postwar poems of the older, established poets. In the major works of Wallace Stevens's final decade for example—*Credences of Summer* (1947), *The Auroras of Autumn* (1948), and *An Ordinary Evening in New Haven* (1949)—the bomb makes no appearance. Indeed, if Helen Vendler is to be believed, this reflected a conscious aesthetic decision. "As Stevens became convinced that poetry, even in world wars, need not be topical or social," Vendler writes, "so he became convinced that the reality of poetry was not given to it by the newspapers, but by the self." (Charles Berger, by contrast, in an important recent reading of these same postwar Stevens poems, argues that they were profoundly shaped by the threat of atomic annihilation, reflecting what Berger calls a "counter-apocalyptic" sensibility "which begins to see the world as saved.")[9]

Only in allusive and tentative ways does the atomic bomb begin to make its appearance in post-1945 American literature. In Carson McCullers's *Member of the Wedding* (1946), for example, a newspaper account of Hiroshima helps illuminate the situation and personality of two principal characters: the isolated, vicarious existence of the unhappy adolescent Frankie; the humanity and practicality of the black housekeeper Berenice. When Frankie uncomprehendingly reads that the new bomb is the equivalent of twenty thousand tons of TNT, Berenice replies:

> Twenty thousand tons? And there ain't but two tons of coal in the coal house. . . . The figures these days have got too high for me. Read in the paper about ten million peoples killed. I can't crowd that many peoples in my mind's eye.[10]

But even such passing references are infrequent. Indeed, it sometimes seemed that the principal function of literature in the immediate post-Hiroshima period was to provide a grabbag of quotations and literary allusions that could be made to seem somehow relevant to the bomb. William L. Borden prefaced his 1946 strategic study *There Will Be No Time* with a quotation from Matthew Arnold. Bernard Brodie began a 1947 essay on nuclear strategy with Milton's account of the epic battle between Heaven and Hell in *Paradise Lost*—a war that escalates until the opposing forces are uprooting mountains and hurling them at each other.[11]

Literary sources from the Greeks onward—with special emphasis on the Bible—were scoured for what seemed anticipations of the atomic bomb, or intimations of the power locked in the atom. Lucretius' discussion of atoms in *De rerum natura* ("And these can nor be sundered from without, by beats and blows, nor from within be torn by penetration, nor be overthrown by any assault soever") was widely quoted, as was the more accurate speculation of the seventh-century mystic Ali Hassam: "Split whatsoever atom you will, and in its heart you will find a sun."[12]

Indeed, from the post-Hiroshima perspective, Western literature seemed suddenly teeming with anticipations of atomic holocaust. Stephen Vincent Benét's 1941 story "By the Waters of Babylon"—in which survivors of a vaguely described holocaust ("the Great Burning") live deep in the Adirondacks, superstitiously avoiding the ruins of New York City, whose very soil has somehow been permanently poisoned—was read with fresh interest four years later. So was Jules Verne's sardonic nineteenth-century observation: "The end of the earth will be when some enormous boiler . . . shall explode and blow up our globe. And [the Americans] are great boiler-makers." Eugene Rabinowitch and many others were struck by Henry Adams's bleak forecast of 1862: "Some day science may have the existence of mankind in its power, and the human race commit suicide by blowing up the world." Reaching still further back, one antiquarian dug up an 1835 *New York Mirror* prediction of transoceanic air travel, underwater tunnels linking Manhattan and New Jersey—and a new weapon that could destroy "a million men . . . in an hour." (Such a nightmarish weapon, the 1835 editorialist had predicted, would surely lead mankind to renounce war forever.) Turning to Shakespeare, a *New York Times* editorial found "new and awful meaning" in Prospero's vision of universal annihilation in Act IV of *The Tempest:*

> The cloud-capp'd towers, the gorgeous palaces,
> The solemn temples, the great globe itself,
> Yea, all which it inherit, shall dissolve
> And, like this insubstantial pageant faded,
> Leave not a wrack behind. [13]

Ferreting out the apt quotation was very different from a vigorous engagement of the literary imagination with the reality of the atomic bomb. The magnitude of this challenge is suggested by the stylistic awkwardness of much post-1945 writing on atomic matters. John Hersey was criticized for the flat tone of *Hiroshima,* but many others had difficulty finding a style appropriate to doomsday. Some scientists and scientific popularizers, eager to explain the bomb in nontechnical terms, affected a breezy, colloquial style embarrassingly ill-suited to the matter at hand. Others feigned an extraterrestrial perspective from which a nuclear holocaust on earth would seem the merest incident. When the atomic end comes, wrote Robert Payne in *Report on America* (1949), "for a few weeks or months or years the clouds of atomic vapor will roll like colored scarves around the body of the earth, and to an inhabitant of Mars looking through a telescope the earth would seem unchanged except for its increasing brightness, for the earth will glow with radioactive vapors." [14]

Still others affected a hearty, scoutmasterish tone as they exhorted

Americans to pull themselves together and rise to the demands of the new era. Civil-defense planning for an atomic war "should not be regarded as an onerous burden," said one writer, but "as a challenge to our democratic way of life and as an opportunity to show that we are able to cope with any situation." David E. Lilienthal spoke with infectious enthusiasm of "the atomic adventure." The Manhattan Project, he insisted, had opened the door to "one of the two or three most vital, most intense and stimulating periods of all history." More exuberant still was John Gunther, who in *Inside USA* described Hiroshima and Nagasaki as simply the latest evidences of America's crazy, endearing, can-do spirit:

> This nation is at once bull shouldered and quick as a ballet dancer on its feet. It is supple and full of nerves and fiber. It is a country capable of spawning 100 thousand airplanes overnight, and that in fifty years or so produced Jack Dempsey, Edna St. Vincent Millay, the Brothers Mayo, both Roosevelts [and on through a dozen more names], and Dr. J. Robert Oppenheimer, who made the atomic bomb go off just where he wanted it, how, and when.[15]

Though hardly a major literary figure, William L. Laurence of the *New York Times* epitomized in his work the problems of tone and style the atomic bomb posed for many writers. The Manhattan Project's official reporter, Laurence wrote the first dispatches about the bomb, and his 1946 account, *Dawn over Zero,* was a best-seller. At times, Laurence was the hard-bitten war reporter, concentrating on the facts at hand, noting the telling detail: "The Atomic Age began at exactly 5:30 Mountain War Time on the morning of July 16, 1945." At Nagasaki, trees miles from ground zero were seared "yellow and brown with brilliant fall colors." But this journalist was clearly shaken by the story that had fallen into his lap. The crew members' accounts after the Hiroshima bomb run, he wrote, "sounded more and more fantastic and awesome, more terrifying than any horror tale in fiction, more like something out of the pages of Dante." With mixed results, he struggled for a style worthy of the subject. Almost compulsively, he suggested new images and personifications for the mushroom-shaped cloud: a decapitated monster, a giant brain, the Statue of Liberty, a squatting totemic creature, a "funeral pyre" for Japan, a work of art so exquisite "that any sculptor would be proud to have created it," a mysterious phenomenon suggesting "the presence of the supranatural."[16]

Laurence's account of the Alamogordo test fluctuated between a gothicism reminiscent of a bad imitation of *Wuthering Heights*—as in the description of the thunder and lightning that rolled across the New Mexico mountains while waiting scientists huddled in the darkness—and a mystic lyricism faintly evocative of Molly Bloom's dreamy soliloquy at the end of

Ulysses: "The hills said yes and the mountains chimed in yes. It was as if the earth had spoken and the suddenly iridescent clouds and sky had joined in one affirmative answer. Atomic energy—yes." [17]

It was easy, of course, to poke fun at the literary deficiencies of such a writer. "The first explosion of the atomic bomb knocked Mr. Laurence breathless," said the *New Yorker* of *Dawn over Zero,* "and, judging by his style, he's been breathless ever since." But more was involved than the stylistic weaknesses of one journalist. The problem confronted all writers and artists. What was the appropriate aesthetic for the bomb? If an air raid on a small Spanish town could inspire one of Picasso's greatest canvases, or the individual brutalities of Napoleon's invasion of Spain Goya's most powerful work, how was one to respond imaginatively to Hiroshima and Nagasaki and, still more, to the prospect of world holocaust? The question haunted writers in 1945, and it would continue to do so. As one linguistic specialist asked in 1965: "Is it possible that in spite of our vast and ever-growing vocabulary we have finally created an object that transcends all possible description . . . ?" [18]

For Gertrude Stein, the very magnitude of the bomb's destructive power was precisely what made it unpromising as a literary subject. In a sad and fragmentary but wholly characteristic statement published posthumously in the *Yale Poetry Review,* the dying Stein wrote in 1946: "They asked me what I thought of the atomic bomb. I said I had not been able to take any interest in it. . . . What is the use, if they are really as destructive as all that there is nothing left and if there is nothing there [is] nobody to be interested and nothing to be interested about. . . . So you see the atomic [bomb] is not at all interesting, not any more interesting than any other machine. . . . Sure it will destroy a lot and kill a lot, but it's the living that are interesting not the way of killing them." [19] A bomb is a bomb is a bomb.

From this perspective, it seems naïve to assess the literary response to the bomb by combing post-Hiroshima poems and novels for explicit references. Why should one expect the most gifted writers immediately to incorporate this shattering new reality into their imaginative world? Silence may have signaled not a failure of imagination, but intensity of imagination—a recognition of the folly of too quickly trying to assimilate this monstrous novelty. Early postwar novels and poems dealt with what writers already knew from experience—in Trilling's case, the radical politics of the 1930s; in Bellow's, the urban immigrant experience; in Mailer's, the Pacific war; for Stevens, the reality of old age and approaching death. Overwhelming as the bomb was, except for a few scientists and several hundred thousand Japanese, it was not lived experience. The central reality of a new era, it was not yet accessible to the creative core of consciousness.

Further, these were also Americans; for them, as for their fellow citizens, the bomb was intimately associated with a war that for four years had dominated the nation's consciousness. A few had opposed the war (Robert Lowell served four months in prison as a conscientious objector), but most patriotically supported it. For them, the bomb's role in bringing that war to a successful conclusion figured importantly in their assessment of its significance. The poet Aaron Kramer, for example, reflecting years later on his failure to respond imaginatively to Hiroshima and Nagasaki, reminded a younger generation of the nearly universal sense in 1941–1945 that World War II was a just struggle against an unambiguous evil. He reprinted his wartime poem "Night Shift, Detroit," in which a war worker lovingly addresses the bombers he is helping build:

> Grow impatiently, children; and when you are
>   grown
> we will teach you to make of your shadow a terrible
>   thing,
> to answer for Guernica deep in the nests of the Rhine,
> and carry the hopes of the nations high on your wing!

This was to illustrate the context of his numbed reaction to Hiroshima and his "inability to feel, as I knew a decent man should feel, when the tidings of horror came." Disgusted by Truman's sanctimony, repelled by the orgy of celebration, uneasily guilty over his own reaction, Kramer nevertheless took years to overcome what he would later call his "hardheartedness" at the atomic annihilation of two cities.[20] He was far from alone.

To William Faulkner, the effect of the bomb seemed numbing rather than energizing. "Our tragedy today," he said in a less frequently quoted section of his 1950 Nobel Prize address,

> is a general and universal physical fear so long sustained by now that we can even bear it. There are no longer problems of the spirit. There is only the question: When will I be blown up? Because of this, the young man or woman writing today has forgotten the problem of the human heart in conflict with itself which alone can make good writing.

For the novelist Mary McCarthy, the bomb offered yet another depressing reminder of the ubiquitous reach and deadening spiritual effect of the modern technocratic order. Anticipating the cultural alienation that would become pervasive among intellectuals in the 1950s, McCarthy wrote in 1947:

> The movies, the radio, the super-highway have softened us up for the atom bomb; we have lived with them without pleasure, feeling them as a coercion on our natures, a coercion coming seemingly from no-

where and expressing nobody's will. The new coercion finds us without the habit of protest; we are dissident but apart.[21]

For the poet John Berryman, the cultural malaise associated with the bomb sprang from a deeper moral uncertainty. "It has been a bad decade so far," he wrote for a 1948 *Partisan Review* symposium on the state of American writing. In the aftermath of the war "and accompanying genocide," he said, "many seem to have lost their nerve. There is a political, perhaps a moral, paralysis." The secret decision to build, use, and stockpile atomic bombs, he went on, had produced "a widespread, violent condition of *bad conscience.*" Surpassing mere guilt, this condition was rooted in the sense of moral impotence Dwight Macdonald and others had articulated: the knowledge that decisions of the utmost moral significance could be made in one's name without one's participation or even knowledge.

If this bad conscience related only to past decisions or even current policy, Berryman contended, one might overcome its deadening effect. One could at least grudgingly accept the argument for using the bomb against Japan, and even for its value as a counterweight to Stalin's ambitions. But what future horror was implicit in the course the power-wielders had chosen?

To be reconciled to *this,* one would have to learn to be reconciled beforehand to an atrocious crime one might well soon commit without having the slightest wish to commit it; and that, I suppose, is out of the question. So that men who can think and are moral must stand ready night and day to the orders of blind evil. . . . It is not a state of mind, this readiness, favorable to writing.[22]

It is not surprising, then, that the most affecting and durable of the first literary works to confront the atomic bomb are not the pontifical and didactic proclamations, but quieter and more tentative works. Often not "about" the atomic bomb in a literal sense, a few fugitive poems and stories nonetheless clearly reflect a post-Hiroshima sensibility.

In "Sonnet to Lise Meitner" (1946), for example, Irene Orgel somewhat uneasily confronted the fact that a woman physicist had played a key theoretical role in bringing the atomic bomb to reality. Using images of conception, gestation, and birth as metaphors for the mind's quantum leap into an unknown and dangerous realm, the sonnet ends:

What has she seen? The embryonic brain
Looks up bewildered at the egg-blue sky,
And prays the hour of birth is not yet nigh,
Or wishes it were unconceived again.
What has she seen? And can she ever tell

(We call on men of science to explain)—
Whether the cracking of the fragile shell
Will free us into heaven or to hell?[23]

Randall Jarrell's "1945: The Death of the Gods" (1948) alludes to the atomic bomb as "the first human sun" and ends with an ambiguous vision of a final holocaust when the gods themselves will vanish with their human creators:

O warring Deities,
Tomorrow when the rockets rise like stars
And earth is blazing with a thousand suns
That set up there within your realms a realm
Whose laws are ecumenical, whose life
Exacts from men a prior obedience—
Must you learn from your makers how to die?[24]

John Berryman's "The Dispossessed" (1948) refers to the bomb in its final lines, offering a sharp new image, the umbrella, for the already hackneyed mushroom-shaped cloud. As in the *Partisan Review* symposium, Berryman ponders the issue of individual versus collective guilt and reflects on the way the bomb had sliced through history, leaving emptiness and deadness in its wake:

That which a captain and a weaponeer
one day and one more day did, we did, *ach*
we did not, *They* did . . . cam slid, the great lock

lodged, and no soul of us all was near was near,—
an evil sky (where the umbrella bloomed)
twirled its mustaches, hissed, the ingenue fumed,

poor virgin, and no hero rides. The race
is done. Drifts through, between the cold black trunks,
the peachblow glory of the perishing sun

in empty houses where old things take place.[25]

One of the best of these early post-Hiroshima poems, Milton Kaplan's "Atomic Bomb" (1948), explores the bomb's effects on the stratagems by which we inure ourselves to inexorable death:

Deep in our fear we think we will escape
Event, for we have wound our days
around

Us till we are inviolate: cocooned
By time and bandaged fleshly out of shape
We are too well disguised to die, though
    one
By one our brothers topple, meagre prey
Gnawed quickly naked to residual bone.

The bomb, profligate, wholesale destroyer, rips away the comforting illusion that one is somehow immune to mankind's common fate:

Never before have so many dead men
    reached
To tear the summer from our muffled brain
And claw us conscious to a season bleached
With danger. . . .

But such knowledge is too threatening; man will soon again clutch about himself the protective blanket of denial:

    No, even when
The focus narrows to the final point
That penetrates the insulated mind
And strips our consciousness of all pretense
To leave us cowering naked, face to face
With imminence, desperately we crawl
Backwards on hands and knees with shrill
    lament:
Not now! till arched against the ticking wall
Pointing the others out, separately
We shriek in unison: *Not me! Not me!*
Not me! [26]

The poems in Robert Lowell's *Lord Weary's Castle* (1946) were mostly written prior to August 1945, but one, "Where the Rainbow Ends," may be a post-Hiroshima work. In a series of harshly etched images, including the city's moldering colonial gravestones, it evokes a nightmare vision of the destruction of Lowell's native Boston:

I saw the sky descending, black and white,
Not blue, on Boston where the winters wore
the skulls to jack-o'-lanterns on the slates.
. . .   .
I saw my city in the Scales, the pans
of judgment rising and descending. Piles

of dead leaves char the air—
And I am a red arrow on this graph
of Revelations.[27]

The poem suggests Lowell's sense of the burden of the artist's prophetic role, as well as the difficulties of such a role in a technological age when graphs, statistics, equations, and the black-and-white of newspaper photographs and newsreels bear the doomsday message.

One of the earliest prose works to reflect a distinctly post-Hiroshima consciousness was Paul Bowles's 1949 short story "Pages from Cold Point." In this story, a recently widowed college professor unexpectedly resigns his position and, over the protests of his Babbitt-like brother, settles with his sixteen-year-old son on Cold Point, a remote corner of a small, unnamed Carribean island. The story begins with the professor's reflections on the bomb and its role in his decisions:

> Our civilization is doomed to a short life: its component parts are too heterogeneous. I personally am content to see everything in the process of decay. The bigger the bombs, the quicker it will be done. Life is visually too hideous for one to make the attempt to preserve it. Let it go. Perhaps some day another form of life will come along. Either way, it is of no consequence. At the same time, I am still a part of life, and I am bound by this to protect myself to whatever extent I am able. And so I am here. . . . It is beautiful here, the trade winds blow all year, and I suspect that bombs are extremely unlikely to be wasted on this unfrequented side of the island, if indeed on any part of it.

At first, life seems idyllic, but the son begins to withdraw amid intimations that all is not well. A local magistrate informs the father that the boy has made sexual advances to several males in the area, and that the populace is angry and restive. Unable to discuss the matter with his son, the father passively acquiesces in the youth's decision to move to Havana. The story ends with an affirmation that rings hollow. Alone now at Cold Point, the father reflects: "I am perfectly happy here in reality, because I still believe that nothing very drastic is likely to befall this part of the island in the near future."[28]

Nuclear fear is not the explicit theme of "Pages from Cold Point." Nevertheless, in an allusive and indirect way, Bowles suggests the interplay of the atomic threat and the other forces shaping his characters' consciousness and behavior. For Milton Kaplan, the atomic bomb was a reminder of inexorable fate and inevitable death; for Paul Bowles's hero, it offers the excuse for a break to a seemingly happier, less time-bound existence. (Interestingly, at just about the time "Pages from Cold Point" was published,

Bowles abandoned his career as a composer in New York City and became an expatriate writer in Morocco.[29]) A slight if well-crafted work, "Pages from Cold Point" is nevertheless of interest as one of the first literary works in which a post-Hiroshima sensibility seeps into the fabric of the story, influencing in fundamental ways its tone, structure, and emotional resonance.

21

Visions of the Atomic Future in Science Fiction and Speculative Fantasy

If the general literary response to the atomic bomb was tentative and muted, the authors of speculative fantasy and science fiction took up the theme with alacrity. In the early post-Hiroshima years, a flood of science fiction, including at least three full-scale novels, offered visions of possible atomic futures.

President Truman's announcement of August 1945 came as no surprise to the writers and readers of science fiction. The reaction of Ray Bradbury, riding a bus in Los Angeles, was typical: "I saw the headline, brought on the bus by a stranger, and thought: Yes, of course, so it's here! I knew it would come, for I had read about it and thought about it for years." H. G. Wells had predicted an atomic bomb in 1914, and in the 1920s and 1930s stories involving atomic weapons had appeared frequently in science-fiction magazines. In March 1944, for instance, *Astounding Science Fiction* published a story that described the construction of an atomic bomb so accurately that both the author and the editor, John W. Campbell, Jr., received visits from War Department security officials. (Thinking fast, Campbell convinced the authorities that his magazine had published so many atomic-bomb stories that suddenly to drop the theme would probably arouse suspicion!)[1]

After August 6, 1945, such stories retrospectively seemed amazingly prophetic, and the status of the genre rose accordingly. As Isaac Asimov later put it, science-fiction writers were "salvaged into respectability" by Hiroshima. Some took lucrative jobs as lecturers, government consultants, or science writers for general publications. Within days of Hiroshima, Campbell was interviewed by the *Wall Street Journal* for his thoughts on the bomb. ("Frankly, I am scared.") Breaking out of its literary ghetto, science fiction began to appear in mass-circulation magazines like *Collier's* and the *Saturday Evening Post.*[2]

But while atomic bombs were old stuff in the world of science fiction by 1945, Hiroshima still had a significant impact. Up to 1945, most science-fiction stories dealing with atomic weapons took place far in the future and often in another galaxy. As one practitioner observed in 1946, even those writers who had used atomic war as a "a limitless source of story materials" had recognized its horrendous potential only "in a delicious drawing-room sort of way, because they couldn't conceive of this Buck Rogers event happening to anything but posterity." Philip Wylie made the same point in September 1945: "All of us who had given real thought and careful imagination to an Atomic Age . . . have assumed it would be the hope and horror of future persons; we never dreamed that we, ourselves, would be asked . . . to sit down and write, 'Here it is. We must now do thus and so.'"[3]

Hiroshima ended the luxury of detachment. The atomic bomb was now reality, and the science-fiction stories that dealt with it amply confirm the familiar insight that for all its exotic trappings, science fiction is best understood as a commentary on contemporary issues.

When science-fiction writers imagined possible social consequences of the development of atomic weapons, the results were, as Albert Berger has documented, almost invariably bleak and pessimistic. In these stories, nuclear holocaust is an ever-present reality—sometimes as a looming or barely averted cataclysm; sometimes as an event that has already occurred. In Theodore Sturgeon's "Memorial" (1946), an idealistic scientist-hero reminiscent of Sinclair Lewis's Martin Arrowsmith tries to warn mankind of the danger of nuclear war by detonating a nuclear explosion that will transform the blast site into a deadly region of perpetual radioactivity: an eternal reminder of the fate of the earth if war should come. In a typical science-fiction twist, the blast that was to save mankind is misread by the military as a hostile attack, and the holocaust the scientist had hoped to forestall is unleashed. Playing upon another pervasive fear of this period, Chandler Davis, in "Nightmare" (1946), has saboteurs smuggle the components of an atomic bomb into New York City. They are captured, but the constant surveillance needed to avoid such incidents in the future transforms the United States into a police state.[4]

Reflecting the controversy over the May-Johnson bill, a number of these stories warned against military control of atomic energy. In Chandler Davis's "To Still the Drums" (1946), yet another heroic atomic scientist struggles against sinister military officers who have deluded Congress into funding an atomic-weapons project the scientist is convinced will lead to war. In a conclusion reminiscent of the movie *Mr. Smith Goes to Washington*, a young pilot courageously flies off to the nation's capital to warn a sympathetic senator. In Theodore Sturgeon's "Thunder and Roses" (1947), after the United States has already been destroyed in a nuclear attack, the military mechanically proceeds with a preprogrammed but utterly meaningless retaliatory strike that will wipe out the remainder of mankind. The crewmen of the nuclear-armed space station are the villains in Kris Neville's "Cold War"

(1949). Unhinged by their isolation, they become homicidal and launch an unprovoked attack on Earth.[5]

One of the more bizarre of these doomsday scenarios was George O. Smith's "The Answer" (1947), in which the secretary-general of the United Nations responds to an aggressor nation's preparations for war with a flood of protesting letters. Contemptuously, the bureaucracy in the hostile capital files away the masses of letters unread. But wait! Each piece of paper has been impregnated with a minute quantity of plutonium; when critical mass is achieved, a nuclear explosion is triggered, obliterating the aggressor government.[6]

The prolific young science-fiction writer Ray Bradbury dealt with the prospect of nuclear war in several stories in these years. In "The Highway" (1950), a Mexican peasant couple watches impassively as American tourists, having learned of the outbreak of war, stream northward to rejoin their families. Bradbury offers a slim ray of hope: perhaps the nonindustrialized regions of the earth will survive. At the end, the peasant turns stoically from the now silent highway to cultivate his fields. Recalling the hysterical scream of one tourist—"It's come, the atom war, the end of the world!"—he mutters to himself: "What do they mean, 'the world'?"[7]

In Bradbury's *The Martian Chronicles* (1950), a collection of stories originally published between 1946 and 1950, human beings who have colonized Mars watch in horror as a giant fireball envelops the Earth. Soon the explanatory message arrives: "AUSTRALIAN CONTINENT ATOMIZED IN PREMATURE EXPLOSION OF ATOMIC STOCKPILE. LOS ANGELES, LONDON BOMBED. WAR. COME HOME. COME HOME. COME HOME." Like the tourists in "The Highway" they dutifully set out for their desolate, incinerated planet.[8]

In the most famous of the *Martian Chronicles* stories, "There Will Come Soft Rains," an automated house continues to prepare meals, draw baths, mix drinks, clean floors, and recite poetry for occupants long since vaporized in a nuclear flash. Only the shadow images of playing children incised on the scorched walls give evidence that human beings had once been in residence.

At least three novels of these years, pervaded by similar intimations of impending doom, reflected and contributed to the national preoccupation with the nuclear menace. The first, *Mr. Adam* (1946), was by Pat Frank, a reporter who had served with the Office of War Information and then as a correspondent in Europe. *Mr. Adam* is set some years in the future, after all the world's males but one have been rendered sterile by a devastating accident at an atomic-power plant in Mississippi. The exception, a geologist named Homer Adam, was deep in a lead mine at the time of the nuclear disaster. Besieged by women, his semen declared a strategic resource by the U.S. government, the painfully shy Homer eventually sterilizes himself deliberately by entering a highly radioactive atomic-research laboratory. But the novel ends happily: a seaweed derivative is developed that restores male potency, and soon the maternity wards are filling up again.

For all its atomic trappings, *Mr. Adam* is essentially a satire on postwar American society. The range of targets is wide: Hollywood starlets, religious and racial prejudice, women politicians, the military mind, media huckster-ism (on one radio network a female quartet warbles: "For all the news of sterilization / Please keep tuned to this station"). A government artificial-insemination agency, the National Refertilization Project, is a nightmare of inefficiency that parodies the proliferating federal bureaucracy of the New Deal and World War II eras—a bureaucracy Frank doubtless knew well from his days at OWI.

In a parody of the national obsession with atomic secrecy, right-wing senators warn against permitting even a drop of what has suddenly become the world's scarcest natural resource to be exported to the Soviet Union. When a rumor circulates that two Soviet miners also escaped sterilization, the American artificial-insemination project goes into high gear, to assure that the world will be repopulated with capitalists.

Occasionally, Frank dropped the satiric mask and confronted directly the prospect of an atomic end to human history. The spokesman for the darker side of Pat Frank's vision is J. C., an elderly newspaper editor whose nihilistic views match those of Mark Twain's grim final years:

> If I were God, and I were forced to risk a time to deprive the human race of the magic power of fertility and creation, I think that time would be now. . . . When Mississippi blew up, God could just as easily have allowed the world to blossom as a nova. Instead, he is going to let it die like the last coal in the grate. Why fight it?

J. C. has nothing but caustic ridicule for the human species' preoccupation with its own survival: "It is as if an ant heap had been stamped down, and all the ants within cried that the world had come to an end."[9]

But such dark reflections clashed with Pat Frank's efforts to sustain a tone of easy humor and fairly lighthearted social satire. Like William L. Lawrence, Frank had trouble finding a style appropriate to his theme. Sharing his uncertainty, the book's publisher, J. P. Lippincott, decided to market it as a comedy, but one with a serious "message." "Readers all over the country will be laughing," predicted the jacket copy, and proceeded to quote reviewers who testified to the book's hilarity while making clear that beneath the fun were weighty issues to be pondered; "It makes you chuckle —yes," the *New York Times* reviewer noted judiciously, "but it also provides food for thought."

Ostensibly concerned with the most sobering theme imaginable, the genetic risks of atomic fission, *Mr. Adam* could manage only an ill-assorted mixture of satire, rather leering humor, and occasional nihilistic flashes. A justifiably forgotten novel, it remains of interest as an illustration of the problems of tone and style that vitiated so much early writing about the bomb—an aesthetic uncertainty that bore witness to a deeper cultural and moral uncertainty.

The sardonic humor of *Mr. Atom* is even more pervasive in *Greener Than You Think,* Ward Moore's 1947 allegorical novel of the world's end. In this story, global destruction comes through a mutant strain of grass, but the allusion to the atomic threat is plain enough. Even the title echoes a slogan of the scientists' movement: "It's Later Than You Think." Just as the atomic bomb was built to further a worthwhile purpose, so the new strain of grass is hybridized for the worthiest of reasons: to solve the world's hunger problem.* But it proliferates uncontrollably, and soon engulfs the entire earth. A few survivors take to the sea, but in the novel's final paragraph, tendrils of the all-consuming grass, having adapted to salt water, snake up through the deck of their boat.

Written in a feverish, surreal style, *Greener Than You Think* offers a bleakly comic vision of human behavior in the face of annihilation. At first, in a bizarre parody of America's actual reaction to the atomic bomb, radio comedians joke about the grass, newspapers publish detailed background stories on its chemical makeup, and a World Congress to Combat the Grass is convened, only to break up in nationalistic bickering. An eager-beaver huckster forms a corporation to develop new uses for the grass, and becomes a rich tycoon in the process. Radio evangelists proclaim that the grass is God's judgment on wicked humanity. Survival schemes include underground cities (similar to proposals actually made from 1945 to 1947) and high towers. The machinery of mass culture quickly turns scary reality into diverting fantasy:

> On the comic page, Superman daily pushed [the grass] back and there was great regret his activities were limited to the four-color process, while Terry Lee and Flash Gordon, ever inspirited by the sharp outlines of mammary glands, also saved the country. Even Li'l Abner and Snuffy Smith battled the vegetation. . . . *The Greengrass Blues* was heard on every radio and came from every adolescent's phonograph until it was succeeded by *Itty Bitty Seed Made Awfoo Nasty Weed.*

* Moore may have gotten his idea from one of Robert M. Hutchins's typical effusions of this period. Writing on the atomic-energy future in the December 1947 *American* magazine ("The Bomb Secret Is Out!") Hutchins predicted: "Lawns and gardens will be luxuriant, for atomic energy promises fertilizers and soil balancers more powerful than any known today."

Artists and writers struggle to respond creatively; an obsessed composer works feverishly on an interminable *Symphony of the Grass.*

But as the killer grass spreads famine, plague, and terror, even this simulation of normality collapses. The framework of civilization totters and "the stigmata of desperation" emerge—from overcrowded churches to an upsurge of crime, drug abuse, alcoholism, and sex orgies. As in Milton Kaplan's 1948 poem "Atomic Bomb," the imminence of mass annihilation disrupts the delicate psychic balance by which people in normal times manage to live with the knowledge of their mortality. People develop a morbid fascination with the grass and hover around its edges; a few throw themselves into it. Strange cults emerge to resist a life force that now seems meaningless: "In secret and impressive ceremonies women scarified their tenderest parts with red hot irons, thus proving themselves forever beyond the lusts of the flesh; men solemnly castrated themselves and threw the symbols of their manhood into a consuming fire."

The social fabric unravels. Starvation increases as farmers stop producing for the market and become self-sufficient survivalists. Only shared terror offers a final, tenuous social link, and it is not enough.

At the very end, a deep passivity that could be mistaken for restored psychic health seeps through society. The febrile activism, the cultural efflorescence, even the crime, cults, and orgies fade away as people seem to forget the grass that was once on every mind. "Tension dissolved into somnolence and the tempo of daily life slackened until it scarcely seemed to move at all. The waves of anxiety, suspicion and distrust of an earlier decade calmed into peaceful ripples, hardly noticeable in a pondlike existence." [10] In a numbed stupor, the handful of survivors await the fate that soon overwhelms them.

The last and best of this trio of post-Hiroshima apocalyptic novels, George R. Stewart's *Earth Abides* (1949), strikes a slightly more hopeful note. The theme is human endurance and continuity at a rudimentary level. An English professor at Berkeley, Stewart was a writer who had already explored human behavior under extreme conditions in *Ordeal by Hunger* (1936), a history of the Donner Party. In *Earth Abides,* the globe has been swept by a deadly plague that has killed all but a few isolated individuals. (Like *Greener Than You Think,* this novel is not explicitly about nuclear holocaust, but it is clearly a product of, and comment upon, the pervasive fears of the early atomic era.)

Taking his title from Ecclesiastes—"Men go and come, but earth abides"—Stewart carries his hero, Isherwood Williams, "Ish," a University of California geography professor, through the first half century or so after the "Great Disaster." Initially, *Earth Abides* seems as bleak as *Greener Than You Think.* Panicky survivors scavenge in supermarkets, copulate randomly, drink themselves into a stupor, or go quietly insane. As religious fanatics shout in empty streets, society's complex and interconnected technological systems fail one by one: tires go flat, batteries die, gasoline pumps stop working; nights are suddenly inky black as power plants cease to function; faucets go dry and toilets no longer flush as water systems break down. Clothes grow ragged; ants, rats, and packs of wild dogs proliferate; the supply of bullets runs out. Inexorably, the survivors are driven back to more and more primitive levels of existence.

On an exploratory automobile trip to the East Coast, Ish finds all the great cities stinking and abandoned. In New York he encounters a couple bizarrely carrying on as though nothing had happened—playing endless rounds of cards, drinking their predinner martinis, cheerfully welcoming the visitor—but it all rings false. "From shock they were walking in a kind of haze. . . . Milt and Ann . . . were city dwellers, and when the city died they would hardly survive without it." He observes the same numbness and lassitude in other survivors. Cut off from job, family, church, and other familiar cultural props, numbed survivors remain physically alive, but "in a kind of emotional death." Ish even observes signs of the same deterioration in himself as he sits motionless for long periods, "conscious but in sheer apathy."

The closest approach to total despair in *Earth Abides* comes as Stewart reflects on how little difference human extinction would make to the larger rhythms of life on earth:

> Of half a million species of insects only a few dozen were appreciably affected by the demise of man, and the only ones actually threatened with extinction were the three species of the human louse. . . . Throughout hundreds of millennia, the lice had adjusted their life nicely to their world . . . and lost the capacity of existing upon any other host.
>
> The overthrow of man was therefore their overthrow. Feeling their world growing cold, they crawled off in search of some new warm world to inhabit, found none, and died. Billions perished most miserably.
>
> At the funeral of *homo sapiens* there will be few mourners. *Canis familiaris* as an individual will perhaps send up a few howls, but as a species, remembering all the kicks and curses, he will soon be comforted and run off to join his wild fellows. *Homo sapiens,* however, may take comfort from the thought that at his funeral there will be three wholly sincere mourners.

But soon *Earth Abides* turns more hopeful. As the modern technological order collapses, a profound peace settles over the land. Unlike the ominous terminal lassitude in *Greener Than You Think,* this is the tranquillity of a species rediscovering its authentic place in the natural order. Men and women are drawn together, babies are conceived, the family is recreated. Ish himself joins up with a mulatto woman of little education but much common sense and a strong will to survive and perpetuate humanity. Soon these families begin to come together to form tribes. No longer unnaturally crowded together, human beings lose their competitive impulses and unite against the common dangers they face. Evil remains, to be sure. A loathsome outsider riddled with venereal disease tries to rape a feebleminded young woman of Ish's tribe. After a solemn council, the intruder is summarily hanged. But the dominant note is harmony and cooperation, not discord and violence.

At first, Ish feels a compulsion to perpetuate the culture he knows. He starts a school, proclaims the university library a sacred place, and institutes rituals to remind the tribe of the passage of the years. "After all," he reflects, "time was history, and history was tradition, and tradition was civilization. If you lost the continuity of time, you lost something that might never be recovered." Gradually, however, the cultural trappings of civilization go the way of its technology; even the language reverts to more rudimentary forms. To his surprise, Ish finds himself accepting this process. His new outlook is reinforced by the death of a particularly bright son in whom he had placed high hopes. Abruptly closing the school, he teaches the young basic survival skills—how to use a bow and arrow, how to build a fire—and simple forms of social organization appropriate to their tribal existence. He pays a final visit to the library, but finds that its hold on him is gone. "Will I dream of a million books passing in endless procession, looking reproachfully upon me," he reflects, "because after so long I have begun to have doubts in them and all they stood for?" [11]

At the end of the novel, the aged Ish is the revered chief of the tribe. He is regarded with superstitious awe by the young as the last of that vanished, half-mythic race called Americans who built the tall buildings and soaring bridges whose ruins brood over the encroaching wilderness, and who made the mysterious round metal objects with faces on them which the hunters of the tribe methodically sharpen into tips for their arrowheads. Ish dies content, gazing at the towers of the Golden Gate Bridge and the abiding hills around San Francisco Bay. A social order had vanished, man had survived.

If the holocaust comes, said George Stewart, modern civilization will surely perish, but with luck the surviving remnant might achieve an existence more in harmony with nature and with each other. *Earth Abides,* with its qualified message of hope—an almost desperate grasping for reassurance —compared to the other postwar speculative writings about possible atomic futures seems a work of soaring optimism. Indeed, it stands practically alone in this respect. At a time when many opinion-molders were arguing briskly that with intelligence, planning, and goodwill the atomic threat could be controlled and atomic energy made a great blessing to mankind, science-fiction writers and the authors of speculative fiction were offering a counter-vision almost unrelieved in its bleakness and despair.

22

Second Thoughts About Prometheus: The Atomic Bomb and Attitudes Toward Science

The Beginning or the End—MGM's 1946 movie about the atomic bomb—offered some very confusing messages about science. Scientists like Einstein and Fermi are presented as heroic, larger-than-life figures, yet a fictional scientist named Matt Cochran, who throughout the movie expresses deep reservations about the bomb, is fatally injured by a radiation leak as he readies the bomb for delivery. In the concluding scene, his pregnant widow visits the Lincoln Memorial as a voice-over recites his final letter to her. "That's what I get for building this thing," he says. Yet he goes on to express confidence in his superiors and hope that his work will benefit mankind.[1]

Is Matt's death Hollywood's revenge on "science"? Or, as the Lincoln imagery suggests, is he a martyr-hero? The movie's ambivalent view of science in fact mirrored a larger ambivalence in post-Hiroshima America. For some, the timely arrival of the atomic bomb—what President Truman hailed in his initial announcement as "the greatest achievement of organized science in history"—offered compelling proof of the beneficence of the scientific enterprise. "Hats off to the men of research," declared the *Milwaukee Journal* in an August 8 editorial titled "A Tribute to the Scholars." The Hiroshima bomb, said the *New York Herald Tribune* the same day, was "a joint product of an international brotherhood which takes little note of national boundaries except those of the enemy." Never again, agreed the *St. Louis Post-Dispatch,* should the nation's "science-explorers . . . be denied anything needful for their adventures."[2]

Science periodicals seized upon such responses to promote goodwill for their enterprise. "However deplorable the human deficiencies that made it necessary for American and British scientists to develop the atomic bomb," observed *Scientific Monthly* in September 1945, "we must admire their glorious achievement. . . . Modern Prometheans have raided Mount Olympus again and have brought back for man the very thunderbolts of Zeus."[3]

Such appeals gave an incalculable boost to the proposals for greater public funding of scientific research. In a September 1945 message to Congress urging support for a National Science Foundation, President Truman used the bomb as his clinching argument: "The events of the past few years are both proof and prophecy of what science can do. . . . The development of atomic energy is a clear-cut indication of what can be accomplished by our universities, industry, and Government working together. Vast scientific fields remain to be conquered in the same way." How the NSF idea "would have fared . . . on [its] own merits we will never know," conceded one supporter, but once the atomic bomb propelled science "to the center of the stage . . . and spotlighted it," he went on, Congress was soon "tumbling over itself with proposals to nourish the roots of discovery."[4]

The campaign to use the bomb project to promote favorable public attitudes toward science and scientists found eloquent expression in the 1947 report of nine Harvard Nieman fellows urging better science reporting in the nation's newspapers: "Science is a universal, unifying language; like music, it makes the whole world kin. Its most momentous achievement, the atomic bomb, was the joint product of Austrian, German, Italian, Danish, British, French, and American scientists. The world-wide fraternity of science gives us an international bond." *Scientific Monthly* heartily agreed:

> If most citizens of the important countries of the world were equal in intellectual and ethical stature to those whose names appear in "American Men of Science," danger of misuse of atomic power would not exist. The most important fruits of science are the character and way of life of scientists; the material results of scientific knowledge are but by-products.

In the same vein, science writer David Dietz declared in *Atomic Energy in the Coming Era:* "The true scientist is motivated by a higher aim than that of making life easier. He wishes to ennoble and to enrich life. . . . Science is the spirit of courage . . . of tolerance. . . . The scientist . . . envisions mankind marching down the ages, with comprehension of the universe growing greater and greater, his mastery of nature and of himself ever increasing."[5]

Calls for broader application of the methods of science were widely heard in the aftermath of Hiroshima. Indeed, some argued that scientists themselves should become society's political and ethical guides. Raymond Gram Swing saw them as "the architect[s] of the future." Philip Wylie urged in *Collier's* that they be brought at once into high government positions, for only they could "fully comprehend the data upon which all future human existence will depend." Thinking still more cosmically, Wylie proposed a "World Chamber of Intelligence" made up of representatives of the major branches of science and scholarship. Through such an advisory body, the internationalism of science and its commitment to truth and "common sense" could be transmitted into the political realm.[6]

Some scientists and cultural observers, however, warned against this tendency to view scientists as miracle workers. "I started this book [in 1944] with the idea of showing people that atomic physics was far from bankrupt," wrote physicist O. R. Frisch in his 1947 popularization *Meet the Atoms.* "After the atomic bomb was launched, I felt that the opposite message was the more urgent, that atomic physicists are not supermen." Edward L. Long, Jr., warned in 1950 that a dialectical process seemed to be shaping public attitudes toward science. The publicity surrounding the Manhattan Project had initially given rise to vastly inflated hopes for the promise of science, but as these unrealistic anticipations were dashed a mood of revulsion might be expected.[7] Such warnings were solidly grounded. For along with admiration and exaggerated expectations, the atomic bomb also brought expressions of deep apprehension and hostility toward science—expressions that became more insistent as the postwar glow of pride gave way to sober second thoughts.

As early as 1914, H. G. Wells had brooded about "the gift of destruction" he saw as "the black complement of all those other gifts science was urging upon unregenerate mankind." In 1945, contemplating the atomic bomb and other developments of the intervening years, the dying Wells completed his final and bleakest book, *Mind at the End of Its Tether,* which concluded that neither science nor human reason could guarantee individual happiness or social progress. As so often in the past, Wells's reaction was remarkably on target. The fear that surged through American culture after August 1945 quickly gave rise to broader apprehensions about science and where it was leading. If Truman's boast was correct that the bomb was "the greatest achievement of organized science in history," wrote Dwight Macdonald in *Politics* a few days after Hiroshima, then "so much the worse for organized science." "News of the bomb," he said, had intensified his "growing doubts about the 'Scientific Progress' which has whelped this monstrosity." Indeed, he said, the prideful descriptions of the bomb as a giant step forward in the onward march of science was for him the episode's most chilling aspect. The "popular suspicion, perhaps only half conscious, that the 19th century trust in science was mistaken"—a suspicion reflected, for example, in the stereotype of the sinister scientist in popular culture—had now, Macdonald concluded, been abundantly confirmed.[8]

Macdonald expressed in a particularly intense way one extreme of a complex and ambivalent public mood. In powerful counterpoint to the almost desperate faith in scientists as technological wonder-workers and political sages, one also finds strong currents of fear, mistrust, and disillusionment. The bomb, wrote Manhattan Project physicist Louis Ridenour in the Spring 1946 *American Scholar,* had "entirely transformed lay thinking regarding science. . . . [People] are beginning to hate and fear [it]. They feel . . . that scientists are somehow warmongers." Much evidence supports Ridenour's generalization. Post-Hiroshima letters-to-the-editor in the nation's newspapers, for example, reflected praise and fear of science in about equal proportions. "Science a Menace" and "Science Moving Too Fast" were typical captions. A letter in the *Portland Oregonian* called the bomb "the idiot child of science and the machine age." A *Louisville Courier-Journal* reader urged a moratorium on research until scientists became more "morally adept." Give science a rest until we spiritually catch up, agreed a *Boston Globe* subscriber.[9]

The view was similarly mixed in newspaper editorial columns. The *St. Louis Post-Dispatch*'s simultaneous praise for science's "triumph" and fear that science had "signed the mammalian world's death warrant" was not unusual. The *Detroit News,* soon after it called for more government-funded scientific research, brooded that a combination of atomic science and German guided-missile technology could bring the human race "to a new pitch of utter terror." W. E. B. DuBois, writing in the *Chicago Defender,* struck the same note: "We have seen . . . to our amazement and distress, a marriage between science and destruction. . . . We have always thought of science as the emancipator. We see it now as the enslaver of mankind." Noting the undercurrent of hostility amidst the plaudits, *Scientific Monthly* observed in September 1945: "Grave doubts are in many minds, and science is being regarded both with greater respect and with greater apprehension than ever before." The enhanced prestige of science, commented a University of Chicago sociologist specializing in popular responses to technological innovations, had deepened the average citizen's sense of helplessness. "All his education in popular science makes him a good audience, but he is convinced that scientists must control matters."[10]

The ambivalence of post-Hiroshima attitudes toward science was also noted by Rockefeller Foundation president Raymond B. Fosdick. "Certainly we laymen are frightened by science as we never were before," said Fosdick in a November 1945 radio address; "It seems as if science were facing a vast dilemma. Science is the search for truth. . . . It springs from the noblest attribute of the human spirit. But . . . this same search for truth . . . has brought our civilization to the brink of destruction." And science's dilemma, warned Fosdick, was society's dilemma as well: "What do we do— curb our science or cling to the pursuit of truth and run the risk of having our society torn to pieces?" Robert M. Hutchins, as usual, put the matter provocatively. "Other civilizations were destroyed by barbarians from without. We breed our own," he declared. "They have marvelous technical skill. They may even be very learned in specific disciplines. But they are barbarians."[11]

Such sentiments found expression at many cultural levels. In post-Hiroshima science fiction, the image of the scientist as idealistic crusader for peace was often balanced by the counterimage of the morally blind, technologically obsessed sociopath. In *Mr. Adam,* for instance, the villains are a cabal of scientists who try to replace the National Refertilization Project with their own mad scheme of genetic engineering to produce a master race of scientific geniuses. Most evil of all is Felix Pell, a Columbia University physicist whose "massive head" is linked by a "thin, wrinkled stem" to his "shrunken body." Observing Pell's cold, detached manner during an interview, the narrator observes: "Up to this moment I had regarded him with a great deal of respect, and even awe, for was he not one of the superior beings who had, in the President's words, tapped the source from which the sun draws its power? But of a sudden I hated him, and I knew that I would not be alone in my hate."[12]

Nor was the portrayal of "science" in post-Hiroshima political cartoons always favorable. The *Philadelphia Inquirer* pictured a scatterbrained hunter firing off "Science's Atomic Shot Gun" in all directions, with the caption: "We've Got to Have More Powerful Game Laws." In the *Louisville Courier-Journal,* the scientist was pictured as a huckster touting atomic energy as a miracle product capable of doing almost anything.[13]

Theologians and churchmen predictably were among the first to insist that in an age of atomic bombs, the uncritical belief in science and its beneficent promise could never again be a pillar of the culture. The scientists' achievement was not only a "triumph of research," declared the president of Fordham University a few days after Hiroshima, but also "a superb symbol for the Age of Efficient Chaos." The threat of nuclear annihilation, wrote Reinhold Niebuhr in October 1945, had decisively ended "the era in which science assumed that all of its discoveries were automatically beneficent to mankind." It was now clear that science had potential for evil as well as good, and "sometimes the evil is more obvious and immediate than the good." Such observations sometimes had a certain "I-told-you-so" quality. "This was the age, you may remember, which was to bring complete security to man, through science's mastery of nature," editorialized one religious periodical late in 1945. "Instead, science produced the atomic bomb and engulfed the nations in an hysteria of fear." All hope for the "redemption of mankind simply through progress in the sciences and technology," declared the Calhoun Commission in 1947, had been "permanently wrecked by the latest achievement in that very progress."[14]

Christian Century, the voice of liberal Protestantism, made the point forcefully in its editorial of August 22, 1945. Washington's atomic-bomb announcement, it said, had aroused "overwhelming fear of the future into which science is leading mankind. . . . The scientist is not so great a figure as he formerly was in the eyes of the common man. His stature is dwarfed by the magnitude of the thing he has done. His is no longer a messianic figure." While warning against an antiscience reaction that could extinguish the "divine fire" of curiosity implanted in man, the magazine insisted that the atomic bomb made essential a reassessment of "the entire scientific enterprise in Western culture." The bomb, it said, was the ultimate product of a centuries-long process by which science and technology had separated from their religious and ethical roots and taken on a powerful momentum as independent historical forces. The quest to subdue nature and pursue knowledge for its own sake had become the age's "ruling passion," relegating to the background the questions of ethics and social good that were at the heart of the Judeo-Christian tradition. Concluding on a note of highly tentative hope, this editorial speculated that "the awe and foreboding" the bomb had aroused in "scientists and common people" alike might conceivably presage "a new era of understanding between science and Christian faith" through which man might become "morally capable of living in a scientific world." [15]

Harry Emerson Fosdick reached the same conclusions by a somewhat different route. The atomic bombing of Japan, he said in a sermon broadcast nationally shortly after Hiroshima, had completed "the most colossal breakdown of optimism in history"—the dissolution of the belief in scientific progress. Speaking autobiographically, Fosdick traced this process, in his own experience, to World War I:

> Younger people who have come to social consciousness since 1918 cannot possibly imagine the mood of optimism in which we were reared. We lived in the days of the first telephones, the first express trains, the first uses of electricity, the first internal combustion engines, the first of so many ingenious devices that we stood on tiptoe wondering what new marvel would appear tomorrow. We were the natural disciples of Herbert Spencer and his gospel of inevitable progress.

But this technological faith, long weakening, had now been shattered: "The high hopes built on these scientific achievements . . . have crashed to the ground as man has proved to be so insane, so corrupt, that the more power you give him the more he will destroy himself. . . . The flash of the atomic bomb lights all that up with frightening clarity." Normally a cheerful preacher, Fosdick on this subject was deeply pessimistic. "We are Frankensteins, who have created a technological civilization that in the hands of sin can literally exterminate us," he declared. "Unless great ethical religion can catch up . . ., our science will be used to destroy us." [16]

From all points of the religious spectrum, spokesmen seized the post-

Hiroshima moment to challenge the exaggerated cultural standing of science and its practitioners. A. J. Muste expressed dismay that atomic scientists whose minds only a short time before had collectively "become a munitions factory, as it were" should enjoy far more "intellectual and spiritual prestige" than the nation's religious leaders. Muste acknowledged that a radical movement of scientists against war and war-making research could dramatically change the nation's "whole spiritual climate," but he saw little prospect for such a development. While some continued to campaign for international control, he pointed out, many were returning to the laboratory to pursue government-sponsored weapons research. The "modern exaltation of science and of scientists," agreed Roman Catholic archbishop Richard J. Cushing of Boston in 1948, "forgets that there are whole areas of human interest, human need, and human activity in which the scientist has no special contribution to make." Indeed, he told students at Boston College, the harnessing of science to nationalistic purposes seemed almost inevitably to produce narrow specialists "insensible to the world of moral values." The "immediate and urgent problem," declared Protestant theologian L. Harold DeWolf that same year, was how mankind could enjoy the benefits of "science the angel of truth and mercy," while avoiding being "crazed, depersonalized, and burned alive by science the monstrous destroyer." [17]

Sensing this post-Hiroshima hostility toward science, a number of leading scientists tried to counteract it. As a loyal man of science, Louis Ridenour was dismayed by the hatred of science he saw building in the culture. To blame the atomic scientists for Hiroshima and Nagasaki, he insisted, was "confusing the weapon with its wielder." Scientists, he said, were growing "impatient with the . . . idea that scientific progress has outstripped man's ability to assimilate technical advance, so that physical science must be stopped to enable the social sciences to catch up." All such suggestions, he insisted—and indeed the entire phenomenon of popular hostility to scientists—reflected an insidious anti-intellectualism that needed to be vigorously resisted: "The keystone of the scientists' creed is that it is good to learn, it is evil to suppress knowledge. . . . The scientist regrets the world's forsaking of the principle that knowledge enriches life. His mind and his emotions hold that to know is good, to refuse to know depraved. He fears a world in which this is no longer true." [18]

A few months earlier, addressing the American Philosophical Society, J. Robert Oppenheimer did concede that Hiroshima had undermined, perhaps fatally, the public's belief in "the unqualified value . . . of scientific power and progress":

We have made a thing, a most terrible weapon, that has altered abruptly and profoundly the nature of the world . . . a thing that by all the standards of the world we grew up in is an evil thing. And by so doing . . . we have raised again the question of whether science is good for man, or whether it is good to learn about the world, to try to understand it, to try to control it.

Society's answers to these questions, Oppenheimer concluded, would determine the future of science as an esteemed cultural pursuit: "Not only the preferences and tastes of scientists are in jeopardy, but the substance of their faith."

> Whatever the individual motivation and belief of the scientist, without that recognition from his fellow men of the value of his work, in the long term science will perish. . . . Because we are scientists, . . . it is our faith and our commitment, seldom made explicit, even more seldom challenged, that knowledge is a good in itself, knowledge and such power as must come with it.[19]

The most refreshingly candid of these early efforts by American science to counteract post-Hiroshima public hostility was an October 1945 editorial in *Natural History,* the publication of the American Museum of Natural History. Acknowledging that the thrill of victory was rapidly yielding to "profound concern about a future exposed to the uses of atomic energy," this editorial warned that any restriction on research in this area could block "the advance of physics along other and more innocent fronts." Science was a seamless web, it suggested. If any areas were "set aside and marked dangerous," the whole enterprise could founder. But rather than rhetorically affirming the nobility of the scientist's faith, in the manner of Oppenheimer and Ridenour, *Natural History* offered a blunter assessment. Whatever the shifting moods of the moment, it said, science and technology were so deeply embedded in the structure of modern life that any reaction against them could be no more than a fleeting and temporary phenomenon: "Mankind is too comfortably installed on a *de luxe* express named 'Science.' There are no stops."[20]

Despite scientists' efforts to reverse the trend, the reaction against "science" intensified as the 1940s wore on. In its most extreme form, it involved proposals for a moratorium on atomic-energy research. Any society with "a modicum of reason and moral discipline," argued Lewis Mumford in 1948, would prohibit such research for at least a decade and concentrate on building agencies of international order. "We have reached a point in history," he said, "where the unchecked pursuit of truth, without regard to its social consequences, will bring to a swift end the pursuit of truth, by wiping out the very civilization that has favored it."[21]

Few went so far, but the trend was clear. "Because a man is a success in physics," observed *New York Times* science editor Waldemar Kaempfert in 1949, "it does not follow that he is qualified to elucidate political issues that perplex able and honest statesmen." Public-opinion pollsters that year found an "anti-scientific sentiment" building in the nation. That same year, the editor of *Scientific American* commented on the paradox of a society built on science that nevertheless regarded scientists "with almost hysterical fear." The reason, he regretfully concluded, was all too clear: "To the average civilized man of 1950, science no longer means primarily the promise of a more abundant life; it means the atomic bomb."[22]

The post-Hiroshima changes in American attitudes toward science may not have been as radical or dramatic as some observers suggested. Such cultural sea changes rarely occur overnight, even under the impact of so shattering a development as the advent of nuclear weapons. When this has been acknowledged, however, it seems clear that the coming of the atomic bomb did influence in important ways the cultural standing of scientists and the scientific enterprise. A useful benchmark is a 1955 lecture at Harvard University in which Manhattan Project veteran I. I. Rabi addressed this question. Down to the 1940s, he said, "science remained almost unchallenged as the source of enlightenment, understanding, and hope for a better, healthier, and safer world." Indeed, "in the person of Albert Einstein, science enjoyed a world-wide respect almost akin to reverence and hardly equalled since the time of Isaac Newton." But since 1945, Rabi continued, a "significant change" had taken place: the pursuit once held in such esteem was now equated in many minds with "the destruction of life and the degradation of the human spirit." Identifying science with atomic destruction and the threat of ultimate annihilation, he said, many had reached the "glib conclusion . . . that science and the intellect are therefore false guides" and were turning elsewhere "for hope and salvation." Rabi clearly deplored this "mood of anti-intellectualism," but he did not deny its reality.[23] Indeed, he saw it as one of the atomic bomb's principal legacies, and in this he was surely correct. It is a legacy that has continued to resonate powerfully in the American culture down to the present.

A few months before Rabi's lecture, the federal government had underscored his central point in the most vivid way imaginable. In 1954, after a grueling administrative trial conducted in the glare of media publicity, J. Robert Oppenheimer—the quintessential "atomic scientist"—was denied his government security clearance on a variety of charges including vaguely defined "defects of character." The Oppenheimer case had many aspects, to be sure, but as a piece of cultural theater, it symbolized in the starkest conceivable way the fear and animosity that had increasingly surfaced as an important component of post-Hiroshima American attitudes toward modern science and its ambiguous gifts.

23

Psychological Fallout: Consciousness and the Bomb

> **For imaginative and for informed minds, the atom bomb has already fallen with a sickening, prolonged explosion in their hearts.**
>
> —Joseph Barth, *The Art of Staying Sane*—(1948) [1]

In 1950, the *New York Times Magazine* invited Michael Amrine, a publicist with the Federation of American Scientists, to survey the first five years of the atomic age. Amrine chose not to concentrate on the scientists' movement, the May-Johnson bill, the Baruch plan, or the rest of the familiar public story. Rather, he tried to assess the impact of the new age on the American consciousness. The atomic bomb's "most important effects," he insisted, "are those in the minds of men." [2]

The relatives of those who died in Hiroshima and Nagasaki would surely not have agreed with this shift of emphasis from the reality of seared flesh and radiation-riddled corpses to the abstract realm of consciousness, yet Amrine had a point. Indeed, a central premise of this book has been that the bomb's larger impact on culture and consciousness demands more attention than it has received. But what was the effect on "the minds of men"? We have explored aspects of this question, but not yet addressed it directly. In part this reflects authorial cowardice, for this is perhaps the most difficult of all the cultural realms to examine. Not only does it overlap frustratingly with other matters already looked at—the bomb's social effects, its ethical implications, its impact on writers and poets—but the evidence is scanty, murky, and indirect, involving impressionistic generalizations by social observers about other people's feelings, or vague speculation about possible future states of collective consciousness.

The question of the bomb's psychological impact is further complicated by the fact that only a handful of psychiatrists or psychologists addressed it in these years. True, in the heady days of 1946, at the urging of the Federation of American Scientists, the "Society for the Psychological Study of Social Issues" of the American Psychological Association issued a brief report that attempted to apply psychological expertise to the problem of avoiding atomic war. ("Neither war nor peacefulness is inborn," it asserted —both were culturally learned. The mutual misunderstanding that underlay conflicts among nations, it advised, could be overcome by cultural and intellectual exchanges aimed at promoting "friendly attitudes and mutual understanding with people of all nations and especially politically important groups in major nations.") However, there was (perhaps mercifully) little follow-up to this one-shot pronouncement. In a 1947 address, for instance, the chairman of the Committee on Social Issues of the Group for the Advancement of Psychiatry, a social-activist subgroup within the American Psychiatric Association, discussed a potpourri of social issues that should concern psychiatrists—the role of women, unemployment, racial and religious prejudice, the problems of the returned veteran—but made only a fleeting and superficial reference to the atomic bomb.[3]

Even the journalists, science-popularizers, and others who speculated so freely about the coming atomic age were significantly less confident in discussing possible alterations in human consciousness. "The psychological effects will be hard to calculate in advance," wrote John J. O'Neill in his 1945 book *Almighty Atom,* "as they may be based on emotional reactions for which there is no rational foundation."[4]

In the absence of extended or systematic discussion by either specialists or laypersons, one must turn to other kinds of evidence: allusions in poetry and fiction, passing comments by journalists, tentative speculations and predictions by cultural observers. Though scattered, there is, in fact, a great deal of such evidence. Collectively, it seems, Americans in these earliest post-Hiroshima months were trying to anticipate, and in a sense steel themselves for, what lay ahead. Piecing together these fragmentary observations, one can assemble a kind of dreamscape of the nuclear future: distorted, luridly exaggerated, at times totally off base—yet in gross outline only too recognizable. In these early speculations, one finds anticipations of almost all the themes later observers would develop when they wrote of the psychic consequences of living with the nuclear threat. In this dreamscape, we find the first rough sketch of the world we, in fact, now inhabit.

What were its contours? Its central motif was the palpable fear that swept American society after Hiroshima—the fear that so many commentators noted. Joseph Barth in 1948 echoed what scores of cultural observers had been saying for three years: "Many people are already minor neurotics, worrying about the falling atom bomb. 'When the atom bomb falls!' 'When the atom bomb falls!' 'When the atom bomb falls!' It echoes through living rooms and lecture halls and over bar tables and on the quiet beach like the tragic refrain of some chorus in a Greek tragedy."[5]

Some deplored this fear, or offered anodynes. The "black cloud of anxiety" and the "hysteria" pervading post-Hiroshima society did not "reflect credit on the United States," insisted William L. Borden in 1946. Certainly the atomic threat would "strain the nerves of any people," he wrote, but the important thing was to "face danger coolly and take those precautions which offer the best protection. . . . The future belongs to the stout of heart." Churchmen, naturally, saw religion as the best antidote to terror. The secular view of the permanence and ultimate importance of life on this earth left one "poorly prepared for the insecurities of our present existence," said one religious journal late in 1945. Only those who grasped the Christian emphasis on the eternal and recognized that "history is not so simply meaningful as modern culture had assumed," this editorial continued, could achieve in a world of atomic bombs that "sublime nonchalance" possible to those "who truly live by faith." Warning against "misdirected panic," the Calhoun Commission in 1946 similarly affirmed that "amid all the perils of earthly life," God was still working "to change men's hearts and win them back from the edge of impending ruin." Even if an atomic war destroyed all but a remnant of humanity, it said, "God could . . . bring to realization through them new stretches of history, perhaps new levels of spiritual community." Indeed, even if all life should perish (what Jonathan Schell would later call the "Second Death") "whatever men have done, whatever of human existence has been good, He will cherish forever."[6] Well intentioned though they were, these efforts to talk Americans out of their atomic fear merely serve, in retrospect, to underscore the pervasiveness and depth of that fear.

A few commentators predicted this fear would be short lived—all would soon return to normal. "As public attention has turned from the implications of atomic power," suggested a writer in *Politics* within weeks of Hiroshima, "so will the brief shock subside and the customary relations of pre-atomic culture continue." Most, however, had little doubt that it would survive and even intensify. "Let there be no delusions . . . ," wrote the editor of the *Christian Advocate* in September 1945, "the atomic bomb is here to stay and is destined, in our opinion, to hold the world in the grip of terror for the next one hundred years." America's post-Hiroshima "sickness of mind and heart," wrote theologian Wesner Fallaw in 1946, was "nothing compared with what is ahead." So long as mankind faced the threat of a holocaust that could obliterate not only individuals and their loved ones but also "signal the doom of . . . civilization," agreed Chicago psychiatrist Jules H. Masserman in 1947, "no sentient man or woman can really find peace of mind and body."[7]

But what was unique in all of this? Fear was pervasive, all agreed, but fear of what? Not just death, surely; there was nothing new about that. As C. S. Lewis observed in his 1945 poem "On the Atomic Bomb":

> What's here to dread? For mortals
> Both hurt and death were certain
> Already; our light-hearted
> Hopes from the first sentenced to final thwarting.

It seems, rather, to have been fear of what Norman Cousins called "irrational death"—death of a new kind, death without warning, death *en masse*. The writings of this period are full of apprehensions of instantaneous, totally unexpected collective annihilation that might at any moment, as one writer put it, "come fluttering out of the skies or be planted as a time bomb in the heart of our cities." Such emotions were played upon endlessly by the campaigners for the international-control plan. Without such an agreement, warned Harold Urey, "the end will be deadly fear everywhere. . . . A world of vast fear and apprehension will be our lot and that of our children. . . . We will eat fear, sleep fear, live in fear and die in fear." Edward Condon's contribution to *One World or None* offered a grim picture of atomic-age sabotage:

> In any room where a file case can be stored, in any district of a great city, near any key building or installation, a determined effort can secrete a bomb capable of killing a hundred thousand people. . . . And we cannot detect this bomb except by stumbling over it, by touching it in the course of our detailed inspection of . . . every room of every house, every office building, and every factory of every city, and every town of our country. . . . Will you look equally at the great sea of roofs around your house in the city? Any one of them may conceal the bomb. . . . We may never know who did it, who planted or smuggled or shipped the bombs.

Asked at a congressional hearing if there were not some instrument that could discover atomic-bomb components being smuggled into the country, J. Robert Oppenheimer replied, yes, there was such an instrument: it was called the screwdriver, and one would have to use it to pry open every single container unloaded from every ship in every port of the nation.[8]

Implicit in the fear of irrational mass death was a less tangible but perhaps even more unsettling source of anxiety: the sense that the meaning of one's existence—at least in social and historical terms—was being radically threatened. Some, like Dwight Macdonald, defined this as a loss of confidence in the idea of "progress." The bomb's fundamental message— "Civilizations can perish"—said Michael Amrine, "attacks directly the belief almost unconsciously accepted by Western man: progress is inevitable." The shattering of this faith was particularly traumatic for America, he went on, where for historical reasons it had taken especially deep root: "It was in the air of the new country; it was taken in by Americans with their mother's milk." So ingrained was the American belief in progress, he said, "that it is very difficult to judge the long-range effects of the largest piece of bad news the race has had since the fall of Rome."[9]

Amrine might have gone on to link the tenacity of American optimism to the fact that in terms of direct physical destruction, the United States had led a charmed existence during two world wars that had spread devastation over so much of the globe. Many American soldiers suffered and died in these wars, to be sure, but not since 1865 had massive physical destruction and bloodletting actually occurred on American soil. The mythology of progress was certainly under heavy challenge in post-World War I America, but hardly to the degree one finds, for example, in Oswald Spengler's *Decline of the West* (1918) or Thomas Mann's *The Magic Mountain* (1924) with their motifs of death and decay. The reality of the bomb, and the stark images of devastated American cities that it evoked, did for many Americans what two grinding wars had done for others.

But more than notions about "progress" were involved. Deeper still lay an even more fundamental question: What now were the prospects for the very *survival* of the human species? In 1859, in the bright midday of the Victorian Age, Charles Darwin had pledged the weight of his scientific reputation to a confidently positive answer to that ultimate question:

> As all the living forms of life are the lineal descendants of those which lived long before the Silurian epoch, we may feel certain that the ordinary succession by generations has never once been broken, and that no cataclysm has desolated the whole world. Hence, we may look with some confidence to a secure future of equally appreciable length.[10]

Yet a mere eighty-six years after Darwin made that declaration in *The Origin of Species,* mankind's "secure future" had vanished in a series of radioactive bursts. Of course, much had happened in the intervening years to cloud and darken Darwin's optimistic vision, but the atomic bomb was the *coup de grâce.* At least some thoughtful Americans of the late 1940s, then, grappled for the first time with the ultimate question that for their children and grandchildren has, perhaps (incredible as it seems, when one thinks about it) lost some of its shattering power through sheer repetition: What meaning can one's individual life have when all human life might vanish at any time?

Such reflections are fragmentary, hesitant, and allusive—but always deeply apprehensive. In *Mr. Adam,* a female character tries to articulate why she finds the continuity of generations—represented in the novel by the National Refertilization Project—so profoundly important: "We are fighting for more than our lives. We are fighting to keep intact the thread that ties us to the hereafter. Man's only link with immortality is through his children. That's why we want the world to keep on having babies." [11]

In his 1946 epic poem about the atomic bomb, Hermann Hagedorn struggled to convey his sense of the radical break in human awareness it represented. The "bomb" that fell on Americans in August 1945, he wrote, unlike those dropped on Japan,

> Erased no church, vaporized no public building, . . . did not dissolve
> their bodies,
> But it dissolved something vitally important to the greatest of them,
> and the least.
> What it dissolved were their links with the past and with the future.
>
> It made the earth, that seemed so solid, Main Street, that seemed so
> well-paved, a kind of vast jelly, quivering and dividing
> underfoot.

A different image suggested itself to A. J. Muste: history had lost its "rationality," he wrote in 1947, and now seemed "like a fluid, rushing cataract on which we toss about impotently." Once "there was comfort in the fact that the life of humanity was bound to outlast that of the individual," observed Edward L. Long, Jr., but in the age of the bomb, one could "no longer take history for granted." [12]

Assuming that atomic fear was in the process of bringing about fundamental changes in consciousness, how would they affect us? On this question, perceptions differed. Some anticipated a sharp upswing in cultural paranoia, as Americans struggled with their fear of a collective menace that was both deadly and impossible to pin down. Dread of a sneak attack from hidden atomic bombs would become so intense, predicted Edward Condon, that only a police state could contain it. If the international-control effort failed, declared Joseph and Stewart Alsop, the "constant, aching, mounting fear, from which we shall all suffer . . . will poison the people, and its inevitable concomitants, mutual hatred and suspicion, will rapidly divide them." The authors of *The Challenge of Atomic Energy* (1948), a high-school instructional manual, offered an equally bleak picture of a culture in the grip of atomic fear: "Class feeling would probably intensify and general social tension . . . become unbearable." Anxieties already at an extreme pitch would be exacerbated by the "artificial stimulation [of] . . . investigations of subversive activities, security rules, press scare headlines, and rumors followed by still more rumors." [13]

The very intensity of this unending fear, some suggested, could itself create the conditions that would lead to cataclysm. The terror generated by a nuclear arms race, wrote Dorothy Thompson in October 1945, would provide the perfect conditions "for a world-wide nervous breakdown." In such a world, agreed the *Wall Street Journal* that December, "tensions and suspicions would mount to fantastic heights" and the mere rumor of war would send millions fleeing the cities in panic. In an era dominated by "a primitive, animal-like fear of the unknown," asserted William L. Laurence in 1946, atomic war could come through the sheer buildup of psychic pressure. "We face increasing tensions, fears, and spiritual blight," wrote Wesner Fallaw, "until, goaded beyond endurance, men's minds snap and the world's structure collapses."[14] First would come the interior holocaust, then the exterior one.

Even if it did not actually trigger war, others suggested, sustained atomic fear would have profound behavioral effects. Some observers anticipated an era of hedonistic self-indulgence. In his 1945 work *God and the Atom,* Ronald Knox predicted an upsurge of aggressive individualism in the atomic era. If the energy bound within the atom could be unleashed, why not also the explosive and contradictory forces within the individual? "Can we expect the rising generation to submit tamely to controls," Knox asked, when "modern science feeds their unconscious minds with . . . a picture not of control, but of release?"[15]

Many American social observers reached similar conclusions. "Faced with a future that might at any moment disintegrate in a series of atomic explosions," speculated New York University sociologist Harvey W. Zorbaugh in a radio lecture on August 10, 1945, "how long would men cling to the long-range values and goals around which . . . we have built our civilization? Living with so drastically uncertain a future must profoundly change man's psychological and social outlook—cause men to live for the present rather than the future, for himself rather than the community." At the February 1946 University of Chicago conference on the bomb's moral implications, one scientist challenged those who were predicting an increase in social consciousness. Just the contrary was possible, he suggested: "People might come to the conclusion that since there is no way to achieve security anyhow, you had better grab while the grabbing is good."[16]

A strongly moralistic tone pervaded some of these prophecies. Theologian Edward L. Long, Jr., warned of a "flight to riotous living in an attempt to forget the seriousness of the times." Psychiatrist Jules Masserman cautioned that a society in full flight from atomic fear could succumb to "the trivia of fashion, the spurious excitements of spectator sports, the false hopes of reckless gambling, the diversions of profligate sensuality, or the numbing haze of alcohol and drugs." The authors of *The Challenge of Atomic Energy* similarly admonished that protracted atomic anxieties could lead to a period of "social decadence" whose reigning creeds would be "Eat, drink, and be merry" and "Why save for the 'rainy day'—spend, for there may be no tomorrow!"[17]

Others, however, foresaw very different social effects: not frantic hedonism, but a lapsing into apathy. Anticipating a theme later developed with imaginative insight by Robert Jay Lifton, they suggested that if atomic fear were sustained long enough, people would simply stop confronting it by dimming their capacity to respond to the evidence of their senses. The novelist Ward Moore described just such a response in *Greener Than You Think,* and other cultural observers offered similar visions. Protracted atomic fear, suggested Wesner Fallaw, could produce "a society of deranged men, gradually and tortuously sinking into futility and frustration." [18]

Indeed, some concluded that this apathetic response was already setting in. As early as 1946, Daniel Lang observed in the *New Yorker,* many Americans were dealing with the atomic threat "by simply refusing to think about it." Another 1946 observer compared Americans' diminishing responsiveness to atomic danger to that of a man lost in a blizzard who gradually loses all will to survive. (If civilization vanished in an atomic war, an Iowa man wrote Robert M. Hutchins that year, "will it really matter very much?") Lewis Mumford marveled at the "glassy calm" with which Americans seemed to accept the Bikini tests and at the diminishing impact of the atomic scientists' warnings. Americans were responding almost "placidly" to the intensifying threat of atomic war, said Mumford, "as a doped policeman might view with a blank, tolerant leer the robbery of a bank or the barehanded killing of a child." So profound was the "state of self-enclosed delusion" by which Americans were collectively blotting out the atomic reality, he wrote in 1950, that if it appeared in a single individual it would demand psychiatric treatment. [19]

The stark post-Hiroshima horror of atomic war had not been sustained, wrote A. J. Muste in 1947: "The human imagination cannot really picture it . . . The nervous frame has stopped trying to react to it." This spreading numbness, Muste suggested, was sapping the human will in alarming ways: "Man no longer believes in himself. . . . Inwardly, men are not sure they want to survive." The mayor of Milwaukee, a strong proponent of civil defense, observed in 1950 that "there appears in many cities a kind of helplessness once they begin to realize that they are objects marked for destruction." [20]

This theme was also central to the analysis of Franz Alexander, one of the few psychiatrists who, in the 1945–1950 period, addressed the psychic aspects of the atomic threat. Director of the Chicago Institute for Psychoanalysis, Alexander was a pioneer in the field of psychosomatic medicine. Like other American Freudians, he was inclined to modify orthodox Freudian theory by giving more weight to cultural factors. In "Mental Hygiene in the Atomic Age" (1946), Alexander saw the bomb's deadening psychic effect as a dramatic intensification of the more long-range impact of technology on consciousness. "Man invented the tool to make life easier for himself; he ends by using it to debase himself to a button-pushing automaton whose last act will be to push the button that will exterminate him." So totally had technological mastery become the "ideological backbone" of the culture that for many, life's only meaning lay in endless work. "Absorbed in producing for the sake of production," Western civilization had forgotten that the point of technology was to free mankind "from the chores of material existence so that we might do something else."[21] The larger cultural challenge whose urgency the atomic bomb had underscored, he said, was to lift the dead hand of technological dominance and restore the machine to its proper role as a means rather than an end.

What then was to be done? Could this bleak dreamscape of the psychic future be avoided? At first, as we have seen, many activists were convinced it could. With international control, both the horror of atomic war and the more insidious horror of atomic "peace" could be escaped. Indeed, many of the predictions we have been looking at were made by polemicists trying to drum up support for international control because the alternative was so depressing. But with the fading of the international-control effort and the onset of the Cold War, what had been presented as a nightmare to be avoided increasingly seemed a prefiguring of the actual future.

Could professional expertise help? John W. Campbell, Jr., suggested in 1947 that "a really mature science of psychology" could surely find "some means of making men more tolerant" of each other, but not many psychologists or psychiatrists shared his optimism.[22] In contrast to the educators, sociologists, city planners, and others who so volubly promoted their areas of expertise in the post-Hiroshima period, few whose specialties touched on the realm of human consciousness stepped forward with bold claims or ready panaceas. Indeed, quite the reverse. Though it was being called for and even predicted in many quarters, said Franz Alexander, there was little hope that man could quickly achieve the "psychological . . . reorientation" necessary to avoid atomic war. Certainly psychiatry, with its individual approach, offered no easy strategies for the kind of radical, large-scale transformations of consciousness necessary to moderate "the power of irrational emotions in shaping the fate of individuals and of nations":

> We psychiatrists . . . know . . . how difficult it is to enforce the rule of reason even in our dealings with a single individual. There is no time to psychoanalyze nations or even their leaders. The tempo of technology is faster than the tempo of psychiatry. . . . The human material we deal with today is the same as that which fought its irrational battles . . . with bows and arrows, with armored phalanxes, with guns, tanks, aëroplanes, rockets, and atomic bombs. The weapons have changed, but those who employ them remain the same.

If through the restraining power of mutual terror mankind got through "the critical years now ahead," Alexander suggested, a long process of cultural change might modify the deep-seated sources of human aggressiveness, but this glimmer of hope did little to lighten a deeply pessimistic essay. "It is more likely," he concluded, "that, paralyzed by mistrust and fear of one another, we shall regress into the darkest phase of human history."[23]

From a different perspective, the same bleak message came from Rushton Coulborn, a historian of ancient civilizations at Atlanta University. Discussing "Survival of the Fittest in the Atomic Age," Coulborn in 1947 compared this newest threat to earlier evolutionary stages when human extinction had loomed as a distinct possibility. The threat to survival now lay in human nature itself rather than in such external forces as glaciers, drought, predators, or plague. This difference, however, was more apparent than real, he said, since human aggressiveness was "a biologically-culturally toughened trait" of such strength that it functioned, in effect, as "a part of the natural environment against which freely thinking man struggles." If, as seemed probable, man destroyed himself, it would be "in his capacity of slave of nature," impelled by drives he could control only partially and fitfully. The one note of optimism in Coulborn's essay must have offered cold comfort to his American readers: among human societies, the Chinese seemed least imbued with the "trait of mutual hostility," and it was they who were therefore most likely to escape atomic annihiliation and "lead in the creation of a new civilized society" in the post-holocaust era.[24]

The most exhaustive post-Hiroshima reflections and predictions regarding the bomb's psychological impact were those of the historian, critic, and regional-planning advocate Lewis Mumford. Fifty years old in 1945, Mumford had a considerable reputation for such cultural and architectural studies as *Sticks and Stones* (1924), *Technics and Civilization* (1934), and *The Culture of Cities* (1938). Mumford's response to the atomic bomb was immediate and passionate. In a series of essays and lectures, he denounced it with unremitting vehemence. In all these works, Mumford focused on the psychological dimension of the crisis. This became most explicit in "Gentlemen, You Are Mad!"—a March 1946 *Saturday Review* article inspired by announcement of the planned Bikini tests. Mumford's title was no mere rhetorical device. "We in America are living among madmen," the essay began:

Madmen govern our affairs in the name of order and security. The chief madmen claim the titles of general, admiral, senator, scientist, administrator, Secretary of State, even President. And the fatal symptom of their madness is this: they have been carrying through a series of acts which will lead eventually to the destruction of mankind, under the solemn conviction that they are normal responsible people, living sane lives, and working for reasonable ends. Soberly, day after day, the madmen continue to go through the undeviating motions of madness: motions so stereotyped, so commonplace, that they seem the normal motions of normal men, not the mass compulsions of people bent on total death.

The American people were mad for passively accepting the irrationality of their leaders; the atomic scientists were madmen who "in the final throes of their dementia, were shocked back into sanity." "The first move toward sanity" must be an act of radical rejection: "Abandon the Atomic Bomb! Give it up! Stop it now! That is the only order of the day." [25]

In several essays in 1947–1948, Mumford turned from the present situation to speculation about the possible future psychological effects of unremitting atomic menace. "If militant genocide does not turn the planet into an extermination camp," he wrote in 1948, ". . . fear and suspicion may turn it into a madhouse, in which the physicians in charge will be as psychotic as the patients." [26] Mumford's most elaborate venture into prophecy was a remarkable 1947 essay in the international journal *Air Affairs* on the atomic bomb's social effects. [27] It was a powerful imaginative tour de force, offering a series of scenarios, each progressively bleaker, of the social and psychological consequences of four possible assumptions about the atomic future.

Mumford's first assumption was that of preemptive war: before the Russians get the bomb, the United States launches a massive and "unbelievably successful" atomic attack, wiping out thirty-six Soviet cities and twenty-five million people. What are the consequences? Millions of survivors pour into Western Europe, swamping its social and economic institutions. Despite hideous losses, the Russians eventually rally for a long and bitter war of revenge—a war that unites most of the world against the United States, where a "deepening moral reaction" and a "general sense of suspicion and guilt" have left the population depressed and divided. What had been planned as a swift and decisive preemptive war in fact produces a nightmare of endless turmoil and conflict.

Mumford's second scenario—a protracted U.S.-Soviet nuclear arms race, leading eventually to war—produces obsessive national security precautions, a breakdown of international trade and travel, and a protracted period of global tension and suspicion. When the atomic war eventually comes after "a succession of feints and withdrawals," the Soviets absorb the initial American attack, destroy the major cities of America's allies in Western Europe, and launch a follow-up attack on the United States mainland "from bomb-proof shelters deep in the Ural Mountains." America's losses are massive, compounded by the breakdown of hospital and medical services. Eventually the conflict settles down to a long war of attrition and "life reverts swiftly to a preindustrial level." "Island cultures" spring up in Africa and

Asia, but "there is a deliberate relapse into primeval ways" as "machines are attacked and disembowelled . . . [or] allowed to fall into complete neglect . . . as symbols of man's . . . will-to-extinction."

Mumford's third assumption involved a drawn-out period of nuclear proliferation and intensifying danger that generates a universal climate of suspicion, fear, mistrust, and ultimately "uncontrolled fantasies of deception and aggression." A police state emerges in America and the FBI grows "to the dimensions of a considerable army." The nation's intellectual resources are channeled entirely into military pursuits: "In every other department of life, there is a slowing down of creativity: worse than that, an active regression":

> Life is now reduced to purely existentialist terms: existence toward death. The classic otherworldly religions undergo a revival; . . . quack religions and astrology, with pretensions to scientific certainty, flourish: . . . The young who grow up in this world are completely demoralized: they characterize themselves as the generation that drew a blank. The belief in continuity, the sense of future that holds promises, disappears: the certainty of sudden obliteration cuts across every long term plan, and every activity is more or less reduced to the time-span of a single day, on the assumption that it may be the last day. To counteract this, a cult of the archaic and the antiquarian becomes popular: the Victorian period is revived as mankind's Golden Age. Suicides become more frequent . . . , and the taking of drugs to produce either exhilaration or sleep becomes practically universal.

For a time, universal danger functions as a deterrent, but eventually the unrelieved tension and fear produce the political equivalent of a psychotic episode, and one of the many nuclear nations, "by accident or deliberate intention," launches an atomic attack that quickly escalates to global cataclysm. Over half the world's population perishes in the initial spasm, and another quarter die eventually of radiation disease or from the radioactive contamination of food and water. For the survivors, existence holds little meaning: "Now, for the first time in history, the disintegration of civilization takes place on a world-wide scale: no 'island cultures' are left to carry on the old processes, even at a reduced level." Man survives as "an animal with the merest remnant of his intelligence, by eliminating every other capacity that identified him as human."

In Mumford's final scenario, atomic war does not occur, but the world lives permanently under its shadow. In a climate of unremitting danger and fear, all power flows to the federal government, which is in turn dominated by the military and "the scientists and technicians responsible for atomic production and anti-atomic defense." Society is entirely geared toward the war that does not come: "By the age of twelve, youths who score high in their aptitude tests are set aside for further training in technological and scientific research along increasingly narrow lines laid down by atomic warfare and its accessory arts." In the obsession with civil defense, the great metropolitan centers are dispersed or transformed into snake-like "Linear Cities." New York City shrinks to under a hundred thousand people. To make radar surveillance more secure, air travel is prohibited. Factories, schools, and public buildings are moved underground, where they are linked by a transcontinental subway system. With productivity falling in all sectors except nuclear weaponry, the standard of living declines precipitously.

By skillful government conditioning, "this state of affairs is characterized as freedom." Nevertheless, the "fear of total catastrophe" leads to "grave psychological disruptions." The preoccupation with civil defense, ironically, intensifies these psychic disorders:

> Every precaution taken to avert atomic disaster, shuts the door to some cherished aspect of normal living and concentrates even the most remote parts of the personality on one theme alone: Fear. . . . As time goes on, the fear becomes more absolute, and . . . the prospect of finding a way out becomes more blank.

Some turn to "fantasy . . . . purposeless sexual promiscuity . . .[and] narcotic indulgence." Others lapse into total apathy and "like Bartleby in Melville's story . . . have nothing further to do with life."

But still others grow rebellious. People calling themselves the "new pioneers" begin to "desert their posts in the underground collective life in order to scratch for a bare, self-centered, insecure, but adventurous living on the surface." The authorities brutally repress this movement, and the "new pioneers" are rounded up and shot. But the rebellion spreads, as a "Let's Die Above Ground" movement takes on international dimensions. All over the earth, people stream to the surface—to be met by the massed troops of their own governments. The stage is set for a final, ironic Armageddon of internecine slaughter.

Lewis Mumford's summary comment on his fourth scenario was grim:

> On the Fourth Assumption, not a single life has been lost in atomic warfare; nevertheless, death has spread everywhere in the cold violence of anticipation, and civilization has been almost as fatally destroyed as it would be [in an actual atomic war] . . . When secrecy, isolation, withdrawal, and preoccupation with mere physical survival dominate in a society, civilization begins to disintegrate. . . . The social order becomes a prison and existence therein is punishment for life. That is why the Fourth Assumption turns out, in some ways, to be the most horrible of all: nothing less than a living death.

Eight

The End of
the Beginning

Settling in for the Long Haul

24 .

Dagwood to the Rescue:
The Campaign to Promote the
"Peaceful Atom"

"The atom bomb, and all it means, does not appear to have sunk in at all. It has bounced off, as it were, or been mentally repelled as a tactless intruder." So wrote the British journalist Wyndham Lewis in 1949 after a visit to the United States. On the matter of the bomb, agreed Robert Payne in his 1949 book *Report on America,* people were behaving much as the medieval Christians who, though "conscious of an impending Day of Judgment, serenely abdicated their responsibilities to the church and to the state." [1]

Whatever the bomb's deeper psychological effects, the surface evidence as the decade ended strongly supported such observations. In contrast to the bomb's massive initial impact, the climate had clearly altered dramatically. There were now fewer expressions of either cosmic despair or euphoric hope, fewer prescriptions for action, fewer pronouncements about the bomb's "larger meaning." As the open sense of urgency faded, the intense discourse of 1945 and 1946 diminished to scattered murmurs and faint echoes. The mood became one of dulled acquiescence. The bomb had come to stay. Represented visually, America's nuclear culture around 1950 would appear as a gray and largely deserted landscape.

To be sure, this cultural shift did not occur overnight. As early as February 1946, Raymond Gram Swing had sensed that the sharp edge of awareness was dulling. Already, he commented, the bomb "seems to have shrunk to something smaller . . . through the corrosion of familiarity." Bernard Baruch made the same point in a December 1946 United Nations speech: "Time is two-edged. It not only forces us nearer to our doom, if we do not save ourselves, but, even more horrendous, it habituates us to existing conditions which, by familiarity, seem less and less threatening. Once our minds have been conditioned to that sort of thinking, the keen edge of danger is blunted, and we are no longer able to see the dark chasm on the brink of which we stand."[2]

By 1947, the shift was clearly evident. In June, summing up a series of recent polls, a public-opinion researcher observed: "On the whole . . . the threat of the bomb does not greatly preoccupy the people." At about the same time the number of entries on the bomb in the *Readers' Guide to Periodical Literature* began a sharp decline that continued with minor fluctuations until the mid-1950s. A content analysis of the nation's fourteen lead-

Percentage of columns mentioning the atomic bomb in the columns of fourteen leading U.S. political columnists, August 1945–December 1948

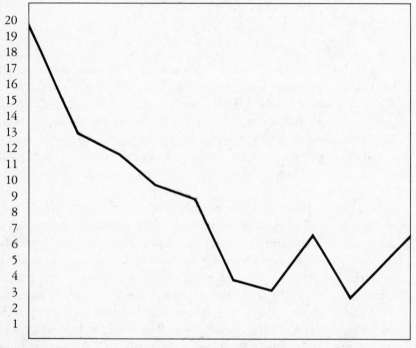

	Aug.–	Jan.–	May–	Sept.–	Jan.–	May–	Sept.–	Jan.–	May–	Sept.–
	Dec.	Apr.	Aug.	Dec.	Apr.	Aug.	Dec.	Apr.	Aug.	Dec.
	1945	1946	1946	1946	1947	1947	1947	1948	1948	1948

SOURCE: Data in Janet Besse and Harold D. Lasswell, "Our Columnists on the A-Bomb," *World Politics,* 3 (October 1950), 74–76.

ing political columns for 1945–1948 reveals a similar pattern, as shown in the accompanying chart. As J. Robert Oppenheimer remarked in a 1948 letter, there was a "surprising lack, both quantitatively and in discernment, in the public discussion of atomic energy."[3]

Some saw this dramatic decline in overt concern about the bomb as a natural cultural reflex, a product of sensory fatigue. For a time after August 1945, the public's capacity to absorb books, articles, speeches, sermons, and discussions about the bomb had seemed boundless. But inevitably (or so this interpretation would suggest) other concerns and interests had reasserted themselves. Awesome in prospect, the atomic threat was simply less immediate than one's job, one's family, the cost of living, even the reviving rhythms of domestic politics and foreign affairs. As one public-opinion expert observed, there were distinct limits on people's capacity to sustain interest in any issue—even atomic war—"not intimately a part of their personal day-to-day preoccupations." Observed Norman Cousins following the Bikini tests: "After four bombs, the mystery dissolves into a pattern. . . . There is almost a standardization of catastrophe."[4] Such explanations help us understand the lull in public attention and concern about the atomic bomb, but they hardly provide the full picture. The conscious manipulation of attitudes by government leaders and opinion-molders was involved as well.

The spontaneous initial surge of post-Hiroshima excitement over the atom's vast promise, quickly debunked by experts, had been short-lived. While it never disappeared entirely, particularly in reference to radioactive isotopes, a clear decline was evident by 1947. The end of the decade, however, brought a sharp quickening of attention to this theme in the media. Magazines once again blossomed with articles on the subject. *Newsweek* in 1949 enthusiastically reported "the new atomic story." The "frenzied wartime patchwork" that had produced the bomb had given way to "an orderly permanent enterprise" involving research and development for peacetime applications as well as weapons production. Under the enthusiastic headline "Plants, Payrolls, and Output Are Shooting Up," *U.S. News and World Report* reported that over sixty-five thousand workers were now employed in the atomic industry, and that the AEC was spending in excess of $600 million per year. While noting in passing that "improved atomic weapons" were being developed, this article left the distinct impression that these tremendous expenditures were primarily for peacetime research. Even weapons research, the magazine noted in 1950, was "certain to turn up scores of new civilian jobs for the atom."[5]

Some expressed skepticism at the new media enthusiasm for "peacetime" atomic development. "Heartening as it is to know" of such programs, wrote Daniel Lang in the *New Yorker* in 1948, "the chilling fact remains that they are merely a by-product and that practically all the [AEC's] fissionable materials are allocated to nuclear weapons. To put it bluntly, more and better bombs are being made." Writing in *Christian Century* in 1949, two physicists noted that in the realm of the atom, "peaceful" research could readily have military applications. So long as the threat of war remained, they wrote, "atomic power will be of greatest benefit to man if it is confined to the sun and the stars."

Significantly, this new media blitz promoting peacetime uses of the atom came just as atomic-energy policymakers realized that such applications were increasingly remote. In a July 1947 report to the AEC, J. Robert Oppenheimer not only (in David Lilienthal's words) "discouraged hope of atomic power in any substantial way for decades, but . . . question[ed] whether it would ever be of consequence." ("Had quite a blow today," commented Lilienthal in his diary.) The AEC's general manager in the late 1940s, Carroll Wilson, later summed up the prevailing mood: "The power thing was pie in the sky, really. . . . All of the other priorities were higher than nuclear power."[6]

Despite such behind-the-scenes gloom, media and public attention to the peacetime promise of atomic energy seemed only to grow as the 1940s ended. Far from being spontaneous, however, this revival was being consciously induced by government, corporate, and media manipulation. The aim was not primarily to publicize peacetime applications per se, but rather to create a more positive—or at least more acquiescent—overall public attitude toward atomic energy. From the beginning, of course, scientific popularizers had tried to convey basic information about nuclear physics in terms not only comprehensible but even appealing to the lay public, by introducing, for example, everyday allusions and reassuring analogies. One 1946 popularization said that the oscillating electrical fields used in isotope separation "make the ion beams dance in the very same way as the electrons dance in the amplifier tubes when some famous crooner sings on the radio." Another called electrons "electrical jitterbugs." *The Atomic Story,* by John W. Campbell, Jr., begins with a Cast of Characters bearing such cute names as "Proton: A plump, positive fellow." Still another early popularization featured illustrations by the young Maurice Sendak, including one picturing atoms as dancing men and women pairing off to form molecules.[7]

A certain innocent exuberance—plus the desire of specialists to demystify their subject—pervades these early popularizations. In the later 1940s, such benign imagery was manipulated much more consciously to allay the public's atomic fears. Central to this effort was the Atomic Energy Commission and its articulate chairman. Often featured in the press as "Mr. Atom," David Lilienthal strove mightily to give a benevolent human face to a reality whose terrifying aspects never lay far beneath the surface. As we have seen, Lilienthal in the privacy of his journals, and occasionally more openly, betrayed deep anxiety over the darkening nuclear weapons situation. In public, at who knows what psychic cost, he usually maintained a determinedly upbeat tone in discussing what he sometimes called "this new critter, the Atom." In articles in the popular press and speeches he wrote himself and delivered in a colloquial, extemporaneous style, Lilienthal (despite occasional cautionary notes) generally extolled the atom's peacetime promise and encouraged positive thinking. In a 1948 high-school graduation address of almost strident optimism delivered at Gettysburg and broadcast nationally, Lilienthal acknowledged that many opinion-makers were in "deepest despair" about the atomic bomb. He urged Americans, however, to ignore their "predictions of dire and utter calamity." Every generation, he said, had its pessimists convinced "the world was going to the dogs." With "knowledge, love [and] faith," he concluded, the atomic age could be "one of the blessed periods of all human history." He sought to ease fears over the bomb itself by insisting—a theme picked up by *U.S. News* and other publications—that research on atomic weapons and development of the atom's "beneficent and creative" potential were "virtually an identical process: two sides of the same coin." The former would inevitably promote the latter.

Another favorite Lilienthal theme was that atomic energy was simply a form of solar energy—and who was afraid of the sun? As he put it in another high-school commencement speech, this one in Crawfordsville, Indiana: "I suppose there is nothing of a physical nature that is more friendly to man, or more necessary to his well-being than the sun. From the sun you and I get . . . the energy that gives life and sustains life, the energy that builds skyscrapers and churches, that writes poems and symphonies." Yet this benevolent, life-giving sun, Lilienthal concluded triumphantly, was nothing but "a huge atomic-energy factory."[8]

Reflecting Lilienthal's upbeat approach, the AEC directed its attention in the late 1940s—when bomb-making was by far its highest priority—to projecting what its official historian called "a peaceful, civilian image." A Division of Public and Technical Information was set up in October 1947 to build favorable public relations through work with "the press, the radio, schools, organized groups and others." In a pilot project that autumn, the AEC organized an Atomic Energy Week in Hyattsville, Maryland, just outside Washington. Sidewalk informational tables were set up, eye-catching exhibits displayed, and ministers and newspaper editors urged to discuss atomic energy in their sermons and editorials. High-school students put on a play featuring such characters as Miss Molecule and Mr. Atomic Energy. Grade-school children were given simplified talks on the atom's peacetime potential and the Baruch plan. The county's seven hundred teachers were lectured by atomic scientists. The whole endeavor was praised by the *New York Times* as "a broad-scale public seminar in just what the atom is all about."[9]

Newspaper accounts of Hyattsville's Atomic Energy Week presented it as a grass-roots undertaking, but the AEC's role became evident in 1948 when communities across the country began organizing similar events. As in Hyattsville, sponsorship by local civic groups was arranged, exhibits were set up, and lectures were given for different age groups. An exhibit was supplied to the Iowa State Fair; Lilienthal himself inaugurated a show in Cincinnati. The overall aim, said one AEC official, was to demonstrate that "atomic energy is already at work for *good*" and to prepare Americans to "assume their atomic-age responsibilities." In 1947 and 1948, the AEC estimated, four million visitors attended exhibits sponsored by the AEC or its corporate contractors. [10]

Prominent in this effort was the Brookhaven National Laboratory, a Long Island facility jointly funded and administered by the AEC and nine large eastern universities. Much of the AEC's limited nonmilitary research was centered at Brookhaven, and its staff frequently spoke to public gatherings "trying to prove, against heavy odds, that atomic energy has its attractive side" (as the skeptical Daniel Lang put it). Brookhaven's public-relations office assembled two traveling exhibits featuring movies, audiovisual displays, and live demonstrations. Exhibitions were held in a number of cities and at the American Museum of Natural History in New York. Reporting a Brookhaven road-show presentation in Stamford, Connecticut, under the title "Main Street Meets the Atom," *Science Illustrated* described the "sober fascination" of adult visitors and the "delighted" reaction of children to such exhibits as a Van de Graaff generator and an "atomic pinball machine"—an atomic-pile simulation complete with gong and blinking lights. [11]

The high point of this exercise in government-inspired positive thinking came in the summer of 1948 with Man and the Atom, a month-long exhibit in New York's Central Park. The show was sponsored by the AEC; its major corporate contractors for nuclear power development, General Electric and Westinghouse; and the New York Committee on Atomic Information—an umbrella organization of local backers. The exhibit's centerpiece was a Theater of Atoms, sponsored by the Westinghouse Corporation. The theater featured such eye-catching exhibits as a "real radiation detector," a "chain reaction" (of sixty mousetraps), and a model of an atomic nucleus which, according to a Westinghouse public-relations spokesman, resembled "a futuristic Christmas tree" and exploded harmlessly with "a blinding flash! an ear-splitting crash!" [12]

Visitors to the General Electric exhibit received free copies of *Dagwood Splits the Atom,* a colorful comic book produced by King Features Syndicate in consultation with the AEC, in which Mandrake the Magician reduces Dagwood and Blondie to molecule size to unfold the wonders of the atom to them while an audience including Popeye and Maggie and Jiggs looks on. (General Groves himself, in yet another of the high-level policy decisions of his career, chose Dagwood as the central character.) Over 250,000 copies were distributed, leading GE to order a further printing of several million. [13]

As the AEC's "public information" campaign gained momentum, it shifted subtly in emphasis. The Hyattsville Atomic Energy Week of 1947, though generally upbeat, did include information on the bomb's destructive power and the need for international control. In the exhibits of 1948, this emphasis largely disappeared, and the focus was almost entirely on soothing public fears. At the Man and the Atom show in Central Park, apart from a single exhibit showing the effects of radiation on blood cells and urging people to give blood in preparation for "any atomic-bomb emergencies," the emphasis was exclusively on stimulating positive attitudes toward atomic energy. In *Dagwood Splits the Atom,* when Mandrake sets off a chain reaction (as silly Dagwood rushes off in a panic shouting "Blondie!"), the "BANG!" in the center of the picture is balanced by drawings of a power plant, a factory, a grain field, a medical lab, and an atomic ship—the many uses of the peaceful atom. Even if most of the peaceful uses featured in the exhibit either lay far in the future or had already been discredited, Westinghouse's public-relations spokesman disingenuously insisted, surely this was "a better note to strike . . . than emphasizing the destruction of bombs." [14]

That the goal of all these Atomic Energy Weeks, Man and the Atom shows, and related activities was less educational than therapeutic and propagandistic emerged in the January 1949 *Journal of Educational Sociology,* a special issue devoted entirely to the previous year's blitz of semiofficial atomic-energy exhibits. The editor emphasized the importance of publicizing the "magnificent story" of the atom. General Groves urged pride in the Manhattan Project and then moved briskly onward:

> Enough of the past—let's talk about the present and future. . . . Much that has been written about atomic energy has inspired fear and confusion. . . . This is not a healthy state of affairs. Atomic energy must be explained. The average American likes new scientific devices. He must learn that nuclear energy, like fire and electricity, can be a good and useful servant.

A Pentagon spokesman complained that too many people regarded atomic energy as "black magic" and that most writers on the subject—"as ill at ease . . . as a Victorian concert audience suddenly subjected to modern jazz" —were merely projecting their own worries. We must, he insisted, "absorb elementary nuclear science into our folklore as soon as possible."

The editor of *Popular Science,* in a similar vein, noted that in 1945–1947 many erroneous and ill-informed notions had been implanted in the public mind, but added that "those days, fortunately, are over now." Scientists, he said, were now inviting journalists into the laboratory to explain "their creed and their work"; Nobel laureates were making themselves "nearly as accessible as politicians"; and the AEC was cooperating "with responsible writers and artists as much as conditions and legal restrictions permit." [15]

Though spearheaded by the AEC, this governmental effort to "domesticate" the atom and play up its peacetime uses took many forms. A 1949 State Department film carried the message to foreign lands. "We have found an increasing need for counteracting some of the effects abroad of the well-known destructive and wartime potentialities of atomic energy," wrote a State Department public-relations staff member. "This short film would be designed to open up some of the peacetime vistas." [16]

Educators played a central role as well. The AEC's public-information office worked closely with the U.S. Office of Education and the American Textbook Publishers Institute, for whom it prepared a *Sourcebook on Atomic Energy*. It also cooperated with the National Education Association in the writing of *Operation Atomic Vision* (1948), a ninety-five page high-school study unit. This handbook urged students to promote interest in atomic energy through discussion groups, lecture series, school projects, letters to the editor, and Community Atomic Energy Councils. The danger of atomic war was discussed, but the clear intent was to supplant this negative image:

> Atomic Energy! What do you think of when you hear these words? The chances are that these words call up in your mind thoughts of war, destruction, the atomic bomb. This is not strange for, after all, the press and radio and prominent people have emphasized the great hazard of war and the A-bomb. . . . You may even wish to bury your head in the sand and resign yourself to fate. But there is a much brighter, a much more constructive, and a much more thrilling side of the atomic energy picture. If we look long enough and hard enough at this side of the picture, we might be able to see a world free from war, strife, poverty, and sickness; a world of hope and of great possibilities for human welfare. . . . Why not keep the bright side of the atomic energy picture in the center of our attention?

Operation Atomic Vision proceeds to picture not only the wonders of isotopes, but an atomic future reminiscent of the most euphoric effusions of the immediate post-Hiroshima period:

> You may live to drive a plastic car powered by an atomic engine and reside in a completely air-conditioned plastic house. Food will be cheap and abundant everywhere in the world. . . . No one will need to work long hours. There will be much leisure and a network of large recreational areas will cover the country, if not the world. [17]

In *The Challenge of Atomic Energy,* a curricular guide published by Teachers College of Columbia University as a supplement to *Operation Atomic Vision,* one finds (despite the apprehensions noted in the last chapter) equally glowing descriptions of an atomic future of boundless food resources, "unlimited, almost automatic, effortless production," and "a fantastic standard of living . . . that might very well abolish what we now call the 'deprived' class in our society." The aim of this curricular project, it was said, was to replace "irrational fears" with "improved attitude and action patterns in this area." [18]

Jumping aboard the bandwagon, the nation's educational journals increasingly touted the atom's peacetime uses of 1948–1949. "Simply to go on repeating that the bomb is awful, that there is no defense against it, and that we must have world control, can only lead to panic and fatalism," said an Iowa teachers' journal in September 1948. "The American people need to be given a new approach to the subject . . . based on calm acceptance of atomic energy as part of our life and one of enormous significance other than for war." "The job of the teacher is not to scare the daylights out of people by regaling them with the horrors of atomic destruction," agreed a University of Illinois education professor. Their emphasis, he said, should be "on the positive aspects of atomic energy control in the service of mankind." [19]

The scientific popularizers joined in as well. In *Energy Unlimited* (1948), Harry N. Davis wrote: "The outlook of this presentation is optimistic. Too many people are counting in advance the possible casualties of future war with the new weapons of atomic power . . . and falling into hopeless despair." The best way to assure peace, he said, was to "keep our eyes on the wonderful goals that are almost within our grasp through the positive use of the forces science has unlocked." While offering a cautious assessment of the possibilities for atomic power, Davis wrote enthusiastically of the medical potential of radioactive isotopes. [20]

The radio networks, too, cooperated with the governmental effort to mute "excessive" fear of the bomb. In 1946, radio had offered such somber fare as Hersey's *Hiroshima* and realistic dramatizations of an atomic attack. In June 1947, by contrast, CBS broadcast an hour-long documentary called "The Sunny Side of the Atom" designed, according to a spokesman, to counteract "the 'scare' approach to atomic education." With Agnes Moorhead in the role of a peripatetic narrator, this pseudo-documentary begins with a "visit" to Oak Ridge, where radioactive isotopes were being produced. The propaganda was not subtle. The looming secret facility at first seems sinister, but "above the eerie whistling of the smokeless stack, I heard the birds, singing." The scene next shifts to a doctor's office, where, thanks to isotopes, a golf pro learns that his foot won't have to be amputated. "You may be out there shooting in the seventies again before too much longer," the kindly doctor tells him. (Only the most attentive listener would have realized that the isotopes did not actually cure the patient, but only facilitated the diagnosis.) On to a great medical research facility, where researchers seek "a cure for cancer with the aid of isotopes."

Shifting to the Southwest, "The Sunny Side of the Atom" next dramatizes the role of isotopes in seeking out residual oil in abandoned wells. Right on cue, a prospector exclaims, "Unless I miss my guess, I think we've struck oil." Ruminates a local: "Guess folks around here won't feel so bad about that atom bomb when they hear about this." (Music "up humorously," directs the script.) After a final visit to an "atom farm" where vast isotope research projects are underway, Agnes Moorhead soliloquizes:

> But that wasn't all, nearly all. The rest of the story was not for our eyes —it was for our hearts and our hopes. It was the personal visions of the hundreds of men and women—scientists, engineers, technicians—who spoke to me frankly at all of our great atomic research centers. They are the custodians of the infant science. And they had bold ideas— about how it can grow and what it can mean tomorrow—for peace and plenty, for health and better living everywhere. If the world will only give them the chance—and the time. (*Music stabs climactically, but quickly broadens and segues into the intimations of a rosy dream.*)

Overwhelmed by all she has seen and heard, the narrator lapses into a trancelike reverie:

> I saw a great light, more luminous than the sun, flooding out over the darkness of the earth. Its rays were lighting up the innermost recesses of life, searching out secrets never revealed by the light of the sun. . . . I saw all men standing straight and tall and confident, facing, without fear, their future, urged forward by a new hope, by the infinite wonder and possibility of a new life.

After a final fleeting reference to the horror of atomic war, optimism triumphs:

> "Everything I have seen, everything I have heard, everything I have felt has given me this faith: We are bigger than the atom, and if we face the future boldly, we will enter a world made bright by the sunny side of the atom."[21]

The psychological intent of this multifaceted campaign of "atomic education" in the late 1940s is quite clear: to implant in the public mind an image of atomic energy associated with health, happiness, and prosperity rather than destruction. Eager to document this shift, CBS's research department assembled a group of test subjects to listen to "The Sunny Side of the Atom." A polygraph hookup measured their moment-by-moment emotional responses, red and green buttons allowed them to indicate approval or disapproval of various segments, and a follow-up questionnaire was administered. "The over-all emotional effect," the researchers reported, "was to lessen fear of atomic energy, with 46 percent of the group less fearful than before the sample broadcast, 3 percent more fearful, and 51 percent with fears unchanged."[22]

A similar improvement in attitude was found among visitors to New York City's Man and the Atom exhibit of 1948. Under the direction of Lillian Wald Kay, a psychologist at New York University, entrance and exit polls were administered to two thousand visitors. When asked to list some uses of atomic energy, only 33 percent of those leaving the exhibit mentioned war, in contrast to 42 percent of those in the entrance poll; while the number mentioning medicine, power, and industrial and agricultural applications increased markedly. Asked to choose from a list of words the one best describing their feelings about atomic energy, 34 percent of the exit-poll subjects selected "Hope," compared to the 27 percent in the entrance poll.[23]

This systematic effort by opinion-molders in government, education, and the media to reshape public attitudes toward atomic energy involved a conscious repudiation of the "fear" strategy of the scientists' movement. This fact was heavily underscored by Lillian Wald Kay in two articles published in professional journals in 1949. The early post-Hiroshima media preoccupation with "the problem of the bomb and its control," she began, had encouraged Americans to think of atomic energy solely as a frightening, destructive power, not as "a possible force for good." As a result, "atomic energy" had become firmly anchored in people's minds with thoughts of "war and the fear of war." This, in turn, had led to "a gradual decrease in enthusiasm" for it and a lack of "clarity" in public perceptions of its potential benefits. Illustrating this progression, Kay cited an interview subject who reported that his initial, spontaneous reaction to the news of Hiroshima had been positive, as he had thought of "the great change in human living atomic energy would bring." But then, fed by a wave of "propaganda" about atomic war, fear had pushed aside hope. Citing public-opinion data, Kay noted that between 1945 and 1947, the percentage of Americans who considered the development of the atomic bomb a "bad thing" had more than doubled. These postwar cultural and attitudinal trends, Kay concluded, posed a clear challenge to "psychologists and educators" who wished to help a worried public "prepare for [the atom's] promise as well as to face its problems." The ambivalence revealed in the polls, she said, made clear that Americans were "ready for well-directed attempts to change their opinions."

Concluding one article on a practical note, Kay reported the discussions of a small "brainstorming" group she had assembled to consider ways of publicizing the positive side of the atomic story. The suggestions included publicizing the pro-atomic-energy views of celebrities and dramatizing the atom's benefits. "Show them a train run by atomic power and they won't worry about the atomic bomb," said one participant; emphasize the medical benefits, suggested another, since "so many people worry about cancer." Whatever the specific strategies, Kay's underlying message was clear: experts must devote their energies to "influencing perception away from the bombs and back to energy." The challenge was no mere "interesting theoretical problem" but "the most vital of our times."[24]

The motives behind this systematic effort to create a more positive public perception of atomic energy were certainly mixed. Many of the educators, psychologists, editors, and radio executives who implemented it doubtless believed they were performing a patriotic public service. For David Lilienthal and others of the AEC, the rhetorical insistence on the atom's exciting peacetime potential helped mask the lack of actual progress in this area. Lilienthal's constant round of speech-making served to build a public constituency for the AEC and also protect him from congressional critics, some of whose personal hostility went back to his days as head of the "socialistic" Tennessee Valley Authority. Theoretically committed to the principle of civilian control of atomic energy, Lilienthal needed to hold out at least the prospect of "peaceful uses" to sustain the rationale for that principle, even as the AEC in practice increasingly became a creature of the military.[25]

Above all, this hoopla for "the sunny side of the atom" must be seen in the context of a deepening Cold War, in which America's military planners were placing increasing strategic reliance on the nation's nuclear weapons program—a rapidly expanding program shrouded in secrecy. With the nuclear arms race entering a dangerous new phase, the public was urged to contemplate the vast and friendly benefits of the peacetime atom. In February 1950, following a meeting with President Truman two weeks after Truman's go-ahead on building the hydrogen bomb, Lilienthal recorded in his diary the president's full agreement "that my theme of Atoms for Peace is just what the country needs."[26]

25

Secrecy and Soft Soap: Soothing Fears of the Bomb

Vannevar Bush was a weighty personage in postwar America. Head of the Carnegie Institution in Washington and former dean of engineering at MIT, this brusque Yankee had served in the war as head of the Office of Scientific Research and Development. Thus when Bush published *Modern Arms and Free Men* in mid-1949, it received a respectful hearing.

One of Bush's themes was that the early postwar burst of atomic fear had been much exaggerated. The shock of Hiroshima had "overwhelmed our calm reason for a time" and even led some "prophets of doom" to predict "the end of the world as we know it," he said, but with the passage of four years it was now possible to "assess the bomb more objectively." In fact, insisted Bush, "we have more breathing time than we once thought." A Soviet bomb was probably far in the future since the Russians lacked not only the "special skills" of American science, but also "the resourcefulness of free men."[1] Shape up, Bush in effect told his countrymen; get over your craven fear of the bomb. American science, if properly supported, would protect the nation.

Vannevar Bush was only one of many opinion-molders preaching this message as the 1940s ended. Along with the systematic effort to portray atomic energy as friendly and nonthreatening, these years also saw a closely related effort to soothe fears of the atomic bomb and its hazards, particularly radiation. This effort had two dimensions. The first was a policy of deep secrecy about atomic-bomb research and stockpiling—a policy that largely withdrew this issue from the arena of public discourse. The second was a pervasive official practice (supported by large segments of the media) of playing down the bomb's dangers and discrediting those who continued to warn of such dangers. Both approaches furthered the deadening of overt nuclear consciousness.

By the late 1940s, the AEC, with its $500 million annual budget and its sixty thousand employees, was operating within a tight cordon of secrecy. Only vague estimates of bomb production filtered into the press, and few specifics about the doomsday strategies that were engaging the Pentagon's war planners—the stockpiles and strategies that historians like David Alan Rosenberg and Gregg Herken have only just begun to document.*

In this context, David Lilienthal played his usual role. On one hand, he endlessly and sometimes eloquently protested the "paralysis of secrecy" that surrounded the military aspects of atomic energy, preventing "people from even thinking about the problem." The "growing tendency in some quarters to act as if atomic energy were none of the American public's business," he said was "plain nonsense."[3] Continually he urged the citizenry to discuss the issues posed by atomic weapons. Knowledge, openness, and the democratic process, he insisted, were the best safeguards against catastrophe.

Yet as the most powerful or at least most visible atomic-energy policymaker in the Truman administration, Lilienthal himself did little to provide information that would have breached the wall of secrecy he so deplored. As the AEC's former general counsel Herbert S. Marks wrote in 1948, the average citizen's natural response to Lilienthal's endless pleas that the public inform itself on atomic-energy issues was: "What is it that they want us to know? Why don't they tell us? Then we may know what to do."[4]

As for atomic testing, the fact of major atmospheric tests, such as the Bikini series of 1946 or Operation Sandstone, the 1948 tests at Eniwetok Atoll, could hardly be concealed, but little further was revealed in the Atomic Energy Commission's bland and generalized news releases. Although a major test series in Nevada in 1951 included detonations bright enough to illuminate the night sky over Los Angeles and San Francisco, no announcement was made by the AEC. *Life* published dramatic photographs of the glowing skies, but could offer no further information. "What was the AEC up to?", asked the magazine; "Clearly something urgent was in the wind."[5] (Though *Life*'s copywriter hardly intended to suggest it, something was indeed "in the wind": radioactive fallout!)

For activists seeking to arouse and sustain public engagement with the atomic threat, this stifling blanket of official secrecy was intensely frustrating. As early as March 1946 Lewis Mumford burst out: "The President, the generals, the admirals, and the administrators have lied to us about their infernal machine: they have lied by their statements and even more they have lied by their silences." The political cartoonist Herblock expressed this frustration visually in a 1948 drawing of a senator exclaiming angrily at a

---

* Not until January 1982, after more than three decades of secrecy, did the government release to Rosenberg figures on the United States stockpile of atomic bombs from 1945 through 1950.[2] Herken's important 1982 book, *The Winning Weapon: The Atomic Bomb in the Cold War, 1945–1950*, is similarly based on long-secret military planning documents only recently declassified.

committee hearing: "How did atomic energy information leak out to the damn scientists in the first place?"[6]

In a penetrating 1948 essay in the *University of Chicago Law Review,* Herbert Marks deplored the "vacuum" in which the AEC was operating, with public discussion "virtually non-existent." The eerie silence on atomic-weapons policy, and on atomic-energy issues generally, he attributed to governmental secrecy and a vague but pervasive public feeling "that to ask questions in this field is unpatriotic." If the situation did not improve, Marks predicted, "our atomic energy program will almost certainly grow so far out of touch with the American environment that when the forces of criticism finally begin to operate . . . they will produce drastic upheavals."[7]

Marks's forebodings were shared by other thoughtful Americans as the decade ended. Even Senator Brien McMahon, framer of the law that had created the Atomic Energy Commission, was dismayed by the secrecy that increasingly enveloped it. The United States had spent $3 billion on atomic weapons, he told the Detroit Economics Club in January 1949, yet even the Joint Congressional Committee on Atomic Energy did not know how many atomic bombs had been built. This lack of public knowledge on such a vital issue, he said, "goes to the very heart of our democratic system." The playwright and onetime FDR speechwriter Robert E. Sherwood, writing in the *Atlantic Monthly*, challenged "the theory that the way to keep the people fearless is to keep them ignorant." It was scandalous, he said, that on so crucial a matter as atomic radiation the public had to rely on either unofficial sources or "the deluding or confusing pronouncements" of far from disinterested military officials. What could the ordinary citizen do, asked *Christian Century,* when basic decisions about atomic-weapons policy were being "made in secret recesses of government where the vaunted democratic process never penetrates?" Telford Taylor, chief counsel at the Nuremberg war crimes trials, writing in the *Nation* in 1950, painted a grim picture of America's nuclear culture five years after Hiroshima:

> Here and there a few scientists and their many assistants are tinkering with these potent machines in surroundings which are more like prisons than laboratories. In a few capitals a few high officials are privy to such of these secrets as they can understand, which may not be so many. . . . The journalist must write his newspaper column on the basis of a guess and a whisper; the rest of us can only grope blindly in an oppressive and baffling murk.[8]

Among those most deeply dismayed were many of the men who had brought the bomb into existence. Repeatedly in these years one finds Manhattan Project veterans and other scientists lamenting the official restrictions on information essential to informed public discourse. Early in 1952, for example, James Conant, a central figure in the wartime bomb project, wrote to J. Robert Oppenheimer:

> The advent of this new weapon has brought an area of secrecy around science that no one would have imagined possible fifteen years ago. . . . As a consequence, governments are forced to say things about technical developments that are not necessarily accurate. . . . Information that "leaks" more or less in a planned fashion is even less reliable. . . . I'm afraid this atmosphere of mystery will continue in this whole area as long as the world remains divided.[9]

Despite such periodic laments or even protests, some from highly influential figures, the policy of strict government secrecy grew, inevitably stifling public discussion and cultural awareness.

Coupled with the official secrecy was a more active governmental effort to soothe public anxiety about the bomb—an effort that neatly complemented the simultaneous campaign to direct public attention to the peacetime uses of atomic energy. Maj. Alexander P. de Seversky kicked off this effort somewhat idiosyncratically with his February 1946 *Reader's Digest* article pooh-poohing the atomic bomb and deploring the public's "near hysteria at the first exhibits of atomic destruction." Hiroshima's devastation, he argued, was because of its shoddy construction. The atomic bomb was like "a great fly swatter two miles broad, slapped down on a city of flimsy, half-rotted wooden houses and rickety brick buildings." Had the atomic bomb been dropped on a solidly built American city, "the property damage might have been limited to broken window glass over a wide area."[10]

Appearing within months of Hiroshima, de Seversky's article ran strongly against the prevailing cultural current. It was universally repudiated and within a few months, as we have seen, *Reader's Digest* itself published a graphic account of an atomic bombing of New York City. Nevertheless, de Seversky's whitewash was reflective of the incipient official impulse to downgrade the bomb's menace—an impulse that found increasing expression as the decade wore on.

One who vigorously took up this theme was Lt. Gen. Leslie R. Groves. Convinced, as he put it in the *Saturday Evening Post* in 1948, that there had been entirely "too much hysteria about the terrible future possibility of America's being scourged by atomic bombs," Groves during his years in the limelight worked strenuously to dispel it. "Mine is not a message of despair, but of hope," he told a nationwide radio audience early in 1949. "America has faced serious situations before. We will come through all right. . . . You don't have to hide under your beds tonight."[11]

As early as 1947 David Lilienthal, too, began lashing out at those who were feeding the public "a publicity diet of almost nothing else but horror stories." Such "hysteria and unreasoning fear," he said, was "scaring the daylights out of everyone, so no one can think." In a 1949 *Collier's* article he urged Americans not to be so "fascinated and preoccupied by atomic weapons," but to take a broader and more hopeful view.[12] When Lilienthal left the AEC early in 1950, many hoped he would speak out on substantive issues related to atomic-bomb policy, but his speeches continued to combine vague invocations of "reason," "democracy," and "faith" with attacks on atomic scientists and other activists for their "extravagant and sensational picturing of the horrors of atomic warfare." In exasperation, *Christian Century* in March 1950 attacked a typical Lilienthal performance as "more of a lullaby than a lecture."[13]

Lilienthal's successor at the AEC, Gordon Dean, continued his policy of offering soothing answers to unsettling questions. Asked in November 1950 whether atomic war could destroy all life on earth, Dean acknowledged that the explosion of "many, many thermonuclear weapons" could "conceivably" contaminate the atmosphere "with elements which are inconsistent with human life," The possibility, he quickly added, was remote and "something that I wouldn't worry about at the moment."[14]

Much of this officially inspired effort to neutralize atomic-bomb fears focused on the frightening, little-understood phenomenon of radiation. In contrast to the more dramatic blast and heat effects, this invisible by-product of atomic fission had received comparatively little public attention in the immediate postwar period. After a flurry of media publicity for Dr. Harold Jacobson's quickly discredited predictions that Hiroshima would be uninhabitable for decades, the issue of radiation receded from the center of public awareness. According to a recent study, not one of more than two hundred letters about the bomb published in a representative group of American newspapers in the early post-Hiroshima weeks mentioned the radiation issue. The death of a young scientist, Harry Daghlian, in a radiation accident at Los Alamos on August 21, 1945, and another, Louis Slotin, on May 30, 1946, were little noticed. Nor did radiation receive much attention in the works of scientific popularization that proliferated after the war. "We will not enter here in the discussion of the unpleasant effects of the radiation of the atomic bomb," wrote George Gamow in *Atomic Energy in Cosmic and Human Life*. "This is a book on physics and not on . . . medicine."[15]

While the effects of radiation figured significantly in the various accounts of hypothetical atomic attacks published or broadcast in the early postwar period, as well as in Hersey's *Hiroshima,* the horrendous immediate toll of death and destruction from blast and fire they described tended to overwhelm the discussion of longer-term radiation effects. Further diminishing public awareness, of course, was the government's initial policy of playing down or seeking to discredit reports of radiation sickness from Hiroshima and Nagasaki. Radiation, then, while certainly a component of the generalized atomic fear of the immediate post-Hiroshima period, was not initially singled out as a clearly defined focus of public worry. While the precise level of radiological knowledge among top government officials and even scientists at successive stages in these early years remains somewhat conjectural, what is clear is that practically none of this knowledge was fully and candidly conveyed to the public. Quite the reverse, in fact: from the first, the hazards of radioactivity were hopelessly obscured in a flurry of vague, optimistic, and downright misleading pronouncements.

All this changed dramatically in 1948, as we have seen, when David Bradley's best-selling *No Place to Hide* sharply focused the public's growing post-Bikini uneasiness about the radiation danger, not only from atomic bombs dropped in war, but from atmospheric tests. Very quickly, a strong governmental countermove took shape. An April 1948 report by the U.S. Surgeon General's office sought to ease public apprehension and debunk the "sensational prophecies" about the dire effects of radioactivity. It denied, for example, that radiation could result in the birth of deformed babies; any fetus that received a sufficient dose to cause a birth defect, it said, would die *in utero*. Visitors to the Westinghouse exhibit at the Man and the Atom show in New York that summer were assured that if any Westinghouse worker became even "slightly radioactive, we put him on another job." At about the same time, the AEC reported progress in research on the treatment of radiation disease: in tests on irradiated dogs, a chemical extracted from buckwheat had reduced internal bleeding dramatically.[16]

Further undercutting Bradley's book were several articles by Austin M. Brues, a University of Chicago radiobiologist and a member of the advisory committee of the Atomic Bomb Casualty Commission, a Hiroshima research center set up by the AEC in 1946 to study bomb survivors. It was time for a "partial debunking" to dispel the "mystery" of radiation, said Brues: certainly it could cause cancer, but so could sunlight; radiation sickness was treatable and "we may reasonably expect to find further means of alleviation"; the genetic risks were "over-rated" and had "not yet been detected at Hiroshima." Radioactive-waste disposal remained a problem, but we "still have years in which we can settle upon a number of feasible methods." Greater than the physical hazards of radiation, Brues suggested, was the danger that the "unreasoning fear" of it aroused by alarmists like Bradley could lead to "an Orson Welles–like panic," should an atomic attack ever become imminent. David Lilienthal added his voice to the soothing chorus: "We have to learn to live with radiation," he said; "Radiation is just as much a natural phenomenon as anything else. . . . It can become one of our best friends as well as one of our direst enemies."[17]

The most elaborate presentation of the government's position on radiation came from Col. James P. Cooney of the U.S. Army Medical Corps. While radioactivity from atomic weapons could indeed be a "diabolical

Domesticating the atom. Many early postwar scientific popularizations sought to make atomic energy seem a nonthreatening, familiar part of the cultural landscape. This illustration is from *Atomics for the Millions* (1947) by Maxwell Eidinoff and Hyman Ruchlis.

Panel from *Splitting the Atom—Starring Dagwood and Blondie*, a 1948 comic book prepared by King Features Syndicate in collaboration with the General Electric Corporation (a major nuclear-power contractor) and the U.S. government. Many thousands of copies were distributed free at "Atomic Energy" exhibits.

By 1950, the Federal Civil Defense Agency had reduced nuclear survival to a series of simple rules, including "jump in any handy ditch or gutter" and "never lose your head."

Fashion tips for the apocalypse. Men should wear wide-brimmed hats, women stockings and long-sleeved dresses. From Richard Gerstell's government-sponsored *How to Survive an Atomic Bomb* (1950).

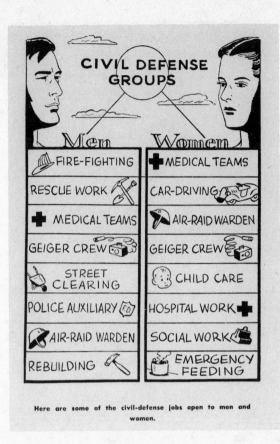

Even after the bomb fell, gender-role distinctions would be carefully preserved, in the view of 1950 civil-defense planners. (From Richard Gerstell, *How to Survive an Atomic Bomb*.)

Flee the city! An early 1950 real estate ad offers "good bomb immunity" in an upstate New York property (*Life*, February 27, 1950).

Redesign the city. Publicizing a plan drafted by MIT's Norbert Wiener and others, *Life* in 1950 proposed eight-lane "Life Belts" around the nation's major cities with camp sites and quonset-hut hospitals for the survivors of nuclear attack (*Life*, December 18, 1950).

"See . . . it's Bead Chain . . . just like yours"

NEW YORK CITY SCHOOLS ORDER IDENTIFICATION NECKLACES FOR ALL STUDENTS

By 1951, with civil defense in full swing, some schoolchildren were being issued dog tags so their bodies could be identified after a nuclear attack. This ad by a Rhode Island bead-chain manufacturer in the April 1951 *School Executive* went on to urge other school districts to follow New York City's lead.

GLOW FROM FOURTH BOMB EXPLODED IN NEVADA SILHOUETTES SPIRES OF ST. JOSEPH'S CHURCH IN DOWNTOWN LOS ANGELES, OVER 200 MILES FROM BLAST

1951: The future unfolds. Against the darkened spires of a church, the glow of a pre-dawn Nevada atomic test illuminates the night sky over Los Angeles, two hundred miles away. "What was the AEC up to?" asked *Life*. "Clearly something urgent was in the wind."

instrument of death and injury to man," Cooney told the American Public Health Association in November, 1948, it was not the unique and mysterious menace some were picturing. Reporting on his recent interviews with Hiroshima and Nagasaki survivors who had experienced radiation sickness after the attack, he said they now "appeared perfectly normal and . . . handicapped in no way toward pursuing their way of living." Cooney's major concern, however, was not the medical aspects of radiation sickness, but the problems that fear of radiation posed for the military. All strategic planning, he noted, involved calculating casualty rates that were not only objectively acceptable but that could be made to appear acceptable to those who would experience them; the key to "battle discipline and military effectiveness," was "not the hazard itself, but the soldiers' estimation of the hazard." If radiation horror stories were allowed to go unchecked, he warned, "the fear reaction of the uninitiated . . . could well interfere with an important military mission in time of war."

The answer, Cooney insisted, was to condition potential radiation victims to perceive it not as a separate category of danger, but as simply another of the many risks of war: "If we are to live with this piece of ordnance and ever have to use it again in the defense of our way of living, we must acquire a practical attitude . . . toward the possible effects and limitations of this 'mysterious' radiation." Illustrating the demystification process he favored, Cooney noted that a spinal wound or even venereal disease picked up behind the lines could cause sterility or impotence just as surely as radiation.[18]

The same message, this time aimed at the general public rather than health professionals, is found in Ralph Lapp's *Must We Hide?* (1949). Lapp was at this time with the Office of Naval Research and his book thus had quasi-official status. Indeed, the preface acknowledges the assistance of the Pentagon, the Public Health Service, and the AEC. (David Bradley has suggested that it was explicitly commissioned by the government as an "answer" to *No Place to Hide.*) The effects of an atomic bomb were indeed terrible, wrote Lapp, but "a complete description of the injuries inflicted by almost any modern weapon would be equally gruesome." The "much publicized burns" of the Hiroshima and Nagasaki victims, for example, were "no worse than those resulting from other forms of modern weapons." As for radiation, Lapp acknowledged that for many people "the mere mention of the word . . . has a numbing effect." He further conceded: "Radiation is dangerous—let there be no mistake about that." But, like Colonel Cooney, he insisted that it was best viewed as "just one more of the hazards of contemporary living." We tolerate the risks of automobile travel in order to enjoy its benefits, he argued; why not adopt the same view toward radiation? Lapp echoed Lilienthal's theme that radiation in the form of sunlight was a familiar part of the everyday environment and added a homely analogy of his own: "Like taxes, radioactivity has long been with us and in increasing amounts; it is not to be hated and feared, but . . . treated with respect, avoided when practicable, and accepted when inevitable." In any event, science and technology would protect us: "We are fortunate in having a nucleus of well-trained scientists who have a thorough understanding of radiation hazards and methods of protection against them. We have adequate instrumentation to permit accurate evaluation of any radiation hazards that may exist." [19]

Further assurance that radiation fears were exaggerated appeared in the first post-Hiroshima civil-defense manual, Richard Gerstell's government-sponsored *How to Survive an Atomic Bomb* (1950), and in articles by Gerstell in the *Saturday Evening Post* and other popular magazines. Atomic radiation could cause "burns" in heavy doses, said Gerstell, but "you can easily protect yourself" and with the proper precautions "it is not likely to hurt you." "Much of the danger of radioactivity is mental," he insisted. Explicitly attacking *No Place to Hide,* he wrote: "To paraphrase in reverse that horrendous book title, there most definitely is some place to hide." The rumor that contact with "'fallout' stuff" would cause cancer, he insisted in an angry burst of italics, was *"absolutely false."* None of the thousands of Hiroshima survivors being studied had contracted cancer that could be traced to radiation exposure, he pointed out. Listing the "foolish stories" about radioactivity that were circulating—loss of hair, blindness, sterility, global environmental damage—Gerstell patiently and confidently dismissed each one. Even during the temporary sterility experienced by some Hiroshima males, he noted, "they were still able to have sexual relations." The radioactivity from an atomic attack, he insisted, would be "no greater a threat . . . than are typhoid fever and other diseases that often follow the ravages of a bombing."

Radioactive fallout, said Gerstell, striking a now-familiar note, was "much the same as sunlight": overexposure to either could cause illness and even death, but in moderation neither would do serious harm. "We've got to learn not to be afraid of those words—'radiation' and 'radioactivity,'" he continued. "We've been living with that stuff all our lives—it's all around us all the time." Like Ralph Lapp, Gerstell played upon the public's will to believe that someone, somewhere, had the problem in hand:

> To combat even the comparatively small but important threat [atomic-bomb radioactivity] does hold, a new and proven military science has arisen. Radiological defense, which consists of the detection and avoidance of radioactive hazards, is something which, in a quiet but effective way, the Government has been perfecting for several years. [20]

In *The Effects of Atomic Weapons,* a 1950 study published for civil-defense workers by the AEC and the Department of Defense, the major emphasis was on the bomb's blast and thermal effects on structures and "Personnel." (The Hiroshima bomb was used as the basis for the data.) As for radiation, the report said: "In the considered opinion of many who have made observations of atomic explosions, the fall-out in the case of a low air burst might be an inconvenience, but it would not, in general, represent a real danger." No attention was given to the long-term radiological effects of an atomic explosion on crops or water supply, though the report did note that radioactive dust generated at the July 1945 Alamogordo test later turned up in strawboard manufactured in Vincennes, Indiana, evidently because the straw had been washed in water from the Wabash River, which drains a wide area. But the radioactivity was "very small" it said, and was discovered only when X-ray film packed in the strawboard fogged up.[21]

The AEC prepared a simplified book for general distribution based on the more technical longer study. Like other government-sponsored material of the period, it played down the danger of radioactivity and stressed preventive measures. At a news conference promoting this booklet, an AEC spokesman insisted that the radiation hazard had been much exaggerated: "If an individual can stand up after the bomb goes off and look around and comment 'This place is really beat up' . . . , he has a pretty good chance of surviving, something like a 90 percent chance." Asked about medical remedies he acknowledged that there was "no specific therapeutic treatment right now. . . . We still depend on the human body to recover on its own accord." But he added: "I think there is much that we can do about it. We don't have to sit back and say that 60,000 people are going to die because a bomb goes off, because that is not the way to look at it."[22]

The soothing message brought by authorities such as Cooney, Lapp, and Gerstell filtered into the culture by many channels. In 1948 a South Dakota man, mentioning an article in *Pathfinder* magazine, popular in rural America, wrote Robert Hutchins to ask if it was true that tobacco and buckwheat could cure radiation disease. In the 1949 Warner Brothers musical *My Dream Is Yours,* Doris Day sang a number called "Tic, Tic, Tic" that poked lighthearted fun at the danger of radioactivity.[23]

The diversity of this quasi-official campaign to soothe the public's atomic-bomb fears is illustrated in the activities of William S. Parsons, the career navy officer who, as a member of the Manhattan Project, had completed final assembly of the atomic bomb aboard the *Enola Gay.* From 1946 to 1949, Parsons was assigned to the Pentagon as assistant chief of naval operations. (Promoted to rear admiral in 1948, he concurrently served as deputy commander of the 1948 atomic tests at Eniwetok.) During his Pentagon years, Parsons worked assiduously to combat the influence of those he believed were dangerously exacerbating the public's atomic fears. He was deeply suspicious of the "articulate scientific propagandists" and the "wild 'liberal' crowd" whose exaggerations and distortions were pushing people toward "a state which could well border on hysteria." (If the activist scientists continued to claim that intercontinental ballistic missiles were imminent, he wrote Adm. Lewis Strauss in 1947, they would quickly be classed with the "crackpots who periodically predict the end of the world.") Parsons's letters and memos of this period are full of references to America's "atomic neurosis" and the need to overcome it. "Continuation of this neurotic approach into the 1950s," he warned in 1948, "could make the United States vulnerable to a war of nerves that would make the Orson Welles Mercury Theater episode pale by comparison." [24]

In speeches, articles, and newspaper interviews, Parsons insisted that "in the uproar after Hiroshima, the potency of the atomic bomb" had been exaggerated. He especially warned against the "unhealthy hysteria" surrounding the issue of radioactivity. Particularly eager to reach young people, he welcomed the National Education Association's "Operation Atomic Vision," and wrote articles for *Boy's Life* and other magazines aimed at this age group. America's "overall national strength in the field of atomic energy in the middle 1950s," he wrote the AEC's public-relations director, "will be greatly enhanced by action taken in the late 1940s to disseminate sound information to children now in high school. This dissemination is made easier by . . . the receptiveness of young people to new ideas." [25]

Parsons carefully monitored and tried to influence the media's coverage of all matters related to atomic weapons. When a New York publisher in 1948 was planning a small book on the atomic bomb aimed at a general audience, the proposal passed through Parsons's office. The staff member who reviewed it wrote Parsons: "I would like to keep it under control, and to make it Navy propaganda as far as is ethical, because sure as shootin', it will become Air Force propaganda otherwise." Parsons's oversight extended to the screen as well as the printed word. As early as 1946, he was asked by MGM to review the script of the movie *The Beginning or the End*. (Pronouncing it generally "in good taste," Parsons found no fault with the movie's propagandistic distortions. He was, however, upset at the prominence given the one fictionalized scientist who expresses moral reservations and "philosophical worries" about the bomb.) Continuing in his role as film critic, Parsons in 1947 sent a sharp memo to the AEC's Military Liaison Committee about a recently released short film based on the book *One World or None*. Raising an issue that particularly preoccupied him in these years, he objected to the film's portrayal, as a theoretical possibility, of highly accurate nuclear-armed missiles landing on American cities. "It is always dangerous to show as fact something which is not fact," Parsons complained. [26]

In February 1949, a few days before a scheduled discussion of the atomic bomb on *Town Meeting of the Air*, Parsons wrote the AEC's public-relations office suggesting efforts to counteract the program's potentially negative effect on public opinion. The program "works like a packed meeting," Parsons noted, urging the AEC to "send someone who knows the facts to keep things from going haywire." Specifically, he urged that a person of "wit and imagination" be placed as a "careful plant" in the studio audience to raise questions aimed at discrediting David Bradley, one of the scheduled panelists.[27]

The sustained and wide-ranging governmental effort—of which Parsons was a part—to downplay the atomic danger had its effect on the media. By the end of the 1940s, one finds few articles describing the horrors of atomic war, but many more suggesting that the fears of the immediate post-Hiroshima period had been overblown. The hope of avoiding atomic war was slim, announced *Life* in October 1949, but humankind would not only survive the coming holocaust but perhaps through it "at last find the secret of peace." Americans still dreaded the bomb, said *Time* that same month, but had accepted "the idea that they must live with it." *Collier's* offers a particularly dramatic instance of this shift. In 1946, as we have seen, *Collier's* had published Harold C. Urey's "I Am a Frightened Man," with its grim warning of atomic holocaust. In January 1949, by contrast, a *Collier's* editorial titled "Our Fears Are False" urged that all the talk of "the atomic bomb and the end of civilization and a number of other fearful things" be taken with a grain of salt. Do not "wallow in the details of horror," *Collier's* advised in an avuncular tone, but "think about the matter calmly and . . . stop being agitated by every speaker and writer with a passion for anxiety." As a contribution to the calming process, *Collier's* offered its analysis of the international situation: "Nobody seems to believe that Russia now has any present supply of bombs or any probable means of making them soon." As for the United States, "we could not use [atomic] bombs without abandoning all our cherished principles. We are simply not that kind of people." Therefore, *Collier's* triumphantly concluded, the atomic situation offered nothing "that men of good will need to fear."[28]

26

The Reassuring Message of Civil Defense

Roger Babson was a Boston economic forecaster who won lasting fame when, in the summer of 1929, he predicted that a stock-market crash lay just around the corner. There was thus a flurry of media attention in 1946 when Babson announced that after a systematic effort to find the safest spot in America, he was shipping his business records to Eureka, Kansas.[1] In 1946, few had yet accepted the notion that the most constructive way to deal with atomic fear was to prepare for attack, but by the late 1940s Babson again seemed a prophet, for the end of the decade brought an intensifying drumfire of official insistence that citizens must prepare for atomic war. "Civil defense" became the kind of panacea that "international control" had represented earlier.

From the earliest days of the atomic era, some opinion-molders had called for defensive efforts against the bomb. Within months of Hiroshima, sociologist William F. Ogburn was urging a massive program of urban dispersal. In 1946, both William L. Borden's *There Will Be No Time* and the report of the United States Strategic Bombing Survey (USSBS) on the atomic bombing of Hiroshima and Nagasaki advocated a large-scale federal civil-defense program involving shelter construction, emergency-evacuation planning, and the stockpiling of medicine and other critical supplies. From the beginning, too, newspapers periodically reported some new civil-defense scheme or carried stories of well-known personages like Babson who were taking refuge in some remote spot. In 1946, a suburban New York contractor attracted brief newspaper notice when he sold his business and moved with his wife and four children to an isolated corner of Montana.[2]

But in the period just after Hiroshima, such stories were treated as isolated "human interest" items, somewhat in the category of flagpole sitters and goldfish swallowers. People could only shake their heads late in 1945 when an eccentric New York City engineer proposed giant subterranean elevators to lower the city's skyscrapers in an atomic emergency. (The Empire State Building, he calculated, could be lowered to the eighty-sixth-floor level in fifty-eight seconds, "leaving only the tower unprotected to avoid expense of added cellar depth.") More serious proposals for defense against atomic attack, particularly those involving urban dispersal, invariably came in for sharp criticism. Only Germany was in a position to disperse its cities, observed Robert M. Hutchins, since Allied bombers had already started the process. E. B. White sarcastically parodied William Ogburn's message: "Disperse, scatter. . . . No use going underground, just go away altogether. Break up. Cities are doomed." Under the atomic threat, White reflected, city dwellers were more likely to draw close together than to disperse. Even Elmer Davis, while sympathetic to some civil-defense proposals, was intensely critical of schemes for mass urban resettlement. "We have been told . . . to rebuild our cities under the mountain ranges; or to string them out along the highways, thirty feet wide on each side of the road for hundreds of miles," observed Davis in December 1945. "Well, that is not going to be done. Either plan would be impossibly expensive; either would require impossible infringements on personal liberty—a military dictatorship telling each of us where to move to and what to do." A life spent "in perpetual fear of the atomic bomb," Davis concluded, "would not be worth living."[3]

Schemes for building vast underground facilities were ridiculed as well. Early in 1947, the New Yorker's Daniel Lang offered a bemused account of a day spent with a team surveying a West Virginia cave as part of a Pentagon effort to find caves and abandoned mines suitable for emergency government use. ("This might even make a good office for the President," says one team member upon entering a particularly capacious room.) Even if an underground city survived the initial blast, argued John W. Campbell, Jr., in 1947, it would likely become "a monstrous tomb . . . , sealed from the upper world by . . . miles of broken, twisted rock." Imagining the end of such a city, Campbell wrote: "It might well be many days before the last of the entombed city's air was exhausted; lights operated by power from atomic piles might still burn for ages thereafter, but no eyes would see them."[4]

True to its tenet "There Is No Defense," the scientists' movement sharply rejected all suggestions of civil defense. The "almost unbelievable" civil-defense proposals of the USSBS, charged W. A. Higinbotham of the Federation of American Scientists, would have the American people "running for cover and burrowing like moles." Even such modest civil-defense measures as school-evacuation drills, he warned, could "poison the American way of life."[5]

But civil defense, the unwanted waif of 1945–1946, came into its own as the decade ended. Instead of There Is No Defense, one now heard talk— much of it officially inspired—of strategies for protecting the populace against atomic attack. Urban dispersal was proposed with new seriousness. "Before World War III, Let's Disperse," urged Science Digest in April 1948, with all the heartiness of a camp counselor cajoling bored teenagers into taking a hike. Among the urban designs for reducing atomic-bomb vulnerability discussed by Ralph Lapp in *Must We Hide?* (1949) were the Rod City (fifty miles long and a mile wide), Satellite City, and Donut City, hollow at the core.

Lapp readily conceded that such radical schemes of urban dispersal would "spell the end of the metropolis as we know it," but like William Ogburn earlier, he insisted that they would also ameliorate many of the nation's most troublesome social problems:

> Indirectly, the atomic bomb offers a rare opportunity for greatly improving the living conditions of millions of our citizens. Our large cities have been growing larger, resulting in more crowded streets and tenement houses. . . . If [dispersal] is done properly, we will at the same time greatly increase our urban attractiveness.

In building his argument, Lapp subtly drew upon a deep-seated belief in American exceptionalism—the conviction that the nation's continental vastness would prove its salvation: "Within our borders . . . we have plenty of space. One of the most decisive things which we as a country can do to reduce our vulnerability to atomic attack is to use this space effectively. . . . Even atomic bombs meet their master in the invincibility of space."

Turning to other, less drastic civil-defense measures, Lapp urged the rehearsal of evacuation procedures to prevent panic when the moment came, and called for the advance training of professionals for their post-attack roles. Physicians should be equipped with Geiger counters, and special fire-fighting teams should be trained for atomic-bomb situations. (These, he noted, should be selected from public-spirited volunteers, since "for the common good, it may . . . be necessary to risk radiation sickness in a few.")

The prerequisite to all effective civil-defense planning, Lapp insisted, was abandonment of "the present defeatist attitude toward the bomb" in favor of "the feeling that something can be done about it after all." The "lurid tales of universal destruction . . . so often blared forth in the press" had to be replaced by a "well-designed program of training and indoctrination . . . to give the general public a more healthy attitude toward atomic warfare."[6]

The warmly favorable reviews of *Must We Hide?* offer a gauge of the changing cultural climate. Hanson W. Baldwin praised it in the *New York Times* as "infinitely superior" to David Bradley's *No Place to Hide*. The *Nation* found it "coolly factual" and "illuminating rather than alarming." *Newsweek* contrasted Lapp's "hopeful" message favorably with earlier works that had portrayed the horror of atomic war in prose "strongly charged with emotion."[7]

The calls for more systematic civil-defense planning and indoctrination as the decade ended reflected developments in Washington. The wartime civil-defense office (directed by Mayor Fiorello La Guardia of New York) had disbanded in 1945, but the later 1940s brought pressures for a revived program. A first step was the creation of the National Security Resources Board in 1947. Its main concern, though, was not civil defense per se, but continued industrial production after an atomic attack. Early in 1948, Defense Secretary James Forrestal set up a temporary office of civil-defense planning under Russell J. Hopley to draft proposals for a more permanent agency. Hopley's November 1948 report, "Civil Defense for National Security," argued for a local and private approach. The government should disseminate information on first aid, fire prevention, radiation detection, and the like; but beyond that "the individual . . . must, in the event of an emergency, take care of himself." Only if a local community were "completely overwhelmed" would state or federal authorities step in. The Hopley report did call for a federal civil-defense office, however, and, in 1950, after considerable foot-dragging, President Truman created the Federal Civil Defense Administration—an agency that despite numerous name changes survives to the present day.[8]

As historian Allan Winkler has written, the FCDA accomplished little of substance in the Truman years, but its activities did have significant ramifications. Under director Millard F. Caldwell, it held conferences, commissioned studies, drew up elaborate plans, and in general infused civil defense with an aura of official bustle. It also, as Winkler notes, did "a good deal of cajoling of the American public." In its early months, the FCDA flooded the country with sixteen million copies of a booklet called *Survival Under Atomic Attack*; distributed a movie of the same title narrated by Edward R. Murrow; prepared a civil-defense exhibit called Alert America that was hauled around the country by a convoy of ten tractor-trailer trucks; and, as a pilot project of a planned national program, gave every citizen of Allentown, Pennsylvania, a metal identification tag.[9]

At the local level, Milwaukee mayor Frank Zeidler had created a Civil Defense and Disaster Committee as early as 1948 to plan "what to do if a possible enemy delivered a 'Sunday punch' in the very near future." In 1950, Zeidler reported that after initial resistance, Milwaukeeans were convinced of the program's urgency. Zeidler urged all big-city mayors to prepare at once for urban dispersal and emergency evacuation, with particular attention to the "lack of harmony" that might develop between urban and rural officials "if a swarm of refugees from a stricken area should pour out into the countryside." In New York City, owners of public buildings were asked to provide space for shelters. (The "vast majority," complained a local civil-defense official, either "refused flatly" or ignored the request.) In Bedford

Hills, N.Y., a civil-defense homeowners' survey inquired: "Would you be willing, in a spirit of patriotism and cooperation, to accept people for temporary shelter in the event of a real war emergency? (Every effort will be made to place people of similar interests with you.)" While there was "not the slightest reason for hysteria or fright," Governor Thomas E. Dewey told New Yorkers, there was "the most desperate and compelling reason for sane and intelligent preparation for a disaster which a ruthless enemy might bring upon us at any hour of the day or night." War would come "whenever the fourteen evil men in Moscow decide to have it break out," he said, "and it could start with . . . atom bombing of New York today, next month, or next year." [10]

An important early contribution to the literature of civil defense was *How to Survive an Atomic Bomb* (1950), by Richard Gerstell, whose comments on radiation we have already noted. A radiologist and former researcher for the Pennsylvania State Game Commission, Gerstell was a consultant with the Pentagon's office of civil defense planning, and his book came with the posthumous blessing of James Forrestal, who had committed suicide shortly before its publication.

How to Survive an Atomic Bomb was widely distributed in a cheap paperback edition, and articles based on it appeared in various popular magazines. Conveyed in simple language, its message was equally basic: "If you want a better chance of living through an atomic attack . . . , read this book." The key, Gerstell insisted, was preparation. None of the 42,000 servicemen at Bikini had been injured, he pointed out, because "those men were prepared. They knew how to take care of themselves." Time and again, Gerstell invoked Bikini. Civil defense after an atomic attack on an American city, he said, would be directed from a well-organized headquarters "not unlike the task-force command ship at Bikini." As for the emotional aftereffects, "psychoneurotic" goats from Bikini were being studied at Cornell for clues to "the human susceptibility to crack-up and panic." The evidence was encouraging: one goat on a ship near ground zero had been filmed munching his food moments after the blast "very much undisturbed. No collapse. No nervous breakdown."

Gingerly and obliquely, Gerstell acknowledged that for millions, there would be little hope: "Let's get a very important matter out of the way first. If you live in an important city or a large seaport or manufacturing town, you ought to think about sending your children away to the country if we get into a big war." But most of the book was more upbeat, with practical, homey advice: buy a first-aid kit; practice lying on the floor. ("Get off in your own room where you won't be laughed at and try it a few times.") In Gerstell's world, the responsible householder was already well on the way toward preparation for atomic war: car windows should always be rolled up and "the car . . . kept in a closed garage"; "Trash should be put in cans and covered tightly, dry leaves should be raked away from the home." Gerstell even included tips on how to dress for the holocaust:

> In the event of an emergency, a person should always wear long trousers or slacks and loose-fitting light-colored blouses with full-length sleeves buttoned at the wrist. A hat, brim down, could help prevent many a face burn. Women should never go bare-legged. . . . During evacuation . . . , wear a hat and, if possible, rubbers.

Above all, Gerstell advised, if the big one falls, keep cool:

> Lots of people have little tricks to help steady their nerves at times like that—like reciting jingles or rhymes or the multiplication table. . . . You'll probably be frightened. But don't be ashamed of being afraid at that moment. It's perfectly normal and healthy to be afraid of danger. Just don't let it make you lose your head and forget the facts in this book. Make sure you've got hold of yourself by the time the all-clear sounds.

Gerstell also sought to prepare his readers for postwar life: "Things are probably going to look different when you get outside. If the bomb hit within a mile and a half of the place where you are, things are going to look very different." But one must function calmly: turn on the radio or TV for instructions; if you feel sick, "get to a doctor or hospital"; if not, help with the cleanup. (Gerstell vehemently denied that corpses would remain highly radioactive after an atomic bombing. The coins in their pockets might be "temporarily heated," he said, but otherwise the dead would pose no radiation danger.) In a question-and-answer section, Gerstell disposed of a variety of practical matters:

> "How about the telephone? Will that work, too?"
> "Yes. Unless, of course, the lines are broken."
>
> "What chance do my animals have of coming through a bombing?"
> "Just about the same chances you have."

In a section that must have confused readers of Lapp's *Must We Hide?*, Gerstell dismissed urban dispersal as a "silly idea." He warned, too, against rushing out of the city to escape attack: "Where are you going to end up? Who's going to take care of you? Who's going to feed and shelter you? Who's going to keep you from running into worse radioactivity than you left?" All such decisions should be left to the authorities: "Your local government may decide to evacuate some people. (That is, move them to a different place. It's pronounced 'ee-VAK-u-ate'). But if they do, they'll do it according to a plan." Shelters offered a more promising option. Every city, Gerstell pointed out, "has *lots* of tall buildings which have deep, safe cellars. . . . So you see, although there is more chance that big cities will be bombed, there is also more protection against bombings in big cities." If properly prepared, Gerstell concluded, even a major city attacked by multiple atomic bombs "should be back to fairly regular life in one or two months." "Just keep *facts* in mind, and forget the fairy stories. Follow the safety rules. Avoid panic. And you'll come through all right." [11]

The media, which now included television, reflected the new emphasis. NBC-TV in 1951 attracted an estimated twelve million viewers to a seven-part series called "Survival," whose message was summed up in its title. "If you think a falling A-bomb means the end of everything, this remarkable report may change your mind," said the *Saturday Evening Post* in introducing a Richard Gerstell article. "Here [is] . . . proof that the blast is not always so fatal and frightful as you think." Describing Washington, D.C., as a "Naked City," *Time* late in 1949 urged dispersal of federal agencies around the country. A 1950 *Collier's* article, "Hiroshima U.S.A.: Can Anything Be Done About It?" began with the kind of vivid description of a hypothetical atomic attack on New York City that had proliferated in 1945–1947, but instead of a plea for international control or political efforts to reduce world tension, *Collier's* now called for a "dependable warning signal" and "properly constructed shelters." This new concern with civil defense, the author wrote, was a "profound relief" after five years of "mysterious mumbo-jumbo" that had "been scaring common people silly . . . with long equation-studded wrangles over how radioactive you are likely to get if you come within mumble feet of the point where an A-bomb explodes." Insisting that the atomic bomb's lethal power had been "grossly exaggerated" and claiming "really hopeful" evidence that an air-raid shelter could assure survival within three hundred feet of ground zero, he called for a major federal push on civil defense. "Keep asking about shelters," he advised. [12]

Proclaiming that "You Can Live Despite A-Bomb," *U.S. News and World Report* in December 1950 downplayed the atomic danger and underscored the emerging theme—not dispersal, but protection in place:

Forget most stories you read about atomic radioactivity, mass evacuation of cities, devastation of whole regions. If there were a 'hydrogen superbomb,' for example, 100 times as powerful as the actual modern atomic bombs, it would reach only [sic] about 9 miles from the center of the explosion—not clear across a State. The new line on atomic attack is to figure on staying and living. The whole country cannot run away and hide.

A thirty-two-inch concrete slab, the magazine claimed, would provide "assured protection from an atomic bomb blast as close as 1,000 feet away." [13]

At about the same time, *Life* published a major feature on "How U.S. Cities Can Prepare for Atomic War." Citing China's entrance into the Korean conflict as evidence of "the growing liklihood of World War III", *Life* described a proposal by three MIT professors for ringing the nation's big cities with "life belts"—circumferential express routes intersected by radial highways providing quick escape in an atomic emergency. The land between the "life belt" and the built-up area, said *Life,* could be "reserved as parks and made ready for large tent cities which could quickly be erected to shelter the refugees." [14]

As in 1945, the press was again full of atomic ephemera, this time with a civil-defense slant. Real estate ads promised "good bomb immunity." *Newsweek* reported growing corporate interest in underground facilities. In upstate New York, an enterprising entrepreneur set up vaults for corporate records deep in an abandoned iron mine. In Chicago, Col. Robert R. McCormick lined the halls of the *Tribune* tower with rolls of newsprint as bomb protection and installed a steamboat whistle as an air-raid alarm. *Science News Letter* warned of hucksters who were peddling backyard shelters, burn ointments, dog tags, flash bags, and "decontaminating agents." [15]

The impact of the civil-defense theme at the decade's end was evident even in the voice of the scientists' movement, the *Bulletin of the Atomic Scientists.* In August 1950, editor Eugene Rabinowitch devoted an entire issue to a sympathetic examination of the subject, with contributions from several well-known advocates including Ralph Lapp, Stuart Symington (chairman of the National Security Resources Board), the director of the NSRB's civil-defense office, and Mayor Zeidler of Milwaukee. In a lengthy introduction, Rabinowitch lamented the loss of "five precious years" in civil-defense planning and called for a "coordinated nationwide program" involving mass evacuation plans and the dispersal of federal agencies and military industries. The nation must be prepared to carry on an atomic war, he said, even if the ports of "New York, Boston, San Francisco, and San Diego were to be suddenly rendered unusable by radioactive contamination." With international-control negotiations "bogged down in the muddy battlefields of the Cold War" and world government no more than the dream of a "powerless *avant garde,*" concluded Rabinowitch, a massive civil-defense program aimed at reducing "the damage to people, industry, and transportation [in] an atomic attack" offered the best hope of preventing such an attack. [16]

By 1950, then, the flag of "international control" had been rung down and the "civil defense" banner unfurled. As a fearful public's attention was directed to Communists, traitors, spies, and "subversives" of all kinds, related and complementary themes now emanated from Washington, from radio and television, and from the editorial offices of the great periodicals.

The effort to prevent an atomic-arms race had been well-intentioned, perhaps, but naïve and misguided; the bomb was not so bad after all, and in any event it was here to stay. The duty of the good citizen was to come to terms with it, and the best way to do that was to show enthusiasm for the peaceful atom and support civil defense.

Professionals of many stripes enlisted under the civil-defense banner. Like the Vicar of Bray, the nation's educators quickly adapted to the altered cultural climate. Educational journals that in 1945–1946 had proclaimed the need for international control and improved social-science education to reduce the risks of war were by the end of the decade, as Charles De Benedetti and JoAnne Brown have noted, stressing patriotism, loyalty, the evils of communism, America's Cold War aims—and civil defense. In 1951, forty educational administrators gathered at the FCDA's "Civil Defense Staff College" in Maryland to discuss means of identifying schoolchildren in high-risk target areas. After rejecting tatooing ("because of its associations and impermanence in the case of severe burns") and marked clothing (fabric was flammable, and children often traded clothes), the educators settled on metal identification tags. In a pilot program reported favorably in the National Education Association *Journal,* the New York City board of education appropriated $159,000 to provide free metal tags to all school children in the city. Professional magazines for school administrators carried ads by companies manufacturing such tags. ("See, it's . . . just like yours," says a proud school boy in one ad as he compares dog tags with a soldier.) [17]

Ever since Hiroshima, city planners had been offering advice on the subject of urban decentralization, and with civil defense now the center of attention, they advanced their claims with redoubled emphasis. Under the deepening shadow of atomic war, insisted *The American City,* a professional journal for municipal administrators, in 1950, the nation must "start to do some genuine city planning." While the older cities could not readily be modified, it said, civil-defense principles should be incorporated in the design of suburbs and expanding newer cities. This article particularly recommended "nucleation"—pockets of concentrated settlement separated by green belts. At the 1951 convention of the American Institute of Architects, a group of shopping-center designers held a news conference to publicize their value as evacuation centers. [18]

As in 1945–1946, some saw the atomic threat as a blessing in disguise that would awaken cities to the need for comprehensive planning. "Nucleation," *The American City* pointed out, would not only save lives in an atomic attack but also stop unplanned suburban sprawl. The proposal of MIT planners to ring America's cities with open spaces, radiating highways, and circumferential "life belts," said *Life,* was "long overdue, war or no war." While protecting America from atomic devastation, it would also relieve traffic congestion and slow cities' "extreme and unhealthy internal growth" by accelerating "the current trend of many city dwellers toward the sub-urbs." [19]

The most comprehensive argument along these lines was that of Tracy B. Augur, a past president of the American Institute of Planners, in "Dispersal is Good Business," his contribution to the *Bulletin of the Atomic Scientists'* 1950 civil-defense issue. Even without the bomb, Augur insisted, the American city was doomed: its streets, buildings, and municipal facilities congested and decaying; its business district "unsuited to the needs of modern merchandising"; its "blighted areas . . . burdens on the public treasury." That they were also vulnerable targets was simply the final nail in the coffin. The atomic emergency, Augur concluded, merely underscored the need for decentralization. Indeed, the process was already underway, as evidenced by "the increasing number of modern, well-planned suburban shopping centers that are being built to replace congested downtown facilities." [20] The exigencies of civil defense having pushed the problem of the city to the top of the national agenda, planners and developers with shopping centers and subdivisions already on the drawing board were more than ready to do their patriotic duty.

The government's concern about the spiritual ramifications of atomic war provided a rich opportunity for experts in these matters. In 1951, the FCDA assembled a group of religious leaders to discuss the clergy's role in the post-attack period. The nation must be "spiritually as well as physically" prepared for "sudden and devastating atomic attack," declared director Caldwell in his opening remarks. The conference report, *The Clergy in Civil Defense,* stressed that churches and pastors could provide "stability and purpose for living" after atomic attack, enabling "the home front to carry on until victory is achieved." On a more down-to-earth level, ministers were urged to plan for mass burials, "counseling of the severely disturbed," and "Bible emergency classes" for upset children. Soon after, the FCDA distributed to radio stations recorded statements in support of civil defense by ten well-known Protestant, Catholic, and Jewish religious leaders. [21]

The medical profession, too, was drawn deeply into civil-defense planning and propaganda. Dr. Howard A. Rusk, a professor at New York University Medical School and a national leader of the profession, chaired the FCDA's medical advisory committee. Beginning in 1947, the American Medical Association's Council on National Emergency Medical Service met periodically to discuss a variety of post-atomic-attack problems, including the disposal of radioactive corpses. (A 1947 article in *Mortuary Science* addressed the same issue. Cremation was out, it said, since radioactive particles would be carried away by the smoke. Wearing lead-lined clothing, the article advised, undertakers should place the tightly sealed coffins in excavations floored by a thick layer of concrete and then filled in with more concrete. The graves should be isolated, with no visitors permitted. A corpse might be exhibited prior to burial "provided the visitors file quickly past the bier.") The AMA also endorsed a joint FCDA–American Red Cross program to stockpile three million pints of blood, the estimated quantity needed during the first three weeks if Hiroshima-type bombs were dropped on fifteen American cities. "With the world a-jitter over the possibility of atomic war," said *Science News Letter,* such a blood program was "essential." [22]

At a 1948 AMA conference on "clinical aspects of atomic energy," the deputy surgeon general of the army, George E. Armstrong, urged medical schools to organize minicourses on radiation disease to "alleviate the worry which pervades the profession." Armstrong also asked his audience's "assistance in 'selling' two concepts to the profession . . . which are contrary to all previous teachings." First, after the bomb fell, doctors must not rush in to aid the victims, but wait until an area had been declared free of radiation hazard. Second, they must recognize that about one-third of the survivors would soon die of radiation exposure whatever the medical steps taken to help them. "The profession must steel itself to make those persons comfortable," he said, and "concentrate every effort to save those who have some chance of survival." [23]

The medical profession's close identification with the emerging civil-defense program culminated in 1950 with the inauguration of a program jointly sponsored by the AEC, AMA, and FCDA under which physicians were brought to leading medical schools throughout the country for brief but intensive training courses in the medical aspects of an atomic attack, including "psychological factors such as mass hysteria." These trainees were then urged to cooperate with local civil-defense authorities in training and organizing the doctors, nurses, and dentists of their area. [24]

Tha AMA also supported civil defense through its popular magazine *Today's Health.* In a 1950 article, an AMA official bearing the appropriate name "Dr. Lull" urged Americans to gird themselves for atomic attack "with skill and foresight, and [to] control fear with reason instead of exaggerating it into hysteria." Certainly, he acknowledged, an atomic attack would produce horrendous medical problems and, without adequate preparation, even "complete chaos and panic." But the answer, he went on, "lies in a smooth-operating civil defense set-up within every community." The medical challenge of atomic war was "stupendous," but "free men with strong hearts and wills" could meet it. [25]

Local and state medical societies also responded with alacrity to Washington's civil-defense call. The Massachusetts Medical Society's "Suggestions for First-Aid Treatment for Casualties from Atomic Bombing," published in the *New England Journal of Medicine* in 1950, was subsequently offered in pamphlet form to the general public. In Colorado, Dr. Thad P. Sears, a professor at the University of Colorado Medical School, gave hundreds of lectures in the Rocky Mountain area trying (in the words of a colleague) to "arouse civilians and his professional colleagues from their unrealistic complacency" about civil defense. The Pennsylvania state medical society set up an Atomic Energy Medical Steering Committee to design a program to "protect the public in event of disaster." Six subcommittees dealt with such matters as radiation measurement, epidemiology, public information, and "strengthening public morale."[26]

Hospital administrators were caught up in the civil-defense boom as well. "The mounting tension in our population makes it imperative that [hospitals] have a workable plan" for coping with atomic war, wrote New York City hospital administrator Marcus D. Kogel, M.D., in *Hospital Management* in 1950. Since most urban hospitals would be wiped out in the initial attack, Kogel urged the establishment of suburban back-up facilities and the training of mobile paramedic teams to set up emergency stations on the perimeter of the bombed-out areas. Kogel's office even offered a list of supplies to be stockpiled for such stations, including a lantern, six sheets and pillowcases, a pint of whiskey, and a bottle of sodium bicarbonate.[27]

Pervading these discussions was the belief that civilian morale required that medical professionals appear totally confident of their ability to cope with atomic attack. As a government doctor told the Florida Medical Association: "It would be impossible to exaggerate the benefits guaranteed by public confidence that prompt and skilled medical services" would be available after the attack. "What the public will believe, as soon as their physicians and health departments tell them at every opportunity," he insisted, was that with advance preparation "most of those resisting attack" would survive.[28] Professionally acculturated to appear masterful and ever-optimistic in dealing with patients, physicians did their best to sustain this manner in their approach to the atomic era.

With disruptive or immobilizing emotional reactions increasingly defined as the central hazards confronting the civilian population in an atomic attack, some psychologists and psychiatrists found themselves drawn into civil-defense planning. Among them was psychiatrist Dale C. Cameron, assistant director of the National Institute of Mental Health from 1945 to 1950. In "Psychiatric Implications of Civil Defense" (1949), a paper read before the American Psychiatric Association and later published in the *American Journal of Psychiatry,* Cameron warned of an atomic attack's potentially dangerous psychological effects on survivors, including "purposeless hyperactivity" and "apathy" characterized by "large numbers of individuals wandering about aimlessly, unable to help themselves or others, adding to the confusion and impeding rescue efforts." But these disruptive behaviors could be minimized if people were psychologically prepared. To this end, he said, Americans should be told authoritatively that the atomic bomb was not as terrible as some were claiming, that the radiation danger had been exaggerated, and that civil-defense planning was well in hand. Cameron's most sweeping proposal was for the organization of the population into small therapy groups under psychiatrically trained leaders who would "assist the group in working through its fears and apprehensions." In the post-attack period, group members would then seek each other out and provide mutual support. Cameron warned, however, that this therapeutic program should not be launched too far in advance of the possible outbreak of atomic war, since "people lose a sense of participation when the situation for which they are preparing does not materialize." [29]

One of the most comprehensive expert contributions to the government's efforts to anticipate and minimize the psychological disruptions of atomic attack was that of Irving L. Janis, a young psychologist at Yale. In 1949, under contract with the RAND Corporation, a California research center funded by the Air Force, Janis prepared a study on "Psychological Aspects of Vulnerability to Atomic Bomb Attacks." Citing evidence of depression, emotional upset, and "an inordinately high degree of apathy" among the Hiroshima survivors, Janis concluded that "inappropriate, disorganized, and maladaptive" behavior would pose "extremely critical problems of disaster control" in any future atomic attack. The risk of catastrophic social breakdown could be reduced, he continued, through advance training and conditioning to teach people "appropriate behavior in an atomic disaster" and through "special psychological devices" to overcome the "emotional excitement" of such an event.

Here Janis demonstrated considerable ingenuity. He proposed, for example, that radio personalities be recruited to record messages for broadcast over portable public-address loudspeakers in the immediate post-attack period: "The calm, authoritative voice of a familiar radio announcer might be extremely effective in reducing confusion and emotional excitement, particularly if reassuring announcements are given about the arrival of rescue and relief teams." To condition people to develop positive associations with these voices, Janis recommended, they should be used during the prewar period to give the welcome all-clear announcement at the end of air-raid drills.

The problem of "distraught and inept performance" among civil-defense workers responsible for "handling large numbers of mutilated human beings" could similarly be minimized by advance conditioning, including service in hospital emergency wards and "increasing doses of graphic sound films (preferably in color) showing actual disasters." (Such films would also be useful, he noted, for weeding out volunteers "who become inordinately upset when exposed to disturbing stimuli." [30])

Even with the best advance preparation, Janis acknowledged, special psychiatric treatment would be necessary for many survivors, including the bereaved, the disfigured, those experiencing "jitteriness about the danger of another A-bomb attack," those "severely apprehensive . . . about the realistic possibility that within a week or two they may die from radiation sickness," and—a catch-all category—everyone "in an extremely anxious or depressed state of mind." All such psychic casualties, he said, would "require calm, reassuring, patient handling." Among his suggestions were the advance stockpiling of "pamphlets and posters . . . containing reassuring information about treatment and the chances of recovery"; the segregation of doomed radiation victims "so that they will not have a demoralizing effect . . . on other patients"; and the preparation of "temporary rest camps" whose "therapeutic atmosphere" would give those "too disturbed to return to productive activity . . . an opportunity to recuperate." With "little likelihood that skilled psychiatric aid [would] be available for all of the temporarily maladjusted persons," Janis urged that all civil-defense workers, whatever their function, be instructed in "elementary psychotherapeutic principles."

Irving Janis was no Pollyanna. He painted a grim picture of possible conditions after an atomic attack, including "thousands of half-starved people . . . wandering about for a long period, seeking for their lost families or friends," and pitched battles between inhabitants of unbombed areas and desperate survivors grimly determined "to obtain shelter and supplies by force if necessary." But he insisted that such horrors could be avoided by careful advance planning: "If the essential needs of the survivors are well provided for, and if there is sound community leadership, there is every reason to expect that within a short period the vast majority will . . . make a fairly adequate adjustment to the deprivational situation." Psychologists could assist this planning, Janis suggested, with predictive studies designed to identify "which types of persons can be relied on and which types are most likely to be uncooperative and demoralized" after an atomic attack.

Turning to the morale problems created by the mere anticipation of atomic war, Janis again argued that careful attention to human psychology could moderate at least some of "the more extreme forms of personal disorganization and inappropriate action." He recommended, for example, that military terminology be used in all post-attack civil-defense directives, such as the ordering of survivors "to a 'battle station' in specified evacuation localities where it is one's 'duty' to be present."

On the question of atomic-bomb shelters, Janis was ambivalent. Until the development of "an effective, inexpensive radioactive-absorbent material," he suggested, they were likely to be of minimal lifesaving value. Further, a program of home-shelter construction could "arouse acute social resentments" among the poor unable to afford their own shelter. At the same time, a shelter program could have great psychological value in combating the public's "strong feelings of insecurity about impending atomic bomb attacks." The "constructive activity" of building a shelter would counteract anxiety and "contribute to the feeling that 'I am really able to do something about it.'" Further, making shelter construction a private responsibility would reduce citizens' inclination to rely on the government for protection and deflect resentment they might otherwise feel over Washington's "apparent 'neglect'" of civil defense. Finally, the mere existence of millions of family shelters could be "an important source of reassurance" as homeowners' pride in owning shelters they themselves had made would invest the shelters "with considerable symbolic value as an anxiety-reducing feature of the environment."[31]

Thus did professionals in various fields contribute their expertise to the civil-defense campaign. The cultural shift this represents is striking indeed. In the volatile months just after Hiroshima, a wide array of professional groups had stepped forward—often naïvely and perhaps self-interestedly—to help the world find its way back from the precipice. Education, psychiatry, psychology, ethics, the humanities, sociology—surely somewhere in all these specialities was the knowledge that could drive back the hovering nightmare of atomic war. As the decade ended, the level of professional involvement with the atomic issue remained high, but the focus was now very different. Experts—from city planners and media specialists to psychologists, psychiatrists, and physicians—now applied themselves to convincing the American people that the atomic threat was not as bad as it had been painted. Fear had been exaggerated: "hysteria" was uncalled for. The "sunny side of the atom" was real and exciting; the radiation scare was overblown; and even if worse came to worst, civil defense offered hope. These reassuring and interconnected messages, emanating from so many authoritative sources as the decade ended, contributed powerfully to the emergence of a decisive and unsettling new stage in America's cultural and political engagement with atomic weapons.

27

1949–1950: Embracing the Bomb

**We are five years away from Hiroshima. We are five years
nearer—what?**

— *Christian Century*, August 2, 1950

Of the many American magazines galvanized into activism by the atomic
bomb, one of the most outspoken had been *Business Week*. Repeatedly in
1945–1946 it warned of the bomb's menace, publicized the scientists'
movement, and campaigned for international control. Within a few short
years, however, all this had changed. In April 1949, *Business Week* reported
that the "technical problems" of atomic-bomb production had been solved,
leaving only "such normal managerial problems as how to reduce costs [and]
. . . speed lagging operations." Bomb output was "now rolling very
smoothly," it said, and "by 1950 or 1951 . . . could be practically doubled."[1]

And so we have come full circle. For a fleeting moment after Hiroshima, American culture had been profoundly affected by atomic fear, by a
dizzying plethora of atomic panaceas and proposals, and by endless speculation on the social and ethical implications of the new reality. By the end of
the 1940s, the cultural discourse had largely stopped. Americans now
seemed not only ready to accept the bomb, but to support any measures
necessary to maintain atomic supremacy.

From the earliest post-Hiroshima days, demands for stockpiling atomic
bombs and even using them against the new postwar enemy, Russia,
emerged as a minority (but far from negligible) position in public-opinion
polls and letters to the editor. "I read Hersey's report," a subscriber wrote
the *New Yorker* in 1946. "It was marvelous. Now let us drop a handful on
Moscow." As we have seen, the nation's atomic-weapons program had continued after the war, and while official secrecy blurred details, this fact was
public knowledge. The Bikini tests made clear, commented I. F. Stone in
1946, that "the atom bomb is part of our active war equipment and an
integral part of our future military strategy."[2]

At first, this program either received little public attention or, if noted at all, was cited to underscore the urgency of international control. By 1948, however, it was being much more openly and even boastfully reported. *Newsweek* described the AEC's success in transforming "a frenzied wartime patchwork . . . into an orderly permanent enterprise" that had put bomb production on "a firm and secure basis." Under the headline "HOW MANY ATOM BOMBS? ENOUGH ON HAND FOR U.S. TO FIGHT MAJOR WAR," *U.S. News and World Report* extrapolated from known figures on plutonium production to estimate the nation's atomic-bomb arsenal at 200 to 250, with a possible increase to 1,000 by 1950. (These numbers were apparently something of an overestimate at the time, if recently released figures are accurate, but the 1,000 total was, of course, soon reached and far surpassed). "What was for the most part a bluff in 1945," wrote Harry Davis in his 1948 popularization *Energy Unlimited,* "has now been replaced by a hand well backed with atomic aces."[3]

At about the same time, in public speeches and articles in *Life* and other magazines, top military leaders like Gen. George C. Kenney of the Strategic Air Command began to discuss openly the Pentagon's strategic plans for a massive atomic attack on Soviet cities and industrial centers in the event of war. Writing in September 1948, Eugene Rabinowitch expressed dismay over this "callous public discussion of plans for atomic warfare." Though part of the war of nerves with the Soviets, he said, it could also have important domestic consequences: "We do not suggest that" such speeches and articles

> arise from a deliberate desire of the military to "condition" American public opinion to the indiscriminate killing and maiming of millions of civilians; but is not their actual effect to soothe in advance all moral revulsion, and to make American people accept the possibility of atomic slaughter as something, perhaps deplorable, but natural in this imperfect world?

In short, Rabinowitch wondered, were such previews of atomic holocaust a way of "asking the American people to acquiesce in advance to the final conversion of war into genocide?" If so, he warned, "the American conscience must refuse to be pacified."[4]

But pacified it was. These same years saw an increase in Americans' expectations of war. The percentage anticipating another war "within the next twenty years or so" grew from 59 percent in October 1945 to 77 percent by late 1947. In 1948, the Gallup poll found 57 percent of Americans expecting war within ten years, and 43 percent within three or four years. "The world has virtually accepted the inevitability of another war," concluded Norman Cousins gloomily that December. But rather than generating support for a redoubled diplomatic effort to reduce the atomic threat, these rising war fears had the reverse effect, leading to an increased reliance on the bomb as the best source of security in a threatening world. The postwar belief that fear would promote the cause of peace, wrote University of Chicago law professor Malcolm Sharp in 1948, had given way to the feeling that "if atomic energy is to be used to destroy people and their works, it had better be the Russians and their works." In a summer 1949 Gallup poll, an overwhelming 70 percent of Americans opposed any U.S. pledge not to be the first to use atomic weapons in a future war.[5] Such, then, was the national mood on the eve of the most unsettling news since August 1945.

On September 24, 1949, a terse announcement from Washington struck a largely unprepared nation: the Soviet Union had tested an atomic bomb! Leading atomic scientists had predicted a Russian bomb within three to five years of Hiroshima, but influential figures like Vannevar Bush and General Groves had dismissed the possibility. "Few atomic people are inclined to think the Russians have made much progress," *Business Week* had said in April 1949. Editorialists and opinion-molders treated the Soviet test as a momentous event. "The prospect of a two-sided atomic war," said Raymond Moley in *Newsweek,* meant a "towering change in the world outlook." "An historic bridge has been crossed," observed a chastened *Business Week.* "From here on, all the rivers run the other way." A Herblock cartoon pictured Uncle Sam as Robinson Crusoe discovering a footprint in the sand.[6]

Given the surprise and the portentous editorializing, public reaction was surprisingly muted. Raymond Moley remarked on "the apparent lack of serious concern"; a Washington journalist found nothing comparable to the "agitation and ferment" the Hiroshima news had caused. "It didn't take long for the shock to wear off," observed *Newsweek* laconically.[7]

In part, this muted response reflected government media manipulation. ("I warn you, don't overplay this," Defense Secretary Louis Johnson had told reporters.) It also reflected the fact that for four years Americans had been imagining vivid scenarios of atomic attack—scenarios that simply assumed that the U.S. atomic monopoly would be brief. Above all, this response reflected the changed political climate of the late 1940s and the shift from the goal of control to the goal of superiority. To be sure, some voices were raised in a familiar refrain, insisting that international control and Big Power agreements on atomic energy were now more urgent than ever. Harold C. Urey called for a "bold political program" to combat the worsening atomic threat. *Christian Century* urged "a new beginning" in disarmament efforts.[8]

The dominant reaction, however, was a grim determination to increase America's lead in nuclear weaponry. The Russian bomb accelerated the shift toward viewing the atomic bomb not as a terrible scourge to be eliminated as quickly as possible, but a winning weapon to be stockpiled with utmost urgency. The United States must "establish unquestioned and unmistakable leadership" in atomic weapons, David Lilienthal declared late in 1949, to "buy time for reason to prevail." The tabloid *New York Daily News* made the point succinctly in a punning headline: "U.S. HAS SUPREMACY, WILL HOLD IT: A-MEN." Rejecting "wishful thoughts . . . about atomic disarmament and control," *Newsweek* columnist Ernest K. Lindley said the Russian bomb meant U.S. nuclear weapons production must remain "as high as is necessary to maintain a great superiority in quantity for a long time to come." If Americans wanted security, said *Time,* they "would have to buy the full, costly package." The Hearst press urged the stockpiling of four atomic bombs for every Soviet one. With the bomb now in the hands of "totalitarians . . . remorselessly driven toward war," said *Life,* America must maintain a "clear, unchallenged, demonstrable" nuclear supremacy and secure its defenses. Russian atomic bombs, warned *Life,* could be delivered by many means, including even commercial freighters that could unload concealed bomb components for ground transport to secret interior sites for assembly. (The latter threat was illustrated with photographs of a Russian freighter unloading and a truck rolling along a highway.)[9]

Senator Brien McMahon, stalwart supporter of the postwar scientists' movement, was driven almost to distraction by the Russian bomb. Only a preemptive atomic attack on Russia, he insisted to David Lilienthal, could prevent an ultimate, world-destroying holocaust. Late in 1949, McMahon's Joint Committee on Atomic Energy lifted all limits on AEC spending and told it to exercise "boldness, initiative, and effort" to "maintain our preeminence in this field." As one journalist who attended the committee's hearings put it, the message boiled down to: "We don't care how or where you spend it; just keep us out in front."[10]

Behind these generalizations lay a very specific objective. Almost from the moment of Hiroshima, there had been hints of a vastly more terrible "superbomb." Edward Condon warned early in 1946 of bombs a thousand times more powerful "in the near future"; diplomat John J. McCloy made the same prediction in a December 1946 speech, specifically mentioning a hydrogen bomb. After September 24, 1949, theoretical speculation became a matter of urgent policy discussion, and on January 31, 1950, President Truman made it official: the AEC would proceed with work "on all forms of atomic weapons, including the so-called hydrogen or superbomb."[11]

The inner history of the hydrogen-bomb decision has been told in the memoirs of participants and in such books as Herbert York's *The Advisors: Oppenheimer, Teller, and the Superbomb* (1976). The conflict between scientists like Edward Teller, Ernest Lawrence, and Luis Alvarez, who favored the hydrogen bomb (who indeed were "drooling" at the prospect, according to Lilienthal), and others who opposed it—including Lilienthal and the eight scientists on the AEC's general advisory committee chaired by Oppenheimer

—is by now familiar. As for the larger cultural context of the decision, discussion has focused mainly on the fact that it was made with no involvement by the American people. "This was a secret debate with only a few participants," McGeorge Bundy has written; "no sermons pro or con, no dire public warnings from defenders of security or Cassandras of nuclear catastrophe—no public discussion at all." If only the public had been consulted, some have suggested, the outcome might have been different. This was what could happen "when decisions of far-reaching national significance are made without public scrutiny of pertinent information," wrote physicist Robert F. Bacher, a former AEC commissioner and hydrogen-bomb critic. "The superbomb issue needed to be put before the American people," agreed Eugene Rabinowitch; "Americans must be given the opportunity to decide whether they want to embark on this course." [12]

Would public participation have led to a different decision? Probably not. In a Gallup poll of early February, 69 percent favored building the hydrogen bomb, 9 percent expressed "reluctant approval," while only 14 percent disapproved. Indeed, Truman's announcement aroused little response of any sort. "Many Americans were by no means ready to think about it," observed *Life,* summing up reports from around the nation; "People wanted to talk about anything else but." [13]

In reflecting on this acquiescent public response, critics of the hydrogen-bomb decision invariably linked it to the larger political climate of 1949–1950. Americans had lost all hope "for international agreements which will have any meaning," said Robert Bacher. "Pumped full of hysteria from Red scares and aggravated by political mudslinging, the average citizen is easily convinced that he can find some security and relief from all of this in the hydrogen bomb." In his 1982 analysis of the hydrogen-bomb decision, McGeorge Bundy, too, stressed the broader political context:

> By the end of 1949 the cold war was raging, the Soviet menace was seen everywhere; . . . the Berlin blockade was a recent and instructive memory; the captive nations were not a slogan but a vivid reality, and Soviet hostility and duplicity were taken for granted. . . . "Who lost China?" was the question of the hour. Alger Hiss was convicted in early January, and [the British atomic spy] Klaus Fuchs confessed just four days before Truman's final decision. [14]

Indeed, influential periodicals trumpeted the Russian menace and soft-pedaled the threat of the hydrogen bomb itself. The bomb made little sense in the "pure economics of destruction," said *Business Week,* but its "psychological and political effects . . . would be tremendous." In a special issue on the communist menace two weeks after the hydrogen-bomb decision, *Life* put a mushroom cloud on its cover; warned that the Soviets were "preparing for war" and would use "any atomic agreement" as a pretext to promote "the victory of Communism throughout the world"; and printed alarming charts showing a supposed "Red Military Advantage." [15]

Fear of the bomb remained, but in the context of the Cold War, the Russian bomb, and repeated assertions of Soviet aggressiveness and perfidy, bigger American bombs seemed to many the only hope. The process that had begun gradually around 1947, in which the image of the bomb as a menace to be eliminated was effaced by its image as a vital asset in the intensifying struggle with the Soviet Union, vastly accelerated after September 1949. Political efforts to diminish the atomic threat were now seen as a snare and a delusion; the best hope lay in keeping ahead. In this competition, *Business Week* wrote reassuringly in July 1950, the Russians were "amateurs competing with professionals." They had built their bomb on a crash basis, and "you don't get a broad, sophisticated technique that way." *Look* reported in November 1950 that the nation's "long-hairs" (that is, scientists) were designing intercontinental ballistic missiles that would open "awesome vistas of mass death and destruction." But rather than using this frightening prospect as an argument for intensified international negotiations, as it surely would have in 1945–1947, *Look* concluded: "What we must do next is apply our vast production facilities to the ideas of our 'long-hairs.' Then we will be ready for the war of tomorrow." In a January 1951 report on the nation's atomic arsenal, *U.S. News* noted that while "city busting" bombs remained the "mainstay," an array of smaller tactical bombs and even atomic artillery had been added as well. America's "headstart in atomic development is being maintained and even extended. If Russia wants an atomic war, she'll get it in more ways than she expects." [16]

Fear of the Russians had driven fear of the bomb into the deeper recesses of consciousness. That the public did not participate in the hydrogen-bomb decision "hardly mattered," said *Business Week*, since Truman's directive so clearly reflected the general will. "In the frightened months right after the Soviet atomic explosion," it said, "the mere public intimation that a [hydrogen bomb] might be possible guaranteed the attempt." In a 1950 poll of 2,700 Cornell University students, 40 percent said "an all-out war to stop communism" would be either "Very Worthwile" (26 percent) or "Fairly Worthwhile" (14 percent). In a July 1950 Gallup poll, 77 percent of Americans said the United States should use the atomic bomb in any future world war. The following January, 66 percent said the U.S. should drop the bomb first in any full-scale war with Russia. [17]

In November 1950, President Truman asked Congress for a billion dollars for nuclear-weapons production. The Du Pont Corporation undertook to build a giant hydrogen-bomb facility for the same "dollar-a-year" fee it had received during the Manhattan Project. Research on the "Super" under Edward Teller again turned Los Alamos into a bustling center where the mood, according to *Business Week,* was "adventurous" and "exuberant." The AEC's contract with General Electric to build a prototype atomic-power plant was terminated to free more scientists and technicians for bomb production. These developments attracted little public attention. The terrible simplifications of the Cold War had seized the American mind, and all issues, even the atomic threat, realigned themselves along the new ideological lines of force. As MIT mathematician Norbert Wiener wrote in July 1950, the probability of atomic annihilation would remain high "so long as we are dominated by a rigid propaganda which makes the destruction of Russia appear more important than our own survival." [18]

The extent to which Cold War obsessions overrode earlier atomic fears is evident in the discussions surrounding the possible use of atomic bombs in the Korean War. Some periodicals advised against it. "The best hope now of preventing the 'police action' from ballooning into a superwar," said the *Saturday Evening Post,* "may lie in a conservative attitude toward the A-bomb." Others, however, discussed the matter quite coolly, as a viable option to be carefully weighed. *Science News Letter* concluded that North Korea's few urban-industrial centers probably did not "warrant" atomic bombing. After an assessment of the tactical pros and cons that ignored any larger considerations, *U.S. News and World Report* concluded that American use of atomic weapons in Korea would probably be "sparing." [19]

"The first flash of the Communist guns," in Korea, wrote William L. Laurence, had unmasked "the Kremlin's ultimate intentions to enslave mankind" and "illuminated for us more clearly than ever before the path we must follow in our policy on atomic weapons": full speed ahead, especially on the hydrogen bomb. On a different cultural front, composer Fred Kirby's 1950 country song "When the Hell Bomb Falls" mingled images of nuclear destruction with the wish that God would "lend a helping hand" in Korea. In Roy Acuff's "Advice to Joe" (1951), the wish became explicit with the warning to the Russians that when Moscow has been obliterated, they will regret their aggressive ambitions. "When atomic bombs start falling," the song asks Stalin, "do you have a place to hide?" [20]

And what of the man in the street? In August 1950, the Gallup poll found 28 percent of Americans in favor of using the atomic bomb in Korea. When Chinese troops entered the war in November, *U.S. News* noted a "wave of demand" for atomic bombing them. By November 1951, with the war in a costly, frustrating stalemate, 51 percent supported dropping the bomb on "military targets." [21]

In this instance, mass culture and popular attitudes mirrored thinking at the highest level of government. In 1952, in two memos evidently drafted for his eyes only, President Truman contemplated a nuclear ultimatum to the Soviets and the Chinese as a way of ending the war. In 1953, President

Eisenhower and the National Security Council seriously considered the direct use of atomic weapons against the Chinese and North Koreans.[22]

The shift in attitudes toward the atomic bomb that culminated in 1950 runs like a fault line through the culture, nearly as visible as the one caused by the Hiroshima bombing itself. A Manhattan Project veteran who had continued to be active in the scientists' movement observed an immediate and dramatic change in his audiences after news of the Soviet bomb. Groups that had formerly generated "spirited questions and comments regarding atomic warfare" now seemed apathetic and silent. Sales of David Bradley's *No Place to Hide* dropped precipitously after September 1949, and Bradley himself, having lectured to large audiences for a year, suddenly found there were no more invitations.[23]

In the schools, emphasis on the atomic threat gave way to Cold War ideology, the "peaceful atom," and civil defense. Among political columnists, declining attention to the menace of the bomb was matched by a sharp increase in discussion of the relative military strength of the U.S. and the Soviet Union. In political cartoons, the powerful images of atomic danger that had proliferated after Hiroshima gave way to variations on the theme of Soviet intransigence and the communist menace. The *Washington Post*'s Herblock, who in 1946–1947 had portrayed the atomic bomb as a sinister thug looking on in amused boredom as statesmen temporized, largely dropped this theme by the end of the decade because, as he explained in 1952, he didn't want his atomic-bomb warnings to get "mixed up with a carefully twisted viewpoint" of communist propaganda. In country music, Charles Wolfe writes, atomic holocaust was now seen as "an inevitable, almost natural occurrence." In fiction, George Stewart's *Earth Abides* of 1949 softened the bleak pessimism of early cataclysmic novels like Ward Moore's *Greener Than You Think* and portrayed the destruction of civilization as a rather desirable development that would restore mankind to a simpler, more harmonious existence.

Atomic fear still found expression, but now more typically in allusive and symbolic ways. At the end of the 1949 Warner Brothers movie *White Heat*, for example, the psychopathic, mother-fixated gangster Cody Jarrett (James Cagney) is trapped in the technological maze of a vast chemical plant, his plan for a master robbery foiled by the police. He climbs to the top of a huge metal cylinder, insanely shouts "Top of the world, Ma!" and fires a random shot into the cylinder, which explodes in a series of mushroom-shaped blasts. The head G-man, watching awestruck as Cody dies amidst the *Götterdämmerung* inferno he himself has created, pronounces an epitaph that echoed the endless somber warnings of 1945–1947: "He finally made it to the top of the world, and it blew up in his face."[24]

Picking up on such cultural signals, psychiatrist Franz Alexander in

"The Bomb and the Human Psyche" (1949) gave a quite literal interpretation to the familiar warning of these years that the human race could now "commit suicide." Having contrived the means of his destruction, Alexander speculated, man might find irresistible the temptation to escape forever the stresses of the atomic age and subconsciously conclude that "a painless end" was preferable to "endless pain." [25]

The events of 1949–1950 also dealt a final blow to the already badly weakened scientists' movement. The best-known scientific spokesman for the new Cold War attitude was, of course, Edward Teller. Summoning his colleagues "Back to the Laboratories" in March 1950, Teller wrote: "It is *not* the scientist's job to determine whether a hydrogen bomb should be constructed, whether it should be used, or how it should be used. This responsibility rests with the American people and with their chosen representatives." The scientist's task was not to meddle in politics, insisted this most political of all scientists, but to understand nature's laws and "find the ways in which these laws can serve the human will." [26] And in 1950, "the human will," as expressed in Harry Truman's decision and the Gallup poll, wanted the hydrogen bomb.

Teller was far from alone. The sharp drop-off in FAS membership in 1948–1950 suggests the degree to which activism was undercut by Cold War compulsions. Said Enrico Fermi somewhat cryptically after the 1949 Soviet atomic-bomb test: "If the United States maintains atomic supremacy over Russia, there will be no war for 20 years. . . . As for me, I expect to sleep as well as my insomnia permits. I am a fatalist by nature anyway." As we have seen, even Eugene Rabinowitch, a staunchly anticommunist Russian émigré, was influenced by the worsening international climate as the decade ended. In 1949 when Rabinowitch's *Bulletin of the Atomic Scientists* published an essay discussing the strategic advantages of America's atomic superiority over the Soviets, one dismayed subscriber wrote in to protest. Stop publishing such material, he urged, and "go back to the practice of printing in large black type face 'There is no defense against the atomic bomb.'" In the *Bulletin's* "civil defense" issue in 1950, Rabinowitch not only called for more attention to civil defense, but for a vastly expanded American military effort generally, including a larger army, military aid to Western Europe and "friendly regimes elsewhere," and "increased production and improvement of our atomic weapons and of the means of their delivery." Any weakening of America's atomic arsenal, he said, would threaten "defeat of the democratic West in its power conflict with the communist totalitarianism." [27] (Rabinowitch never ceased, however, to open the *Bulletin of Atomic Scientists* to discussions of the atomic danger or proposals for new political initiatives.)

Some scientists resisted the shift from activism to Cold War acquiescence. Leo Szilard continued to speak out, warning in 1950 that the spreading radioactivity of a thermonuclear war could destroy all human life on earth. A somewhat lonely Hans Bethe sought to reawaken the activist spirit of 1945–1946: the introduction of the atomic bomb had given rise to a "general feeling" that this vast increase in destructive power "required and made possible a new approach" to international relations, he said, and "the step from atomic to hydrogen bombs is just as great again, so we have again an equally strong reason to seek a new approach. We have to think how we can save humanity from this last disaster." That the effort to control the atomic bomb had so far failed, Bethe insisted, was "no reason to introduce a bomb which is a thousand times worse." [28]

As the scientists' movement faded, the new field of nuclear strategy emerged. In the early postwar period, as Gregg Herken has shown, "strategic thinking" in the Pentagon consisted mainly of doomsday scenarios for hitting Russian cities with as many atomic bombs as were available at the moment. As the decade ended, though, nuclear strategy increasingly became the domain of civilian specialists, many of them drawn from the social sciences. The bright hopes of social-science publicists in 1945–1947 that with sufficient funding these disciplines could help man achieve a more harmonious and peaceful world were quickly transformed into something quite different. Bernard Brodie of Yale's Institute of International Studies signaled the shift in an October 1948 article in *Foreign Affairs.* Nuclear strategy, he said, was "much too important to be left to the generals—or to the politicians either for that matter." In dealing with the atomic bomb, he went on, it was time to move beyond "high moral protestation" and the "frenetic pursuit" of international control. Policymakers and the public alike must "develop the habit of living with the atomic bomb" and view it not as "a visitation of a wrathful deity" but "as an instrument of war—and hence of international politics." Even after the Soviets developed the bomb, he said, American atomic superiority would continue for many years, and policymakers must take that fact into account in all their calculations. In 1951, Brodie joined the staff of the RAND Corporation, where he and other political scientists, mathematicians, and logicians systematically pursued strategic analysis of an increasingly sophisticated and arcane variety. [29]

The waning of activism and cultural attention directed to the atomic threat also resulted in a distinct muting of, and subtle shifts of emphasis in, discussions of the bomb's moral implications. Again, the change was not absolute, but one of degree. One still finds explorations of these issues in 1949–1950. In *Some Quaker Proposals for Peace* (1949), the American Friends Service Committee restated the moral case against nuclear weapons and offered concrete ideas for slowing the arms race. An editor of the Jesuit journal *America* in September 1949 described the U.S. strategy of massive atomic attacks on Soviet cities as "utterly reprehensible" and "against all fundamental moralities." [30]

The moral case against America's atomic strategy gained support from an unlikely quarter in October 1949 when Rear Adm. Ralph A. Ofstie, the navy's liaison officer with the AEC, in testimony before the House Armed Services Committee, denounced as "morally wrong" air force plans for the atomic destruction of Russia's civilian population in the event of war. Such a "ruthless and barbaric policy," said Ofstie, would lead directly to "the breakdown of those standards of morality which have been a guiding force in this democracy since its inception." *Christian Century* welcomed "The Moral Revolt of the Admirals." The issues raised in Ofstie's testimony, it declared, were ones "the Christian Churches of the United States, and American citizens who are striving to be Christians, must face with a profound seriousness." [31]

Truman's hydrogen-bomb announcement aroused isolated moral protest. "We prepare to make this wanton decision with no readiness to accept moral responsibility for our act," declared *Christian Century*. "Worse than that, we are not willing to admit that we *have* any moral responsibility. We are about to act as gods in a world from which we insist that moral responsibility has departed. And so we become devil-gods." The response of the Federal Council of Churches' Executive Committee was another of the carefully balanced tripartite pronouncements with which Protestants were becoming familiar:

> Some of us feel deeply that the hydrogen bomb does not present a new and different moral issue, but sheds vivid light on the wickedness of war itself. Some of us oppose the construction of hydrogen bombs, which could be used only for the mass destruction of populations. Some of us, on the other hand, believing that our people and the other free societies should not be left without the means of defense through the threat of retaliation, support the attempt to construct the new weapon. All of us unite in the prayer that it may never be used. [32]

In a February 1950 manifesto, twelve prominent physicists, all Manhattan Project veterans, declared: "No nation has the right to use such a bomb, no matter how righteous its cause. This bomb is no longer a weapon of war, but a means of extermination of whole populations. Its use would be a betrayal of all standards of morality." The organizer of this protest, Hans Bethe, poured forth his forebodings in an anguished essay. "Can we, who have always insisted on morality and human decency between nations as well as inside our own country, introduce this weapon of total annihilation into the world?" A war fought with such weapons, Bethe went on, would be both a physical and a moral catastrophe of unfathomable proportions. Even if the United States "won" such a conflict, history would remember "*not* the ideals we were fighting for, but the method we used to accomplish them." [33]

The leadership of American Judaism wrestled with the issue of the bomb in the aftermath of the Russian test and President Truman's H-Bomb decision. In 1950, the Central Conference of American Rabbis adopted a bleak and somewhat contradictory resolution drafted by a committee on atomic energy chaired by Rabbi Julius Mark of New York's Temple Emanu-El, the world's largest Reform congregation. Only those who placed "their confidence in superior and more diabolic armaments," it said, could find reason for hope in Truman's decision. But, like earlier pronouncements, this resolution did not address the ethics of thermonuclear weapons or of mass and indiscriminate destruction through such weapons. The central moral issue, it said (echoing a point often made by military leaders in these years) was not any particular category of weapons, but war itself:

> Why is an instrument that destroys a thousand or ten thousand human beings more immoral than a gun which snuffs out the life of a single individual? The immorality lies not in the weapon, but in the killing. The attempt to outlaw the means of war is useless so long as war itself remains a legal means to settle international disputes.

Nevertheless (and despite a preamble noting that hopes for achieving peace through the United Nations "appear to have vanished"), this resolution ended with yet another call for United Nations control of atomic energy.[34]

But, though such moral discourse continued, it was much muted. "The churches have been nibbliing at the problem of the morality of atomic warfare at intervals ever since Hiroshima, and so far they have gotten exactly nowhere," said *Christian Century* in October 1949. "Perplexed by doubt and divided in mind, . . . they have reached a tacit understanding among themselves to blanket in silence this most crucial of all the political issues affecting the fate of mankind."[35]

Those who did raise the ethical issues were often, for one reason or another, treated dismissively. The "Moral Revolt of the Admirals" was widely ridiculed as merely reflecting navy resentment at the air force's dominant role in atomic strategy. To the navy, some cynics observed, an immoral weapon was one they couldn't use. The 1949 peace proposals of the American Friends Service Committee were generally ignored because of their pacifist origins. As *Christian Century* summed up a prevailing response: "The Quakers? Oh yes; fine people, but so naïve. Of course, if the men around Stalin were all Quakers. . . ."[36]

One finds, too, in the ethical writings of this early Cold War period, an increasing inclination to defend the moral legitimacy, under certain circumstances, of using atomic bombs. An American first strike would be morally justified if the government had "sound reason to believe" an enemy attack was imminent, argued Jesuit theologian Edmund A. Walsh of

Georgetown University in 1950. "Neither reason nor theology nor morals requires men or nations to commit suicide by requiring that we must await the first blow." That same year, the dean of theology at Catholic University, Francis J. Connell, similarly defended the use of the atomic bomb under certain conditions. Ethically, he asserted, the atomic bomb was "not essentially different from a TNT bomb, a cannon, a hand grenade, or a rifle."[37]

Father Connell's argument was vigorously challenged by Gordon C. Zahn, a Catholic pacifist and World War II conscientious objector who insisted that the bomb was, indeed, "essentially different," and that unless the Church adopted the total-war philosophy "which treats of whole cities and their inhabitants as an impersonal mass, this essential distinction between the A-Bomb and the rifle must be recognized and our moral judgments revised accordingly." In a testy and defensive reply, Father Connell again insisted that morally the rifle and the atomic bomb were "essentially" the same: both could kill. Rejecting Zahn's characterization of the atomic bomb as an "indiscriminate" weapon, Connell asserted that like the rifle it could be directed at legitimate targets whose "destruction would involve the death of no civilians, such as a fleet at sea." Catholic theology offered no basis, Connell concluded, for a categorical condemnation of the bomb.[38]

The somewhat greater tolerance for atomic war in the ethical discourse at the end of the decade is illustrated in *The Christian Conscience and Weapons of Mass Destruction,* the 1950 report of a Federal Council of Churches commission set up to resolve the disarray so blatantly evident in its hydrogen-bomb statements. In both its makeup and the substance of its report, this commission provides a benchmark for the cultural and political changes between 1946 and 1950. The membership, while overlapping with that of the earlier Calhoun Commission was subtly shifted to reflect a position more sympathetic to the stockpiling and possible use of atomic weapons. Among those dropped were Douglas Steere, a Quaker, and Ernest Fremont Tittle, the Illinois Methodist leader who had taken an uncompromising stand against the bomb in 1946. Replacing them were several prominent laymen identified with the government's nuclear program, including physicist Arthur Compton and William W. Waymack of the U.S. Atomic Energy Commission, and the theologian Reinhold Niebuhr, who was at this time emerging as a militant Cold Warrior.[39] The chairman was Bishop Angus Dun of the Washington Diocese of the Protestant Episcopal Church.

The Christian Conscience and Weapons of Mass Destruction contained many strong and unambiguous passages deploring war, the moral effects of advancing military technology, and wanton civilian destruction unjustified by legitimate military objectives; and it warned against any first use of atomic weapons by the United States since this would almost surely be met by retaliation in kind. In contrast to the Calhoun Commission, however, the Dun Commission offered no explicit expression of guilt for the atomic bombing of Hiroshima and Nagasaki, and issued no call for repentance. On the general question of future use, it temporized. While atomic weapons raised ethical issues of "terrible dimensions," it said, these could not be isolated "as belonging to an absolutely different moral category." The essential moral question, it said (echoing Father Connell), was not the weapon, but the motive, and one could not "draw this moral line in advance, apart from all the actual circumstances": "What can and cannot be done under God can be known only in relation to the whole concrete situation by those responsibly involved in it. We can find no moral hiding place in legalistic definitions." In its key passages, the commission implicitly endorsed current American strategic policy:

> For the United States to abandon its atomic weapons, or to give the impression that they would not be used, would leave the non-Communist world with totally inadequate defense. For Christians to advocate such a policy would be for them to share responsibility for the worldwide tyranny that might result. We believe that American military strength, which must include atomic weapons as long as any other nation may possess them, is an essential factor in the possibility of preventing both world war and tyranny. If atomic weapons or other weapons of parallel destructiveness are used against us or our friends in Europe or Asia, we believe that it could be justifiable for our government to use them in retaliation with all possible restraint.[40]

Two of the commission's nineteen members dissented: Robert L. Calhoun of Yale and the sole woman, Georgia Harkness, professor of theology at Garrett Biblical Institute, a Methodist seminary in Chicago. The majority's insistence that "if 'we' are attacked 'we' must do whatever is needed to win," while defensible on "political and cultural grounds," said Calhoun, could "scarcely be regarded as distinctively Christian." In Harkness's view, the majority report neither did justice to the pacifist position nor provided any "distinctive moral guidance from the Christian gospel." Further, she suggested, when one was speaking of thermonuclear war, "retaliation with all possible restraint" was a contradiction in terms.[41] In the 1946 Calhoun Commission report, the "pro-bomb" position had been relegated to an uneasy footnote. In the FCC's 1950 report it was far more explicitly and vigorously articulated, with the two lonely dissenters consigned to a footnote.

In May 1950, a small group of pacifists gathered in Detroit to form a Church Peace Mission to promote a dialogue between pacifists and nonpacifists. The delegates included representatives of the so-called "historic peace churches" (Quaker, Mennonite, Brethren); A. J. Muste's Fellowship of Reconciliation; and individual pacifists from the mainstream Protestant denominations. Their report, *The Christian Conscience and War,* drafted in large part by Muste and Edward L. Long, Jr., challenged not only the "cultural jingoism and conventional patriotism" with which secular opinion-molders were approaching atomic-weapons questions, but also the muffled and tentative response of the churches, as symbolized by the Dun Commission report. The Dun report was explicitly criticized for its reliance on arguments of military expediency and American national interest in justifying the possible future use of atomic weapons, and for its failure to recognize that the United States' decision to drop the atomic bomb in 1945 was a critical determinant of postwar world politics; one that helped explain, for example, the unwillingness of a large part of the world "to attach much credence to American protestations that we shall never be first to use atomic weapons again."

The prospect of atomic war, this report went on, gave a "new and terrible urgency" to a rethinking of war as part of a larger social pathology. "War is not a neutral or aseptic tool," it insisted, "but a symptom of sickness, . . . the outer expression of inner conflict in society." Social disintegration and injustice led to war, which in turn produced further disintegration and injustice, and so on in an endless and now potentially catastrophic spiral. In an age of thermonuclear weapons, war could no longer be viewed as a value-free instrument for achieving other "objectives" or protecting other "interests." The nuclear arms race, supposedly undertaken to protect American cultural and political values, was in fact perverting those values: "War *is* the culture of our age and the culture *is* war." Only an "amiable optimism," it said, could see in atomic war "not the maniac who will destroy democracy but the slave who will obediently serve it."

The doctrines of love and redemption, *The Christian Conscience and War* went on, must be the essential beginning point for any religious engagement with the issue of the atomic bomb. "No political or cultural achievement of man should lure Christians into the belief that history no longer needs redemption," it said. "No historic catastrophe should cause them to despair and believe that history cannot be redeemed." It ended with a plea to nonpacifist Christians to "consider whether the hour has not struck for the Church to issue a condemnation of war as an instrument of policy."[42]

This appeal went largely unnoticed and unanswered. *The Christian Conscience and War* represented the statement of a tiny minority resisting a powerful tide. As the 1950s began and the Cold War deepened, such religious or ethically based resistance to the nuclear arms race increasingly became the domain of a distinct group that could be easily encapsulated and dismissed as "pacifist" and thus by definition out of touch with hard political realities. The sometimes anguished documents this minority produced served at the time primarily to reveal how unrepresentative they were of the prevailing cultural and political drift.

The dread destroyer of 1945 had become the shield of the Republic by 1950; America must have as many nuclear weapons as possible, and the bigger the better, for the death struggle with communism that lay ahead. Early in 1950, in a mood of deep despair that he continued to keep out of his public utterances, David Lilienthal resigned from the AEC. The agency, he confessed to an aide, had become "nothing more than a major contractor to the Department of Defense." The new pattern of thought was nowhere better illustrated than in *The Hell Bomb* (1950) by William L. Laurence, chronicler of the Manhattan Project and the leading journalistic authority on atomic weapons. After a simplified introduction to the physics of the hydrogen bomb, Laurence turned to his real theme: an impassioned plea for a vastly expanded atomic-weapons program, and a dire warning against any efforts to restrain that program. International control, he said, had been a "noble ideal" but was now "completely out of tune with the times." In a world "threatened by a savage dictatorship," all schemes for outlawing, restricting, or controlling atomic weapons posed an "extreme danger." Proposals such as Hans Bethe's for an American no-first-use pledge would deny the military access to "the principal weapon standing between us and possible defeat." The awe at the atomic bomb's vast force, which in Laurence's account of the Alamogordo test had taken an almost poetic and even quasi-religious turn, became little more than sheer bloodlust as he contemplated the still greater power of the hydrogen bomb:

> As a blast weapon . . . it can cause total destruction of everything within an area of more than 300 square miles. As an incinerator it would severely burn everything within an area of more than 1200 square miles. It is thus the tactical weapon par excellence. No army in the field or on the march could stand up against it. Had we possessed it at the Battle of the Bulge, just one could have wiped out the entire Bulge.

Cease the "futile debate" and "flood of verbiage" about atomic weapons, exhorted Laurence, and "be done with all visionary plans for destroying the shield that now protects civilization as we know it."[43]

At some level, though, Americans did seem to understand and shudder at what was happening. "We are less complacent than we seem," said Edward L. Long, Jr. "We live in a crisis, and it runs deeper than we commonly suppose. . . . Despair lies close to the surface." Cultural observers vied in the bleakness of their imagery. "We find ourselves more and more in the position of the hanged man who leaps and contorts his body in a desperate effort to escape," wrote Robert Payne in 1949, "but . . . all his contortions only make his death more certain."[44]

"Like the shadow of an eclipse of the sun," wrote *Christian Century* early in 1950, "atomic darkness is racing across the world. . . . The nations are proceeding as though caught in the vicious closed cycle of an inescapable atomic arms race—weapon, counterweapon; threat, counterthreat—the end whereof is horror." Even *Life* magazine, in its February 1950 special issue on the forthcoming showdown with world communism, gave the last word to a fourteen-year-old Los Angeles schoolboy who in a class assignment on the hydrogen-bomb decision had written in a compulsively reiterative outburst:

> The hydrogen bomb reeks with death. Death, death to thousands. A burning, searing death, a death that is horrible, lasting death. The most horrible death man has invented; the destroying annihilating death of atomic energy. The poisoning, killing, destroying death. Death of the ages, of man, the lasting death.[45]

Images of dreaming and nightmares drift through the writings of those who sought to capture the national mood in these years. "We fear terribly that what we do in a new war will be as wrong and stupid as much of what we did in the last one," editorialized the *Saturday Evening Post* in November 1949, "but like a man in a dream, we see no way to reverse the field." Like the compulsions of the alcoholic, wrote David Bradley in 1951, the quest for ever more potent atomic weapons "promises only to bring the nightmares, the hallucinations, the convulsions of a final global dementia."[46]

Only a few years earlier, opinion-molders of all kinds had insisted that an informed citizenry, sensitized to the magnitude of the danger, could play a decisive role in banishing the atomic threat. And, indeed, many Americans had responded to that message with desperate eagerness. Hope had been the frail child of terror. By the end of the decade, all had changed. In its discouragement, *Christian Century* concluded that the entire post-Hiroshima surge of cultural engagement and political activism had been ephemeral and illusory; "From the beginning," it declared in 1949, "the American people . . . reacted to the atomic threat as a sleepwalker would react to the edge of a roof toward which he was walking." Certainly in 1949–1950 the evidence for such a conclusion seemed overwhelming—as it would be more than thirty years later to George Kennan when he described Americans' response to the bomb in almost identical terms.[47] In the brutal and strident climate of the early Cold War, hope shriveled. What remained was fear—muted, throbbing, only half acknowledged—and a dull sense of grim inevitability as humankind stumbled toward the nothingness that almost surely lay somewhere down the road—no one knew how far.

While Billy Graham exploited this half-submerged atomic fear to bring sinners to repentence, Norman Vincent Peale chose a different approach. The world was full of "worried, anxious people," Peale acknowledged in his best-selling *A Guide to Confident Living* (1948)—people were "afraid of the future." But there was a "cure for fear," he insisted: "Say confidently to yourself: 'Through God's help and the application of simple techniques, I will be free from fear.' Believe that—practice it, and it will be so." We should "develop the habit of not talking about our anxieties and worries," he added in *Faith is the Answer* (1950); "Get your anxiety out of your general conversation, and it will tend to drop out of your mind." Millions took Peale's message to heart. The prevailing cultural mood, concluded I. I. Rabi in 1955, was best characterized as "the complacency of despair."[48]

A few lonely voices of muted hope remained. Lewis Mumford, writing in 1950, conceded the picture was bleak: the nation's leaders were "living in a one-dimension world of the immediate present." Seeking "security," they were fashioning a world "of total insecurity"; worse, the American people, sealed in their delusions, supported these policies.[49] But one must still struggle, against all odds, to reverse the downward drift. "Our first obligation," he wrote, "is the restoration of our own capacity to be human: to think and feel as whole men, not as specialists." To achieve this restoration would be to "challenge the automisms we have submitted to and evaluate both the near and the remote consequences of the forces that we have helped to set in motion. Above all, we must conquer our moral numbness and inertia." Was it a dream to expect such a transformation? he asked, falling into the prevailing imagery. "Naturally it is a dream," he answered, "for all challenges to animal lethargy and inertia begin in a dream. . . . But it is better to sink one's last hopes in such a dream than to be destroyed by a nightmare."

Epilogue

From the H-Bomb to Star Wars: The Continuing Cycles of Activism and Apathy

Histories end; history goes on. This study closes in the early 1950s, a moment in our forty-year encounter with the bomb dramatically different from the immediate postwar period. By 1950, the obsessive post-Hiroshima awareness of the horror of the atomic bomb had given way to an interval of diminished cultural attention and uneasy acquiescence in the goal of maintaining atomic superiority over the Russians.

But the story of this cultural shift is only the prelude to a much longer one. In the decades that followed, two more such cycles of activism and apathy would play themselves out. To tell that longer story would require another book; but in order to place the developments of 1945–1950 in perspective and suggest how an understanding of that five-year period can contribute to a deeper understanding of our present situation, one must at least sketch in the contours of what followed.

The early 1950s mood of diminished awareness and acquiescence in the developing nuclear arms race soon gave way to a new and very different stage. In the mid-1950s the issue of nuclear weapons again surged dramatically to the forefront, once more becoming a central cultural theme. As in 1945–1946, the reason was fear—this time, fear of radioactive fallout. As we have seen, such fears had surfaced after the Bikini test of 1946, but when the United States in 1952 and the Russians soon after began atmospheric testing of multimegaton thermonuclear bombs, they increased dramatically. It was the United States' 1954 test series that really aroused alarm, spreading radioactive ash over seven thousand square miles of the Pacific, forcing the emergency evacuation of nearby islanders, and bringing illness and death to Japanese fishermen eighty miles away. In 1955, radioactive rain fell on Chicago. In 1959, deadly strontium-90 began to show up in milk. The *Saturday Evening Post* ran a feature called "Fallout: The Silent Killer." A new group of scientists and physicians warned of the health hazards of fallout, including leukemia, bone cancer, and long-term genetic damage. A full-blown fallout scare gripped the nation.[1]

This in turn spawned a national movement against nuclear testing. Adlai Stevenson raised the issue in the 1956 presidential campaign. Soon it was taken up by such groups as Leo Szilard's Council for a Liveable World; Bernard Lown's Physicians for Social Responsibility; and SANE, the National Committe for a Sane Nuclear Policy, founded in 1957. One memorable SANE ad in the *New York Times* featured the famed pediatrician Benjamin Spock gazing with furrowed brow at a young girl under the caption: DR. SPOCK IS WORRIED.[2]

The revived nuclear anxieties of these years were also fed by a renewed emphasis on civil defense, including radio alerts (remember "CONELRAD"?) and wailing warning sirens. In a practice test in 1956, ten thousand Washington government workers scattered to secret relocation centers and President Eisenhower was helicoptered to an underground command post in Maryland. Civil defense hit the big time in 1961 as part of President Kennedy's sparring with the Russians over Berlin. With little advance preparation Kennedy went on television, warned of the danger of nuclear war, and called for a massive fallout-shelter program. Soon, black-and-yellow "Fallout Shelter" signs were adorning schools and public buildings across America. Few homeowners actually built shelters, but a lot of publicity was given to those who did. Schoolchildren hid under their desks in air-raid drills. In one civil-defense film, Bert the Turtle taught schoolchildren to "Duck and Cover."[3]

Not surprisingly, American culture in these years was once again pervaded by the nuclear theme. Books, essays, sermons, and symposia explored the medical, psychological, and ethical implications of nuclear weapons. Novels like Nevil Shute's *On the Beach* (1957), Helen Clarkson's *The Last Day* (1959), Walter Miller's *A Canticle for Leibowitz* (1959), Eugene Burdick and Harvey Wheeler's *Fail-Safe* (1962), and Kurt Vonnegut's *Cat's Cradle* (1963) imagined scenarios of nuclear war and human extinction. The film versions of *On the Beach* and *Fail-Safe*—not to mention the Stanley Kubrick classic *Dr. Strangelove*—were highly successful. In Frank and Eleanor Perry's *Ladybug, Ladybug* (1963), a terrified little girl sent home from school in an air-raid drill becomes so frightened she hides in an abandoned refrigerator and asphyxiates.[4]

This revived nuclear awareness surfaced at all cultural levels. Tom Lehrer's satirical song about a nuclear-age cowboy roaming the test sites of the Southwest in his lead BVDs was a hit on college campuses. *Mad* magazine published a nuclear war "Hit Parade" featuring post-holocaust parodies of current popular songs. If nuclear testing continued, said *Mad,* these were the songs "young lovers of future generations will be singing as they walk down moonlit lanes arm in arm in arm in arm . . ."[5]

A spate of mutant movies—*The H-Man, The Blob, It, Attack of the Crab Monsters, The Incredible Shrinking Man, Them!*—had obvious psychological roots in the fear of genetic damage from radiation. This is quite explicit in *Them!* (1954), in which mutant ants big enough to ruin any picnic emerge from an atomic-bomb test site in New Mexico. At the end, the scientist-hero draws the moral: in the atomic age, this sort of thing must be expected.[6]

Science fiction as usual mirrored the preoccupations of the larger culture. In Isaac Asimov's "The Gentle Vultures" (1957), representatives of a sophisticated alien civilization, observing earth from their base on the far side of the moon, patiently await the nuclear war that has enabled them to establish their rule over numerous other technologically advanced civilizations throughout the galaxy. In Mordecai Roshwald's *Level 7* (1959), the inhabitants of a vast seven-level underground shelter die, level by level, as the radiation from a nuclear war penetrates deeper into the earth. As the longest-lived survivors, in Level Seven, await their end they invent a new religion in which strontium represents the elemental force of evil.[7]

TV science-fiction series like *The Outer Limits* and Rod Serling's *Twilight Zone* frequently dealt with nuclear war, radioactivity, and the psychological effect of atomic fears. In a 1961 *Twilight Zone* episode called "The Shelter," the warning sirens go off and the people of a typical suburban neighborhood rush to the home of the one man who has built a shelter. He barricades himself and his family inside, refusing their pleas. As panic mounts, the neighbors turn on each other. What had been a tranquil community disintegrates into a screaming mob. Eventually the all-clear signal sounds, but the shaken neighbors recognize they have been destroyed as a community almost as surely as if the bomb had actually fallen.[8]

Like the mutant movies, these TV science-fiction shows also reflected the culture's fear of genetic damage from radiation. In a 1962 *Outer Limits* episode, genetically enhanced bees bent on world domination transform their queen into a beautiful young female humanoid. She insinuates herself into the home of a cozy suburban couple and nearly seduces the weak-willed husband. But the wife becomes suspicious when she sees the newcomer in the garden one night, pollinating flowers. A swarm of bees stings the wife to death and the bee-girl seductively offers herself to the grieving husband. In a surge of revulsion he kills her, and the bees' master plan is foiled—for the moment.

In these years, too, the nation's imaginative writers and poets began to find their voice. Thomas Merton's *Original Child Bomb* (1962), subtitled *Points for Meditation to be Scratched on the Walls of a Cave*, offered a series of terse and sardonic observations on America's development and use of the atomic bomb in World War II. In "Fall 1961," Robert Lowell conveyed his mood in a series of images and impressions:

All autumn, the chafe and jar
of nuclear war;
We have talked our extinction to death.
I swim like a minnow
behind my studio window.

Our end drifts nearer,
the moon lifts,
radiant with terror
The state
is a diver under a glass bell.

A father's no shield
for his child.
We are like a lot of wild
spiders crying together
but without tears.[9]

This second period of nuclear fear and activism ended abruptly in 1963.
After the Cuban missile crisis of 1962, when the United States and the
Soviets went to the nuclear brink and pulled back, it was widely hoped that
they would cooperate to avoid such confrontations in the future. Then in
1963 the United States, the Soviet Union, and Great Britain signed a treaty
banning atmospheric nuclear testing. A mood of euphoria swept the country. Almost overnight, the nuclear fear that had been building since the
mid-1950s seemed to dissipate. "Writers rarely write about this subject
anymore, and people hardly ever talk about it," the columnist Stewart Alsop
observed in 1967. "In recent years there has been something like a conspiracy of silence about the threat of nuclear holocaust."[10]

This is not to suggest that nuclear fear ceased to be a significant cultural
force in these years. Robert Jay Lifton may well be right in his speculation
that the denial of nuclear awareness—like the massive underwater mountain
chains that influence ocean currents, marine life, and weather patterns in all
kinds of hidden ways—affects a culture as profoundly as acknowledging it
does. Psychiatrist John Mack may be correct in suggesting that deep-seated
fear of nuclear war is a pervasive constant in children.[11]

What one does see after 1963, however, as in 1947–1954, is a sharp
decline in culturally expressed engagement with the issue. With apologies
to Raymond Chandler, one might call this the Era of the Big Sleep. Public-
opinion data reflect the shift. In 1959, 64 percent of Americans listed
nuclear war as the nation's most urgent problem. By 1964, the figure had
dropped to 16 percent. Soon it vanished entirely from the surveys. An early
1970s study of the treatment of the nuclear arms race in American educational journals found the subject almost totally ignored. "The atom bomb is

a dead issue," concluded a sociologist studying student attitudes in 1973. Soon after, the editor of the *Bulletin of Atomic Scientists* lamented the ubiquitous "public apathy" on the issue. In 1976 a political journalist observed: "Any politician who would now speak, as President Kennedy once did, about the 'nuclear sword of Damocles' poised above our collective head, would be dismissed out of hand as an anachronism. The fear of nuclear war, once so great, has steadily receded." [12]

In the later 1960s, it is true, Pentagon proposals to build a city-based antiballistic missile system aroused a flurry of activism and media attention. Like the atomic obliteration of two cities in 1945 and the fallout of 1954–1963, such talk forced the nuclear danger unavoidably to the forefront of public awareness, as citizens contemplated the prospect of defensive missile systems practically in their backyards. [13] But apart from this issue (which faded with the signing of the ABM Treaty in 1972), the prevailing American stance toward the nuclear war threat from 1963 until well into the 1970s was one of apathy and neglect.

After 1963, the nuclear theme largely disappeared from TV and the movies, emerging only fleetingly in fiction and popular music—little subsurface tremors, one might say: the 1965 rock hit "Eve of Destruction"; Randy Newman's song "Political Science" with its insinuating refrain, "Let's drop the big one and see what happens"; the young man in Ann Beattie's novel *Falling in Place,* who won't let his girlfriend use the bug killer Raid in their apartment because it gives him nightmares of nuclear tests and radioactive fallout; the middle-aged man in Charles McCarry's *The Tears of Autumn,* who recalls growing up "thinking uranium was good for curing cancer"; the minor character in Stephen Greenleaf's mystery *Death Bed,* a garrulous ex-jockey, who fantasizes about how the computers of the United States and the Soviet Union could begin a nuclear war without human intervention: "Two of those babies are going to get mad at each other one of these days, one of ours and one of theirs, and before they're through we'll all be dead." [14]

Why this sharp decline in cultural attention to the bomb? Why this Big Sleep? The most reassuring explanation would be that the complacency was justified—that the nuclear threat did diminish in these years. Unfortunately, this was not the case. Taking advantage of a gaping loophole in the 1963 test-ban treaty, both sides developed sophisticated techniques of underground testing. The United States tested more nuclear weapons in the five years after the "test ban" treaty than in the five years before. And despite various arms-control agreements culminating in SALT I (1972), the nation's nuclear weapons program went forward at a rapid rate. Despite minor fluctuations as new systems were introduced and old ones retired, the United States' stockpile of nuclear warheads and bombs never fell below twenty-four thousand during the years of the Big Sleep (1963–1980). Indeed, these years brought a number of highly dangerous innovations in nuclear technology, most notably MIRV, the American technological breakout of the 1970s, by which a single missile could carry up to sixteen independently targeted nuclear warheads.[15]

If this long period of nuclear apathy and cultural neglect had so little basis in objective facts, why did it happen? Several reasons might be at least briefly suggested.

First, the *illusion of diminished risk.* The 1963 treaty did not stop nuclear tests, but it did put them underground, out of sight. The various arms-limitation negotiations and treaties of these years did not stop the nuclear arms race, but they gave the appearance that something was being done about the hazard of nuclear war, reassuring a public only too ready to grasp at hopeful straws suggesting that the experts had the problem in hand.

Second, the *loss of immediacy.* With atmospheric tests no longer dominating newspapers and TV screens, the world's massive nuclear arsenals seemed increasingly unreal. As one journalist wrote in 1966: "Familiarity takes the sting out of practically anything, even Armageddon." Nuclear weapons "constitute a danger so theoretical, so remote, as to be almost nonexistent."[16] This loss of immediacy was furthered by an increasingly sanitized, impersonal strategic vocabulary and by the names of doomsday missile systems that evoked comfortable associations with the stars, classical mythology, American history, even popular slang: Polaris, Poseidon, Tomahawk, Pershing, David Crockett, Honest John, Hound Dog. As George Orwell wrote in another context: "The revolution will be complete when the language is perfect." The nuclear arms race—theoretical, remote, largely invisible—was ill-suited to the insatiable visual demands of television. After 1963, the mushroom-shaped cloud, the corporate logo of the nuclear age, became a tired visual cliché, embalmed in the pages of history textbooks where it had little more emotional impact than the lithographs of shivering soldiers at Valley Forge.

Third, in the 1960s and early 1970s, *the promise of a world transformed by atomic energy.* Once again, as in the late 1940s, this helped mute concern about nuclear weapons. This time the utopian dream was focused on nuclear power, reinforced by the reality of power plants springing up from Maine to California. By the mid-1970s these plants would become the focus of demonstrations and protest, but initially, thanks to heavy promotion by the nuclear power industry, they were viewed in a hopeful light. Indeed, a kind of psychological balancing act seems to have occurred, with images of the peaceful atom once again counteracting and to a degree neutralizing images of the destroying atom. As nuclear strategist Albert Wohlstetter observed in 1967, "bright hopes for civilian nuclear energy" offered "an emotional counterweight to . . . nuclear destruction." Implicitly, the policy issue was often posed as a kind of zero-sum game: support peaceful development enthusiastically enough, and the destroying atom would somehow wither away. In a 1967 speech entitled "Need We Fear Our Nuclear Future?" the chairman of the Atomic Energy Commission, Glenn T. Seaborg, managed a resounding "no" by the simple expedient of never once mentioning nuclear weapons.[17]

Of course, it was not a zero-sum game. Military and civilian uses of atomic energy were deeply interwoven, as the Reagan administration would later remind the nation with its proposals to recycle plutonium from nuclear power plants for weapons production. But for a time, the delicate psychological balancing act seemed to have worked.

Fourth, the Big Sleep was linked to the *complexity and comfort of deterrence theory*. In the immediate postwar years, American nuclear strategy, such as it was, involved a simple if chilling premise: if war came, the United States would simply rain all its available atomic bombs upon Russia's urban and military centers. By the 1960s, nuclear strategy had become an esoteric, complex pursuit involving computers, game theory, and a specialized technical vocabulary. This had a chilling effect on public engagement with the issue. It all seemed—and was clearly meant to seem—too arcane for the average citizen. It also seemed, at least superficially, reassuring. As promulgated by Secretary of Defense Robert McNamara in 1967–1968, the basic logic of deterrence theory was seductive: in a nuclear world, security lay in maintaining a retaliatory capacity so powerful and so invulnerable that no nation would dare attack us or our allies. To tinker carelessly with this arsenal, even to diminish it, could heighten rather than reduce the risk of nuclear war.[18]

A fifth and final explanation for the nuclear apathy of these years is perhaps the most obvious of all: in the later 1960s, *the Vietnam War* absorbed nearly every available drop of antiwar energy. From the major escalation of February 1965 to the final helicopter evacuation from Saigon a little over ten years later, Vietnam obsessed the national consciousness. From the first "teach-in" at the University of Michigan in March 1965 through successive "mobilizations" and "moratoriums" to the final convulsive demonstration against the Cambodian invasion of May 1970, the war was *the* focus of activist energy. For radicals, peace activists, many religious leaders, college students facing the draft, and ultimately countless Americans of no strong ideological bent, opposition to a war that was claiming thousands of lives, devastating entire regions, turning hundreds of thousands of peasants into refugees, and draining the national treasury with no sign of "victory" in sight had an urgency that could not be denied.

Even as media events and as the source of powerful television images, the war and the domestic turmoil it engendered had an immediacy the more abstract nuclear weapons issue could not begin to match. "The second round of Strategic Arms Limitation Talks have started in Geneva," the *Wall Street*

Journal could report as late as 1973, "though even an attentive newspaper reader would scarcely have noticed amid the distractions of Vietnam hopes and fears."[19]

From this perspective, the nuclear issue seems not so much to have been set aside as forcibly pushed to the background. The bomb was a potential menace; Vietnam was actuality. This is vividly illustrated in the history of SANE, the major voice against the nuclear arms race in the late 1950s and early 1960s. In the mid-1960s some SANE directors, including co-chairman Benjamin Spock, shifted their energies entirely to opposing the Vietnam War, while a minority tried to keep the nuclear weapons issue paramount. At a SANE executive board meeting in 1966, a catch-all entry called "Disarmament—Nuclear Tests—Non-Proliferation" appeared far down on a long agenda otherwise given over to Vietnam and related issues. The minutes for this item are revealing: "The Board discussed these issues briefly, recognizing the necessity for continued attention and action, but noted that the Vietnam issue must receive the major emphasis until the war is ended." Torn by resignations and dissension, SANE in 1969 even dropped the word "Nuclear" from its name.[20]

As for the New Left—the most dynamic political force in America in the late 1960s—it was not well positioned ideologically to deal with the nuclear arms race. Pointing to Vietnam, to Third World revolutions, and to America's exploited poor, oppressed minorities, and masses of alienated workers numbed by media-induced "false consciousness," New Left ideologues argued that there lay the future arena of a revolutionary struggle that would be pursued through liberation conflicts abroad and mobilization of the masses at home. Impressed by the cool managerial style of Robert McNamara and his computer experts, New Left ideologues shared with the deterrence theorists the tacit assumption that the technocrats could be counted on to "manage" the nuclear arms competition while radicals turned their energies elsewhere. One finds many rhetorical allusions to "the Bomb" in New Left literature, but not much hard analysis of the nuclear arms race as a complex and immensely threatening global phenomenon.[21]

By the later 1970s, however, the nexus of circumstances that had sustained the Big Sleep for some fifteen years was beginning to break up. India's explosion of a "nuclear device" in 1974, after a decade when the "nuclear club" had held steady at five, revived concerns about proliferation. The arms-control process—never notably successful at best—lost momentum after 1972 and ground to a halt in 1979 when President Carter withdrew the SALT II treaty from the Senate after the Soviet invasion of Afghanistan. The Vietnam War faded at last from the spotlight, as did Watergate, OPEC, the Iranian hostage crisis, and the grinding inflation of the Carter years.

Two further developments—one originating abroad and the other in the American heartland—also played a decisive role in the late-1970s revival of nuclear awareness. A vigorous anti-nuclear-weapons movement in Western Europe, focused on the planned NATO deployment of Pershing and cruise missiles, provided both a stimulus and model for Americans growing increasingly uneasy about the bomb.

Simultaneously, without much media attention, opposition to nuclear power had been spreading in grass-roots America. This movement gained massive visibility in 1979 with the release of the Jane Fonda movie *China Syndrome* and the accident at Three Mile Island, but in fact it had been building for several years at the local level. For decades government officials had urged Americans to focus on the peacetime promise of atomic energy as a reassuring alternative to worrying about nuclear war. In the 1970s they succeeded beyond their wildest dreams, but with results far different than they had anticipated. For when people at last did begin to think seriously about the "peaceful" atom—now symbolized by the nuclear power industry —they concluded that it was not reassuring at all, but deeply alarming. Local activists, students, church groups, and concerned citizens began to focus heavy publicity on nuclear power plants that not only were failing in their economic promise but also raising grave doubts about public health and safety. [22]

Unconsciously influenced by the long-standing official insistence that nuclear weapons and nuclear power were two totally distinct realms, these "Anti-Nuke" activists of the 1970s initially paid little attention to the remote and theoretical issue of nuclear war and focused instead on the local, immediate, and highly visible issue of nuclear power. But by the end of the decade, as other developments forced the nuclear weapons issue once again into public awareness, the always unstable distinction between the "peaceful" atom and the "destroying" atom rapidly collapsed, and activists who had been focusing only on nuclear power began to confront the entire issue in its full and disturbing interconnectedness.

By 1980, then, the stage was already set for a return to the oldest item on the agenda: the threat of nuclear war. The accession of Ronald Reagan, with his bellicose rhetoric, his vast military buildup, his elaborate and heavily publicized civil-defense programs, his proposals to push the nuclear arms race into space, and the barely concealed contempt of powerful administration figures for the whole concept of arms control provided the final decisive push back toward antinuclear activism and revived cultural awareness.

By late 1981, a dramatic shift in the nation's political consciousness was beginning to be felt. Town meetings in rural New England passed resolutions calling for a halt to nuclear weapons production. On November 11—Veterans' Day—students on college campuses turned out in unexpectedly large numbers for speeches and panel discussions on the nuclear threat.

"After several decades in which scarcely anyone but a few indestructible peaceniks and the limited fraternity of arms-control specialists gave any sustained attention to the peril of nuclear destruction in war," observed the president of the Rockefeller Foundation in March 1982, "it is being written about and talked about on every side." That April, towns and colleges across America observed Ground Zero Week with films, lectures, and such consciousness-raising events as a Race for Life, in which runners set out from the center of a hypothetical nuclear blast and ran out of town, passing successive mile markers describing the destruction at that point. That same month, historian Barbara Tuchman wrote in the *New York Times Magazine* of "the remarkable change in this country from the recent indifference to the new deep and widespread concern."[23] On June 12, 1982, over seven hundred thousand antinuclear demonstrators—the largest such assembly in American history—marched in New York City. In November, voters in eight states overwhelmingly approved a referendum calling for a mutual and verifiable freeze on the production and deployment of nuclear weapons. Moribund organizations dating from the days of the test-ban movement—SANE, Physicians for Social Responsibility, the Council for a Liveable World, the Union of Concerned Scientists—dusted off their mailing lists and reemerged with new vigor and visibility. Aging veterans of the Manhattan Project and the postwar scientists' movement found themselves once more in demand.

As in the earlier cycles of activism, this Reagan-induced wave of nuclear awareness found dramatic expression not only in the political arena but also in the mass media and the cultural realm. On March 29, 1982, *Time* presented its 4.5 million readers with a particularly sinister mushroom cloud on its cover. Ann Landers devoted one of her popular advice columns to the nuclear threat and wrote at the end: "I implore every person to sign his or her name across this column and mail it to President Reagan." The comic strip *Bloom County* pictured Norma the Nuke as a jaded but alluring prostitute at the bedside of a sorely tempted man. In Gary Trudeau's ever-topical *Doonesbury*, a trendy young minister pondered the ethical issues of nuclear deterrence with the aid of his new home computer. In a popular newspaper cartoon series, an irritated bartender asked a gloomy patron to stop talking about nuclear war until Happy Hour was over.[24]

After years of neglect, the movies and television rediscovered nuclear war in the early 1980s, dramatizing the ways such a conflict might begin— *World War III, War Games, Countdown to Looking Glass*—and its effect on specific communities ranging from Sheffield, England (*Threads*) to Boston (*The Apocalypse Game*) to Kansas City (*The Day After*) to northern California (*Testament*). An episode of the NBC dramatic series *Lou Grant* challenged the administration's vision of orderly urban dispersal in a nuclear crisis by portraying the confusion and panic that even the rumor of a nuclear attack would create in a city like Los Angeles. (The administration struck back. One official criticized the media's "appeal to emotionalism" and its obsession with "the pornography of violence." Television, complained Senator Barry Goldwater, was showing only "the negative side of nuclear weapons."[25])

Having for years been ignored, the issue of nuclear war suddenly seemed in danger of trivialization. Theodore Gesell produced a Dr. Seuss book comparing the Cold War and the nuclear arms race to a quarrel over how bread should be buttered. A small book of drawings of balloons, bicycle riders, and animal tracks in snow was entitled *Fifty-Seven Reasons Not to Have a Nuclear War*. *The Little Black Book of Atomic War* answered such pressing questions as which actor starred as the atomic scientist in *Them!* (James Arness). A poster at the University of Wisconsin invited students to "Boogie Against Nuclear War"; the Nuclear Polka Band of Denton, Texas, appeared on public radio's *Prairie Home Companion*. In "Be in My Video" (1984), a song satirizing the TV promotional films that in the early 1980s became a major marketing force on the pop-music scene, Frank Zappa wrote:

There's a cheesy atom bomb explosion
all the big groups use—
atomic light will shine
through an old venetian blind
making patterns on your face,
then it cuts to outer space.[26]

"Be in My Video," by Frank Zappa,
© 1984. Munchkin Music, ASCAP.

Nuclear fear, it seemed, was becoming simply another advertising gimmick, helping sell the latest songs of Van Halen and Iron Maiden. As Vartan Gregorian put it in December 1984, the apocalypse was becoming a "bland cliché." Even serious and well-intentioned TV productions like *The Day After* had less impact than predicted, as viewers long since inured to the tube's make-believe violence and faked disasters of the *Towering Inferno* variety readily took them in stride.[27] Perhaps the only adequate television treatment of nuclear war would be two hours of a totally blank screen in prime time. But who would sponsor it?

Yet, this was far from the whole story. At a very different point on the cultural landscape, journals of opinion as politically diverse as *Dissent*, the *Nation*, the *New York Review of Books*, the *New Republic*, *Commentary*, and the *National Review* all published major essays in 1981–1983 on nuclear-related issues. The American Psychiatric Association, whose last major pronouncement on the subject, *Psychiatric Aspects of the Prevention of Nuclear War*, had come in 1964, published a volume warning of the unsettling *Psychosocial Aspects of Nuclear Developments*. A Washington conference of higher-education leaders in March 1982 considered "The Role of the Academy in Addressing the Issues of Nuclear War." On college and university campuses across the country, courses were introduced, and public-affairs symposia conducted, on the nuclear issue. Emulating the physicians, concerned teachers formed Educators for Social Responsibility.[28]

The nuclear theme also found increasing expression in the realm of imaginative literature. In Russell Hoban's *Riddley Walker* (1980), the inhabitants of a post-nuclear-war England try to make sense of the vanished civilization whose ruins clutter the landscape and whose culture survives in garbled and fragmentary oral traditions. Bernard Malamud's *God's Grace* (1982) is set on a remote Pacific island after civilization has destroyed itself in a nuclear war.

From all across the cultural landscape came a babble of voices as Americans—in novels, in letters to the editor, in classrooms, at dinner parties—began to unlock the closed door of nuclear memory. In Mary Gordon's *The Company of Women* (1982), a character recalls the time she spent in fallout shelters in the 1950s. In Leslie Epstein's *Regina* (1982), the heroine remembers the air-raid drills of her school days, her activism in SANE, and a friend's skepticism about the 1963 test-ban treaty: "'Watch' he'd said during the debate on the test ban treaty. 'They'll push everything underground, which means under the rug, and go right on testing. Better to keep the filth exposed so we have to taste it.' He'd been right, she imagined. The treaty *had* made the difference. They'd all buried the bomb blasts inside themselves. She had to drag even these thoughts from herself, against the force of repression."[29]

Poets, too, began to write of the nuclear threat—or wrestle with their inability to do so. Introducing the Summer 1983 *New England Review and Bread Loaf Quarterly,* an issue devoted to Writers in the Nuclear Age, the editor noted the wave of nuclear awareness sweeping the nation and went on: "It is clear that writers struggle to reconcile political necessities with artistic forms, and sometimes feel blocked when turning their minds to 'subjects' such as the threat of global annihilation—as though our hard-won skills were unsuited for travel on this rough ground." Carolyn Forché put the matter succinctly in the October 1984 issue of *Mother Jones*: "We are the poets of the Nuclear Age, perhaps the last poets, and some of us fear what the Muse is telling us. Some of are finding it harder to write. . . . There is no metaphor for the end of the world and it is horrible to search for one."[30]

The resurgence of cultural attention to the nuclear threat also brought a renewed effort to confront the ethical issues posed by the bomb. The major Protestant denominations appointed commissions and drafted statements, while individual congregations wrestled with the question at the grass-roots level. Even on the Protestant evangelical front, stamping ground of Jerry Falwell, Armageddon prophet Hal Lindsay, and the flag-waving National

Association of Evangelicals (to which President Reagan delivered his speech branding the Soviet Union as "the focus of evil" in the world), a moral critique of American nuclear policy could be heard. Through an organization called Evangelicals for Social Action and such books as *Nuclear Holocaust and Christian Hope* (written with Richard K. Taylor), the Rev. Ronald Sider, an evangelical of unimpeachable credentials, called those who shared his beliefs to a radical rejection of nuclear weapons on biblical principles. In May 1985 a Washington-based evangelical group called Sojourners organized a major demonstration involving nonviolent civil disobedience reminiscent of the early civil-rights movement, to protest the administration's nuclear weapons policy. Within the Roman Catholic Church, the renewed engagement with this issue culminated in *The Challenge of Peace* (1983), the powerful pastoral letter of the National Conference of Catholic Bishops calling on Catholics and non-Catholics alike, both ordinary citizens and those in power, to re-think the morality of American nuclear-weapons policies in the light of Christian teaching and the natural law.[31]

Nor was this ethical discourse confined to the churches. With Jonathan Schell's enormously influential *The Fate of the Earth* leading the way, such diverse books as *Nuclear Culture* by Paul Loeb, *Weapons and Hope* by physicist Freeman Dyson, *The Nuclear Delusion* by diplomat George Kennan, and *Late Night Thoughts on Listening to Mahler's Ninth Symphony* by biologist Lewis Thomas were linked by a common thread of moral concern about the nuclear arms competition and its effect on our lives.

To the historian immersed in studying the bomb's cultural and intellectual impact in the earliest postwar years, this latest upsurge of awareness brings a powerful sense of *déjà vu*. Once again the possibility of nuclear annihilation looms large in the national consciousness, and once again the agencies of culture and the media both resonate to and amplify that awareness. Indeed, the parallels are striking. Except for a post-holocaust "Nuclear Winter," every theme and image by which we express our nuclear fear today has its counterpart in the immediate post-Hiroshima period. The concentric circles of hypothetical destruction we superimpose upon maps of our cities appeared in American newspapers within hours of August 6, 1945. (On today's maps, of course, there are a great many more circles.) Jonathan Schell's graphic description of what a nuclear attack would do to New York City would have been familiar to any reader of *Life, Collier's,* or *Reader's Digest* in the late 1940s. Even images like Schell's arresting "Republic of Insects and Grass" appeared in newspaper editorials within days of the atomic-bomb announcement. Those critics of the Reagan Strategic Defense Initiative who point out that even if it worked the United States would still be vulnerable to nuclear weapons smuggled into the country are resurrecting one of the major themes of the scientists' campaign of 1945–1947.

And again, as in the later 1940s, voices of reassurance are to be heard. Once more we hear of security through civil defense (crisis relocation in rural hamlets now, rather than fallout shelters or redesigned cities), new missile systems, new modes of defense, new technological marvels. (Just as one turns from the more bizarre civil-defense schemes of the late 1940s, congratulating oneself that at least we're not *that* naïve anymore, NASA scientists seriously consider research on putting large quantities of human bone marrow into orbit, for retrieval after a nuclear war for the treatment of radiation victims![32])

But for all the similarities, there is also a major, and depressing, difference between the current wave of nuclear awareness and that of the late 1940s. The first time around, the images of mass destruction were anticipatory. By a remarkable leap, Americans in the earliest days of the atomic era summoned up vivid scenes of their great cities in smouldering ruins—scenes that would not, in fact, become real possibilities for another twenty years. The holocaust scenarios of the 1980s, by contrast, are only too plausible. Indeed, our stabs at imagining possible nuclear futures are continually outdistanced by actual developments. In the 1940s, imagination raced ahead of reality; in the 1980s, reality races ahead of imagination.

A further discouraging dimension to one's sense of *déjà vu* is the fact that today's activists have so little awareness of the long history to which they are contributing the latest chapter. We extemporize everything, from strategy and tactics to metaphors and images, as though it had not all been done before—several times, in fact. We debate the wisdom of the scare tactics of a Helen Caldicott with little apparent awareness that this very issue was the subject of massive discussion—and some bitter lessons—a generation ago.

Certainly there is in all this ample reason for pessimism. Viewed in historical perspective, this latest upsurge of activism could easily be seen as simply the latest convolution of a long cyclical process—the most recent swing of a pendulum that since 1945 has oscillated several times between political activism and cultural attention on the one hand and political apathy and cultural neglect on the other. More depressing still is the realization that after each of those earlier periods of activism, the nuclear arms race in fact entered a new and more deadly upward spiral. Will the same be true this time? Certainly by mid-decade, activism seemed already distinctly on the wane, and it was not at all clear that a new cycle of nuclear competition, burdening the earth and perhaps even the heavens above with still more horrible instruments of mass death, would not be our long-term fate.

But it would be wrong to conclude that this cyclical pattern must inexorably shape the trajectory of the future. This fallacy could be as potentially dangerous as its opposite: the comforting assumption that since forty years have now passed without a nuclear war, such a war can be avoided indefinitely in the future. Such a view of historical inevitability, based on a projection of past trends into the future, reckons without the factor of human unpredictability. History never repeats itself mechanically, like a stuck record. There are always novel twists, in the interstices of which one may sometimes find reason for hope. Our breathing space may be periously small, and diminishing day by day, but it still remains. Those who warn of the danger of nuclear war rightly point out how readily unpredictable human factors—whether individual miscalculation or some surge of collective madness—could propel us down the road to holocaust despite all efforts to rationalize the technology of decision-making. Yet this same unpredictable human factor can work in the opposite way as well, introducing new forces for sanity and survival in a situation that seems increasingly structured toward a catastrophic denouement.

Of course the past influences the future, even if it does not determine it absolutely; yet even this fact offers cause for hope as well as pessimism. To some, each successive cycle of nuclear awareness has seemed unique and *sui generis*—"like an abrupt, unexpected change in the weather," as one observer characterized the early 1980s surge of activism.[33] In reality, despite our obliviousness, this current wave of political activism and cultural attention is intimately linked to the earlier periods of heightened sensitivity to the nuclear threat. From one vantage point, of course, the cultural world of 1945–1950 has vanished irretrievably. The great media outlets of those days —*Life, Collier's,* the *Saturday Evening Post,* the radio networks with their vast national audiences—have fallen by the wayside, victims of that brash upstart, television. Most of the opinion-molders who figure so prominently in this book—Oppenheimer, Rabinowitch, Compton, Muste, Hutchins, Swing, Laurence, Lilienthal, and the others—are long since dead. But there are continuities as well as discontinuities. John Hersey still visits college campuses, still warning that what happened to Hiroshima could happen to us. George F. Kennan, who opposed the hydrogen-bomb decision as a policy-maker in 1949, now publicly summons Americans to resist the spiraling nuclear arms race. The *Bulletin of the Atomic Scientists,* that idealistic product of the postwar scientists' movement, remains an influential forum.

At a more fundamental level, the continuity is not a matter of specific individuals or publications, but of themes and concerns. Even when the intensity of an activist cycle fades, a residuum remains, working itself out in the culture in ways no one can predict. Like the heroine of *Regina,* many Americans who were stirred into protest in 1981 gradually recalled dim memories or historical accounts of the test-ban campaign, or even the international-control activism of 1945–1946. If each upward spiral of the nuclear arms race has spawned its progeny of ever more terrible weapons, so has each cycle of antinuclear activism bequeathed to the future its legacy of cultural documents and political experience. Books like *Hiroshima* and *A Canticle for*

Leibowitz remain powerful today; the somber 1945 pronouncements of Einstein, Oppenheimer, and the others have not lost their resonance after the passage of many years. Philip Morrison's haunting 1946 description of what an atomic bomb would do to New York City can still chill the blood. Movies like *Dr. Strangelove* possess the same quality; at the first or the fifth viewing, one still watched in hypnotized fascination as the steps toward Armageddon unfold.

Such products of the past remain part of the culture. The moral eloquence of A. J. Muste in 1947 flows into and blends with that of the Catholic bishops in 1983. The somber reflections of Lewis Mumford on the psychological and social effects of nuclear fear remain part of an ongoing cultural discourse to which Robert Jay Lifton, Jonathan Schell, and many others continue to contribute. The poets and writers of the 1980s struggling to find a voice adequate to the nuclear danger do so in the knowledge that the same challenge was faced by the Agees, Berrymans, Jarrells, and Lowells of an earlier generation.

This is why I have explored in such detail the "vanished" cultural moment of 1945–1950, the years when Americans first confronted the prospect of atomic annihilation. This has not been an exercise in antiquarianism—and certainly not a venture in nostalgia—but an effort to deepen our understanding of the world in which we live. For it was in that era which now seems so distant that the fundamental perceptions which continue to influence our response to the nuclear menace were first articulated, discussed, and absorbed into the living tissue of the culture.

Will the political energies of the antinuclear cause once again be dissipated, and cultural awareness muted, as in the late 1940s, as in 1963? Or this time, will there be genuine progress, as opposed to mere cosmetic tinkering, toward driving back the shadow of global death? Can the destroyer be destroyed?

The historian has no crystal ball. As he approaches the cresting edge of history's wave, he must fall silent. It is up to all of us caught up in that wave to do what we can to shape its course and direction.

Notes

A Note on the Sources

While this book was written primarily on the basis of research in contemporary books, newspapers, and other print materials, the following manuscript collections proved helpful as well:

The Library of Congress, Manuscript Division
    Joseph and Stewart Alsop Papers
    Elmer Davis Papers
    Archibald MacLeish Papers
    Robert Oppenheimer Papers
    G. Bromley Oxnam Papers
    William S. Parsons Papers
    Raymond Gram Swing Papers
The University of Chicago, Regenstein Library
    Papers of the Atomic Scientists of Chicago
    Papers of the *Bulletin of the Atomic Scientists*
    James M. Franck Papers
    Robert Maynard Hutchins Papers
Massachusetts Institute of Technology
    Vannevar Bush Papers
State Historical Society of Wisconsin (Madison)
    H. V. Kaltenborn Papers
    Rod Serling Papers
University of Wisconsin Archives
    Farrington Daniels Papers
Swarthmore College Peace Collection
    Papers of SANE, The National Committee for a Sane Nuclear Policy

I should also like to acknowledge with gratitude the following persons who, through interviews or correspondence, helped illuminate my understanding of the early days of the atomic era: Ruth Adams, Hans Bethe, Ray Bradbury, David Bradley, Bernard Feld, Jerome Frank, John Hersey, Sidney Hook, David Inglis, Homer Jack, Alfred Kazin, Ralph Lapp, Max Lerner, Edward L. Long, Jr., Philip Morrison, Edward Shils, Alice Kimball Smith, Cyril Smith, I. F. Stone, Paul Warnke, and Victor Weisskopf.

Introduction

1. Robert Karl Manoff, "The Media: Nuclear Security vs. Democracy," *Bulletin of the Atomic Scientists,* January 1984, p. 29.

2. "Bikini," *New Yorker*, March 9, 1946, reprinted in E. B. White, *The Wild*

Flag: Editorials from the New Yorker *on Federal World Government and Other Matters* (New York, 1946), p. 161.

3. "Dayton Counting on Military," *New York Times,* January 14, 1985, business section, p. 1.

4. "As Our End Drifts Nearer . . . Editor's Afterword," *New Boston Review,* December 1981, p. 26.

5. Anne O'Hare McCormick, "The Promethean Role of the United States," *New York Times,* August 8, 1945, p. 22.

6. *Washington Post,* August 26, 1945, pp. 3B (column by Howard W. Blakeslee, Associated Press Science Editor), 4B (editorial: "Last Judgment").

7. Henry Adams, *The Education of Henry Adams,* ed. Ernest Samuels, (Boston, 1973), p. 447.

1. *"The Whole World Gasped"*

1. *New York Times,* August 7, 1945, p. 2; *Editor and Publisher,* August 11, 1945, p. 7; John Haynes Holmes, "Editorial Comment," *Unity,* September 1945, p. 99; Stanley N. Katz to author, December 18, 1984.

2. *Atomic War/Atomic Peace: Life in the Nuclear Age* (Visual Education Corp., Princeton, N.J., 1975), Cassette 2, side 2.

3. Lowell Thomas, *History as You Heard It* (Garden City, N.Y., 1957), p. 296; *Milwaukee Journal,* August 6, 1945.

4. H. V. Kaltenborn Papers, State Historical Society of Wisconsin, Madison, Broadcast transcripts.

5. *Atomic War/Atomic Peace,* Cassette 2, side 2 (Goddard); "A Decision for Mankind," *St. Louis Post-Dispatch,* August 7, 1945; "The Beginning or the End?" *Milwaukee Journal,* August 7, 1945, p. 12.

6. "War Department Called *Times* Reporter to Explain Bomb's Intricacies to Public," *New York Times,* August 7, 1945, p. 5; *Atomic War/Atomic Peace,* Cassette 2, side 1, side 2; Donald Porter Geddes, ed., *The Atomic Age Opens* (New York, 1945), p. 31.

7. John Gunther, *Inside USA* (New York, 1947), p. 119; "Peace and Mrs. Roosevelt," *New Yorker,* August 25, 1945, pp. 16–17; "Key Man's Wife Not in on Secret," *New York Times,* August 7, 1945, p. 7; *Santa Fe New Mexican,* August 6, 1945, p. 1; "More Atom Plants Rise at Oak Ridge," *New York Times,* August 8, 1945, p. 6; "Gen. Groves, 48, Guided Job on Atomic Bomb," *New York Herald Tribune,* August 7, 1945, p. 6.

8. "Bomb's Fury Shown in Test," *Milwaukee Journal,* August 6, 1945; Edward Teller, *The Legacy of Hiroshima* (Garden City, N.Y., 1962), p. 5; *The Decades: The 1940s* (Visual Education Corp., Princeton, N.J., 1975), Cassette 3, side 1.

9. Geddes, *Atomic Age Opens,* p. 38.

10. Fitzpatrick cartoon reprinted in *The Rotarian,* October 1945, p. 9; "The Atomic Bomb," *New York Herald Tribune,* August 7, 1945, p. 22; "Man and the Atom," *Christian Century,* August 22, 1945, p. 951; "Atomic Bomb Poses Problem," *New York Times,* August 9, 1945, p. 20; Adams quoted in "The Atom Bomb," *Catholic World,* September 1945, p. 452.

11. Joseph H. Willits, "Social Adjustments to Atomic Energy," *Proceedings of*

the American Philosophical Society 90 (January 1946): 51 (address delivered November 16, 1945); "Atomic Anxieties," *New Republic,* August 20, 1945, p. 222.

12. *In Search of Light: The Broadcasts of Edward R. Murrow, 1938–1961* (New York, 1967), p. 102.

13. "The Bomb," *Time,* August 20, 1945, p. 19; "A Strange Place," ibid., p. 29; Kaltenborn broadcasts, August 17, September 6, 1945, Kaltenborn Papers.

14. [Norman Cousins], "Modern Man Is Obsolete," *Saturday Review of Literature,* August 18, 1945, p. 5.

15. Geddes, *Atomic Age Opens,* pp. 38, 40.

16. "The Atomic Age," *Life,* August 20, 1945, p. 32; "The Atomic Bomb: Its First Explosion Opens a New Era," ibid., pp. 87B–93, quoted passage, p. 87B; Hanson W. Baldwin, "The Atom Bomb and Future War," ibid., pp. 19–20; ibid., pp. 27, 28, 29, 30, 31; John Kieran, ed., *Information Please Almanac, 1948* (Garden City, N.Y., 1948), p. 330 (magazine circulation statistics).

17. George E. Eustis, Aiken, S.C., Letter to the Editor, *Life,* September 10, 1945, p. 6.

18. "Gags Away," *New Yorker,* August 18, 1945, p. 16; *Atomic Cafe* (Movie soundtrack album, Rounder Records No. 1034, Somerville, Mass., 1982).

19. "Gags Away," p. 16; *Editor and Publisher,* August 11, 1945, p. 59; *Philadelphia Inquirer,* August 26, 1945; *Time,* August 20, 1945, p. 36; *Life,* August 20, 1945, p. 93; *Milwaukee Journal,* August 8, 1945; *Stars and Stripes/Pacific,* August 9, 1945, quoted in Herbert Mitgang, ed., *Civilians Under Arms* (New York, 1959), pp. 181–182; *Chicago Tribune,* August 13, 1945.

20. Jean Toll, Corporate Archivist, General Mills, Inc., to author, April 15, 1985; William R. Foulkes, "The Atom: Death—or Life Abundant?" *Vital Speeches of the Day,* March 15, 1948, p. 345; *Time,* July 15, 1946, p. 29; *Life,* August 27, 1945, p. 32; *Editor and Publisher,* September 15, 1945, p. 16; J. C. Furnas, "A Scientist Tells Us What We May Expect," *Ladies' Home Journal,* February 1946, p. 175; "Another Atom Magazine," *Business Week,* September 1, 1945, p. 54; Joseph C. Goulden, *The Best Years, 1945–1950* (New York, 1976), p. 261; Daniel Lang, *From Hiroshima to the Moon: Chronicles of Life in the Atomic Age* (New York, 1959), p. 102.

21. Charles Wolfe, "Nuclear Country: The Atomic Bomb in Country Music," *Journal of Country Music,* 7 (January 1978); 14; *Atomic Cafe* soundtrack record.

22. Wolfe, "Nuclear Country," p. 14; Goulden, *Best Years,* p. 261; "Anatomic Bomb," *Life,* September 3, 1945, p. 53.

23. Erich Kahler, "The Reality of Utopia," *American Scholar,* 15 (Spring 1946): 176; William Fielding Ogburn, "Sociology and the Atom," *American Journal of Sociology,* 51 (January 1946): 269.

24. William Liscum Borden, *There Will Be No Time: The Revolution in Strategy* (New York, 1946), p. 222.

25. Geddes, *Atomic Age Opens,* pp. 116, 120, 121, 176; John Joseph O'Neill, *Almighty Atom: The Real Story of Atomic Energy* (New York, 1945), p. 48; Rudolph Meyer Langer, "Fast New World," *Collier's,* January 6, 1940, pp. 18–19ff.

26. Karl Davis and Harty Taylor, "When the Atom Bomb Fell," recorded December 4, 1945, *Atomic Cafe* soundtrack album, Charles Wolfe liner notes;

Chicago Tribune, August 11, 1945; David Dietz, *Atomic Energy in the Coming Era* (New York, 1945), p. 176 (Truman); "We Are Not Proud of It," *Omaha Morning World Herald*, August 8, 1945; "Our Answer to Japan," *New York Times*, August 7, 1945, p. 22; *Daily Worker*, August 8, 1945, quoted in Paul F. Boller, Jr., "Hiroshima and the American Left," *International Social Science Review* 57 (Winter 1982): 14; *Los Angeles Times*, August 8, 1945; *Philadelphia Inquirer*, August 11, 1945; "The Jap Must Choose," *Newsweek*, August 18, 1945, p. 30; Freda Kirchwey, "One World or None," *Nation*, August 18, 1945, p. 149.

27. *Atlanta Constitution*, August 8, 1945; *Philadelphia Inquirer*, August 7, 1945; *Editor and Publisher*, August 11, 1945, p. 7 (PM); *Chicago Tribune*, August 12, 1945.

28. Hanson W. Baldwin, "The Atomic Weapon," *New York Times*, August 7, 1945, p. 10.

29. Herbert E. Benton, "The Present Challenge," *Christian Leader*, September 15, 1945, p. 420.

30. J. D. Bernal, "Everybody's Atom," *Nation*, September 1, 1945, p. 201 (Churchill); "Vatican Deplores Use of Atom Bomb," *New York Times*, August 8, 1945, p. 6.

31. "Last Judgment," *Washington Post*, August 26, 1945, p. 4B. James Reston, "Dawn of the Atom Era Perplexes Washington," *New York Times*, August 12, 1945, "News of the Week in Review," p. 6; *Milwaukee Journal*, August 8, 1945, p. 12; "One Victory Not Yet Won," *New York Times*, August 12, 1945, p. 8; "Answer to Atomic Bomb," *Detroit News*, August 17, 1945; "1945 Cassandra," *New Yorker*, August 25, 1945, p. 16; Geddes, *Atomic Age Opens*, p. 174 (Zorbaugh); *Who Was Who in America* 4 (Chicago, 1968): 1047 (Zorbaugh).

32. "The Bomb and the Future," *New Republic*, August 20, 1945, p. 210; Arthur H. Compton, "Now That We've Burst the Atom," *Rotarian*, October 1945, p. 53 (*Chicago Tribune* quote).

33. United States Strategic Bombing Survey, *The Effects of Atomic Bombs on Hiroshima and Nagasaki* (Washington, D.C., 1946), p. 36; Reinhold Niebuhr, "Our Relations to Japan," *Christianity and Crisis*, September 17, 1945, p. 5; Eugene Rabinowitch, "Five Years After," *Bulletin of the Atomic Scientists*, January 1951, p. 3.

34. Elmer Davis, ABC radio newscast, December 30, 1945, Davis Papers, Library of Congress; Phelps Adams in the *New York Sun*, quoted in "The Atom Bomb," *Catholic World*, September 1945, p. 452; "The Bomb and the Future," *New Republic*, August 20, 1945, p. 212.

35. Foulkes, "The Atom: Death—or Life Abundant?" p. 345; "Adjustment," *New Yorker*, August 18, 1945, p. 17.

36. Patricia E. Munk, Pelham Manor, N.Y., to H. V. Kaltenborn, August 9, 1945, Kaltenborn Papers; Kahler, "The Reality of Utopia," p. 179; Dwight Macdonald, "Note by Editor," *Politics*, May 1946, p. 150.

37. John Hersey, *Hiroshima* (New York, 1946), p. 118.

38. "The Bomb and the Man," *Time*, December 31, 1945, pp. 15, 16; Robert Redfield, "Consequences of Atomic Energy," *Phi Delta Kappan* 27 (April 1946): 221 (report of November 1945 symposium); Sydnor H. Walker, ed., *The First One*

Hundred Days of the Atomic Age (Washington, D.C., 1945), p. 3; Hertha Pauli, "Nobel's Prizes and the Atom Bomb," *Commentary* 1 (December 1945): 26.

39. Foulkes, "The Atom: Death—or Life Abundant?" p. 345; Sumner Welles, "The Atomic Bomb and World Government," *Atlantic Monthly,* January 1946, p. 39; Kahler, "The Reality of Utopia," p. 176; A. M. Meerloo, *Aftermath of Peace: Psychological Essays* (New York, 1946), pp. 163, 164; "Atomic Valentine," *Phi Delta Kappan,* 27 (April 1946): 224.

40. "The Fortune Survey," *Fortune,* December 1945, p. 305.

41. Leonard S. Cottrell, Jr., and Sylvia Eberhart, *American Opinion on World Affairs in the Atomic Age* (Princeton, N.J., 1948), p. 15; Walker, *First One Hundred Days of the Atomic Age,* p. 36 (Gallup poll); "Unforgettable," *Time,* December 24, 1945, p. 19.

42. "The Fortune Poll," p. 206; Lillian Wald Kay, "Public Opinion and the Atom," *Journal of Educational Sociology* 22 (January 1949): 357 (September 1945 Gallup poll).

43. Cottrell and Eberhart, *American Opinion on World Affairs,* pp. 26, 109.

44. Ibid., pp. 24, 101, 103, 107 (Nearly 40 percent of the in-depth interviewees expressed no opinion on how soon other nations would develop the bomb); George H. Gallup, ed., *The Gallup Poll: Public Opinion, 1935–1971,* 3 vols. (New York, 1972), 1: 566.

45. Cottrell and Eberhart, *American Opinion on World Affairs,* pp. 19 (quote), 28, 104.

46. Ibid., pp. 28, 78, 79, 88.

47. Kay, "Public Opinion and the Atom," pp. 357–58; *Gallup Poll* 1:680.

48. "Unforgettable," *Time,* December 24, 1945, p. 19; Cottrell and Eberhart, *American Opinion on World Affairs,* p. 29 fn. 13.

49. Wolfe, "Nuclear Country," pp. 7, 9, 10–11, 12–13.

50. Ibid., p. 11.

2. The Summons to Action

1. "What Others Say," *NEA Journal,* March 1946, p. 117.

2. Elmer Davis, ABC radio newscast, December 23, 1945, Davis Papers, Library of Congress.

3. William L. Laurence, *Dawn Over Zero: The Story of the Atomic Bomb* (New York, 1946), p. 270; [Norman Cousins], "Modern Man is Obsolete," *Saturday Review of Literature,* August 18, 1945, p. 5; Dorothy Thompson, "Atomic Science and World Organization," *Ladies' Home Journal,* October 1945, p. 6.

4. Merrill E. Bush, "World Organization or Atomic Destruction?" *School and Society* 64 (November 23, 1946): 355; Robert M. Hutchins, "The Atomic Bomb Versus Civilization," *NEA Journal,* March 1946, p. 114.

5. David E. Lilienthal, "Science and Man's Fate," *Nation,* July 13, 1946, pp. 40–41.

6. Harold C. Urey, "The Atom and Humanity," *Science,* 102 (November 2, 1945): 437, 438.

7. "Exploring the Unknown," Mutual radio broadcast, June 30, 1946, script

in Papers of the Atomic Scientists of Chicago, Regenstein Library, University of Chicago, box 12, folder 2; Struthers Burt, "A Man Tells Us What We Must Do," *Ladies' Home Journal,* February 1946, p. 173; C. Dale Fuller, "America's Choice: Atomic War or Atomic Peace," April 13, 1946, University of Denver radio series broadcast over seven midwestern stations, ibid., box 19, folder 14.

8. Rob Paarlberg, "Forgetting About the Unthinkable," *Foreign Policy* 10 (Spring 1973): 132.

9. Raymond Gram Swing, *"Good Evening!": A Professional Memoir* (New York, 1964), p. 242; idem., *In the Name of Sanity* (collection of radio newscasts, New York, 1946), p. 1.

10. Joseph H. Willits, "Social Adjustments to Atomic Energy," *Proceedings of the American Philosophical Society* 90 (January 1946): 49 (address delivered November 16, 1945); Max Lerner, "Ms. to be Put in a Bottle," *PM* (November 14, 1945), reprinted in Lerner, *Actions and Passions: Notes on the Multiple Revolution of Our Time* (New York, 1949), p. 260.

11. C. W. Boyer, "I Met Dr. Einstein," *The Sunday School Herald* (Nappanee, Ind.), January 25, 1948, pp. 5–6; C. W. Boyer to author, personal reminiscence; "Educational," *New Yorker,* January 3, 1948, pp. 18–19.

12. Swing, *In the Name of Sanity,* p. 104.

13. Harold C. Urey, "How Does It All Add Up?" in Dexter Masters and Katharine Way, eds., *One World or None: A Report to the Public on the Full Meaning of the Atomic Bomb* (New York, 1946), pp. 57, 58.

3. Atomic-Bomb Nightmares and World-Government Dreams

1. Raymond Gram Swing, *"Good Evening!": A Professional Memoir* (New York, 1964), pp. 1–16; Stanley J. Kunitz, ed., *Twentieth Century Authors: First Supplement* (New York, 1955), pp. 974–75.

2. Swing, *"Good Evening!"* pp. 242, 243, 247–49; idem., *In the Name of Sanity* (New York, 1946), pp. vii, viii, 20; Albert Einstein as told to Raymond Gram Swing, "Einstein on the Atomic Bomb," *Atlantic Monthly,* November 1945, pp. 43–45; Raymond Gram Swing, ABC radio newscasts, August 24, 1945; January 25, March 22, April 26, 1946, Swing Papers, Library of Congress.

3. Max Lerner, to author, March 11, 1985; idem., "World State and World Society," *PM,* August 20, 1945, reprinted in Lerner, *Actions and Passions: Notes on the Multiple Revolution of Our Time* (New York, 1949), p. 257; J. Robert Oppenheimer, "The New Weapon: The Turn of the Screw," in Dexter Masters and Katharine Way, eds., *One World or None: A Report to the Public on the Full Meaning of the Atomic Bomb* (New York, 1946), p. 22; G. Bromley Oxnam Papers, Library of Congress, box 14; Anne O'Hare McCormick, "The Promethean Role of the United States," *New York Times,* August 8, 1945, p. 22; E. B. White, *The Wild Flag: Editorials From the New Yorker on Federal World Government and Other Matters* (New York, 1946), p. 136 (quoting Dorothy Thompson).

4. Harrison Brown, "The World Government Movement in the United States," *Bulletin of the Atomic Scientists,* June 1947, p. 156; James Marshall, "Old Adam and the Atom," *American Scholar,* 15 (Winter 1945–1946): pp. 13, 21, 23. For the view that America's atomic monopoloy created a propitious moment for the

imposition of world government see Cord Meyer, *Facing Reality: From World Federalism to the CIA* (New York, 1980), p. 44.

5. Meyer, *Facing Reality*, p. 44; Charles DeBenedetti, *The Peace Reform in American History* (Bloomington, Ind., 1980), p. 149; "Perilous Fusion," *Time*, October 29, 1945, p. 31; Sydnor H. Walker, ed., *The First One Hundred Days of the Atomic Age* (Washington, D.C., 1945), p. 43.

6. Walter Lippmann, "International Control of Atomic Energy," in Masters and Way, *One World or None*, p. 75; White, *Wild Flag*, pp. x, 109; "Editorial," *Antioch Review* 5 (Winter 1945–1946): 462.

7. "The Ultimate Weapon," *Commonweal*, November 23, 1945, p. 131.

8. Stephen King-Hall, "World Government or World Destruction?" *Reader's Digest*, November 1945, pp. 14, 16; Freda Kirchwey, "One World or None," *Nation*, August 18, 1945, p. 150; *New York Herald Tribune*, October 30, 1945, p. 16.

9. Harold C. Urey, "The Atom and Humanity," address of October 21, 1945, reprinted in *Science* 102 (November 2, 1945): 439; Alice Kimball Smith, *A Peril and a Hope: The Scientists' Movement in America, 1945–47*, rev. ed., (Cambridge, Mass., 1970), pp. 86–87.

10. Leo Szilard, "The Physicist Invades Politics," *Saturday Review of Literature*, May 3, 1947, pp. 8, 31, 32, 34.

11. Einstein as told to Swing, "Einstein on the Atomic Bomb," pp. 43, 44; Albert Einstein, "The Way Out," in Masters and Way, *One World or None*, pp. 76, 77; idem., "The Real Problem is in the Hearts of Men," *New York Times Magazine*, June 23, 1946, p. 7.

12. Dorothy Thompson, "Atomic Science and World Organization," *Ladies' Home Journal*, October 1945, p. 6; Walker, *First One Hundred Days of the Atomic Age*, pp. 39–40 (Fosdick); Meyer, *Facing Reality*, p. 40; White, *Wild Flag*, p. 109 (originally published in "Notes and Comments," *New Yorker*, August 18, 1945).

13. Leonard S. Cottrell, Jr., and Sylvia Eberhart, *American Opinion on World Affairs* (Princeton, N.J., 1948), pp. 40–41; DeBenedetti, *Peace Reform in American History*, p. 150.

14. Michael R. Harris, "Robert Maynard Hutchins," in *Five Counter-revolutionists in Higher Education* (Corvallis, Ore., 1970), pp. 133–62.

15. "The Third Year of the Atomic Age: What Should We Do Now?" *Chicago Roundtable* radio broadcast, August 24, 1947, in Harold F. Harding, ed., *The Age of Danger: Major Speeches on American Problems* (New York, 1952), p. 35; "Atomic Force: Its Meaning for Mankind," *Chicago Roundtable*, August 12, 1945, ibid., p. 23; Robert M. Hutchins, *The Atom Bomb and Education* (London, 1947), p. 5; Walker, *First One Hundred Days of the Atomic Age*, p. 14; "And What of the Future? A Symposium of Opinion," *Reader's Digest*, October 1945, p. 11.

16. See, e.g., John Gunther, *Inside USA* (New York, 1947), p. 378. Sociologist Edward Shils, who knew Hutchins well in these years, vigorously rejects the suggestion that the desire to counteract Chicago's close identification with the atomic bomb influenced Hutchins's postwar activities. Shils to author, January 30, 1985.

17. *Who's Who in America, 1982–83* (Chicago, 1982) 1: 689.

18. "Modern Man Is Obsolete," *Saturday Review of Literature,* August 18, 1945, p. 8; idem., *Modern Man Is Obsolete* (New York, 1945), pp. 42, 43.

19. *New York Times,* November 4, 1945, p. 4 (John Davenport review, quoting Roberts); *New Yorker,* November 3, 1945, p. 106; review by D. W. Robinson, *Social Studies,* February 1946, p. 91; review by Hans Bethe, *Chemical and Engineering News,* March 25, 1946, p. 849.

20. *New York Times,* November 4, 1945, p. 4; "The Rooster," *Time,* October 29, 1945, p. 30; Ernest K. Lindley, "Our Gropings on the Atom," *Newsweek,* November 19, 1945, p. 43; David Lawrence, "The Right to Kill," *U.S. News and World Report,* October 5, 1945, p. 34; John W. Campbell, Jr., *The Atomic Story* (New York, 1947), p. 291.

21. David E. Lilienthal, *Atomic Energy Years* (New York, 1964), p. 261 (November 29, 1947, diary entry); Elmer Davis, "No World, If Necessary," *Saturday Review of Literature,* March 30, 1946, pp. 7ff. (quoted passage, p. 50).

22. Herbert W. Briggs, "World Government and the Control of Atomic Energy," *Annals of the American Academy of Political and Social Science,* 249 (January 1947): 42–53, quoted passages, pp. 42, 45, 46.

23. Robert Warshow, "Melancholy to the End," *Partisan Review* 14 (January–February 1947), reprinted as "E. B. White and the *New Yorker"* in Warshow, *The Immediate Experience: Movies, Comics, Theatre and Other Aspects of Popular Culture* (New York, 1974), pp. 105, 107, 108.

24. Jacob Viner, "The Implications of the Atomic Bomb for International Relations," *Proceedings of the American Philosophical Society* 90 (January 1946): 55, 57; Joseph H. Willits, "Social Adjustment to Atomic Energy," ibid., pp. 48, 49.

25. Nathaniel Peffer, "Politics is Peace," *American Scholar* 15 (Spring 1946): 160–66, quoted passages pp. 160, 161, 162; Sumner Welles, "The Atomic Bomb and World Government," *Atlantic Monthly,* January 1946, pp. 39–42, quoted passages, p. 40. See also, idem., "One Practical Chance—the UNO," *American Scholar* 15 (Spring 1946): 127–29.

26. "Changing the World," *United Evangelical Action,* October 15, 1945, p. 12; Justin Wroe Nixon, "Amos and the Bomb," *Christian Century,* December 12, 1945, p. 1383; Federal Council of the Churches of Christ in America, Commission on the Relation of the Church to the War in the Light of Christian Faith, *Atomic Warfare and the Christian Faith* (New York, [1946]), p. 15.

27. Richard M. Fagley, "The Atomic Bomb and the Crisis of Man," *Christianity and Crisis,* October 1, 1945, p. 5; Reinhold Niebuhr, "The Atomic Issue," ibid., pp. 5–7, quoted passages, p. 6.

28. DeBenedetti, *Peace Reform in American History,* p. 151.

29. Reinhold Niebuhr, "The Illusion of World Government," *Foreign Affairs* 27 (April, 1949): 379, 380, 382, 385, 388.

30. Swing, *"Good Evening!"* pp. 243–44; Michael R. Harris, "Hutchins, Robert Maynard," in John A. Garraty, ed., *Encyclopedia of American Biography* (New York, 1974), pp. 558–59.

31.. Meyer, *Facing Reality,* pp. 56, 59.

32. Norman Cousins, *In Place of Folly* (New York, Washington Square Press paperback ed., 1962), pp. 147–48.

4. The Political Agenda of the Scientists' Movement

1. Alice Kimball Smith, *A Peril and a Hope: The Scientists' Movement in America, 1945–47,* rev. ed., (Cambridge, Mass., 1971), p. 88; Raymond Gram Swing, *In the Name of Sanity* (New York, 1946), p. 26.

2. Dexter Masters and Katharine Way, eds., *One World or None: A Report to the Public on the Full Meaning of the Atomic Bomb* (New York, 1946), pp. ix–x; Smith, *Peril and Hope,* pp. 58, 371–83.

3. Edward Shils, "Freedom and Influence: Observations on the Scientists' Movement in the United States," *Bulletin of the Atomic Scientists* (hereafter: *BAS*), January 1957, p. 13; Peter J. Kuznick, "Beyond the Laboratory: Scientists as Political Activists in 1930s America" (Ph.D. dissertation, Rutgers University, 1984).

4. Harold C. Urey, "I'm a Frightened Man," *Collier's,* January 5, 1946, p. 19; David L. Hill, Eugene Rabinowitch, and John A. Simpson, "The Atomic Scientists Speak Up," *Life,* October 29, 1945, p. 45.

5. *Chemical and Engineering News,* August 10, 1946, p. 2112.

6. Christian Gauss, "Is Einstein Right?" *American Scholar* 15 (Autumn 1946): 475, 476; author interview with David R. Inglis, November 7, 1982; James Franck, "The Social Task of the Scientist," *BAS,* March 1947, p. 70.

7. Smith, *Peril and Hope,* pp. 114, 203–11.

8. Ibid., pp. 128–31; "Scientists' Warning," *Time,* October 29, 1945, p. 31 (quoted passage).

9. Smith, *Peril and Hope,* pp. 131–200, 269.

10. Ibid., pp. 271–75, 301–27, quoted phrase, p. 325; Gregg Herken, *The Winning Weapon: The Atomic Bomb in the Cold War, 1945–1950* (New York, 1980), p. 148.

11. Sydnor H. Walker, ed., *The First One Hundred Days of the Atomic Age* (Washington, D.C., 1945), p. 44.

12. *Report on the International Control of Atomic Energy* (Washington, D.C., Department of State, March 16, 1946); Norman Cousins and Thomas K. Finletter, "A Beginning for Sanity," *Saturday Review of Literature,* June 15, 1946, pp. 5–9, 38–40; Joseph I. Lieberman, *The Scorpion and the Tarantula* (Boston, 1970), pp. 254–55.

13. Lieberman, *Scorpion and Tarantula,* p. 254; Smith, *Peril and Hope,* p. 332.

14. Author interview with David R. Inglis, November 7, 1982; Smith, *Peril and Hope,* p. 335; Edward Teller, "The State Department Report—A Ray of Hope," *BAS,* April 1, 1946, p. 10; "H. C. Urey on State Department Report," ibid., p. 13.

15. "Baruch's Speech at Opening Session of U.N. Atomic Energy Commission," *New York Times,* June 15, 1946, p. 4.

16. Lieberman, *Scorpion and Tarantula,* pp. 270, 303–4, 305; *Saturday Review of Literature,* June 15, 1946, p. 5 (Fitzpatrick cartoon).

17. Daniel Yergin, *Shattered Peace: The Origins of the Cold War and the National Security State* (Boston, 1977), pp. 238–39; Lloyd Gardner, *Architects of Illusion* (Chicago, 1972), p. 193; I. F. Stone, "Atomic Pie in the Sky," *Nation,* April 6, 1946, pp. 390–91; Lieberman, *Scorpion and Tarantula,* pp. 256–57.

18. Stone, "Atomic Pie in the Sky," p. 391, Interview with I. F. Stone, April 27, 1984 (interview conducted for author by Andrew Patner).

19. *Compete Poems of Robert Frost, 1949* (New York, 1949), p. 569.

20. "The Politics of the Atom," *New Republic,* April 3, 1950, pp. 5–11; *New York Times,* June 20, 1946, p. 1; Herken, *Winning Weapon,* pp. 159–62; Lieberman, *Scorpion and Tarantula,* pp. 272, 282–88, 305–10; Jordan A. Schwartz, *The Speculator: Bernard M. Baruch in Washington, 1917–1965* (Chapel Hill, N.C., 1981).

21. "Atom Control: The Door Is Still Open," *Business Weeek,* July 6, 1946, p. 112; "Man vs. the Atom—Year I," ibid., p. 65; "Bomb Control: The Two Plans," *New York Times* editorial, June 21, 1946, p. 22.

22. Leonard S. Cottrell, Jr. and Sylvia Eberhart, *American Opinion on World Affairs* (Princeton, N.J., 1948), pp. 32, 113; Walker, *First One Hundred Days of the Atomic Age,* p. 35 (1945 Gallup poll).

23. Cottrell and Eberhart, *American Opinion on World Affairs,* pp. 33–35.

24. Ibid., pp. 20, 56–57, 58, 59.

5. *"To the Village Square"*

1. Albert Einstein, "The Real Problem Is in the Hearts of Men," *New York Times Magazine,* June 23, 1946, p. 44.

2. Alice Kimball Smith, *A Peril and a Hope: The Scientists' Movement in America, 1945–47,* rev. ed. (Cambridge, Mass., 1970), p. 288.

3. *New Republic,* February 11, 1946, p. 179 (Fitzpatrick cartoon); Robert Redfield, "Consequences of Atomic Energy," *Phi Delta Kappan* 27 (April 1946): 223; Smith, *Peril and Hope,* p. 358; *Chicago Daily Tribune,* August 11, 1945.

4. Author interview with Bernard Feld, April 27, 1984; Max Lerner, "Ms. to be Put in a Bottle," *PM,* November 14, 1945, reprinted in Lerner, *Actions and Passions: Notes on the Multiple Revolution of Our Time* (New York, 1949), p. 260; Lewis Mumford, "Gentlemen: You Are Mad!" *Saturday Review of Literature,* March 2, 1946, p. 5; Raymond Gram Swing, *In the Name of Sanity* (ABC radio newscast, New York, 1946), p. 47; Samuel K. Allison, "The State of Physics: or The Perils of Being Important," *Bulletin of the Atomic Scientists* (Hereafter *BAS*), January 1950, p. 3.

5. Arthur H. Compton, "The Atomic Crusade and Its Social Significance," *Annals of the American Academy of Political and Social Science* 249 (January 1947) 9, 10, 11.

6. Leo Szilard, "The Physicist Invades Politics," *Saturday Review of Literature,* May 3, 1947, p. 7.

7. Author interview with Ralph Lapp, December 28, 1982; Sidney Hook, "The Scientist in Politics," *New York Times Magazine,* April 9, 1950, p. 27; "Atom Held Peace Agent," *New York Times,* August 9, 1945, p. 8.

8. *Atomic Information,* March 20, 1947, pp. 9–10; Smith, *Peril and Hope,* pp. 227–28, 293–98.

9. Smith, *Peril and Hope,* pp. 104, 282, 295–97; Volta Torrey (managing editor, *Popular Science*), "Magazines and Nuclear-Energy Education," *Journal of Educational Sociology* 22 (January 1949): 325.

10. "How to Live with the Atom," *New York Times Magazine*, June 9, 1946, pp. 8–9; "To Prevent the Utter Destruction of Urban Civilization," *American City*, February 1946, p. 5; "Psychologists Advise on Atomic Bomb Peril," *School and Society*, June 8, 1946, p. 405; Smith, *Peril and Hope*, p. 263; "Hold That Monster," *Time*, November 19, 1945, p. 20.

11. Papers of the Atomic Scientists of Chicago (hereafter ASC Papers), Regenstein Library, University of Chicago. See especially boxes 2, 3, 4, 7, 10, 12, and 19. Author interview with Alice Kimball Smith, April 27, 1984.

12. Smith, *Peril and Hope*, pp. 284–85.

13. "Hyman H. Goldsmith," *BAS*, August-September 1949, p. 206; Smith, *Peril and Hope*, p. 22.

6. The Uses of Fear

1. "Exploring the Unknown," radio script, Papers of the Atomic Scientists of Chicago (hereafter ASC Papers), Regenstein Library, University of Chicago, box 12, folder 2.

2. Robert DeVore, "What the Atomic Bomb Really Did," *Collier's*, March 2, 1946, pp. 19ff; "Outlook for 1946—Second Year of Atomic Age May Be Complacent but Bomb Race Looms," *Wall Street Journal*, December 27, 1945, pp. 1, 6; "Atom Bomb Force in Big City Argued," *New York Times*, February 16, 1946, p. 15.

3. John J. O'Neill, "The Blasts That Shook the World," *Reader's Digest*, October 1945, p. 8; Francis Vivian Drake, "Let's Be Realistic About the Atom Bomb," *Reader's Digest*, December 1945, pp. 109–10.

4. Robert Littell, "What the Atomic Bomb Would Do to *Us*," *Reader's Digest*, May 1946, p. 125; Alexander P. de Seversky, "Atomic Bomb Hysteria," *Reader's Digest*, February 1946, p. 121.

5. David B. Parker, "Mist of Death Over New York," *Reader's Digest*, April 1947, pp. 7–10, quoted passages, p. 9.

6. Francis Vivian Drake to J. Robert Oppenheimer, May 16, 1947, Oppenheimer Papers, Library of Congress, box 60.

7. "The 36-Hour War," *Life*, November 19, 1945, pp. 22ff., quoted passages pp. 29, 34, 35.

8. Harold C. Urey as told to Michael Amrine, "I'm a Frightened Man," *Collier's*, January 5, 1946, p. 18; W. A. Higinbotham, "There Is No Defense Against Atomic Bombs," *New York Times Magazine*, November 3, 1946, pp. 11, 49.

9. *Atomic Cafe* soundtrack album (Rounder Records No. 1034); Parker, "Mist of Death Over New York," p. 10.

10. "The War That Must Not Come," WMAQ (Chicago) radio broadcast, April 16, 1946, script, ASC Papers, box 4, folder 9; John Skinner to Seymour Katcoff, May 7, 1946, ibid., box 19, folder 14.

11. Mrs. Ogden Reid, quoted in *New York Herald Tribune*, October 20, 1945, p. 16; "Morals and the Bomb," *Commonweal*, October 28, 1949, p. 60; Franz Alexander, "Mental Hygiene in the Atomic Age," *Mental Hygiene* 30 (October 1946): 532.

12. [Norman Cousins], "Modern Man Is Obsolete," *Saturday Review of Literature,* August 18, 1945, pp. 5, 6; Robert M. Hutchins, *Chicago Roundtable* radio broadcast, August 12, 1945, quoted in Sydnor H. Walker, ed., *The First One Hundred Days of the Atomic Age* (Washington, D.C., 1945), p. 32.

13. Arthur H. Compton, "Now That We've Burst the Atom," *Rotarian,* October 1945, pp. 8, 9, 52, 53; Philip Morrison, "Beyond Imagination," *New Republic,* February 11, 1946, p. 180; Eugene Rabinowitch, "Five Years After," *Bulletin of the Atomic Scientists,* January 1951, p. 3; Albert Einstein as told to Raymond Gram Swing, "Einstein on the Atomic Bomb," *Atlantic Monthly,* November 1945, p. 45.

14. Bernard Iddings Bell to Dr. Katherine Chamberlain, July 17, 1946, ASC Papers, box 4, folder 3; M. C. Otto, "With All Our Learning," *Antioch Review* 5 (December 1945): 469; Daniel Lang, "A Reporter at Large: 'That's Four Times 10^{-4} Ergs, Old Man,'" *New Yorker,* November 16, 1945, p. 98.

15. John H. Skinner to "John," undated memo, ASC Papers, box 3, folder 12; Skinner to Howdy Myers, NBC (Chicago), October 21, 1946, ibid., box 19, folder 14; "The Meaning of the Atomic Bomb to People Who Work for Wages," mimeographed draft, ibid., box 3, folder 3; Beth Olds to Reuben Gustavson, March 27, 1946, ibid.; Beth Olds to Louis Ridenour, May 29, 1946, ibid., box 3, folder 12.

16. Cyril Smith, interview with author, April 27, 1984.

17. Niels Bohr, "A Challenge to Civilization," *Science* 102 (October 12, 1945): 363, 364.

18. J. Robert Oppenheimer, "Atomic Weapons," *Proceedings of the American Philosophical Society* 90 (January 1946) 9.

19. Reinhold Niebuhr, "The Atomic Issue," *Christianity and Crisis,* October 15, 1945, p. 7; Stefan T. Possony, "The Atomic Bomb," *Review of Politics* 8 (April 1946): 147; idem., "The Lessons of the First Atomic Year," *Review of Politics* 9 (April 1947): 131.

20. G. A. Borgese, "Of Atomic Fear and Two 'Utopias,'" *Common Cause,* September 1947, p. 87; Harry Emerson Fosdick, *On Being Fit to Live With: Sermons on Postwar Christianity* (New York, 1946), p. 8; Eduard C. Lindeman, "Morality for the Atomic Age," *Forum,* November 1945, p. 231; "Not Peace but a Sword," *Fortune,* January 1946, p. 97; Elbert D. Thomas, "Atomic Bombs in International Society," *American Journal of International Law* 39 (October 1945): 739.

21. F. R. Shonka, "Conference of Religious Leaders and Scientists Sponsored by the Atomic Scientists of Chicago, Inc., February 7–9, 1946," p. 39, typescript, ASC Papers, box 3, folder 15; Lewis Mumford, "Gentlemen: You Are Mad!" *Saturday Review of Literature,* March 2, 1946, p. 5; Truman P. Kohman, "One Year in the Atomic Age," typescript, ASC Papers, box 12, folder 2; *Newsweek,* December 17, 1945, p. 37; Erich Kahler, "The Reality of Utopia," *American Scholar* 15 (Spring 1946): 179.

22. David E. Lilienthal, "Atomic Energy is Your Business," *BAS,* November 1947, p. 335; John W. Campbell, Jr., *The Atomic Story* (New York, 1947), p. 250.

23. Oppenheimer to William A. Higinbotham, (March 1946), quoted in Alice Kimball Smith, *A Peril and a Hope: The Scientists' Movement in America, 1945–47,* rev. ed. (Cambridge, Mass., 1971), p. 350; Robert M. Hutchins, "The Atomic

Bomb Versus Civilization," *National Education Association Journal*, March 1946, p. 115.

24. "When H. G. Wells Split the Atom: A 1914 Preview of 1945," *Nation*, August 18, 1945, pp. 154–56, quoted passages, p. 154.

7. *Representative Text:* One World or None

1. Freda Kirchwey, "One World or None," *Nation*, August 18, 1945, p. 149; *In Search of Light: The Broadcasts of Edward R. Murrow, 1938–1961* (New York, 1967), p. 102.

2. Lou Frankel, "In One Ear," *Nation*, March 22, 1947, p. 334; "World War III Preview," *Time*, March 25, 1946, p. 90; *Weekly Book Review*, March 17, 1946, p. 1; "A-Bomb Warning," *Business Week*, March 16, 1946, p. 20; Leigh Maxwell and Hyman Ruchlis, *Atomics for the Millions* (New York, 1947), pp. 268–69.

3. Edward U. Condon, "The New Technique of Private War," in Dexter Masters and Katharine Way, eds., *One World or None: A Report to the Public on the Full Meaning of the Atomic Bomb* (New York, 1946), p. 40; Arthur H. Compton, "Introduction," ibid., p. v; Louis Ridenour, "There Is No Defense," in ibid., pp. 33–38.

4. Harlow Shapley, "It's an Old Story with the Stars," in ibid., p. 10; Frederick Seitz and Hans Bethe, "How Close Is the Danger?" in ibid., p. 46; Irving Langmuir, "An Atomic Arms Race and Its Alternatives," in ibid., p. 48; H. H. Arnold, "Air Force in the Atomic Age," in ibid., pp. 26–32.

5. Philip Morrison, "Beyond Imagination," *New Republic*, February 11, 1946, pp. 177–80, quoted passages, pp. 178, 179, 180; Raymond Gram Swing, *In the Name of Sanity* (ABC radio newscasts, New York, 1946), p. 90; "Black Lesson of the Atom Bomb: Its Awful Fury Kills Even Hope," *Newsweek*, December 17, 1945, p. 37.

6. Philip Morrison, "If the Bomb Gets out of Hand," in Masters and Way, *One World or None*, pp. 1–6, quoted passage, p. 3.

7. Ibid., pp. 5, 6.

8. Federation of American (Atomic) Scientists (hereafter FAS), "Survival Is at Stake," ibid., pp. 78–79; Compton, "Introduction," ibid., p. v; J. Robert Oppenheimer, "The New Weapon: The Turn of the Screw," ibid., p. 22.

9. Walter Lippmann, "International Control of Atomic Energy," ibid., pp. 66–75, quoted passages, p. 74; Albert Einstein, "The Way Out," ibid., pp. 76–77.

10. Leo Szilard, "Can We Avert an Arms Race by an Inspection System?" ibid., pp. 61–65, quoted passages, pp. 62, 63; Alice Kimball Smith, *A Peril and a Hope: The Scientists' Movement in America, 1945–47*, rev. ed. (Cambridge, Mass., 1971), p. 283.

11. FAS, "Survival Is at Stake," in Masters and Way, *One World or None*, pp. 78–79 (italics added); Urey, "How Does It All Add Up?" ibid., p. 56.

12. John Gunther, *Inside USA* (New York, 1947), p. 544 (*New York Daily News* letter quoted); "The Rooster," *Time*, October 29, 1945, p. 30 (*Chicago Tribune* quoted).

13. Elmer Davis, "No World, If Necessary," *Saturday Review of Literature*, March 30, 1946, pp. 7, 8, 51.

8. The Mixed Message of Bikini

1. "The Broken Mirror," *Time,* July 15, 1946, pp. 28–29; "Bikini," *New Yorker,* March 9, 1946, reprinted in E. B. White, *The Wild Flag: Editorials From the* New Yorker *on Federal World Government and Other Matters* (New York, 1946), p. 161; Ralph E. Lapp, *Must We Hide?* (Cambridge, Mass., 1949), p. 33.

2. White, *Wild Flag,* p. 161.

3. "The Broken Mirror," *Time,* July 15, 1946, pp. 28–29; Mrs. Marjorie E. Harvey, Vancouver, to H. V. Kaltenborn, April 2, 1946, Kaltenborn Papers, State Historical Society of Wisconsin, Madison.

4. Raymond Gram Swing, ABC radio newscasts, June 28, 1946, Swing Papers, Library of Congress, box 30.

5. John Crosby, "Bikini: The Build-Up," *New York Times,* July 2, 1946, reprinted in Crosby, *Out of the Blue: A Book About Radio and Television* (New York, 1952), quoted passages, p. 2.

6. Leonard S. Cottrell, Jr. and Sylvia Eberhart, *American Opinion on World Affairs in the Atomic Age* (Princeton, N.J., 1948), p. 16; Crosby, "Bikini: The Build-Up," in *Out of the Blue,* pp. 4, 5; idem., "Bikini: The Let-Down," *New York Times,* July 3, 1946, reprinted in Crosby, *Out of the Blue,* p. 7; Lloyd J. Graybar and Ruth Flint Graybar, "America Faces the Atomic Age: 1946," *Air Force Review,* January-February, 1984, p. 68; Norman Cousins, "The Standardization of Catastrophe," *Saturday Review,* August 10, 1946, p. 17.

7. Graybar and Graybar, "American Faces the Atomic Age," p. 72; Joseph C. Goulden, *The Best Years, 1945–50* (New York, 1976), p. 264; Crosby, "Bikini: The Let-Down," in *Out of the Blue,* p. 8; "Bomb Ridiculed in Argentina," *New York Times,* July 2, 1946, p. 19.

8. Goulden, *Best Years,* p. 264; Elmer Davis, ABC radio newscast, July 1, 1946, Davis Papers, Library of Congress, box 14; "The Broken Mirror," *Time,* July 15, 1946, pp. 28, 29; David Bradley, *No Place to Hide* (Boston, 1948), p. 167; Alice Kimball Smith, *A Peril and a Hope: The Scientists' Movement in America, 1945–47,* rev. ed. (Cambridge, Mass., 1971), p. 339; "Angel Food," *Time,* November 18, 1946, p. 31.

9. Richard Gerstell, Ph.D., *How to Survive an Atomic Bomb* (Washington, D.C., 1950), p. 6.

10. William L. Laurence, "Bikini 'Dud' Decried for Lifting Fears," *New York Times,* August 4, 1946, p. 3.

11. Cousins, "Standardization of Catastrophe," p. 18; W. A. Higinbotham, "There Is No Defense Against Atomic Bomb," *New York Times Magazine,* November 3, 1946, p. 48; Anne O'Hare McCormick, "The Human Atom at Operation Crossroads," *New York Times,* July 1, 1946, p. 30.

12. "Bikini Breath of Death," *Science News Letter,* August 10, 1946, p. 84.

13. Edward P. Morgan, "The A-Bomb's Invisible Offspring," *Collier's,* August 9, 1947, pp. 18–19, 61; Stefan T. Possony, "The Lessons of the First Atomic Year," *Review of Politics* 9 (April 1947): 132; David B. Parker, "Mist of Death Over New York," *Reader's Digest,* April 1947, pp. 7–10.

14. "What Science Learned at Bikini," *Life,* August 11, 1947, pp. 78, 80.

15. Ibid., pp. 77–78, 83–84, quoted passage, p. 83; Stafford L. Warren,

"Conclusions: Tests Proved Irresistible Spread of Radioactivity," ibid., pp. 86, 88, condensed in "A Report on Bikini a Year Later," *Reader's Digest,* November 1947; "1946 Warning on Fallout Danger in Bomb Tests Disclosed in Report," *New York Times,* May 25, 1983.

16. E. B. White, "Journal of a Contaminated Man," *New Yorker,* December 4, 1948, pp. 171–77, quoted passage, p. 171; "Books," *Bulletin of the Atomic Scientists,* April 1949, p. 128 (review by Austin M. Brues); author interview with David Bradley, May 5, 1984.

17. Ibid.; Norman Cousins, "Bikini's Real Story," *Saturday Review of Literature,* Dec. 11, 1948, p. 15.

18. Bradley, *No Place to Hide,* p. 147; Alexander Hammond, review of reissue of *No Place to Hide,* in *Bulletin of the Atomic Scientists,* November 1983, p. 37.

19. Bradley, *No Place to Hide,* p. 163.

20. Ibid., pp. 165–66.

9. The Scientists' Movement in Eclipse

1. Eugene Rabinowitch, "Five Years After," *Bulletin of the Atomic Scientists* (hereafter *BAS*) January 1951, pp. 3–5, 12.

2. Alice Kimball Smith, *A Peril and a Hope: The Scientists' Movement in America, 1945–47,* rev. ed. (Cambridge, Mass., 1971), pp. 228, 310; "Topics of the Times," *New York Times,* October 21, 1945, section E, p. 8, quoted in ibid., p. 176.

3. Bernard Brodie, "The Atomic Dilemma," *Annals of the American Academy of Political and Social Science* 249 (January 1947): 41; Frederick S. Dunn, "The Common Problem," in Bernard Brodie, ed., *The Absolute Weapon: Atomic Power and World Order* (New York, 1946), p. 4; William L. Borden, *There Will Be No Time: The Revolution in Strategy* (New York, 1946), p. 155.

4. "The Smiling Scientists," *Commonweal,* November 29, 1946, pp. 157–58 (quoted passages, p. 158); Reinhold Niebuhr, "The Atomic Issue," *Christianity and Crisis,* October 15, 1945, p. 6.

5. P. W. Bridgman, "Scientists and Social Responsibility," *BAS,* February 1948, pp. 69–72, quoted passages, pp. 70, 71.

6. James R. Newman and Byron S. Miller, *The Control of Atomic Energy* (New York, 1948), pp. 5–6, quoted in Smith, *Peril and Hope,* p. 270; Max Lerner, "Ms. to be Put in a Bottle," *PM,* November 14, 1945, reprinted in Lerner, *Actions and Passions: Notes on the Multiple Revolution of Our Time* (New York, 1949), p. 260; "Editorial," *Antioch Review* 5 (Winter 1945–1946): 459.

7. Smith, *Peril and Hope,* pp. 265, 270, 282, 349, 350 (Oppenheimer to William A. Higinbotham, [March 1947] quoted); David E. Lilienthal, *The Atomic Energy Years* (New York, 1964), p. 69 (diary entry, July 24, 1946, on Oppenheimer's mood).

8. Robert Jungk, *Brighter than a Thousand Suns: A Personal History of the Atomic Scientists* (New York, 1958), p. 253; Michael Amrine to J. Robert Oppenheimer (May 1947), Oppenheimer Papers, Library of Congress, box 15.

9. Leo Szilard, "The Physicist Invades Politics," *Saturday Review of Literature,* May 3, 1947, pp. 33, 34.

10. J. Robert Oppenheimer to Niels Bohr, September 3, 1947, Oppenheimer

Papers, box 21; John A. Simpson, "The Scientists as Public Educators: A Two-Year Summary," *BAS,* September 1947, p. 246.

11. Lilienthal, *Atomic Energy Years,* p. 297 (diary entry, February 23, 1948).

12. David E. Lilienthal, "Democracy and the Atom," *NEA Journal,* February 1948, p. 80 (Einstein quoted); Lewis Mumford, "Kindling for a Global Gehenna," *Saturday Review of Literature,* June 26, 1948, p. 29.

13. Ralph E. Lapp, *Must We Hide?* (Cambridge, Mass., 1949), p. 3.

14. Edward L. Long, Jr., *The Christian Response to the Atomic Crisis* (Philadelphia, 1950), pp. 14, 16, 38, 97.

15. Sidney Hook, "The Scientist in Politics," *New York Times Magazine,* April 9, 1950, pp. 10, 25–30.

16. Clifford Grobstein and A. H. Shapley, "The Federation of American Scientists," *BAS,* January 1951, pp. 23–25, quoted passages, p. 23; Charles DeBenedetti, *The Peace Reform in American History* (Bloomington, Ind., 1980), p. 147.

17. J. Robert Oppenheimer, "Encouragement of Science," *BAS,* January 1951, p. 7; Samuel K. Allison, "The State of Physics, or The Perils of Being Important," *BAS,* January 1950, p. 3.

18. Edward Shils, "Freedom and Influence: Observations on the Scientists' Movement in the United States," *BAS,* January 1957, pp. 13–18, quoted passages, pp. 14, 15.

19. Henry DeWolf Smyth, "The Pattern of Destruction," *Nation,* December 22, 1945, p. 701.

20. Michael Mandelbaum, *The Nuclear Question: The United States and Nuclear Weapons, 1946–1976* (Cambridge, England, 1979), pp. vii, 23–40.

21. Ibid., p. 6.

22. Ibid., p. 18.

23. Shils, "Freedom and Influence," p. 13.

24. Edward Teller with Allen Brown, *The Legacy of Hiroshima* (New York, 1962), pp. 23–24.

25. Daniel Yergin, *Shattered Peace: The Origins of the Cold War and the National Security State* (Boston, 1977), pp. 174, 240; Stephen E. Ambrose, *Rise to Globalism: American Foreign Policy Since 1938* (New York, 1971); Lloyd C. Gardner, *Architects of Illusion: Men and Ideas in American Foreign Policy, 1941–1949* (New York, 1970); Walter LaFeber, *America, Russia and the Cold War,* 3rd ed. (New York, 1976).

26. Gregg Herken, *The Winning Weapon: The Atomic Bomb in the Cold War, 1945–1950* (New York, 1980), pp. 193–337, especially pp. 214 (Groves), 219–29; David Alan Rosenberg, "U.S. Nuclear Stockpile, 1945 to 1950," *BAS,* May 1982, pp. 25–30.

27. Yergin, *Shattered Peace,* pp. 282–84; Walter LaFeber, ed., *The Origins of the Cold War* (New York, 1971), pp. 151–56 (text of Truman speech).

28. Jane Pease, Orono, Maine, communication to author, April 30, 1984; Yergin, *Shattered Peace,* p. 285; David Caute, *The Great Fear: The Anti-Communist Purge Under Truman and Eisenhower* (New York, 1978); Athan F. Theoharis, *Seeds of Repression: Harry Truman and the Origins of McCarthyism* (New York, 1971).

29. James Gilbert, *Another Chance: Postwar America, 1945–1968* (New York, 1981), p. 97.

30. Ibid.; Peter Biskind, *Seeing Is Believing: How Hollywood Taught Us to Stop Worrying and Love the Fifties* (New York, 1983), pp. 145–59; Yergin, *Shattered Peace,* p. 285 (opinion polls); Carl N. Degler, *Affluence and Anxiety: America Since 1945,* 2nd ed. (New York, 1975), p. 33.

31. *New York Times,* September 2, 1948, p. 1; September 4, 1948, p. 26; June 12, 1949, p. 1; "In Defense of Science and Freedom—Speeches at the Condon Dinner," *BAS,* June 1948, p. 173; T. H. Davies, " 'Security Risk' Cases—A Vexed Question," *BAS,* July 1948, pp. 193–94; "Condon Is Cleared by Atomic Energy Commission," *BAS,* August 1948, pp. 226, 255; "Some Individual Cases of Clearance Procedures," *BAS,* September 1948, pp. 281–85; Theoharis, *Seeds of Repression,* p. 131.

32. "In Defense of Science and Freedom—Speeches at the Condon Dinner," p. 173; Karl T. Compton, "Science and Security," *BAS,* December 1948, pp. 375–76; "FAS Forms a Scientists' Committee on Loyalty," ibid., p. 342; *New York Times,* September 7, 1948, p. 20.

33. Struthers Burt, "A Man Tells Us What We Must Do," *Ladies' Home Journal,* February 1946, p. 173; Harold C. Urey, "The Atom and Humanity," *Science* 102 (November 2, 1945): 439.

10. Atomic Cars, Artificial Suns, Cancer-Curing Isotopes

1. "A Decision for Mankind," *St. Louis Post-Dispatch,* August 7, 1945; Donald Porter Geddes, ed., *The Atomic Age Opens* (New York, 1945), pp. 185–86. Editorial cartoons: *Dallas Morning News,* August 12, 1945, section 4, p. 8; *Detroit News,* August 12, 1945; *San Francisco Chronicle,* August 9 and 27, 1945.

2. Gale Young, "The New Power," in Dexter Maxters and Katharine Way, eds., *One World or None: A Report to the Public on the Full Meaning of the Atomic Bomb* (New York, 1946), p. 16.

3. L. R. Koller, "The Radioactive Elements," *Scientific Monthly,* July 1928, p. 56.

4. John J. O'Neill, "Enter Atomic Power," *Harper's,* June 1940, pp. 1–10; William L. Laurence, "Possible Fabulous Power From Uranium," *Science Digest,* July 1940, pp. 83–87; idem., "Atom Gives Up," *Saturday Evening Post,* September 7, 1940, pp. 12–13; "Vast Power Source in Atomic Energy Opened by Science," *New York Times,* May 5, 1940, p. 1; Bruce Bliven, "World-Shaking Promise of Atomic Research," *Reader's Digest,* July 1941, pp. 103–6. See also "Science and the Future: Man and Nature Both Split Atoms," *Life,* October 20, 1941, pp. 76–77.

5. Rudolph M. Langer, "Fast New World," *Collier's,* July 6, 1940, pp. 18–19ff. See also, idem., "Miracle of U-235," *Popular Mechanics,* January 1941, pp. 1–5ff.

6. Geddes, *Atomic Age Opens,* p. 185.

7. "Bombing Polar Ice," *Science Digest,* May 1946, pp. 69–70; John J. O'Neill, *Almighty Atom: The Real Story of Atomic Energy* (New York, 1945), pp. 59, 60, 73, 75, 90.

8. Frank Sullivan, "Cliché Expert Testifies on the Atom," *New Yorker,* November 17, 1945, pp. 27–29; David Dietz, *Atomic Energy in the Coming Era* (New York, 1947), preface and pp. 12, 13, 166.

9. Dietz, *Atomic Energy,* pp. 16–17, 18, 19.

10. Boris Pregel, "Power and Progress," *Nation,* December 22, 1945, p. 711; Robert M. Hutchins, "The State of the University" (Sept. 25, 1945), Hutchins Papers, Regenstein Library, University of Chicago, box 26, folder 6.

11. Geddes, *Atomic Age Opens,* p. 184 (*New York Times*); "The Beginning or the End?" *Milwaukee Journal,* August 7, 1945, p. 12; "For the Future," *Newsweek,* August 20, 1945, pp. 59–60.

12. Geddes, *Atomic Age Opens,* pp. 176, 177.

13. Stuart Chase, "The New Energy," *Nation,* December 22, 1945, p. 709; J. D. Bernal, "Everybody's Atom," *Nation,* September 1, 1945, p. 203; Joseph C. Goulden, *The Best Years, 1945–1950* (New York, 1976), p. 262 (Hutchins); Philip Wylie, "Deliverance or Doom?" *Collier's,* September 29, 1945, pp. 18, 19.

14. "Enter: The Atomic Age," *Business Week,* August 11, 1945, p. 16; Aaron Levenstein, "The Atomic Age: Suicide, Slavery, or Socialism?" (New York, [1946]), p. 3. For the after-history of the atomic airplane see John Tierney, "Take the A-Plane: The $1,000,000,000 Nuclear Bird That Never Flew," *Science 82,* January-February 1982, pp. 46–55.

15. "Enter: The Atomic Age," p. 16; "What to Expect from Atomic Energy," *Business Week,* September 1, 1945, p. 22; Max Lerner, "The Stakes of Power," *PM,* August 19, 1945, reprinted in Lerner, *Actions and Passions: Notes on the Multiple Revolution of Our Time* (New York, 1949), p. 255; Geddes, *Atomic Age Opens,* p. 192 (*Journal of Commerce*).

16. Walter Isard and Vincent H. Whitney, "The Atom and the Economy," *American Scholar* 17 (Winter 1947–1948): 45–55, quoted passages, pp. 45, 46, 50, 55. See also Walter Isard, "Some Economic Implications of Atomic Energy," *Quarterly Journal of Economics* 62 (February 1948): 202–28.

17. Dietz, *Atomic Energy,* p. 179.

18. *Chemical and Metallurgical Journal,* November 1945, p. 285; Albert Einstein as told to Raymond Gram Swing, "Albert Einstein on the Atomic Bomb," *Atlantic Monthly,* November 1945, p. 45; Chase, "The New Energy," p. 709 (Compton).

19. "1945 Cassandra," *New Yorker,* August 25, 1945, p. 16.

20. "Bombing Polar Ice," p. 69; George Gamow, *Atomic Energy in Cosmic and Human Life* (New York, 1946), p. 153; Young, "The New Power," in Masters and Way, *One World or None,* pp. 16, 17; Harold C. Urey, "How Does It All Add Up?", ibid., p. 56.

21. Leonard I. Katzin, "Industrial Uses of Atomic Energy," *Scientific American,* February 1946, pp. 74–78, quoted passages, pp. 75, 78.

22. O. R. Frisch, *Meet the Atom: A Popular Guide to Modern Physics* (New York, 1947), pp. 220–21; David E. Lilienthal, "Atomic Energy and American Industry," *Bulletin of the Atomic Scientists,* November 1947, p. 339.

23. John W. Campbell, Jr., *The Atomic Story,* (New York, 1947), p. 261; Chase, "The New Energy," p. 709; Maxwell Leigh Eidinoff and Hyman Ruchlis, *Atomics for the Millions* (New York, 1947), pp. 224, 230, 231.

24. "Elusive Dream," *Time,* August 23, 1948, p. 38; Lester Velie, "Inertia —USA," *Collier's,* May 3, 1947, p. 13.

25. "The Coming Atomic Age Offers Some Awesome Possibilities," *Science*

Illustrated, February 1949, pp. 12–13; R. Bretnor, "Maybe Just a Little One," *Harper's,* August 1947, pp. 137–44, quoted passages, p. 141.

26. Leon Svirsky, "The Atom in Peace and War," *New Republic,* September 18, 1950, pp. 11, 12, 14.

27. William L. Laurence, "Is Atomic Energy the Key to Our Dreams?" *Saturday Evening Post,* April 13, 1946, pp. 9–10, 37.

28. Vernon Snodgrass, Tularoosa, N.M., to Robert M. Hutchins, October 31, 1948, Hutchins Papers, Regenstein Library, University of Chicago, box 7; William F. Russell, "Recreation and the Atomic Age," *Recreation,* December 1947, pp. 421–24, quoted passages, p. 421; Joseph Barth, *The Art of Staying Sane* (Boston, 1948), p. 180.

29. "Atom-Driven Planes," *Time,* July 5, 1948, p. 44; "Atomic Hints," *Time,* October 25, 1948, p. 87.

30. Laurence, "Is Atomic Energy the Key to Our Dreams?" pp. 39, 41.

31. Robert M. Hutchins, "The Bomb Secret Is Out!" *American Magazine,* December 1947, p. 137; Alvin W. Weinberg, "Peacetime Uses of Nuclear Power," *New Republic,* February 25, 1946, p. 276; "Tracers," *Life,* December 2, 1946, p. 100; Albert Q. Maisel, "Medical Dividend," *Collier's,* May 3, 1947, pp. 14, 44.

32. "Atom: Key to Better Farming," *U.S. News and World Report,* June 4, 1948, pp. 26–27, quoted passage, p. 27; Hubert M. Evans, Ryland W. Crary, and C. Glen Hass, *Operation Atomic Vision* (Washington, D.C., 1948), pp. 6–7.

33. Harold Wolff, "A World Worth Waiting For," *Coronet,* November 1948, pp. 31–38.

34. George N. Gallup, ed., *The Gallup Poll: Public Opinion, 1935–1971,* 3 vols. (New York, 1972), 1: 767.

11. Bright Dreams and Disturbing Realities

1. "One Victory Not Yet Won," *New York Times,* "News of the Week in Review," August 12, 1945, p. 8.

2. "Control of Cancer Instead of Atomic Bombs," *Science News Letter,* April 6, 1946, p. 213; Robley D. Evans, "Medical Uses of Atomic Energy," *Atlantic Monthly,* January 1946, pp. 68–73, quoted passage, p. 68; "Atomic Research May End World's Hunger," *Christian Century,* July 28, 1948, p. 749.

3. Harold C. Lueth, M.D., "Medical Care in the Atomic Age," *West Virginia Medical Journal* 46 (February 1950): 35; William F. Russell, "Recreation and the Atomic Age," *Recreation,* December 1947, p. 421; Austin M. Brues, M.D., "Nature of Trauma in Atomic Warfare," *American Journal of Surgery* 78 (November 1948): 563; Harold Wolff, "A World Worth Waiting For," *Coronet,* November 1948, pp. 37, 38.

4. Arthur H. Compton, "The Atomic Crusade and Its Social Implications," *Annals of the American Academy of Political and Social Science* 249 (January 1947): 10, 11.

5. Bruce Bliven, "The Bomb and the Future," *New Republic,* August 20, 1945, p. 212.

6. Boris Pregel, "Power and Progress," *Nation,* December 22, 1945, p. 710.

7. Joseph Barth, *The Art of Staying Sane* (Boston, 1948), p. 180; Lillian Wald Kay and Irving J. Gitlin, "Atomic Energy or the Atomic Bomb: A Problem in the Development of Morale and Opinion," *Journal of Social Psychology* 29 (February

1949), p. 79; Gerald W. Johnson, "The Liberal of 1946," *American Scholar* 15 (Spring 1946): 156.

8. R. Will Burnett, "The Teacher and Atomic Energy," *Education,* May 1948, p. 545; Philip Wylie, "Deliverance or Doom?" *Collier's,* September 29, 1945, p. 18 (emphasis in original); "Psychologists Advise on the Atomic-Bomb Peril," *School and Society,* June 8, 1946, p. 406.

9. David E. Lilienthal, *The Atomic Energy Years* (New York, 1964), pp. 160, 269 (March 15 and December 16, 1947, diary entries); "Good in the Atom," *Life,* December 5, 1949, p. 50.

10. Dwight Macdonald, "The Bomb," *Politics,* September 1945, p. 258.

11. Wylie, "Deliverance or Doom?" p. 18; "Science and the Bomb," *New York Times,* August 7, 1945, p. 22; "Terrifying Event," *Dallas Morning News,* August 9, 1945; Raymond Gram Swing, ABC radio newscast, August 13, 1945, Swing Papers, Library of Congress, box 27.

12. Federation of American (Atomic) Scientists (FAS), "Survival Is at Stake," in Dexter Masters and Katharine Way, eds., *One World or None: A Report to the Public on the Full Meaning of the Atomic Bomb* (New York, 1946), p. 78.

13. William L. Laurence, *Dawn over Zero: The Story of the Atomic Bomb* (New York, 1946), pp. 237, 265, 270, 271.

14. Quoted in David E. Lilienthal, "Science and Man's Fate," *Nation,* July 13, 1946, p. 41.

15. Lilienthal, "The Atomic Adventure," *Collier's,* May 3, 1947, pp. 11, 12; idem., Oct. 28, 1946, address, *Atomic Cafe* (movie soundtrack album, Rounder Records, no. 1034, Somerville, Mass., 1982).

16. W. W. Waymack, "A Letter to Judith and Dickie," *National Education Association Journal,* March 1947, p. 214.

17. "Atomic Age Up to Now," *Science News Letter,* August 10, 1946, p. 85.

18. *Collier's,* May 3, 1947, pp. 12, 13, 14.

19. William R. Foulkes, "The Atom: Death—or the Life Abundant?" *Vital Speeches of the Day,* March 15, 1948, p. 346.

20. Bernard Brodie, "The Atomic Bomb as Policy Maker," *Foreign Affairs,* October 1948, p. 17; "The Fateful Atom Can Serve Man or Destroy Him," *Business Week,* July 6, 1946, p. 68; Walter Isard and Vincent H. Whitney, "The Atom and the Economy," *American Scholar* 17 (Winter 1947–1948): 45; David Bradley, *No Place to Hide* (Boston, 1948), p. 168.

21. John K. Jacobs, "Communication," *Science and Society* 10 (1946): 297.

22. J. Robert Oppenheimer, "The Atom as a Great Force for Peace," *New York Times Magazine,* June 9, 1946, p. 7; Albert Einstein as told to Raymond Swing, "Einstein on the Atomic Bomb," *Atlantic Monthly,* November 1945, p. 45; J. Robert Oppenheimer, "Atomic Weapons," *Proceedings of the American Philosophical Society* 90 (January 1946): 8.

23. Richard M. Fagley, "The Atomic Bomb and the Crisis of Man," *Christianity and Crisis,* October 1, 1945, p. 5.

24. "Second Milestone on the Road to Destruction," *Christian Century,* August 13, 1947, p. 965.

25. "Three Tenses," *Commonweal,* January 4, 1946, p. 300.

26. Edward L. Long, Jr., *The Christian Response to the Atomic Crisis* (Philadelphia, 1950), pp. 39, 93–94, 94–95.

12. Optimistic Forecasts

1. E. B. White, *The Wild Flag: Editorials from the* New Yorker *on Federal World Government and Other Matters* (New York, 1946), p. 108.

2. William L. Laurence, *Dawn over Zero: The Story of the Atomic Bomb* (New York, 1946), p. 270; "The Bomb," *Time,* August 20, 1945, p. 19; Allan Nevins, "How We Felt About the War," in Jack Goodman, ed., *While You Were Gone: A Report on Wartime Life in the United States* (New York, 1946), p. 26.

3. Louis Wirth, "Responsibility of Social Science," *Annals of the American Academy of Political and Social Science* 249 (January 1947): 143.

4. Boris Pregel, "Power and Progress," *Nation,* December 22, 1945, p. 711; Joseph H. Willits, "Social Adjustments to Atomic Energy," *Proceedings of the American Philosophical Society* 90 (January 1946): 48 (address delivered November 16, 1945).

5. Homer Metz, "Atomic Dawn," *Christian Science Monitor,* magazine section, February 21, 1947, p. 2; Gerald Wendt, "What Happened in Science," in Goodman, *While You Were Gone,* p. 250; Franz Alexander, "Mental Health in the Atomic Age," *Mental Hygiene* 30 (October 1946): 531 (address delivered March 1946).

6. J. Robert Oppenheimer, "The New Weapon: The Turn of the Screw," in Dexter Masters and Katharine Way, eds., *One World or None: A Report to the Public on the Full Meaning of the Atomic Bomb* (New York, 1946), p. 22 (quoting Truman); John H. O'Neill, *Almighty Atom: The Real Story of Atomic Energy* (New York, 1945), p. 81.

7. John A. Simpson, "The Scientists as Public Educators: A Two-Year Summary," *Bulletin of the Atomic Scientists,* September 1947, p. 245; Nevins, "How We Felt About the War," p. 63; "Man vs. Atom—Year I," *Business Week,* July 6, 1946, p. 70; Leonard S. Cottrell, Jr. and Sylvia Eberhart, *American Opinion on World Affairs in the Atomic Age* (Princeton, N.J., 1948), p. xv.

8. Oliver S. Loud, "Social Control of Atomic Energy," *Antioch Review* 5 (December 1945): 523.

9. Gerald W. Johnson, "The Liberal of 1946," *American Scholar* 15 (Spring 1946): 154, 155; Metz, "Atomic Dawn," p. 2; Editorial, *Antioch Review* 5 (Winter 1945–1946): 459; Harold C. Urey, "How Does It All Add Up?" in Masters and Way, *One World or None,* pp. 57, 58.

10. Editorial, *Antioch Review* 5 (Winter 1945–1946): 459.

11. O'Neill, *Almighty Atom,* p. 94; J. D. Ratcliff, "Your Servant the Atom in the World of Tomorrow," *Coronet,* June 1946, p. 43; Pregel, "Power and Progress," p. 711; Metz, "Atomic Dawn," p. 2.

12. Lewis Paul Todd, "Atomic Energy and the Coming Revolution in Education," *School and Society,* October 27, 1945, p. 258; Norman Cousins, "Modern Man Is Obsolete," *Saturday Review of Literature,* August 18, 1945, p. 7.

13. Wendt, "What Happened in Science," p. 254.

14. Philip Wylie, "Deliverance or Doom?" *Collier's,* September 29, 1945, p. 80.

15. John F. Sembower, "Democracy and Science Fused by the Atomic Bomb," *Antioch Review* 5 (December 1945): 493–500, quoted passages, pp. 493, 498, 500.

16. "Origins," *Time,* August 20, 1945, p. 35; *New York Times* and Eleanor Roosevelt (on NBC radio broadcast) quoted in Donald Porter Geddes, ed., *The Atomic Age Opens* (New York, 1945), p. 53.

17. "Enter the Atomic Age," *Business Week,* August 11, 1945, pp. 16–17; Sembower, "Democracy and Science Fused by the Atomic Bomb," p. 498.

18. Arthur H. Compton, "The Atomic Crusade and Its Social Implications," *Annals of the American Academy of Political and Social Science* 249 (January 1947): 9, 15, 18, 19; idem., "Atomic Energy as a Human Asset," *Nature* 157 (February 9, 1946): 149, 150.

13. Darker Social Visions

1. *Letters of James Agee to Father Flye,* 2nd ed. (New York, 1971), p. 155.

2. Max Lerner, "The Atomic Bomb and the Human Heart," *PM,* August 21, 1945, quoted in Paul F. Boller, Jr., "Hiroshima and the American Left: August 1945," *International Social Science Review* 57 (Winter 1982): 19.

3. Bruce Bliven, "The Bomb and the Future," *New Republic,* Aug. 20, 1945, p. 212.

4. Gerald W. Johnson, "The Liberal of 1946," *American Scholar* 15 (Spring 1946): 156, 157; James Reston, "Dawn of the Atomic Era Perplexes Washington," *New York Times,* "News of the Week in Review," August 12, 1945, p. 6; "The Bomb," *Time,* August 20, 1945, p. 19.

5. Robert M. Hutchins, *The Atom Bomb and Education* (London, 1947), pp. 3, 4; John Gunther, *Inside USA* (New York, 1947), p. 378.

6. Max Lerner, "The Stakes of Power," *PM,* August 19, 1945, reprinted in Lerner, *Actions and Passions: Notes on the Multiple Revolution of Our Time* (New York, 1949), p. 256; Robert M. Hutchins, Reuben Gustavson, and William F. Ogburn, "Atomic Force: Its Meaning for Mankind," *Chicago Roundtable* radio broadcast, August 12, 1945, in Harold F. Harding, ed., *The Age of Danger: Major Speeches on American Problems* (New York, 1952), p. 26; Aaron Levenstein, "The Atomic Age: Suicide, Slavery, or Socialism?" (New York [1946]), pp. 19, 20.

7. Virgil Jordan, *Manifesto for the Atomic Age* (New Brunswick, N.J., 1946); Joseph H. Willits, "Social Adjustments to Atomic Energy," *Proceedings of the American Philosophical Society* 90 (January 1946): 51.

8. Charles Edison, "The Atom in Local Democracy," *National Municipal Review,* December 1947, pp. 608, 610.

9. Robert DeVore, "Passport to the Golden Age," *Collier's,* May 3, 1947, p. 15.

10. Norman Cousins and Thomas K. Finletter, "A Beginning for Sanity," *Saturday Review of Literature,* June 15, 1946, pp. 5, 6; Donald Porter Geddes, ed., *The Atomic Age Opens* (New York, 1945), p. 174 (Harvey W. Zorbaugh on WNEW radio, New York City, August 10, 1945); S. Colum Gilfillan, "The Atomic Bombshell," *Survey Graphic,* September 1945, p. 357. For similar views, see Robert Redfield, "Consequences of Atomic Energy," *Phi Delta Kappan* 27 (April 1946): 223.

11. Harold C. Urey, "How Does It All Add Up?" in Dexter Masters and Katharine Way, eds., *One World or None: A Report to the Public on the Full Meaning of the Atomic Bomb* (New York, 1946), pp. 56, 57; Joseph C. Goulden, *The Best Years, 1945–1950* (New York, 1976), p. 265 (quoting *Time*).

12. Albert Berger, "The Triumph of Prophecy: Science Fiction and Nuclear Power in the Post-Hiroshima Period," *Science-Fiction Studies* 3 (July 1976): 145; Edward U. Condon, "The New Technique of Private War," in Masters and Way, *One World or None,* p. 40.

13. Ryland W. Crary et al., *The Challenge of Atomic Energy* (New York, 1948), pp. 38, 39, 40; Joseph H. Willits, "Social Adjustments to Atomic Energy," *Proceedings of the American Philosophical Society* 90 (January 1946): 51.

14. Edward L. Long, Jr., *The Christian Response to the Atomic Crisis* (Philadelphia, 1950), pp. 56–58.

15. E. L. Woodward, "How Can We Prevent Atomic War?" *New York Times Magazine,* January 13, 1946, p. 40; Garet Garrett, "Introduction," in Jordan, *Manifesto for the Atomic Age,* pp. 7–8.

16. Charles E. Merriam, "The Atom and World Community," *Christian Century,* March 6, 1946, p. 298.

17. William L. Borden, *There Will Be No Time: The Revolution in Strategy* (New York, 1946), pp. 64, 139, 141, 142; Peter Goodchild, *J. Robert Oppenheimer: Shatterer of Worlds* (Boston, 1981), pp. 208–23, 256–57.

18. Joseph and Stewart Alsop, "Your Flesh Should Creep," *Saturday Evening Post,* July 13, 1946, pp. 9, 49, 50.

14. Experts and Ideologues Offer Their Prescriptions

1. Frank G. Tyrrell, "Is the Use of the Atomic Bomb Justified?" *Vital Speeches of the Day,* October 1, 1945, p. 768.

2. Leonard S. Cottrell, Jr., and Sylvia Eberhart, *American Opinion on World Affairs in the Atomic Age* (Princeton, N.J., 1948), pp. 57, 58.

3. "Newspapers and the Bomb," *Saturday Review of Literature,* October 4, 1947, pp. 9, 10, 41.

4. "Planning Cities for the Atomic Age: Mere Survival Is Not Enough," *American City,* August 1946, p. 75, 76.

5. William F. Russell, "Recreation and the Atomic Age," *Recreation,* December 1947, pp. 421–24, quoted passages, pp. 422, 423, 424.

6. Hutchins on ABC radio program *Headline Edition,* January 14, 1946, transcript in Hutchins Papers, Regenstein Library, University of Chicago, box 26, folder 7; Christian Gauss, "Is Einstein Right?" *American Scholar* 15 (Autumn 1946): 476; Marjorie Hope Nicholson, "The American Scholar 1932–1945," *American Scholar* 15 (Winter 1945–1946): 12.

7. Florence Gelbond, "The Impact of the Atomic Bomb on Education," *The Social Studies* 65 (March 1974): 110, 111; Charles L. DeBenedetti, "Educators and Armaments in Cold War America," unpublished essay, courtesy of Professor DeBenedetti.

8. Merrill E. Bush, "World Organization or Atomic Destruction?" *School and Society,* November 23, 1946, p. 355; Walker D. Wyman, "Foreign Affairs in the Atomic Age," *Social Education* 10 (February 1946): 66.

9. Charles Edison, "The Atom in Local Democracy," *National Municipal Review,* December 1947, p. 611.

10. Wesner Fallaw, "Atomic Apocalypse," *Christian Century,* September 25, 1946, pp. 1146–48.

11. Alonzo B. May, "Atomic Energy and the Liberal Arts," *School and Society,* August 24, 1946, p. 132.

12. Goodwin B. Beach, "Liberal Education and Leisure in the Atomic Age," *Education,* June 1947, pp. 595, 600, 601.

13. Gauss, "Is Einstein Right?" pp. 469–76, quoted passages pp. 471, 473, 474, 475, 476.

14. Robert M. Hutchins, *The Atom Bomb and Education* (London, 1947), pp. 4, 7, 8, 10; idem., "The Atomic Bomb Versus Civilization," *NEA Journal,* March 1946, p. 117; "Hutchins, Robert Maynard," by Michael R. Harris in John A. Garraty, ed., *Encyclopedia of American Biography* (New York, 1974), pp. 558–60.

15. John K. Jacobs, "Communication," *Science and Society,* 10 (1946), 298, 299.

16. Aaron Levenstein, "The Atomic Age: Suicide, Slavery, or Socialism?" (New York, [1946]), pp. 18, 20, 24, 29, 31.

17. Freda Kirchwey, "One World or None," *Nation,* August 18, 1945, p. 150; Raymond Gram Swing, *In the Name of Sanity* (ABC radio broadcasts, New York, 1946), p. vii; Max Lerner, "World State or World Security," *PM,* August 20, 1945, reprinted in Lerner, *Actions and Passions: Notes on the Multiple Revolution of Our Time* (New York, 1949), 258.

18. Stuart Chase, "The New Energy," *Nation,* December 22, 1945, pp. 709, 710; Oliver S. Loud, "Social Control of Atomic Energy," *Antioch Review* 5 (December 1945): 522.

19. Edison, "The Atom in Local Democracy," pp. 609, 624.

20. "Mr. Dewey and Atomic Control," *Christian Century,* November 10, 1948, pp. 1199–201; Dewey quoted p. 1200; "Atom Becomes Big Business," *U.S. News and World Report,* Februrary 10, 1950, pp. 11–13; David E. Lilienthal, "Free the Atom," *Collier's,* June 17, 1950, pp. 13–15ff.

21. Gerald W. Johnson, "The Liberal of 1946," *American Scholar* 15 (Spring 1946): 154–59, quoted passages, pp. 156, 157, 158, 159.

15. Social Science into the Breach

1. Lewis Paul Todd, "Atomic Energy and the Coming Revolution in Education," *School and Society,* October 27, 1945, p. 258.

2. Sidney B. Fay, "The Idea of Progress," *American Historical Review,* 52 (January 1947): 245; Lyman Bryson, CBS radio broadcast, August 12, 1945, in Sydnor H. Walker, ed., *The First One Hundred Days of the Atomic Age* (New York, 1945), p. 15; "Atomic and Human Energy," *New Republic,* August 27, 1945, p. 241; editorial, *Antioch Review* 5 (Winter 1945–1946): 461; John Dewey, "The Crisis in Human History," *Commentary* 1 (March 1946): 9.

3. Christian Gauss, "Is Einstein Right?" *American Scholar* 15 (Autumn 1946): 474, 475; E. B. White, *The Wild Flag: Editorials from the* New Yorker *on Federal World Government and Other Matters* (New York, 1946), pp. ix, x.

4. Todd, "Atomic Energy and the Coming Revolution in Education," p. 258; Alonzo B. May, "Atomic Energy and the Liberal Arts," *School and Society*, August 24, 1946, p. 133; John H. Starie, "Schools and the Atom," *Education*, April 1946, p. 591.

5. Stuart Chase, "The New Energy," *Nation*, December 22, 1945, p. 710; George S. Pettee, Talcott Parsons, H. Van B. Cleveland, Lincoln Gordon, and John Lydenberg, "Atomic Power: A Communication, August 8, 1945," *Washington Post*, August 19, 1945.

6. John S. Perkins, "Where Is the Social Sciences' Atomic Bomb?" *School And Society*, November 17, 1945, pp. 316, 317.

7. A. M. Meerloo, "We Need a New Kind of Leader," *New York Times Magazine*, May 26, 1946, p. 42.

8. Kenneth B. Clark, "Social Science and Social Tensions," *Mental Hygiene* 32 (January 1948): 15, 16; Bruce L. Melvin, "Science and Man's Dilemma," *Science*, March 1, 1946, pp. 241, 243, 244.

9. William Fielding Ogburn, "Sociology and the Atom," *American Journal of Sociology* 51 (January 1946): 267, 268, 272, 274; Robert Redfield, "Consequences of Atomic Energy," *Phi Delta Kappan* 27 (April 1946): 223, 224.

10. Donald R. Taft, "The Atom and Sociology," *American Journal of Sociology* 51 (May 1946): 558, 559.

11. Louis Wirth, "Responsibility of Social Science," *Annals of the American Academy of Political and Social Science* 249 (January 1947): 143, 144, 145, 146, 147, 150, 151.

12. Gene M. Lyons, *The Uneasy Partnership: Social Science and the Federal Government in the Twentieth Century* (New York, 1969), pp. 47–123 (pre-1945 background), 130–36; James L. Penick et al., eds., *The Politics of American Science, 1939 to the Present* (Chicago, 1965), pp. 72–89.

13. *Hearings on the Science Legislation (S. 1297 and Related Bills) . . . Before a Subcommittee of the Committee on Military Affairs, U.S. Senate, 79th Cong. 1st sess.* (Washington, D.C., 1945 [parts I–III] and 1946 [parts IV–VI]), I, 92 (testimony of Howard A. Meyerhoff, executive secretary, American Assn. for the Advancement of Science); Meyerhoff, "The National Science Foundation: S. 1850, Final Senate Bill," *Science* 103 (March 1, 1946): 271; "The Committee for a National Science Foundation," *Science* 103 (January 4, 1946): 11, and 103 (Jan. 11, 1946): 45, 62–63 (list of signers); Lyons, *Uneasy Partnership*, 130.

14. *Hearings on Science Legislation*, IV, 738–95; II, 301; III, 632; V, 984; Penick et al., *Politics of American Science*, p. 81.

15. *Hearings on Science Legislation*, I, 145; III, 654; V, 946.

16. Talcott Parsons, "The Science Legislation and the Role of the Social Sciences," *American Sociological Review* 2 (December 1946): 653–66, quoted passages, 662, 663, 665.

17. Idem., "The Case for the Social Sciences," *Bulletin of the Atomic Scientists* (henceforth *BAS*), 3 (January 1947): 3–5.

18. David E. Lilienthal, *The Atomic Energy Years* (New York, 1964), pp. 112–13, 295 (November 24, 1946, and February 12, 1948, diary entries); Joseph E. Willits, "Social Adjustments to Atomic Energy," *Proceedings of the American Philosophical Society* 90 (January 1946): 48.

19. L. Harold DeWolf, "Religion in an Age of Science," *Journal of Bible and Religion* 16 (October 1948): 202, 203.

20. Lyons, *Uneasy Partnership,* p. 136; Penick et al., *Politics of American Science,* pp. 72–89; "The National Science Foundation Act of 1950," *BAS,* June 1950, p. 186.

21. Ogburn, "Sociology and the Atom," pp. 270, 271, 272.

22. Ogburn's critic Donald R. Taft was unimpressed by his speculations about urban dispersal, calling them "very much of the 'duck and cover' variety"—Taft, "Atom and Sociology," p. 558. According to sociologist Edward B. Shils, Ogburn's post–World War II writings had little impact in the profession (Edward B. Shils to author, January 30, 1985).

23. Ansley J. Coale, *The Problem of Reducing Vulnerability to Atomic Bombs* (Princeton, N.J., 1947), foreword.

24. Dorothy McClure, "Social-Studies Textbooks and Atomic Energy," *The School Review* 57 (December 1949): 542; Michael Amrine, "What the Atomic Age Has Done to Us," *New York Times Magazine,* August 6, 1950, 27; Edward Shils, "Freedom and Influence: Observations on the Scientists' Movement in the United States," *BAS* 13 (January 1957), p. 16; Shils to author, January 30, 1985.

16. Justifications, Rationalizatons, Evasions

1. "Coliseum Throng Views Tableau of War Scenes," *Los Angeles Times,* October 28, 1945, pp. 2, 12.

2. Author interview with Ralph Lapp, December 28, 1982; A. J. Muste, "Sketches for an Autobiography," in Nat Hentoff, ed., *The Essays of A. J. Muste* (New York, 1970), p. 12; James B. Conant to J. Robert Oppenheimer, March 14, 1947, Oppenheimer Papers, Library of Congress, box 27; National Conference of Catholic Bishops, *The Challenge of Peace: God's Promise and Our Response* (Washington, D.C., 1983), p. 92.

3. A. M. Meerloo, *Aftermath of Peace: Psychological Essays* (New York, 1946), p. 163.

4. Edward Teller with Allen Brown, *The Legacy of Hiroshima* (New York, 1962), p. 310; Michael J. Yavenditti, "The American People and the Use of Atomic Bombs on Japan: The 1940s," *Historian* 36 (February 1974): 224; Elbert D. Thomas, "Atomic Warfare and International Law," *Proceedings of the American Society of International Law, . . . April 25–27, 1946* (Washington, D.C., 1946), p. 85; Mary McCarthy, "The Hiroshima '*New Yorker,*'" *Politics,* November 1946, p. 367.

5. "The Fortune Survey," *Fortune,* December 1945, p. 305; Sydnor H. Walker, ed., *The First One Hundred Days of the Atomic Age* (New York, 1945), p. 35.

6. Maureen Fitzgerald, " 'Sixteen Hours Ago . . .': America at the Threshold of the Atomic Age" (unpublished seminar paper, University of Wisconsin, 1984).

7. Lillian Wald Kay, "Public Opinion and the Bomb," *Journal of Educational Sociology* 22 (January 1949): 357 (Gallup poll data), 358–60.

8. Yavenditti, "The American People and the Use of the Atomic Bombs," p. 225; Janet Besse and Harold D. Lasswell, "Our Columnists on the A-Bomb," *World Politics* 3 (October 1950): 78.

9. Eunice M. Knapp to editor, *Washington Post,* August 17, 1945, and follow-

up letters, August 23–29; W. J. Rademacher, New Leipzig, N.D., to H. V. Kaltenborn, August 12, 1945, Kaltenborn Papers, State Historical Society of Wisconsin, Madison, box 107; "Unconditional Surrender," letter to editor, *Philadelphia Inquirer*, August 23, 1945; B. F. Berry to editor, *Louisville Courier-Journal*, August 26, 1945; Leonie M. Cole to editor, *Milwaukee Journal*, August 16, 1945; Fitzgerald, "'Sixteen Hours Ago,'" Appendix.

10. William L. Laurence, *Dawn over Zero: The Story of the Atomic Bomb* (New York, 1946), p. 234; "The Fellow Who Lighted the Fuse" (cartoon), *Chicago Daily Tribune*, August 8, 1945, p. 1; *Atlanta Constitution* editorial, September 1, 1945, quoted in Yavenditti, "The American People and the Use of the Atomic Bombs," p. 229. For other editorials in this vein see *Los Angeles Times*, August 30, 1945, and *New Orleans Times Picayune*, August 21, 1945.

11. Allan Nevins, "How We Felt About the War" in Jack Goodman, ed., *While You Were Gone: A Report on Wartime Life in the United States* (New York, 1946), p. 25; Robert Jay Lifton and Richard Falk, *Indefensible Weapons: The Political and Psychological Case Against Nuclearism* (New York, 1982), p. 57; "But for the Grace of God" (cartoon), *Louisville Courier-Journal*, August 30, 1945.

12. "For This We Fight," *Chicago Daily Tribune*, August 11, 1945; *New York Times*, August 30, 1945, p. 4 (Byrnes); Freda Kirchwey, "One World or None," *Nation*, August 18, 1945, p. 149; Bruce Bliven, "The Bomb and the Future," *New Republic*, August 20, 1945, p. 212; Paul Fussell, "Hiroshima: A Soldier's View," *New Republic*, August 22–29, 1981, pp. 26–30.

13. Harold C. Urey, "I'm a Frightened Man," *Collier's*, January 5, 1946, p. 19; Ellery C. Stowell, "The Laws of War and the Atomic Bomb," *American Journal of International Law* 39, (1945): 786; Vannevar Bush, *Modern Arms and Free Men* (New York, 1949), p. 40.

14. United States Strategic Bombing Survey, *Japan's Struggle to End the War* (Washington D.C., 1946), p. 13; Robert C. Batchelder, *The Irreversible Decision, 1939–1950* (Boston, 1962), p. 120.

15. Wilfred Burchett, *Shadows of Hiroshima* (London, 1983), pp. 7–24, quoted passages, pp. 18–19, 22–23, 34, 44–45; "U.S. Atom Bomb Site Belies Tokyo Tales," *New York Times*, September 12, 1945; "No Radioactivity in Hiroshima Ruin," *New York Times*, September 13, 1945; "A-Test 'Confusion' Laid to Eisenhower," *New York Times*, April 20, 1979. Burchett's leftist politics and pro-Soviet position after the war eased the task of those seeking to discredit his report of what he had observed in Hiroshima.

16. *Atlanta Constitution*, August 8, 1945, pp. 1, 3; "Atomic Bomb, Russian War Blast Way into Front Page," *Editor and Publisher*, August 11, 1945, pp. 7, 59.

17. "A Job for Hirohito," *New Republic*, September 24, 1945, pp. 365–66; "70-Year Effect of Bombs Denied," *New York Times*, August 9, 1945, p. 8; "After Effect of the Bomb" (editorial); *New York Times*, August 25, 1945; "That Atom," editorial, *Boston Globe*, August 25, 1945; Yavenditti, "The American People and the Use of the Atomic Bombs," p. 233; "Plants Springing Up in Atom-Blasted Cities," *Science News Letter*, September 15, 1945, p. 168.

18. H. V. Kaltenborn, NBC radio newscast, August 6, 1945, p. 2, Kaltenborn Papers, box 176; Donald Porter Geddes, ed., *The Atomic Age Opens* (New York,

1945), p. 45. The 1946 report of the U.S. Strategic Bombing Survey stated flatly: "Hiroshima and Nagasaki were chosen as targets because of their concentration of activities and population." United States Strategic Bombing Survey, *The Effects of Atomic Bombs on Hiroshima and Nagasaki:* (Washington, D.C., 1946), p. 41.

19. Robert H. Ferrell, *American Diplomacy: A History,* 3rd ed. (New York, 1975), p. 623; Lowell Thomas, CBS radio newscast, August 7, 1945, extract in Thomas, *History as You Heard It* (Garden City, N.Y., 1957), p. 296.

20. A. P. Peck, "Atomic Bombs," *Scientific American,* October 1945, p. 241; Louis Espitallier to the editor, *New Orleans Times Picayune,* August 10, 1945.

21. Karl T. Compton, "If the Atomic Bomb Had Not Been Used," *Atlantic Monthly,* December 1946, pp. 54, 55, 56.

22. Henry L. Stimson to Harry S. Truman, Jan. 7, 1947, Stimson Papers, Yale University Library, quoted in Michael J. Yavenditti, "John Hersey and the American Conscience: The Reception of 'Hiroshima,'" *Pacific Historical Review* 43 (February 1974) 44; Henry L. Stimson, "The Decision to Use the Atomic Bomb," *Harper's,* February 1947, p. 97.

23. Ibid., pp. 99, 101, 102, 105, 106, 107.

24. A. J. Muste, *Not by Might: Christianity, the Way to Human Decency* (New York, 1947), p. 28; Raymond Gram Swing, ABC radio newscast, April 26, 1946, p. 1, Swing Papers, Library of Congress, box 30; Norman Cousins and Thomas K. Finletter, "A Beginning for Sanity," *Saturday Review of Literature,* June 15, 1946, p. 7.

25. P. M. S. Blackett, *Fear, War, and the Bomb* (New York, 1948), p. 135.

26. I. I. Rabi, "Playing Down the Bomb," *Atlantic Monthly,* April 1949, pp. 21, 23; Philip Morrison, "Blackett's Analysis of the Issues," *Bulletin of the Atomic Scientists* (hereafter *BAS*), February 1949, pp. 37–40, quoted passages, p. 40.

27. Leslie R. Groves, "People Should Learn About Nuclear Energy," *Journal of Educational Sociology* 22 (January 1949): 318.

28. Merle Miller, *Plain Speaking: An Oral Biography of Harry S. Truman* (New York, 1974), p. 248; Author interview with Ralph Lapp, December 28, 1982. For another version of the Truman-Oppenheimer encounter see Peter Goodchild, *J. Robert Oppenheimer, Shatterer of Worlds* (Boston, 1981), p. 180.

29. Richard M. Fagley to A. J. Muste, September 1945, Fellowship of Reconciliation Papers, Swarthmore College Peace Collection, quoted in Yaveneditti, "The American People and the Use of Atomic Bombs," p. 242; ibid., p. 238; "Before Hiroshima," *BAS,* May 1946, p. 1.

30. Mary McCarthy, "The Hiroshima 'New Yorker'"; H. V. Kaltenborn, NBC radio newscast, August 6, 1945, p. 3, Kaltenborn Papers, box 176; "A Tide in the Affairs of Men," *Business Week,* September 1, 1945, p. 57; Elbert D. Thomas, "Atomic Bombs in International Society," *American Journal of International Law* 39 (October 1945): 741; Carter Holmes, Dallas, to the editor, *Time,* September 17, 1945, p. 5.

31. "Atomic Bombs," *Scientific American,* October 1945, p. 238; George Gamow, *Atomic Energy in Cosmic and Human Life* (New York, 1946), p. 150.

32. James Marshall, "Old Adam and the Atom," *American Scholar* 15 (Winter 1945–1946): 13, 18.

33. Stephen King-Hall, "World Government or World Destruction?" *Reader's Digest*, November 1945, p. 14.

34. Yavenditti, "John Hersey and the American Conscience," p. 46; William S. Parsons to Leslie R. Groves, December 12, 1946, Parsons Papers, Library of Congress, box 1; Jack G. Shaheen and Richard Taylor, *"The Beginning or the End"* in Jack G. Shaheen, ed., *Nuclear War Films* (Carbondale, Ill., 1978), pp. 3-10; Harrison Brown, *"The Beginning or the End:* A Review," *BAS,* March 1947, p. 99; Nathan Reingold, "MGM Meets the Atomic Bomb," *Wilson Quarterly,* Autumn 1984, p. 158.

35. *Ibid.,* p. 163; Brown, *"The Beginning or the End:* A Review," p. 99.

17. *"Victory for What?"*

1. Fred Eastman, Letter to the Editor, *Christian Century,* August 29, 1945, p. 983; Randall Jarrell to Margaret Marshall, September 1945, in *Randall Jarrell's Letters: An Autobiographical and Literary Selection,* edited by Mary Jarrell with Stuart Wright (Boston, 1985), p. 130.

2. "Stuart Chase Says," *Common Sense,* October 1945, p. 29, quoted in Paul F. Boller, Jr., "Hiroshima and the American Left: August 1945," *International Social Science Review* 57 (Winter 1982): 24; Norman Thomas, *The Call,* August 13, 1945, pp. 4, 5, quoted in ibid., p. 24; Norman Thomas, "When Cruelty Becomes Pleasurable," *Human Events,* September 26, 1945.

3. "We Are Not Proud of It," *Omaha Morning World Herald,* August 8, 1945; Donald Porter Geddes, ed., *The Atomic Age Opens* (New York, 1945), p. 44; "The Annihilation of Hiroshima," *New York Herald Tribune,* August 9, 1945, p. 22.

4. "A Moral Calamity," *Progressive,* August 20, 1945, p. 3 (Strout); Marquis W. Childs, "The State of the Nation," *New York Post,* August 10, 1945; David Lawrence, "What Hath Man Wrought!" *U.S. News and World Report,* August 17, 1945, pp. 38–39.

5. Walter G. Taylor, New York City, to the editor, *Time,* August 27, 1945, p. 2; "Doubts and Fears," *Time,* August 20, 1945, p. 36 (quoting *New York Times* letter); Geddes, *Atomic Age Opens,* p. 42; Maureen Fitzgerald, "'Sixteen Hours Ago . . .' America at the Threshold of the Atomic Age," unpublished seminar paper, University of Wisconsin, Spring 1984, appendix.

6. Letters to H. V. Kaltenborn from A. M. Hendrickson, St. Paul, August 13, 1945; K. F. Scallan, East Rutherford, N.J., August 9, 1945; and Charles May (undated)—Kaltenborn Papers, State Historical Society of Wisconsin, Madison, box 107.

7. Hermann Hagedorn, *The Bomb That Fell on America* (Santa Barbara, Cal., 1946), p. 33.

8. *Chicago Defender,* August 18, 1945, p. 1; *Washington Afro-American,* August 11, 1945; "Colored Scientists Aided Atom Study," *Washington Afro-American,* August 18, 1945, p. 1; "The Front Page," *Race Relations: A Monthly Summary of Events and Trends,* August–September, 1945, p. 53.

9. "Splitting the Atom of Race Hate," *Chicago Defender,* August 18, 1945, p. 12; *Washington Afro-American,* August 11, 1945, photo captions.

10. "The Atomic Bomb," *The Crisis,* September 1945, p. 249; Walter White, "Atom Bomb and Lasting Peace," *Chicago Defender,* September 8, 1945;

W. E. B. DuBois, "Negro's War Gains and Losses," *Chicago Defender*, September 15, 1945.

11. "Are We Prepared for Peace?" *Washington Afro-American*, August 18, 1945, p. 1.

12. Langston Hughes, "Simple and the Atom Bomb," *Chicago Defender*, August 18, 1945, p. 12.

13. "Roving Reporter," *United Evangelical Action*, September 1, 1945, p. 8; Editor's Note, *United Evangelical Action*, September 15, 1945, p. 2.

14. "Churchmen Speak on Atomic Bomb," *Federal Council Bulletin*, September 1945, p. 6. See also "Statement on Control of the Atomic Bomb," *Federal Council Bulletin*, October 1945, p. 6 (Statement of the Federal Council of Churches Executive Committee).

15. Harry Emerson Fosdick, *On Being Fit to Live With: Sermons on Postwar Christianity* (New York, 1946), pp. 20, 76, 77; "Godless Götterdämmerung," *Time*, October 15, 1945, p. 62.

16. John Haynes Holmes, "Editorial Comment," *Unity*, September 1945, pp. 99–100.

17. Roy L. Smith, "In My Opinion," *Christian Advocate*, September 27, 1945, p. 3; "Let's Rebuild Hiroshima," *Christian Advocate*, March 28, 1946, p. 4; *Watchman-Examiner*, August 16, 1945, quoted in Robert C. Batchelder, *The Irreversible Decision, 1939–1950* (Boston, 1962), p. 171.

18. Robert H. Hamill, "The Atom Explodes, or Those Blasted Japs," *Motive*, November 1945, pp. 44, 45; "The New Bomb," *Central Christian Advocate*, August 30, 1945, p. 3; "We Have Sinned," *Motive*, October 1945, p. 19; William Watkins Reid, "Hiroshima and Nagasaki Methodists," *Motive*, November 1945, p. 44.

19. *Christian Century*: Editorial, August 15, 1945, p. 923; "America's Atomic Atrocity," August 29, 1945, pp. 974–75; "Atrocities and War," Sept. 26, 1945, p. 1086; "On the Atomic Bomb," August 29, 1945, pp. 982–84 (letters).

20. Federal Council of the Churches of Christ in America, Commission on the Relation of the Church to the War in the Light of the Christian Faith, *Atomic Warfare and the Christian Faith* (New York, 1946), pp. 11, 12, 19; Edward L. Long, Jr., *The Christian Response to the Atomic Crisis* (Philadelphia, 1950), p. 16.

21. "Horror and Shame," *Commonweal*, August 24, 1945, pp. 443–44; Batchelder, *Irreversible Decision*, p. 170.

22. "The Atom Bomb," *Catholic World*, September 1945, pp. 449–51, quoted passages pp. 449, 450.

23. Edgar R. Smothers, S.J., "An Opinion on Hiroshima," *America*, July 5, 1947, pp. 379–80.

24. Michael J. Yavenditti, "John Hersey and the American Conscience: The Reception of 'Hiroshima,'" *Pacific Historical Review* 43 (February 1974): 32, 34.

25. Irving J. Gitlin, "Radio and Atomic-Energy Education," *Journal of Educational Sociology* 22 (January 1949): 327; Joseph C. Goulden, *The Best Years, 1945–1950* (New York, 1976), p. 181.

26. John Hersey, *A Bell for Adano* (New York, 1965), pp. 5–6, advertising copy on flyleaf; Yavenditti, "Hersey and the American Conscience," p. 34.

27. John Hersey, *Hiroshima* (New York, 1946), pp. 3, 68.

28. Russell S. Hutchinson, "Hiroshima," *Christian Century,* September 25, 1946, p. 1151; Charles Poore review, *New York Times,* November 10, 1946, p. 7.

29. Dwight Macdonald, "Hersey's 'Hiroshima,'" *Politics,* October 1946, p. 308; *Times Literary Supplement* (London), December 7, 1946, p. 605; Ruth Benedict, "The Past and the Future: *Hiroshima* by John Hersey," *Nation,* December 7, 1946, p. 656.

30. Mary McCarthy, "The Hiroshima 'New Yorker,' " *Politics,* October 1946, p. 367. For a more recent criticism in a similar vein see Kingsley Widmer, "American Apocalypse: Notes on the Bomb and the Failure of Imagination," in Warren French, ed., *The Forties: Fiction, Poetry, Drama* (Deland, Fla., 1969), p. 143.

31. Hutchinson, "Hiroshima," p. 1151.

32. Hersey, *Hiroshima,* pp. 4, 33.

33. Ibid., pp. 37–38, 40, 50, 54, 76, 90, 118 (quoted passages).

34. John A. Siemes, S.J., "Hiroshima: Eye-Witness," *Saturday Review of Literature,* May 11, 1946, pp. 24–25, 40–44; Robert DeVore, "What the Atomic Bomb Really Did," *Collier's,* March 2, 1946, pp. 19ff.

35. John Leonard, "Looking Back at Hiroshima Makes Uneasy Viewing," *New York Times,* August 1, 1976.

36. Hersey, *Hiroshima,* pp. 23, 48.

37. Ibid., pp. 49–50, 88, 116; John Hersey to author, January 24, 1985.

38. Hersey, *Hiroshima,* p. 61; Natalie Mochlmann to *New Yorker,* September 3, 1946, quoted in Yavenditti, "Hersey and the American Conscience," p. 38; Alice Kimball Smith, *A Peril and a Hope: The Scientists' Movement in America, 1945–1947,* rev. ed. (Cambridge, Mass., 1971), p. 80; "*New Yorker* and the Soul," *America,* September 14, 1946, p. 569.

39. Ruth Benedict, "The Past and the Future," *Nation,* December 7, 1946, pp. 656–57.

18. Atomic Weapons and Judeo-Christian Ethics

1. "Awful Responsibility," *Time,* August 20, 1945, p. 29.

2. *New York Journal American,* October 21, 1945, reprinted in Sydnor H. Walker, ed., *The First One Hundred Days of the Atomic Age* (New York, 1945), p. 24; Edgar A. Guest, "Atomic Bomb," *Detroit Free Press,* September 17, 1945, quoted in Michael J. Yavenditti, "The American People and the Use of Atomic Bombs on Japan: The 1940s," *Historian* 49 (February 1974): 229.

3. *Milwaukee Journal,* August 10, 1945, p. 16; James Rivers, New Orleans, and Delmar Lewis, Camp Shelby, Miss., to the editor, *Life,* September 10, 1945, p. 8; Bert S. Heintzelman, to the editor, *Time,* September 17, 1945, p. 5.

4. "Not Peace but a Sword," *Fortune,* January 1946, p. 99; M. C. Otto, "With All Our Learning," *Antioch Review* 5 (December 1945): 471.

5. Arthur H. Compton, "The Moral Meaning of the Atomic Bomb," in William Scarlett, ed., *Christianity Takes a Stand: An Approach to the Issues of Today* (New York, 1946), pp. 57–71, quoted passages pp. 58, 66–67, 68, 70, 71.

6. Ronald Schaffer, "American Military Ethics in World War II: The Bombing of German Civilians," *Journal of American History* 67 (September 1980): 318–

34; *St. Louis Post-Dispatch,* February 18, 1945, p. 1, quoted in ibid., p. 331; Richard B. Morris, ed., *Encyclopedia of American History* (New York, 1976), pp. 443–44, 446, 447; Michael Walzer, *Just and Unjust Wars: A Moral Argument with Historical Illustrations* (New York, 1977), pp. 255–56; Ralph E. Lapp, *Must We Hide?* (Cambridge, Mass., 1949), p. 56; "A February Firestorm Dresden Cannot Forget," *New York Times,* January 30, 1985, p. 4

7. "Firebirds' Flight," *Time,* March 19, 1945, p. 32; Homer C. Wolfe, "Japan's Nightmare: A Reminder to Our High Command," *Harper's,* January 1943, p. 187; George E. Hopkins, "Bombing and the American Conscience During World War II," *Historian* 28 (May 1966): 462, 463, 471.

8. "Bombers Over Tokyo," *Christian Century,* April 29, 1942, p. 550; "Bombing Civilians," *Christian Century,* April 21, 1943, p. 478, quoted in Hopkins, "Bombing and the American Conscience," pp. 465, 466.

9. Federal Council of the Churches of Christ in America, "The Relation of the Church to the War in the Light of the Christian Faith," *Social Action* 10 (December 19, 1944): 68, 69.

10. John C. Ford, S.J., "The Morality of Obliteration Bombing," *Theological Studies* 5 (September 1944): 261–309; "Tentative Essay on Morals," *Commonweal,* August 28, 1942, p. 435; "The Bombing of Hamburg," *America,* August 14, 1943, p. 505, quoted in Hopkins, "Bombing and the American Conscience," p. 466; "Massacre by Bombing," *Catholic World,* May 1944, pp. 97–104; "Massacre by Bombing: Again," *Catholic World,* August 1944, pp. 391–93; Erwin N. Hiebert, *The Impact of Atomic Energy* (Newton, Kansas, 1961), p. 237 (quoting Pope Pius XII).

11. *New York Times,* March 18, 1944, p. 5 (McIntyre); *New York Times,* March 9, 1944, p. 16 (Ockenga); "Obliteration Bombing," *Christian Century,* March 22, 1944, p. 359; "Area Bombing," *Commonweal,* March 17, 1944, p. 531; Hopkins, "Bombing and the American Conscience," pp. 467–69.

12. Author interview with Philip Morrison, April 27, 1984; "The Atomic Age," *Life,* August 20, 1945, p. 32; "The New Bomb," *Central Christian Advocate,* August 30, 1945, p. 3; J. Robert Oppenheimer, "The New Weapon: The Turn of the Screw," in Dexter Masters and Katharine Way, eds., *One World or None: A Report to the Public on the Full Meaning of the Atomic Bomb* (New York, 1946), p. 22.

13. William V. O'Brien, *Nuclear War, Deterrence, and Morality* (New York, 1967), p. 6; Dieter Georgi, "The Bombings of Hiroshima," *Harvard Magazine,* March-April 1985, p. 64.

14. Vannevar Bush, *Modern Arms and Free Men* (New York, 1949), p. 39; *Chicago Sun,* August 9, 1945, quoted in Yavenditti, "The American People and the Use of the Atomic Bombs," p. 231; "Atomic and Human Energy," *New Republic,* August 27, 1945, p. 1066; Frank G. Tyrrell, "Is the Use of the Atomic Bomb Justified?" *Vital Speeches of the Day,* October 1, 1945, p. 767.

15. A. E. Bruce, Claremont, Calif., to the editor, *Christian Century,* September 19, 1945, p. 1066.

16. "Atrocities and War," *Christian Century,* September 26, 1945, p. 1087.

17. William Liscum Borden, *There Will Be No Time: The Revolution in Strategy* (New York, 1946), pp. 141, 148, 151.

18. Rudolph A. Winnecker, "The Debate About Hiroshima," *Military Af-*

fairs 11 (Spring 1947): 29–30; Max Lerner, "The Atomic Bomb and the Human Heart," *PM,* August 21, 1945, quoted in Paul F. Boller, Jr., "Hiroshima and the American Left: August 1945," *International Social Science Review* 57 (Winter 1982): 20.

19. "The Atom Bomb," *Catholic World,* September 1945, p. 450; Richard M. Sutton, "Transmuting Atoms and Men," *Christian Century,* July 24, 1946, p. 916; Ronald A. Knox, *God and the Atom* (New York, 1945), p. 57.

20. Arthur M. Crawford, Erie, Pa., and David D. Rose, Orono, Maine, to the editor, *Christian Century,* August 29, 1945, pp. 983, 984.

21. Reinhold Niebuhr, "Our Relations to Japan," *Christianity and Crisis,* September 17, 1945, p. 6; Raymond Gram Swing, ABC radio newscast, April 5, 1946, p. 2, Swing Papers, Library of Congress, box 30; David Lawrence, "What Hath Man Wrought!" *U.S. News and World Report,* August 17, 1945, pp. 38–39.

22. David E. Lilienthal, *Atomic Energy Years* (New York, 1964), pp. 271, 347, 476 (December 21, 1947, May 20, 1948, and February 15, 1949 diary entries); Herbert Hoover, *Addresses upon the American Road, 1945–1948* (New York, 1949), p. 14.

23. Lewis Mumford, "Atom Bomb: 'Miracle' or Catastrophe?" *Air Affairs,* July 1948, pp. 327, 328.

24. Women's International League for Peace and Freedom, *Statement of the National Board,* October 1945, in Walker, *First One Hundred Days of the Atomic Age,* p. 15.

25. A. J. Muste, *Not by Might: Christianity the Way to Human Decency* (New York, 1947), pp. 18, 47, 51, 54, 55, 74, 91, 105, 109, 149–150, 158, 169; A. J. Muste, "Sketches for an Autobiography," in Nat Hentoff, ed., *The Essays of A. J. Muste* (New York, 1970), pp. 1–123, 136–39, 169.

26. John A. Siemes, S. J., "Hiroshima: Eye-Witness," *Saturday Review of Literature,* May 11, 1946, p. 44.

27. Bruce Gould, "Last Trump," *Ladies' Home Journal,* January 1946, p. 5; Erich Kahler, "The Reality of Utopia," *American Scholar,* 15 (Spring 1946): 179; Lawrence, "What Hath Man Wrought!"

28. Archie H. Greenberg, "JWV statement on V-J Day," *Jewish Advocate,* August 16, 1945, p. 5.

29. Jerome D. Folkman, "A Rabbi Views Atomic Age," *National Jewish Monthly,* March 1946, pp. 238–39; Elliot E. Cohen, "An Act of Affirmation: Editorial Statement," *Commentary,* November 1945, p. 1.

30. "Jewish Scientists and the Atom," *National Jewish Monthly,* February 1946, p. 200; Ahron Opher, "Religious Activities," in American Jewish Committee, *American Jewish Yearbook,* ed. Harry Schneiderman and Julius B. Maller, 48, 1946–1947 (Philadelphia, 1946): 121–22; Central Conference of American Rabbis (henceforth CCAR), *Yearbook,* 56 (1946): 102–03.

31. Bernard Postal, "In the Atomic Vanguard," *Liberal Judaism,* reprinted in *Jewish Advocate,* October 10, 1945, p. 7.

32. Boris Smolar, "Between You and Me," *Jewish Record,* August 17, 1945, p. 8.

33. "Excerpts from Yom Kippur Sermons," *Jewish Advocate,* September 30, 1945, p. 11.

34. Mordecai M. Kaplan, "The Atomic Bomb and the Peace," *The Reconstructionist*, October 5, 1945, pp. 3–5.

35. Trude Weiss-Rosmarin, "Judaism in the Atomic Age," *Jewish Spectator*, December 1945, p. 11.

36. Postal, "In the Atomic Vanguard," p. 7; David Schwartz, "Weekly Panorama," *Jewish Record*, August 17, 1945, p. 4.

37. "Atomic Power and the Human Race," *National Jewish Monthly*, October 1945, p. 56.

38. Cohen, "An Act of Affirmation," pp. 1, 2.

39. CCAR, *Yearbook*, 59 (1949): 128.

40. CCAR, *Yearbook*, 59 (1949): 128; Federal Council of the Churches of Christ in America, Commission on the Relation of the Church to the War in the Light of the Christian Faith, *Atomic Warfare and the Christian Faith*, (New York, 1946), pp. 12, 13.

41. Ernest Fremont Tittle, "Reconciliation or Atomic Destruction," *Christian Century*, May 1, 1946, p. 557.

42. Muste, *Not by Might*, pp. 163, 164, 166, 167.

43. Edward L. Long, Jr., *The Christian Response to the Atomic Crisis* (Philadelphia, 1950), pp. 82, 112.

44. Francis X. Murphy, "God, Man and the Atom Bomb," *Catholic World*, May 1946, pp. 148, 150, 151; *America*, August 18, 1945, p. 394.

45. Wilfred Parsons, S.J., and the Ethics Committee, "The Ethics of Atomic War," in Catholic Association for International Peace, *Peace in the Atomic Age* (Washington, D.C., 1947), pp. 9, 10, 11, 12, 13.

19. Human Nature, Technical Man, the Apocalyptic Tradition

1. Edward L. Long, Jr., *The Christian Response to the Atomic Crisis* (Philadelphia, 1950), p. 110.

2. E. Kendall Scouten, "The Bomb's Blast: A Call to Repentance," *Christian Advocate*, September 6, 1945, p. 8.

3. John Haynes Holmes, "Editorial Comment," *Unity*, September 1945, pp. 99–100; Elbert D. Thomas, "Atomic Bombs in International Society," *American Journal of International Law* 39 (October 1945): 739, 740.

4. Richard M. Fagley, "The Atomic Bomb and the Crisis of Man," *Christianity and Crisis*, October 1, 1945, p. 102; Robert H. Hamill, "The Atom Explodes: or, Those Blasted Japs," *Motive*, November 1945, p. 45; "Atomic Hopes," *Commonweal*, February 18, 1949, p. 459.

5. William E. Hocking, "The Atom as Moral Dictator," *Saturday Review of Literature*, February 2, 1946, pp. 7, 8, 9.

6. Richard J. Cushing, "A Spiritual Approach to the Atomic Age," *Bulletin of the Atomic Scientists*, July 1948, p. 223; "The Atom Bomb," *Catholic World*, September 1945, pp. 450, 451.

7. A. J. Muste, *Not by Might: Christianity, the Way to Human Decency* (New York, 1947), pp. 149, 150, 151, 157.

8. Long, *Christian Response to the Atomic Crisis*, pp. 29 (Milton Mayer), 32, 34, 43, 57, 58, 63, 72; "Hiroshima Tops Atlanta in Size," *Atlanta Constitution*,

August 8, 1945, p. 3 (Parsons); Edward L. Long, Jr., to author, February 10, 1985.

9. Dwight Macdonald, *Politics Past: Essays in Political Criticism* (New York), pp. 6–31.

10. Dwight Macdonald: Editorial, *Politics,* August 1945, reprinted in *Politics Past,* p. 169; "The Bomb," *Politics,* September 1945, reprinted in *Politics Past,* pp. 170–79, quoted passages, pp. 171, 172, 173, 175 (Smyth), 177, 178; "The Root Is Man, Part II," *Politics,* July 1946, p. 205; "Manhattan Project: Its Scientists Have Harnessed Nature's Basic Force," *Life,* August 20, 1945, p. 101.

11. Macdonald, "The Root Is Man: Part II," pp. 195, 197, 205; Macdonald, "The Bomb," p. 179; A. Dwight Culler, "Man—Piltdown to Fermi," *Politics,* May 1946, p. 150.

12. Ernest Fremont Tittle, "Reconciliation or Atomic Destruction?" *Christian Century,* May 1, 1946, p. 556; Wesner Fallaw, "Atomic Apocalypse," *Christian Century,* September 25, 1946, p. 1146; Long, *Christian Response to the Atomic Crisis,* p. 88.

13. Tittle, "Reconciliation or Atomic Destruction?" p. 556; James Agee to James Flye, September 19, 1945, in *Letters of James Agee to Father Flye,* 2nd ed., (New York, 1971), p. 154; Fallaw, "Atomic Apocalypse," p. 1147.

14. Fallow, "Atomic Apocalypse," p. 1147; Fagley, "The Atomic Bomb and the Crisis of War," p. 5; Philip Wylie, "Blunder: A Story of the End of the World," *Collier's,* January 12, 1946, pp. 11–12, 63–64, quoted passage, p. 12.

15. Long, *Christian Response to the Atomic Crisis,* pp. 88, 93, 95, 101, 106, 109.

16. Billy Graham, "We Need Revival" and "Prepare to Meet Thy God!" in *Revival in Our Time: The Story of the Billy Graham Evangelistic Campaigns, Including Six of His Sermons* (Wheaton, Ill., 1950), pp. 70, 73, 75, 122, 125.

17. Perry Miller, "The End of the World," *William and Mary Quarterly* 8 (April 1951): 171–91, reprinted in Miller, *Errand Into the Wilderness* (New York, 1956), 217–39, quoted passages, p. 239.

20. Words Fail: The Bomb and the Literary Imagination

1. James Agee, "Dedication Day," in *The Collected Short Prose of James Agee,* ed. Robert Fitzgerald (London, 1972), pp. 103–117, quoted passages pp. 106, 116; Agee to James Flye, November 19, 1945, in *Letter of James Agee to Father Flye,* 2nd ed., (New York, 1971), pp. 156–57.

2. William L. Laurence, *Dawn over Zero: The Story of the Atomic Bomb* (New York, 1946), p. 225.

3. Philip Wylie, "Blunder: A Story of the End of the World," *Collier's,* January 12, 1946, pp. 11–12, 63–64; R. Bretnor, "Maybe Just a Little One," *Harper's,* August 1947, pp. 137–44; Louis N. Ridenour, "Pilot Lights of the Apocalypse," *Fortune,* January 1946, pp. 13–15.

4. Hermann Hagedorn, *The Bomb That Fell on America* (Santa Barbara, 1946), pp. 28, 34.

5. Karl Shapiro, "The Progress of Faust," in *Trial of a Poet* (New York, 1947),

pp. 51–52; Aaron Kramer, "Hiroshima: A 37–Year Failure to Respond," *New England Review and Bread Loaf Quarterly* 5 (Summer 1983): 535 (Kramer, "On the Harnessing of Atomic Energy"), 536 (Benét, "God's Fire").

6. "William Faulkner's Speech of Acceptance upon the Award of the Nobel Prize for Literature," December 10, 1950, in Malcolm Cowley, ed., *The Faulkner Reader* (New York, 1954), p. 4; Lewis Mumford, "Mirrors of a Violent Half Century," *New York Times Book Review,* January 15, 1950, reprinted in Mumford, *In the Name of Sanity* (New York, 1954), pp. 100–110; Lewis Mumford, "Renewal in the Arts," Lecture, University of Pennsylvania, April 1950, reprinted in ibid., pp. 111–41, quoted passages, pp. 109, 110, 141.

7. Alfred Kazin, "The Alone Generation" (1959), reprinted in Kazin, *Contemporaries* (New York, 1962), pp. 212, 213; Kingsley Widmer, "American Apocalypse: Notes on the Bomb and the Failure of Imagination," in Warren French, ed., *The Forties: Fiction, Poetry, Drama* (Deland, Fla., 1969), p. 141.

8. Edmund Wilson, *The Forties: From Notebooks and Diaries of the Period,* ed. Leon Edel (New York, 1983), p. 144; Malcolm Cowley to William Faulkner, August 9, 1945, in Cowley, *The Faulkner-Cowley File: Letters and Memories, 1944–1962* (New York, 1966), pp. 21–24; Archibald MacLeish to T. S. Eliot, August 13, 1945, in R. H. Winnick, ed., *Letters of Archibald MacLeish* (Boston, 1983), p. 330.

9. Charles Berger, *Forms of Farewell: The Late Poetry of Wallace Stevens* (Madison, 1985), pp. xi–xii; Helen Hennesy Vendler, *On Extended Wings: Wallace Stevens' Longer Poems* (Cambridge, 1969), p. 218.

10. Carson McCullers, *The Member of the Wedding* (New York, 1951), p. 90.

11. William L. Borden, *There Will Be No Time* (New York, 1946); Bernard Brodie, "The Atomic Dilemma," *Annals of the American Academy of Political and Social Science* 249 (January 1947): 32.

12. John J. O'Neill, *Almighty Atom: The Real Story of Atomic Energy* (New York, 1945), p. 5; Donald Porter Geddes, ed., *The Atomic Age Opens* (New York, 1945).

13. "One Victory Not Yet Won," *New York Times,* August 12, 1945, p. 8; Stephen Vincent Benét, "By the Waters of Babylon," in *Selected Works,* (New York, 1942), vol. 2, pp. 471–83; Ralph E. Lapp, *Must We Hide?* (Cambridge, Mass., 1949), p. 31 (Verne); Eugene Rabinowitch, "Ten Years That Changed the World," *Bulletin of the Atomic Scientists,* January 1956, reprinted in Rabinowitch, *The Dawn of a New Age* (Chicago, 1963), p. 131; "Atom Bomb Foretold in 1835," *Science Digest,* January 1946, p. 72.

14. Robert Payne, *Report on America* (New York, 1949), p. 93.

15. John Gunther, *Inside USA* (New York, 1947), pp. xii–xiii.

16. Laurence, *Dawn over Zero,* pp. 3, 187, 194, 216, 224, 237, 252, 271.

17. Ibid., p. 4.

18. Blossom Grayer Feinstein, "The 'Purr' and the 'Snarl' of the Atom," *War/Peace Report,* May 1965, p. 20; *New Yorker,* September 7, 1946, p. 100.

19. Gertrude Stein, "Reflections on the Atomic Bomb," *Yale Poetry Review* 7 (1947): 3–4.

20. Kramer, "Hiroshima," pp. 534, 535.

21. Mary McCarthy, "America the Beautiful: Humanist in the Bathtub,"

Commentary 4 (July–December 1947): 205; Faulkner, "Speech of Acceptance," p. 3.

22. John Berryman, in "The State of American Writing, 1948: Seven Questions," *Partisan Review* 15 (August 1948): 856–57.

23. Irene Orgel, "Sonnet to Lise Meitner," *American Scholar* 146 (Spring 1946): 146.

24. Randall Jarrell, *The Complete Poems* (New York, 1969), p. 183. See also Suzanne Ferguson, *The Poetry of Randall Jarrell* (Baton Rouge, 1971), p. 73.

25. Gary Q. Aripin, *The Poetry of John Berryman* (Port Washington, N.Y., 1978), p. 24.

26. Milton Kaplan, "Atomic Bomb," *Commentary,* March 1948, p. 262.

27. Robert Lowell, "Where the Rainbow Ends," *Lord Weary's Castle* (New York, 1946), p. 69.

28. Paul Bowles, "Pages from Cold Point" [1949], reprinted in John Hollander, ed., *American Short Stories Since 1945* (New York, 1968), pp. 95–118, quoted passages, pp. 95, 113–14, 118.

29. "Bowles, Paul," in James D. Hart, *The Oxford Companion to American Literature,* 4th ed., (New York, 1969), pp. 97–98.

21. Visions of the Atomic Future in Science Fiction and Speculative Fantasy

1. Albert I. Berger, "The Triumph of Prophecy: Science Fiction and Nuclear Power in the Post-Hiroshima Period," *Science-Fiction Studies* 3 (July 1976): 144; "1945 Cassandra," *New Yorker,* August 25, 1945, p. 15; Ray Bradbury to author, February 14, 1985.

2. Ibid.; Donald Porter Geddes, ed., *The Atomic Age Opens* (New York, 1945), p. 159; Isaac Asimov, *Opus 100* (Boston, 1969), p. 148; Berger, "Triumph of Prophecy," pp. 143–44.

3. Philip Wylie, "Deliverance or Doom?" *Collier's,* September 29, 1945; Theodore Sturgeon, quoted in Berger, "Triumph of Prophecy," p. 143.

4. Theodore Sturgeon, "Memorial," *Astounding Science Fiction,* April 1946; Chandler Davis, "Nightmare," *Astounding Science Fiction,* May 1946, cited in Berger, *Triumph of Prophecy,* pp. 144, 145.

5. In *Astounding Science Fiction:* Chandler Davis, "To Still the Drums," October 1946; Theodore Sturgeon, "Thunder and Roses," November 1947; Kris Neville, "Cold War," October 1949. Berger, "Triumph of Prophecy," pp. 145–47.

6. George O. Smith, "The Answer," *Astounding Science Fiction,* February 1947; Berger, "Triumph of Prophecy," p. 145.

7. Ray Bradbury, "The Highway" [1950], in Bradbury, *The Illustrated Man* (New York, 1951), pp. 39–51.

8. Ray Bradbury, *The Martian Chronicles* (Garden City, N.Y., 1950), p. 180.

9. Pat Frank, *Mr. Adam* (Philadelphia, 1946), pp. 16, 31, 32, 51, 113, 126, 144, 145.

10. Ward Moore, *Greener Than You Think* (New York, 1947), pp. 220–23, 224, 227–28, 279, 303.

11. George R. Stewart, *Earth Abides* (New York, 1949), pp. 64–65, 81, 85, 90, 113, 133, 275–79, 363.

22. Second Thoughts About Prometheus

1. Jack G. Shaheen and Richard Taylor, *"The Beginning or the End,"* in Jack G. Shaheen, ed., *Nuclear War Films* (Carbondale, Ill., 1978), pp. 3–10.

2. "A Tribute to the Scholars," *Milwaukee Journal,* August 8, 1945, p. 10; "An International Product," *New York Herald Tribune,* August 8, 1945, p. 22; "A Decision for Mankind," *St. Louis Post-Dispatch,* August 7, 1945.

3. F. L. Campbell, "Science on the March," *Scientific Monthly,* September 1945, p. 234.

4. R. W. Gerard, "A National Science Foundation and the Scientific Worker," *Science,* January 4, 1946, p. 4; Harry S. Truman, "Special Message to Congress Presenting a 21-Point Program for the Reconversion Period," September 6, 1945, *Public Papers of the Presidents of the United States, Harry S. Truman, 1946* (Washington, D.C., 1962), p. 292.

5. David Dietz, *Atomic Energy in the Coming Era* (New York, 1947), pp. 174, 175; Nine Nieman Fellows, "Newspapers and the Bomb," *Saturday Review of Literature,* October 4, 1947, p. 41; Campbell, "Science on the March," p. 233.

6. Philip Wylie, "Deliverance or Doom?" *Collier's,* September 29, 1945, p. 476; Raymond Gram Swing, ABC radio newscast, September 21, 1945, Swing Papers, Library of Congress, box 27.

7. Edward L. Long, Jr., *The Christian Response to the Atomic Crisis* (Philadelphia, 1950), p. 41; O. R. Frisch, *Meet the Atoms: A Popular Guide to Modern Physics* (New York, 1947), p. viii.

8. Dwight Macdonald, "Editorial," *Politics,* August 1945, pp. 225–27; *idem.,* "The Bomb," *Politics,* September 1945, pp. 257–58, reprinted in Macdonald, *Politics Past: Essays in Political Criticism* (New York, 1970), pp. 169–79, quoted passages, pp. 169, 173, 174; H. G. Wells, *Mind at the End of Its Tether* (London, 1945); idem., "The World Set Free" (1914), quoted in "When H. G. Wells Split the Atom," *Nation,* August 18, 1945, p. 154.

9. Louis N. Ridenour, "Science and Secrecy," *American Scholar,* Spring 1946, p. 151; *Portland Oregonian,* August 12, 1945; *Louisville Courier-Journal,* August 17, 1945; *Boston Globe,* August 15, 1945; Maureen Fitzgerald, "'Sixteen Hours Ago . . .': America at the Threshold of the Atomic Age," unpublished seminar paper, University of Wisconsin, spring 1984, appendix.

10. "A Decision for Mankind," *St. Louis Post-Dispatch,* August 7, 1945; "Answer to Atomic Bomb," *Detroit News,* August 17, 1945; Campbell, "Science on the March," p. 233; W. E. B. DuBois, "Negro's War Gains and Losses," *Chicago Defender,* September 15, 1945.

11. Robert M. Hutchins, *The Atom Bomb and Education* (London, 1947), p. 12; Raymond B. Fosdick, "A Layman Looks at Science," radio address, New York Philharmonic intermission feature, November 4, 1945, extracts in Sydnor H. Walker, ed., *The First One Hundred Days of the Atomic Age* (New York, 1945), p. 62, and in M. C. Otto, "With All Our Learning," *Antioch Review* 5 (December 1945): 477; Albert I. Berger, "The Triumph of Prophecy: Science Fiction and Nuclear Power in the PostHiroshina Period," *Science-Fiction Studies,* 3 (July 1976): 143–50.

12. Pat Frank, *Mr. Adam* (New York, 1946), pp. 25, 26.

13. *Philadelphia Inquirer,* August 14, 1945; *Louisville Courier-Journal,* August 9, 1945.

14. The Rev. Robert I. Gannon, S.J., quoted in "What the Atomic Bomb Means—A Digest of Opinion," *New York Times* "News of the Week in Review," August 12, 1945, p. 4; Reinhold Niebuhr, "The Atomic Issue," *Christianity and Crisis,* October 15, 1945, p. 6; "The Atomic Bomb," *Christianity and Society* 11 (Fall 1945): 3; Federal Council of the Churches of Christ in America. Commission on the Relation of the Church to the War in the Light of the Christian Faith, *Atomic Warfare and the Christian Faith* (New York, 1946), p. 8.

15. "Man and the Atom," *Christian Century,* August 22, 1945, pp. 951–53.

16. Harry Emerson Fosdick, "Science Demands Religion" and "On Worshipping Things We Manufacture" in Fosdick, *On Being Fit to Live With: Sermons on Post-War Christianity* (New York, 1946), pp. 21, 22, 23, 121, 123.

17. L. Harold DeWolf, "Religion in an Age of Science," *Journal of Bible and Religion* 16 (October 1948): 202; A. J. Muste, *Not by Might: Christianity, the Way to Human Decency* (New York, 1947), pp. 43, 179, 195; Richard J. Cushing, D.D., "A Spiritual Approach to the Atomic Age," *Bulletin of the Atomic Scientists,* July 1948, p. 224.

18. Ridenour, "Science and Secrecy," pp. 151, 153.

19. J. Robert Oppenheimer, "Atomic Weapons," *Proceedings of the American Philosophical Society* 90 (January 1946): 7, 9, 10 (address delivered November 16, 1945.

20. H. L. Shapiro, "Man and the Atom," *Natural History,* October 1945, p. 349.

21. Lewis Mumford, "Kindling for Global Gehenna," *Saturday Review of Literature,* June 26, 1948, p. 30.

22. Leon Svirsky, "The Atom in Peace and War," *New Republic,* September 18, 1950, p. 11; Waldemar Kaempfert, "The Atom's Power in War and Peace," *New York Times Book Review,* February 13, 1949, p. 32; Lillian Wald Kay and Irving J. Gitlin, "Atomic Energy or the Atomic Bomb: A Problem in the Development of Morale and Opinion," *Journal of Social Psychology* 29 (February 1949): 78.

23. I. I. Rabi, "Science and the Humanities," typescript in I. I. Rabi to J. Robert Oppenheimer, December 6, 1955, Oppenheimer Papers, Library of Congress, box 59.

23. *Psychological Fallout*

1. Joseph Barth, *The Art of Staying Sane* (Boston, 1948), pp. 184–85.

2. Michael Amrine, "What the Atomic Age Has Done to Us," *New York Times Magazine,* August 6, 1950, p. 26.

3. Sol Wiener Ginsburg, M.D., "Psychiatry and the Social Order," *Mental Hygiene* 32 (July 1948): 392–406; "Psychologists Advise on the Atomic-Bomb Peril," *School and Society* 63 (June 8, 1946): 406.

4. John J. O'Neill, *Almighty Atom: The Real Story of Atomic Energy* (New York, 1945), p. 93.

5. Barth, *The Art of Staying Sane,* pp. 184–85.

6. Federal Council of the Churches of Christ in America, Commission on the

Relation of the Church to the War in the Light of the Christian Faith, *Atomic Warfare and the Christian Faith* (New York, 1946), pp. 6, 22, 23, 24; William L. Borden, *There Will Be No Time: The Revolution in Strategy* (New York, 1946), pp. 147, 221, 222; "The Atomic Bomb," *Christianity and Society,* Fall 1945, p. 9.

7. Jules H. Masserman, M.D., "Mental Hygiene in a World Crisis," Papers of the *Bulletin of the Atomic Scientists,* Regenstein Library, University of Chicago, box 29; (read before the Women's Auxiliary of the American Medical Association, Chicago, November 7, 1947); Harold Orlansky, "The Bomb (3): Observations from an Asylum," *Politics,* September 1945, p. 263; Roy L. Smith, "In My Opinion," *Christian Advocate,* September 27, 1945, p. 3; Wesner Fallaw, "Atomic Apocalypse," *Christian Century,* September 25, 1946, p. 1147.

8. John W. Campbell, Jr., *The Atomic Story* (New York, 1947), p. 249; C. S. Lewis, "On the Atomic Bomb (Metrical Experiment)," *The Spectator,* December 28, 1945, p. 619; Aaron Levenstein, "The Atomic Age: Suicide, Slavery, or Socialism," (New York, [1946]), p. 12; Harold C. Urey, "I'm a Frightened Man," *Collier's,* January 5, 1946, p. 51; Edward U. Condon, "The New Technique of Private War," in Dexter Masters and Katharine Way, eds., *One World or None: A Report to the Public on the Full Meaning of the Atomic Bomb* (New York, 1946), pp. 40, 41.

9. Amrine, "What the Atomic Age Has Done to Us," p. 26.

10. Charles Darwin, *On the Origin of Species* (Cambridge, Mass., 1964), p. 489.

11. Pat Frank, *Mr. Adam* (Philadelphia, 1946), p. 145.

12. Edward L. Long, Jr., *The Christian Response to the Atomic Crisis* (Philadelphia, 1950), pp. 88, 93; A. J. Muste, *Not By Might: Christianity, the Way to Human Decency* (New York, 1947), p. 54; Hermann Hagedorn, *The Bomb That Fell on America* (Santa Barbara, Cal., 1946), pp. 9, 10, 11.

13. Ryland W. Crary et al., *The Challenge of Atomic Energy* (New York, 1948), p. 41; Joseph and Stewart Alsop, "Your Flesh *Should* Creep," *Saturday Evening Post,* July 13, 1946, p. 50.

14. Fallaw, "Atomic Apocalypse," p. 1147; Dorothy Thompson, "Atomic Science and World Organization," *Ladies' Home Journal,* October 1945, p. 128; "Outlook for 1946: Second Year of Atomic Age May Be Complacent, but Bomb Race Looms," *Wall Street Journal,* December 27, 1945, pp. 1, 6; William L. Laurence, *Dawn over Zero: The Story of the Atomic Bomb* (New York, 1946), p. 174.

15. Ronald A. Knox, *God and the Atom* (New York, 1945), p. 117.

16. F. R. Shonka comment, "Conference of Religious Leaders and Scientists Sponsored by the Atomic Scientists of Chicago, February 7–9, 1946," p. 39, transcript, Atomic Scientists of Chicago Papers, Regenstein Library, University of Chicago, box 3, folder 15; Harvey W. Zorbaugh, radio lecture, WNEW, New York City, August 10, 1945, reprinted in Donald Porter Geddes, ed., *The Atomic Age Opens* (New York, 1945), p. 174.

17. Crary et al., *Challenge of Atomic Energy,* pp. 6, 40–41; Long, *Christian Response to the Atomic Crisis,* p. 99; Masserman, "Mental Hygiene in World Crisis," p. 7.

18. Fallaw, "Atomic Apocalypse," p. 1147.

19. Lewis Mumford, "Gentlemen: You Are Mad!" *Saturday Review of Literature,* March 2, 1946, p. 5; idem., "In the Name of Sanity," January 1950, reprinted

in Mumford, *In the Name of Sanity* (New York, 1954), p. 3; Daniel Lang, "A Reporter at Large: That's Four Times 10^{-4} Ergs, Old Man," *New Yorker,* November 16, 1946, reprinted as "The Unscientific Lobby" in Daniel Lang, *From Hiroshima to the Moon: Chronicles of Life in the Atomic Age* (New York, 1959), p. 65; Raymond Gram Swing, *In the Name of Sanity* (New York, 1946), p. xi; Louis Benedict, Dubuque, Iowa, to Robert M. Hutchins, December 18, 1946, Hutchins Papers, Regenstein Library, University of Chicago, box 7, folder 4.

20. Muste, *Not by Might,* pp. 8, 47; Frank P. Zeidler, "A Mayor Looks at the Civil Defense Problem," *Bulletin of the Atomic Scientists,* August–September, 1950, p. 286.

21. Franz Alexander, M.D., "Mental Hygiene in the Atomic Age," *Mental Hygiene* 30 (October 1946): 529–44, quoted passages, pp. 534, 537; J. A. C. Brown, *Freud and the Post-Freudians* (Baltimore, 1961), pp. 87–88

22. Campbell, *Atomic Story,* pp. 292, 295.

23. Alexander, "Mental Hygiene in the Atomic Age," pp. 530, 531–32.

24. Rushton Coulborn, "Survival of the Fittest in the Atomic Age," *Ethics: An International Journal of Social, Political, and Legal Philosophy,* July 1947, pp. 235–58, quoted passages, pp. 256, 257.

25. Mumford, "Gentlemen: You are Mad!" pp. 5, 6.

26. Idem., "Atom Bomb: 'Miracle' or Catastrophe?" *Air Affairs,* July 1948, p. 329.

27. Idem., "Social Effects," *Air Affairs,* March 1947, pp. 370–82, quoted passages, pp. 371–81, passim.

24. Dagwood to the Rescue

1. Robert Payne, *Report on America* (New York, 1949), p. 219; Wyndham Lewis, *America and Cosmic Man* (New York, 1949), p. 244.

2. Address by Bernard M. Baruch . . . to the [United Nations] Atomic Energy Commission . . . December 5, 1946," mimeographed copy in William S. Parsons Papers, Library of Congress, box 1; Raymond Gram Swing, *In the Name of Sanity* (New York, 1946), pp. x, xi.

3. J. Robert Oppenheimer to Joseph Alsop, July 28, 1948, Oppenheimer Papers, Library of Congress, box 15; Sylvia Eberhart, "How the American People Feel About the Atomic Bomb," *Bulletin of the Atomic Scientists* (hereafter *BAS*), June 1947, p. 147; Rob Paarlberg, "Forgetting About the Unthinkable," *Foreign Policy* 10 (Spring 1973): 132–40; Janet Besse and Harold D. Lasswell, "Our Columnists on the A-Bomb," *World Politics* 3 (October 1950: 74–76.

4. Norman Cousins, "The Standardization of Catastrophe," *Saturday Review of Literature,* August 10, 1946, p. 18; Eberhart, "How the American People Feel About the Atomic Bomb," p. 147.

5. "Atom Becomes Big Business at Billion Dollars a Year," *U.S. News and World Report,* February 10, 1950, pp. 11–13, quoted passages, p. 13; "Atom Man," *Newsweek,* February 7, 1949, pp. 50, 52; "Atom: Biggest New Business," *U.S. News and World Report,* February 11, 1949, p. 22.

6. Daniel Ford, *The Cult of the Atom* (New York, 1982), pp. 32–33; Daniel Lang, "The Center of Reality," *New Yorker,* March 20, 1948, p. 67; Cuthbert Daniel and Arthur M Squires, "How to Break the Atomic Deadlock," *Christian*

Century, May 18, 1949, p. 620; Richard G. Hewlett and Francis Duncan, *Atomic Shield: History of the United States Atomic Energy Commission,* vol. 2 (College Park, Pa., 1969), p. 100.

7. Maxwell Leigh Eidinoff and Hyman Ruchlis, *Atomics for the Millions* (New York, 1947), p. 13; George Gamow, *Atomic Energy in Cosmic and Human Life* (New York, 1946), p. 121; Harry M. Davis, *Energy Unlimited: The Electron and the Atom in Everyday Life* (New York, 1947), p. 5; John W. Campbell, Jr., *The Atomic Story* (New York, 1947), frontispiece.

8. David E. Lilienthal, "Youth in the Atomic Age," *NEA Journal,* September 1948, pp. 370–71 (Gettysburg speech), quoted passages, p. 371; idem., "Atomic Energy Is Your Business," *BAS,* November 1947, pp. 335, 336, (Crawfordsville speech); "To Those of Little Thought," *Time,* February 16, 1948, p. 24 (report of Lilienthal address to Radio Executives Club, New York City); David E. Lilienthal, *Atomic Energy Years* (New York, 1964), pp. 347, 553 (May 20, 1948, and July 23, 1949, diary entries); Ford, *Cult of the Atom,* p. 35.

9. "Main Street vs. the Atom," *New York Times Magazine,* November 2, 1947, pp. 12–13; Richard G. Hewlett and Francis Duncan, *Atomic Shield, 1947–1952. History of the United States Atomic Energy Commission,* vol. 2 (University Park, Pa., 1969), pp. 96, 126, 350; United States Atomic Energy Commission, *Atomic Energy Development, 1947–48* (Washington, D.C., [1948]), p. 116.

10. Ibid., p. 117, 118; George L. Glasheen (Assistant Director of Educational Services for the AEC), "The Adult Tries to Understand the Atom," *Journal of Educational Sociology* 22 (January 1949): 339–43, quoted passages, p. 340; "Atomic Energy Exhibit Biggest of Its Kind in U.S.," *Science News Letter,* January 31, 1948, p. 69; Lilienthal, *Atomic Energy Years,* p. 426 (November 10, 1948, diary entry).

11. "Main Street Meets the Atom," *Science Illustrated,* April 1948, pp. 19–23, 68–69; Daniel Lang, "The Long Island Atoms," *New Yorker,* December 20, 1947, p. 33; Michael Amrine, "Exhibits as a Technique in Atomic Education," *Journal of Educational Sociology* 22 (January 1949): 343–47, quoted passage, p. 347.

12. Richard C. Hitchcock, "Westinghouse Theater of Atoms," *Journal of Educational Sociology* 22 (January, 1949): 353–56; Max Spitalny, "New York Committee on Atomic Information," *BAS,* February 1950, p. 60.

13. Richard C. Robin, "Power from the Atom," *Journal of Educational Sociology* 22 (January 1949): 350–53; Louis M. Heil and Joe Musial, "'Splitting the Atom' Starring Dagwood and Blondie: How It Developed," ibid., 331–36.

14. Hitchcock, "Westinghouse Theater of Atoms," 354, 355; idem., "The Atomic World and Blood Development," ibid., 348–50, quoted passages, p. 349; Heil and Musial, "'Splitting the Atom,'" 355.

15. Volta Torrey, "Magazines and Nuclear Energy Education," *Journal of Educational Sociology,* 22 (January 1949): 324–27, quoted passages, pp. 324, 325; Dan W. Dodson, "Editorial," ibid., 317; Lt. Gen. Leslie R. Groves, "People Should Learn About Nuclear Energy—I," ibid., 318–20; Rear Adm. William S. Parsons, "People Should Learn About Nuclear Energy—II," ibid., 320–22.

16. Howland H. Sargeant, deputy assistant secretary of state for public affairs, to Rear Adm. William S. Parsons, chief of naval operations, January 27, 1949, Parsons Papers, Library of Congress, box 1.

17. Hubert M. Evans, Ryland W. Crary, and C. Glen Hass, *Operation Atomic*

Vision: A Teaching-Learning Unit for High School Students (Washington, D.C., 1948), pp. 5, 6, 7; USAEC, *Atomic Energy Development, 1947–1948,* pp. 6–7, 116.

18. Ryland W. Crary et al., *The Challenge of Atomic Energy* (New York, 1948), pp. 5, 44, and preface.

19. R. Will Burnett, "The Teacher and Atomic Energy," *Education,* May 1948, p. 545; Robert J. Blakely, "Public Understanding of Atomic Energy," *Midland Schools,* 63 (September 1948): p. 17; JoAnne Brown, "Education and Acquiescence: The Political Rehabilitation of Atomic Energy in the Educational Press, 1945–1950," unpublished seminar paper, University of Wisconsin, 1982.

20. Davis, *Energy Unlimited,* pp. vi (quoted passages), 198.

21. "The Sunny Side of the Atom," CBS radio broadcast, June 30, 1947, transcript in Papers of the Atomic Scientists of Chicago, Regenstein Library, University of Chicago, box 19, folder 14, pp. 4, 6, 8–9, 12, 20, 24, 26, 30; Irving J. Gitlin, "Radio and Atomic-Energy Education," *Journal of Educational Sociology,* 22 (January 1949): 329.

22. Gitlin, "Radio and Atomic-Energy Education," 328–30, quoted passages, p. 329.

23. Lillian Wald Kay, "Public Opinion and the Atom," *Journal of Educational Sociology,* 22 (January 1949): 358–60.

24. Ibid., pp. 356, 357, 358, 359; Lillian Wald Kay and Irving J. Gitlin, "Atomic Energy or the Atomic Bomb: A Problem in the Development of Morale and Opinion," *Journal of Social Psychology,* 29 (February 1949): 57–84, quoted passages, pp. 58, 61, 75, 76, 77, 79. Gitlin was in CBS Radio's Public Affairs Division.

25. Ford, *Cult of the Atom,* pp. 33–35; Lilienthal, *Atomic Energy Years,* p. 291 (February 8, 1948, diary entry).

26. Lilienthal, *Atomic Energy Years,* p. 635 (Feb. 14, 1950, diary entry); Gregg Herken, *The Winning Weapon: The Atomic Bomb in the Cold War, 1945–1950* (New York, 1980).

25. Secrecy and Soft Soap

1. Vannevar Bush, *Modern Arms and Free Men* (New York, 1949), p. 40.

2. David Alan Rosenberg, "U.S. Nuclear Stockpiles, 1945 to 1950," *Bulletin of the Atomic Scientists,* (hereafter *BAS*), May 1982; Gregg Herken, *The Winning Weapon: The Atomic Bomb in the Cold War, 1945–1950* (New York, 1980), pp. 193–337.

3. R. Will Burnett, "The Teacher and Atomic Energy," *Education,* May 1948, p. 540 (quoting Lilienthal).

4. Herbert S. Marks, "The Atomic Energy Act: Public Administration Without Public Debate," *University of Chicago Law Review* 15 (Summer 1948): 843.

5. "Atomic Tests Light Up Four States," *Life,* February 12, 1951, p. 25.

6. Herbert Block, *The Herblock Book* (Boston, 1952), p. 62; Lewis Mumford, "Gentlemen: You Are Mad!" *Saturday Review of Literature,* March 2, 1946, p. 5.

7. Marks, "Atomic Energy Act," pp. 840, 842, 843, 849, 854.

8. Telford Taylor, "The Trouble is Fear," *Nation,* May 20, 1950, p. 507; Brien McMahon, "Atomic Energy Publicity," *Vital Speeches of the Day,* February 15, 1949, p. 265; Robert E. Sherwood, "'Please Don't Frighten Us,'" *Atlantic Monthly,*

February 1949, pp. 77, 78; "Men as Devil-Gods," *Christian Century,* February 8, 1950, p. 168.

9. James B. Conant to J. Robert Oppenheimer, January 15, 1952, Oppenheimer Papers, Library of Congress, box 27.

10. Maj. Alexander P. de Seversky, "Atomic Bomb Hysteria," *Reader's Digest,* May 1946, pp. 121–26, quoted passages, pp. 123, 124, 125.

11. Remarks of Lt. Gen. Leslie R. Groves, *Town Meeting of the Air* radio broadcast, February 15, 1949, transcript attached to memorandum of William S. Parsons to E. R. Trapnell, February 11, 1949, Parsons Papers, Library of Congress, box 1; Lt. Gen. Leslie R. Groves, "The Atom General Answers His Critics," *Saturday Evening Post,* June 19, 1948, p. 101.

12. David Lilienthal, "What *Good* Is the Atom?" *Collier's,* June 11, 1949, p. 57; idem., "Atomic Energy Is *Your* Business," *BAS,* November 1947, p. 335.

13. "The Lilienthal Lullaby," *Christian Century,* March 22, 1950, pp. 358, 359 (Lilienthal lecture at Town Hall, New York City, March 1950, quoted in *BAS,* November 1947, p. 358).

14. "All A-Bombs Can Be Converted to Peacetime Uses: An Interview with Gordon Dean," *U.S. News and World Report,* Nov. 3, 1950, p. 37.

15. George Gamow, *Atomic Energy in Cosmic and Human Life* (New York, 1946), p. 150; Peter Goodchild, *J. Robert Oppenheimer: Shatterer of Worlds* (Boston, 1981), pp. 153, 170–71. For a fictional treatment of Louis Slotin's death, see Dexter Masters, *The Accident* (New York, 1955).

16. "Feel Better Now?" *Time,* April 19, 1948, p. 77; Richard C. Hitchcock, "Westinghouse Theater of Atoms," *Journal of Educational Sociology,* 22 (January 1949): p. 354.

17. Austin M. Brues, "The 'Mystery' of Biological Radiation Effects," *BAS,* November 1948, pp. 341–42; Brues, review of *No Place to Hide, BAS,* April 1949, p. 128.

18. Col. James P. Cooney, "Psychological Factors in Atomic Warfare" (address to American Public Health Association, November 12, 1948), *American Journal of Public Health,* 39 (August 1949): 969–73, quoted passages, pp. 969, 971, 972, 973.

19. Ralph E. Lapp, *Must We Hide?* (Cambridge, Mass., 1949), pp. v, 10, 11, 14, 15, 44, 48, 49; author interview with David Bradley, May 5, 1984.

20. Richard Gerstell, Ph.D., *How to Survive an Atomic Bomb* (Washington, D.C., 1950), pp. 5, 15, 17, 19, 20, 23; idem., "How You Can Survive an A-Bomb Blast," *Saturday Evening Post,* January 7, 1950, pp. 23, 74, 73, 76.

21. J. O. Hirschfelder, ed., *The Effects of Atomic Weapons, Prepared for and in Cooperation with the U.S. Department of Defense and the U.S. Atomic Energy Commission Under the Direction of the Los Alamos Scientific Laboratory* (New York, 1950), pp. 273, 274.

22. "Atomic Bombing," *Journal of the American Medical Association,* 143 (August 19, 1950): 1419.

23. Carrie Rickey, "'Do You Think the End of the World Will Come at Night or at Dawn?'" *Village Voice,* June 15, 1982, p. 68; F. A. DeWolf, Letche, S.D., to Robert M. Hutchins, February 10, 1948, Hutchins Papers, University of Chicago, box 7, folder 3.

24. William S. Parsons, Memorandum to "Op-00," March 11, 1947; Parsons to Lewis L. Strauss, March 10, 1947; Parsons, "Memorandum for Captain Smedley," May 13, 1947, p. 2; Parsons to Robert Sibley, Boston, Mass., July 10, 1948, p. 3; Parsons, "Memorandum for Op-004," August 18, 1948 (all from Parsons Papers, Library of Congress, box 1); *Who Was Who in America,* 3 (Chicago, 1960): 668.

25. William S. Parsons to Morse Salisbury, July 8, 1948, Parsons Papers, box 1.

26. Walter Karig, Memorandum to Parsons, August 9, 1948, ibid.; Parsons to Norman Ramsey, October 30, 1946, ibid.; Parsons, Memorandum to Chairman of the Military Liaison Committee of the Atomic Energy Commission, March 3, 1947, ibid.

27. Parsons, Memorandum to E. R. Trapnell, February 11, 1949, ibid.

28. *"Collier's* Believes," *Collier's,* January 8, 1949, p. 74; "Bomb to Bomb," *Life,* October 3, 1949, p. 22; "The Other Bomb," *Time,* October 3, 1949, p. 16.

26. The Reassuring Message of Civil Defense

1. Albert Perry, "Before World War III, Let's Disperse!" *Science Digest,* April 1948, p. 53.

2. Ibid.; William L. Borden, *There Will Be No Time: The Revolution in Strategy* (New York, 1946), pp. 75, 76, 221; United States Strategic Bombing Survey, *The Effects of Atomic Bombs on Hiroshima and Nagasaki* (Washington, D.C., 1946), pp. 41–42.

3. Elmer Davis, ABC radio newscast, December 30, 1945, p. 4, Davis Papers, box 14; "Atom Bomb Antidote—Sink N.Y.C.," *New York Post,* September 4, 1945; Robert M. Hutchins, "The Atomic Bomb Versus Civilization," *NEA Journal,* March 1946, p. 115; E. B. White, *New Yorker,* November 10, 1945, reprinted in White, *The Wild Flag: Editorials from the* New Yorker *on Federal World Government and Other Matters* (New York, 1946), p. 127.

4. John W. Campbell, Jr., *The Atomic Story* (New York, 1947), p. 246; Daniel Lang, "A Reporter at Large: Mission to Trout," *New Yorker,* May 17, 1947, p. 89.

5. "Control Fear, Not Fission," *Science News Letter,* July 27, 1947, p. 51; Higinbotham, "There Is No Defense Against Atomic Bombs," *New York Times Magazine,* November 3, 1946, p. 50.

6. Ralph E. Lapp, *Must We Hide?* (Cambridge, Mass., 1949), pp. 8–9, 151, 153, 154, 156, 157, 159; idem., "The Strategy of Civil Defense," *Bulletin of the Atomic Scientists* (hereafter *BAS*), August–September 1950, pp. 242, 243. Ralph Lapp has subsequently stated that he deliberately wrote about civil defense in these years as a politically acceptable means of awakening Americans to the larger nuclear threat. Author interview with Lapp, December 28, 1982.

7. Hanson W. Baldwin, *New York Times Book Review,* July 3, 1949, p. 1; *Nation,* July 2, 1949, p. 19; "Young Man with a Bomb," *Newsweek,* April 25, 1949, p. 56

8. Allan M. Winkler, "A 40-Year History of Civil Defense," *BAS,* June–July 1984, pp. 16–23; Russell J. Hopley, "Planning for Civil Defense," *BAS,* April 1949, pp. 111, 126 (quoted passage); Lapp, *Must We Hide?* p. 166.

9. "You Can Live Despite A-Bomb," *U.S. News and World Report*, December 15, 1950, p. 27; Winkler, "40-Year History of Civil Defense," pp. 17–18; William M. Lamers, "Identification for School Children," *NEA Journal*, February 1952, p. 99.

10. "Dewey Bids Public Back Civil Defense," *New York Times*, June 21, 1951; "Questionnaire on Shelter Space," *New York Herald Tribune*, January 12, 1951; "City Hall Bomb Shelter Will be Built for Mayor," *New York Herald Tribune*, Jan. 13, 1951; Frank P. Zeidler, "A Mayor Looks at the Civil Defense Problem," *BAS*, August-September, 1950, pp. 249–51, 286 (quoted passages, pp. 250, 251).

11. Richard H. Gerstell, Ph.D., *How to Survive an Atomic Bomb* (Washington, D.C., 1950), acknowledgments, and pp. 1, 6, 23, 27, 54, 63, 65, 72, 76, 81, 82–83, 85, 90, 93, 112, 118; idem., "How You Can Survive an A-Bomb Blast," *Saturday Evening Post*, January 7, 1950, pp. 23, 73, 74, 75, 76.

12. John Lear, "Hiroshima, U.S.A.—Can Anything Be Done About It?" and "Something CAN Be Done About It," *Collier's*, August 5, 1950, pp. 16, 64, 69; Winkler, "40-Year History of Civil Defense," p. 18; Gerstell, "How You Can Survive an A-Bomb Blast," p. 23; "Naked City," *Time*, November 28, 1949, p. 66.

13. *U.S. News and World Report*, "You Can Live Despite A-Bomb," pp. 26–27.

14. "How U.S. Cities Can Prepare for Atomic War," *Life*, December 18, 1950, pp. 77, 79.

15. "Defense Gadget Racket," *Science News Letter*, January 13, 1951; "Dodging Atom Bombs," *Newsweek*, August 9, 1948, pp. 54–56; *Wall Street Journal* real estate advertisement, reprinted in "A-Bombs on a U.S. City," *Life*, February 27, 1950, p. 89; "Iron Mountain a Third Ready as Bomb Vault," *New York Herald Tribune*, June 1, 1951, *BAS* Papers, box 25; A. J. Liebling, "Aspirins for Atoms, Down with Babuskas!" *New Yorker*, January 7, 1950, p. 53.

16. Eugene Rabinowitch, "Civil Defense: The Long-Range View," *BAS*, August-September 1950, pp. 226–30, quoted passages, pp. 226, 227, 228.

17. *The School Executive*, August 1951, p. 92; Charles DeBenedetti, University of Toledo, "Educators and Armaments in Cold War America," unpublished paper, 1983; William M. Lamers, "Identification for School Children," *NEA Journal*, February 1952, p. 99; JoAnne Brown, " 'A' Is for 'Atom,' 'B' Is for 'Bomb': Civil Defense in American Public Education, 1950–1964," unpublished seminar paper, University of Wisconsin, spring 1982.

18. "Private Suburban Shopping Centers Urged as Defense Points," news release, American Institute of Architects, May 8, 1951, *BAS* Papers, Regenstein Library, University of Chicago, box 25, "Shelters" folder; Donald and Astrid Monson, "How Can We Disperse Our Large Cities?" *American City*, December 1950, pp. 90–92, quoted passage, p. 90.

19. "How U.S. Cities Can Prepare for Atomic War," *Life*, pp. 79, 85; Monson and Monson, "How Can We Disperse Our Large Cities?", p. 92.

20. Tracy B. Augur, "Dispersal Is Good Business," *BAS*, August-September 1950, pp. 244–45.

21. National Religious Advisory Committee, "The Clergy in Civil Defense" (Preliminary Draft, for Official Use Only, Washington, D.C. [1951]), mimeo-

graphed copy in *BAS* Papers, box 25, "Religion" folder; "Churches to Study Civil Defense Role," *New York Times,* June 2, 1951, p. 20.

22. Jane Stafford, "Blood Against the Atom Bomb," *Science News Letter,* July 3, 1948, p. 10; Joseph C. Goulden, *The Best Years, 1945–1950* (New York, 1976), p. 265; Howard A. Rusk, M.D., "Medicine, Mobilization and Manpower," *Virginia Medical Monthly,* 77 (December 1950): 625–26.

23. Gen. George E. Armstrong, comment on Andrew H. Dowdy and Stafford L. Warren, "Teaching the Clinic Aspects of Atomic Energy," *Journal of the American Medical Association* (henceforth *JAMA*), 137 (May 1, 1948): 105–6.

24. "Physicians Training Against Atomic Warfare," *JAMA,* 142 (April 8, 1950): 1090,

25. George F. Lull, M.D., "Burns in Atomic Warfare," *Today's Health,* October 1950, pp. 19, 44.

26. "Disaster Committees Appointed," *JAMA,* 137 (May 8, 1948): 205; "Suggestions for First-Aid Treatment of Casualties From Atomic Bombing," *New England Journal of Medicine,* November 2, 1950, pp. 696–98; James J. Waring, foreword to Thad P. Sears, *The Physician in Atomic Defense: Atomic Principles, Biologic Reaction, and Organization for Medical Defense* (Chicago, 1953).

27. Marcus D. Kogel, M.D., "What Hospitals Can Do When the A-Bomb Falls," *Hospital Management,* 70 (August 1950): 25–27, quoted passage, p. 25; Oscar Schneidenbach, "Civilian Defense is Back in the Hospital Limelight," *Modern Hospital,* 75 (September 1950): 72.

28. Col. William L. Wilson, "Medical Planning for Atomic Disaster," *Journal of the Florida Medical Association,* 37 (October 1950): 203.

29. Dale C. Cameron, M.D., "Psychiatric Implications of Civil Defense," *American Journal of Psychiatry,* 106 (February 1950): 587–93, quoted passages, pp. 588, 590, 591; *World Who's Who in Science* (New York, 1968), pp. 291–92.

30. Irving L. Janis, "Psychological Problems of A-Bomb Defense," *BAS,* August-September 1950, pp. 257, 258, 259. For Janis's full report, "Psychological Aspects of Vulnerability to Atomic Bomb Attack," presented to the RAND Corporation January 15, 1949, see *BAS* Papers, box 24.

31. Janis, "Psychological Problems of A-Bomb Defense," pp. 258, 259, 260–61, 262.

27. 1949–1950: Embracing the Bomb

1. "Atomic Energy 1949," *Business Week,* April 30, 1949, pp. 67, 70.

2. Lloyd J. Graybar and Ruth Flint Graybar, "America Faces the Atomic Age: 1946," *Air Force Review,* January-February, 1984, p. 74 (Stone quoted); Joseph Luft and W. M. Wheeler, "Reaction to John Hersey's 'Hiroshima,'" *Journal of Social Psychology,* 28 (August 1948): 138.

3. Harry M. Davis, *Energy Unlimited: The Electron and Atom in Everyday Life* (New York, [1947]), p. 181; "Atom Man," *Newsweek,* February 7, 1949, p. 50; *U.S. News and World Report,* July 1, 1949, p. 22.

4. Eugene Rabinowitch, "Previews of Armageddon," *Bulletin of the Atomic Scientists* (hereafter *BAS*), September 1948, pp. 258–60.

5. George H. Gallup, ed. *The Gallup Poll: Public Opinion, 1935–1971,* 3 vols. (New York, 1972), I, 680, 759; II, 197, 839; Norman Cousins, "Bikini's Real

Story," *Saturday Review of Literature,* December 11, 1949, p. 15; Malcolm Sharp, "Death Against Life," *University of Chicago Law Review* 15 (Summer 1948): 902.

6. Herbert Block, *The Herblock Book* (Boston, 1952), p. 132; "Did the Soviet Bomb Come Sooner Than Expected?" *BAS,* October 1949, pp. 262–64; "Atomic Energy 1949," *Business Week,* April 30, 1949, p. 71; Raymond Moley, "An Atomic Balance of Power," *Newsweek,* October 10, 1949, p. 96; "The Atomic Era-Second Phase," *Business Week,* July 8, 1950, p. 58.

7. "Reactions of 150,000,000," *Newsweek,* October 3, 1949, p. 25; Moley, "Atomic Balance of Power," p. 96; Anne Wilson Marks, "Washington Notes," *BAS,* December 1949, p. 327.

8. Harold C. Urey, "Needed: Less Witch Hunting and More Work," *BAS,* October 1949, p. 265; "A Little Something," *Time,* October 3, 1949, p. 55 (Johnson).

9. "Bomb to Bomb," *Life,* October 3, 1949, p. 22; "Can Russia Deliver the Bomb?" *Life,* October 10, 1949, p. 45; Michael Amrine and Edward A. Conway, "The Price of Our Survival," *BAS,* November 1949, p. 300 (quoting Lilienthal and a Hearst newspaper editorial); "A Little Something," *Time,* October 3, 1949, p. 55; Ernest K. Lindley, "The Atomic Timetable," *Newsweek,* October 10, 1949, p. 29; "Red Alert," *Time,* October 3, 1949, p. 8.

10. Marks, "Washington Notes," p. 327; David E. Lilienthal, *The Atomic Energy Years* (New York, 1964), p. 584, November 1, 1949, p. 584.

11. McGeorge Bundy, "The Missed Chance to Stop the H-Bomb," *New York Review of Books,* May 13, 1982, p. 13; Raymond Gram Swing, ABC radio newscast, March 8, 1946, Swing Papers, Library of Congress, box 29 (quoting Condon); "McCloy Predicts Super Atomic Bombs Within Decade," *BAS,* January 1947, p. 5; Watson Davis, "Superbomb Is Possible," *Science News Letter,* July 17, 1948, p. 35.

12. "Secrets Will Out," *BAS,* March 1950, p. 67; Lilienthal, *Atomic Energy Years,* p. 582 (October 30, 1949, diary entry); Bundy, "Missed Chance," p. 13; Robert F. Bacher, "The Hydrogen Bomb," *BAS,* May 1950, p. 137.

13. *Gallup Poll,* II, 894–95; "The Soul-Searchers Find No Answer," and "War Can Come, Will We Be Ready!" *Life,* February 27, 1950.

14. Bundy, "Missed Chance," p. 18; "Alternative to Atomic Chaos," *Christian Century,* February 15, 1950, p. 199; Bacher, "Hydrogen Bomb," pp. 133, 137.

15. *Life,* February 27, 1950, pp. 21, 30; "Where the Superbomb Stands," *Business Week,* July 8, 1950, p. 62.

16. "Army, Navy, Air Can Use A-Bomb," *U.S. News and World Report,* January 26, 1951, pp. 16–17; "Where the Russians Stand," *Business Week,* July 8, 1950, p. 61; "Weird Machines of 'Next' War," *U.S. News and World Report,* May 12, 1950, pp. 18–19; Fletcher Knebel, "Remote Control War: Are We Ready for It?" *Look,* November 21, 1950, pp. 33, 37.

17. *Gallup Poll,* II, 965; "The Limits of Atomic Energy," *Business Week,* July 8, 1950, p. 60; Rose K. Goldson, et al., *What College Students Think* (Princeton, N.J., 1960), p. 143.

18. Norbert Wiener, "Too Damn Close," *Atlantic Monthly,* July 1950, p. 52; "Atom-Bomb Program to Expand Again," *Business Week,* December 2, 1950, p.

21; "How to Make a Buck," *Time,* November 6, 1950, p. 93; *Business Week,* "Where the Superbomb Stands," p. 62; "Atom for Power," ibid., pp. 64–65.

19. "A-Bomb Will Not Beat China: Crowded Military Targets Scarce in Far East," *U.S. News and World Report,* December 8, 1950, p. 23; "America Mustn't Open the Way to Atomic Conflict," *Saturday Evening Post,* August 5, 1950, p. 10; "No Worthwile Target for A-Bomb in North Korea," *Science News Letter,* July 22, 1950, p. 50.

20. Charles Wolfe, "Nuclear Country: The Atomic Bomb in Country Music," *Journal of Country Music* 7 (January 1978): 19; William L. Laurence, *The Hell Bomb* (New York, 1951), pp. 88, 100.

21. *Gallup Poll,* II, 938, 1027 (in the November poll, 41 percent of those questioned favored using the atomic bomb on military targets without qualification; 10 percent qualified their answer in various ways); see note 19 above, *U.S. News and World Report.*

22. "Truman Considered All-Out War in 1952," *New York Times,* August 3, 1980, p. 20; "U.S. Files Tell of '53 Policy on Using A-Bomb in Korea," *New York Times,* June 8, 1984, p. 9.

23. Farrington Daniels to Morse Salisbury, December 23, 1949, Farrington Daniels Papers, University of Wisconsin Archives, cited in Brian Ohm, "The Silence Before the Storm: Student Activism at the University of Wisconsin, 1945–1963," unpublished seminar paper, University of Wisconsin, spring 1982; author interview with David Bradley, May 5, 1984.

24. Carolyn Brooks, "Visions of Excess: *Film Noir* and the A-Bomb," unpublished seminar paper, University of Wisconsin, May 1985; Wolfe, "Nuclear Country," p. 18; Charles DeBenedetti, "Educators and Armaments in Cold War America" (unpublished paper, courtesy Professor DeBenedetti); JoAnne Brown, "Education and Acquiescence: The Political Rehabilitation of Atomic Energy in the Educational Press, 1945–1950," unpublished seminar paper, University of Wisconsin, 1982; Block, *Herblock Book,* p. 35.

25. Franz Alexander, "The Bomb and the Human Psyche," *United Nations World,* November 1949, pp. 30–32.

26. Edward Teller, "Back to the Laboratories," *BAS,* March 1950, pp. 71–72.

27. Eugene Rabinowitch, "Civil Defense: The Long-Range View," *BAS,* August-September, 1950, pp. 226, 227; "More Scientists Comment on Soviet Bomb," *BAS,* November 1949, p. 324 (Fermi); Bernard Brodie, "The Atomic Bomb as Policy Maker," *BAS,* December 1948, pp. 377–83 (reprinted from October 1948 *Foreign Affairs*); Zenas Potter to the editor, *BAS,* April 1949, pp. 127–28; author interview with Ruth Adams, June 30, 1983.

28. Hans A. Bethe to author, February 26, 1985; Bethe, "The Hydrogen Bomb," *BAS,* April 1950, p. 103; "The Mathematics of Doom," *Scientific American,* December 1950, pp. 27–28 (Szilard).

29. Brodie, "Atom Bomb as Policy Maker," pp. 377, 380, 381, 382; Arthur Herzog, *The War-Peace Establishment* (New York, 1965), pp. 72, 302; Fred Kaplan, "Strategic Thinkers," *BAS,* December 1982, pp. 51–56; Gregg Herken, *The Winning Weapon: The Atomic Bomb in the Cold War, 1945–1950* (New York, 1980); idem., *Counsels of War* (New York, 1985), pp. 7–110.

30. "Jesuit Editor Protests Plans for Atomic Bombing," *Christian Century*, September 7, 1949, p. 1028; American Friends Service Committee, *The United States and the Soviet Union: Some Quaker Proposals for Peace* (New Haven, 1949), especially pp. 14–17, 34–37.

31. "The Moral Revolt of the Admirals," *Christian Century*, October 26, 1949, pp. 1255–57; Herken, *Winning Weapon*, pp. 308–10.

32. Quoted in "Protestants and the Bomb," *Time*, April 3, 1950; "Men as Devil-Gods," *Christian Century*, Feb. 8, 1950, p. 168.

33. Bethe, "Hydrogen Bomb," p. 102; "The Soul-Searchers Find No Answers," *Life*, February 27, 1950, p. 37; William L. Laurence, *The Hell Bomb* (New York, 1951), p. 57.

34. "Report of Commission on Justice and Peace," Central Conference of American Rabbis, *Yearbook*, 60 (1950): 154, 168–69 (quoted passages).

35. "Moral Revolt of the Admirals," pp. 1256, 1257.

36. Ibid., p. 1255; "Men as Devil-Gods," *Christian Century*, February 8, 1950, p. 169; Herken, *Winning Weapon*, p. 309.

37. Gordon C. Zahn, "The A-Bomb: Moral or Not?" *Commonweal*, September 29, 1950, p. 607 (quoting Rev. Connell); "How About the Bomb?" *Time*, December 18, 1950, p. 50.

38. Zahn, "The A-Bomb: Moral or Not?" p. 607.

39. "The Christian Conscience and Weapons of Mass Destruction: Report of a Commission Appointed by the Federal Council of the Churches of Christ in America," extract in *Christian Century*, December 13, 1950, p. 1489 (list of members). Cf. Federal Council of the Churches of Christ in America, Commission on the Relation of the Church to the War in the Light of the Christian Faith, *Atomic Warfare and the Christian Faith* (New York, 1946), p. 3 (list of members).

40. "Christian Conscience and Weapons," pp. 1489, 1490, 1491.

41. Ibid., p. 1491.

42. The Church Peace Mission, *The Christian Conscience and War* (New York, 1950), pp. 2, 8, 14, 16, 27, 40; Edward L. Long, Jr., to author, February 10, 1985.

43. Laurence, *Hell Bomb*, pp. 73, 102, 104, 105, 113; Herken, *Winning Weapon*, p. 320 (Lilienthal).

44. Robert Payne, *Report on America* (New York, 1949), p. 89; Long, *Christian Response to the Atomic Crisis*, pp. 16, 19.

45. "A General Deplores Ignorance and a Schoolboy Sees Death," *Life*, February 27, 1950, p. 40; "Spreading Atomic Eclipse?" *Christian Century*, January 18, 1950, p. 70.

46. David Bradley, "The Road to Global Dementia," *Saturday Review of Literature*, January 6, 1951, p. 33; "If New Wars Come, They Will Be More 'Total' Than Ever," *Saturday Evening Post*, November 19, 1949, p. 10.

47. George F. Kennan, "A Modest Proposal," *New York Review of Books*, July 16, 1981, p. 14; "Cities of Destruction," *Christian Century*, October 12, 1949, p. 1192.

48. I. I. Rabi, "Science and the Humanities" (1955 Loeb Lectures, Harvard University), typescript enclosed in I. I. Rabi to J. Robert Oppenheimer, December 6, 1955, Oppenheimer Papers, Library of Congress, box 59, p. 2; Norman Vincent

Peale, *A Guide to Confident Living* (New York, 1948), pp. 133, 146; Norman Vincent Peale and Smiley Blanton, *Faith is the Answer* (New York, 1950), p. 71.

49. Lewis Mumford, "In the Name of Sanity," *Common Cause,* January 1950, abridged in Mumford, *In the Name of Sanity* (New York, 1954), pp. 3, 4, 5, 8–9.

Epilogue

1. Steven M. Spencer, "Fallout: The Silent Killer," *Saturday Evening Post,* August 29, 1959, pp. 26, 89, and September 5, 1959, p. 86; Robert A. Divine, *Blowing on the Wind: The Nuclear Test Ban Debate, 1954–1960* (New York, 1978), pp. 4, 42, 127, 262–80.

2. Divine, *Blowing on the Wind,* pp. 72–73, 165–69, 196, 203; Lawrence S. Wittner, *Rebels Against War: The American Peace Movement, 1941–1960* (New York, 1969), pp. 240–48, 257–58; D. F. K. [Donald F. Keys], "Seven Years for a Sane Nuclear Policy," *Sane World,* April 15, 1964, n.p.; Barbara Deming, "The Ordeal of SANE," *Nation,* March 11, 1961, pp. 200, 204–5.

3. Allan M. Winkler, "A 40-Year History of Civil Defense," *Bulletin of the Atomic Scientists* (hereafter *BAS*), June-July 1984, pp. 16–22; Neal Fitzsimmons, "Brief History of American Civil Defense" in Eugene P. Wigner, ed., *Who Speaks for Civil Defense?* (New York, 1968), pp. 28–46; Roy Bongartz, "Remember Bomb Shelters?" *Esquire,* May 1970, pp. 130ff.

4. Ramey Elliot and Jack G. Shaheen, "Ladybug, Ladybug," in Jack G. Shaheen, ed., *Nuclear War Films* (Carbondale, Ill., 1978), pp. 51–57.

5. *Like Mad* (New York, 1973), p. 16 (paperback collection of *Mad* magazine features from 1956 to 1960).

6. Andrew Dowdy, *The Films of the Fifties* (New York, 1975), pp. 159–71 (especially p. 160 on *Them!*); Susan Sontag, "The Imagination of Disaster," in *Against Interpretation and Other Essays* (New York, 1965), pp. 200–225; Stephen King, *Danse Macabre* (New York, 1979), pp. 153–60; Robin Cross, *The Big Book of B Movies* (New York, 1982), pp. 112–33.

7. W. Warren Wagar, *Terminal Visions: The Literature of Last Things* (Bloomington, Ind., 1982), p. 70.

8. Marc Scott Zicree, *The Twilight Zone Companion* (New York, 1982), pp. 66–70, 72–73, 90–92, 226–27, 263–65; "Research on 'The Shelter' " typescript, Rod Serling Papers, State Historical Society of Wisconsin, Madison.

9. Robert Lowell, *For the Union Dead* (New York, 1964), p. 11.

10. Stewart Alsop, "Neither Will I Again Smite Every Thing Living," *Saturday Evening Post,* June 17, 1967, p. 16; idem., "MIRV and FOBS Spell DEATH," *Reader's Digest,* July 1968, p. 134.

11. Evidence on subconscious nuclear fear remains fragmentary and somewhat politicized, but see Hans J. Morgenthau, "Death in the Nuclear Age," in Nathan A. Scott, Jr., ed., *The Modern Vision of Death* (New York, 1967), pp. 69–77; Ron Rosenbaum, "The Subterranean World of the Bomb," *Harper's,* March 1978, pp. 85–88; John E. Mack, M.D., "Psychosocial Trauma," in Ruth Adams and Susan Cullen, eds., *The Final Epidemic: Physicians and Scientists on Nuclear War* (Chicago, 1981), pp. 21–34; Michael J. Carey, "Psychological Fallout," *BAS,* January 1982,

pp. 20–24; and the work of Robert Jay Lifton, especially *Death in Life: Survivors of Hiroshima* (New York, 1968); *The Broken Connection: On Death and the Continuity of Life* (New York, 1979), pp. 337–87; and *Boundaries: Psychological Man in Revolution* (New York, 1971), 339–52.

12. Peter J. Ognibene, "Nuclear Game Plans at the Pentagon," *Saturday Review of Literature,* April 17, 1976, p. 14; Albert H. Cantril and Charles W. Roll, Jr., *Hopes and Fears of the American People* (New York, 1971), pp. 22–23, Table IV; George H. Gallup, ed., *The Gallup Poll: Public Opinion, 1935–1971,* 3 vols. (New York, 1972), III, p. 1944; Florence Gelbond, "The Impact of the Atomic Bomb on Education," *Social Studies* 65 (March 1974): 112; Mary P. Lowther, "The Decline of Public Concern Over the Atom Bomb," *Kansas Journal of Sociology* 9 (Spring 1973): 77; Samuel H. Day, Jr., "Our Unfinished Business," *BAS,* December 1975, p. 9.

13. Michael Mandelbaum, *The Nuclear Question: The United States and Nuclear Weapons, 1946–1976* (Cambridge, England, 1979), pp. 113–19; *War/Peace Report,* February 1969, p. 20; April 1969, p. 21; June-July 1969, p. 22 (on ABM protests); Jerome B. Wiesner, "The Cold War is Dead, But the Arms Race Rumbles on," *BAS,* June 1967, p. 9.

14. Stephen Greenleaf, *Death Bed* (New York, 1980), p. 127; Charles Mc-Carry, *The Tears of Autumn* (New York, 1974), p. 58.

15. William M. Arkin, Thoms B. Cochran, and Milton M. Hoenig, "Resource Paper on the U.S. Nuclear Arsenal," *BAS,* August–September 1984, pp. 4s, 5s; Milton Leitenberg, "The Present State of the World's Arms Race," *BAS,* January 1972, pp. 15–21; Chalmers M. Roberts, *The Nuclear Years: The Arms Race and Arms Control, 1945–1970* (New York, 1970), pp. 79–94; Gladwin Hill, "About 355 of 'Those Things' Have Exploded in Nevada," *New York Times Magazine,* July 27, 1969, pp. 6–7, 27–38.

16. P. E. Schneider, "What We Can't Cover with Plants, We'll Paint," *New York Times Magazine,* August 14, 1966, p. 19.

17. Glenn T. Seaborg, "Need We Fear Our Nuclear Future?" *BAS,* January 1968, pp. 36–42; Albert Wohlstetter, "Perspective on Nuclear Energy," *BAS,* April 1968, pp. 2, 3.

18. Albert Wohlstetter, "The Delicate Balance of Terror," *Foreign Affairs* 37 (January 1959): 211–34; "Remarks by Secretary of Defense Robert S. McNamara, September 18, 1967," *BAS,* December 1967, pp. 26–31; Gregg Herken, *Counsels of War* (New York, 1985), pp. 163–252; Roy E. Licklider, *The Private Nuclear Strategists* (Columbus, Ohio, 1971), especially p. 161; Arthur Herzog, *The War-Peace Establishment* (New York, 1965); Ralph E. Lapp, *The New Priesthood: The Scientific Elite and the Uses of Power* (New York, 1965).

19. "Mutual Genocide?" *Wall Street Journal* editorial, January 11, 1973.

20. Donald Keys, "SANE's Wayward Drift to the Left," *War/Peace Report,* January 1968, pp. 14–16; Minutes of July 21, 1966 board meeting, "National Board Minutes, 1965–1967," SANE Papers, Swarthmore College Peace Collection.

21. For a more extended discussion of this theme see Paul Boyer, "From Activism to Apathy: The American People and Nuclear Weapons, 1963–1980," *Journal of American History,* 70 (March 1984): 837–44.

22. Connie de Boer, "The Polls: Nuclear Energy," *Public Opinion Quarterly,*

41 (Fall 1977): 402–11; Sheldon Novick, *The Careless Atom* (Boston, 1969); Nuclear Energy Policy Study Group, *Nuclear Power: Issues and Choices* (Cambridge, Mass., 1977). In a 1976 Gallup poll, 40 percent of the respondents said that "the operations of nuclear power plants should be cut back until more strict safety regulations can be put into practice;"—de Boer, "The Polls," p. 403. On the European movement see Nigel Young, "The Contemporary European Anti-Nuclear Movement: Experiments in the Mobilization of Public Power," *Peace and Change* 9 (Spring 1983): 1–16.

23. Barbara W. Tuchman, "The Alternative to Arms Control," *The New York Times Magazine*, April 18, 1982, p. 98; Richard W. Lyman, "The Role of the Academy," in *Proceedings of the Symposium: The Role of the Academy in Addressing the Issues of Nuclear War, Washington D.C., March 25–26, 1982* (Geneva, N.Y., 1982), p. 96; "Thinking About the Unthinkable," *Time*, March 29, 1982, pp. 10–26; Fox Butterfield, "Anatomy of the Nuclear Protest," *New York Times Magazine*, July 11, 1982, pp. 14–17, 32–39. For perceptive observations on the early 1980s nuclear freeze movement see Michael Kazin, "Politics and the New Peace Movement," *Socialist Review* 1–2 (1983): 109–121, and "The Freeze: From Strategy to Social Movement," in Paul Joseph and Simon Rosenblum, eds., *Search for Sanity: The Politics of Nuclear Weapons and Disarmament* (Boston, 1984), pp. 445–61.

24. Ann Landers, "A Plea to Stop Nuclear Holocaust," *Wisconsin State Journal* (Madison, Wisc.), May 17, 1982; "Doonesbury," *Capital Times* (Madison, Wisc.), December 21, 22, 1982; "Bloom County," *Capital Times*, April 7, 1983.

25. Howard Kohn, "Nuclear War and TV: Are the Networks Playing Fair?" *TV Guide*, January 15–21, 1983, pp. 6, 8.

26. Frank Zappa, "Be in My Video," from *Them or Us* album (1984).

27. Margaret R. Miles, "Voyeurism and Visual Images of Violence," *Christian Century*, March 21–28, 1984, p. 306; *New York Times Book Review*, December 2, 1984, p. 43 (Gregorian).

28. Dick Ringler, ed., "Nuclear War: A Teaching Guide," *BAS*, December 1984, supplement; H. A. Feiveson, "Thinking About Nuclear Weapons," *Dissent*, Spring 1982, pp. 183–94; Michael Kazin, "How the Freeze Campaign Was Born," *Nation*, May 1, 1982, pp. 523–24; George F. Kennan, "A Modest Proposal," *New York Review of Books*, July 16, 1981, pp. 14, 16; Leon Wieseltier, "Nuclear War, Nuclear Peace," *New Republic*, January 10 and 17, 1983, pp. 7–38; Michael Novak, "Arms and the Church," *Commentary*, March 1982, pp. 37–41; Michael Novak, "Moral Clarity in the Nuclear Age," *National Review*, April 1, 1983; pp. 358–92; American Psychiatric Association, *Psychosocial Aspects of Nuclear Developments* (Washington, D.C., 1982).

29. Leslie Epstein, *Regina* (New York, 1982), p. 35.

30. Carolyn Forché, "Imagine the Worst," *Mother Jones*, October 1984, p. 39; "The Front Pages," *New England Review and Bread Loaf Quarterly* 5 (Summer 1983), n.p.

31. National Conference of Catholic Bishops, *The Challenge of Peace: God's Promise and Our Response* (Washington, D.C., 1983); Ronald J. Sider and Richard K. Taylor, *Nuclear Holocaust and Christian Hope* (Downers Grove, Ill., 1982); "Evangelical Group Sets Prayer Protest of Federal Policies," *New York Times*, May 25, 1985, p. 8.

32. "Shuttle May Take Bone Marrow into Space in Radiation Study," *New York Times,* February 11, 1985, p. 11.

33. Michael Mandelbaum, "The Anti-Nuclear Movements," *PS* (American Political Science Association) 17 (Winter 1984): 25.

Index

Lindsay, Malvina, 29
Lippmann, Walter, 35, 79, 169
Littel, Robert, 66
Loeb, Paul, 364
Long, Edward L., Jr., 235
  on scientists' movement, 97
  on "peaceful atom," 130
  on Manhattan Project, 146
  on public mood, 268, 280, 349
  on ethical and theological issues,
    227–28, 230, 232–33, 238–39,
    281, 348
Look, 339
Los Angeles, visions of destruction of,
  239
Los Angeles Times, 13, 181
Lou Grant (TV series), 361
Louisville Courier-Journal, 185, 269, 270
Lowell, Robert, 251, 254–55, 354–55,
  367
Lown, Bernard, 353
loyalty oaths, 103
Lucretius, 247
Lynd, Robert S., 168

MacArthur, Douglas, 181
McCarry, Charles, 356
McCarthy, Joseph R., 103
McCarthy, Mary, 183, 206, 207–08,
  251–52
McCloy, John J., 337
McCormick, Anne O'Hare, *xix,* 34, 84
McCormick, Robert R., 36, 326
McCullers, Carson, 247
Macdonald, Dwight, 125, 206, 208,
  226, 233–37, 252, 268, 278
McIntyre, Carl, 214
Mack, John R., 355
MacLeish, Archibald, 246
McLuhan, Marshall, 136
McMahon, Brien, 52, 305, 337
McMahon Act: *see* Atomic Energy Act of
  1946
McMahon Committee, 66, 70, 73, 78
McNamara, Robert, 358, 359
Mad Magazine, 353
Magnuson, Warren, 172
Mailer, Norman, 246, 250
Malamud, Bernard, 363

"Man and the Atom" exhibit, 296–97,
  301, 308
Mandelbaum, Michael, 99–100
Manhattan Project, 6, 10, 297
  as model for society, 61, 123, 138, 140
  as foretaste of technological future, 146
  as model for social-science research,
    168, 170, 198
  black comment on, 198
  Dwight Macdonald, on, 234–35
Manifesto for the Atomic Age (V. Jordan),
  143
Mann, Thomas, 279
Manoff, Robert, *xv*
Mark, Rabbi Julian, 345
Marks, Herbert S., 304, 305
Marschak, Jacob, 176
Martian Chronicles (R. Bradbury), 259
Maruki, Iri and Toshi, 226
Marxists, response to atomic bomb, 13,
  161
Massachusetts Medical Society, 329
"Massacre by Bombing" (V. Brittain),
  214
Masserman, Jules H., 277
Masters, Dexter, 77
Mauldin, Bill, 204
May, Alonzo B., 167
May-Johnson Bill, 51–52, 100, 145
Mayer, Louis B., 195
medical profession:
  and civil defense, 328–331
  and anti-nuclear activism, 353, 361
medical applications of atomic energy:
  see isotopes
Meerloo, A.M., 169, 182
Meet the Atoms (O. Frisch), 116, 268
Meitner, Lise, 223
Member of the Wedding (C. McCullers), 247
"Memorial" (T. Sturgeon), 258
Mennonite Church, 347
"Mental Hygiene in the Atomic Age" (F.
  Alexander), 282–83
Merriam, Charles E., 146–47
Merton, Thomas, 354
Methodist response to atomic bomb, 201,
  217, 227, 230–31, 347
Methodist Student Movement, 201
Meyer, Cord, 34, 37, 44
Military Affairs, 217

Miller, Perry, 240
Miller, Walter, Jr., 353
Milton, John, 247
Milwaukee Journal, 5, 10, 14, 112, 185,
    211, 266
Mind at the End of Its Tether (H.G. Wells),
    268
MIRV, 357
Mr. Adam (P. Frank), 259–61, 270,
    279–80
Modern Arms and Free Men (V. Bush), 303
Modern Man Is Obsolete (N. Cousins), 8,
    39–40, 70
Moley, Raymond, 336
Moore, Ward, 261–62, 282, 341
Moorhead, Agnes, 299, 300
Moral Man and Immoral Society (R.
    Niebuhr), 43
"Moral Meaning of the Atomic Bomb"
    (A. Compton), 212
Morgan, Edward P., 90
Morrison, Philip, 68, 70, 77–78, 95,
    192, 215, 367
Mortuary Science, 328
Mother Jones, 363
motion pictures related to atomic bomb,
    11, 104, 194–95, 266, 298, 341,
    353, 354, 356, 360, 367
    see also individual movie titles
Motive, 201, 230–31
Mumford, Lewis, 284, 367
    on scientists and science, 60, 273
    on public mood, 73, 97, 104
    on moral aspects, 218–19
    on artists and the bomb, 246
    on Bikini, 282
    scenarios of nuclear future, 284–87
    on official lies, 304
    on need to resist inertia, 351
Murphy, Francis X., 228
Murray, John Courtney, 228
Murrow, Edward R., 7, 76, 204, 322
music, popular, atomic theme in, 11, 12,
    13, 25, 68, 316, 340, 341, 353,
    356, 362
    see also individual song titles
Must We Hide? (R. Lapp), 97, 321
Muste, A.J., 226, 229, 232, 367
    on atomic bombing of Japan, 181–82,
    192, 193

on ethics of nuclear war, 219–21
on Calhoun Commission report, 227
on science, 272
on cultural and psychological effects of
    atomic fear, 280, 282
Church Peace Mission, 347, 348

Nagasaki, 6, 7, 8
    see also Hiroshima and Nagasaki
Nation, 62, 76, 134, 214, 362
    supports atomic bombing of Japan, 13,
    186
    calls for world government, 35
    critiques Acheson-Lilienthal Plan, 55
    on promise of atomic energy, 113, 124
    on public ownership of atomic energy,
    162
    rev. of *Hiroshima,* 205
    on political climate in 1950, 305
    rev. of *Must We Hide?* 321
National Aeronautics and Space
    Administration, 365
National Association for the Advancement
    of Colored People, 198, 199
National Association of Evangelicals,
    42–43, 199–200, 214, 363–64
National Committee for Atomic
    Information, 62, 98
National Committee for Mental Hygiene,
    169
National Committee for a Sane Nuclear
    Policy, 353, 359, 361, 363
National Education Association, 30, 103,
    119, 298, 317, 327
National Institute of Mental Health, 330
National Jewish Monthly, 222, 225
National Municipal League, 143, 154
National Planning Resources Board, 162
National Recreation Association, 152
National Review, 362
National Science Foundation, 172–73,
    175, 267
National Security Council, 341
National Security Resources Board, 322,
    326
Nation's Business, 163
Natural History, 273
Nevins, Allan, 133, 135,185
Nevins, Kris, 258–59

Popular Science, 62, 297
Portland Oregonian, 269
Possony, Stefan T., 72, 90, 104
Postal, Bernard, 223, 224
Potsdam Declaration, 12, 189, 191
Potter, John Milton, 173
Pound, Ezra, 246
Problem of Reducing Vulnerability to Atomic
    Bombs (A. Coale), 176–77
"Progress of Faust" (K. Shapiro), 245–46
Project ELF, xvi
Protestant comment:
    on atomic bombing of Japan, 199,
        202–3
    on firebombing raids, 213, 215, 216
    on ethics of nuclear war, 226–28, 345,
        348, 363–64
    on implications for view of man,
        230–33
    calls for religious revival, 239–40, 277
    view of science, 270–71
    on hydrogen bomb, 344
psychiatrists and psychiatry, 283–84,
    330–31, 341–42, 362
Psychiatric Aspects of Prevention of Nuclear
    War, 362
psychologists, 63, 124, 275–76
    and civil defense 331–33
"Psychological Aspects of Vulnerability to
    Atomic Bomb Attacks" (I. Janis),
    331–33
Psychosocial Aspects of Nuclear Development,
    362
Public-opinion experts, role in atomic era,
    151
Public-opinion polls:
    on impact of atomic bomb, 22–25
    on attitudes toward bomb project, 22,
        24
    on nuclear war expectations and worry,
        23, 335, 355
    on world government, 37–38
    on international-control plan, 56–58
    on Soviet Union as threat, 103
    on uses of atomic energy, 120–21,
        301
    on atomic bombing of Japan, 183–84
    on science, 274
    on level of awareness, 293
    on hydrogen bomb, 338

on anti-Soviet war, 339
on use of atomic bomb in Korea, 340
Pyle, Ernie, 204

Quakers: see Society of Friends

Rabi, I.I., 176, 192, 274, 351
Rabinowitch, Eugene, 99, 105, 248, 366
    visions of atomic holocaust, 15
    on world government, 35
    on public role of scientists, 50, 93–94
    founds Bulletin of Atomic Scientists,
        63–64
    on the uses of fear, 70
    on civil defense, 326
    on public acquiescence in idea of
        nuclear war, 335
    urges public voice in hydrogen bomb
        decision, 338
    urges military build-up (1950), 342
racism, as factor in atomic bombing of
    Japan, 13, 183, 184, 199
radiation, effects of, 78–79, 111, 115,
    116, 123, 286, 325
    at Bikini, 90–92
    at Hiroshima, 187–88, 207
    in hypothetical attack on New York
        City, 187–88
    governmental cover-up of dangers,
        187–88, 307–08, 314–18, 329–30
    in thermonuclear tests, 305
radio, 15, 30, 31, 166, 366
    first reports of atomic bomb, 3–7
    dramatizations of atomic attack on
        U.S., 5, 14, 65, 68–69, 76
    comedians, 6, 21
    role in international-control campaign,
        31, 62
    reading of One World or None, 76
    at Bikini, 83
    reading of Hiroshima, 204
    promotes "peaceful atom" theme,
        299–301
    Gen. Groves soothes atomic fears on,
        306
    government efforts to influence,
        317–18
RAND Corporation, 331, 343

About the Author

Paul Boyer is a professor of history at the University of
Wisconsin in Madison.
Professor Boyer's books include *Urban Masses and Moral
Order; Purity in Print: Book Censorship in America;* and
(with Stephen Nissenbaum) *Salem Possessed: The Social
Origins of Witchcraft,* which received the John H.
Dunning prize of the American Historical Association.
Professor Boyer has been both a Rockefeller Foundation
Humanities Fellow and a John Simon Guggenheim
Memorial Fellow.